History of Costume

HISTORY
OF COSTUME

From the Ancient Egyptians to the Twentieth Century

BLANCHE PAYNE

University of Washington

drawings by Elizabeth Curtis

HARPER & ROW, PUBLISHERS, NEW YORK

To
Helen Payne

Contents

List of Plates

Preface

To study the history of costume is to engage in an adventure of vast and absorbing dimension. It is to embark upon a journey through time and space to civilizations long past, for costume records live not only in clothing itself, but in the arts of every civilization. The indelible record is found in sculpture, mosaics, pottery, manuscripts, frescoes, and paintings.

In ferreting out this record, the researcher is led to fascinating places, close at hand and far away. Museums come to mind first. When studying Egypt, for example, the great collections of the Louvre, the British, the Metropolitan, the Brooklyn, the Berlin, the Boston, and the Cairo museums are invaluable. Exploration of the tombs and temples of Sakkara, Giza, and those in the vicinity of Luxor naturally follows. The journey to Knossus rewards the researcher of Cretan costume with a view of the Cup Bearer in its original setting. Constantinople and Ravenna sing the story of Byzantine splendor. So it goes, through all the realms of glory, from Greece and Rome to the Renaissance and the later stately courts of Europe.

It is not the glorious alone, however, that brings the past to life; the humble calls it forth as vividly: an athlete's strigil, a family altar, a grist mill, or a deeply worn step on the Acropolis. With this sense of the past comes a shock of recognition that real people—not stone and marble statues—lived in these places and adorned themselves with costume that was as pertinent and timely to them as ours is to us.

This book involved three trips to Europe for the express purpose of studying original source material. Most illuminating, most evocative are the actual garments and accessories that people have worn: the pleated linen fragments and golden ornaments of the Egyptians; the more complete, tapestry-enriched tunics of the Copts; such exquisitely wrought vestments as Charlemagne's dalmatic; the highly perfected cut of Charles of Blois' gold and ivory brocade pourpoint; the blackened shoes of the ordinary folk of Henry's London; the shining splendor of Elizabeth's golden doublet; the character and quality of the suit of Gustavus II, Adolphus the Great; the rich pageantry of the royal costumes of Denmark; the floating, lustrous, silken gowns of the eighteenth century; the in turn revealing, absurd, romantic, distorted, elegant gowns of the nineteenth century.

Considerate and courteous cooperation, beyond one's fondest hopes, made possible in-the-hand examination of the rarest treasures in many of the outstanding costume collections. One royal garment after another, from storage and gallery installations, was placed on my study table for close observation and precise measurement. Photographs and patterns of many of these are included in this book.

In any publication on costume, however, there must be some limitations. Not even Racinet, who managed to cover a vast area both in time and scope, gives us all we need to know about any given age or people. This work will have many lacunae.

The time element imposes two restrictions. In the first place, the task of covering the 5000 years involved in the history of costume of ancient civilizations and western Europe with any degree of meaning is Herculean. To include national and folk costume would have reduced the whole to a superficial review.

Secondly, the complete story of primitive costume alone would require a lifetime study by an accomplished anthropologist. Staffs of ethnographic museums are usually the best authorities on national costume. Working with museum curators in Jugoslavia and searching the country from boundary to boundary for a year convinced me of the impossibility of mastering the subject of national costumes within one incarnation. Much the same is true of military uniforms and ecclesiastical vestments. Children's wear would be another intriguing subject for years of research. None of these will be dealt with except as it impinges upon the main flow of fashion.

Throughout the book, I have used photographs of primary source material as the most reliable evidence. I believe that readers will be guided to make their own observations and analyses and to draw rational conclusions. If they note the great variety of loin skirts worn during the course of ancient Egypt and associate a given type with the status of the wearer and his place in history, they will retain far more than if simply told such was the case.

I have relied heavily upon many authors. On origins of dress and primitive costume there is nothing that can compete with Hilaire Hiler's *From Nudity to Raiment*. If one wishes to learn of Egyptian costumes in a most delightful manner, he should sit at a large table with Davies' *Ancient Egyptian Paintings*. Illuminating information is also to be found in Abraham's *Greek Dress* and Lady Evans' *Chapters on Greek Dress*. For years to come students of Roman costume will be obligated to Lillian Wilson for her scholarly *Clothing of the Ancient Romans* and *The Roman Toga*.

Max von Boehn early in this century contributed eight compact volumes unequaled for their correlation of historic costumes with their social background. Herbert Norris' five volumes and Kelly and Schwabe's two volumes are excellent for the periods they cover, while the Cunningtons' handbooks of costume from the Middle Ages to the present should be within easy reach of every student of costume.

Leloir's published volumes on costume of the seventeenth and eighteenth centuries are invaluable. And Millia Davenport in her *Book of Costume* has provided background and documentation of source material such as was never before so readily available.

For all the privileges extended to me I am indebted to innumerable people: the staffs of the costume collections at the Victoria and Albert Museum, Musée Carnavalet and Musée des Arts Decoratifs; Gudmund Boesen, Director of the collection of Rosenborg Palace; Ellen Anderson, National Museum, Copenhagen; Gudrun Ekstrand, and the late Dr. Torsten Lenk, Director of the Royal Armoury, Stockholm; Mrs. Hazelius of the staff of Nordiska Museet, Stockholm; Robert Riley and Dassah Saulpaugh of the Design Laboratory, Brooklyn Museum; Gertrude Townsend, for many years Curator of Textiles in the Museum of Fine Arts, Boston; Alice Beer, Curator of Textiles in the Cooper Union Museum; Edith Standen, Curator of Textiles, Metropolitan Museum of Art; and Polaire Weissman, administrator of the Costume Institute, Metropolitan Museum of Art.

To the staffs of the New York Public Library's Art and Architecture Department and Prints Room, the Metropolitan Museum of Art's Print Room, the J. Pierpont Morgan Library, the Index of American Design in the National Gallery, Washington, D.C., and librarians of the collection of manuscripts in the British Museum, I shall always be profoundly thankful.

Most grateful acknowledgement is made to Mrs. Lois Keeler for her precise preparation of the pattern drafts and to Elizabeth Curtis, formerly of the Art Faculty of the University of Washington, for the illuminating line drawings throughout the book.

BLANCHE PAYNE

History of Costume

Introduction

The Origin of Clothing

The clothing industry today represents a sizable portion of our economy. From fiber productions, to Fifth Avenue, and out to the chain stores, we are given further evidence of the fascination and importance costume has held for men and women since the Eviction.

Social scientists have given the subject much thought and analysis. The two most obvious functions of clothing are to provide concealment in the name of modesty and to protect the body against inclement weather and other unpleasant or dangerous contacts. Respecting the first, we know that the conception of modesty in dress differs widely the world over, and some of us have seen it change within our lifetime from almost complete coverage to the Bikini bathing suit. As to the second, the general consensus is that man probably evolved in a salubrious climate where little or no protection was necessary.

Skin decoration probably preceded clothing as we conceive it. Staining or painting the body may have been motivated by the impulses to beautify, to terrify the enemy, or to serve in amuletic capacity in warding off evil or danger. Whatever the purpose, it began man's effort to transform his natural appearance. Today we are again in a cycle of accelerated activity in the application of cosmetics.

Mutilation stems from another custom: public proof of the tribesman's ability to endure pain stoically. Among primitives, it is usually associated with puberty rites and may involve scarification of the skin in definite patterns, filing of the teeth, tattooing, or flagellation—permanent records to be borne proudly through life. However, mutilation has sartorial as well as tribal implications. Tattooing, though inerasable, was widely practiced even recently, and is probably no more unnatural than the long, blood-red fingernails fashionable among the female of the species. The Ubangi woman's lip plug is in the same category as pierced ears in our society; the difference is a matter of degree.

Primitives do wear clothing for functional purposes, however, and their use of native resources is clever and ingenious. Eskimos have exploited the advantages of fur. Though Mama's teeth are often worn down

almost to the gums from chewing the leather
to make it pliable, certainly her work fa-
cilitates the construction of her garments
and makes them much more comfortable to
wear. The woman's parka is enlarged through
the shoulders to provide space for baby
to be carried piggyback within the garment,
safe, secure, and loved. Elongated coattails
serve as extra padding and insulation on long
Arctic journeys, and an undersuit worn
with the fur next to the skin creates an im-
pervious barrier to wind and freezing cold
(Figs. 1 and 2). The finest specimens of
Eskimo fur garments, employing intricate fur
mosaic, are remarkable in design and technique, reflecting the makers' feeling for
beauty, their skill as craftsmen, and their
social status as well (Fig. 2).

The walrus or seal-gut parka of the
Eskimo, by which he can bind himself into

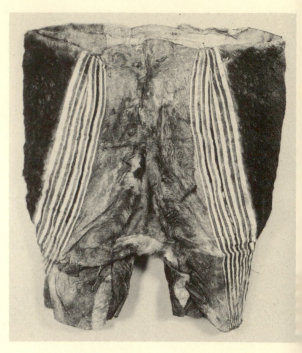

FIG. 2. *Eskimo Woman's Trousers. Coronation
Gulf. (Thomas Burke Memorial, Washington State
Museum)*

FIG. 1. *Eskimo Woman's Parka. Coronation Gulf.
(Thomas Burke Memorial, Washington State
Museum)*

his kayak so that man and boat operate as
a unit, predates modern plastic raincoats and
skin-diving equipment by many centuries.
The Eskimo learned long ago that his breath
would not condense and freeze on wolverine
fur—hence the picturesque border of this
fur about his face. He learned also to carve
wooden goggles with mere slits for the eyes
and eyeshades to cut down the glare from
the snow.

The Indians of the Puget Sound area,
in a totally different climate and environment, became resourceful in the use of cedar
bark. A large tassel of shredded bark hung
beside the doorway doubled for a roller
towel. Spreading cone-shaped skirts and
capes of it in that rain belt furnished a water-
shedding surface that rivaled the proverbial
duck's back. Collecting enough mountain
goat wool for a skirt or blanket was a long
and hazardous process and cedar bark became
a welcome extender.

But man seems always to have asked

more of his clothing than mere protection. Searching for motives among the primitives to help clarify our own, we find indication of prowess or rank high on the list. The temptation to wear the teeth, claws, feathers, or tail of a dangerous or rare animal he killed was more than most hunters could resist. In ancient Egypt the lion's tail became so symbolic as an index of bravery, strength, and shrewdness that it was an important appendage in the king's regalia throughout the history of that civilization.

Veblen, in his *Theory of the Leisure Class*, suggests that the wife's clothing is the showcase through which the husband displays his wealth. The higher the income, the more he or she can afford to indulge in conspicuous waste—thus mink coats, far more costly than needed for modest coverage, warmth, or chic. Chinchilla, by virtue of its rarity and cost, even though less attractive, outranks mink in exclusiveness. The lion's tail and the chinchilla coat serve much the same purpose.

Among primitive peoples understanding and respect for the animals with which they come in contact lead, in part at least, to totemism; and here is another incentive to bedeck the human form. Beguiled by the adulation evoked by his trophy, the hunter might easily feel gratitude and a sort of comradeship for the animal itself. Possibly, also, wearing the hoofs or horns might transmit to him some of the enviable qualities of the animal. Eventually, through auspicious association, he might adopt the animal as his symbol, and these became permanent family totems or crests through inheritance. As a means of identification they appeared on all artifacts created by the family, from ladle to totem pole. What could be more effective in dramatizing and publicizing the family crest than the dance apron and blanket of the Chilcat Indians (Figs. 3 and 4)? The jupon of Edward, the Black Prince, is related in cut and function to the apron, as are all the heraldic devices from the Crusades onward, and all the helms, surcoats, mantles, and

horse trappings displaying them. Vestiges of totemism exist even today in coronation robes and military uniforms.

Combining both economic and totemistic significance is the headdress of the Chilcat Indians. The rings forming part of the slender crown of these ceremonial hats indicate the number of potlatches the owner has given. In Fig. 3 he has accumulated enough worldly wealth to make it worth his while to give

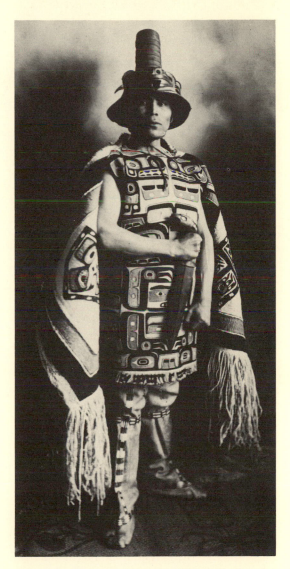

FIG. 3. *Louis Shotridge in Chilcat Ceremonial Costume. (Museum of the University of Pennsylvania)*

Fig. 4. *Chilcat Blanket. (Thomas Burke Memorial, Washington State Museum)*

most of it away (reinvest it) on eight occasions. A potlatch is far from an ordinary feast. It is a grand celebration to which many are invited, climaxed by the presentation of gifts. But the host in this case is truly an Indian giver. He expects, and the recipients know it, that the full value of the gifts plus high interest will be returned to him at the potlatches to which he will be invited in the future. The hat is the record of his investment; the higher the crown the greater his prestige.

Religion plays an important part in the history of costume. Early in human history the man of insight must have been set apart from his fellows as definitely as was the man of brawn. In the hands of such a man certain objects seemed to be endowed with supernatural power to cure the sick and expel evil. Symbols of these fearful and beneficent agents were adopted, the one to appease, the other to revere, and there we have the beginning of religious vestments and ritual. American Indian medicine men strengthened their position in the tribe by painting their bodies, wearing special garments and accessories, and carrying bundles of objects containing magical properties.

Man has always dedicated his best efforts to his religion, whether it was the sacred paintings of the Indian's Kiva, the Parthenon, or the Sainte Chapelle. Vestments have always been among the finest achievements of the costume art. In ancient Greece, only the most skilled maidens were worthy of the honor of creating the peplos of Athena, described later.

Anthropological and ethnological collections are generally rich in weird, frightening, amusing, and regal headdresses, all having some tribal, military, or religious significance; they may even have economic implications, as in the case of the Chilcat hat. Even today they confer a certain dignity, mood, a sense of fulfillment upon the wearer.

Today, possibly more than ever before, both men and women consciously choose their clothing to create and substantiate the image they wish to present to the public; "role playing" is the current term. Our wardrobes range from simple to complex, depending upon the extent of our social contacts and the diversity of situations and audiences we foresee for ourselves. Primitive man is well aware that he most nearly realizes his potentialities when he is arrayed in full panoply. The very swish of swinging fabrics, grasses, and pelts against and in rhythm with his body, raises his spirits and increases his confidence. The girl who changes from jeans to evening gown knows what it does to her ego.

There is a possibility that, lacking the kangaroo's pouch and not yet having invented the pocket, primitive man knotted a thong about his waist to which he could attach the day's take. If a pretty flower or bright feather attracted his eye, what more natural than to add it to his collection? The fish or rabbit would be consumed, the feather become a treasured ornament. One of the most imposing headdresses ever devised is the Indian chieftain's war bonnet of eagle feathers. In the same casual way a pretty pebble —say an agate or a bit of turquoise—might, by patient drilling, be added to a string. The desire to possess an object of beauty and to have it within sight is compelling and can account for much that we wear. The urge to beautify self and surroundings did not arrive with modern advertising. The noted anthropologist Franz Boaz[1] says: "The desire for artistic expression is universal. We may even say that the mass of population in primitive society feels the need of beautifying their lives more keenly than civilized man."

Sexual attraction is probably as old as cell life. That it is the supreme motive in the origin and continuance of dress is questionable, but that it is present is undeniable. The young buck returning from the foray doubtless was aware of the impression he was making on the women. The first girl who put a hibiscus blossom in her hair or stained her lips with berry juice probably appreciated the aesthetic effect herself, but she also hoped it would catch the wandering eye of Pithecanthropus, Jr.

[1] Franz Boas, *Primitive Art*, Dover, New York, 1955, p. 356.

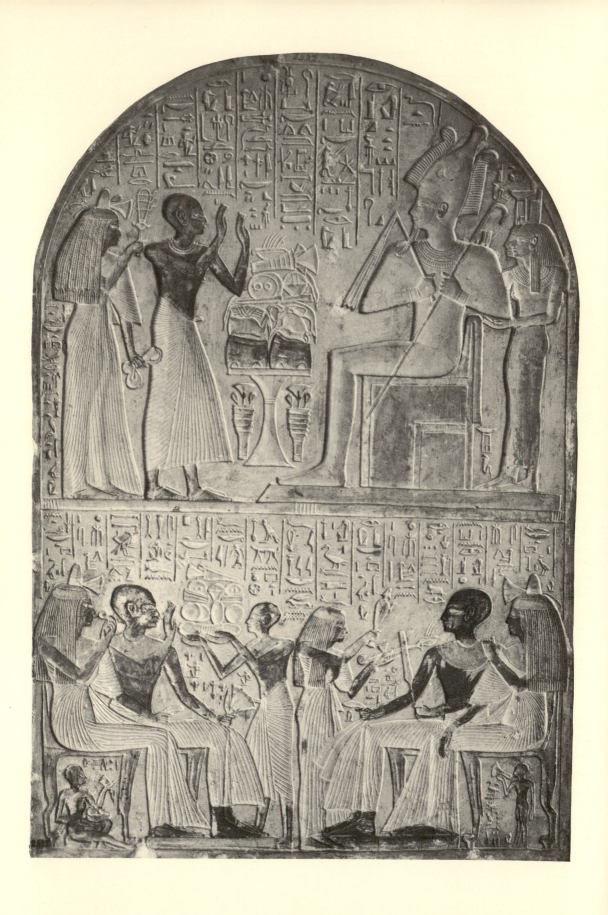

1

Egypt

Ancient Egypt with its strange customs and aura of mystery still casts a spell over the observer of its culture. Intermingled and closely integrated elements contributed to this unique expression, such as geography, religion, social customs, including home life and recreation, and the peoples round about the Egyptians.

The long narrow Nile valley and its delta provide the setting. Since the arable land is confined to the floor of the valley and the productiveness of the soil is sharply limited by the farthest irrigation canal, the river has always played a major role in the lives of the people along its course. In the almost rainless climate of the lower Nile, that is, from the Cataracts north to the Mediterranean, the untutuored early residents were ignorant of the cause of the annual inundations. Snow was unknown to them, and only some benign mystical source seemed responsible. The other omnipresent force, then as now, was the sun. The Egyptians had no knowledge of the solar system, and the daily journey of that life-giving heavenly body was awesome and wonderful to them. Much of their worship centered around a sun god of various guises and names.

The Nile then as now supplied water for irrigation and provided natural transportation and communication facilities. The two plant forms which repeatedly occur in Egyptian architecture, art, and costume accessories are the lotus and the papyrus, both aquatic in nature. The lotus symbolizes upper Egypt, papyrus the lower or delta region.

From early times these two geographical divisions seem to have been distinct, with the more aggressive southern or upper Nile peoples dominating the whole of Egypt throughout most of the historical period. Though little is known of predynastic Egypt, that is, before 2900 B.C., the level of culture of the early dynasties is evidence of a long period of development.

DYNASTIES I AND II, 2900–2700 B.C.

Men's Costumes

One of the earliest personalities to emerge from the Nile valley is Narmer (2900 B.C.). Archeologists now agree that he is probably the legendary Menes who suc-

7

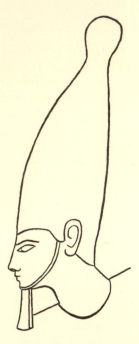

FIG. 5. *Crown of Upper Egypt. Nineteenth Dynasty. 1292–1225 B.C. Redrawn from Relief of Ramses II. (Temple of Abu Simbel)*

FIG. 6. *Crown of Lower Egypt. Eleventh Dynasty. 2100–2000 B.C. Redrawn from Relief of Menthuhotep IV. (Brooklyn Museum)*

ceeded in uniting upper and lower Egypt; he therefore takes his place as the first king of the first dynasty. In that stellar position he had the right to wear both crowns, the high white crown of upper Egypt, shaped somewhat like a tenpin (Fig. 5), and the low red wicker crown of lower Egypt, with its high panel at the back (Fig. 6). On his famous slate palette with its round cavity for mixing cosmetics, Narmer is seen wearing both crowns, but not simultaneously as became customary later.

The drawing shown in Fig. 7 looks as if the cloth of his costume were wrapped around the body once, passed under the right arm, and tied in front of the left shoulder. A belt confines the garment at the waist. Heuzey[1] believes that the artist omitted many of the drapery lines in the interest of simplified design and that actually the long strip of cloth started with one corner held at the left shoulder, draped downward across the back, under the right arm, then straight

FIG. 7. *Narmer, First King of First Dynasty. c.2900 B.C. Redrawn from Palette of Narmer. (Cairo Museum)*

[1] Leon and Jacques Heuzey, *Histoire du costume dans l'antiquité classique*, Paris, Les Belles Lettres, 1935, plate 3.

around the body under the right arm a second time, thence upward across the chest to the left shoulder, where the last corner was tied to the initial one. An elaborate girdle held this drapery in place. Experiment proves that this method produces the main peripheral lines carved on the relief.

The girdle shown here is significant as the possible forerunner of the royal apron. From the front hang four long beaded pendants mounted with horned cow heads, symbolic of the goddess Hathor. The lion's tail, hanging down from the waistline to the ankles, was probably originally worn by chieftains as a symbol of prowess. At any rate, it was worn as a symbol of rank by all kings from Narmer's time onward.

The British Museum contains a little ivory statuette of a king listed as reigning during the First Dynasty. Much argument has arisen as to the texture and fabric of his costume: Mrs. Antrobus[2] exclaims over the needlework of the quilting; others praise the pattern weavers of his day. Through it all he remains calm and dignified, wearing the tall white crown of upper Egypt, his body cloaked in a diaper patterned shawl of admirable technique, whatever craft it may represent.

THE OLD KINGDOM, 2700–2200 B.C.
DYNASTIES III, IV, V, AND VI

Men's Costumes

King Zozer, famous for his step pyramid at Sakkara, was the outstanding king of the Third Dynasty. His statue in the Cairo Museum shows him in an all-enveloping cloak which, though seldom illustrated, was probably worn throughout Egyptian history. His headdress deserves special attention. A very full wig reaches to the chest in front

and is a little longer in back. Over that is a striped headcloth, its front corners hanging free, the back ones caught and bound with a cord. Zozer's wig is much larger than those usually worn during the Old and Middle Kingdoms. In fact, only the women's wigs exceeded it in size. His headcloth does not envelop the wig as it does on later kings. For an excellent reconstruction of Zozer's costume see the *National Geographic Magazine* of October, 1941.

EVERYDAY COSTUMES

From the tombs of the Old Kingdom have come a wealth of documents concerning the costumes and customs of the Egyptians. To any student of historic art or architecture, not only are the Great Sphinx and pyramids of Giza impressive, but the people who built them or lived near them become very real and familiar characters.

Thanks to the Egyptians' belief in an afterlife patterned closely after the earthly one, daily activities are recorded on tomb walls, this being considered sufficient guarantee of their provision in the world to come. While the occupant of the tomb sits in lordly state or associates with various gods, his servants are shown busily occupied with the harvest, hunting, fishing, fowling, herding, laundry, vintage, and metal crafts.

The people engaged in these occupations are scantily dressed. The simplest costume consists of a narrow girdle tied in center front (Fig. 8). Rather strangely, the ends most often fall as three streamers. That this arrangement was not for modesty's sake is clearly proved by the fact that on several figures the streamers are tucked into the waistband for greater convenience while working. Examination of reliefs and paintings shows this costume frequently, but not invariably, worn by boatmen, fishermen, or workmen in and about water.

Closely related to this costume is a wider girdle with a single broader pendant in front. The shortest hip covering shown

[2] Mary Symonds Antrobus, *Needlecraft Through the Ages*, Hodder, London, 1928, p. 40.

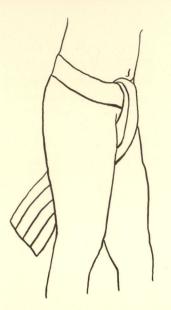 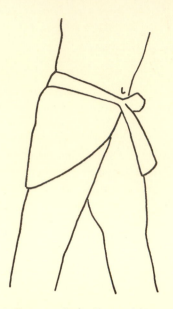 

FIG. 8. *Girdle with Front Streamers, Simplest Form of Clothing of Old Kingdom. 2700–2200 B.C. Redrawn from Bas-Relief. (Tomb of Ptahotep, Sakkara)*

FIG. 9. *Early Form of Loin Skirt with Ends Meeting at Center Front. c.2650 B.C. Redrawn from Bas-Relief. (Tomb of Ti, Sakkara)*

FIG. 10. *Wraparound Loin Skirt with Edge of End Folded Back. c.2650 B.C. Redrawn from Bas-Relief. (Tomb of Ti, Sakkara)*

is a strip of cloth 8 to 10 inches wide placed about the loins, with the ends caught together at the waistline in center front (Fig. 9). Again there is no concern with modesty in dress as we conceive it. Similar to this outline is the true diaper, which was probably put on as a triangle with the base at the waistline and the apex brought between the legs and fastened with the other corners at center front. This continued in use throughout the empire period.

True loin skirts were of varying length, though in the early dynasties they ended above the knee. The series of drawings reproduced here, taken from reliefs in tombs and in outstanding museum collections, are self-explanatory (Figs. 10, 11, and 12). Figure 13, the so-called Sheik-el-Beled, shows the easy natural way in which the end of the loin skirt curled forward when it was tucked into the waistline. The butcher's costume (Fig. 12) included a whetstone tied by a cord to one corner of the skirt and thrust into the waistband when not in use. Men leading cattle are shown in several instances

with the square end of the loin skirt projecting sharply forward (Fig. 14).

KINGS AND UPPER CLASSES

A study of a series of statues of the Old Kingdom gives convincing evidence of the gradual evolution of the triangular projection, a costume feature peculiar to the Egyptians, and peculiar from any point of view. One figure from the Rawer tomb of the Fifth Dynasty in the Cairo Museum has the overlapping end of his loin skirt rounding out in front with no sharp angles; another has a sharp angular fold on the left side only; on a third there is a fully formed triangular projection, shaped like a half-pyramid, extending beyond the body in what seems to be a solid, almost architectural structure (Fig. 15). On other statues (Figs. 16 and 17) a striped or plaid design is indicated in the fabric of the skirt, the lines continuing in logical fashion across the angles of the projection suggesting that it was formed of a single piece of cloth; what held it in shape

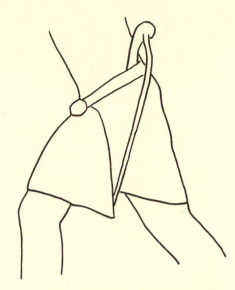

Fig. 11. *Loin Skirt in Action. c.2500 B.C. Redrawn from Bas-Relief. (Tomb of Pehenu-ka, Sakkara, Egyptian Museum, Berlin)*

Fig. 12. *Loin Skirt of Butcher with Whetstone Tucked into Girdle. Fifth Dynasty. 2565–2420 B.C. Redrawn from Bas-Relief. (Tomb of Akhuhotep, Louvre)*

is a matter of conjecture. On the earlier figures the extension may have been due to the stiffness and bulkiness of the fabric itself, but on the fully developed triangles there must have been a framework of some kind to provide support. A seated figure wearing this costume looks as if he were provided with a lectern.

The so-called gala skirt wraps at least one and a half times around the body, beginning probably at the left hip, proceeding thence across the back, around the right hip, and continuing in this direction, to end with a gold pleated section over the right half of the body. This last section rounds upward from the hemline to the belt at center front. Painted statues invariably show it as accordion pleated (sometimes in herringbone pattern) and gold in color. We do not know how the gold was applied in real life; fine gold thread could have been woven in with the linen, or gold leaf applied. Certainly it added to the richness of the costume, which seems to have been reserved for festive occasions. The square knotted girdle and pro-

jecting tab almost always accompany it (Fig. 18).

In the shendot both ends of the loin skirt are rounded, and the overlap in front is so slight that the tab from the girdle shows plainly, forming an integral part of the costume (see Fig. 23). This loin skirt is pleated all the way around and the front panel is usually represented with horizontal pleats. During the Old Kingdom the right to wear the shendot was restricted to royalty. During the Middle Kingdom this privilege was conferred upon a deserving few as a great favor. By the time of the empire period, it had lost much of its social significance.

With these upper-class costumes the belt was an important accessory; it is sometimes knotted in the back with falling ends, sometimes tied in a square knot, especially in connection with the gala skirt, and in other instances a single loop projects outward from the girdle. There has been much surmising concerning the tab, which often projects above the belt. This could be one end of the girdle or it might be the hilt of a weapon.

FIG. 13. *Sheik-el-Beled. c.2600 B.C. Sakkara. (Cairo Museum)*

the bare shaven head and a leopard skin draped about the body. Later, during the empire period, the priests became less ascetic and donned the sheer pleated costume and wig of the upper class. The leopard skin, however, was retained.

WIGS. When costume is as basic as it was during the Old Kingdom, accessories form an all-important part of the ensemble. Some of these have already been mentioned. Since the Egyptians had a high standard of cleanliness and in addition had to contend with great heat, it became the custom to shave or clip the hair close to the scalp and to wear wigs. This promoted cleanliness and coolness indoors and the wig lent dignity and provided insulation from the sun out of doors. During the Old Kingdom, men's wigs were usually small and followed the contour of the head. Short curls are indicated on the statues by close horizontal lines (Fig. 18). Slightly fuller wigs were constructed with straight hair. Zozer's wig, as noted earlier, was unusually large. Wigs recovered from the tombs were not always made of human

During the Sixth Dynasty, toward the end of the Old Kingdom, the loin skirt of the upper class lengthened perceptibly. On a wooden statue in the Metropolitan Museum it reaches almost to the ankles; in other cases it extends to midcalf. The triangular arrangement is retained, but modified in size.

PRIESTS

Figures of priests occur often in Egyptian art, since they officiated at so many ceremonies concerned with worship and burial. Two features help to identify them:

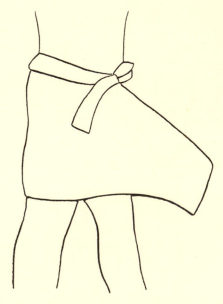

FIG. 14. *Loin Skirt on Men Leading Cattle. c.2500 B.C. Redrawn from Bas-Relief. (Tomb of Ptahotep, Sakkara)*

hair; some received much of their bulk from the addition of sheep's wool.

THE HEADCLOTH. The headcloth was in use as a headdress at an early date. Statues of Mykerinus show it in its familiar formal arrangement, which was retained throughout Egyptian history. The headcloth completely enveloped the wig (Fig. 19). Judging from the direction of the stripes, a straight edge of the headcloth was bound about the head, covering the hairline, and was secured at the nape of the neck. Traditionally shaped folds, starting at precise matching angles on each side of the head, were brought forward over each shoulder. The rest of the cloth was drawn to the back and bound about the wig in a pigtail, similar to the arrangement of the eighteenth-century wig. Kretschmer and Rohrbach[3] make an interesting comparison between the arrangement of this headcloth and that of the present-day desert dweller, suggesting that the same climatic conditions

[3] Albert Kretschmer and Carl Rohrbach, *Die Trachten der Völker*, J. G. Bach, Leipzig, 1864, vol. I, pp. 8–9.

of heat, wind, and dust have produced the same type of protection against them. The cloth furnishes shade but allows circulation of air; the traveler can arrange one corner over his nostrils and mouth to screen out choking dust. In royal Egyptian costume this kerchief is referred to as the Nemes headdress. It was generally a plain square of linen.

THE PSCHENT. When the two royal crowns mentioned in connection with Narmer were worn at the same time, the combination was called the "pschent." The sacred uraeus poised on the front of the royal headdress was the symbol of the king's power over life and death and was designed to strike terror in the beholder. Since the king was looked upon as the son of the god Horus, and later of Ra, he was considered one of the gods and was worshiped as such after his death. Accordingly he had the privilege of wearing the symbols of the gods: the two straight upright feathers of the god Amon, the curling ostrich feathers of Osiris, the ram's horns of Khnum, the sun disc of

FIG. 15. *Early Form of Loin Skirt with Triangular Projection. c.2650 B.C. Redrawn from Bas-Relief. (Tomb of Ti, Sakkara)*

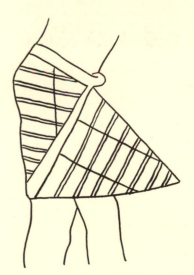

FIG. 16. *Loin Skirt with Triangular Projection. c.2300 B.C. Redrawn from an Old Kingdom Figure. (Egyptian Museum, Berlin)*

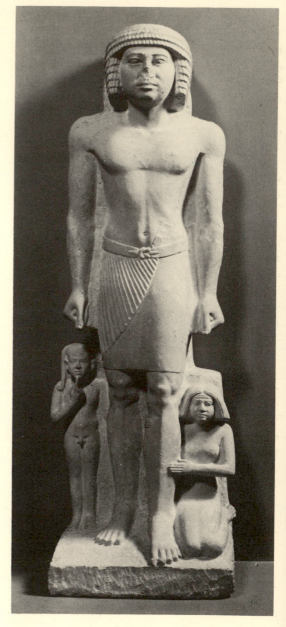

FIG. 17. *High Official, Methethy, Wearing Lengthened Loin Skirt of Late Fifth Dynasty.* c.2420 B.C. (*Brooklyn Museum*)

FIG. 18. *Superintendent of Granaries Wearing Gala Costume. Fifth Dynasty.* 2565–2420 B.C. (*Brooklyn Museum*)

Ra. Combinations of these symbols are referred to as "diadems of the gods."

THE BEARD. The beard was considered admirable for its manly significance. However, since it was hot and unclean, in every-

day life the Egyptians were clean shaven. The king reserved the right to wear an artificial beard, which he donned for state occasions. Beards were of three sorts. A short stubby beard could be worn by men of royal rank. The king's beard was much longer, but straight and thick. The beards of the gods resembled the king's, but could be distinguished from it by a more slender form and an upward curving crook at the end. When the king appeared in the guise of a god he wore the curved beard.

THE LOCK OF YOUTH. In the Old Kingdom children of the king were distinguished by the lock of youth (Fig. 18). The child Horus is usually depicted wearing this enormous braid jutting from the right side of the head over the ear. This mark of identification was retained in the empire period but a decorative panel was substituted for the braid of hair. Other youngsters ran about with their heads shaved, except for a few locks falling to one side.

COLLARS AND NECKLACES. Collars or necklaces have been associated with Egyptian costumes from earliest times. Predynastic finds include strings of small shells, faïence beads, and crystal, carnelian, and amethyst carved in both round and oblong forms. Collars were the most common article of adornment and were worn by both men and women. They were most often made of faïence beads, sometimes of semiprecious stones. Rahotep in Fig. 20 wears a simple necklace of small beads.

FOOTWEAR. Footwear was of little importance in Egypt until the empire period. Although Narmer is shown accompanied by a sandal bearer, which proves at least that sandals were manufactured that early, all Egyptians, including royalty, are shown barefooted during the Old Kingdom. The sandals were made of papyrus and palm fiber and sometimes of tanned goatskin.

Women's Costumes

Women's costumes were simpler than men's. Women of all classes are portrayed in straight sheath gowns, which were probably not as tight as the artists show them.

Dancing figures are able to take quite a natural stride and at least one sculptured figure is represented with a herringbone pleated dress (Nanupkau and wife from his tomb at Giza, collection of the Oriental Art Institute, University of Chicago). A slim young woman in the Louvre has additional elegance in the surface design of her straps which may be bead work.

These ladies were the earliest sponsors of the empire line. One or two tapered shoulder straps form the upper part of the garment. Women servants enjoyed unimpeded action

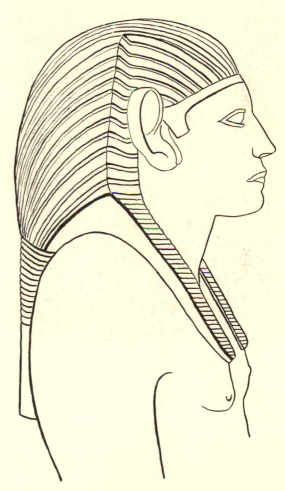

FIG. 19. *Side View of Nemes Headdress, Showing Pigtail Effect at Back. Twelfth Dynasty. 2000–1788* B.C. *Redrawn from Statue of Sesostris III.* (*British Museum*)

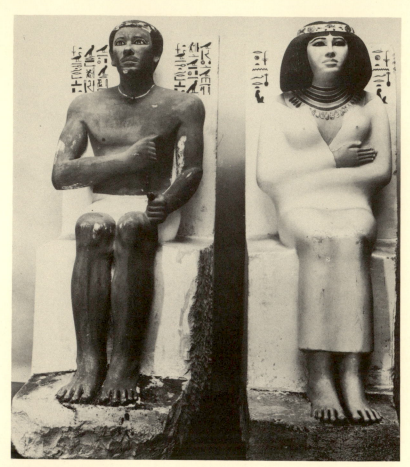

FIG. 20. *Rahotep and Nofret from Meydum. Early Fourth Dynasty. 2650–2500 B.C. (Cairo Museum)*

FIG. 21. *Gardener. Twelfth Dynasty. 2000–1788 B.C. (Museum of the University of Pennsylvania)*

in short skirts. Fig. 20 shows Nofret, wife of the high priest Rahotep, wearing a light-weight shawl draped far out on the shoulders.

ACCESSORIES. Women as well as men wore wigs during the Old Kingdom. Many of these wigs revealed the natural hairline, indicating that the women had their hair clipped less closely than the men. In Nofret's hairdress in Fig. 20 the center part visible on the forehead is made of her own hair. Her wig, bushy but quite smooth, is shoulder length; that of the young girl is short and close, made up of horizontal rows of tight little curls; a third form, as bulky as Nofret's, falls forward over the shoulders to the armpits. For the working class a crew cut sufficed.

During this period the use of jewelry is quite restrained. Nofret's coronet and collar add much style to her costume. The shape of the collar is typical throughout ancient Egyptian history. The collar of the young girl mentioned above is wider and consists of five rows of tubular beads. She also wears wide bracelets and anklets of beads. A woman of the Third Dynasty wears matching bracelets about 5 inches wide, which appear to be in the form of closely spiraled metal bands.

THE MIDDLE KINGDOM, 2100–1788 B.C.
DYNASTIES XI AND XII

Men's Costumes

The Middle Kingdom is more renowned for accomplishments in the fields of engineering, literature, and applied art than for any change in the customs of everyday living. Costume continued very much as it had been in the Old Kingdom. The costume of men of upper rank was long but, as we have seen, it had lengthened during the Old Kingdom (Fig. 17). The triangular projection became

less exaggerated in the Middle Kingdom. Several figures in the important museum collections wear a long narrow skirt wrapped closely about the body and extending well above the waistline (Fig. 21). Shawled figures are also seen (Fig. 22). Erman states that a small shoulder shawl came into use at this time.[4] The royal costume consisting of

[4] Adolf Erman, *Life in Ancient Egypt*, Macmillan, London, 1894, p. 206.

FIG. 22. *Statuette of Seated Figure. Twelfth Dynasty, 2000–1788* B.C. *(Metropolitan Museum of Art)*

became more bushy in appearance, and reached to the shoulders (Fig. 22).

Women's Costumes

Women in the Middle Kingdom continued to wear the sheath gown of the Old Kingdom. The painted wooden figures of the offering bearers in the Louvre, Metro-

Fig. 24. *Offering Bearer.* c.2000 B.C. *(Louvre)*

FIG. 23. *King Sesostris III Wearing Shendot, Nemes Headdress, and Lion's Tail. Twelfth Dynasty.* 2000–1788 B.C. *(Brooklyn Museum)*

shendot, Nemes headdress, and lion's tail continued in the traditional form. King Sesostris III (Fig. 23) wears a necklace with a small pectoral (an ornament worn on the chest or breast), a bracelet on his right wrist, and a patterned girdle. The wig increased in bulk,

politan, and Cairo Museums are outstanding examples of this period (Fig. 24). Here too, are examples of the feather-patterned fabric of the gowns, whose fresh lovely hues attest to the Egyptian's love of color. Note the queen's costume in Fig. 25. Figure 26 shows women occupied with spinning and weaving. One wears a skirt similar to that of the bread maker in the Old Kingdom. The spinner is scantily clad in a diaper type of covering. The others wear sheath skirts of varying lengths, supported by single shoulder straps.

ACCESSORIES. A new style of wig, shown in Fig. 27, seems peculiar to this period; it was excessively bulky and the hair brought forward over the shoulders tapered rapidly to form a coil on each side of the chest.

FIG. 25. *Goddess Buto Dressed in Queen's Costume of Middle Kingdom: Sheath Dress with Feather Design, Decorated Shoulder Straps, and Vulture Headdress.* c.2000 B.C. (Brooklyn Museum)

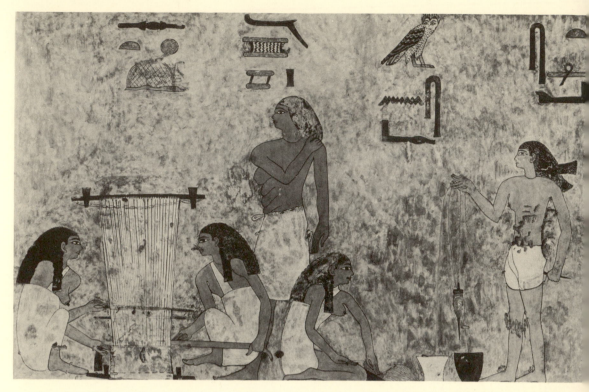

FIG. 26. *Women Spinning and Weaving. Twelfth Dynasty.* 2000–1788 B.C. *Reproduction of Wall Painting.* (Metropolitan Museum of Art)

The vulture headdress illustrated in Fig. 25 was the prerogative of queens. It fitted the head smoothly, the tips of the wings resting on the chest. The sacred cobra, the uraeus, rears its head above the forehead. The wearing of the vulture headdress by the queen was believed to afford her husband protection when he was absent.

Jewelry was the most important women's accessory in the Middle Kingdom. Outstanding examples of it include the cloisonné crown and floral diadem of fine gold wire in the Cairo collection and the marvelous jewelry of Princess Sit-Hat-Hor-Yunet in the Metropolitan Museum—especially the cloisonné crown with its accompanying golden tubes (Fig. 28) and the pectoral, which has enjoyed much publicity. A girdle of gold cowrie shells combined with carnelian and green feldspar beads and armlets of gold,

carnelian, and turquoise are included in the collection.

THE EMPIRE, 1580–1090 B.C., DYNASTIES XVIII, XIX, AND XX

Men's Costumes

Many innovations in dress marked the empire period. Contact with peoples of the eastern Mediterranean, Syria, and Palestine, and an upsurge of wealth in the form of loot from conquered lands, were responsible for a great elaboration of costume.

THE WORKING CLASS

The dress of working men and women remained static, was simple, functional, and comfortable. One dress item of which we have ample evidence is a leather loincloth, worn diaper fashion. Well-tanned skin was cut into a fine lattice design—no doubt both for greater suppleness and for ventilation—except for a rectangle in the center and a border around the edge (Fig. 29). The wall painting reproduced in Fig. 30 shows how the slashed leather garment was worn.

THE UPPER CLASS

The costume of the upper class was marked by great variety. For state occasions the royal shendot was still in use. The figures

FIG. 28. *Crown of Princess Sit-Hat-Hor-Yunet. Twelfth Dynasty. 2000–1788* B.C. *(Metropolitan Museum of Art, Circlet and Half of Tubing Are Reproductions of Originals in Cairo Museum)*

guarding the door to Tutankhamen's tomb chamber wear loin skirts with great triangular projections. Covering the upper part of the body was one of the innovations of the empire period.

A kimono style of garment, the most common type worn by men, consisted of a length of cloth twice the height of the wearer (or a little less) and wide enough to reach from elbow to elbow. A small hole in the center to fit the neck and a vertical slit down the center front enabled the wearer to draw it on over his head. The fabric fell in a broad panel to the floor, front and back. When not joined under the arms, the edges of the front panel were wrapped around the sides toward the center back and the edges of the back panel were brought forward, overlapping the front panel and closing the

FIG. 27. *Woman's Wig, Peculiar to Middle Kingdom. c.1850* B.C. *Redrawn from Statue of Queen Nofret, Wife of Sesostris IV. (British Museum)*

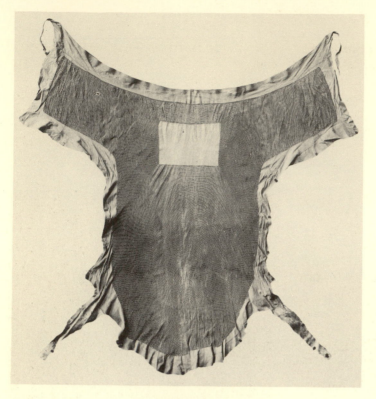

FIG. 29. *Egyptian Loin Covering of Gazelle Skin. Eighteenth Dynasty. 1580–1350 B.C. (Courtesy, Museum of Fine Arts, Boston)*

FIG. 30. *Leather Loin Covering. c.1450 B.C. Redrawn from Reproduction of Wall Painting in Tomb of Rek-Mi-Re. (Metropolitan Museum of Art)*

sides. The panels were held in this position by ingenious arrangements of girdles. Sometimes a girdle resembling the old loin skirt was wrapped once around the body, drawn taut and tied, the ends left hanging down the front. Longer girdles encircled the body twice and reached almost to the ankles in back. In Fig. 31 the girdle is long enough to be tied with a great loop which falls to the knee. Both ends of the girdle are visible, a short one at the left of the waistline and the other appearing as a point beneath the loop. The basic kimono of this costume is short; its lower edge is covered by the girdle.

This kimono type of garment could also be secured in place without a girdle. The front and back edges were overlapped as described above. The selvages of the back panel were then caught at waist level or

slightly above and twisted into points a few inches long; these points could be knotted in front to hold the garment in place, as shown in Fig. 32.

Another fashion of the empire period consisted of a long, sheer skirt worn over an opaque short loin skirt. It often fell to the bend of the knee or to the calf in the back, but was pulled upward in a sharply slanting line toward the front. The cloth of the outer skirt is customarily represented as pleated.

At times this medium-length skirt is pictured with a full end hanging like an apron down the front, as if the wide girdle of the kimono costume were worn with nothing under it. A relief of the Amarna period (1375–1358 B.C.) in the Metropolitan Museum suggests such a practice. A second figure in the same composition wears the falling end in a puff above the knees, the other end reaching to the bottom of the skirt. This puffed detail, which was a characteristic fashion of Akhenaten's reign, must have continued in use, since the Metropolitan statue of the kneeling Haremhab records it. During the Twentieth Dynasty the resem-

blance to an apron became more pronounced, and gayly colored ribbons edged the sides of the spreading panel.

A shirt and skirt combination was also worn during the empire period, the short sleeved kimono-cut shirt being tucked under a loin skirt of variable length. Sometimes these shirts were transparent. In one example

FIG. 31. *Basic Kimono Type Garment with Elaborate Girdling. Relief from Tomb of Eighteenth Dynasty. 1580–1350 B.C. (Gulbenkian Foundation)*

FIG. 32. *King Seti I Wearing Kimono-Cut Garment with Royal Apron. 1313–1292 B.C. (Archeological Museum, Florence, Alinari Photograph)*

a shirt of a subtle delphinium blue is worn with a long sheer skirt over the traditional short loin skirt.

THE MILITARY

Military dress at this time had considerable variety. What might be called a battle jacket, short sleeved and kimono-cut, was worn by kings of the empire. Wide bands extending from the front edges crossed and wrapped around the body and tied in center front. These were highly decorated, the enfolding bands giving the effect of sheltering wings of the sacred hawk or vulture; other religious symbols appeared in the decorative patterns. Since the queen wore the vulture headdress to ensure protection to her husband while he was engaged in war, the designs on his costume probably were placed there for the same purpose. A loin skirt in feather pattern and the royal apron were worn with this jacket. The blue military helmet was restricted to royalty but not to active warfare. Ramses II, otherwise fash-

Fig. 33. *Ramses II in Draped Sheer Pleated Costume and Royal War Helmet. 1292–1225 B.C. (Turin Museum, Anderson Photograph—Alinari)*

ionably dressed, wears the helmet as an accessory in Fig. 33.

The soldier in the ranks during the empire period wore a short skirt for mobility, with an elongated heart-shaped device, probably made of leather, suspended from the waist in front for protection.[5]

OTHER FASHION FEATURES

The empire period brought with it changes in accessories and more frequent use of articles from previous periods.

THE ROYAL APRON. The royal apron, which is possibly related to the tasseled ornament of Narmer (Fig. 7), became a ubiquitous symbol of authority during the empire period (Fig. 32). It consisted of a group of narrow tapered and patterned panels, flanked by shorter streamers on each side, ending sometimes with a border of uraei across the bottom or a single uraeus at each lower corner. These aprons were richly colored but their real nature is unknown. Judging by the marvelous flexible woman's headdress in the Metropolitan Museum, the aprons might well have been a jeweler's handiwork, employing gold and inlay of glass and semiprecious stones. This royal symbol was suspended from a wide belt of harmonizing color and design.

At this time also, the king often posed with other symbols of power: the crook, an indication of his authority over the shepherds of his realm, and the flail, a comparable sign of his authority over the agricultural citizens. In Fig. 33 Ramses II carries the crook in his right hand; the flail, originally in his left hand, has disappeared.

FANS. The king's fanbearers were chosen from his closest friends and were usually of royal rank; they carried fans of two sorts: (1) a simple feather held aloft on a long staff; this was also a symbol of rank and was employed not only by the king but also by other high officials such as governors of

[5] *Ibid.*, p. 544.

provinces; (2) a large semicircular fan of ostrich feathers carried in royal processions; this was not only a beautiful insignia of power but provided a welcome relief from heat and insects.

WIGS. Wigs changed in form in the empire period, employing greater detail in the arrangement of the forepart; the lower edge characteristically dipped toward the front (Figs. 31 and 32). The revolutionary king Akhenaten wore a cloth headdress made in the form of a snood which completely enclosed his wig (Fig. 34).

SANDALS. Sandals came into more common use during this period, especially by kings and noblemen. The man's sandal, slightly pointed at the toe, is shown on the statue of Ramses II (Fig. 33). The upturned points of the sandals of Seti I (Fig. 32) probably reflected eastern Mediterranean influence. Tutankhamen's sandals were encrusted with gold.

JEWELRY. As can be readily observed in the illustrations, jewelry was worn more frequently and the designs were heavier, wider, and bolder than during the Old and

FIG. 34. *Akhenaten, 1375–1358* B.C. *Redrawn from Sculptured Figure of the King.* (*Cairo Museum*)

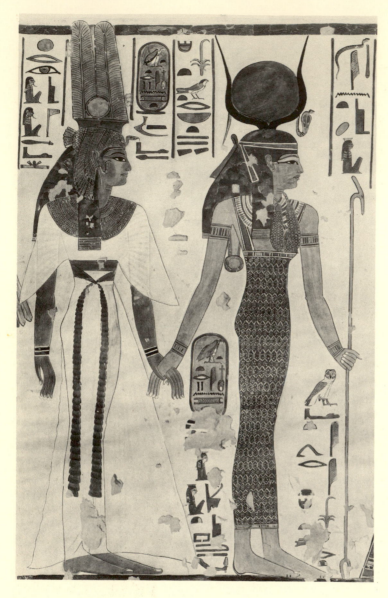

FIG. 35. *Queen Nefretiri, Wife of Ramses II, Wearing Kimono Costume with Narrow Girdle Placed High. 1292–1225 B.C. Reproduction of a Wall Painting in Her Tomb. (Metropolitan Museum of Art)*

Middle Kingdoms. The jewelry found in King Tutankhamen's tomb is truly fabulous.

Women's Costumes

During the empire period, the women, like the men, continued to wear the simple costume of earlier periods on state occasions. But this sheath gown was not an artless little dress, as proven by the statue of Queen Ahmose-Nofretere, first queen of the Eighteenth Dynasty, in the Oriental Institute of the University of Chicago. The material bears an imbricated design of overlapping feathers, and the head of a lioness adorns the midriff. A deep collar and broad armlets add to the rich effect.

No doubt the women of lower rank continued to wear the plain sheath gown, and women engaged in arduous labor retained the short skirt noted earlier. But queens and wives of the nobility indulged themselves with a variety of draped costumes of hand-pleated white linen that must have kept a battery of laundries occupied continuously.

The kimono arrangement was worn by women as well as men, except that instead of the wide girdle women wore a narrow sash tied at a high waist level, with long streamers falling below the knees. Figure 35 shows Queen Nefretiri, favorite wife of Ramses II, thus costumed. In another painting in her tomb, she wears the kimono costume with overlapping edges, the selvages of the back being twisted and knotted between her breasts.

A two-piece costume of the empire period consisted of a skirt and shawl combination that was relatively easy to arrange and wear. But many of the sheer pleated costumes were complicated in drapery, studied and beautiful in line, and must have required trained lady's maids to arrange them. The procedure seems to have been comparable to that still employed in draping Indian saris. These draped costumes are distinguishable from the kimono type by the arm coverage. In the kimono style both arms are covered to the same length and width. But the draped costume, where the simplest method required the least yardage, was usually unpleated and left the right arm and breast bare. More complicated styles employed much greater lengths of fabric and were pleated; one arm was covered as in the kimono costume, but the end of the yardage fell over and down from the other arm, its free fringed edge often reaching below the hip.

A brief explanation of both the simple and more complex types may help to make clear how these effects were achieved. The statuette of Lady Tuty shown in Fig. 36 exemplifies the simpler arrangement. Starting below the right breast the cloth encircles the body at that level, passes under the right arm a second time, angles upward across the back and over the left shoulder, and then slants downward across the front, where it is knotted to the initial corner of the fabric. This gives coverage to the left shoulder and arm but leaves the right arm and breast bare.

A second painting of Queen Nefretiri (Fig. 37) depicts her in a more involved draped costume. Again starting below the right breast the cloth is brought around the back under the left arm to center front. As in draping the Indian sari, a group of pleats is placed in the upper edge and fastened

FIG. 36. *Statuette of Lady Tuty Wearing Simply Draped Costume and Ointment Cone. 1411–1375* B.C. *(Brooklyn Museum)*

with pins or an inconspicuous belt. The cloth is then continued under the right arm, across the back and under the left arm a second time. It is then drawn upward toward the right shoulder with the fullness placed in studied pleats. At high waist level the fabric is completely reversed so that the edge which has formed the hem line now faces toward center front. This edge is then brought around the neck and over the left shoulder back to the starting point. The two corners are tied near the left breast. Figure 38 shows a reconstruction of such a draped costume.

Reversing the cloth in this way balances the lengths of the two long edges, providing

FIG. 37. *Queen Nefretiri Wearing Elaborately Draped Costume of Empire Period. 1292–1225* B.C. *Reproduction of Wall Painting in Her Tomb. (Metropolitan Museum of Art)*

greater length and thus more ease to the outer edge of the cape-like portion. A similar procedure may be followed in draping a wide girdle which encircles the body twice.

Both Houston[6] and Heuzey[7] have done much research on the reconstruction of these

[6] Mary Houston, *Ancient Egyptian, Mesopotamian and Persian Costume and Decoration*, 2nd ed., A. & C. Black, London, 1954, pp. 88–93.
[7] Leon Heuzey, *op. cit.*, plates XXVI–XXIX.

FIG. 38. *Reconstruction of Draped Costume of Queen Nefretiri (Fig. 37) Without Sash.*

draped costumes. Their books are recommended for a more complete understanding of the full range of costumes of the empire period.

WIGS AND HEADDRESSES. Women's wigs reached their greatest volume during this period, often enveloping the shoulders (Fig. 36). Ornamentation became more elaborate and as diverse as that illustrated in Fig. 32. The decoration of the wig of the goddess Isis probably reflected the fashion of the time. In Fig. 35, Queen Nefretiri and the goddess Isis make a startling note with their deep bright blue wigs. The elegant and beautiful flexible gold headdress inlaid with carnelian and colored glass is one of the wonders of the Metropolitan Egyptian collection (Fig. 39).

Figure 35 illustrates the vulture headdress with the two feathers of Amon and the sun disc of Ra superimposed. On the same plate the goddess Isis wears the horns of the sacred cow Hathor encircling the moon disc.

The most beautiful queen in Egyptian history was Queen Nefertiti, wife of Akhenaten, the religious reformer (Fig. 40). She wore a crown unlike any other royal headdress of ancient Egypt. Moreover, she had the courage to wear it without a wig. Her blue crown is banded with a polychromatic ribbon and highlighted with an upturned band of gold across the front. The uraeus head is missing; only the design of the snake's body remains.

NECKLACES. Necklaces were enlarged in the empire period, as Figs. 35 and 37 show. Made of semiprecious stones and faïence beads, they were very heavy, even though they usually extended only from shoulder to shoulder. To hold them in place and to make them more comfortable to wear, they were often supplied with a counterpoise, an example of which is shown hanging below the shoulder of the goddess in Fig. 35. A thick necklace of multiple strands of round

Fig. 39. *Headdress of Lady at Court During Reign of Thuthmosis III. 1501–1447 B.C. Gold Inlaid with Carnelian and Glass. (Metropolitan Museum of Art)*

beads was one of the symbols of the goddess Isis. She also holds a staff with a top patterned after a jackal's head. Erman[8] says that this was originally the sceptre of the gods but later was used by individuals as a walking stick.

COSMETICS. The Egyptians were fastidious to a high degree. Cleanliness of both body and linen was regarded as a social necessity. Incense and myrrh, the perfumes of Araby, attar of lotus and jasmine have long been associated with Egypt. Their ointment jars and mirrors are beautifully

8 Erman, *op. cit.*, p. 229.

wrought. Wall paintings show guests amusing themselves by applying cosmetics.

One well-known cartoon shows an Egyptian using her lipstick. It was common practice to make up the eyes heavily, both to accent the expression and to afford protection from the sun. The use of kohl is evidenced by its presence in containers found in the tombs. Although the hair was clipped short, formulas have been found purporting to prevent the hair from turning gray or falling out.

Unguents were necessary to keep the skin from parching in the hot dry climate.

Erman points out that laborers were paid in oil as well as grain.[9] Unguents were so much a part of their lives that on festive occasions seated guests are shown with cones saturated with perfumed ointment on their heads. (Lady Tuty is provided with one in Fig. 36.) As the evening progressed the melting unguent oozed down over the scalp onto the body, releasing its fragrance.[10]

It has been suggested that the golden color of the tops of the costumes at these festivities was due to saturation with oil.

[9] *Ibid.*, p. 230.
[10] *Ibid.*, p. 231.

Fabrics of Ancient Egypt

Costumes of the early Egyptians were largely made of linen, matting and leather being used to supplement the products of flax. Wool-bearing sheep were brought into Egypt only in the empire period. The early Egyptians, like the Hebrews, probably considered wool unclean.

Linen was used from the earliest recorded time; by 3000 B.C. cloth was produced with a warp count of 160 and weft of 120 per inch. The fabric was not only fine in texture but was amazingly wide. The

Cairo Museum exhibits a tunic made of material which measures 60 inches from selvage to selvage. Fabrics were woven many yards in length.

Although such colors as red, yellow, blue, and blue-green were used in the textiles of the Old Kingdom, white seems to have predominated. Linen is difficult to dye in fast color, and the fact that the Egyptians did not know the use of mordants may account for the predominance of white. Laundering was, therefore, an important service, and skill in hand pleating was developed to a high degree. The Cairo Museum possesses an example of pleating on cross grain in groups of four $\frac{1}{8}$ inch pleats. Another piece is pleated solidly in $\frac{3}{16}$ inch pleats. The most elaborate specimen has a combination of vertical pleats with horizontal herringbone pleating superimposed at intervals. The cross pleating of a tunic of the Sixth Dynasty in the Boston Museum also affords eloquent evidence of the launderer's skill.

Some pattern weaving in the form of simple plaids is shown on several Old Kingdom statues, though it is impossible to tell whether the interesting stripes were made of contrasting color or of heavier cordlike threads. The technique of weaving fabric with a looped pile was practiced by the Egyptians during the empire period, though it started as early as the Middle Kingdom. From Tutankhamen's tomb come examples of embroidered and tapestry-woven designs on garments, as well as the application of thin gold motifs, forerunners of sequins. Much beading was done on both fabric and netting which was worn as an overskirt or wide girdle.

In Egypt, as in all other civilizations, the textile arts largely determined and molded the style of the costumes of the people. The history of Egypt beyond the empire period was for the most part that of foreign domination. The Libyans, neighbors to the northwest, were the first to gain control of the Nile. Their rule was followed for a brief period by that of the Ethiopians to the south and the Assyrians from upper Mesopotamia. The Twenty-sixth Dynasty (663–525 B.C.) brought a renaissance of the arts of the Old and Middle Kingdoms, but nothing new or vital. Persians, Greeks, and Romans conquered Egypt in turn. Thus, with little opportunity or incentive to create, Egypt's unique cultural contribution to the world ended with the empire period.

2

Mesopotamia

Mesopotamia, the land of the two historic rivers, the Tigris and the Euphrates, has long been known as the fertile crescent. Within its borders lay the garden of Eden[1] and the setting of many Old Testament incidents. Its cultural development parallels rather closely that of the Nile valley and some archeologists believe there may have been communication between the two at an early date.

Settled by invaders from the highlands of Persia, from Cilicia within the territory of modern Turkey, and from Syria, the lower area near the Persian Gulf was, by 3000 B.C., already known as Sumer. The Biblical flood, leaving a deposit as thick as 11 feet in some areas, obscured this early phase from recorded history.[2] In the Babylonian account of this event in the British Museum, Noah's role was enacted by Uta-Napishtim and the locale was Shurippak instead of Babylon.[3]

Our rich and diverse heritage from this region has come down to us through devious channels via the successive empires of the Babylonians, Assyrians, Persians, Greeks, and Romans. Various phases of Mesopotamian art, religion, law, and language have been absorbed and transmitted until it is difficult to trace specific ingredients. The division of our day into multiples of six and ten is certainly one obvious legacy.

Dates within the 1500 years following the flood are chaotic at best, and modern archeological discoveries continue to upset one chronological table after another. The dates given by Dr. Svend Pallis,[4] based on information revealed by most recent finds, together with careful synchronization of new evidence with proven dating, are used in this chapter. For the most part, however, the sequence of the fashion story remains undisturbed by these shifts in date. The one important exception is the date assigned to the magnificent contents of the Royal Tombs of Ur. There is now general agreement that they belong near the middle of the third millennium B.C.

[1] Genesis 2, 8–14.
[2] C. Leonard Woolley, *The Development of Sumerian Art*, Scribner, New York, 1935, p. 32.
[3] British Museum, *A Guide to the Babylonian and Assyrian Antiquities*, 3rd ed., Harrison and Sons, Ltd., London, 1922, p. 220.

[4] Svend Pallis, *The Antiquity of Irak*, Ejnar Munksgaard, Ltd., Copenhagen, 1956, pp. 483–484.

Out of the confusion of long, unfamiliar, and unpronounceable names, a few Sumerian notables project themselves, either because of important political achievements or because some unknown sculptor left a memorable monument. The list includes, from the Royal Tombs of Ur, King Meskalamdug and Queen Shubad; from among the rulers of Ur and Lagash, Urnina and Eannatum I; from the third dynasty of Uruk (Erech), Lugalzaggisi, who conquered the last of Urnina's line; from the third dynasty of Kish, Queen Kuban and her grandson, Ur-Ilbaba. To students of costume, among the most

FIG. 42. *Mother Goddess from Tell Asmar, Iraq. c.2800 B.C. (Iraq Museum, Baghdad, Photograph, Oriental Institute, University of Chicago)*

significant items of the period are the little statuettes of Tell Asmar and Khafaje, which Frankfort[5] dates between 2900 and 2700 B.C. Following the Sumerians came the great Sargon of the Agade dynasty, Gudea of Lagash (Neo-Sumerian), Hammurabi of the First Babylonian Dynasty, and the conquerors and builders of Assyria.

As with the Egyptians, the surviving record of the Mesopotamians is closely related to their religious observances. For example, the statuettes of Tell Asmar include a god of fertility, a goddess and a priest, as well as lay citizens. These last were created in the belief that their presence in the temple would be a constant reminder to the gods of

FIG. 41. *God of Fertility from Tell Asmar, Iraq. c.2800 B.C. (Iraq Museum, Baghdad, Photograph, Oriental Institute, University of Chicago)*

[5] Henri Frankfort, *Sculpture of the 3rd Millennium B.C.*, University of Chicago Press, 1939, p. 9.

FIG. 43. *Female Head Dressed with Turban.* c.2800–2675 B.C. *From Shara Temple. (Iraq Museum, Baghdad, Photograph, Oriental Institute, University of Chicago)*

the existence of the people represented, in whose behalf they would serve as petitioners. Water, earth, and sky were deified. Iananna, Sumerian goddess of love and war, is more familiar as Ishtar of the Bible. Gilgamish was the great hero, capable of performing the impossible, even as Hercules, who may have been fashioned after him.

Such sacrifices as burying alive dozens of retainers with deceased royal personages is shocking to us, but less so than modern warfare. Hammurabi's code of laws, based in part at least upon previous codes, clarified practices of long standing and made them official and available to the public. Its provisions for such matters as property rights, burglary, military service, agriculture (water rights and responsibilities), commerce, dowries, adultery, divorce, adoption, debts, and wages reveal these people as quite similar to citizenry anywhere.

SUMERIAN COSTUME, 3000–2300 B.C.

The earliest costume of the Sumerians, as with the Egyptians, was a waist string wrapped around the body one or more times, ending in hanging tabs. This was succeeded by an intercrural cloth which, however, gave little more coverage than the string.

One of the first carefully recorded fashions is the Man with Feathers, a bas-relief dated about 3000 B.C., now in the Louvre. Two upright feathers and a headband give the gentleman an air of distinction; a bordered diamond-patterned wraparound skirt reaches from waist to ankles. Following him closely are three large-eyed bearded gentlemen in spreading knee-length skirts decorated with a deep border of fringe.

Tell Asmar and Khafaje, 2900–2700 B.C.

Frankfort's finds at Tell Asmar and Khafaje pick up the fashions described above, with several variations.[6] The statuettes, he believes, predate the Royal Tombs of Ur, that is they are before 2500 B.C. (Figs. 41 and 42). This means that a smoothly fitting, obviously sewed garment was worn earlier than the tiered skirts usually associated with Sumerians. Frankfort points out that weaving was a well-known craft at the beginning of this period. Copper axes wrapped in cloth, dating from the fourth millennium B.C., were found at Susa. These few fragments of linen are almost as fine as the best we produce today. The elaborately wrapped turbans on female heads (Fig. 43) could have been achieved only with lightweight finely woven fabric. Coarse needles have been found—proof of the practice of sewing.

[6] *Ibid.,* pp. 49–55.

Men's Costume

The usual costume in the earlier part of the Sumerian period was a wraparound skirt reaching to mid-calf or farther, overlapping at left back and closed with three to five fastenings. The god of fertility, shown in Fig. 41, wears a costume identical with that of the petitioners, his divine nature being indicated by enormous eyes and his symbols on the base upon which he stands. The skirts were finished with fringe or petal-like tabs of material which vary in depth from rather narrow, as those carved on a statue in Copenhagen, to over half the length of the skirt. The nature of the fringe is uncertain, though it is obviously a separate ornamental finish sewn onto the lower edge of the garment on the Copenhagen sculpture. It might, however, be long and adjustable. The front fringe is sometimes tucked into the girdle.

A few instances have been found where the fringe hangs hula-skirt fashion, from the waist down. Other variations include an allover overlapping diamond or triangle design. The seated figure of the steward Ebih-il in the Louvre wears a skirt closely resembling a fleece. One of the most interesting statues shows a combination of deep fringe topped by a peplum of allover triangular design (Fig. 44).

Nearly all of these skirts were cinched with a thick round girdle fastened at the back, with short ends hanging to the hipline. There seems to be no distinction in dress which might indicate rank or function except in the case of the kneeling priest, who wears only the multiple-wrapped waist string.

Men usually wore their hair long and parted in the center, with the ends brought forward over the shoulders; sometimes they appear bald or shaven. Frankfort thinks they probably clipped their hair for participation in religious rites and wore wigs on other occasions, for the same man is shown in both styles. Some faces are bearded and some beardless, the latter probably youths. As in Egypt, a mustache is rarely seen. No footwear is shown.

Women's Wear

The women wore a simple costume but gave their imaginations free reign regarding hair and headdress. Their single garment ap-

Fig. 44. *Male Figure from Khafaje, First Half of Third Millennium*, B.C. *(Iraq Museum, Baghdad, Photograph, Oriental Institute, University of Chicago)*

pears to be a shawl, one corner of which is thrown backward over the left shoulder, the main part being drawn across the chest under the right arm, thence upward across the back and over the left shoulder, covering the left arm but allowing comfortable use of the left hand. A simple band or hem seems to be the only finish, as shown on Fig. 42, a statue of the mother goddess. On another statue draped in the same way, the entire surface of the shawl is covered with the triangle design shown in Fig. 44, which might be either a woven fabric with a fleeced surface or fur.

The Sumerian woman's hairdress of this period was extremely complex. On a female head from Khafaje the hair seems to have been drawn up to the crown of the head, then braided into four to six braids from the crown to the base of the skull. Here the small braids were combined into one huge one which was wound around the head, passing across the top as a coronet, the ends being disposed of in a variety of ways. There are numerous examples of this style, which is both dignified and flattering. The turbans worn by the women were masterpieces of draping; it seems impossible that the wearer could have arranged her own (Fig. 43).

Cosmetic containers were also found at Khafaje.

LAGASH, UR, URUK,
2459–2289 B.C.

Men's Costume

THE KAUNAKES. This garment with many tiers of fringe has aroused much con-

FIG. 45. *Urnina, King of Lagash, and Family. Ur Dynasty I. 2459–2443* B.C. (*Louvre*)

troversy. Frankfort[7] has simplified matters by declaring it a late arrival in the costume story, associated with a more realistic form of sculpture, which places it later than the Tell Asmar and Khafaje figures. This automatically puts Urnina, who wears such a garment, at a later date. Pallis[8] dates the beginning of Urnina's reign as 2459 B.C. (Fig. 45).

The construction of the kaunakes is another bone of contention. Before discovery of the earlier, simpler, yet undeniably woven garments of Tell Asmar and Khafaje, it was thought that the kaunakes was made by draping a sheepskin or two around the loins, the tiered effect resulting from the primitive sculptor's method of indicating fleece. We now know that the wearers knew how to weave, make fringe, and sew. It is possible, then, that the tiered garment had a smoothly woven foundation to which rows of fringe were attached; or the fringe may have been knotted in during the weaving process in the manner of oriental and modern rugs. That would explain the four-, five-, and six-tiered skirts. Still, when the fringe suddenly spirals from the upper row of the skirt across the chest and over the left shoulder, we wish the sculptor had been more realistic. Is the model wearing a two-piece garment consisting of tiered skirt and fringed stole? Eannatum, son of Urnina, is clearly represented on his stele (sculptured monument) wearing a tiered skirt and a separate animal skin draped diagonally from shoulder to hem.

The backs of some kaunakes-clad statues show a bunching, bustle effect, which might result from the draping of a stiff, bulky fabric as it was drawn upward from the back under the right arm and thence across the chest over the left shoulder. However, the tiers would certainly be disarranged in such case. People of the intelligence and experience of these early Sumerians were surely capable of cutting a garment to the desired shape and attaching the fringe in orderly rows.

In the lower register of Eannatum's Stele of the Vultures the soldiers wear the kaunakes and well-shaped helmets. In the upper register they advance in perfect formation, their huge overlapping shields reaching from neck to ankle for maximum protection. The king's helmet is distinguished by a false chignon, bound in place by a band which surrounds the crown of the helmet. Parrot describes both helmets and shields as made of leather.[9]

Another war scene, the Mosaic Standard, now in the British Museum, came from the Royal Cemetery of Ur. (In the Pallis chronology the tombs are dated about 2400 B.C.)[10] The soldiers in this wonderful composition wear helmets with chin straps, dagged skirts similar to those of Tell Asmar, and capes, probably of leather, fastened by a strap across the chest. In the banquet scene on the opposite side of the Standard, the king alone wears the kaunakes, the guests being clad in deeply tabbed skirts. King and guests are clean shaven, including their heads. Here is evidence of the long duration of the skirt style seen first at Khafaje (2900–2400 B.C.); at least during part of that period this style and the kaunakes were worn contemporaneously.

The most elegant accessory of male attire found in the Royal Tombs is the gold wig-helmet of King Meskalamdug, fashioned in the form of the leather helmet with a false chignon; in fact it appears to be a copy of the fashionable hairdress meticulously wrought in gold. Holes pierced in the outer edge indicate that some sort of lining had been attached to it.

Women's Costumes

When we examine the tiered costumes of Sumerian women we are forced to as-

---

[7] *Ibid.*, p. 51.
[8] Pallis, *op. cit.*, p. 483.

[9] André Parrot, *Sumer*, Thames and Hudson, London, 1960, pp. 135–136.
[10] Pallis, *op. cit.*, p. 483.

FIG. 46. *Woman Holding Aryballus from Tello.* c.2500 B.C. (*Louvre*)

FIG. 47. *Head (Reconstruction). Diadem, Hair Ornament, and Earrings from Royal Tombs of Ur.* c.2400 B.C. (*Museum of the University of Pennsylvania*)

sume that cutting and sewing were employed, especially when the fringe forms a perfect yoke pattern about the neck and covers both arms with what may be a cape, though on the statue it gives the appearance of sleeves (Fig. 46). A bust of a Sumerian woman in the Louvre shows a fringed garment with a high V-shaped neck, finished with a corded and decorated edge. Her hair is dressed compactly with a broad headband and a chignon at the back of the neck. Parrot refers to her as the woman with a kaunakes.[11] In an intermediate stage between the goddess of Fig. 42 and the female worshiper from Tello (Fig. 46), the fringe spirals from the upper tier of the skirt over the left shoulder

[11] Parrot, *op. cit.,* pp. 142–143.

and arm as on the men's costume (See Urnina's wife in Fig. 45).

The jewelry of the Sumerians is more familiar to us than their costumes. Many excellent examples have been recovered. From Khafaje came beads of alabaster, rock crystal, lapis lazuli, carnelian, and gold. Pendants in the form of animals predate our charm bracelets by some 4500 years. The Royal Tombs of Ur held the richest hoard of jewelry yet discovered in Sumeria. The University of Pennsylvania has many of the items, including one of Queen Shubad's diadems, a regal hair ornament, and a pair of dramatic earrings, each composed of two large hollow gold crescents (Fig. 47). Woolley's official report of the excavation of the

FIG. 48. *Bronze Head, Possibly Sargon I. c.2300 B.C. (Iraq Museum, Baghdad, Photograph, Oriental Institute Univerity of Chicago)*

Royal Cemetery[12] shows page after page of colorful necklaces of gold and semiprecious stones, rings, pins topped with balls of lapis lazuli mounted in gold, and miniature gold animals which decorated one of Queen Shubad's diadems. A shoulder cape composed of strands of beads covered the queen's shoulders and upper arms.

THE AKKADIAN DYNASTY, 2303–2108 B.C.

Queen Kuban and her grandson Ur-Ilbaba represent the last of the Sumerian Dynasty III of Kish. The Queen, the only woman in Sumerian history to rule in her own right, began as an ale seller—about the only career open to women at that time. Although women, other than priestesses, were free to patronize taverns, such an occupation was not held in high repute. How Kuban managed the leap from tavern to throne is not known, but it must have been a fascinating bit of history. The great Sargon appears upon the scene as cupbearer to Ur-Ilbaba. Dissatisfied with the status of his people, who were of Semitic origin, Sargon led a successful revolt against the reigning house and thus initiated the Akkadian Dy-

[12] C. Leonard Woolley, *Ur Excavations*, Oxford, London, 1934, vol. II, plates 128–147.

nasty. In his own words, "Ishtar looked upon me and found me good and I reigned for fifty years."

The bronze head shown in Fig. 48, thought by some authorities to be a likeness of King Sargon, displays a hair arrangement comparable to the design of the gold helmet of the Sumerian king, Meskalamdug. A knot of hair juts out at the back, while a braid and band simulate a crown. Sargon's grandson, Naramsin, wears kaunakes in one likeness; on his stele, however, as leader of his army, he seems to be wearing little more than a sash, its broad fringed end hanging down in front. A peaked helmet protects his head while a pair of bull's horns springing upward from the sides of his helmet declare his affinity with the gods. Well-designed sandals protect his feet—one of the earliest representations of footwear in Mesopotamia. His long hair falls back of his shoulders and he must have taken pride in his luxuriant beard. Heavy bracelets and a cone-shaped tiara are worn as accessories with his kaunakes costume.

NEO-SUMERIAN PERIOD, 2130–2016 B.C.

Under the light touch of Akkadian rule some of the city-states asserted themselves.

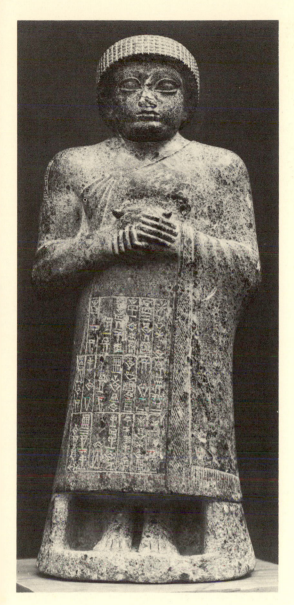

the right chest indicate where the opposite corner of the shawl was tucked into the neckline.

the right chest indicate where the opposite corner of the shawl was tucked into the neckline.

Gudea's cap represents quite an innovation also. It seems to be of sheepskin and is probably of the finest quality of Persian lamb, with a tight curl. It consists of a low, round, comfortable fitting crown with a sharply upturned brim, not unlike our sailor caps, but larger and less casual. The allover pattern of coils has also been explained as an applied decoration, possibly in the nature of small gold discs.

A woman contemporary with Gudea, sometimes identified as his wife, displays a comparable reserve in both line and ornamentation (Fig. 50). Heuzey[13] interprets the sculptured lines of this statue as follows: the center of one edge of the shawl is placed high on the chest; the material is then drawn under both arms to center back, where the two corners are crossed and thence brought forward over the shoulders. This creates the two vertical edges of the front design. Experimentation will show that it is well-nigh impossible to reproduce the neckline of the statue by this method without some means of anchoring it in place.

The dog-collar fashion shown in Fig. 50, consisting of several metal bands, has a precedent in a real one of different design found by Frankfort. A sheer head scarf confines the hair.

FIG. 49. *Gudea of Lagash.* 2130 B.C. *(Ny Carlsberg Glyptotek, Copenhagen)*

Thus Gudea of Lagash, 2130 B.C., became a distinguished leader of the Neo-Sumerian period. The many statues we have of him indicate the adoption of the shawl as practically Neo-Sumerian uniform (Fig. 49). With one corner of the shawl falling forward over the left shoulder, the bulk of the fabric was wrapped around the body under the right arm, over the left shoulder, and again under the right arm. Draped lines on

THE FIRST BABYLONIAN DYNASTY, 1894–1595 B.C.

Hammurabi's costume shown in Fig. 51 shows no change from Gudea's except that his cap is plain. Small figurine plaques in the Louvre portray the average citizen. A musician wears a wraparound loin skirt with a hemline slanting from above the knee in front to the top of the calf in back. His

[13] Leon and Jacques Heuzey, *Histoire du costume dans l'antiquité classique*, Paris, Les Belle Lettres, 1935, plate 42.

short hair and beard are also characteristic of two wrestlers and a carpenter. Recently discovered wall paintings of Mari, from the eighteenth century B.C., do much to bring this period to life. Here a fisherman wears a pale-blue loin skirt, knee length and tabbed along the diagonal overlapping edge and hemline. A painting depicting the investiture of a king shows his majesty in a short white loin skirt and white folded shawl draped from the left shoulder across the back, under the right arm and over the left upper arm. The king pouring a libation before a god wears a gay costume like the tiered garment of the god Shamash shown in Fig. 51. The exciting difference is supplied by color. The rows of fringe employ sequences of tile red, grey, gold, and white yarns repeated regu-

FIG. 50. *Female Figure of Era of Gudea. (Louvre)*

larly, but no two rows of fringe match vertically in color. The headdress consists of a white cap with high round crown and narrow upturned brim.

Our information regarding women's costume in this period is limited to that worn by goddesses. Those participating in the investiture mentioned above wear the kaunakes in the same bizarre color scheme the king wears. An outstanding statue of a goddess from Mari has an arresting personality and her dress is quite modern in appearance: kimono-cut bodice with short tabbed sleeves, fitted midriff, and slim sheath-like skirt. Her hair and headdress suggest her importance. The ends of her abundant hair are massed on her shoulders. Her large, bulky headdress has a space-age look, due to the huge horns

FIG. 51. *Hammurabi Before the Sun God Shamash. 1790–1750 B.C. Top of Column on Which Hammurabi's Code Is Inscribed. (Louvre)*

which form the base and jut upward at center front. A five-strand necklace of large beads forms a dog collar and bib.

ASSYRIA, 1380–612 B.C.

Asserting herself first under Ashur-Uballit in the fourteenth century B.C., Assyria had become a strong political power by the end of the twelfth century B.C., with the accession of Tiglath Pileser I, 1116–1093 B.C. The Assyrians dominated Mesopotamia, extending their empire from the Persian Gulf to the Mediterranean and southward into Egypt. According to their own boastful accounts, they dealt with the conquered tribes most cruelly and burned city after city to the ground, not even sparing Babylon. Whole populations were tortured and murdered or deported to foreign soil—the fate of the ten lost tribes of Israel. The Assyrians must have had great organizational ability to have raised, equipped, and maintained such large and efficient military and governing forces. They left remains of vast building projects at Nimrud (Ashurnasirpal II, 883–859 B.C.), Khorsobad (Sargon II, 722–705 B.C.) and Nineveh (Sennacherib, 705–681 B.C. and Ashurbanipal, 668–625 B.C.), whence came the sculptures which are our chief source of information about what they wore.

FIG. 52. *King Ashurnasirpal II. 883–859 B.C.* (British Museum)

Men's Costume

From the austere draped shawl of Hammurabi, taste changed to ostentation in ornamentation, though the basic shapes were simple. The kings are shown wearing tunics and shawls completely covered with pattern, which many have been tapestry-woven or embroidered. The tunic appears to be of kimono cut: the sleeves are short and the body of the garment is tubular, reaching to the ankles among the upper class but shortened to knee length for active military duty, hunting, and day labor.

Fringed shawls or yardage of fringe used as girdles or insignia of office are the trademark of formal Assyrian costume. Elaborately mounted tassels hang from corners of shawls and baldrics (shoulder straps from which swords were suspended). Carefully groomed masses of curled hair and beards give the Assyrians a heavy hirsute look which contrasts sharply with the lithe, linen-clad Egyptians.

In Fig. 52 King Ashurnasirpal II is dressed for participation in a religious ritual, one of his functions as king. His shawl is folded off-center lengthwise; after being draped about the body from waist to ankle it is brought upward in a spiral to cover his figure from waist to shoulders, forming a sling for the left arm. A girdle steadies the unsewn fabric. Crook and dagger are symbols of his office. The heavy bracelet is typical of Assyrian jewelry.

King Sargon II is shown wearing a short-sleeved tunic finished with fringe at the hemline. The pattern is marked off in squares. The shawl which envelops his body, the corners falling over the shoulders toward the front, has an allover rosette design. Wool is the fabric most often recorded throughout Mesopotamian history, and the Assyrians favored rich and brilliant colors.

The tiara, symbol of office, was a high fez-shaped headdress formed by alternating rows of patterned and plain bands. An inverted cone on top (Fig. 53), provided extra height. Infulae, or ribbon-like streamers, fell from the headdress down the back. Large earrings, bulky bracelets, and armlets harmonize with the heavy, muscular, masculine forms. Swords and sheaths were handsomely

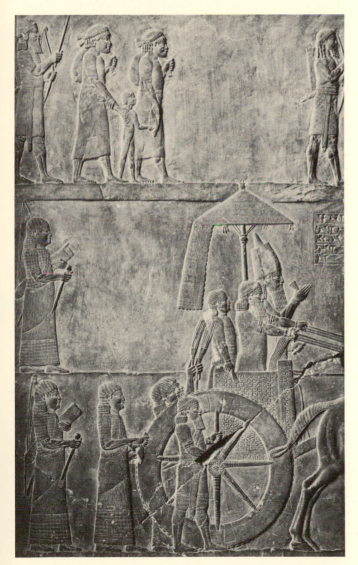

Fig. 53. *King Ashurbanipal in His War Chariot. 668–625 B.C. (British Museum)*

wrought. Sandals with functional counters are typical of Assyrian design.

On the Sargon relief referred to above the king's vizier wears a costume befitting his rank.. His long tunic is fringed at the hem and a deep band of fringe, after encircling his body from waist to knees, is drawn upward across his chest and over the left shoulder. His broad coronet is also indicative of his position. Lloyd[14] shows the fringe as red, worn over a white basic costume.

King Ashurbanipal in his royal war chariot, complete with curtained parasol and accompanied by carriers of fly whisks, is shown in Fig. 53. Note the costume of the attendant beside the chariot wheel: knee-length tunic, strip of fringe hanging from his girdle, decorated baldric, high laced boots, which appear later than sandals in Assyrian history, and fitted long hose, cross-gartered above the boot and bound below the knee. An archer in an upper register of this same relief wears a peaked helmet with ear flaps, a coat of mail made with overlapping metal scales (such scales have been found), and boots and hose similar to those just described.

Assyrian men below the rank of the officials who are profusely fringed and long-skirted are often shown with a small fringed shawl reaching from waist to kneecap. This was held in place with a leather girdle about 6 inches wide, secured in turn by a narrow belt, through which might be thrust one or two swords. A similar use of double girdling was current in southern Serbia prior to World War II.

Women's Costume

Our knowledge of the costume of Assyrian women comes from the very few likenesses which occur in Assyrian art; their rarity suggests the low status of women in this society. Women were the property of

[14] Seton Lloyd, *The Art of the Ancient Near East*, Frederick A. Praeger, Inc., New York, 1961, p. 199.

their fathers until marriage, when ownership passed to their husbands. According to Pallis,[15] wives were veiled, but not prostitutes or slave women, the purpose being to protect the husband's interest.

One of the rare scenes in sculpture featuring an Assyrian woman shows Ashurbanipal dining with his queen, Ashur-Sharrat. She wears a long fringe-trimmed tunic (Fig. 54) similar to that of her husband but with longer sleeves. A matching shawl is so draped that the final edge falls off the right arm, leaving it unhampered. She wears a dog collar, which had been fashionable as far back as Akkadian times, jeweled coronet,

[15] Pallis, *op. cit.*, p. 612.

FIG. 54. *Queen Ashur-Sharrat Dining with Husband, King Ashurbanipal. (British Museum)*

and bulky earrings and bracelets. Her low shoes completely cover her feet, the front part being patterned, the back appearing to be shaped and held in place by a thong such as is seen on primitive moccasins.

PERSIA, 600–300 B.C.

Though the fall of the Assyrian Empire in 612 B.C. was accomplished by combined forces of Medes and Babylonians, it was the Persians under the leadership of Cyrus II, the great, who reigned from 550–530 B.C., who conquered Media, Lydia, and Babylonia and so came into possession of the great empire amassed by the Assyrians. We are familiar with some of the rulers of the Achaemenian Dynasty (600–330 B.C.) through their wars with the Greeks: Darius I and the battle of Marathon; Xerxes (Ahasuerus of the Bible, associated with Esther), defeated at Salamis; and Darius III, killed in 330 B.C. after his defeat by Alexander the Great.

Men's Costume

Though they were masters of the Medes, the Persians respected them and treated them with more leniency than their other subjects. The Achaemenian kings even adopted the long flowing robe of the Medes, making it difficult to distinguish one from the other in the processions of the great Apadana stairway at Persepolis. The north side of the stairway, for instance, shows Median dignitaries alternating with Persians. The central figure (in Fig. 55) is a Mede in a kimono-cut costume similar to that of the Egyptians, that is, made of two lengths of cloth, but with selvages closed only from waist to hem. The carefully centered fullness is held by a narrow knotted sash. The generous width of the fabric provides full-length sleeves and the open selvages from shoulder to waist create a wide opening at the wrist. A handsome fluted cap lends an aristocratic air. However,

in another section of the same stairway, Persians are dressed in the same fashion as the Medes. This may be accounted for by the fact that the uniform of the king's 10,000 guards was an exact copy of the Median style. Judging from the frieze of archers found at Susa, both pattern and color were freely used.

Persia's contribution to the history of costume lies elsewhere. For example, Fig. 55 shows a gentleman from Media flanked by Persians. At the left is the national costume, consisting of a knee-length belted tunic with long set-in sleeves worn over trousers which fit within the low shoe tops. These are the first examples of trousers and set-in sleeves encountered in history.

The theory is that the Persians, living in rugged mountainous country and adept at horsemanship and hunting, first used animal skins for clothing. Adapting the shape of the pelt to the contour of his body, he learned gradually to make a second protective skin, as it were, for himself. In the process he evolved the craft of tailoring: the ability to cut shapes which would closely follow the lines of his body and sew them securely in place. The third man in the picture is wearing the first true coat. It is ankle length and has well-shaped sleeves and a tuxedo collar.

Probably it is presuming too much to give all the credit to one nationality, for among the tributary peoples being conducted by the Persians are to be seen the Bactrians (a Bactrian camel in tow) wearing costumes with similar tunics. Their trousers are fuller than those of the Persians and they blouse over boots which reach to mid-calf. Only a thick bandeau is worn on the head. The Armenians in the procession are clad in trousers. So are the men in tall peaked helmets from Saka Tigraxauda (Fig. 56), shown carrying coats and trousers with feet (the first leotards?) as tribute.

Persians wore a variety of headdresses. As noted above, the king's guards aped the Medes. But the high, rounding, slightly

FIG. 55. *Detail from North Side of Apadana Stairway. Mede Between Two Persians.* 500–350 B.C.
(*Persepolis, Photograph, Oriental Institute, University of Chicago*)

Fig. 56. *Detail of Eastern Side of Apadana Stairway. Tribute Bearers from Saka Tigraxauda Carrying Articles of Clothing.* 500–350 B.C. (Persepolis, Photograph, Oriental Institute, University of Chicago)

FIG. 57. *Statue of Napir-Azu, Queen of Elam.* C.1200 B.C. (*Louvre*)

FIG. 58. *Seated Woman Spinning. Susa. Early First Millennium* B.C. (*Louvre*)

bulging caps which sit primly but securely on their bushy curled hair seem to be uniquely theirs. Their helmet was designed on similar lines but had in addition cheek plates which curved forward to protect the chin and a back panel which guarded the neck. The headdress of the king was shaped like that of the Medes (Fig. 55), but it was without the fluting, and flat on top.

Low shoes seem to have been skillfully constructed. Well-preserved low reliefs show what appear to be three form-fitting, carefully modeled latchets over each instep. The shoe reached to the anklebone.

Women's Costume

As for the ladies, the Persians were even more reticent than the Assyrians. However, a marvelous work of art provides some background for the period under discussion, 600–330 B.C. Dated until recently about 1500 B.C., it is now assigned the date of about 1250 B.C.[16] The statue, cast in bronze, is that of Queen Napir-Asu of Susa (Fig. 57). She was an Elamite, from the land later known as

[16] Parrot, op. cit., p. 322.

Persia. Her costume is astonishing in the modernity of its appearance. It is precisely cut and fitted as blouse and skirt; it is professionally sewed and decorated with deep fringe and possibly sequins and/or an embroidered design covering most of the surface. She would have been quite at ease with our late nineteenth-century society women. The only comparable costume this early is that of the Minoans of 1600 B.C. and their followers, the Mycenaeans.

A relief, also from Susa, gives a clue to what the Achaemenian women may have worn, though this rare bit of ivory sculpture is rather vaguely dated early first millennium B.C. (Fig. 58). A seated woman, spinning, is attended by a companion wielding a flag-shaped fan. The companion is wearing a plain short-sleeved dress; her accessories consist of an ornamental belt and either an exceedingly wide bracelet or multiple bracelets. Her hair is in short curls. The barefooted spinner seems to be similarly dressed, but also has a shawl brought over her shoulders. Her hair is elaborately dressed with a chignon at the nape and a fillet around the crown of her head.

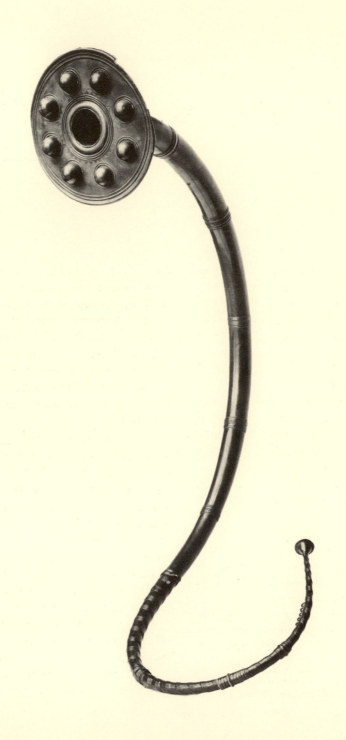

3

The Bronze Age in Denmark

Since there exists a truly remarkable collection of actual garments worn during the Bronze Age in Jutland, it seems worthwhile to discuss them in some detail rather than consider European costumes of the migration period (300–500 A.D.) and the centuries immediately following, where our knowledge is largely suppositional.

A unique combination of circumstances connected with Bronze Age burials resulted in the preservation to an astonishing degree of both bodies and clothing. The National Museum of Copenhagen houses this wonderful material and any student of costume would be amply repaid by a close scrutiny of the original garments. Next to a trip to Copenhagen, a study of Broholm and Hald's *Costumes of the Bronze Age in Denmark*[1] is recommended. The present discussion is based largely upon their work, as well as upon a study of the costumes themselves.

Dr. Broholm has placed most of the costumes in the early period of the early Bronze Age—1500–1100 B.C. By the late

Stone Age (2000–1500 B.C.) sheep had been domesticated and evidence of spinning and weaving makes it certain that primitive woolen garments were worn then. By the time of Tutankhamen (1350 B.C.), Moses (1225–1200 B.C.) and the Trojan War (1184 B.C.), the early Danes were going about in garments of definite style, with accessories which might well inspire our costume jewelers today.

All of these Danish garments are of wool, rather coarsely woven; in some cases the cloth has been fulled or felted until the weave is obscured. The natural color of the wool, brown for the most part, prevails; only a blanket from Trindhøj is white. Perhaps the most amazing thing concerning the fabric itself is its width. The cloak of the Muldbjerg costume measures 7 feet 8 inches by 3 feet 11 inches, without a seam. The widest piece that has been found is fully 7 feet, and that after much shrinkage has taken place. The logical explanation is that the cloth was woven on an upright loom, the warp threads held taut by loom weights, and that two or more people worked simul-

[1] H. C. Broholm and Margrethe Hald, *Costumes of the Bronze Age in Denmark*, Nyt Nordisk Forlag, Arnold Busck, Copenhagen, 1940.

taneously, passing the weft threads from one to another.

The needlework, though obviously not fine, is admirable. Blanket stitch is used to finish edges; it also forms the basis of the clever open joining of the crown to the side of the cap from Trindhøj. The pile of these smart little caps, it has been determined, was made with the needle rather than by weaving. To insert the threads stitch by stitch and knot each one to form the rich decorative pile must have required both skill and patience.

Men's Costume

Four quite complete men's costumes have been preserved. Typical of the group is the costume from Muldbjerg (Fig. 59). The Muldbjerg costume includes a cloak, cap, wraparound body garment, and foot cloths. The cloak is roughly semicircular in shape with selvage forming the straight edge. The ends of this straight edge are rounded off, as is the lower edge of the cloak. This was done after fulling, which was sufficient to render any other finish unnecessary. The

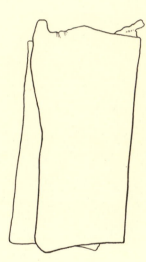

Fig. 60. *Wraparound Body Garment from Muldbjerg.* (*Danish National Museum, Copenhagen*) *Redrawn from Broholm and Hald,* Costumes of the Bronze Age in Denmark, *Figure 16.*

Fig. 59. *Man's Costume from Muldbjerg. 1400–1200* B.C. (*Danish National Museum, Copenhagen*)

fold for the roll collar is parallel to the selvage. A pair of two-piece fibulae (an early but ornamental form of safety pin) was inserted at center back in the fold forming the collar.

The wraparound garment is best understood by a drawing (Fig. 60). The order of wrapping was from the left front across the chest, around the body and back across the chest a second time. Extensions at the upper corners helped to anchor the costume. The right-hand corner was attached to a leather strap which extended over the shoulder and fastened by means of a bronze button to the upper edge of the garment. The left extension, it is believed, went under the left arm to fasten to a similar button at the left of center back. A leather belt further secured the garment in place and held the dagger, while the sword hung from a leather baldric. The raw edges of the garment were blanket-stitched and reinforced by a row of overcasting caught in the loops.

The cap, as already remarked, was a

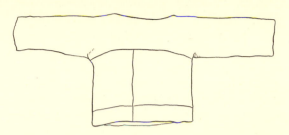

FIG. 62. *Egtved Jacket, Back View.* (*Danish National Museum, Copenhagen*) *Redrawn from Broholm and Hald,* Costumes of the Bronze Age in Denmark, *Figure 111.*

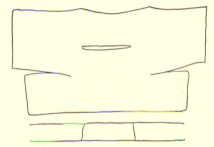

FIG. 63. *Pattern of Egtved Jacket.* (*Danish National Museum, Copenhagen*) *Redrawn from Broholm and Hald,* Costumes of the Bronze Age in Denmark, *Figure 112*)

FIG. 61. *Cap from Muldbjerg.* (*Danish National Museum, Copenhagen*)

work of art (Fig. 61). A circular, slightly domed crown is attached to the side piece with blanket stitches and the edge finished with two or three rows of blanket stitches oversewn with overcasting to form a firm cord-like finish. Several layers of cloth were used to give it firmness and sixteen horizontal rows of stitches inside the cap gave further reinforcement. The cap is 6⅓ inches high with a 22 inch headsize.

Two strips of cloth, measuring approxi-

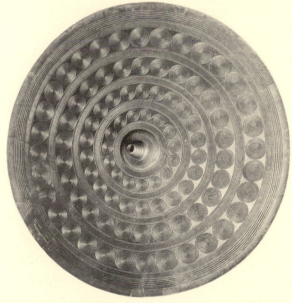

FIG. 64. *Belt Disc from Langstrup. 1400–1200 B.C.* (*Danish National Museum, Copenhagen*)

mately 20 inches by 8 inches were wound around the feet, their edges raw except for one selvage.

Women's Costume

The most outstanding woman's costume comes from Egtved. It consists of a jacket, fringed skirt, belt, belt disc, and other accessories. Figures 62 and 63 show the cut of the jacket, which is clever and might well be adapted to modern clothing. The band at the bottom seems merely to afford greater length, and the edges of the sleeves and the neck opening are finished with blanket stitches. A narrow woven belt with fringed ends, worn over the blouse and tied in front, supports the horn comb and belt disc (Fig. 64).

The *pièce de résistance* of the costume, however, is the corded skirt, unique and yet reminiscent of the grass skirts of the Pacific islands (Fig. 65). This skirt is composed of wool cords made by twisting together two two-ply threads; these are separated at the lower edge, where they are tied once, and the ends overlapped to form small rings which are wrapped with wool, creating an interesting oval contour. A cord strung through the loops thus formed prevents the fringe from flying loose. The waist edge is controlled by a border of weaving which extends to form belt ends. Measurements indicate that the wearer had a waist of 24 inches and the skirt was large enough (48 inches) to encircle the waist twice, thus giving a coverage of double fringe. It might be added that the climate of this region was milder during the Bronze Age than it is today. In fact, all evidence of such skirts disappears after the Bronze Age, probably because of the decided drop in temperature that came at the beginning of the Iron Age (400 B.C.).

The fringe on the end of the belt is finished in the same manner as the lower edge of the skirt. The great bronze belt disc shown here is from Langstrup instead of Egtved. It is more handsome, larger, and in better condition than the one from Egtved. It is, however, contemporary with the Egtved costume. It is at least 8¾ inches in diameter, with a central spike extending 2 inches outward.

The young girl who wore these gar-

FIG. 65. *Corded Skirt from Egtved. 1400–1200 B.C. (Danish National Museum, Copenhagen)*

ments had short blonde hair bound with a woolen cord. She wore two bronze arm rings, a broad flat one which fastened with simple hooks and a rigid circlet ¼ inch thick. A simple slender bronze ring served as an earring. An awl in the same find suggests the type of tools with which she worked.

A jacket from Skrydstrup of the same period offers some interesting elaborations (Fig. 66). Its more detailed ornamentation shows that even at this early date needlework had already developed beyond the purely functional. Rows of the Kensington outline stitch pulled to a tight tension create the transverse ridges on the sleeves. The borders on the sleeve edges are made by interlacing three threads under a row of small stitches spaced well apart. The neck finish is more involved, the seamstress first forming a narrow yoke by eleven rows of interlocked blanket stitches—the same method as that involved in making needlepoint lace. Into each of these rows of blanket stitches she laced three rows of extra threads.

In the grave the lower part of the body was covered by a voluminous wrapping, 4 yards and 12 inches in circumference and 4 feet 8 inches in length, placed about the figure like a skirt and held in place by a narrow belt. The excess length was wrapped about the feet. This is not illustrated here, since authorities differ regarding whether it was really a skirt. Dr. Broholm argues logically that as a skirt it would have been of excessive length and quite out of keeping with the life of the time. But certainly some sort of skirt was necessary to complete the costume. This Skrydstrup woman also had a cap of interesting construction, made in the same manner as headdresses recently worn by Croatian women near Karlovac, by a form of plaiting or braiding.

The horn comb tied to the belt was similar in shape and design to others of the same period. The feet were protected by wrappings of cloth and leather shoes, the latter largely destroyed by time. In spite of the 3000 years since she was laid to rest, this young woman manages to present a rather brave and jaunty effect, with her fine features, perfect teeth, and elaborate coiffure. Her hairdress is a cleverly made wig built up to an impressive pompadour encased in a net of horsehair. A soft cord of wool is

FIG. 66. *Jacket from Skrydstrup. 1400–1200 B.C. (Danish National Museum, Copenhagen)*

wound many times around her head, covering her brow. Her earrings are great circles
of fine gold wire. All in all, she elicits admiration. Another accessory of the Bronze
Age, a little hanging bronze vessel suspended
from the wearer's belt, is a likely forerunner
of the modern purse.

Another important find of the early
Bronze Age was a woman's grave at Olby
in which 125 bronze tubes were arranged
about the hips in two rows, as they would
appear if they were the terminals of fringes
of a corded skirt. Remnants of wool thread
were found in the tubes. Such a skirt would
have somewhat the appearance of the garment seen on a kneeling figure of Faardal,
which dates from the late Bronze Age (800–
400 B.C.). Broholm's deduction is that the
corded skirt was worn throughout the
Bronze Age.

Costume accessories were important to
the well-dressed belles of the Bronze Age
and earlier. Early in the Stone Age necklaces
of animal teeth were used. Because of the
rich deposits of amber along the shores of
the North and Baltic Seas, the earliest settlers
there decked themselves lavishly with amber.
Later, when amber became the most important export of the region, its trade value led
to a more conservative display of it at home.
However, it remained in continuous use.
Torques—rigid necklaces seen in many varia-

tions among the Celts and early Teutons—
appeared early in the Bronze Age as heavy
wires ending in small spirals, curved to the
shape of the neck. By the late Bronze Age
(800–400 B.C.) they had become more ornate (see Fig. 149, Chap. 7).

Armlets and bracelets were popular
from the late Stone Age onward. They
ranged from simple spirals of bronze to exquisitely modeled circlets of gold.

A treatise could be written on fibulae
alone. No doubt pins of wood and bone
were ancestors of the finely formed bronze
pins found in the burials, the more elaborate
of which date from the late Bronze Age.

Both men and women used horn combs.
Since the women wore them attached to
their belts, they must have been proud both
of the comb and of the appearance of their
hair. Razors have been found from the early
Bronze Age onward and tweezers appear in
a wide variety of patterns.

The costumes described above no doubt
belonged to the more important people in
the community. Reconstructions demonstrate that they were pleasing in line, practical, and, with the handsome bronze and
gold jewelry, deserving of respect and admiration. A large percentage of the population, however, undoubtedly continued to
wear garments of skin throughout the
Bronze Age. The many scrapers found are
evidence of the preparation of skins.

4

Crete and Greece

With the recent translation of Linear B inscriptions found in the palaces of Knossus, Mycenae, Pylos, and elsewhere, previous conceptions of the ancient relationships between Crete and Greece have been drastically revised. However, the fashion record remains the same whether the haute couture was located on the island of Crete or on the Greek mainland.

It is now generally agreed that Greek invaders from north of present-day Greece arrived in the Peloponnesus by 2000 B.C., and that the achitecture and artifacts found at the sites of Mycenae, Tiryns, Pylos, etc., were probably of Greek workmanship, undoubtedly influenced by the Minoans of Crete.

CRETE

A high point in Cretan culture had been reached by 2000 B.C., the beginning of the middle Minoan period, about the time the wandering Greeks reached their future homeland. Though these early Greeks showed little promise of the marvelous achievements they would attain in the classic period, the Cretans were already building great palaces and their artisans in pottery, jewelry, engraving, and fresco painting were well advanced in their fields.

Men's Costume

At this point, also, Cretan costume assumes importance. The earliest male figurines of middle Minoan I (2000 B.C.) show the Minoan sheath already in general use, accompanied by a rope-like girdle which at times supported scabbard and sword. The Minoan sheath, unlike other early loin coverings, was definitely shaped of rigid material to afford protection to the male organs. It evolved into the prominent, carefully designed, and expertly executed form seen on the Priest-King in Fig. 67. That it symbolized more than a vain bit of haberdashery is suggested by the fact that both male and female participants in the bull games wore it. Furthermore, a statue of the mother goddess as patroness of these performances is realistically dressed in an elaborately wrought corselet and sheath of gold.

Attention should be called again to the Priest-King, since his is the most striking figure to be found among the frescoes. He belongs to the late Minoan I period, 1500–1450 B.C. From his iris crown spring three feathers, rose, purple, and blue. The larger of his two necklaces carries out a lily motif. His red and white girdle is topped by a thick blue roll. His cutaway loin skirt is scarcely visible, though it dips downward in the back. Much more prominent than on any other figure is the white panel with horizontal accent, suggestive of cross pleating, which falls to the right of the sheath. Evans[1] refers to this as a kind of descending sash.

After the simple sheath of middle Minoan I, male costume progressed to a loin skirt, very abbreviated but still featuring the sheath. Evidence has been found, too, of a double loin skirt. A short bordered skirt worn with a wide belt, probably of metal and seemingly no more than an incredible 12 inches in circumference, constituted the uniform of the captain of the blacks.[2] By late Minoan I, 1550–1450 B.C., the Cretan loin skirt took on the form which has since identified it wherever seen. Reaching to mid-thigh at the sides, it dipped sharply to a point in front, where it was often weighted with a beaded tassel, as on the fresco of the Cup Bearer of Knossus. His patterned gold- and tile-colored skirt is bordered by a bold deep-blue band. Similar loin skirts are worn by men in the procession fresco (Fig. 68). The Egyptians of the empire period recorded that these skirts were characteristically gayly colored (Fig. 69).

Men of the late Minoan I period wore their hair long and waved or, as in the case of the captain, cut short. A round-edged beret-like cap is shown on the men of the Harvester vase from the palace of Hagia Triada, 1550–1500 B.C.

Footwear was often elaborate and well made. The Cretan offering bearers depicted

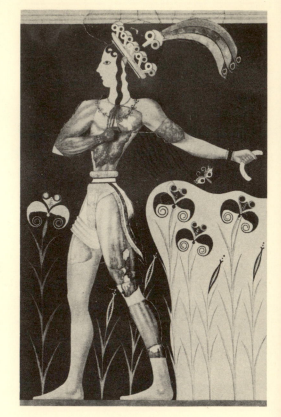

FIG. 67. *Priest-King from Knossus. Late Minoan I. 1500–1450 B.C. (Palace of Minos, Knossus) From Evans, The Palace of Minos, Vol. II, Part II, Frontispiece.*

in Egypt (Fig. 69) are shod quite conspicuously in possibly patterned socks bound in place by the thongs of their low shoes. The toreadors of the bull games appear to wear cushioned soles to lessen the jar of alighting. Their legs are wrapped closely up to the lower calf, and palms and wrists are taped for increased strength. These leaping athletes must have been among the most graceful, agile, and quick-witted in the history of sports.

Women's Costume

Female statuettes of about 2000 B.C. wear skirts of definite bell shape, and male figures show evidence of a brief loin skirt or phallustache.

[1] Sir Arthur Evans, *Palace of Minos*, Macmillan, London, 1925–1935, vol. II, p. 775.
[2] *Ibid.*

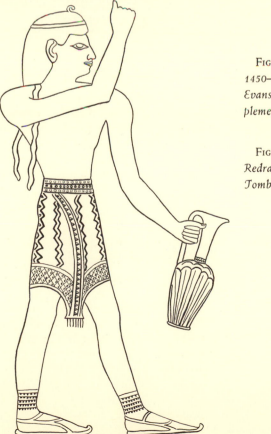

FIG. 68. *Procession Fresco. Late Minoan II. 1450–1375* B.C. *(Palace of Minos, Knossus) From Evans, The Palace of Minos, Vol. II, Part II, Supplementary Plate XXVII.*

FIG. 69. *Offering Bearer from Crete.* C.1450 B.C. *Redrawn from Reproduction of Wall Painting in Tomb of Rek-mi-re. (Metropolitan Museum of Art)*

Evans[3] develops a good case for a shawl as the origin of the feminine silhouette. He points to figures wrapped in shawls from the early Minoan period as the genesis of the style, and the smartly robed little lady from Petsofa (Fig. 70), middle Minoan I (2000–1850 B.C.), as the intermediate step between the draped technique and the elaborately conceived and executed costume of middle Minoan III (about 1600 B.C.). The Evans theory is that a full-length shawl of crisp texture was wrapped around the body and girdled tightly at the waist. The stiffness of the fabric kept the shawl in an upright position, spreading outward somewhat like the Medici collar, covering the arms but leaving the breasts bare. In the Petsofa figurine there is a great difference between the girth of the

[3] *Ibid.*, vol. 1, p. 152.

FIG. 70. *Petsofa Figurine from Votive Station of Petsofa. (Mountain Sanctuary of Petsofa) Redrawn from Evans,* The Palace of Minos, *Vol. I, Figure 111a.*

FIG. 71. *Snake Goddess and Votary, Crete. Middle Minoan III. 1700–1550 B.C. (Metropolitan Museum of Art Reproductions)*

bodice and the sweep of the skirt. The photograph (Fig. 70) reveals a definite sharp point at center back, rather close to the head, a bell-shaped skirt, and a cord-like girdle, which, after encircling the waist twice, falls in two long pendants. The skirt is boldly patterned, a characteristic of Cretan fashions. The lady has real style. Her headdress, tall and peaked, could be a fifteenth-century hennin which suddenly abandoned its rigidity and tilted rakishly forward.

By middle Minoan III (1700–1550 B.C.) the waistline on men and women alike had become diminutive; this was achieved by soldering a metal girdle in place during early childhood. Such girdles appear throughout the rest of Cretan history, their edges usually rolled to reduce abrasion (Fig. 71).

The form-revealing bodice associated with Cretan feminine attire from middle Minoan III onward was cleverly cut to shape. The sleeves reached well toward the elbow and the front edges were laced together below the breasts. The silhouette of the skirt changed from a full rounded bell shape to cone-like. The characteristic horizontal emphasis—an effect achieved by lines—is illustrated on the left and central statuettes of Fig. 71. The skirt of the goddess at the right shows a definite flounced effect. Early representations suggest that the series of horizontal lines may have originated from superimposing one skirt above another, each shorter than the one beneath it, as seen until recently in the costume on the island of Skyros. However, the fully developed style seen on the goddess in Fig. 71 leaves little doubt that a series of ruffles or flounces has been mounted to a shaped skirt.

On figurines of religious import a noticeable feature of the costume is a shaped peplum which curves upward over the hips from front and back. However, on the Hagia Triada sarcophagus of about 1400 B.C. (Fig. 72), the participants in what are evidently ritual scenes are dressed more simply. A priestess at the left is pouring a liba-

tion into a vessel beside a column supporting the sacred double axe. She wears the fashionable tight bodice with wide neckline and short sleeves, but her fur skirt with broad scallops at the lower edge is in an older tradition, probably an adaptation of the natural shape of an animal skin used in an earlier, more primitive period. The figure at the right is dressed more in keeping with the mode of the day: the usual bodice combined with a slightly flared skirt. The chief deviation is a vertical border down center front—a feature repeated on other figures of the same sarcophagus. Since the theme of the paintings is religious, this style may be a heritage from an earlier period also, before the elaborate horizontal flounces were designed. The iris crown must be important, as it closely resembles that of the Priest-King in Fig. 67.

The high style of strictly social circles is elegantly represented by the fresco of the Ladies in Blue shown in Fig. 73. Here is the ultimate in sophistication of this period in history, about 1600 B.C. The carefully coiffed hair is entwined with exquisitely wrought gold jewelry. The bodices, fitted to perfection, would do credit to a Parisian coutourière. In fact, one fresco of a Cretan lady is called the Parisiènne because of her chic appearance. We can only conjecture

FIG. 72. *Figures from Hagia Triada Sarcophagus, Crete. c.1400 B.C. (Archeological Museum, Heraklion) Redrawn from Evans*, The Palace of Minos, *Vol. I, Figure 317.*

FIG. 73. *Ladies in Blue. Middle Minoan III. 1700–1550 B.C. (Palace of Minos, Knossus) From Evans, The Palace of Minos, Vol. I, Figure 397.*

that flounced skirts completed the ensemble.

Metal work reached a high degree of proficiency in the late Minoan period. Necklaces recovered from Phaestus, Knossus, and Hagia Triada attest to the beauty of design and delicacy of workmanship. Rosette, lily, and small papyrus motifs are employed, while miniature bull's heads, ducks, and lions form pendants. Note the armlets and anklets of Fig. 68 and the hair ornaments and necklaces of Fig. 73.

GREEK MYCENAEAN COSTUME, 1600–1100 B.C.

The citizens of Mycenae and her contemporaries on the Greek mainland, such as Tiryns, Argos, and Pylos, were strongly influenced by Minoan art and architecture. They employed the Minoan tapered column and many decorative motifs which had appeared earlier in Crete.

Men's Costume

Men's wear differed more from the Minoan than women's did. A fresco from Tiryns shows a man dressed for a boar hunt in a short-sleeved tunic of mid-thigh length rather than a loin skirt; and his legs are protected to the knees. Though his waist is slim, it could be so naturally, not the result of wearing a girdle. On the other hand, the bull hunters on the famous golden cups of Vaphio, about 1500 B.C., are dressed much the same as the Cretan youths engaged in the bull games. A vase from Mycenae in the Metropolitan Museum, known as the Warrior vase because of its procession of soldiers, shows the military uniform, which in some ways resembles the costume of the boar hunter (Fig. 74). A fringed tunic reaches only to mid-thigh but covers the upper part of the bodice completely. The long sleeves are most unusual. Long hose seem to be gartered above the knees and high footwear supports the ankles. Dotted helmets, both horned and crested, conceal the hair. Beards are a fashionable and practical feature of the soldier's grooming. The vase is dated about 1200 B.C., that is, the time of the Trojan war. Compare these costumes with that of Achilles in Fig. 82.

Women's Costume

Similarly, the costumes found in the frescoes of Tiryns and the carved ivories and gold signet rings of Mycenae reveal how closely related these people were in the fashion world. For example, the Lady with the Casket, dated between 1375 and 1200

B.C. could certainly pass as a young matron of Crete (Fig. 75). The dividing line down the center of her skirt has caused the garment to be interpreted as a pair of trousers. A similar division appears on engraved seals and ivory carvings. It is doubtful, however, that the Mycenaeans wore a trousered costume. The line is more likely to be the artist's method of indicating excessive fullness. The cut of the bodice is certainly Minoan, as is the hair style. If we accept the dates of the Trojan War as 1194–1184 B.C. and the end of the Mycenaean era as 1100 B.C.,[4] Helen of Troy, whose home town was really Sparta, and Penelope, the patient loyal wife of Ulysses, may well have been dressed in Mycenaean fashions, though it seems irreverent even to imagine it.

GREEK ARCHAIC PERIOD, 1100–460 B.C.

Men's Costume

Evidence of men's costume of this

[4] Spyridon Marinatos, *Crete and Mycenae*, Harry N. Abrams, Inc., New York, 1961, p. 84.

FIG. 74. *Warrior Vase from Mycenae. 1375–1200 B.C. (Metropolitan Museum of Art)*

FIG. 75. *Woman Carrying Casket. Copy of Fresco Found at Tiryns. Mycenaen. Late Minoan III. 1375–1200* B.C. *(Metropolitan Museum of Art)*

clining on couches, are draped in himations which leave the upper part of the body exposed. Soldiers in combat are equipped with only their armor: helmet, shield, greaves, and corselet. Horsemen are dressed in short sleeveless chitons which reach to the upper thigh.

Under one handle of the vase, two men are engaged in preparing the feast. Figure 76 shows one of these men with a large cleaver used in cutting up meat. The simple chiton depicted here is the standard garment seen most often during the archaic period. It consisted of two rectangles joined at the shoulders and down the sides, leaving openings for the head and arms. Usually if the drawing is detailed, a border appears along the upper edge both front and back, around the arm openings, and at the hemline. The chiton might also have been made by folding a larger rectangle in half, the fold line falling at the side under one arm and a seam joining the opposite edges. In this case, a slit at the

period is scant and for the first few centuries practically nonexistent. The early sculptured figures of men and boys are nude; the early vase paintings are in the geometric style with the few human figures rendered in such abstract form that they reveal little concerning costume. It is not, therefore, until the seventh century B.C. that the details of the vase paintings are clear enough to indicate the nature of the costumes represented.

A late seventh-century B.C. Corinthian vase in the Louvre shows men taking part in various activities and illustrates diversity of dress. In the top register on one side of the vase, men from the upper class are shown at a feast honoring Hercules. The guests, re-

FIG. 76. *Greek Man Typical of Seventh and Sixth Centuries* B.C. *Redrawn from Corinthian Vase. Late Seventh Century* B.C. *(Louvre)*

FIG. 77. *Scene from Francois Vase. First Half of Sixth Century* B.C. *(Archeological Museum, Florence) From Fürtwangler and Reichhold,* Griechische Vasenmalerei.

athletic prowess, are wearing short chitons to mid-thigh.

The full-length chiton seems to have been the correct wear for charioteers from the earliest records on through Greek history (Figs. 77 and 78). Certain of the gods are usually vested in this manner as are musicians, older men, and officials of high rank. These long chitons are full and modeled on the Ionic order, that is, without an apotygma.

top of the fold would have to be made to serve as an armhole.

Richter[5] points out that this design with side openings for the arms was characteristic of the archaic period while the placement of the arm openings at the extremities of the upper edges when the chiton was much wider, was the practice during the classic period.

In addition to the short chiton, a longer or full-length chiton was in use from the seventh century onward. A mid-seventh-century Greek breastplate found at Olympia, cited by Richter[6] presents both Zeus and Apollo appareled in richly patterned garments. The chiton of Zeus reaches to mid-calf; that of Apollo is slightly shorter. On an Attic vase of mid-sixth century in the Louvre, Poseidon is shown in an ankle-length chiton with a small allover pattern while Hermes and Hercules, both noted for their

[5] Gisela Richter, *The Sculpture and Sculptors of the Greeks,* Yale, New Haven, Conn., 1930, pp. 88–89.
[6] Gisela Richter, *A Handbook of Greek Art,* Phaidon, London, 1959, p. 195.

FIG. 78. *Charioteer of Delphi. 500–450* B.C. *(Museum of Delphi, Alinari Photograph)*

A handsome little bronze figure of Hermes from Sparta dated between 525 and 500 B.C. (Fig. 79) indicates that the short chiton had changed little during the previous century in this conservative part of Greece. The neckline is too small to be slipped over the head, necessitating shoulder openings. These are fastened with buttons or round brooches. A knotted girdle defines the waistline.

However, by the turn of the sixth century B.C. changes occurred in men's fashions which reflected influences similar to those observed in women's costumes. Chitons became fuller; the fabrics were of lighter weight and often were covered with small allover designs. On a late sixth-century cup in Tarquinia the gods are clothed in long pleated Ionic chitons.

FIG. 79. *Bronze Statuette of Hermes.* 525–500 B.C. *(Courtesy, Museum of Fine Arts, Boston)*

On vases dated in the first half of the fifth century B.C. soldiers are shown in pleated chitons extending to mid-thigh. Sometimes a short sleeve appears beyond the shoulder of the armor but not invariably. On a vase in the Louvre dated early fifth century B.C. Theseus is dressed in a sheer sleeveless pleated chiton which is probably the counterpart of those worn by the soldiers. Note the chiton on the hunter in Fig. 80. An old man from this same period wears a long pleated Ionic chiton with elbow-length sleeves—the same design as the women's Ionic chiton (Fig. 84). The most famous and beautiful statue which illustrates this fashion for men is the charioteer of Delphi (Fig. 78).

Workmen wore a minimum of clothing. On a vase in the Louvre from the second half of the sixth century B.C. the plowmen and a man sowing grain are nude, while a man behind a mule-drawn cart has a short wrap draped around his shoulders. A bird-catcher on another vase is shown in a short skirt which allows a generous stride, and a servant carrying a wine jug wears a narrow cloth bound about his loins.

The outer wraps of the seventh and sixth centuries B.C. include the himation and the chlamys. The himation was the more basic of the two, serving often as the only garment worn by men of the upper class and the intelligentsia. The early himation was of smaller dimensions than the later ones. In Fig. 77 it seems to have the proportions of a square which has been folded diagonally and placed around the shoulders like a shawl. The corners hang symmetrically down the front. The alternate method of draping is the one usually associated with Greek dress and was used throughout much of the rest of Greek history (Fig. 81). Starting with one end hanging down the left side-front, the himation was placed over the left shoulder, drawn diagonally across the back, under the right arm and then upward and over the left shoulder a second time. The method of draping varied with the wearer and the oc-

Fig. 80. *Hunter with Dog. Vase by Pan Painter. 470–460 B.C. (Courtesy, Museum of Fine Arts, Boston)*

Fig. 81. *Sophocles. Fourth Century B.C. (Lateran Museum, Rome, Alinari Photograph)*

casion. The himation might cover the right shoulder and envelop the right arm or the end might be placed over the left forearm. Artful draping and seemingly effortless control of the himation were indicative of social status.

Greek garments evidently were woven to the proportions of the wearer. Since they were based on a rectangular shape it was possible to finish all edges on the loom. The absence of hems lent grace to the draping quality of the fabric. Weights often appear at free corners.

The second type of wrap, the chlamys, was designed for active pursuits and was smaller than the himation. In the early centuries it was approximately square and was most often worn around the left shoulder with the upper edges brought together and pinned with a fibula on the right shoulder. If the wearer wished both arms free, the chlamys was fastened on the chest. In Fig. 82 Achilles seems to have tied the two upper corners together at the throat. This is an unusually splendid example, covered as it is with intricate design. Fig. 83 shows the bold pattern typical of the chlamys worn in Thrace while Fig. 80 illustrates the fuller, lighter weight chlamys fashionable from this time onward.

Men's hair in the seventh century B.C. was long and curly, groomed to hang down the back. A narrow fillet was bound around the crown of the head. In the sixth century B.C., the hair was sometimes brought to the back and wound with a band or cord in a single compact club shape which hung between the shoulders. Or it might be formed

FIG. 82. *Achilles. From an Amphora by Exekias. 550–540 B.C. (Vatican Museum, Rome) From Fürtwangler and Reichbold, Griechische Vasenmalerei.*

into two braids which crossed at the back and encircled the head. Another popular fashion is shown in Fig. 82 where the ends of the hair have been reversed and are held in place by the fillet. A variation of this style was to place the fillet around the head and then tuck the ends of the hair over the fillet, thus forming a roll which followed the hairline.

The earliest beards were long and jutted outward in a sharp point (Fig. 77). This style was followed by older men until mid-fifth century B.C. Young men favored a shorter, more rounded contour than their elders in the sixth century. From the fifth century onward they are usually beardless.

The two types of Greek hats—the petasos and pilos—were in use during this era. The petasos was a broad-brimmed low-crowned hat worn quite level on the head, as in Fig. 80; but often it was pushed off to hang at the back by a neck cord. Adopted later as the official symbol of a cardinal, it has inspired many a milliner.

The pilos was narrow brimmed or brimless (Fig. 79). The pilos of the working man resembled a fez with a round or pointed top and was probably made by felting wool fibers in the hand. Hat makers of south Serbia were still creating such headgear prior to World War II by soaking the wool fibers, then rubbing and molding them in the hollow palm until they became felted and assumed the desired shape. Hephaestus, the god of fire and metal working is usually portrayed wearing a pilos.

As in Egypt, footwear rarely appears in the early Greek records. It was the custom to go barefooted indoors. In general, Greek footwear may be classified as sandals, shoes or boots. The sandal, closely associated with the Greeks, is seldom represented until the classic period (Fig. 81). By this time it had become quite elaborate. Earlier sandals consisted of a sole cut to the shape of the foot. The Greeks distinguished right from left in footwear. A single thong fastened to the sole passed between the great toe and the

next and was caught at the ankle by thongs coming from the sides of the sole.

A closed shoe affording more protection is worn in Fig. 80. The coloring on a vase painting of fifth century B.C. clearly defines shoes, socks, and thongs bound spirally from the shoes to the top of the socks. This form is often seen on Greek hunters, travelers, and other men engaged in active pursuits. It may be descended from an old Cretan custom.

Another type of foot covering was introduced by the close of this period. It combined the height of the shoe with the open look of the sandal (Fig. 86). A lattice design achieved by interweaving strips of leather or by cutting the openwork design from a single piece of leather formed the counter and vamp. Lacings through the front loops formed by the reversed strips of leather held the shoe in place. The laces spiraled above the ankle as in Fig. 80.

Hermes, the messenger of the gods, is consistently shown in winged boots (Fig.

Fig. 83. *Man from Thrace Wearing Boldly Patterned Chlamys. c.500 B.C. Redrawn from Vase Painting by Euphronios. (Antikensammlung, Munich) From Fürtwangler and Reichhold, Griechische Vasenmalerei.*

79). Boots were fastened by lacings passed around the double row of buttons as in this case or by lacing through eyelets provided for the purpose. Hunters, travelers, horsemen and other outdoor enthusiasts preferred this sturdy footgear (Fig. 83). The boots were often cuffed with fur cut into deep tabs. Usually reaching to mid-calf, they are sometimes shown as high as the knee.

Jewelry as such is seldom seen in men's costuming. A fibula—a form of clasp or brooch—was essential for fastening the chlamys and some forms of the chiton. Fibulae would vary with the taste and wealth of the wearer. Rings were largely limited to engraved metal or stone for the purpose of signing or sealing letters and documents. The earliest seal rings were of iron. Later they were of gold with the insignia carved in sunken design (intaglio) on sardonyx, chalcedony, carnelian, or other semiprecious stones.

Women's Costume

When the Greeks emerged from their temporary oblivion following the Dorian invasions of the eleventh and tenth centuries B.C., their wearing apparel had become drastically simplified. A truly Greek garment, the peplos, had replaced the pinched waistlines and flounces. This was a straight tubular dress woven in one piece, long enough to reach from shoulder to ankle with a generous overfold at the top, and wide enough to encircle the body comfortably. The fold at the upper edge, which must have been 12 to 15 inches deep, formed a bolero-like line on the figure. The folded edges were overlapped on the shoulders, back over front, and fastened with large pins resembling hat pins. Figure 77 illustrates the method of overlapping and fastening. On the second figure from the right note the chain connecting the two pins. A rather wide belt defined the waistline.

The importance of the peplos to the Greeks is illustrated in the great frieze of the Parthenon, whose theme is the Panathenaic festival, held every four years. The heart and climax of this celebration was the offering of a peplos to the revered statue of Athena on the Acropolis—the life-sized statue in the chapel dedicated to her worship in the Erectheum. The most highly skilled maidens were chosen to work on this peplos. The yarns had to be fine and even, and the

FIG. 84. *Archaic Maiden from Acropolis, Athens. Second Half of Sixth Century* B.C. *(Metropolitan Museum of Art Reproduction)*

weaving of the designs, which extolled the exploits of Zeus and Athena, nothing less than perfect. For the great Athena, in addition to her role as goddess of wisdom, watched over craftsmen as well as warriors.

From the vase paintings it appears that the peplos was colored, opaque, and often decorated with an allover pattern or borders. The wearer's hair was either allowed to fall in ringlets down the back or looped and bound at the back of the head as in Fig. 77. A fillet served as both decoration and control. These women wore shawls, doubtless the early himation. They are represented with it folded diagonally and worn about the shoulders, with the corners hanging evenly down each side of the front, as shown on the man in Fig. 77.

During the sixth century B.C. there was a great dress innovation in Athens, the best illustrations of which are the Archaic Maidens of the Acropolis in Athens (Fig. 84), most of them dated between 530 and 500 B.C. Through contacts with Asia Minor, the Greeks, especially the Athenians, had become familiar with the more sophisticated, sheer, full dress known as the Ionic chiton, which they adopted in preference to the peplos. Legend says that Greek women were sentenced to wear this foreign costume, the Ionic chiton, as punishment for having murdered the lone survivor of a military expedition. Grief-stricken at the loss of their own men, and infuriated at what they considered the treason or cowardice which enabled just one man to return safely, they tore the huge pins from their shoulders and stabbed the man to death.

From its adoption in the sixth century B.C. until the Persian wars early in the fifth century, the Ionic chiton enjoyed wide popularity among the Greeks. It is shown on the fashionable figures of the Acropolis Maidens and in many vase paintings. The upper part of the chiton is in fine wavy pleats, and hence is often referred to as the crinkled Ionic chiton, to distinguish it from the fashion of later periods. Since this chiton

must have been over 3 yards in circumference (twice the distance from finger tip to finger tip with arms outstretched) some form of pleating was essential to control so much fullness. Unlike the peplos and the Doric chiton, the Ionic chiton, in its pure form, had no overfold, but was held together along the shoulders and down the upper arms by brooches or seaming. During this early period the extra length was controlled by low girdling, which was usually hidden by the fold formed by adjusting the hemline to ankle length. The bloused edge reached to the hips, and below this line the skirt portion fell in flat folds.

Because the upper part of the costume is crinkled and the skirt smooth, it is sometimes described as two separate garments, skirt and blouse. This is not likely, however. We know that the Egyptians were masters of intricate pleating and it is probable that the Greeks learned the art from the people whose clothing inspired their new fashion. An Etruscan maiden whose ancestors came from Asia Minor is shown wearing the same crinkled costume. Furthermore, the importance of controlling the excessive fullness of the blouse portion does not apply to the skirt. Anyone who has ever watched a Croatian or Slovakian woman hand pleat her costume can understand that the time and skill involved might well limit the area to be pleated.

The himation of the Archaic Maidens is more widely disputed. What they wear is the so-called narrow himation, draped under the left or right arm, with the ends crossing or hanging from the opposite shoulder. On the Acropolis Maidens it often looks as if the cloth had been pleated and sewed in regular folds with a heading comparable to that of window drapery. Certainly the carving indicates some such formal treatment. However, Lady Evans, wife of the Sir Arthur Evans quoted earlier in this chapter, advances the theory that "these folds occur everywhere in Greek art of a certain period and are the results of a rigid archaism and

Fig. 85. *Demeter and Persephone. From Greek Vase by Makron. 490–480 B.C. (British Museum)*

conventionality."[7] There are many discrepancies between the sculptors' representations and reality. For example, usually there is no connection between the design of the heading and the vertical folds that fall from it (Fig. 84). On some of the figures the himation is worn shawl-wise about the shoulders. Vase paintings, too, support Lady Evans' theory (Fig. 85).

The ringlets of the Archaic Maidens are as set and formal as their pleating and their smiles; they are arranged across the forehead and cascade down the back.

These maidens must originally have been very colorful; vestiges of the bright rich colors have been preserved in grooves and other protected areas of the figurines.

That the Bikini bathing suit may not be as modern as we think is confirmed by the costume of Atalanta, famed for her fleetness, as she appears on the interior of a Greek vase

[7] Maria Millington Evans, *Chapters on Greek Dress*, Macmillan, London, 1893, pp. 41–42.

in the Louvre. Dated first half of the fifth century B.C., the painting shows Atalanta as a girl athlete clad in a brassiere-shaped upper garment barely concealing the breasts and a diaper-like loin covering 6 to 8 inches in depth. The upper edge of the short shorts rests at hipbone level. A close round cap similar to a modern bathing cap is tied under her chin.

Parasols, probably copied from models in the Near East, were used extensively throughout Greek history.

THE AGE OF PERICLES, 460–332 B.C., TO THE FALL OF CORINTH, 146 B.C.

Men's Costume

The changes in men's costume during the latter part of this period are for the most part toward simplification. As in earlier periods, the most important gods continue to be dressed in long pleated Ionic chitons with sleeves—an indication perhaps of the costume of men of high status. The short sleeveless chiton worn by Theseus continued in use. Euphorbus with the child Oedipus (Fig. 86) exemplifies the height of fashion at mid-fifth century B.C.

Relaxing after the suffering and austerity imposed by the Persian Wars, the Greeks turned to the most complicated styles in their history. Doric and Ionic details were combined and executed in full pleated costumes of fine fabric; even the Doric chitons were pleated. Braids instead of fibulae joined front and back shoulder sections, and the girdle became decorative as well as functional.

Fourth-century funerary scenes record more conservative garments than those seen on vases. A young horseman wears a plain chiton a few inches above the knee, a chlamys fastened on the right shoulder and boots to lower calf. His hair is short, giving much the same effect as modern hair styling.

Philosophers and such men as Demosthenes, the statesman and orator, considered himation and sandals the only essential garments (Fig. 81).

As in women's costume during the Hellenistic period (338–146 B.C.) long sleeves for men are assumed to have been copied from the Persians, but they are seldom represented in art and were probably as seldom worn.

A man at active work is often shown with his chiton unfastened on the right side, the so-called exomis, which freed his arm and shoulder. Or he abandoned the chiton and wore his chlamys wrapped about his hips in lieu of a loin skirt.

As the power of Rome increased and the strength of Greece waned, pleats disappeared, the sleeves were extended to mid-upper arm, and the chiton was lengthened to the kneecap. The versatile clasped chlamys and the stately draped himation continued to serve as outer wraps.

Footwear was designed, as previously, to suit the occasion. Sandals were most popular (Fig. 81). They varied from the simple though beautiful sandal of the Hermes of Praxiteles (mid-fourth century B.C.), which has an interestingly fashioned plaque of leather over the instep, to a sturdier style, sometimes made with a wooden sole and with leather counter and side pieces added to afford more protection to the feet. On the latter type a long tongue was often folded forward, extending from the fastening at the ankle to the toes (Fig. 81). Boots ranging in height from mid- to high-calf were laced up the front.

The petasos and pilos remained in use.

Hair was worn short except for a relatively brief period during the reign of

FIG. 86. *Euphorbus with Child Oedipus. From Greek Vase. Mid-Fifth Century* B.C. *(Cabinet des Medailles, Paris) Redrawn from Fürtwangler and Reichhold,* Griechische Vasenmalerei.

Alexander the Great when men adopted the longer fashion of their hero (Fig. 87).

Women's Costume

The great upsurge of nationalism after the Persian invasions of the early fifth century revived the popularity of the native Doric chiton. Classic examples of this style include the Porch Maidens or Caryatids of the Erectheum and the Dancing Girls of Herculaneum (Fig. 88), done between 480 and 450 B.C. The Doric chiton was a direct descendant of the archaic peplos and, it might be added, had been worn continuously in regions of Greece in less direct contact with Asia Minor than Athens.

The Doric chiton was folded and worn in the same manner as the peplos, but was of larger dimensions (in girth, approximately

FIG. 88. *Dancing Maiden of Herculaneum. Roman Copy of Bronze Greek Statue.* c.480–450 B.C. *(National Museum, Naples, Anderson Photograph—Alinari)*

twice the width from elbow to elbow with arms bent and lifted to a horizontal position). It is shown either closed or open down the right side. Davenport[8] states that it was worn closed in Corinth and Attica. The chief variation in design was in the depth of the overfold, the apotygma. On the peplos it ended well above the waistline, but on the Doric chiton it was longer. In fact, here the waistline dropped so decidedly that the lower edge of the blouse which was formed by pulling the excess length above the girdle could reach the hipbones. This

FIG. 87. *Alexander the Great.* c.330 B.C. *Redrawn from Bust. (Capitoline Museum, Rome)*

[8] Millia Davenport, *The Book of Costume,* Crown, New York, 1948, vol. 1, p. 46.

bloused portion is called the kolpos. In later years the apotygma was lengthened to hip or thigh level and the girdle was placed in normal position over it. The Mourning Athena furnishes an excellent example of this mode.

When the Persian Wars ended, the Ionic chiton returned to favor. Possibly the most beautiful version of it in this classic period is the relief, The Birth of Aphrodite, now in the Terme Museum, Rome, dated between 470 and 460 B.C. (Fig. 89). The sheerness and draping quality of the linen are wonderfully expressed.

From this time onward, the changes which took place involved new ideas in girdling, combinations of features of the two types of chitons in one garment and the superimposing of the Doric over the Ionic. There are instances of the apotygma on the Ionic chiton and of double girdling with one belt at the waist and another at hip level.

Cutting and sewing must have gradually become increasingly intricate. Neck bindings appear, and there are shirred seams down the shoulders and sleeves of the Ionic chiton. A braided shoulder strap similar to that of Fig. 86 is occasionally seen on the Doric style.

During the Hellenistic period, 338 to 146 B.C., girdling became more complicated, with bands passing in front of the armscye (armhole) position (Fig. 90) or crossing between the breasts. The waistline was moved upward, producing the proportions revived in the Napoleonic era, familiar to us

FIG. 89. *Birth of Aphrodite. Greek Bas-Relief.* c.470 B.C. *(Terme Museum, Rome, Alinari Photograph)*

FIG. 90. *Themis of Rhamnus.* 300–250 B.C. *(National Museum of Greece, Athens)*

der, down across the back and under the right arm, thence upward and over the left shoulder again. Sometimes it was drawn over the right shoulder. For greater protection it enveloped the head. The Tanagra figurines, which represent the chic Greeks of their day, demonstrate the finesse and feeling for line involved in the infinite number of ways of tucking in the excess length over and about the arms; of pulling certain sections taut to emphasize a given line direction; of

as the empire line. There are rare instances of long tight sleeves, an idea borrowed from the Persians but never popular.

The garment which permitted and invited countless variations in arrangement was the himation. Probably woven to the proportions of the wearer, it seems to have been 12 to 15 feet long and 5 to 6 feet wide. Supple in texture, it readily lent itself to skillful manipulation. Since social prestige depended to a degree upon the ease and grace with which it was worn, many an hour must have been spent in practice and experimentation.

Traditionally the draping started with one end at the left ankle or higher. The cloth was carried up and over the left shoul-

FIG. 91. *Greek Woman Donning Her Diplax Redrawn from Diana of Gabii. Mid-Fourth Century* B.C. *(Louvre)*

controlling by elbow pressure as well as by hand this mass of uncut, unpinned, slippery material.

Made of linen or wool, the early himations were enriched with bands of decoration covering the entire surface. The figure of Demeter on a vase dated in the early fifth century B.C. demonstrates this (Fig. 85). Later himations were bordered in such classic patterns as the Greek key, the wave, and the palmette.

Ladies as well as men possessed a second type of wrap which allowed greater freedom of movement. A rectangle more nearly square than the himation was folded off-center and draped from under the right or left arm up to the opposite shoulder, where it was pinned with a fibula. This was called the diplax (Fig. 91).

An infrequent but, from the historic standpoint, important piece of apparel was an overgarment shown in a vase painting in the Metropolitan Museum. Richter refers to it as a sleeveless jacket or overtunic and says it was worn during the fifth and fourth centuries B.C.[9] The vase is dated 420–410 B.C., and its subject is the scenting of costumes in preparation for a festival.

Greek hairdress is best explained by the following illustrations: drawings from the Francois vase (Fig. 77) dated 600 to 550 B.C.; Archaic Maiden (Fig. 84), 550 to 500 B.C.; Demeter (Fig. 85), 490 to 480 B.C.; and Maiden from Herculaneum (Fig. 88), 480 to 450 B.C.

Headdresses include the fillet wound one to three times about the head; the sphendone, a scarf bound about the head (Fig. 92); a cap, sometimes tasseled at the tip, called the sakkos (Fig. 93); snoods of various sorts which enclosed or supported the hair at the back or enveloped the entire hair arrangement (Fig. 94), and coronets such as those seen on Demeter (Fig. 85a), which were probably the Tiffany products of their

[9] Gisela Richter, *Red Figured Athenian Vases in The Metropolitan Museum of Art*, Yale, New Haven, Conn., 1936, vol. I, p. 199.

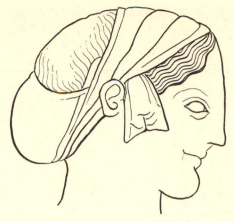

FIG. 92. *Sphendone. Early Fifth Century* B.C. *Redrawn from Bas-Relief, Girls with Flowers. (Louvre)*

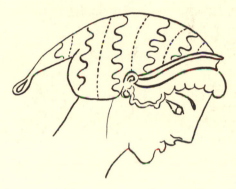

FIG. 93. *Sakkos.* 500 B.C. *Redrawn from Vase Painting. (British Museum)*

FIG. 94. *Hair Enclosed by Draped Covering.* 510–500 B.C. *Redrawn from Vase Painting by Euthymides. (Antikensammlung, Munich) From Abrahams,* Greek Dress, *London: John Murray, 1908, Figure 28)*

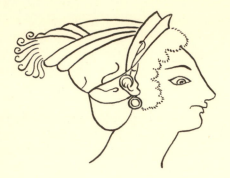

FIG. 95. *Stephane. Redrawn from Hope,* Costume of the Ancients, *London: William Miller, 1812, Vol. II, p. 178.*

FIG. 96. *Phrygian Bonnet. Redrawn from Hope,* Costume of the Ancients, *London: William Miller, 1812, Vol. I, p. 29.*

day. The stephane, an elegant crescent-shaped diadem, was the most regal of all (Fig. 95). The Tanagra hats with their pointed crowns are among the world's famous chapeaus.

Also recorded in Greek art is the Phrygian cap (Fig. 96). The Phrygian kingdom in Asia Minor dated from 1000 to 700 B.C. King Midas (about 715 B.C.) is the most famous Phrygian. The Phrygian cap is important historically because it has been copied or adapted so many times. It was the inspiration for the official headdress of the Doges of Venice. It was the model for the identifying headdress of the French Revolutionists and hence became the symbol of

freedom. In the United States our goddess of Liberty wears it, and until recently we carried it constantly in our purses on the lowly dime.

Though women are most often shown barefooted, light open sandals were worn; these are shown in Fig. 91 and also appear on the seated figure of Penelope in the Vatican Museum. An early version of the platform sole is shown in Fig. 90.

Other Aspects of Greek Fashion

As is to be expected, the Greeks practiced moderation in their use of jewelry, yet some remarkable pieces survive to prove their goldsmith's skill (Fig. 97). Brooches or fibulae were a necessary accessory. The early large and lethal pins used to fasten the peplos were eventually replaced by a safety pin, in principle and appearance closely akin to our own. Through the centuries designs became more decorative; some of the fibulae must have been collec-

FIG. 97. *Gold Earring. Greek. Fourth Century* B.C. *(Courtesy, Museum of Fine Arts, Boston)*

tor's items among the Greeks. Gems were carved using intaglio and cameo techniques.

The high regard in which the Greeks held the human body ensured both cleanliness and careful grooming. One of their methods of using fragrance has been cited. It is quite certain that they used some sort of foundation garment which provided both support and control for the figure.

Contrary to what is generally supposed, the Greeks were great lovers of color and used it lavishly. The disappearance of paint from their architecture, the unrelieved whiteness of marble statues, and the failure of Greek paintings to survive as have the Roman paintings in Pompeii and Herculaneum, have led us to think of the Greeks as eternally robed in white. Actually their early costumes were probably glowing with color and there is reason to believe that they continued to use it in the later periods. The

Archaic Maidens still retain remnants of their original paint. The most attractive one is dressed in an olive green chiton with polychromatic designs all over the himation. Norris mentions the possibility that blue dye was unknown to the Greeks.[10] If so, blue was about the only color missing from their wardrobes.

Richter quotes a list of descriptive terms applied to bed covers which suggest qualities and colors of costume fabrics also: ". . . delicate, well-woven, glistening, beautifully colored, of many flowers, covered with ornaments, purple, dark green, scarlet, violet, with scarlet flowers, with a purple border, shot with gold, with figures of animals, with stars gleaming upon them."[11]

[10] Herbert Norris, *Costume and Fashion*, Dent, London, 1924, vol. I, p. 58.
[11] Gisela Richter, *A Handbook of Greek Art*, Phaidon, London, 1959, p. 369.

5

Etruscans and Romans

THE ETRUSCANS

When the Etruscans arrived in northern Italy, the peninsula was already well populated. The same great stirring of tribes which propelled the Dorians into southern Greece had already led the Villanovans, workers of iron from the Danube basin, across the Alps and into this area. These last invaders to settle in Italy before the Etruscans were already skilled in metal craft and became apt apprentices and assistants to their future masters.

The importance of the Etruscans in developing and spreading Mediterranean civilization has only recently been fully recognized. It is now established that they migrated from Asia Minor to the Italian peninsula toward the end of the ninth century B.C.;[1] that they brought a heritage of culture derived from Mesopotamia, Egypt, and Crete; and that the Romans were deeply indebted to them in every phase of daily living—economic, social, political, and religious.

[1] William Langer, *An Encyclopedia of World History*, Houghton Mifflin, Boston, 1948, p. 68.

The Etruscan colonization of northern Italy may be compared to the English colonization of America during the seventeenth century. In both cases the colonists arrived with many material objects of high quality from the homeland, with skills well developed, and with appreciations and standards that led to a steady stream of both production and importation.

By the sixth century B.C., when they had conquered Corsica, the Etruscans ruled from the Po River to the southernmost part of Campania. Though their kings did much for Rome, they won the cordial hatred of the old Roman aristocracy. The last king, Tarquinius Superbus, was expelled in 509 B.C. and a republic was established. This date marked the peak of Etruscan power; the defeat of their fleet in 474 B.C. by the combined efforts of the Greeks and Sicilians signaled the beginning of their loss of power. Early in the following century they were attacked simultaneously by Gauls, Samnites, and Romans. Unable to fight successfully on three fronts, their greatest disaster was the loss of Veii to the Romans in 392 B.C. From

then on Rome increased in power and
Etruria declined. Finally, military colonists
were sent by the Roman consul Sulla in re-
venge after the Etruscans sided with another
Roman, Marius; this brought the Etruscans
completely under the domination of Rome.

Although the political power of the
Etruscans ceased, in numberless ways their
influence continued. A powerful hold was
maintained by the haruspices, who forecast
the future by interpreting the flights of birds
and judged the auspiciousness of an occasion
by the appearance of the livers of sacrificed
animals—practices relayed from the Mesopotamians. Etruscan soothsayers continued
in the active and respected service of the
emperors of Rome until the beginning of the
Christian Era, and their language was retained in rituals hundreds of years after it
had ceased to be used by laymen.

The Etruscans are most famous as metal
workers; a brief survey of their accomplishments in bronze is sufficient to prove their
stature as artists and craftsmen in that medium. A bronze chariot dated 550–540 B.C.
and a statuette of a girl from late in the same
century are two superb examples of their
work. Other contributions which survived
included the development of a system of
highways, later extended and improved by
the Romans; the use of the curule chair, the
official seat of the magistrate; and the procession of 12 lictors bearing fasces. Two of
their deities were adopted as Juno and
Jupiter. In the realm of clothing they contributed footwear, the tutulus, the decorative and significant clavi, the bulla, and even
the toga praetexta, all of which are described
later in this chapter.

Men's Costume

On a bronze bowl of the early seventh
century B.C., figures representing a plowman,
a hunter, and a warrior show little class or
occupational differentiation. The short loin
skirt is common to all. One young man wears
also a short T-shirt. By the middle of the

century a one-piece tunic extending from
shoulder to lower thigh appears on a warrior,
though the shorter version seen on the
chariot in Fig. 104 was more prevalent, occurring on many male figures throughout
the fifth and sixth centuries B.C.

As we have observed in other early
civilizations, an ankle-length garment appears on men of dignity or importance. The
gentlemen shown in Fig. 98 is a contemporary of the little lady in Fig. 105 about
600 B.C. Like hers, his garment shows a
geometric design, possibly plaid. His wrap,
fastened with a fibula instead of being
draped, is related to the chlamys.

FIG. 98. *Etruscan Male Figure.* c.600 B.C. *Redrawn from Seated Figure.* (British Museum)

FIG. 99. *Male Dancer. Redrawn from Etruscan Wall Painting. Early Fifth Century* B.C. *(Tomb of Triclinium, Tarquinia)*

Male dancers usually appear nude except for the semicircular tebenna or rectangular wrap, which they often wear centered in front with the ends thrown to the back and then looped through to the front again under the arms, as shown in Fig. 99. This would keep the drapery in position even during fairly strenuous activity. Their color schemes are fully as bold as those of the female dancers.

The bronze situla (vessel) of Certosa, late sixth or early fifth century B.C., reveals a wide range of costume. The theme of the design is a burial with all the pomp of a military guard of honor, production of food, preparations for the sacrifice, and procession of dignified nobles.

The country life depicted on this vessel probably includes earlier settlers of the lower class who had become subject to the Etruscans. A plowman, for example, wears a knee-length sleeveless tunic and a close-fitting cap; a man dragging a pig is bareheaded, and his tunic has elbow-length sleeves; other workingmen wear only abbreviated loin skirts bound closely about the hips or knotted in center front. Two huntsmen wear ankle-length tunics and berets are set primly on their heads. Most of the men of dignity, the nobles, are wrapped in long plaid mantles extending to the insteps, though one is wearing a plain mantle over a longer tunic. Their picturesque wide hats with upturned brims and low crowns are comparable to the Greek petasos, but the Etruscan brim is broader and differently shaped.

Clavi (vertical borders), which became so important in Roman costume first as status symbols and later for pure decoration, were worn on the longer tunics of the Etruscans. An example is shown in Fig. 100 and they are discussed later in this chapter as part of Roman costume.

The statue known as Apollo from Veii and often referred to as the ultimate achievement of Etruscan art (500 B.C.) serves also

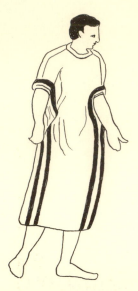

FIG. 100. *Clavi on Etruscan Tunic. Fourth Century* B.C. *Redrawn from Etruscan Wall Painting. (Tomba dei Sette Camini, Orvieto, Alinari Photograph)*

the period of the Republic. His garments consist of tunic and toga—really the toga praetexta, for the broad border of the circular edge is clearly shown. These are described in the next section of this chapter. The cut of his tunic is clear also, since the right arm emerges from the side seam opening. His boots, the Roman calceus, are so

as a document of costume (Fig. 101). He is wearing a knee-length tunic, over which the tebenna is draped in the usual fashion, that is, under the right shoulder and over the left. Though rather soft and natural in appearance as they pass under the right arm, the folds take on an impossible geometric accuracy as they ascend the chest and again as they fall from the left shoulder toward the floor. This statue supports the theory that the drapery of the narrow himation of the Archaic Maidens of the Acropolis is a flight of fancy of the sculptor rather than an accurate record of what the well dressed Athenian lady wore.

For outer wear, the Etruscan wardrobe included the fastened wrap akin to the chlamys shown in Fig. 98, the draped semicircular wrap seen in Figs. 101 and 102, and the long rectangular shawl similar to the himation clearly represented in the fourth-century tomb painting shown in Fig. 103.

Although the famous statue of the orator shown in Fig. 113 is of Etruscan workmanship, it is usually cited as a classic example of the Roman citizen's costume of

FIG. 101. *Apollo of Veii.* C.500 B.C. *(Villa Guilia Rome, Alinari Photograph)*

meticulously cast that copies could be accurately made from them. This, then, seems to represent the transition from Etruscan to Roman costume.

Hair styles are often repetitive from culture to culture. In the early Etruscan period the hair was usually long and was accompanied by a beard; from the fifth cen-

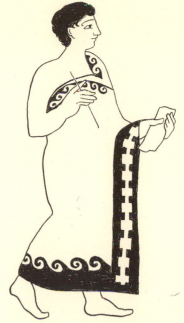

FIG. 103. *Etruscan Wearing Rectangular Mantle Similar to Greek Himation. Redrawn from Wall Painting. (Tomba dei Sette Camini, Archeological Museum, Florence, Alinari Photograph)*

FIG. 102. *Back View of Etruscan Statue from Orvieto. c.500 B.C. (Ny Carlsberg Glyptotek, Copenhagen)*

tury B.C. onward, the barbering had quite a modern look. As we have seen, Etruscan head coverings ranged from a simple close cap to the beret shape and from a rather narrow brim to the imposing scale of the Certosa nobles.

Space does not permit discussion of armor here but Fig. 104 gives some idea of its excellence, with the sleek fitting greaves, huge shield, and magnificent helmet. The towering helmet with ram's head and crest resembles the recently reconstructed silver masterpiece in the City Art Museum of St. Louis.

In the seventh century B.C., the Etruscans are shown barefooted, but a sixth-century painting shows the men wearing elaborately designed and constructed footwear. The toes are pointed, a Near Eastern feature, and the back rises upward in a peak which reaches mid-calf. A tongue of the same extreme height is held in place by a strap with a decorative fastening, and other straps bind

the ankle. Low shoes covering the anklebone had either a center front lacing or an
angular overlap. Some low boots laced all
the way up center front. Numerous varieties
of sandals are shown, from very open strap
construction with minimum protection, to
intricate interlacing which would lend support and give adequate coverage to the foot.
Red was a favorite color. No doubt the
Romans inherited their love of fine footwear
from the Etruscans.

Women's Costume

Small figurines dating from the seventh
century B.C. wear dresses with short sleeves
and long skirts girdled once or twice. The
detail that lends them distinction is the
hairdress: the hair is pulled smoothly to the
back, where it is sometimes braided in one
long plait ending at the hem line, and sometimes divided into double strands which
must have been augmented artificially and
redivided into multiple strands which
reached the ankle.

A female standing figure from an ossuary (Fig. 105) has been interpreted as a
goddess but seems much more human than
divine; her puzzled expression belies om-
niscience. Her dress is similar to those of the
other early figurines, except for its allover
geometric pattern. Whether woven or embroidered, the surface is greatly enriched.

Figure 104, which shows the front panel
of the bronze chariot referred to earlier, portrays a mother's gift of armor to her son.
Her long dress or chiton is handsomely
decorated with a lotus border above the hem
and a wide vertical band featuring the Greek
key. An enlarged, isolated Greek key motif
just below knee level is balanced by a design
composed of four palmettes. It is quite
probable that the mother is wearing two
chitons, one of which reaches to her ankles.
The sleeve of the outer one is unusually long,
coming almost to the wrist. Her shawl is
worn over her head in a manner which occurs so frequently that it must have been

FIG. 104. *Bronze Chariot from Monteleone. 550–
540 B.C. (Metropolitan Museum of Art, Rogers Fund)*

typical throughout much of Etruscan history.

The Etruscan girl from the second half
of the sixth century B.C., shown in Fig. 106,
would have been quite at home with the
Acropolis maiden illustrated in Fig. 84. At
least they are contemporary, suggesting that
the fashions were either derived from the
same source, that is, Asia Minor, or that one
was a copy of the other. The flowers on her
headdress and the pointed toes of her shoes
proclaim her Etruscan identity.

But our richest source of information
about Etruscan costume is their tomb paintings. Here they left a gay, spirited, colorful
account of their manner of living, which,
if it did not assure them the same pleasures
in the next world as they hoped, at least
suggests the good and often hilarious life

they enjoyed on earth. Athletic games, chariot racing, dancing, symposia, combining the satisfactions of fine food, drink, and stimulating conversation, are all depicted. Then as now hours were whiled away with wine, women, and music. In fact, a flute accompaniment was apparently necessary to all activities, from chastising the slaves, to cooking a meal, to mourning the death of a relative.

Women represented in the paintings seem to have been accorded a position of confidence and honor in the Etruscan home. The typical costume consists of a long, full,

FIG. 105. *Female Figure from Ossuary Found at Chiusi. Seventh Century* B.C. *(Civic Museum, Chiusi, Alinari Photograph)*

FIG. 106. *Bronze Statuette. Second Half of Sixth Century* B.C. *(Metropolitan Museum of Art, Gift of J. Pierpont Morgan)*

sheer chiton and an outer, dark, more closely cut overdress with elbow-length sleeves, decorated with borders around the neck, ends of sleeves, down center front, and around the hem. The wrap was draped in the conventional manner of the himation— under the right shoulder and over the left.

The paintings of the dancers in the tomb of Triclinium, early fifth century B.C., are among the most delightful of all the Etruscan frescoes. A female dancer, Fig. 107, could almost double for a modern co-ed in sweater and skirt. However, her costume is peculiar to the première danseuse: a darker overblouse with straps of bells crossing in front of the shoulders is her special prerogative. A similar dancer from another tomb, moves with great restraint because of a pillar-like object balanced on her head. Straps of bells and wreaths resembling Hawaiian leis occur often on the tomb walls,

FIG. 107. *Etruscan Dancer. Redrawn from Wall Painting. Early Fifth Century* B.C. *(Tomb of Triclinium, Tarquinia)*

and were evidently a favorite accompaniment to merrymaking.

The colors of the costumes are as gay as the dancers themselves. The ballerina's costume in Fig. 107 consists of a sheer light-yellow dress with a dark brick-red pattern of dots and zig-zag lines, and solid border at neck and sleeves. Her overblouse is dark red with cerulean blue borders. Wraps were usually dark red with either golden yellow or blue borders.

Shoes were usually red, blue and black being occasional alternates. Etruscans seem to have been expert cobblers, for their footwear was popular among the Romans. Some of the dancers are shod in sandals, others in shoes with more surface coverage.

Spiral bracelets were commonly worn, along with disc earrings and necklaces.

Figure 108 gives a good idea of the appearance of women of wealth and position of that day. This is Velia, wife of Arnth Velca, and the date is within the fourth century B.C. Her red hair is confined at the back by a figured snood and adorned by a coronet of golden leaves. Several of these coronets have been retrieved (Fig. 112). Velia wears two necklaces, the smaller one of golden beads, the other probably of mounted amber, a trade article of high value. Her wrap, with its wide crenelated border, crosses the left shoulder. She is a true patrician.

The tutulus, mentioned above, seems to have been a headdress peculiar to the Etruscans, though it was also worn by Roman women when Rome was under Etruscan domination. Figures 109 and 110 illustrate its basic shape: a high cone, either with or without an upturned brim or coronet across the front.

The bronze figure from the Vatican shown in Fig. 110 wears the tutulus with an engraved coronet, a dress, and a semicircular wrap instead of the rectangular one most often observed. This is the tebenna, which is said to have been worn by all Roman women in their early history. Often illus-

FIG. 108. *Velia, Wife of Arnth Velca. Fourth Century* B.C. *Reproduction of Wall Painting. (Tomb of Orcus, Tarquinia, Archeological Museum, Florence, Alinari Photograph)*

FIG. 109. *Head of Woman Wearing Tutulus.* c.500 B.C. (*Ny Carlsberg Glyptotek, Copenhagen*)

THE ROMANS

Men's Costume

Rome's contribution to law and government was great and far reaching, but her role in the arts was more of borrower and adapter than of creator. This fact is especially apparent in costume. Thus the toga, usually considered the most Roman of Roman garments, came from the Etruscans as did var-

trated in men's costume, it is the forerunner of the Roman toga.

Etruscan society women had a wide choice of magnificent jewelry. Fibulae from the earliest times were available in a variety of sizes and designs. The precision of the repoussé designs, the delicacy of the granular outlines, and the charming little three-dimensional animals are typical of Etruscan design and workmanship. Figure 111 shows the bulla, a hollow circular locket or pendant, worn in multiples by both men and women; this was adopted by the Romans, who gave it more than decorative significance. Figure 112 shows a magnificent golden diadem worn as illustrated on the portrait of Velia in Fig. 108.

FIG. 110. *Bronze Statuette.* (*Museo Etrusco Gregoriano, Vatican, Anderson Photograph—Alinari*)

ious accessory details. From the Greek chiton and himation the women took the stola and the palla, dress and wrap, while men copied one article after another. The Greek himation became their pallium, the chlamys their paludamentum. The chlamys was also probably the inspiration for two other wraps, the laena and the lacerna. Through military contact with the Gauls, Roman soldiers came to see the wisdom of close leg coverings in a cold climate and calf-length trousers became part of their G.I. issue. But in spite of all this pilfering the Romans nevertheless managed to develop a style of their own.

THE EARLY ROMAN TUNIC. We have little documentation in regard to Roman costume during the period from 750 B.C. to 510 B.C., when the Etruscans were dominant and one of their outstanding families, the Tarquins, were ruling as kings. It may safely be assumed that Etruscan influence was strongest during the kingdom and the early republican period. (The kingdom lasted from 750 B.C. to 510 B.C.; the republic from

FIG. 111. *Bulla. Fifth Century* B.C. *(Museo Etrusco Gregoriano, Vatican, Anderson Photograph—Alinari)*

510 B.C. to 30 B.C.; the empire period from 30 B.C. to 476 A.D.) The Roman tunic was a simple affair made of two squares of cloth seamed together on the shoulders and down the sides, openings being left for neck and arms. The first tunics were quite narrow, barely capping the shoulders (Fig. 113). A statue of Marcellus dated 211 B.C. shows the sleeve reaching the biceps; one of Augustus as Pontifex Maximus 27 B.C.–14 A.D., shows

FIG. 112. *Gold Diadem. Third Century* B.C. *(Museo Etrusco Gregoriano, Vatican, Anderson Photograph—Alinari)*

FIG. 113. *The Orator. Late Third or Early Second Century* B.C. *(Archeological Museum, Florence, Alinari Photograph)*

FIG. 114. *Augustus Caesar.* 27 B.C.–14 A.D. *(Terme Museum, Rome, Alinari Photograph)*

it coming to the bend of the elbow (Fig. 114). On a relief of Claudius Caesar (emperor from 41 to 54 A.D.) receiving the symbol of power, his sleeve covers the elbow and reaches onto the forearm, a length maintained until Commodus introduced the full-length sleeve (Fig. 117). Commodus reigned from 180 to 192 A.D.

THE CLAVI. During the republic the clavi—the vertical borders over the shoulders of the tunic—were significant of rank, but this distinction disappeared early in the Empire. Christian paintings in the catacombs represent worshipers in tunics with clavi, certain proof of their general use. A little Roman boy in the Metropolitan Museum and the Camillus in the Capitoline Museum in Rome (Fig. 115) furnish good illustrations of the narrowest clavi—approximately ⅜ inch wide and running the full length from shoulder to hem on each side. No design is

men who could afford to contribute a horse and its upkeep as well as their own services. This custom was retained long after its original significance was obsolete. These were the moneyed class, the plutocrats, and they had the right to wear clavi three times as wide as that of freeborn boys. A painting in Pompeii shows a horseman wearing clavi of this width.

The widest of the three common types of clavi, the latus clavus, was the symbol of highest rank and was therefore reserved for government officials—senators or higher. The tunic with the wide clavi was known as the tunica lato clavo, later the tunica palmata. The width of the latus clavus varied from 3 to 4 inches, more modest officials preferring less ostentation. This is illustrated in the wall painting from the first century house of the Vetii in Pompeii (Fig. 116).

Except during mourning the Roman

FIG. 115. *Camillus. Early Empire. (Capitoline Museum, Rome, Alinari Photograph)*

FIG. 116. *Roman Wearing Tunic with Widest Clavi and Toga Praetexta. First Century A.D. (House of Vettii, Pompeii, Alinari Photograph)*

indicated within the band. Wilson believes that this ornamentation was the right of every son of a Roman citizen.[2] The color was no doubt purple, or at least the Roman conception of that color.

Since one of the great enterprises of the early Romans was war, military costumes were important. The equites or equestrian order, which originated in the days of universal military duty, at first comprised only

[2] Lillian Wilson, *The Clothing of the Ancient Romans*, Johns Hopkins, Baltimore, 1938, p. 62.

tunic was girdled, and much store was set on the manner of girdling. Wilson quotes Quintilian, a Roman authority on the subject:

He who has not the right to the lati clavi should be so girt that the front edge of the tunic will come a little below the knee; in the back to the middle of the knees, for below this point it is the dress of a woman; above that of a centurion. For those having the lati clavi,

he adds, it was the fashion to be girt a little lower.[3]

Neatness of girdling was considered an index of character.

ROMAN TUNICS OF THE EMPIRE PERIOD. During the empire period the tunic lengthened, sleeves were added, clavi became mere ornamentation, and other forms of decoration developed. Most of these changes occurred during the third century. Commodus aroused much criticism by appearing in a long-sleeved tunic (Fig. 117). Soon the tunic itself was lengthened to the form called tunica talaris, a fashion retained through the remaining years of the empire.

Fortunately tunics dating from the empire period have been recovered from graves in Egypt. The Copts, an early Christian sect in Egypt, were expert weavers and embroiderers. When Egypt fell under the dominion of Rome, Roman fashions were set by the Roman official group and were followed in Alexandria as they were in Athens, Antioch, and Constantinople. Kendrick describes the textiles from Egyptian burying grounds of the early Christian centuries as follows:

. . . products of that Graeco-Roman art which then dominated the Mediterranean region and we must not expect them to bear the local stamp of the land where they were made.[4]

We are on safe ground in assuming that these remarkable stuffs from Egypt give us a correct idea of the woven and embroidered decoration of Graeco-Roman costume, not only in Egypt but also in other parts of the Empire from the first century onward.[5]

Garments in the third and fourth centuries had continuous clavi, as described above, but patterned with Greek fretwork

FIG. 117. *Commodus. 180–192* A.D. *(Vatican Museum, Rome, Anderson Photograph—Alinari)*

[3] Wilson, *op. cit.,* pp. 58–59.
[4] A. F. Kendrick, *Catalogue of Textiles from Burying-Grounds in Egypt,* Victoria and Albert Museum, published under the authority of His Majesty's Stationery Office, London, 1920, vol. I, p. 2.
[5] *Ibid.,* p. 20.

(Fig. 118). In the fourth century designs in the clavi became more open and included running animals—lions, antelopes, and hares. Foliage was also employed and the grapevine, long the symbol of Bacchus, became a popular design. Eventually it was given deeply religious significance by Christians.

In addition to the clavi, segmentae (isolated squares and roundels) filled with pattern were placed on the shoulders and front of the tunic. Bands of dancing figures, Greek in feeling, were sometimes placed below the horizontal slit forming the neckline. As early as the third century the clavi were sometimes broken, leaving a space between shoulder and skirt sections, the ends being finished in a leaf design.

Early Coptic tunics were decorated in monochromatic color, purple clavi with a design formed by a fine line of undyed linen embroidery. Later the patterns employed many colors and were tapestry woven.

THE DALMATIC. The dalmatic was a wide ungirdled outer garment, worn over the tunica talaris (Fig. 118). It was cut with full straight open sleeves and its clavi extended from shoulder to hem; usually two broad bands paralleled the bottom edge of the sleeves. A fresco from the fourth century shows a Christian in the attitude of prayer wearing a dalmatic (Fig. 119). The dalmatic survives today as a church vestment of the same name.

The fact that generals and emperors often came from distant parts of the Empire accounts for many of the fashion changes during the Empire. Thus Heliogabalus, who

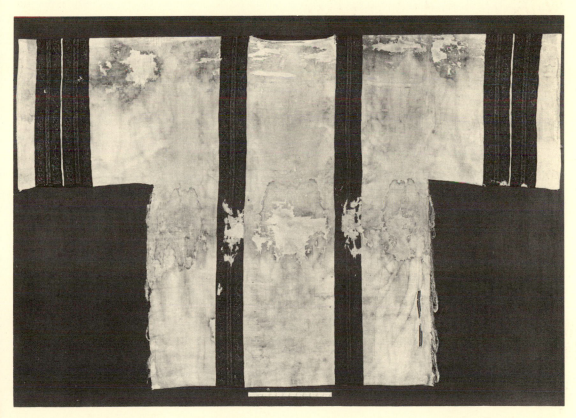

FIG. 118. *Dalmatic. Coptic. Egypt. Third to Fourth Century* A.D. *(Victoria & Albert Museum, Crown Copyright)*

Fig. 119.   *Early Christian Wearing Dalmatic. End of Fourth Century* A.D. *(Catacomb of Priscilla, Rome) Redrawn from Pierce and Tyler,* L'Art Byzantin, *Vol. I, Plate 51.*

ruled from 218 to 222 A.D. is said to have introduced the dalmatic, a garment which took its name if not its origin from Dalmatia. It probably appealed to him because of its loose flowing lines, akin to the dress of his native Syria. His Near East origin also explains his use of make-up, his lavish display of jewelry, and his addiction to silken garments. His debauched and effeminate appearance would have horrified Romans of the old school.

UNDERWEAR. Roman men customarily wore an under-tunic shorter and narrower than the outer one, called the subucula. Augustus must have been supersensitive to the cold for he is said to have worn four tunics and a subucula, plus extra protection for chest, thighs, and ankles.[6] A loincloth,

[6] William Ramsay, *A Manual of Roman Antiquities*, revised by Rodolfo Lanciani, Scribner, New York, 1895, p. 506.

designated as the subligaculum, was considered necessary for decency.

LEG COVERING. A garment called the feminalia covered the area of the femur (thigh bone) and was visible below the knee-length tunic (Fig. 120). This was a sort of close-fitting breeches which sometimes even covered a portion of the upper calf. The Romans long resisted anything resembling trousers or close leg coverings, associating them with such people as the Gauls, enemies of long standing, and the Dacians of Trajanic times. However, even though they were considered a symbol of barbarism, Roman campaigns in the rigorous northern climate compelled their adoption for both cavalry and foot soldiers, and even generals and emperors appeared in them. Figure 123 shows Trajan in the role of Roman emperor wearing feminalia as he offers a sacrifice. Prejudice against them seems finally to have broken down, for Wilson claims they were worn by Roman citizens of high rank when hunting or riding.[7]

THE TOGA. The garment usually associated with the Romans is, of course, the toga. Though it has come to be symbolic of their civilization, there is evidence that it too was based on an Etruscan counterpart. (See,

[7] Wilson, *op. cit.*, p. 74.

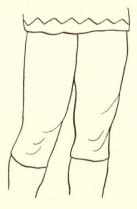

Fig. 120.   *Feminalia, Type of Trousers Worn by Roman Soldiers. Redrawn. (Trajan's Column, Rome)*

for example, the back view of the Etruscan statue in Fig. 102.) A clear early example of the Roman toga is also seen on the bronze statue of the Orator (Fig. 113), an Etruscan masterpiece of late third or early second century B.C. This Roman toga was doubtless a blend of the modes of the two peoples. The toga was evidently semicircular in shape and had a wide border (3 or 4 inches) on the outer curved edge. This bordered toga was known as the toga praetexta. The same order of draping persisted in all periods of Roman history except the very last. Starting with one point just above the left ankle, the straight edge facing toward center front, the mass of material was carried up over the left shoulder, downward under the right arm, upward across the chest to cover the left shoulder a second time, and downward to ankle length in back.

A later representation of the toga on the relief of a mother and her two sons (see Fig. 127), second century B.C., shows its tendency to increase both in length and width, throwing more bulk under the right arm and over the left shoulder.

That the change in size of the toga was rapid is proved by the statue in Fig. 114 of Augustus Caesar as Pontifex Maximus toward the end of his reign, which extended from 27 B.C. to 14 A.D. Here he is wearing the fully developed *imperial toga*, complete with the wide overfold which created the sinus (the outer layer of drapery under the right arm), the pouch at the waist called the umbo, and a mound of folds on the shoulder. These dimensions necessitated folding the toga before it was draped. The border was then changed from the outer lower edge to the edge of the overfold, as illustrated in Fig. 116. Later changes were in the direction of better control of the fullness and eventually toward mathematical arrangement and diminished size of the toga.

Only the emperor could wear the purple toga. In the days of grandeur this was probably made of the finest, sheerest wool, or a mixture of wool and silk, and embroidered in gold. The addition of embroidery, or pictures, gave it the name of *toga picta*. Tyrian purple, the richest in hue as well as the most costly of purple dyes, was no doubt reserved for the emperors. Students of Roman costume owe a great debt to Lillian Wilson for her detailed and annotated account of the subject.[8] Her research on dyes reveals that, from the Roman point of view, purple covered a wide range of hues, many of which we would call red. A dark toga was worn for mourning, a bleached white one (symbol of purity, no doubt) by a candidate for office.

The toga is not to be dismissed as a utility garment, casually changing in size and shape during the centuries. It was the Roman garment most fraught with meaning. Every freeborn son of a Roman citizen was entitled to wear, not just the ordinary toga of citizenship, but the *toga praetexta* of the governing class, a white toga with a purple border (Figs. 113 and 116). At the age of 16, when such a lad reached maturity, this toga as well as the bulla—a round pendant suspended from a ribbon (shown in Fig. 128), another symbol of his Roman birth—was ceremoniously laid aside and dedicated to the household gods. He then donned the plain white toga which was the badge of all Roman citizens. To wear the toga praetexta again he had to earn the right by becoming a senator or one of the higher magistrates.

Once impressiveness in size had reached its limit, subsequent changes came in the manner of wearing the toga, especially in controlling the sliding fabric. This did not modify the order of draping but employed a series of folds parallel to the original fold which formed the sinus (Fig. 121). In the *banded toga* many layers of cloth must have been pinned or sewed invisibly to hold them in position. In order to give further security to the drapery, as the end of the toga was thrown over the shoulder a second time, the set folds of the first or under portion of the

8 Wilson, *op. cit.*, frontispiece.

toga were sometimes brought over the bands of the latter section, covering them and binding them in place.

Because the many folded layers were cumbersome, heavy, and no doubt awkward to manage, an additional logical change eventually took place: the under layers were cut away, leaving only the visible top layer as a panel. Consuls are shown on their diptychs (commemorative panels of ivory

carved with the likeness of the consul in his state robes) wearing togas of this form (Fig. 122). In the *consular toga* all excess cloth was cut away, leaving only a panel, except as the wrap was brought forward under the right arm to spread over the front of the wearer.

At this point the order of draping must have changed, for the panel comes from the right shoulder down toward the waist, a line unknown in the republican and early imperial periods. Norris suggests that the panel started at ankle length in center front, went over the right shoulder and down to the waistline in the back where it formed a loop, came up over the left shoulder, crossed the chest, and proceeded under the right arm to center back.[9] From there it went through the waist loop and back under the right arm again, to be held across the lap of the seated consul. This toga is in the form of a panel until it passes through the waist loop, when it spreads into a semicircular shape.

Another possible order of draping is this: it went up over the right shoulder, circled the right arm, went across the chest and over the left shoulder, then angled downward across the back, under the right arm again and across the front to the left forearm. It would have helped us solve this problem if the sculptors of the ivory diptychs had carved a back view. These panel togas were elaborately embroidered, an offshoot of the richly decorated imperial toga picta.

OTHER ROMAN WRAPS. Although the toga is the outer garment most usually associated with the Romans, many other more practical wraps were in use, among which were the following:

1. The *pallium*, a Roman copy of the Greek himation and practically indistinguishable from it. Norris explains that the himation was worn wherever Greek culture was spread and that by the beginning of the

FIG. 121. *Statue of Edile. Early Fourth Century* A.D. *(Conservatori Museum, Rome, Alinari Photograph)*

[9] Herbert Norris, *Costume and Fashion*, Dent, London, 1924, vol. I, p. 162.

Fig. 122. *Leaf of Consular Diptych of Flavius Anastasius.* 517 A.D. (*Victoria & Albert Museum, Crown Copyright*)

FIG. 123. *Relief of Trajan Wearing Laena Drawn Over His Head, the Custom When Officiating at a Sacrifice. Early Second Century* A.D. *(Arch of Constantine, Rome, Originally from Trajan's Arch, Anderson Photograph—Alinari)*

Christian Era it had become universal among intellectual people.[10] By the second century A.D., possibly because it was the sole garment of Greek philosophers, it became the badge of all learned men, including the Roman literati. It was also adopted by the Christians, and in the later centuries of the Empire went through much the same order of folding and change as the toga, though it seems to have been folded through its full length. It survives today as the archbishop's pallium, a

narrow panel forming an elliptical yoke with front and back pendants. Before it reached this form it was a long panel draped about the shoulders. (Note its appearance in the mosaic of Justinian in Fig. 140.) As an accessory of the lay costume, it became the heavily jeweled and ornamented lorum, which was part of the regalia of the Byzantine emperors (shown in Fig. 143).

2. The *paludamentum*, an adaptation of the Greek chlamys, which was worn fastened on the right shoulder with a fibula.

[10] *Ibid.*, p. 107.

This was the military cloak of generals as early as the republican era and was worn by emperors and generals throughout the empire period. In the fifth century it became the imperial mantle of Byzantine emperors.

3. The *laena*, defined by Servius as a double toga and described by Wilson as possibly either folded or lined or made of a double-faced fabric.[11] Large, heavy, and often gayly colored, it was semicircular and was fastened at the right shoulder with a fibula. It is referred to in Latin literature from the first century B.C. through the empire period (Fig. 123).

4. The *lacerna*, another semicircular wrap, also fastened at the shoulder, and worn more frequently than the laena. It was made of light-weight material in a variety of colors from white to purple, and provided a protective wrap to be worn in case of rain or over the toga for added warmth. Worn by all classes, it varied in length from a hip-length riding version to mid-calf length on dignitaries. Its popularity extended from the first century B.C. through the empire period.

5. The *sagum*, a sort of blanket wrap adopted by Roman soldiers from the Gauls during the republican era. A versatile affair, it served as blanket, tent, overcoat or knapsack. It was never accepted for general wear by the Roman populace and even the army abandoned it by the end of the second century A.D.

6. The *paenula*, probably worn by Romans more than any other wrap. It was a cape-like garment, open down center front, with its own peaked hood usually attached. Though some paenulae were made of quite fine fabric, for ordinary men heavy wool homespun was used in natural colors—gray, brown, or black. They are mentioned in literature as early as the third century B.C. and probably have never completely disappeared since then. The peasants of Albania and Jugoslavia still weave such fabric for men's garments and many of their jackets

11 Wilson, *op. cit.*, p. 113.

and capes are provided with sailor collars which can be quickly converted into hoods.

7. The *casula*, a poncho-like wrap which slipped over the head. In case of storm it could be used as a miniature tent, hence the name casula, which means little house. It survives to this day as the chasuble of ecclesiastical vestments.

HEADDRESS. A hood or cucullus was usually worn with the casula, but it could also be combined with the laena or lacerna. The cucullus had its own small shoulder cape and when worn with draped wraps formed a welcome and efficient protection in inclement weather (Fig. 124). This hood no doubt is one of Rome's gifts to posterity. It seems never to have entirely disappeared, coming back into prominence during the Middle Ages as the chaperon.

The Romans also wore a cap similar to the Greek pilos and a brimmed hat copied from the petasos.

FOOTWEAR. The Romans were expert tanners and cobblers. While some of their

FIG. 124. *Roman Cucullus. Redrawn from Relief on Tomb of Noviomagus. (Rheinisches Landesmuseum, Trier)*

footwear is similar to that of the Greeks and the Etruscans, the Romans were given to greater variety and elaboration. The four types most often observed are the solea or sandal (Figs. 115 and 125); the calceus or shoe (Figs. 113 and 121); the crepida, which was a combination of these two (Fig. 126); and the cothurnus (Fig. 117), a high laced boot. In Fig. 123 Trajan and the man just back of him are wearing shoes laced in the modern manner over the instep.

Sandals were worn less by the Romans than by the Greeks; the calceus was more popular with the Romans. This shoe completely covered the foot; it was cut about the height of men's shoes today. A pair of straps came from the back part of the uppers, wrapped about the ankle, and tied in front. A second pair of straps was attached at each side of the sole near the ball of the foot, crossed at the instep and circled the ankle, being tied below the first pair. Sometimes only one pair of straps was used.

The cothurnus was higher in cut, coming well up on the leg. The most elaborate

examples are to be seen in the footgear of conquering generals, whose boots were ornamented with lions' heads and tooled designs. Many statues show what seems to be a folded cloth inside the top of the shoe, often rolled over the edge to protect the leg from abrasion. We know that the Copts were knitting hose by the fourth or fifth century. Possibly the Romans knew something about this craft also.

HAIRDRESS.   The haircut of the Roman man stayed much the same throughout Roman history. During the kingdom, no doubt, the hair was worn longer. However, on extant statues and reliefs the hair is short and allowed to take its own direction. Ramsay, in his manual of Roman antiquities, says that hairdressers came from Sicily as early as 300 B.C., the younger Scipio (about 200 B.C.) being the first person of note who shaved every day.[12] During the Empire, Hadrian revived the custom of wearing beards. The barber's shop seems to have been a favorite lounging place, and its equipment

[12] Ramsay, *op. cit.*, p. 509.

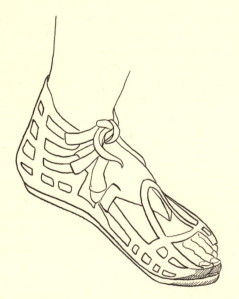

FIG. 125. *Roman Sandal. Redrawn from Statue of Charioteer. (Vatican Museum, Rome)*

FIG. 126. *Roman Crepida. Redrawn from Statue of Marcellus. (Capitoline Museum, Rome)*

was not unlike our own: knife and razor for nails and beard, scissors, comb, tweezers, curling tongs, mirror, towels, and dressing gown.

The popularity of the Roman bath is too well known to require discussion here, but it does indicate an extremely high standard of cleanliness.

JEWELRY. Except for fibulae, a necessary fastening device, rings were the only ornaments worn by men during the republic. Originally made of iron, they were used in sealing letters and documents. An exception to this was the right of certain government officials to wear gold rings, a right also granted to members of the equestrian order in the second century B.C. Like everything else, this custom changed during the Empire. Rings became ornamental and it was not uncommon for men to wear a ring on every finger or several on the same finger. Instead of a congressional medal, bracelets as well as gold rings were bestowed as a military honor and worn with pride. Heliogabalus probably set an all-time record for male adornment when he appeared with a necklace of pearls, his arms covered with bracelets, his hands heavy with rings. However, he was not typical of the ordinary Roman citizen.

The imperial crown of the first four Roman emperors consisted of a wreath of laurel leaves in gold. Nero adopted the corona radiata, inspired by the sun's rays. Heliogabalus was the first to wear a crown of pearls; this was a circlet of two or three strands fastened in front with another precious gem. It was Diocletian who had the courage—or effrontery—to assume an imperial diadem based on the crowns of the eastern rulers: a broad band of gold set with pearls, prototype of all subsequent royal crowns.

Women's Costume

THE STOLA. The mother with two sons shown in the relief in Fig. 127 (second century B.C.) suggests the intelligence, strength of character, and restrained taste of the women of early Rome. But when we read of the licentiousness of such women as Messalina, first wife of Claudius, who ruled from 41 to 54 A.D., of Agrippina the younger, niece and second wife of Claudius and appropriately the mother of Nero, and of Poppaea, who matched her husband Nero in criminal activity, we can be quite sure that they did not overlook the possibilities of enhancing their charms by their costumes.

Basically the Roman woman's costume was the same garment as that worn by Greek ladies of fashion. The Greek chiton became the stola in Rome, and the himation became the palla. Both styles of chiton are to be observed, the Doric often worn over the Ionic. The latter seems at times to have been cut fuller than its Greek ancestor, though the amount of fabric used must have varied widely. Examination of statues shows stolas of Ionic form clasped on the shoulders with brooches or buttons which produced a sleeve. These buttons could be increased in number from two to eight, the sleeve then extending beyond the elbow. Yardage probably differed with the texture of the cloth, sheerer fabrics utilizing more widths of material. Wilson suggests that sleeve length also varied with the season.[13] Many statues show excessive sweep at the hem; this has been interpreted as a flounce or ruffle, but no evidence of the mounting of such a feature is to be found. Literary references to an instita or border probably mean just that: a border rather than an additional gathered portion. The statue of Livia at Naples shows her wearing an elbow-length Ionic sleeve under a stola of Doric style. A shoulder strap about 6 inches long joins the neckline edges of the outer garment instead of the pinned closing used by the Greeks. A braided shoulder support is clearly visible on the bust of Julia, daughter of Augustus, in the Uffizi Gallery.

Variations inevitably occur in the costume of Roman women; it is only surprising

[13] Wilson, op. cit., p. 152.

that there are not more of them. Agrippina in the middle of the first century A.D. wore the Ionic type of stola, girdled high as was the custom during the Alexandrian period in Greece (Fig. 128). A relief of the second century A.D. shows a simple shoulder seam forming a short cap sleeve comparable to that of the men's tunic. In the famous Pompeian painting of the punishment of Eros (first century A.D.) the lady is wearing a sleeveless stola of the Doric order that has no overfold (Fig. 129). It is caught on the shoulder with a single brooch.

On the other hand, the seated figure of another Agrippina, wife of Germanicus, first century A.D., wears a stola which combines the Ionic fastening of many buttons with a waist-depth overfold, a detail of Doric design (Fig. 130). This is also a notable example of that extreme fullness at the

FIG. 127. *Mother and Sons. Second Century* B.C. (*Gallery Borghese, Rome, Alinari Photograph*)

bottom of the stola, mentioned a moment ago, which has been interpreted as a ruffle.

WRAPS. In the earliest years of Roman history women were supposed to have worn the toga, but no extant statues or reliefs confirm that supposition. Instead the palla is the omnipresent wrap. Wilson quotes Nonius, writing in the fourth century A.D., as stating that the palla was the garment of respectable women, and matrons were not supposed to appear in public without it.[14] The palla was the Roman copy of the Greek himation, and was worn in much the same manner; however, Roman statues lack the ingenuity and grace of arrangement achieved by the Greeks. In time the voluminous palla, like the toga, made way for a more practical

[14] *Ibid.*, p. 148.

FIG. 128. *Agrippina with Son Nero. Mid-First Century* A.D. *(Capitoline Museum, Rome, Anderson Photograph—Alinari)*

FIG. 129. *Punishment of Eros. Fresco from Pompeii. First Century* A.D. *(National Museum, Naples, Anderson Photograph—Alinari)*

Fig. 130. *Agrippina, Wife of Germanicus. First Century A.D. (Capitoline Museum, Rome, Alinari Photograph)*

wrap; by the latter part of the third century a much smaller and more manageable palla was in vogue. This, like the larger one before it, could be drawn up over the head for protection.

UNDERGARMENTS. For underwear a Roman woman wore a tunica interior, a short camisia (chemise) fitting close to the body, over which she placed a wide girdle. Called the strophium, this was the foundation garment of the time and gave support to the breasts.

HAIRDRESS. If the garments themselves remained fairly constant in form during these 800 years of Roman history, the hair-

dress varied enough that a close study of its change in fashion helps to date many a portrait bust and statue.

As would be expected, the hairdress during the republic was based on the Greek mode: the hair was parted in the middle, softly waved, and drawn to the back, where it was formed into a knot or long club-like chignon at the nape of the neck. The first deviation from this came during the latter part of the first century B.C. A small puff or pompadour was formed by bringing the center front section of the hair forward onto the forehead and then abruptly reversing it. Sometimes this portion was braided; when plaited in two sections the little pigtails were carried toward the ears and back into the knot; if one large braid was made it was taken straight back over the crown of the head. The latter fashion was still followed by unmarried girls in the Bosnian Village of Mrkonic Grad as late as 1937.

During the Empire, however, and especially by the last half of the first century, a great change took place. From the simplest of arrangements hairdress veered to the most elaborate—the very high pompadour, consisting of a front framework supporting a mass of short curls. The rest of the hair was braided and formed into a huge knot above the neck. The Flavian lady sometimes identified as Julia, daughter of Titus, who reigned from 79 to 81 A.D., wears this fantastic coiffure with grace (Fig. 131). This fashion held well into the second century. By the end of the first century, during Trajan's

FIG. 131. *Julia, Daughter of Titus. First Century* A.D. *(Capitoline Museum, Rome, Alinari Photograph)*

FIG. 132. *Faustina, Wife of Antoninus Pius. Second Century* A.D. *(Vatican Museum, Rome, Alinari Photograph)*

reign, 98–117 A.D., a turban-like silhouette was created by coiling the braids around the crown of the head in an upward and outward slanting line. The mass of hair involved makes one wonder if hair-growing nostrums were more effective then than now. In this connection it might be added that contact with the blonde Gauls brought blonde hair into fashion; if bleaching was not effective, wigs were worn.

The hair styling of Faustina the elder, wife of Antoninus Pius, emperor from 138 to 161 A.D. is dignified in contrast to all this elaboration (Fig. 132). She has drawn her loosely waved hair to the back, braided it, and arranged the braids in a dignified elongated knot over the crown of her head.

During the third century it became fashionable to show masses of hair below and back of the ears, sometimes covering them.

FIG. 133. *Julia Pia. Third Century* A.D. *(National Museum, Naples, Alinari Photograph)*

FIG. 134. *Vestal Virgin. Second Century* A.D. *(National Museum, Rome, Alinari Photograph)*

Some portrait busts show the hair cut and curled in quite modern fashion. On most of them the hair is reversed, that is, brought upward either to form a knot or braided in a broad flat braid which covers the crown of the head like a cap, as on the bust of Guilia Pia at Naples (Fig. 133). This style was still

practiced by young girls of Baranja, Jugoslavia, before World War II. Their braids had as many as forty strands and of course required a hairdresser and tedious hours of work. This fashion was followed by the roll or tire fashion of the Byzantine mode (see Fig. 139).

(a)   (b)

The hairdresses of brides and vestal virgins were quite similar, each producing the effect of a high crown, over which a veil was draped. According to both Ramsay[15] and Wilson[16] the hair was divided into six locks with a pointed instrument such as a sword. These locks were formed into six braids which were bound about the head in coronet fashion. Over this was placed the vitta, a symbol of purity, made of three wool cords joined together. This was bound over the braids, circled the head twice, and was fastened in the back; the ends were brought forward onto the shoulders. This formed a high bulky crown over which the veil was placed. Figure 134 shows a vestal virgin. The bride's veil was orange or flame color, sheer,

and as large as the palla. As late as the twentieth century a veil similar in color and size was worn by the brides of Astapylaea, one of the Cyclades group of islands.

HEADDRESS. In general, head coverings ranged from a kerchief the size of a square neck scarf to a bridal veil as large as the early palla. Materials varied from sheer to heavy textures.

FOOTWEAR. Women's footwear resembled that of men. Solae or sandals (Fig. 130) were most frequently worn, but the calceus appears also (Fig. 128). Brides shoes were golden or yellow.

JEWELRY. The first wedding rings, of iron, were in use well through the republic, when they were replaced by gold. As wealth from conquered nations poured into Rome,

[15] Ramsay, *op. cit.*, pp. 477–478.
[16] Wilson, *op. cit.*, p. 140.

(c)

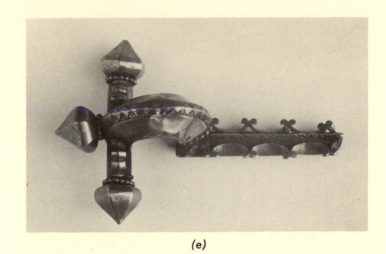

(e)

(d)

Fig. 135. a. *Gold Necklace, Third Century* A.D. b. *Cameo, Late Third Century.* c. *Wedding Ring, Early Fifth Century.* d. *Earrings, Early Fourth Century.* (a–d, *Dumbarton Oaks Collection*) e. *Fibula, Late Fourth Century.* (*British Museum*)

including precious metals from the mines of newly acquired provinces, taste in jewelry as in everything else turned toward elaboration. Amber from the Baltic was long a coveted trade item and ladies carried it in their hands both for tactile pleasure and for the faint fragrant perfume the warmth of the body released. Diamonds from Bengal, pearls from the Near East, emeralds and rubies became available. Pliny says that the Empress Paulina, wife of Caligula, who ruled from 37 to 41 A.D., appeared at a supper party with neck, arms, hands, and girdle covered with emeralds and pearls. Sabina, wife of Emperor Hadrian (117–138 A.D.), possessed a diadem of stephane design valued at nearly a million dollars.

Figure 135 shows outstanding examples of Roman jewelry: The necklace of paired golden birds (*a*) ends with dolphins and shell motifs. Renowned for both intaglio and cameo engravings, Roman jewelers produced such pendants as (*b*) the design of which includes the busts of Emperor Diocletian and Emperor Maximian Herculius. Wedding rings were often set with an engraving of the heads of bride and groom (*c*). Surely ranking among the most superb earrings in the world is the pair of gold, pearl, and sapphire pendants in the Dumbarton Oaks collection (*d*) from the fourth century A.D. The typical Roman fibula (*e*) was an indispensable accessory throughout Roman history.

6

The Byzantine Empire

When Constantine moved the capital of the Roman Empire to the small Greek town of Byzantium and renamed it Constantinople in 330 A.D., he probably had little conception of what long-lasting and wide-ranging effects would follow his action. Although Rome fell to the barbarians in 476, Constantinople held out until 1453, almost a thousand years longer. In these centuries she kept in trust her heritage from Greece, Rome, and the Orient, combining, assimilating, and evolving a culture of her own whose enormous influence was world wide. Her indomitable resistance to one foe after another and the loyalty and bravery displayed still excite admiration.

In creating a court in keeping with the supreme power, both religious and political, which they assumed, Byzantine emperors freely adapted to their own use settings and customs from the East. It is difficult in these days of democracy to imagine the splendor in which they moved. The choicest marbles were combined with gold and jewels to bedazzle the eye. Silver lions stationed at each side of the throne rose and roared at propitious moments to reduce a visitor to an attitude even lower than his prostrate form.

During the eighth and ninth centuries, the iconoclastic controversy so reduced the output of Byzantine artists that the record of costume during these centuries is decidedly meager.

Byzantine Fabrics

The regalia prescribed for rulers and their attendants equaled in magnificence the settings in which they moved. Sumptuous silken fabrics, which were produced by imperial looms, became easily available when Justinian established the silk industry in Constantinople in the sixth century. Before that time silk had been imported from the Far East, much of it routed through Persia and Syria. During the Graeco-Roman period, from the first century onward, it had been customary to ravel out these heavy imported silks and reweave the filaments into sheer fabrics, more suited to the climate and fashions of the Mediterranean area. These fabrics were also varied by combinations with other fibers. Heliogabalus is said to have been the first Roman emperor to appear entirely

Fig. 136. *Charlemagne's Dalmatic. c.800. (Sacristy, St. Peters, Rome) From Lady Alford,* Needlework as Art, *1886, Plate 54.*

clothed in silk. Since the supply was definitely limited at that time, it was easily worth its weight in gold.

But from Justinian onward the Byzantine emperors suffered no such restrictions. Monopolizing the output of the looms, they reserved the best for themselves. With wily discretion, they distributed the magnificent fabric as coveted and persuasive gifts to royalty far and near. Mrs. Antrobus relates

that some of Charlemagne's magnificent state ceremonial garments were gifts from the imperial workshops at Constantinople.[1] Possibly the dalmatic associated with Charlemagne's name was one of these garments (Fig. 136). Mrs. Antrobus says of it:

It is universally agreed that the well-

[1] Mary Symonds Antrobus, *Needlecraft Through the Ages,* Hodder, London, 1928, p. 171.

Fig. 137. *Early Byzantine Costume. Mid-Fourth Century* A.D. *Redrawn from Silver Plate from Kertch.* (*Hermitage Museum, Leningrad*)

known dalmatic of Charlemagne in the sacristy of St. Peter's, Rome, for its marvelous composition and beauty must be ranked amongst the highest and best of Byzantine embroideries.[2]

Its date has been disputed but the one assigned to it in the sacristy is within Charlemagne's reign, 771–814.

Such exports not only spread Byzantine

fashion but whetted the desire for more. One important effect of the Crusades was the impact of eastern fabrics and fashions upon the European invaders.

Under Byzantine dominance, fabrics became stiffer, heavier, and more richly patterned. The Persians, as the silk passed through their hands, put their imprint upon it, especially during the Sassanian Dynasty (226–651 A.D.). The familiar designs of con-

[2] *Ibid.*, p. 183.

fronted animals separated by the sacred tree, of hunters on horseback, and the Gilgamish motif of a heroic figure strangling a lion with each hand, are all traceable to Mesopotamia. These in turn were copied in Egypt, Syria, and Constantinople. Some of the extant examples of Byzantine fabrics employ single animals on a grand scale, such as the eagle and elephant silks.

Important weaving centers arose at Thebes and Corinth in Greece, and it was from there that the Norman, Roger II, secured weavers for his Sicilian industries. The twelfth century coronation robes of the Holy Roman Emperors furnish ample proof of the skill of Sicilian craftsmen. They also illustrate the use of eastern designs in the embroidered motifs.

FIG. 138. *Coptic Tunic. Seventh to Eighth Century. (Brooklyn Museum)*

Men's Costume

The discussion of Coptic tunics in the chapter on Roman costume is also applicable to Byzantine fashions. Tunics ornamented with clavi, segmentae, and borders at wrist and hem were common to both eastern and western divisions of the Roman Empire (Figs. 137 and 138). Important extant examples of tunics of the later centuries of the Coptic period, that is, sixth to eighth, are made of colored wool—green, yellow, red, and purple—with polychromatic decoration. The most exquisite examples of Coptic embroidery and tapestry work were done in silk.

Tunics of the working class were much simpler in style and without decoration.

Fig. 139.   *Diptych of Stilicho and Serena.* 395 A.D. (*Monza Cathedral, Alinari Photograph*)

FIG. 140. *Justinian and His Court.* 547 A.D. (*Choir of San Vitale, Ravenna, Alinari Photograph*)

They fitted more loosely, were shorter, and might have sleeves of elbow length. In the case of fishermen, represented by Andrew and Peter, the tunic might be sleeveless and worn with the right shoulder exposed in the manner of the Greek exomis (see p. 79). Evidence of long, rather loose, open-legged trousers worn under knee-length tunics is found on an ivory panel of the fifth century. In the scenes illustrating the episode of Joseph and Potiphar's wife in a manuscript of the late fifth century, the men in the employ of Potiphar wear short white tunics with long sleeves over white fitted trousers.

Their black hose reach the knee, where a bit of brilliant red indicates a colored lining.

Greater variety appeared in the tunics of the upper classes. The Vandal Stilicho, commander in chief of the Roman army and for a while virtual ruler of the Eastern Empire (395 A.D.) wore a long-sleeved knee-length design made of patterned silk and girdled below the normal waistline (Fig. 139). On the other hand, Emperor Justinian (sixth century) could well have ordered the tunic he wears in Fig. 140 from Alexandria. The ornamentation is highlighted with gold.

As David presents himself before Saul on one of the plates of the Cypress Treasure (seventh century) he and one of the soldiers standing by wear short-sleeved short tunics; the long-sleeved ankle-length garment is more in keeping with the dignity of Saul and his companion.

The Emperor Nicephoras Botaniates (eleventh century) wore a long formal tunic, made of the finest purple fabric and emblazoned with gold and jewels (Fig. 141). Around 1342 the high admiral Apocaucos posed in a full-length tunic with long sleeves made of Byzantine silk showing addorsed lions (turned back to back) framed in roundels (Fig. 142).

WRAPS. Outer wraps are not as fully represented in art as tunics are, but there is

FIG. 141. *Nicephoras Botaniates with St. John Chrysostom and Archangel Gabriel. 1078-1081. From Coislin MS. 79. (Bibliothèque Nationale, Paris)*

FIG. 142. *Portrait of High Admiral Apocaucos, Prefect of Constantinople. c.1342 From Greek MS. 2144, Folio 11. (Bibliothèque Nationale, Paris)*

evidence that in addition to draped and pinned wraps the Byzantines adopted some of the sleeved coats of the Persians. Thus in Fig. 139 Stilicho wears a paludamentum which falls as if it were made of silk. The fibula is classic Roman. In his Psalter, Basil II (963–1025) is shown wearing a blue chlamys.

THE PALUDAMENTUM. In Byzantium the paludamentum replaced the Roman toga as a state garment. Its color and decoration were set by rank, purple being reserved for the emperor and empress. All during Byzantine history it remained much the same, the chief change occurring in the shape and

FIG. 143. *Nicephoras Botaniates and Wife Marie. 1078–1081. From Coislin MS. 79.* (*Bibliothèque Nationale, Paris*)

placement of the "tablions," the excessively rich ornamental plaques placed on the open back and front edges of the paludamentum and illustrated in Figs. 140 and 141. Justinian's tablions employ a design of green birds on a gold ground. Note the elongated shape on Fig. 141. The paludamentum of the late Byzantine Empire became quite stiff and heavy and the tablion was set with jewels.

THE LORUM. The lorum was a panel which resulted from the folding and eventual elimination of the excess material of the Roman pallium. The lorum is the royal counterpart of the ecclesiastical pallium: just as the pallium was a mark of distinction reserved for archbishops, the lorum was the prerogative of the emperor and empress. In Fig. 140 the archbishop, Maximian, standing at Justinian's left, is vested in albe, dalmatic, chasuble, and pallium. The pallium at this period was a long, narrow band draped about the shoulders.

The lorum changed somewhat with the centuries. At least three versions are represented in Byzantine art: (1) a very long narrow panel of even width with its full length decorated (Fig. 143); (2) a panel of greater width which, instead of being draped about the body, had an aperture for the head permitting it to be worn poncho style; and (3) a version worn in conjunction with the broad Byzantine collar, worn in Fig. 143 by an empress but appearing on emperors also.

FOOTWEAR. The Roman tradition of fine footwear was observed also by the Byzantines. Justinian made long hose respectable by adopting them. In Fig. 140 they are purple and worn with low shoes fastened with jeweled clasps. However, as early as the fourth century, with complete disregard for Roman opinion, Stilicho, whose ancestors had been accustomed to leg coverings for centuries, wore long, well-fitted hose (Fig. 139). His pointed, low-cut shoe is eastern rather than classic in origin. A laced boot is clearly detailed on one of the soldiers of a silver plate in the Metropolitan Museum. Basil II was more impressive because of his high red military boots, sewed with pearls (Fig. 144). The Roman calceus remained in use, but the open-toed crepida, laced to lower calf, was apparently preferred for more active pursuits. In pastoral scenes shepherds wrapped their legs to the knee and in many outdoor activities men appear to be wearing socks and low shoes with thongs binding the leg to boot height. This custom was still predominant among the Serbians up to World War II.

ACCESSORIES. One accessory which was practically nonexistent among the Byzantines is the headdress. Except for royalty, men went bareheaded. In early reigns the crown consisted of a double row of pearls. By Justinian's era (527–565) it had become rigid and more imposing (Fig. 140): a slightly flaring gold band, edged with pearls, encircled with precious stones, with pear-shaped pearls suspended from the sides. In later centuries an enormous precious stone occupied the center front panel, with other stones subordinate to it (Figs. 141 and 143). The crown of Constantine IX (1042–1054) was made of enameled panels linked together.

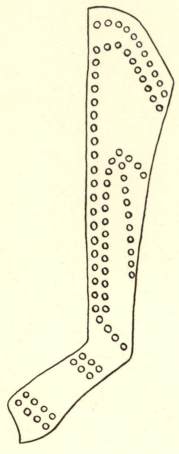

FIG. 144. *Red Boot of Emperor Basil II. 976–1025. Redrawn from Psalter of Basil II. (Marcian Library, Venice)*

Figure 148 is from a photograph of one of the panels now in the National Museum of Budapest. By the twelfth century the emperor's crown had become dome-shaped and two centuries later the dome above the circular band had become bulbous (Fig. 142).

The honored Roman fibula gave way in Byzantium to the fabulous jeweled brooch worn by Justinian in Fig. 140. The torques worn by his bodyguards are similar to those in Fig. 149.

Women's Costume

Costumes of Byzantine women, like those of the men, depended for interest upon sumptuous fabrics, lavish ornamentation, and jewels unlimited, rather than originality of design. The simply cut long-sleeved stola was the fundamental garment throughout the thousand years of Byzantine history. Sometimes the revived Ionic chiton, the dalmatic, or, in later centuries, an overdress or supertunic was combined with it.

The palla continued in practical use, the right of women to wear the paludamentum being limited to empresses. The same restrictions applied to the lorum when it became part of the royal regalia.

The dalmatic was adopted by the early Christians, both men and women, but by the seventh century it had practically disappeared as a garment for the laity. When it was again seen in the eleventh and twelfth centuries, it was as part of the empress' regal attire.

Another garment entered the fashion picture about the eleventh century. This was a contrasting overdress varying in length from hip to knee level.

These fashions can be seen in ivory reliefs, mosaics, frescoes, and in the designs of actual fabrics. Figure 139 shows Serena (395 A.D.), wife of Stilicho, wearing the stola, the revived Ionic chiton, the palla, the characteristic turban, and pointed shoes. Her earrings and double strand of jewels, both on a grandiose scale, are significant of Byzantine taste.

Though the garment worn directly over the stola is usually referred to as the Ionic chiton, in reality it seems to have been more nearly akin to the early Roman tunic. The chief difference is in the size of the arm opening. The wonderful procession of fe-

Fig. 145. *St. Cecilia. Sixth Century. (Basilica of Saint Apollinare Nuovo, Ravenna, Alinari Photograph)*

male saints in St. Apollinare Nuovo in Ravenna shows that this overdress was worn as late as the sixth century. Each saint wears such a garment almost covering her stola (Fig. 145). Only the lower part of the long sleeve of the latter is visible.

These saints also illustrate one of the first steps in the alteration of the pallium. The colorful narrow panel visible above the hem at center front replaced the full width of the original pallium (or, in the case of the women's wrap, the palla). The panel at this time probably extended to the waist, where it was attached to the palla proper. From there it spread out to drape around the shoulders, enveloped the right upper arm, and was then brought diagonally upward again over the left shoulder. A wide belt fastened with a prominent jeweled buckle was worn over the palla to secure it in place. The Empress Ariane, shown in Fig. 146 (about 500), is a typical example of Byzantine ostentation. Her paludamentum is weighted with a double border of pearls which even Hollywood would describe as colossal. Her tablion encrusted with pearls bears a likeness of her son in consular attire. Her broad collar drips pear-shaped pearls, and her crown has masses of pearls in front as well as perpendulia—long jeweled pendants—suspended from the sides. One noteworthy feature is the lovely soft suppleness of the fabric. This quality will disappear later.

The mosaic of Theodora and her suite shown in Fig. 147 suggests the rich and glowing atmosphere of court functions in the sixth century. The Empress was a woman of strong character and wore her regal finery with ease and assurance. Her white stola is adorned with gold; her purple paludamentum is symbolically embroidered with the three magi bearing gifts. Beside her stands her closest friend, Antonina, wife of the great general, Belisarius. Antonina's purple stola is arresting because of the broad gold clavi embroidered with red, white, and green floral designs. The accompanying white palla bears large gold segmentae in

FIG. 146. *Empress Ariane. Ivory Diptych.* 500 A.D. *(Bargello, Florence, Alinari Photograph)*

the corners. Other color combinations in the group include a white stola patterned in blue under a gleaming gold palla with red and green motifs, and a green stola combined with an orange-red palla. Little scarlet shoes add a gay note.

Figure 143 shows Marie, wife of Nicephoras Botaniates (eleventh century) wearing the very wide-sleeved dalmatic, with a broad collar matching the lorum, the front panel of which hangs from under the collar. The back panel, widening at the end, is brought forward under the right arm and spreads across the lower front of her costume. The dominating areas of jeweled cloth of gold produce an effect of inflexibility. Note the higher crown with three circlets of jewels.

A Byzantine fashion which will be seen repeatedly in Western Europe during the Middle Ages is illustrated in Fig. 148. This is a panel from the crown of Constantine IX who ruled in the eleventh century. Over her full-length dress the dancing maiden is wearing a fitted tunic which reaches her upper thigh, richly decorated with jewels and em-

broidery. Two other panels from the same crown show women in tunics extending well toward the knee. Jeweled girdles confine the waistline. All of the tunics have long tight sleeves.

Judging by the few examples of women of middle or lower class which appear in Byzantine art, their clothing was conservative, consisting of stola and palla. The portrait of David's bride on a seventh-century silver plate shows her wearing a long-sleeved high-girdled stola with a remarkable resemblance to the empire gown of early nineteenth century. Even the smooth manner in which the fabric falls from the high waistline looks familiar. On the other hand, maids as-

FIG. 147. *Empress Theodora and Suite. 547 A.D. (Choir of San Vitale, Ravenna, Alinari Photograph)*

sisting in such scenes as the Nativity appear in sleeveless or short-sleeved stolas.

For outdoor wear the palla was universal. It was drawn up over the head, muffling the upper part of the figure and thus concealing details of neckline and sleeves. Varied

FIG. 148. *Panel of Crown of Constantine IX, Monomachos. Eleventh Century. (National Museum, Budapest)*

colors contributed to the liveliness of the scenes.

HAIRDRESS AND HEADDRESS. The headdress was the Byzantine woman's most distinctive accessory. At the end of the fourth century it had a turban shape formed by a tire-like roll surmounted by a soft round crown and entirely concealed the hair (Fig. 139). To this basic shape empresses added jeweled bands and upon it they set their crowns (Figs. 146 and 147). Gold, pearls, and precious stones were used with lavish abandon, encircling, standing upright, and hanging in long perpendulia from the sides. Figure 145 shows St. Cecilia's hair arranged with softness about her face and a knot on top of her head. A jeweled diadem helps to project her sublimity and at the same time secures the long floating white veil which reaches to her ankles. By the eleventh and twelfth centuries, empresses were allowing their hair to show, the only difference in appearance being single curls which fell from each side to the shoulder or chest. Sometimes they wore tiered crowns with serrated or battlemented edges which were compatible in height with the domed crowns of the emperors (Fig. 143).

FOOTWEAR. Since women's costumes in the art works of the Byzantine period usually obscure their feet, little can be discerned about their footwear. We know that the Empress Theodora wore shoes of purple and gold and her ladies-in-waiting red shoes (Fig. 147). In fact wherever shoes are visible they are usually red, whether upper or lower class is indicated. In an adoration scene of the twelfth century the Virgin Mary is shown in low-cut red slippers quite modern in effect. In a detail of this same mosaic a young woman assisting with the bath of the Christ child deviates from the general practice by wearing black slippers with orange hose. Pointed toes such as those of Empress Ariane in Fig. 146 suggest eastern influence.

JEWELRY. As fabrics lost their supple quality and emphasis shifted to dazzling splendor, jewels were used profusely on tablions and lorums; they even outlined embroidered designs on the tunics. Though jewelry as we think of it would hardly be noticed in the face of such competition, some beautiful examples exist. A gold bracelet set with pearls and sapphires in the Metropolitan Museum and an earring combining pearls and precious stones in the Cleveland Museum of Art are typical examples.

7

Western Europe to the Twelfth Century

BACKGROUND

As early as the second millennium B.C., the Germans or Teutons, who appeared briefly in our discussion of the Bronze Age in Northern Europe, were established in Scandinavia and on the continent between the Elbe and Oder rivers. To the west of the Elbe were the Celts, who spread into France and England during the Bronze Age, 2000–1000 B.C. In the sixth and fifth centuries B.C. pressures from the Teutonic tribes stirred them to migrate. Some branches of them had settled as far away as Asia Minor by the third century B.C. These were the Galatians of the Bible. Other Celts, or Gauls, as they were known to the Romans, poured into northern Italy and early in the fourth century B.C. succeeded in sacking Rome. A westward contingent reached the British Isles, though some Celts had invaded Britain even earlier, occupying the area where England is now. These earlier Celts, the Gaels, were pushed to the extremities of the islands and into Ireland and Scotland, by the newly arrived Celts, the Brythons. During that westward movement what are now France and Belgium were also occupied.

As early as 1000 B.C. the western Germans had begun to exert pressure on the Celts by moving up the Elbe and Rhine rivers, and southern Germany was occupied by 100 B.C. The eastern Germans, those in Scandinavia, crossed the Baltic and followed the Vistula to the Carpathian Mountains and onward to the Black Sea, which they reached in the third century A.D.

On the move also were the Huns, of Mongolian origin, who began their conquests and depredations in eastern Europe during the fourth century A.D. These contributed largely to the continental migrations of the Germanic (or Teutonic) tribes. Attila, greatest of the Huns, died in 453 A.D., and the following year a united force under Roman direction defeated the Huns and scattered them to be absorbed into the general population.

The Teutons, in a vast outpouring of peoples bent on conquest, looting, and colonization, did their bit in hastening the fall of Rome and resettled most of Europe during the fourth, fifth, and sixth centuries A.D. Of the eastern group which reached the Black Sea, the Goths, including both Ostrogoths and Visigoths, were outstanding. The Ostrogoths (eastern Goths), to whom Theodoric the Great belonged, occupied much of Italy; the Visigoths (western Goths) under Alaric threatened Constantinople, sacked Rome, and, having conquered Spain, enjoyed supremacy there until the Mohammedans took over. Of the western wanderers, the Franks gave their name to the great French nation and the Alemanni and Saxons became major elements in Germany. Other areas were occupied by Teutonic groups during this migration period: northern Africa by the Vandals, east-central France by the Burgundians, northern Italy by the Lombards, and Britain by the Angles, Saxons, and Jutes.

COSTUME ON THE MAINLAND

During these centuries of unrest and almost constant movement, costume undoubtedly received little more than utilitarian consideration. Skin garments probably predominated among the masses and jewelry no doubt played the major role in satisfying personal pride.

The Gundestrup bowl, a Celtic masterpiece found in Denmark (Fig. 149), gives a clue to the costume of central and western Europe at this time. One of the silver plates which cover the vessel shows a seated male figure grasping a torque in one hand and a serpent in the other. Though the antlers springing from the top of his head help to identify him as a fertility god, his costume, which resembles a form-fitting pullover sweater tucked into or continuous with skin-tight Bermuda shorts, must have some basis in fact. The texture or surface of the material of the costume is rendered in the same manner as the wearer's hair and the fur of the animals in the composition. Note his trim footwear. Another plate shows a group of soldiers similarly dressed. Two women

shown wear sleeveless one-piece garments cut slightly low in front, one ankle-length and belted, the other longer and hanging loose. The dresses seem to be fastened on the shoulders in the manner of the Greek peplos.

Concerning the provenance and date of the Gundestrup bowl, the unidentified author of the text of the Museum publication *National Museum of Denmark* says: "We are far from understanding of the imagery on the Gundestrup Bowl. Both its age and its origin are still disputed. Most scholars consider it to be of Northern French workmanship dating from shortly before the Birth of Christ."[1]

Tacitus, the Roman historian, writes thus of the Germans of about 98 B.C.:

The clothing common to all is a sagum fastened by a clasp or, in want of that, a thorn. With no other covering they pass whole days on the hearth, before the fire. The more wealthy are distinguished by a vest, not flowing loose, like those of the Sarmatians and Pathians, but girt close, and exhibiting the shape of every limb. [Compare this with the costume of the Gundestrup bowl.] They also wear the skins of beasts, which the people near the borders are less curious in selecting or preparing than the more remote inhabitants, who cannot by commerce procure other clothing. These make choice of particular skins, which they variegate with spots and strips of the furs of marine animals, the produce of the exterior ocean; and seas to us unknown. The dress of the women does not differ from that of the men; except that they more frequently wear linen, which they stain with purple; and do not lengthen their upper garment into sleeves but leave exposed the whole arm and part of the breast.[2]

In another passage Tacitus speaks of the Suebi who twist back their hair and often tie it in a knot on top of the head, to make them look taller and to terrify the enemy

---

[1] *The National Museum of Denmark*, Copenhagen, 1957, p. 58.
[2] Cornelius Tacitus, *The Germany and the Agricola of Tacitus* (Oxford translation revised), McKay, Philadelphia, 1897, pp. 37–38.

as they engage in battle, while another tribe lets their hair and beard grow until they have killed a man.

Only a few actual examples of clothing of the first centuries of the Christian Era have been preserved. Among them are a famous man's costume found in the Thorsberg bog in Germany and the woman's garments from Denmark in the National Museum in Copenhagen. The Thorsberg costume, now in the Schleswig-Holstein Museum, consists of shirt and trousers (Fig. 150). The diaper weave gives added interest, and the cut shows quite an advanced understanding of pattern making. The set-in sleeves of the shirt, the shaping of the seat of the trousers, and the design of the foot portion attached to the bottom of the

FIG. 149. *Gundestrup Bowl. Detail. Celtic. Near Time of Christ. (Danish National Museum, Copenhagen)*

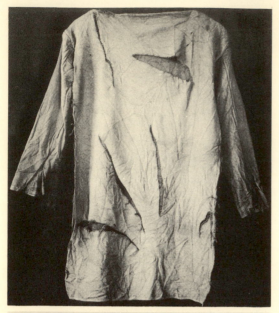

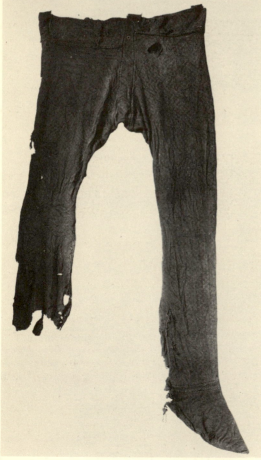

FIG. 150. *Thorsberg Costume Found in Germany. First to Third Centuries* A.D. *(Schleswig-Holstein Museum)*

trouser leg, all exhibit a genuine sense of fitting. The trousers are provided with belt loops. The Schleswig-Holstein Museum dates the costume between the first and third centuries A.D.

Replicas in the National Museum in Copenhagen are in a rust-colored wool, much more finely spun and woven than fabrics of the Bronze Age.

The woman's costume from Denmark consists of a full skirt made of wool plaid in monochromatic browns and a skin cape (Fig. 151). A length of plaid wool which might have been used as a stole was found in the same place. Another costume of plaid wool displayed by the Museum is in the style of a Doric chiton with a narrow overfold; that is, it is made in one length, with the upper edges caught together on the shoulders and a girdle confining the waist. Both costumes bear similarities to those of the Gundestrup bowl.

Jewelry of the Gauls and Germans of the Roman and migration periods shows a predilection for torques and heavy bracelets, akin in feeling to Bronze Age products (Fig. 149).

COSTUME OF THE BRITONS

Our knowledge of the costume of the ancient Britons, the people who inhabited England before the invasion of the Angles, Saxons, and Jutes, is largely literary.

Julius Caesar was the earliest Roman author whose comments upon these people have been preserved. He wrote:

The most civilized people among them are the Kentish men, whose country lies altogether upon the seacoasts; and whose customs are much the same with those of the Gauls. The inland people seldom trouble themselves with agriculture, living on milk and flesh meat, and are clad with skin; but all of them paint themselves blue with woad [a herbaceous plant from which they extracted blue dye], that they may look the more dreadful to their enemies in battle. The hair of their heads they wear very long, but shave all the rest of their bodies, except the upper lip.[3]

Herodianus wrote of the more northern people of England who were less civilized than the Kentish folk. Speed quotes him thus:

The Britaines knew no use of garments at all, but about their waistes and necks wore chains of iron, supporting them a goodly ornament, and a proofe of their wealth; and their bare bodies they marked with sundry pictures representing all manner of living creatures, and therefore they would not be clad, for hiding the gay paintings of their bodies.[4]

Although Julius Caesar invaded Britain in 55 B.C. the conquest of that portion of the British Isles now known as England was not completed until the reign of Hadrian, who led the final campaign and marked his success by building Hadrian's wall in 123 A.D. Romanization, however, went on in the meantime. One decisive step was the suppression of the rebellion led by the great heroine Boadicea in 61 A.D., who inspired the Britons to revolt against their harsh treatment by the Romans. As a widowed queen Boadicea and her two daughters had suffered the most cruel indignities at the hands of their masters. The revolt was unsuccessful and rather than be taken prisoner to Rome, Boadicea committed suicide. Tacitus relates that "the Britons fought not only under the conduct of men but also of women, who were admitted into their councils both of peace and war and great deference was paid to their opinions; of which sex Boadicea was a wonderful example of courage and greatness of soul."[5]

The Roman historian Cassius Dio described Boadicea as follows:

In person she was very tall, with the most sturdy figure and a piercing glance; her voice was harsh; a great mass of yellow hair fell below her waist and a large golden necklace clasped her throat; wound about her was a tunic of every conceivable color [possibly plaid] and over it a thick chlamys had been

FIG. 151. *Woman's Costume from Huldremose. Second Century* A.D. *(Danish National Museum, Copenhagen)*

[3] G. Julius Caesar, *Commentaries of his Wars in Gaul and Civil War with Pompey*, 7th ed., trans. Martin Bladen; P. and P. Knapton, London, 1750, p. 84.

[4] John Speed, *The Historie of Great Britaine under the Conquests of the Romans, Saxons, Danes and Normans*, 3rd ed., John Dawson for George Humble, London, 1632, p. 21.

[5] Joseph Strutt, *A Compleate View of the Manners, Customs, Arms, Habits, Etc. of the Inhabitants of England from the Arrival of the Saxons till the Reign of Henry VIII*, London, 1775, vol. I, p. 4.

fastened with a brooch. This was her constant attire.[6]

The Roman occupation was further described by Tacitus in his biography of his father-in-law, Agricola, proconsul of Britain from 78 to 84:

Agricola held forth the baits of pleasure, encouraging the natives, as well by public assistance as by warm exhortations, to build temples, courts of justice, and commodious dwelling houses. He bestowed encomiums on such as cheerfully obeyed. . . . To establish a plan of education, and give the sons of the leading chiefs a tincture of letters, was part of his policy. . . . The consequence was, that they, who had always disdained the Roman language, began to cultivate its beauties. The Roman apparel was seen without prejudice, and the toga became a fashionable part of dress. . . . Baths, and porticoes, and elegant banquets grew in vogue. [Evidently one would be justified in imagining the outstanding citizens of leading communities dressed in the mode of Rome itself.][7]

By his wisdom and tact Agricola was able to raise the standard of living of the Britons and to implant Roman customs and culture so firmly that they survived to a certain degree the inundation of Britain by the Germanic Angles, Saxons, and Jutes during the fifth century.

THE SAXONS IN BRITAIN

The Anglo-Saxons were a stout and hardy people. They delighted chiefly in war, which was part of their religion, and they considered it dishonorable to die of a disease or in bed.[8] Prudence and valor they esteemed most highly and evidently women were accorded respect. The men would not go into battle or undertake any great expedition

without first consulting their wives, whose advice they regarded highly.

The Saxons, as these Germanic invaders were called in England, lived simply, even the ruling class. Women of higher rank spent their leisure hours spinning and were not above helping the maids in their household duties, while the lords supervised and assisted their men at their work.

Strutt throws additional light upon their clothing after their conquest of England:

The kings and nobles when in their state dress, were habited in a loose coat which reached down to their ankles, and over that, a long robe fastened over both shoulders, on the middle of the breast, with a clasp or buckle. . . . The edges and bottom of their coats, as well as their robes were often trimmed with a broad gold edging, or else flowered with different colors.

The soldiers and common people wore close coats reaching only to the knee, and a short cloak over the left shoulder, which buckled on the right; this cloak was often trimmed with an edging of gold. The kings and nobles also in common, were habited in a dress very similar to this, only more richer and more elegant. . . . From the form of it, it appears to have been put on over the head like a shirt; the bottom edge of these garments were also ornamented in various manners according to history; those of the richer were adorned with pearles and precious stones.

The women were habited in a long loose robe reaching down to the ground and large loose sleeves; besides this they added a hood (or vail) over the head, which falling down before, was wrapped round the neck with great order; their robe was often ornamented with broad borders of different colors, as well at the knees as at the bottom. The women do not appear to have any other covering for their heads than the vail; but the men wore caps which came to a point before; perhaps they might be made of the skins of some beasts dressed with the fur part turned outward.

Both men and women wore shoes or rather slippers, the legs of the men were covered half way up with a kind of bandage bound round, or else a straight stocking reaching above the knee; while the commoner sort went naked-

[6] Cassius Dio, *Rome*, trans. Herbert Baldwin Foster, Pafraets Book Co., Troy, N.Y., 1906, vol. 5, p. 30.
[7] Arthur Murray, *The Works of Cornelia Tacitus*, John Stockdale, London, 1811, vol. 7, p. 114.
[8] Strutt, *op. cit.*, p. 17.

legged and often barefooted: they also wore a sort of boots which were curiously ornamented at the top.[9]

He adds that a bracelet, presumably Saxon, had been found in eastern Kent "of massy gold and big enough to be put upon the arm of the shoulder of a middling sized man."

THE DARK AGES

With the occupation of western Europe by the Germanic tribes, the culture disseminated by the Romans was submerged and was either destroyed, lay dormant, or, with the Christianization of the barbaric tribes, was nourished and kept alive in the monasteries, where Latin remained the language of the educated few. An outstanding leader in this Christianizing movement was St. Patrick (389–461), who converted Ireland. The organization of the church effected there led to the establishment of monasteries which became renowned throughout Europe. Art found expression in such manuscripts as the eighth century Book of Kells, one of the most beautiful books of all time. From Ireland, missionaries such as St. Columba (521–597) went to Britain, Wales, and Scotland. The famous Lindesfarne Gospels, dating from about 700, was produced in a monastery on the island of Lindesfarne, just off the northeast coast of England.

From the British Isles missionaries made their way to Brittany and on into Europe, converting, teaching and establishing monasteries as centers of religion and learning. One such was the monastery of St. Gall in Switzerland, named for a disciple of St. Columban (543–615) who had done much to inspire this eastward mission. It was here that the magnificent Golden Psalter was produced in the ninth century.

Talented and inspired monks, devoted and dedicated, created the great art of the

[9] *Ibid.*, pp. 45–47.

so-called Dark Ages and it is to them that we are largely indebted for what information we have concerning secular customs and costumes of the time. The earliest manuscripts however, such as the Book of Kells, contain few, if any, illustrations which can be construed as typical of lay costume. The period from the fifth century to the ninth is almost a total vacuum as far as knowledge of costume in western Europe is concerned. Sculpture, mosaics, and frescoes were almost nonexistent, so we can only surmise that the barbarian costumes recorded by Latin authors were gradually replaced by more sophisticated garments, copied from the peoples whom they conquered or influenced by trade with the Byzantine Empire.

From the ninth century onward the manuscripts are relatively rich in illustrations of men's costumes. Women, however, received scant attention prior to the twelfth century and the story of their costume is thus necessarily brief.

EIGHTH TO TWELFTH CENTURIES

Men's Costume: General Characteristics

Medieval costume seems simple and rather uniform compared with modern clothing, yet such features as quality of fabric and richness of decoration distinguished one class from another or indicated the nationality of the wearer.

Basically men's costume of the early medieval period consisted of an under and an outer tunic, long or short—depending largely upon the occasion or the rank of the wearer—and a mantle, rectangular or circular, which might be fastened on the shoulder or the chest. Since the greatest variety was exhibited by the legwear, an explanation of the terms used to designate legwear may help to visualize medieval costume. Leg coverings were divided into two groups according to their position on the body. Drawers and trousers, also called breeches, braies, or bracco, were pulled on over the feet and hung from the waist downward. Hose, socks, pedules (combination sock and boot named by the French), and leg bands extending upward from the feet were worn throughout the period from the eighth to the twelfth centuries.

The term *drawers* was used to indicate underwear. They were made of linen for the upper class and varied in length from above to below the knee. Trousers, already observed on the early Celts and Germans, remained in use and assumed different forms. They were made of wool or linen for the upper class, of wool for the common man. The sleekness of the fitting also varied with rank. On the Bayeux Tapestry the Normans appear in open-legged trousers. Although this remarkable piece of needlework probably dates from the last quarter of the eleventh century it is quite likely that the fashions recorded on it existed for some time previous to that date. Strutt dates a drawing of full-length loose trousers as being worn in the ninth and tenth centuries.[10]

Hose were long or short, often coming to just below the knee, and were either smooth or wrinkled in appearance (see Fig. 161). Long hose are almost indistinguishable from trousers since their tops were covered by the tunic and do not show unless the skirt of the tunic is slit or pulled high over the girdle. They sometimes spread out from the leg at the top, indicating that they were made of stiff, firm fabric and they might be rolled, scalloped, or embroidered on the upper edge. Shorter hose reached to lower or mid-calf. Socks were only slightly higher than shoes. Some illustrations show men wearing trousers, hose, and socks simultaneously.

Throughout this period there was a practice of wrapping the legs with one or more bands of varying widths. Sometimes

one band is indicated by the angling of a single band out of sight behind the knee (as shown in Fig. 157). Knotting of the ends at the top of the bound section implies the use of two bands. In lay costume narrow bands, often gilded, criss-crossing the legs in an open pattern were an indication of royal rank (see Fig. 153). The bands were made of wool, linen, or leather. Peasants are shown with rectangles of cloth tied around their legs for protection.

EIGHTH AND NINTH CENTURIES

Men's Costume

The eighth-century frescoes in Santa Maria Antigua, Rome, give valuable infor-

FIG. 152. *David. Redrawn from Golden Psalter of St. Gall. Ninth Century. (Library of Monastery of St. Gall, Switzerland)*

[10] Joseph Strutt, *A Complete View of the Dress and Habits of the People of England*, rev. J. R. Planché, Henry G. Bohn, London, 1842, vol. I, plate 18.

FIG. 153.   *Emperor Lothaire. 840–855. Additional MS. 37768, Folio 4. (British Museum)*

mation on men's wear. They show a short tunic and hose costume which is similar to that of Justinian, but different in the shape and placement of decoration on the tunic. A wide embroidered panel runs from neckline to waist.

Illuminations in ninth-century manuscripts begin to include more lay figures. David was a favorite subject and a few distinguished rulers of the time are represented.

The Golden Psalter of St. Gall, illustrated with the familiar David and his companions, is awe-inspiring in its richness and beauty. David's tunic is deep ivory with green borders on the skirt and gold at the wrist; note its very short length in Fig. 152. His mantle is grayish red. His legwear is very gay: the long breeches are vermillion, and over them he wears calf-height buff hose trimmed with green and gold scallops; on his feet are purple shoes.

In a British Museum manuscript, Emperor Lothaire wears a short tunic, girdled and bloused, and a short mantle of gold, either embroidered or set with stones (Fig. 153). His hose are deep red; the shoes are gold with spurs attached, and his legs are wrapped to the knees with bright orange-red bands. His heavy crown of gold is richly jeweled, as is the handsome brooch which fastens his mantle on the right shoulder. In the same manuscript, Folio 5 shows a man with a musical instrument wearing loose red breeches which cover the feet like the Thorsberg trousers. His greenish-blue tunic has long close-fitting sleeves rucked or wrinkled on the forearms. His red mantle, fastened with a gold clasp on the left shoulder, is longer than Lothaire's. His hair is short.

Illustrations of the lower classes include a shepherd wearing a long-sleeved knee-length girdled tunic under a shaggy cloak fastened on the right shoulder, and olive-green hose and black shoes. Two other men wear knee-length tunics, one with short sleeves, the other with long. Both are made with a close round neckline and center front slit. The short-sleeved tunic is blue, and grayish-red hose and gray shoes are worn with it.

Fortunately for our story there are some written records of eighth- and early ninth-century costume. Einhard, writing of his lord and master, Charlemagne, described his clothing as follows:

He used to wear the national, that is to say, the Frank dress: next his skin a linen shirt and linen breeches and above these a tunic fringed with silk, while hose fastened by bands covered his lower limbs and shoes, his feet, and he protected his shoulders and chest in winter by a close fitting coat of otter or marten skins. Over all he flung a blue cloak and he always had a sword girt about him, usually one with a gold or silver hilt and belt. He sometimes carried a jeweled sword but only on great feast days, or at the reception of ambassadors from foreign nations. He despised foreign costumes, however handsome, and never allowed himself to be robed in them except twice in Rome when he donned the Roman tunic, chlamys [paludamentum] and shoes. [Charlemagne was crowned in such regalia in 800 A.D. as a revival of the tradition of Roman emperors.] On great

feast days he made use of embroidered clothes and shoes bedecked with precious stones; his cloak was fastened by a golden buckle and he appeared crowned with a diadem of gold and gems; but on other days his dress varied little from the common dress of the people.[11]

Although Einhard took great pains to list the four wives, the four concubines, and all the daughters of Charlemagne, he said nothing of their finery. A monk of St. Gall, writing about the Franks of Charlemagne's time, reported that they wore long red linen hose, over which were bound the laces of their boots and red thongs.[12] With these they wore a rich linen shirt, sword belt, and a blue or white cloak formed in a double square so that when it was placed on the shoulders the corners touched the feet in front and back while it hardly reached the knees at the side.

Charles the Bald, grandson of Charlemagne, who ruled France from 843 to 877, seems to have enjoyed his robes of state more than his great ancestor did. Two paintings of this king add to our information on ninth-century costume. His tunics, both blue, embroidered or woven in a gold allover pattern, are of mid-calf length and are bordered at hem, wrist, and probably neck, in gold set with precious stones. His large rectangular purple mantle is also bordered in gold, and it is fastened on the right shoulder with an elaborately jeweled gold brooch. His crimson hose are cross-banded to the knees with narrow gold strips—a privilege accorded only to royalty and high ecclesiastics.[13] He wears a short mustache.

In both these paintings the young men in attendance wear short tunics devoid of decoration. These end well above the knees

[11] Einhard, *Life of Charlemagne*, Harper's School Classics, American Book Co., New York, 1880, pp. 58–59.

[12] Einhard and the Monk of St. Gall, *Early Lives of Charlemagne*, Chatto & Windus, Ltd., London, 1922, p. 102.

[13] C. Willet and Phillis Cunnington, *Handbook of English Mediaeval Costume*. Dufour Editions, Albert Saifer, Philadelphia, 1953, p. 13.

FIG. 154. *Group of Frankish Women. Ninth Century. Bible of Charles le Chauve. (Bibliothèque Nationale, Paris)*

and are girdled low, with blousing concealing the girdle. Short mantles are clasped on the right shoulder. Long hose or trousers fit neatly and over them are drawn pedules (sock boots) with rolled tops which come to mid-calf. Their short hair radiates from the crown, forming bangs on the forehead.

NINTH CENTURY

Women's Costume

The typical woman's costume of this period consisted of an ankle-length under-tunic or gown, with long closely fitted sleeves, over which was placed a second gown with open sleeves, either shorter than the first or folded back to reveal the under-sleeves. Though the girdling and neckline were often concealed by the mantle, one portrait of Charles the Bald shows women in gowns with wide necklines of medium

height bordered in gold. Bands of gold embroidery sometimes set with jewels, decorated the hemlines and ends of sleeves of the royal ladies. Color combinations were pleasing: a red and gold gown under a white and gold mantle, a rose gown under a grayish-blue mantle. The hair was entirely concealed by drawing the mantle up over the head or by a closely worn veil. One illustration shows long earrings reaching to the shoulders, made of four circles joined edge to edge and ending in small pendants. This lady also wore heavy gold bracelets.

Figure 154 is the classic illustration of ninth-century Frankish women's costume. Arrayed in outer tunics with embroidered borders at neck, center front, and in one case at the hemline, these women reflect the far-reaching influence of Byzantium. Their long fitted sleeves emerge below the wider, shorter ones of the outer tunic. Large mantles serve as both wrap and headdress. The allover pattern of groups of three dots recurs later in textiles of the Near East. Footwear appears pointed and possibly jeweled.

Women of the lower class wore plain simple gowns which covered them from neck to wrists and ankles.

Anglo-Saxon women of the ninth century are shown wearing a floor-length underdress with long fitted sleeves and a shorter girdled outer tunic with wide three-quarter length sleeves. Byzantine influence is apparent in the gold-embroidered borders. A mantle shaped like a chasuble and a head-kerchief complete the costume. Figure 155 shows a typical costume. The original painting shows their love of color: blue under-dress, purple outer tunic, purplish red man-tle, and blue head scarf. Women of the upper class probably also wore a linen under-garment. Their footwear was similar to that of the men.

TENTH CENTURY

Men's Costume

During the tenth century garments be-gan to be more fitted, a tendency which grew stronger in the eleventh century and developed into the sleek body line of the twelfth.

The German court of this era came under strong Byzantine influence through the marriage of Otto II, Holy Roman Em-peror from 980 to 983, to Theophano, daughter of Romanus II, Byzantine emperor from 959 to 963. Otto must have had a strong predilection for the grandeur of the Byzantine court, judging from a richly orna-mented costume in which he was painted. The deep embroidery at the neckline of his long silk tunic suggests the decoration on royal Byzantine robes. Similar embellishment forms a wide plaque on the front of his tunic, borders the hemline, ascends the open sides toward the knees, finishes the sleeves at the wrist, and encircles the upper arm.

FIG. 155. *The Virgin Mary in Costume Typical of Anglo-Saxon Dress. Ninth Century. Redrawn from Harley MS. 2908, Folio 123. (British Museum)*

His mantle has an allover design and is fas-tened on the right shoulder with a large circular jeweled brooch. His crown, like that of his successor, Otto III, is square, the corners placed at center front, center back, and over the ears. Jeweled projections ex-tended above these angles. His shoes cover the ankles and are jeweled down the center from top to toe.

Tenth-century Anglo-Saxon manuscripts give a vivid picture of the styles on the other side of the English channel. A similar trend toward a more fitted tunic is shown there: the upper part of the costume conforms to the body while the skirt has flared fullness; the upper part of the costume is red, the lower blue. If the illuminator was realistic, this is an early form of a pullover jacket. Strutt[14] shows a comparable illustra-

[14] Joseph Strutt, *A Complete View of the Dress and Habits of the People of England*, rev. J. R. Planché, Henry G. Bohn, London, 1842, vol. I, plate VII, p. 7.

tion of a tunic supplemented by a hip-length surcoat. He also considers the blue hair and forked beard dyed, in keeping with the current mode. A purple mantle fastened on the chest with a large brooch is an innovation. White hose, brown shoes, and a red crown complete this costume.

Figure 156 reveals a tunic in which the side seams are left open quite a distance above the hem. A handsome gold-embroidered border emphasizes the hem and open seam edges. The custom of cutting the sleeves excessively long and wrinkling them

FIG. 156. *English Costume. Tenth Century. From Claudius MS. B IV, Folio 13. (British Museum)*

on the forearm was followed by both men
and women. The tunic on the central figure
in this illustration is grayed orange-red, the
mantle olive-green, the hair and beard blue.
Although Fig. 156 shows the mantle closed
at center front, note that the king in Fig.
157 has adjusted his mantle to clasp on the
right shoulder. Note also the form of leg
wear. A long band, which might be of linen,
wool, or leather, is wrapped closely almost
to the bend of the knee. (The king's posture
in this drawing seems impossible, though it
was copied line for line from the original:
the position of the hands indicates a back
view; of the feet, a front one.)

Though men are usually represented
bareheaded, the head-covering most frequently illustrated is a cone-shaped cap with

Fig. 158. *English Costume. Tenth Century. From
Claudius MS. B IV, Folio 66ᵇ, (British Museum)*

Fig. 157. *English King. Tenth Century. Redrawn
from Vespasian MS. A VIII, Folio 2ᵇ. (British Museum)*

a softly rounded point falling forward. A
narrow upturned brim was sometimes added.
The design was based on the Phrygian bonnet.

Women's Costume

Women's clothing in tenth-century
England, contrary to the tendency in men's
costume, seems to have been looser and more
voluminous than during the ninth century.
Sleeves were lengthened and widened. Head
scarves concealed the hair and muffled the
shoulders while mantles shrouded the whole

figure. Decoration was restrained but colors were often gay and brilliant.

By modern standards the gown of the lady in Fig. 158 looks as if it were several sizes too large for her. Such is not the case, however. The loose look and knee-length sleeves were fashionable. Sleeves could be anchored at the wrist with bracelets; in cold weather they could serve as a muff. This fashion, however, was not followed to the exclusion of all others, for even in the same manuscript another woman wears wide elbow-length sleeves.

Headdress was an important feature of medieval costume. In most instances a head scarf (which the Normans called the couvre-chef) was worn, the ends crossing about the throat or fluttering in the wind. In Fig. 159 they are entwined about the dancer's arms. The headdress in Fig. 158, which shows no break about the face opening, might be an early form of the hood. The consistent style feature throughout English illuminations of this period is that the throat is swathed in cloth.

Women's mantles of the tenth century were predominantly of chasuble shape, that is, closed circles with an opening which allowed the garment to be slipped on over the

FIG. 159. *Woman Dancing. English. Tenth Century. Redrawn from MS. 24199, Folio 18. (British Museum)*

FIG. 160. *English Woman. Tenth Century. Redrawn from MS. 24199, Folio 5ᵇ. (British Museum)*

head. Often this opening was off-center, and then the shorter side was worn in front. The hands were often used in gesturing while covered by the mantle. Figure 160 illustrates this tent-like wrap, but at the same time poses a problem in interpretation: the girdling over the mantle must pass through slits provided for it or else the arms would be pinioned to the body.

Shoes received little attention at this time. When they are visible in illustrations they are plain and pointed much like men's shoes.

Theophano, the Byzantine princess who married Otto II (the German Holy Roman Emperor), must certainly have influenced women's fashions. However, examples of continental fashions of the tenth century are rare. Probably the female figures representing France, Italy, and Germany, paying homage to Otto II in the painting referred to earlier were dressed in royal attire. An underdress extending to the floor is covered as far as the knees by an outer gown with lavish embroidery about a rounded neckline in the shape of the Byzantine collar. Matching embroidery forms a band down center front and around the wrists. This gown is girdled low and bloused so as to conceal the girdle. The hair is covered by a long light veil which hangs down the back almost to the floor. A square crown, modeled after that of the Emperor, though of course less grand, rests upon the veil.

ELEVENTH CENTURY

Men's Costume

A British manuscript of the eleventh century indicates a trend toward a more closely fitted tunic with sleeves of normal cut and full short skirts. In some cases skirts were slashed from hem to hip, revealing the hose ending at mid-thigh where they were probably fastened to the drawers. Simply designed shoes were of ankle height, and

Fig. 161. *Eleventh Century Costume. Redrawn from Saxon Calendar, Tiberius MS. BV. (British Museum)*

bands wrapped the leg to lower calf. The hair was short and the face either clean shaven, slightly bearded as in Fig. 161, or more heavily bearded on older men. Mustaches were seldom seen. The cap of Phrygian origin remained in fashion.

The full-length tunic continued in use as regal regalia, worn with a large mantle fastened on the right shoulder. Harpists also wore the full-length tunic. But except for the most important occasions, tunics were short and full skirted; for unimpeded action they were girdled and drawn upward well above the knees. The girdling was comparatively low.

Figure 161, from a Saxon manuscript, shows a man of the upper class in a tunic with embroidered band at neckline, sleeve mounting, and near the hem, with separate motifs on the left side of the skirt. In addition to long hose or trousers he wears short hose, which fall in wrinkles. His shoes are nicely shaped, with slightly pointed toes and slits from the instep toward the toe. His sharply pointed cone-shaped helmet is military in style. A farmer is shown in a short tunic and mantle, hatted but barefooted. He carries the seed he is sowing in a loop of his mantle.

Since they were within the sphere of Byzantine influence, the Italians of the eleventh century dressed in the mode of the Eastern Empire. Shown in a fresco in the church of St. Angelo in Formis near Naples, King Solomon is dressed with the splendor of the Near East: broad jeweled borders, two tunics, and patterned hose (Fig. 162). His boots bear a resemblance to those of Basil II, Byzantine emperor from 976 to 1025.

Another figure from the same source wears a long tunic with similar elaborate embroidery. The central panel on these two tunics, and on those of Otto II and Otto III mentioned earlier, should not be confused with the Roman clavi. The latter were regularly used in pairs, reaching from the shoulder downward. The single centered border illustrated here is eastern in origin; when seen in Roman art, it is worn by a foreigner.

Henry II of Germany, Holy Roman Emperor from 1014 to 1024, continued the grand manner of the Ottos. In one royal portrait he wears a gold-colored tunic reaching to the lower calf, with broad borders of gold embroidery studded with jewels. His blue mantle, fastened on the right shoulder, is equally magnificent. His patterned hose are not as bold in design as those of King Solomon (Fig. 162), but the idea was probably derived from the same source. His shoes are gilded. The royal crown is round with a single arch over the top.

A second portrait shows him in a tunic of silver cloth, purple mantle, patterned purple hose, and gilded and jeweled shoes. The embroidery is more ostentatious in design than that in the other portrait. In an illumi-

nation where Henry and his Empress Cunigunda are making an offering of a model of a basilica, the Emperor is more conserva-

Fig. 162. *King Solomon. Eleventh Century. Italian. (St. Angelo in Formis, Anderson Photograph—Alinari)*

tively dressed. Here he is wearing a short green tunic banded at the hem in gold, a small plain red mantle, purple hose with matching cross-gartering, and gold shoes, open at each side of the ankle.

Women's Costume

Although information on eleventh-century women's costume is meager, we know that there was a definite change in the silhouette—at least the loose rather shapeless cut of the gown was replaced by a fitted upper section which outlined the body. This was laced either up center back or under the arms, while the skirt was left free to fall in full folds about the feet. In contrast with the new sleekness of the body lines, the sleeves of the outer garment began to assume greater importance. Sometimes they widened gradually from the armscye downward to very generous proportions; at other times they retained a slender cut to the forearm or wrist and then dropped suddenly in a long loop to the knees. The underdress remained visible on the lower arm and below the hemline of the outer gown.

Figure 163, from a manuscript in the Benedictine monastery of St. Peter in Salzburg, illustrates many features of this era. In this case the costume is ungirdled, as was that of the Byzantine dancer on the crown of Constantine IX in Fig. 148. With communication open to the Near East via trade with the Byzantine Empire, it took only a short time for the turban to spread from Persia westward.

Byzantine modes continued to influence the German royal wardrobe. Empress Cunigunda, wife of Henry II, who ruled Germany from 1002 to 1024, was pictured in a magnificent outer tunic of purple which reaches to mid-calf and has sleeves which widen sharply on the forearm. Gold embroidery highlighted with jewels is placed at the hemline, in a border above the knees, and on the edges and upper-arm sections of the sleeves. A golden girdle harmonizes with

the embroidery. The long underdress and narrow veil are blue. A high round jeweled crown rests on the veil. Her gilded shoes are plain in design.

Another illumination shows a German queen in tunic and underdress of matching

Fig. 163. *Job's Wife. Late Eleventh Century. Redrawn from MS. in Library of Benedictine Cloister of St. Peter, Salzburg. After J. H. von Hefner—Alteneck, Trachten, Kunstwerke und Gerathschaften, Frankfurt am Main: Heinrich Keller, 1879, Vol. I, Plate 64G.*

deep rose tone, the outer sleeves excessively widened from the armscye. An important new fashion noted here is her long green mantle lined with fur, showing that women shared with men the beauty and luxury of fur. The mantle is unfastened but it has a loop of cloth and small gold brooch at the left shoulder which might well function as a clasp when necessary. The queen's small white head scarf conceals her hair and passes under her chin but has no floating ends. A wide gold crown seems deceptively simple, with only three pearls at the upper edge.

Young girls seldom appear in medieval art, hence it is refreshing to find a bride and her contemporaries beautifully drawn.[15] This royal bride of the latter half of the eleventh century wears a long white under-dress and an ungirdled, sleekly fitted over-tunic of blue patterned in red circles and bordered at the hem in gold. Her open sleeves fall below her knees. She also wears a fur-lined mantle, crimson in hue. Her wavy golden hair falls down her back and a round red jeweled cap fits snugly over the top of her head. In the same illumination another young girl is dressed in much the same manner, but with less ornamentation. Her green mantle, fur-lined, is worn over a red tunic. Her hair, parted in center, falls unconfined. A plain little red cap rests on her head. No fastening device is indicated on either mantle.

In England, women's costume was more voluminous, more loosely fitted, and less ostentatious than the German. In comparison with the elaborate Byzantine embroidery on German robes, English garments seem modest in decoration if not starkly plain. Large veils covered the heads, concealing the hair and shrouding the shoulders. Mantles were full and long and had a cord arrangement for fastening on the chest.

[15] J. H. von Hefner-Altenek, *Trachten, Kunstwerke und Gerathschaften*, Heinrich Keller, Frankfort, 1879, vol. I, plate 60 (Manuscript in University Library, Leipzig).

THE VIKINGS

Inevitably the story of the Vikings must be mentioned because they played an important role in the history of Europe and were directly or indirectly connected with the development of costume, especially in fostering the textile industry. And where would costume be without textiles?

Vikings from Norway, Sweden, and Denmark began their raids in the eighth century. It must be admitted that they were glorified pirates; periods of raiding, looting, and conquest preceded their colonization. On the other hand, we cannot help but admire them for their boldness, courage, and wonderful seamanship. They discovered and colonized Iceland in the late ninth century; Eric the Red sailed from Iceland to discover Greenland in 981, and America was reached by the year 1000. The Swedish adventurers followed the eastern rivers across what is now Russia to the Black Sea and Constantinople, founding the cities of Novgorod and Kiev on the way. Norsemen (a general name for the Vikings) formed the valiant and fearful Varangian guard of the Byzantine emperors. The Danes gave England a bad time in the ninth and tenth centuries, though King Canute, in the early eleventh century, was a competent ruler and his reign was one of conciliation and efficient organization.

Other Vikings were attracted by the opportunity of plunder and the conquest of Italy. By the middle of the eleventh century they had conquered southern Italy and before the end of the century Sicily was under their control. Robert Guiscard led the main attack, leaving to his illegitimate brother Roger the glory of wresting Sicily from the Mohammedans, who had held the island since the ninth century. Exploiting the skill in weaving already developed by the Mohammedans, the Normans went further and encouraged weavers to come from Greece, Byzantium, and the Near East. Roger II is said to have used force when persuasion

failed to interest the highly skilled weavers
he wanted. At any rate, by the twelfth century the reputation of Sicilian fabrics had
spread far and wide. Silk and gold figured
largely in their textiles, and designs were
adapted from all the countries represented
by the weavers. As a result, Sicily became
the source, not only of magnificent fabrics,
but of the knowledge needed to produce
them. In turn Sicilian weavers emigrated to
Italy, teaching their craft first in Lucca. The
Lucchese spread these intricate techniques
to Venice, Genoa, and Florence, the great
textile centers of the Renaissance.

Following their early raids on France,
Charles the Bald granted the Norsemen the
earldom of Chartres in the latter part of the
ninth century; later Charles the Simple
ceded to them the portion of France now
known as Normandy.

In 1066, William, Duke of Normandy,
led his forces across the English Channel to
claim the English crown, declaring it had
been promised him by his late cousin, King
Edward the Confessor. In the meantime
Harold, brother-in-law of King Edward and
the most powerful earl in England, had been
elected to the throne and crowned. The two
contestants met at the Battle of Hastings,
where Harold was killed and William was
victorious. The Normans, as they were then
called, had in their century and a half of
residence in France been strongly influenced
by their environment and so brought to
England another contribution of language
and customs.

The story of the Norman invasion and
conquest has been uniquely and brilliantly
recorded, both in Latin and pictorially on
the Bayeux Tapestry—a misnomer because
the technique of the design is embroidery,
not weaving. The events leading up to the
invasion and the Battle of Hastings are
vividly delineated in a series of 76 scenes.
The date of this masterpiece has been widely
disputed but it is now generally thought to
have been made in the last quarter of the
eleventh century. Since there are literally

FIG. 164. *A Norman. Late Eleventh Century.
(Bayeux Cathedral) Redrawn from Hilaire Belloc,
The Book of the Bayeux Tapestry, London: Chatto
& Windus Ltd., 1913, Illustration 12.*

hundreds of figures involved, it is a store-
house of information on costume.

The Normans on the Bayeux Tapestry
wear exceptional costumes. They have retained the trousers of the early Germanic
tribes but the Norman variety is looser in
the leg and just caps the knee. The shirt is
quite like the top of the tunic then current.
Many of the men wear spiral leg bands, but
in several instances the bands are separated
and horizontal as if they were some form of
decoration. Their most startling feature is
their hair style. The hair is cut short and
combed forward onto the forehead, while

the back of the head is shaved to the ears and up onto the crown (Fig. 164). William's robes of state include a long tunic and large mantle clasped on the right shoulder. His legs are wrapped but not cross-gartered.

The English men on the tapestry wear a tunic, knee-length or shorter and quite smart in line, with a fitted top and flared skirt. The neckline is high and round, but a central vertical slit facilitated dressing. The sleeves are long and fitted. A narrow girdle is placed rather low. A short mantle fastened with a round brooch on the right shoulder completes the costume. The men are bare-headed except in battle array, when they wear a cone-shaped helmet with a nasal extension. They also wear chain mail. In the introductory scene, King Edward wears a long green tunic with decoration at neck, center front, and at knee level of the skirt, and a wide gold girdle. His hair is cut short and he wears a long mustache and forked beard. Some of the younger men wear mustaches but many are clean-shaven.

8

Twelfth and Thirteenth Centuries

BACKGROUND

Two great movements mark the twelfth century, the Crusades and the introduction of Gothic architecture. Both were expressions of deeply religious faith and dedication to the church in western Europe at this time.

The Crusades

Pilgrimages in themselves were nothing new. Devoted adherents of Christianity had been visiting the holy places in Palestine for centuries. During the early Mohammedan domination of the Holy Land pilgrims were free to come and go. But when the Seljuk Turks, after crushing the Byzantine army in 1071, pushed on to rule over Syria and Palestine, Christians found their way to Jerusalem dangerous if not impossible.

Both Pope Urban II and Peter the Hermit urged the peoples of Europe to unite in a crusade to rescue the Holy Land from the Turks. Their eloquence was heeded. The first crusade was under way by 1096 and Jerusalem was captured in 1099. How-

ever, the conditions and events leading up to the Crusades were not as simple as this account implies. No doubt most of the people enrolled in this first great army were motivated by religious zeal but from the first crusade to the last many mundane motives existed also. The Crusades became struggles for political power and opportunities for adventure and booty, as well as for grand tours of cities of older and richer cultures than most of the crusaders had ever seen before. The Italian cities of Genoa, Pisa, and especially Venice profited materially through the maritime transportation they furnished and the excessive prices they demanded. Venice diverted the fourth crusade to an attack on Constantinople in her name. St. Mark's Cathedral in Venice stands as a monument to the plundering which followed that enterprise.

All these experiences had a profound effect upon those engaged in the Crusades. They returned far more sophisticated than when they set forth. Their contact with the ancient culture of the Near East must have been enlightening in many ways, not the least of which was the knowledge they gained of foreign dress. The sumptuous fabrics, the jewels and embroidery employed, the designs of the garments themselves had a far-reaching effect upon the costumes of western Europe. Some immediate results appeared in the twelfth century; others developed more gradually as eastern ideas were adapted to the western way of life.

Because it was necessary to have some way of distinguishing ally from enemy, heraldry came into widespread use among the crusaders, and eventually it became the smart thing to employ heraldic devices in the decoration of outer garments of the nobility and in the livery which set apart their liegemen.

A minor custom of the crusaders was the wearing of a purse suspended from the girdle. There were two reasons for this: (1) A purse, along with a pilgrim's staff and cross, was given each recruit by his priest. (2) He needed a convenient means of carrying negotiable articles of value.

A more important effect of the Crusades was the adoption of the cyclas (see p. 162) for general use; it had first served as an overgarment to protect armor from rain and dust and eyes from the glare of sun upon metal. The many derivatives of the cyclas make up a large part of thirteenth- and fourteenth-century outer clothing.

These developments did not occur all at once, but the contact of many thousands of Europeans of all classes with the older, richer culture of the eastern Mediterranean set up a chain reaction in all phases of fine and applied art that is probably still in progress.

Gothic Architecture

In the meantime, there arose in France the style of architecture known as Gothic, first expressed in the great cathedrals at Chartres, Amiens, and Rheims, to name only a few, and later seen in the palaces of the nobility and the rising merchant class. The inspired and inspiring beauty and grandeur of these structures hastened the spread of the style to other countries of Europe.

Many conditions contributed to the achievement of the architects and builders of these centers of worship, including the religious ardor which stirred the whole populace from serfs to king. Cathedrals such as Chartres were the result of the combined efforts of all classes—from the sturdy laborers who moved the stones to the kings and nobles who contributed handsomely to the cost. Hundreds of unknown artists designed the intricate tracery of iron, skillfully carved the choir stalls, created the marvelous jeweled lighting of the stained glass windows, and sculptured the hundreds of figures, large and small. Architects conceived the soaring vaults and devised the means of uniting these infinite works of beauty into the magnificent structures which are still a source of wonder and reverence.

It is, of course, only incidentally that Gothic architecture contributes to our knowledge of costume, for the designs on the stained glass windows and the numerous sculptured figures which frame the portals and fill the arches had a more serious purpose. In a time when a large portion of every congregation was illiterate, the most impressive way to affirm the Christian faith and teach the contents of the Bible was through the media of art: sculpture, stained glass, paintings, embroidered vestments, and altar furnishings. Gothic architecture left little wall space for paintings but the other media were fully exploited. Liturgical needlework in thirteenth-century England, for example, reached a perfection that has seldom been equaled.

On the exteriors of the cathedrals the figures of the Virgin Mary and Christ testified to their importance in Christian doctrine, and the spacing of figures within a given composition was done with symbolic meaning. Scenes in the lives of the Virgin Mary and Christ were of paramount interest and occupied strategic positions. But the stories of the Old Testament were illustrated also.

Such themes as the Creation, the Flood, the sacrifice of Isaac, David and Goliath, and the Queen of Sheba and Solomon appear over and over again. Prophets and angels, disciples and saints, blend the Old Testament with the New.

Lacking information about costumes worn at the time of these various events or personages, the artist or artisan who created the figures almost invariably dressed them in the costume of his own period. Thus we have a record not only of royal costume but also of a cross section of the population. Stained glass windows donated by guilds often included scenes of guild members practicing their trade, be it baking, preparing pelts, or weaving cloth. Fitted in among the more important scenes on the facade of the cathedral, sculptured figures might represent the seasons or months of the year.

As the history of architecture, painting, or sculpture unfolds, the themes remain much the same but the costumes change to conform with the period of the work of art. Thus we could compile quite a complete history of men's costume by studying the consecutive representations of David, a popular subject through the centuries. In like manner, the many statues and paintings of the Queen of Sheba contribute to the changing story of fashion. But to the worshiper of the time, she was much more than a fashion model. She brought the Old Testament to life.

TWELFTH CENTURY

Men's Wear

Men's costumes of the twelfth century were characterized by increased yardage, voluminous flowing cloth, lengthening to the point where it became a hazard in battle.

The bliaut, the new long outer body garment, was a combination of separate upper and lower sections joined with a seam at a low waistline. The skirt consisted of two

Fig. 165. *King Solomon from Notre Dame de Corbeil. Twelfth Century. (Louvre)*

semicircles, only the central sections of the straight edges being joined to the upper part of the garment. The unattached portions of these edges hung free, either down center front and center back, as in Fig. 165, or down the sides, as in Fig. 166. The visible tunic beneath remained an important part of the ensemble. Bands of embroidery at

FIG. 166. *King and Queen from Royal Portal. Twelfth Century. (Chartres Cathedral)*

neck, wrist, and hemline reflected eastern influence.

Another innovation during the twelfth century was the cyclas, a garment adopted during the Crusades to protect eyes from the glare of the sun upon armor, to furnish a certain amount of insulation against the oppressive heat of the Near East, and to shield the armor itself. This early cyclas was really a long panel widening slightly from the center, which was shoulder width, toward the two ends. In the center of the panel was an opening for the head; the front and back sections hung from the shoulders to about knee level. Directly related to the cyclas was the tabard, the official garment of heralds, still seen in such royal ceremonies as a coronation. The tabard was open at the sides and emblazoned with the arms of the sovereign, while the cyclas was girdled and slit from the hem upward—at center front and back—to accommodate the wearer's activity. The cyclas was first adopted in France as a lay costume, and was lengthened to conform to the long garments then in fashion. The thirteenth century brought more significant changes to the cyclas, as we shall see, and thus greater variety to the wardrobe.

A practice which seemed innocuous at the time was that of cutting slashes upward from the hemline, producing a petaled or scalloped effect. This method of ornamentation is called *dagging* and the scallops are *dagges*. A few examples are to be found in the twelfth century, but in the fourteenth and fifteenth centuries dagging was carried to the limits of absurdity.

In the first half of the twelfth century, English royalty dressed more simply than French royalty. Eleventh-century fashions continued, except that the long sleeves were turned back in a deep-cuff effect instead of being wrinkled on the forearm. Figure 167 shows an English king wearing his long tunic slashed to the hip and the top of his hose at mid-thigh. The royal mantle, lined and bordered with fur, was clasped either on the shoulder or on the chest. Crowns were

either round or square, and were tipped with recurring leaf motifs.

The low shoes shown in Figs. 167 and 168, cut away at the instep and fastened at the ankle, were new in design.

Doctors appear frequently in medical manuscripts. Figure 169 shows a seated physician wearing the conventional double tunic of the Middle Ages, dignified by a jeweled border at the hem and wrists, and a broad, ornate, rather loose girdle. His cap is of Phrygian inspiration and his haircut and beard are conservatively short. But when the doctor was treating a patient, his tunic was knee-length, his sleeves close, and his head

FIG. 167. *English King. First Half of Twelfth Century. Redrawn from Nero MS. CIV, Folio 6. (British Museum)*

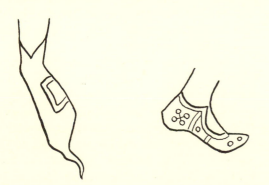

FIG. 168. *Royal Footwear. English. Twelfth Century. Redrawn from Harley MS. Roll Y.6. (British Museum)*

FIG. 169. *English Physician. Twelfth Century. Redrawn from Harley MS. 1585, Folio 7ᵇ. (British Museum)*

FIG. 171. *Shepherd Wearing Hood. French. Twelfth Century. Redrawn from Detail of Royal Portal. (Chartres Cathedral)*

From the time of the Romans the hood no doubt remained in use among shepherds and peasants, even as it does today, but the twelfth century ushered in its revival as an article of fashion. Figure 171 shows it worn by shepherds, the peaked shape in combination with a shoulder cape being similar to the cucullus (see p. 107). A longer hooded cape resembled the paenula (see p. 107). It

FIG. 170. *French Physician Treating a Patient. Twelfth Century. Redrawn from Sloane MS. 1975, Folio 95. (British Museum)*

bare; oddly, though, he retained the mantle (Fig. 170).

In most illustrations the patient's costume varies little from that of the doctor, though a round yoke on the tunic is characteristic; this might have been suggested by the round Byzantine collar. Soft boots wrinkled about the lower leg.

Apparently few men wore head coverings, either indoors or out. An exception was the farmer. He is shown in a knee-length blue tunic, over open-legged brown pants reaching almost to the ankle, and a brimmed hat.

FIG. 172. *Early Example of Coif. English. Twelfth Century. Redrawn from Harley MS. Roll Y.6. (British Museum)*

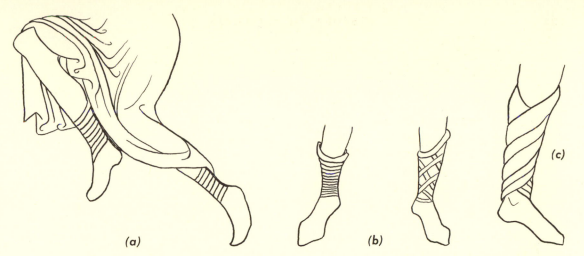

FIG. 173. *Footwear of Twelfth Century. a. Redrawn from Harley MS. Roll Y.6. b. Redrawn from Nero MS. CIV, Folio 21. c. Redrawn from Nero MS. CIV, Folio 11. (a–c, British Museum)*

was the shorter form that captured the fancy in the latter part of the twelfth century.

Another type of hood was introduced in this century, but so late that its association with the thirteenth century has almost made it a symbol of that period. This is the coif, a small plain white hood, tied under the chin for all the world like a baby's hood (Fig. 172). Nevertheless, it was worn by men of

great dignity. It has survived in the legal profession in the title of their honorary society, "The Order of the Coif."

Figure 173 shows prevalent types of footwear of the twelfth century.

The most convincing evidence of the splendor of this period is the coronation robes of Holy Roman Emperors (Figs. 174 and 175). The blue tunic and royal mantle,

FIG. 174. *Coronation Mantle of Holy Roman Emperors. Twelfth Century. Made in Palermo, Sicily. (Weltliche Schatzkammer, Vienna) From De Farcy,* La Broderie, *1890, Plate 86.*

made in Sicily, probably for the coronation of the Norman king, Roger II, are definitely twelfth century. (These robes probably passed to the German emperors following the marriage in 1186 of Emperor Henry VI to Constantina, sister of William I, King of Sicily.) The outer tunic, also richly embroidered, is not illustrated. These historic garments are evidence of the success of the Norman conquerors in expanding the crafts of weaving and needlework in Sicily previously established there by the Mohammedans. The design on the coronation mantle is cosmopolitan, to say the least. The lion represents the Normans, the camel, the Mohammedans whom the Normans had conquered. This victory is emphasized by the fact that the lion stands triumphant over the recumbent camel. The palm tree in the center of the mantle is taken practically intact from the Assyrian tree of life. The Arabic inscription around the outer edge states that the mantle was made in Palermo in 1133.

The embroidery on the mantle is done in couched gold thread on a crimson silk background. Pearls outline the main designs and figure prominently in the border along the front edges and neck line. In Fig. 175, a drawing of the tunic of the coronation robes, pearls again are used profusely in the decoration. The quality of the silks, the finesse of the embroidery, the resplendence of shimmering gold on glowing color, and the prodigal use of pearls combine to create an impression of great magnificence.

Women's Costume

IN FRANCE

The outstanding new features of women's twelfth-century costumes were the accent on vertical lines and the sheer supple texture of the fabric which made those lines possible. Evidently the same ideas which revolutionized Egyptian costume during the empire period and lured the Athenians from the simple peplos to the Ionic chiton were responsible for the stately bliauts of the twelfth-century European courts, which required the most compliant fabrics and the most exquisite workmanship. Extant embroideries are proof that the skill existed at a time when the Crusades exposed large

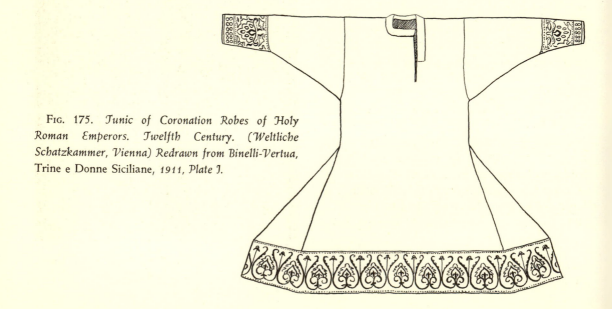

FIG. 175. Tunic of Coronation Robes of Holy Roman Emperors. Twelfth Century. (Weltliche Schatzkammer, Vienna) Redrawn from Binelli-Vertua, Trine e Donne Siciliane, 1911, Plate 7.

numbers of Europeans to the finest of fabrics for the first time.

In essence, the bliaut was a two-piece dress—an important innovation since previous to this time, with few exceptions such as Crete, women's garments had been cut in one length from shoulder to hem. The bliaut consisted of a closely fitted elongated bodice to which a very full skirt was sewed. The sleeves were excessively wide and long.

The Queen of Sheba from the Church of Notre Dame de Corbeil and the queens of the West Portal of Chartres Cathedral, both dating from mid-century, furnish classic examples of the bliaut. Its vertical lines are in perfect harmony with the soaring columns and spires of the Gothic cathedrals.

The bliaut, which for a time replaced the gown of previous centuries, has had numerous interpretations. Viollet-le-Duc's conception of bliaut, corsage or corselet, and broad girdle has long been accepted.[1] However, close examination of the sculptured figures from Chartres suggests a simpler explanation. The queens' costumes reproduced in Figs. 166 and 176 show no evidence of the armscye of a corselet and no indication of the wide, fitted, corset-like girdle. The smooth cloth over the queen's bust merges naturally and without a break into the horizontal folds of the fabric. In Fig. 166 the queen's mantle covers her shoulders, but there is no reason to suppose that she is wearing the wide constricting girdle over her bliaut. The general consensus is that she was wearing some sort of firm foundation garment under it.

In Fig. 176 it seems likely that the horizontal folds are produced by shirring along the underarm seams. The garment would have to fit tightly to produce such even folds, and there is little doubt that it does. A center back fastening, probably lacing, is logical. On the Queen of Sheba (Fig. 177) the fullness is represented in regularly

[1] Viollet-le-Duc, *Dictionnaire Raisonné du Mobilier Francais*, Bance, Editeur, Paris, 1858, vol. III, p. 43.

Fig. 176. *Queen and King from Royal Portal. Twelfth Century. (Chartres Cathedral)*

broken lines of dominantly horizontal direction resembling smocking. This occurs also on the sleeves of the queen in Fig. 166 and on other figures there. The perfection of the embroidered borders would indicate that French ladies were expert at needlework and no doubt they could smock if they wished. Smocking would give much more even control of fullness than shirring. It has also been suggested that the diamond pattern represents an intricate form of pleating. Another possible explanation, however, is that the sculptor wished to produce variety in texture or a more interesting line direction and chose this means of accomplishing it. The same treatment appearing on the hose of one of the shepherds in the nativity scene seems to bear this out.

In the sculptured figure of the Queen of Sheba (Fig. 177) she is quite the most elegant of twelfth-century royal ladies. Her costume exemplifies the unique features of that century's fashions. Her bliaut is made with a seam joining a tight, extended bodice to a very full long skirt. Sleeves of great width fall in fine folds, a heritage from the Medes and the Persians. A round jeweled brooch clasps the throat opening. The floor-length mantle adds little bulk, as the clinging fabric falls softly from the shoulders. Emphasizing the impression of height, her two plaits of hair are intertwined with ribbons which descend to her knees. Her high crown, the position of her hands, the direction of the scroll, and her pointed shoes all contribute to the elongated effect.

The queen in Fig. 166 furnishes additional information about women's twelfth-century costume. A girdle at least 4 yards in length encircles her body at a low waistline; crossing at center back, it returns at hip depth to the front and is tied there. The ends, made of many strands of silk knotted at intervals, fall to her ankles. Her sleeves are so long they must be knotted to keep them from dragging on the ground. Her mantle has the conventional fastening by means of cords across the chest. Jeweled

FIG. 178. *Woman's Costume. England. Twelfth Century. Redrawn from Nero MS. CIV, Folio 24. (British Museum)*

FIG. 179. *English Woman. Twelfth Century. Redrawn from Titus MS. D XVI, Folio 17ᵇ. (British Museum)*

plaques often served to anchor these cords. The embroidery at neck opening, waistline seam, and on the mantle deserves a salaam.

The costumes of these ladies are French and royal. They surpass in elegance all other costumes of the medieval period. The middle and lower classes followed as best they could —and sometimes their best made the nobility a bit uneasy.

IN ENGLAND

In the first half of the twelfth century in England sleeves were fitted easily from shoulder to forearm and then widened abruptly into a long pendant. The hair, as shown in Fig. 178, was divided into two strands and encased in silken tubes wrapped spirally with a narrow ribbon. The bliaut or gown of country women was seamed at the low waistline but without the shirred fullness of the bodice or the column-like folds of the skirt (Fig. 179). The appealing apple gath-

FIG. 180. *Apple Gatherer. English. Twelfth Century. Redrawn from Titus MS. D XVI, Folio 20ᵇ. (British Museum)*

erer in Fig. 180 wears a gay little red cap and old-fashioned tunic as she fills the bags suspended from her girdle with fruit. Her parted hair is combed back over her ears and allowed to fall naturally.

The head scarf continued in use throughout the century. Figure 181 shows a small hat worn over a hood to which a shoulder cape is attached. Norris states that mantles for common use had hoods for covering the head when required.[2]

FIG. 181. *Twelfth-Century English Hood with Shoulder Cape Worn under Small Hat with Upturned Brim. Redrawn from Harley MS. 1585, Folio 22. (British Museum)*

Another innovation in England at this time was the wimple, an accessory which remained long in use by widows and is still part of the habit of many sisterhoods. Introduced late in the twelfth century, the wimple was a shaped piece of linen which was draped about the throat and drawn upward around the face, concealing the hairline, the ends being overlapped on top of the head and secured there. Usually the lower edge extended under the neckline of the gown. In Fig. 182 the ends of the wimple are draped over the headdress; the usual custom, however, was to don the veil after the wimple was in place. A circlet often served to steady the arrangement.

Jewelry took the form of brooches, plaques on mantles, and enrichment of gir-

[2] Herbert Norris, *Costume and Fashion*, Dent, London, 1927, vol. II, p. 50.

dles. Examples of women's footwear are shown in Figs. 166, 177, and 182.

As we have seen, the quality of European fabrics improved rapidly during this century. Coupled with increased importation of Near Eastern silks and liberal use of fine furs, they produced a degree of sophistication among the costumes of the upper classes that had been missing since the Teutonic invasions.

THIRTEENTH CENTURY

Men's Costume

The thirteenth century marks the culmination of the religious fervor of the Middle Ages. Louis IX, Saint Louis, probably the most consecrated of the millions of crusaders, ruled France from 1226 to 1270. At a time when the finest products of all crafts were dedicated to the church, man himself assumed a role of humility. The craze for the exotic in dress which had been aroused by contact with the East gave way in the thirteenth century to a simplification of form in costume that is unique.

Apparel remained quite uniform over Europe, with but slight variations. Basically men's costume consisted of tunic or cotte and one of many kinds of surcoats which included the cyclas, already familiar to us, and the ganache and gardcorp, which will be described presently. The mantle was still the formal wrap for the man of distinction. He also wore hose, shoes, and one of several kinds of headdress.

Royal costume relied upon richness of fabric and luxuriousness of fur to set it apart. A long tunic, usually girdled, with dolman sleeves tapering to a fitted wrist, might be worn alone or with a shorter supertunic or cyclas over it. A fur-lined or trimmed mantle was the usual wrap.

Hair and beard were of moderate length, the hair often being arranged in a single curl across the back of the neck.

FIG. 182. *Adoration. Relief in Whalebone. English. Early Twelfth Century. (Victoria & Albert Museum, Crown Copyright)*

Solomon's crown on the North Portal of Chartres Cathedral is less ornate than the one he wore in the twelfth century. A cap of Phrygian derivation served for less formal occasions.

Footwear remained pointed, though not excessively so. Higher clergy and royalty are shown with embroidered shoes, often in diaper pattern.

Figure 183 shows the investiture of an English knight. His costume for this solemn occasion consisted of two long tunics, an angular neckline accenting the outer one. Pages buckle his golden spurs in place while the king girds him with a sword—an honor which gave rise to the expression "belted earl." His hair style is typical of thirteenth-century barbering.

The cyclas of the Crusades, which was adopted by all classes, is well illustrated on the statue of St. Theodore, on the South Portal of Chartres Cathedral (Fig. 184). By this time it had become closed under the arms. The lad in Fig. 185 is also wearing this garment, which is shown frequently throughout the thirteenth century on both men and women.

Extending the shoulder line of this sleeveless garment created a cap-sleeved surcoat called the ganache (garnache) (Fig. 186). The fourteenth-century ganache often had two rounded tabs on the chest, turning back from a center opening; that of the thirteenth century seldom if ever had such detail. The ganache is usually shown with hood of matching color, which indicates that it was attached to it. The color range of the ganache was wide: white lined with green, red lined with orange, etc.

When a long sleeve of generous dimensions was mounted to the armscye of the cyclas, a third protective garment, the gardcorp, resulted (Fig. 187). It was widely used by both sexes, especially for travel. The extra fullness in the width of the sleeve was controlled by several rows of shirring which formed vertical ridges at the top. A lengthwise slit in the sleeve or an opening in the armscye itself provided freedom for the arms. The gardcorp bears a striking resemblance to our academic gown today, especially the ridged mounting of the sleeves, the slash in the sleeves of the master's gown, and

FIG. 183. *Investiture of a Knight. English. Thirteenth Century. Redrawn from* Strutt, A Compleate View of the Manners, Arms, Habits, Etc., *London, 1775. Vol. I, Plate 37, from Original by Matthew Paris in* Lives of the Offas, *Royal Library, 14CVII. (British Museum)*

the fullness and length of both sleeve and robe. Even the hood of modern academic regalia had its origin in medieval headdress, or, if you will, the Roman cucullus.

Another type of surcoat which appears repeatedly is shown in Fig. 188. The sleeve was of ordinary fullness but often curtailed in length, the arms emerging through the unsewed front armscye.

THE WORKING CLASS

Working men wore the short cotte, girdled, and with a center front slit which enabled them to tuck the corners into their belts when uninhibited action was called for (Fig. 189). A man representing February on the North Portal of Chartres Cathedral wears two tunics for warmth, and long hose which apparently are without feet, as the shoeless foot is bare. His hood has a square front panel instead of the usual shoulder cape.

Artists of the thirteenth century have given us a better idea of men's nether garments than we usually find recorded. When outer clothing was suddenly lengthened to

FIG. 184. *Queen of Sheba (Left), North Portal. St. Theodore (Right), South Portal. Thirteenth Century. (Chartres Cathedral)*

about his body and legs in diaper fashion. The outer corners are knotted to a cord, and this in turn is fastened to the drawstring or belt at the waist. The hose on the man at the left are drawn up over the drawers and also secured to the waist string. Modesty doesn't seem to be involved, for the front opening of the tunic reveals the underwear in numerous illuminations. Shoes are most clearly delineated in Fig. 187.

The various types of headgear included the round cap with a slight brim, a beret similar to the current French version, even to the little tab on top, the pointed hat of Abraham, a typical Hebrew headdress (Fig. 188*a*), the coif (Fig. 189), the straw hat,

FIG. 185. *Young Man Wearing Cyclas. Thirteenth Century. Redrawn from Sloane MS. 2435, Folio 23. (British Museum)*

the ground in the twelfth century, the breeches, or braies, tended to disappear, leaving hose and drawers as leg coverings. As tunics shortened the hose lengthened; evidence of this was pointed out earlier (p. 150). Drawers varied in cut and in length, as shown in Figs. 189 and 190. In the well-loved drawing of St. Christopher carrying the Christ Child, the drawers shown are comfortably full and the leg opening is mounted to a band tied just below the knee. The thresher at the right in Fig. 189 wears an undergarment which appears to be draped

FIG. 186. *Man Wearing Ganache with Hood and Coif. 1279. (Bibliothèque Nationale, Paris, Gaignières Collection)*

FIG. 187. *Man Wearing Gardcorp with Hood, Coif, and Beret. 1258. (Bibliothèque Nationale, Paris, Gaignières Collection)*

FIG. 188. *a. Abraham and Isaac; Rebecca and the Beasts. b. Father and Mother of Samson, Sacrificing. From The Psalter of St. Louis. Latin MS. 10525, Folio 11. 1252–1270. (Bibliothèque Nationale, Paris)*

FIG. 189. *Ruth and Naomi; The Threshers. Thirteenth Century. From The Maciejowski Bible. (The Pierpont Morgan Library)*

which doubtless had widespread use among the farming folk down through the centuries (Fig. 189), and the hood (Fig. 188*b*).

Women's Costume

The most remarkable and admirable woman of the thirteenth century was undoubtedly Blanche of Castile, who deserves much credit for the development of the character of her son, Louis IX, that revered monarch who was canonized in the same century he ruled. Her idealism was in sharp contrast to the earthy philosophy of Eleanor of Aquitaine, who, with her ladies, was

FIG. 190. *St. Christopher Carrying the Christ Child. c.1240. Redrawn from Royal MS. 2A XXII. (British Museum)*

really a glorified camp follower and more of a hindrance than a help. Marguerite of Provence, wife of Louis IX, and her sister Eleanor, wife of Henry III of England, were both estimable women.

The thirteenth century is a quiet, refreshing interlude between the elaboration of twelfth-century fashions and the fantastic vagaries of the late fourteenth and fifteenth centuries. Thirteenth-century dress could hardly have been more restrained. A floor-length gown, loosely fitted and girdled with a long narrow belt, was practically a uniform for most of the period. The costume of the Queen of Sheba of the North Portal of Chartres Cathedral (Fig. 184) seems puritanical by comparison with that of her counterpart from Notre Dame de Corbeil (Fig. 177). Her dress has embroidery at the neck and a modest brooch clasps the opening of her chemise at the throat. Her mantle is held in place by a cord across the chest. The carving on the narrow turnover collar suggests that it was made of fur. The strap closing was the prevailing style for women; the gesture of the right hand is also characteristic of the period.

As already noted, the cyclas or sleeveless surcoat was worn by both sexes. In its original form the cyclas was a long panel with an opening at the center for the head. Widening the panel to the dimensions of a skirt was one of the first changes made in it. The woman in Fig. 191 is wearing a blue gown; her cyclas is red lined with orange. The side edges of the cyclas were often closed, forming a sleeveless surcoat. The women on Chartres Cathedral working with wool and flax and Ruth in Fig. 189 wear this sleeveless surcoat. The illustration of Rebecca and her companion from the Psalter of St. Louis (Fig. 188*a*) shows them wearing surcoats with close armscyes, ungirdled.

Women expressed their individuality in their hairdress and headdress. The woman in Fig. 188*b* wears the headdress which was as distinctive of the thirteenth century as the long braids were of the twelfth. It consisted

FIG. 191. *Woman's Cyclas and Headdress. Thirteenth Century. Redrawn from Harley MS. 1527, Folio 97. (British Museum)*

of a chin band, or barbette, fastened on top of the head, and a pillbox hat, usually referred to as the woman's coif, though it had nothing in common with the man's coif except the name. Sometimes the cloth enveloping the chin was soft and arranged with a fold; sometimes it was cut to a definite shape (Fig. 191). In some cases the crown of the coif was higher than the brim, and vice versa. At times it was a true pillbox, with no brim; sometimes it was simply a band (Fig. 192); in either case it was severely plain or fluted (Fig. 184).

In addition to barbette and coif, a net called the crespine or crespinette often confined the hair; most of the time it was visible only at the back. Later in the century, when bulkiness over the ears became fashionable, the entire hairdress might be covered with the crespine, the barbette and coif being reduced to narrow strips of cloth (Fig. 192). Barbette and coif were quite consistently white but the crespine might be colored or of gold. In Fig. 192 the crespine is green.

The wimple continued to be worn in conjunction with a veil, but it was more apt to be seen on older women and widows (Naomi, Fig. 189).

Ladies' footwear was seldom visible. However, in Fig. 189, Ruth, holding her gleanings in the front of her costume, shows horizontally striped hose and low dark shoes.

FIG. 192. *Woman's Headdress. Late Thirteenth Century. Redrawn from Additional MS. 17341, Folio 33. (British Museum)*

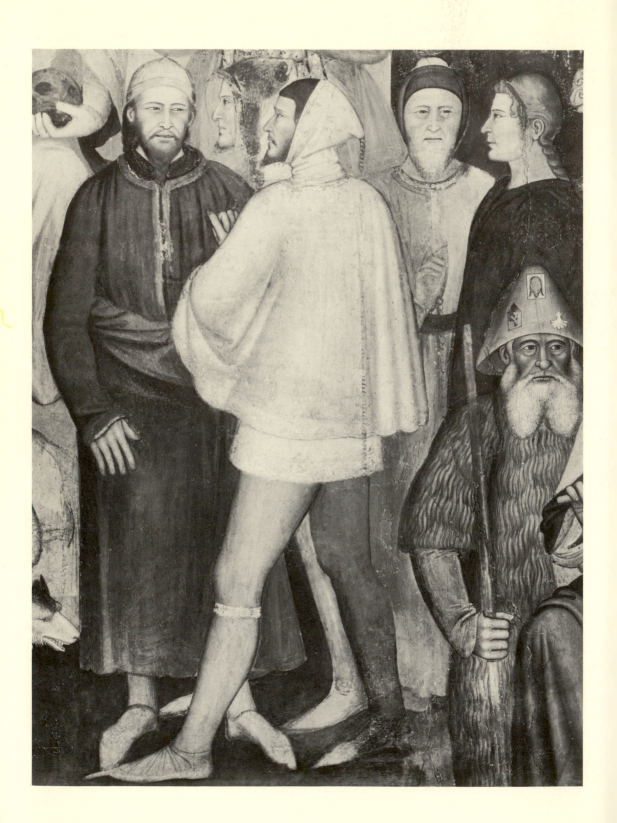

9

The Fourteenth Century

In the fourteenth century men again began to seek their own pleasure, and not the least of their diversions was dress. With the establishment of skilled weavers in Italy, particularly in Lucca, fabrics rich in hue and texture and spirited in design became more readily available. Velvet and gold brocades, inspired by the Far East, added elegance to the foppishness of extreme styles. Cotehardies, to be described shortly, surcoats, and mantles, lined with ermine and trimmed with sable, are mentioned in one record after another. Goldsmiths were hard pressed to satisfy the demand for massive girdles of gold or silver gilt, studded with precious stones.

We have four primary sources of information concerning costume in the fourteenth century: (1) the burials in Greenland; (2) the paintings of such artists as Lorenzetti, Taddeo Gaddi, and Simone Martini; (3) memorial brasses covering burial places within the churches of England and on the continent; and (4) illuminated manuscripts glowing in jewel tones and highlighted with gold. Literary references are also revealing. This was the century of Chaucer, whose characterizations of the Canterbury pilgrims are realistic and diverting with such descriptions as that of the wife of Bath, who was "wimpled well and on her head a hat as broad as a buckler," and the carpenter's wife, whose "apron was as white as morning milk."

Other writers were less complimentary, and their mention of the long gowns which swept the filthy streets makes us realize that standards of sanitation were pretty primitive.

Housekeeping approved such practices as spreading fresh rushes over the floors in the fall and removing them the following spring, along with all manner of refuse from people and animals. Castles, located on the highest hills for observation and defense against enemies, were buffeted by all the storms and winds that blew. Dark, drafty, stone-cold interiors made furs and multiple layers of clothing most desirable. The usual heating facility consisted of an open fire in the middle of a packed-earth floor, the smoke escaping as best it might.

And yet the great halls with their minstrel galleries and long tables accommodating any and all visitors—above or below the salt as their station merited—evoked scenes of conviviality, laughter, and romance.

The Greenland Finds

As noted earlier, Eric the Red, sailing from Iceland in 981, discovered Greenland. Upon his return to Iceland, his enthusiasm led to colonization of Greenland in 985. Three main settlements were made, which lasted about 500 years. At first the colonists were able to maintain a comfortable standard of living by trading furs, whale oil and ivory for grain and other necessities from Norway. But when the fur trade shifted to Russia and ivory could be procured from Africa with much less effort and danger than were involved on the Greenland route, Norwegian ships came less and less frequently; malnutrition of the settlers was the result.

An abrupt and severe change in climate in the fourteenth century brought on the final tragedy. The glaciers pushed southward, covering fields and pastures. The indigenous primitives living far north of the settlements were driven southward as their hunting grounds disappeared. When they reached the villages of the Norsemen, they destroyed them. The first village was overwhelmed in 1360; in 1500 the last of the Norsemen were burned in their church.

Bodies which had been buried previous to these disasters were preserved by the constant freezing temperature. Systematic excavations were begun in 1921 under the leadership of Poul Nørlund,[1] whose report is a thrilling and enlightening account of the Vikings and their fate.

Costumes found in the graves were damaged, but they are complete enough to

[1] Poul Nørlund, *Viking Settlers in Greenland,* Cambridge, New York, 1936.

FIG. 193. *Sir Geoffrey Luttrell, His Wife, and Daughter-in-Law. Fourteenth Century. The Luttrell Psalter, Folio 202*[b]. *(British Museum)*

FIG. 194. *Front View of Pourpoint of Charles of Blois. 1367. (Le Musée Historique des Tissus, Lyon)*

show the fabric, style, and cut of men's and women's clothing, including tunics and dresses, surcoat, hose, hoods with liripipes, and even the fashionable fifteenth-century sugar-loaf hat. These were costumes of common folk. However, as long as contact with Europe was maintained, fashion news arrived with the ships and had its usual effect.

These rare items of clothing are in the National Museum in Copenhagen and are invaluable as a guide in interpreting the costumes displayed in paintings and sculpture of the time.

Men's Costume

A major factor contributing to the bizarre look of the fourteenth-century pageant was the widespread adoption of heraldic devices on both the costumes of the nobility and the livery of their servants (Fig. 193). Since coats of arms were often designed in brilliant color and unique patterns, their enlargement for use on costumes and the divisions recording the quarterings resulting from successive marriages among titled familities were startling, to say the least. The two halves of the surcoat might be of different colors. One hose might be of two colors and the other a third color. These garments are referred to as parti-colored or mi-parti. The court jester's costume perpetuated this practice, and our circus clowns continue it. Another custom which made the tournaments so picturesque was that of caparisoning the horses in matching trappings (Fig. 193).

THE POURPOINT. Although space does not allow the inclusion here of a study of armor, its influence on fashion cannot be ignored. As noted in the discussion of the crusaders, they originally wore the cyclas over their armor, partly to cut out the sun's glare on the chain mail then in use. The change to plate armor in the fourteenth century necessitated further adjustments. The closely fitted and relatively sharp edges of the metal called for a smooth thick protection against abrasion. The solution was the padded and quilted pourpoint or jupon, expertly cut and fitted to body contour. With metal encasing the legs, hose became more shapely. When knights appeared unarmored after centuries of flowing gowns, the effect was so sleek and smart that no fashion promotion was needed for its enthusiastic acceptance.

The finest, and possibly the only, extant example of a pourpoint is that of Charles of Blois, dated 1367, in Le Musée Historique des Tissus in Lyon (Fig. 194). Draft 1 presents the pattern for it. (Pattern Drafts are grouped after Chapter 19.) It will be seen from an examination of the photograph and draft that the pourpoint was a form of jacket, long enough to extend down over the thighs, tapered to fit the waistline and provided with sleeves so cleverly designed that the wearer could move his arms freely in a full circle—a highly desirable advantage in time

of danger. The cut is surprisingly sophisticated; in fact nothing approaches it in finesse until the work of Madeleine Vionnet in the twentieth century. The outer fabric is of ivory silk brocaded in a gold pattern of alternating lions and eagles set in a framework of octagons. The lining is of fine linen canvas and the interlining of cotton wadding is quilted to both materials in horizontal rows. A notable feature, and one characteristic of the fourteenth century, is the use of dozens of buttons. The pourpoint served a second important function, that of supporting the hose, by means of ties or points attached to the lining (Fig. 195).

THE COTEHARDIE.   The well-dressed man of the fourteenth century wore over the pourpoint a cotehardie, which was an abbreviated derivative of the cotte or tunic. The earlier versions were sometimes skirted, as illustrated in Fig. 196, but the shorter

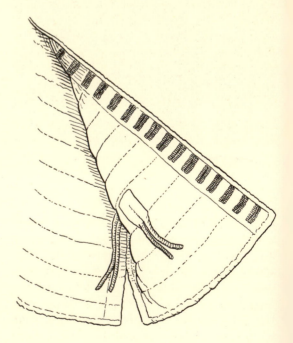

FIG. 195. *Inside of Pourpoint (Fig. 194) Showing Attachment of Laces or Points Which Held up Hose. (Le Musée Historique des Tissus, Lyon)*

FIG. 196. *Taddeo Gaddi, The Martyrdom of St. Peter. Detail. 1334–1366. (Spanish Chapel, Cathedral of Santa Maria Novella, Florence, Alinari Photograph)*

body-clinging style shown in Fig. 197 prevailed among the more fashion-conscious (see also Fig. 204). The cotehardie often had elbow-length sleeves, from which long narrow streamers called tippets hung to the knees. As the hemline of the cotehardie rose, the hose necessarily were lengthened. The clergy and other conservative critics considered the overlap of the two insufficient for decency. A belt worn low about the hips over the cotehardie was probably the most

costly single item in the wardrobe, sometimes representing the sacrifice of a portion of the family estate.

SURCOATS AND MANTLES. The gardcorp and ganache changed little from the thirteenth century, remaining an important part of the wardrobe (Figs. 187 and 198). The typical rounded tabs are to be seen on the ganache in the latter illustration. The plain surcoat with three-quarter or elbow-length sleeves is the outergarment worn by the three most prominent horsemen in Fig. 199. Two of the men wear narrow belts from which their swords are suspended. Shorter surcoats reaching to upper calf were also popular. Jaunty shorter capes were worn by the younger blades.

Toward the end of the century, when fashion interest quickened and exaggeration became the order of the day, the houppelande, another form of surcoat, began its reign of popularity. Usually attributed to Spain, it was soon adopted throughout most of Western Europe. This garment required an extravagant amount of fabric: the collar pushed up against the ears and back of the head; the full skirt trailed the ground; the excessively wide sleeves often reached the floor. In Fig. 200, dated 1377, King Edmund and Richard II of England are wearing magnificent houppelandes; Edmund's is made of a brocade typical of Lucchese design, while Richard's is patterned in his heraldic device.

Fig. 201 shows the houppelande in its extreme dimensions as well as a knee-length alternate which is already available. The early sixteenth-century ruff and the armscye wings of the early seventeenth century show marked similarities to fourteenth-century details.

Mantles of the fourteenth century are distinguished from those of other periods by being fastened on the right shoulder, typically by a series of buttons (Fig. 202). In his effigy in Westminster Abbey, Edward III wears a full ankle-length mantle with rounded dagging at the lower edge, and

FIG. 197. *Feast Given in 1377 by King Charles V of France for Emperor Charles IV. From Grand Chronique de France, 1380, French MS. 2813, Folio 470. (Bibliothèque Nationale, Paris)*

FIG. 198. *Man with Axe Wearing Ganache. Fourteenth Century. Redrawn from The Luttrell Psalter, Folio 66ᵇ. (British Museum)*

FIG. 199. *Orcagna, The Triumph of Death. c.1375. (Campo santo, Pisa, Alinari Photograph)*

fastened on the right shoulder by two large buttons. These mantles were circular in shape, long and full; those for the upper classes were made of the finest fabrics and were lined with fur.

Dagging, which we observed as early as the twelfth century, became general in the fourteenth, and hardly an edge escaped the scissors. The bottom of the cotehardie, tippets, the cape of the hood, sleeve edges, and surcoat hems were dagged—that is, cut into scallops of all shapes and sizes, some of them taking on indented leaf outlines.

Fur was used lavishly. Ermine, sable, lamb, and squirrel (minevair, or miniver, the white fur of the squirrel's belly) were considered the choicest, and sumptuary laws attempted to limit them to the upper classes. The merchant class, however, prospering in the expanding trade of Europe, competed with the nobility in finery.

HOSE. Hose, already mentioned in connection with the pourpoint, gained importance as they lengthened, and more care was devoted to their contour. The finds in Greenland help to explain the nature of these accessories. Only the longer one shown in Fig. 203a would serve as a basis for reconstructing the hose of the ultrafashionable. Bias cut provided the elasticity necessary for movement and at the same time contributed to the desired sleekness. The long point reached practically to the waist and was tied either to the pourpoint or to the waist belt which held the drawers in place. The Greenland hose are clumsy about the ankle and the feet are seamed in what must have been an uncomfortable fashion, yet the essential method of shaping is there and given a little more skill in fitting and fabric of finer texture, a very creditable leg covering could be made. Often the hose also per-

FIG. 200. *Richard II with King Edmund, Edward the Confessor, and John the Baptist. Artist Unknown. Detail. 1380–1385. (National Gallery, London)*

FIG. 201. *Coronation Ceremony. French. 1395–1400. Chronicles of St. Denis. (British Museum)*

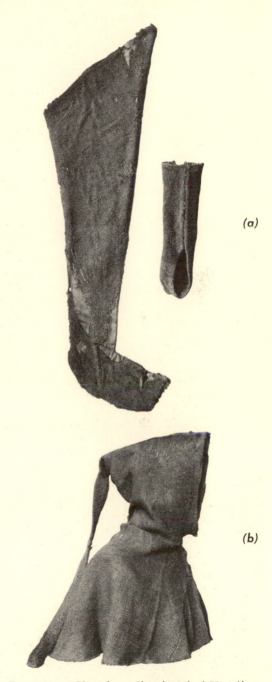

(a)

(b)

FIG. 202. *Agnolo Gaddi, Annunciation with Donor. Detail. Late Fourteenth Century. (Samuel H. Kress Foundation)*

FIG. 203. a. *Hose from Churchyard of Herjolfnes and b. Hood. Greenland. Fourteenth Century. (Danish National Museum, Copenhagen)*

formed the function of a shoe, in which case a leather sole or fabric reinforcement must have been used (Fig. 197).

SHOES. Men's shoes in the fourteenth century were generally low in cut and those of the elite were embellished with embroidery. They were either cut out over the instep and fastened with a button or buckle, or laced up the side. The abnormally long points on both hose and shoes were exceeded only in the fifteenth century. They are referred to as *crackowes*, after Crakow in Poland, or as *poulaines*, from the word Poland, and are believed to have been introduced into western Europe via the marriage of Richard II to Anne of Bohemia. Poland at that time was part of the kingdom of Bohemia.

Though much is written about the tips of the points having been attached to the knee garter by a gold or silver chain, there is little evidence of such a practice in contemporary illustration. Figure 204 shows a rare example of extremely extended points. On the man at the far right the total length of the foot covering seems to be about two and a half times the length of the foot. Below his knee is a garter with a pendant to which it might be possible to attach the tip of the point. Planché[2] describes an original example of a point as 6 inches in length and stuffed with moss. That they were a hazard in battle and a nuisance when kneeling is obvious.

Another foible, indicative of the increasing levity of the period, was the use of small bells mounted upon baldrics, collars, and belts. These were worn, not only by gay fops, but also by men of high rank.

HAIRDRESS AND HEADDRESS. Figures 197 and 201 show some of the fourteenth-century hair styles. Bearded men are seen about as often as are clean-shaven. Toward the end

[2] James Robinson Planché, *Cyclopaedia of Costume*, Chatto & Windus, Ltd., London, 1876, vol. I, p. 460.

FIG. 204. *Men Wearing Cotehardies and Long Poulaines. Late Fourteenth Century. Royal MS. 20B VI, Folio 2. (British Museum)*

of the century, shoulder-length hair gave way to the short bowl crop and shaved occiput, as collars of houppelandes pushed upward. This hair style which continued well into the fifteenth century, resembles the Norman barbering observed on the Bayeux tapestry (Fig. 201).

Though many types of headdress were worn in this period, the hood was by far the most common (Fig. 202). Actual fourteenth-century hoods found in Greenland clarify the contour and patterns in use at that time (Fig. 203*b*). The peak of the hood, called the liripipe, suddenly lengthened to compete with the tippets on the sleeves (Fig. 202). A back view of such a hood shows the slender liripipe reaching to the thigh; Viollet-le-Duc includes one of floor length.[3] About the same time some exuberant wag undoubtedly drew applause by putting the face opening of the hood on the crown of his head, allowing the shoulder cape to fall to one side and the liripipe to the other (Fig. 199). This was merely the beginning and many variations were played on this theme. A turban was formed by pushing the cape section upward and binding it in position by winding the liripipe about the head. In the coronation series of which Fig. 201 shows the final act of crowning the king, the hood is in the fully developed turban stage. Note the dagged edge of the cape which forms a decorative cockade.

Hats in this period were more modern in design than they had been in previous centuries. They included the Robin Hood shape, with high crown and upturned brim projecting into a point in front (Fig. 199). A hat with a single ostrich feather was contemporary with the adoption of three plumes as the symbol of the Prince of Wales. Another form observed in Fig. 201 is the true turban, enlarged by the addition of overlapping leaves. Also significant was the high-crowned hat flaring outward at the top (Fig. 201).

[3] Viollet-le-Duc, *Dictionnaire Raisonné du Mobilier Francais*, Bance, Editeur, Paris, 1858, vol. IV, p. 368.

KNIGHTLY ORDERS

Some mention should be made of such honorary organizations as the Order of the Garter, founded by Edward III in 1348, which is to this day the highest order of knighthood in England. From the fourteenth century onward, elaborate collars, devised from the symbols of their respective orders, were worn about members' shoulders.

The Order of the Golden Fleece was founded in 1429 by Philip the Good of Burgundy, its name signifying the wealth which the wool trade had brought to his country.

COMMON FOLK

One of the most informative and delightful illuminated manuscripts in the British

FIG. 205. *Organist. 1340. Redrawn from The Luttrell Psalter, Folio 55. (British Museum)*

Museum is the Luttrell Psalter of 1340. Its illuminations present the nobility in all their splendor (Fig. 193) but manage to poke fun at the pompous. At the same time they show farmers and their womenfolk, musicians, wandering entertainers, and craftsmen as if life were well worth the living sans bath tubs and electricity.

As to be expected, there is a definite fashion lag in the costumes of the people of this class. Thus the organist in Fig. 205 wears a cyclas over his tunic, and his footwear is rather shapeless. The farmer sowing grain in Fig. 206 is dressed in knee-length tunic girdled with a sturdy belt, his head protected by both hood and brimmed hat. His surprising accessory is a pair of gloves, made with two fingers and a thumb. The right glove is tucked into his belt, since it would interfere, if worn, with the even distribution of the grain. The upper classes were provided with gloves having the usual quota of fingers (Fig. 199).

FIG. 207. *Man in Tunic and Hose. 1340. Redrawn from The Luttrell Psalter, Folio 60. (British Museum)*

FIG. 206.   *Farmer Sowing Grain. 1340. Redrawn from The Luttrell Psalter, Folio 170. (British Museum)*

The young man in knee-length tunic in Fig. 207 indicates the continuation of the deep slit up center front of the skirt, the pointed top of the hose fastened to the underwear and gartering below the knee. The two cloaked men in Figs. 198 and 208 wear longer tunics and both have hoods under their broad-brimmed hats. The latter, carrying a pitchfork, is mantled by a cape, a distant relative of the paenula, and the other wears the common man's ganache. The footwear of the latter seems to be a combination of hose and shoes.

Women's Costume

COTEHARDIE AND SIDELESS GOWN. In the fourteenth century women's costume consisted basically of two garments: the cote-hardie and the sideless gown. The cote-hardie would today be described as a well-fitted one-piece dress with flaring skirt and long tight sleeves which often reached to the knuckles. It was usually fastened down the back. The neckline was wide and low. The girdle, if any, was ornate and was placed at hip level, much as on men's costumes.

Over the cotehardie the woman of fashion wore the sideless gown, one of the many variants of the cyclas. In the modern sense it was a form of jumper. To convert the cyclas into a sideless gown, the long floating panels were widened to skirt proportions and sewed together from hip to hem. From shoulder to hip the edges were free. As the century advanced the edges of the front panel were cut in deep concave curves reaching from the outer edge of the shoulder to the top of the underarm seam. The back was either left to hang in a slanting line or cut less severely.

Although the illumination depicting the Luttrell family in the Psalter of that name is damaged, it is still clear enough to give an excellent idea of the noblewoman's costume of the time (Fig. 193). Lady Luttrell, who is handing the great helm to her husband, is wearing a cotehardie and sideless gown. The cotehardie is, by virtue of its low broad neckline, of the latest vogue. The practice of blazoning the family coat of arms on articles of civilian wear reached its peak of popularity at this time. The husband's coat of arms appears on the right side of the sideless gown, the father's on the left. The daughter-in-law, who holds the shield, is dressed in the same fashion. Both ladies wear the gorget, a shaped sheer linen accessory, related to the wimple, which covers the throat and chin and disappears under the hair. A long sheer veil placed over the back of the head is held in place by a fillet.

Another use of heraldic devices was as an allover pattern. Still a third method was to employ one's father's coat-of-arms on the gown and the husband's on the mantle.

The combination of cotehardie and sideless gown, the fourteenth-century version of

FIG. 208.   *Farmer Riding an Ox. 1340. Redrawn from The Luttrell Psalter, Folio 62. (British Museum)*

the cyclas, continued throughout the century and well into the next, though several changes took place: the arm openings of the outer garment became deeper, reaching well below the hips; they were often cut so far in toward the front that only a narrow central strip was left; an elaborate hip girdle corresponded to that worn by the men; the decoration became more elaborate, with fur the usual finish about the enormous armscyes and a plastron of fur in front. Sleeves of the cotehardie were lengthened, often reaching to the knuckles. The statue of Jeanne de Bourbon, wife of Charles V of France (Fig. 209) illustrates several of these features.

When the sideless gown is omitted, the cotehardie is revealed to better advantage. The effigy of Joan de la Tour on the tomb of her father, Edward III of England, wears a short-sleeved cotehardie buttoned down center front (it was often laced). Tippets reaching to her ankles are attached to the sleeves. The skin-tight sleeves of her kirtle or underdress reach well down onto her hands. Long sleeves of this period were usually closed with dozens of pea-sized buttons. Fitchets—vertical slits in the side front of the skirt—gave access to a purse which hung from an inside belt (Fig. 210). Figure 211, from the Luttrell Psalter, shows a back view of a cotehardie in which the elbow-length sleeve suddenly widens into a trumpet shape.

A detail from *The Deposition* by Giottino (Fig. 212) illustrates fourteenth-century Italian fashion, which featured the same very low neckline, the tight many-buttoned sleeve, and the hip girdle. Rich borders of embroidery are reminiscent of Byzantine decoration. The women in Orcagna's *Triumph of Death* (Fig. 213) wear similarly cut costumes, loosely fitted and ungirdled, but made of richly colored and patterned fabrics.

None of these illustrations shows a horizontal seam in the cotehardie or gown, though fullness is quite evenly distributed about the hips. Here again the Greenland garments help us account for this (Figs. 214 and 215). The many gores placed at the

Fig. 209. *French School, Jeanne of Bourbon, Wife of Charles V of France. 1364–1380. (Louvre)*

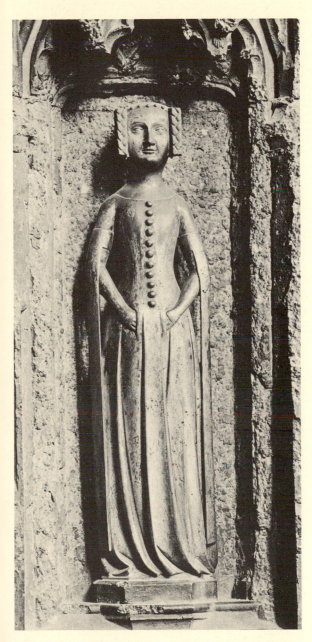

Fig. 210. Joan de la Tour, Daughter of Edward III of England, from His Tomb. 1377. (Courtesy of the Dean and Chapter of Westminster Abbey)

Fig. 211. Back View of Woman's Cotehardie. 1340. Redrawn from The Luttrell Psalter, Folio 68. (British Museum)

sides and the godets inserted at front and back of the Greenland garments explain how the bodice part could be fitted smoothly, yet without a waist seam the skirt expanded into uniformly flared fullness.

Sculptors and painters were seldom concerned with seam lines. However, a fresco in the church of Santa Maria Novella in Florence indicates that the Italian method of cutting was sometimes different from that in Greenland. Here there can be no doubt about the joining of skirt to bodice at a low hip line. Sometimes contrasting fabrics were used for the top and bottom of the costume.

HAIRDRESS AND HEADDRESS. As in the thirteenth century, women's hairdress and headdress showed more imagination in the fourteenth century than the costume itself, and the emphasis continued to be placed on width rather than height. The hair was usually parted in the middle and formed into two braids. It is in the arrangement of these braids that the fourteenth century is unique. Figure 216, from the Luttrell Psalter, shows hairdressing in progress, the braid here being wound into a coil over the ear in what has been called the ram's horn hairdress.

The brass rubbing showing Lady Northwood reproduced in Fig. 217 shows that she brought her braids forward, faced them to the front, and carried the tapering ends back to the crown of her head. Figure 209 showed Jeanne de Bourbon wearing much the same arrangement, but her braids were wrapped in a caul or net. Possibly, since she was a queen, this was of gold. The effigy of Queen Philippa, wife of Edward III of England, shows how the side and back of the head looked with such a hair style. Her braids are brought forward onto the cheeks, exposing the hairline above and back of the ears. A jeweled caul encloses the braids and covers the entire crown of her head. Figure 210 shows Queen Philippa's daughter, Joan de la Tour, wearing her hair in similar fashion; the second daughter, Mary, Duchess of Brittany, wears hers in a pompadour-

FIG. 213.   Orcagna, The Triumph of Death. Detail. c.1375. (Camposanto, Pisa, Anderson Photograph—Alinari)

FIG. 215.   Pattern of Greenland Dress (Fig. 214). Redrawn from Nørlund, Viking Settlers in Greenland, p. 112.

FIG. 214.   Greenland Dress. (Danish National Museum, Copenhagen, No. 38)

shaped roll covered by a jeweled caul. These cauls were modifications of the thirteenth-century cauls or crespinettes, as well as fore-runners of the reticulated headdresses of the fifteenth century.

The woman in Fig. 218, again from the Luttrell Psalter, wears a caul or crespinette held by a green fillet; a transparent veil lies across her forehead, and she wears a gorget and a purple hood which matches her gown. Another headdress, sometimes referred to as the *nebulé*, is illustrated in Fig. 219. There are conflicting interpretations of it, but a study of the headdress in the Van Eyck portraits of the early fifteenth century helps us understand it. It is surely made of cloth, though it is not clear whether it is several separate layers or one cloth folded as in the Van Eyck paintings. Ruffles frame the face and finish the edge or edges, which lie across the back from shoulder to shoulder.

The gorget is perfectly illustrated in Fig. 217 on Lady Northwood. It envelops her throat and chin up to the ears. The wimple, as distinguished from the gorget, extended on upward and was fastened on

FIG. 217. *Lady Northwood. Brass Rubbing. Minster, Sheppey. 1330. (Victoria & Albert Museum, Crown Copyright)*

FIG. 216. *Fourteenth-Century Hair Arrangement. Redrawn from The Luttrell Psalter, Folio 63. (British Museum)*

FIG. 218. *Woman Wearing Gorget, Crespine, and Hood. 1340. Redrawn from The Luttrell Psalter, Folio 33. (British Museum)*

FIG. 219. *Wife of Reginald de Malyns. Brass Rubbing. Chinnor, Oxon. 1385. (Victoria & Albert Museum, Crown Copyright)*

pleating and it is this pleating which sets it apart. Figure 220 shows Alianora de Bohun wearing this mark of widowhood. Norris[4] states that sumptuary laws, although of the fifteenth century, applied also to the wimple

[4] Herbert Norris, *Costume and Fashion*, Dent, London, 1927, vol. II, p. 192.

FIG. 220. *Alianora de Bohun, Duchess of Glouces-ter. Brass Rubbing. Westminster Abbey. 1399. (Victoria & Albert Museum, Crown Copyright)*

top of the head (see Fig. 182). Sometimes, when a veil or couvrechef has been added it is difficult to distinguish one from the other. These throat coverings, together with the elaborate hair and headdresses, were symbols of wifehood, and their counterparts are to be found among the peasants of Europe today. Just prior to World War II the matrons at Kossovo Polje, in Serbia, were still wearing their braids in the manner of Lady Northwood, and women at the market in Karlovać, Croatia, wore their hair encased in vertical coverings shaped like those of Jeanne de Bourbon.

The widow's barbe was closely allied to the wimple. Fullness inserted in the chin section was controlled by regular gathers or

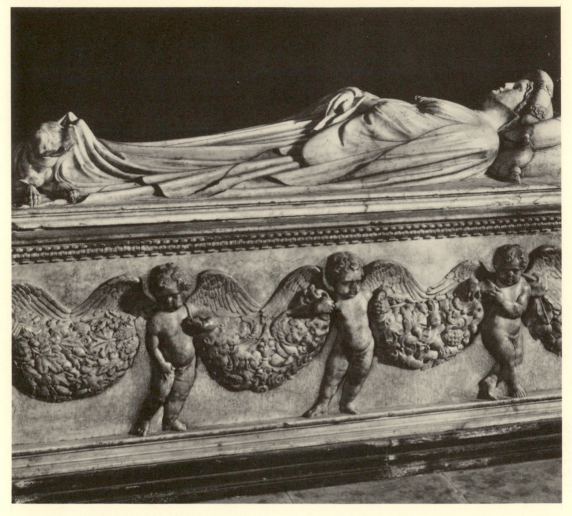

FIG. 221. *Sepulchral Figure of Ilaria del Carretto. Late Fourteenth Century. (Lucca Cathedral, Alinari Photograph)*

of thirteenth-century widows and the barbe of fourteenth-century widows. The law stated that the queen and all ladies down to the degree of baroness were licensed to wear the barbe above the chin. Baronesses and women beneath that rank were ordered to wear the barbe beneath it. So important was the wimple that sumptuary laws reserved to queens the right to cover the chin, and prescribed the height or amount of coverage allowed those of lesser rank. Like all other sumptuary laws, however, it was often violated.

Women's hats—when they were worn—followed men's styles (Figs. 199 and 213).

OUTER WRAPS. Women's outer wraps showed little change from the thirteenth to the fourteenth century. Lady Northwood was shown in Fig. 217 wearing a closed circular mantle, fur-lined, with bordered slits at a convenient height for her arms. About her shoulders and falling down over her chest is a large fur-lined hood, with its face edges folded in toward the neck. Alianora de Bohun (in Fig. 220) wears a mantle with a cord fastening much like those worn in the thirteenth century. Figure 219 illustrates a surcoat buttoning all the way down center front. Women also wore the gardcorps combined with the hood as a practical outdoor garment.

Women as well as men wore the houppelande (Fig. 221), with the same high collar and exuberant flowing sleeves. A radical change in the waistline has here raised it above its normal position. The cotehardie, too, was affected by the urge toward greater volume. Note the very long full sleeve gathered into a deep fitted cuff.

ACCESSORIES. Women's feet are seldom visible in the art works of the time. When they can be seen they are usually wearing pointed footwear like that of the men. Well-shaped gloves are frequently shown (Fig. 213). Jewelry usually took the form of elaborate belts and large jeweled buttons or ornaments on the front of the sideless gowns (Figs. 212 and 209).

10

Men's Costume of the Fifteenth Century

Early Renaissance

The fifteenth century is both one of the most richly documented and one of the most mystifying periods in the history of costume. Suddenly, it seemed, a host of artists appeared in Italy, France, and Flanders. Illuminated manuscripts, frescoed walls, canvas and tapestry, as well as brasses and wood, record the whimsical to outlandish costumes which resulted from the great creative urge pervading much of Europe. Cimabue, Giotto, Lorenzetti, Orcagna, and other painters were followed by a great profusion of artists whose history is confusing.

The invention of printing, increased travel leading to the age of discovery, and scientific advancements were outgrowths of the adventurous questing spirit which produced the Renaissance.

General Characteristics

The fifteenth century was a very important period in the major countries of Europe, especially Italy, France and the Duchy of Burgundy, which was not then part of France. Costumes of specific countries and changes during the century are discussed in the pages that follow.

In general, certain characteristics of men's costume, that were common in Europe in the early fifteenth century were continuations of fourteenth-century styles. The houppelande, for example, continued in fashion, recognizable by its high collar, voluminous cut, and the huge sleeves—wide-mouthed and knee- to floor-length or shaped into a somewhat fitted wrist (bagpipe or poky sleeves). In the earlier part of the fifteenth century houppelandes were made in three practical lengths: full, mid-calf, or to the knee. Later they lost their distinguishing features and became robes, their fullness carefully controlled by long vertical organ-pipe pleats, the girdle moved from the hips to the normal waistline.

Throughout the century both long and short surcoats were worn side by side. A full-length outer garment usually indicated a man of high position, a ceremonial occasion, or an elder citizen. Shorter surcoats were less formal and preferred by the younger set. The fourteenth-century cotehardie merged into the fifteenth-century jacket, which appeared in a myriad of designs. Probably each had its own name at the time, but only a few of these have survived: journade and courtepy were short outer jackets of the middle century: paltock, jupon, and pourpoint were close body garments which supported the hose. Around the middle of the century the term doublet was used in England for these last three jackets. From around 1480 the doublet became an outer garment in its own right, with a long and colorful future ahead of it.

Our difficulty in getting a clear picture of the varied costumes of this period may be understood by comparing it with our own time: 400 years from now, a student of costume may have considerable difficulty distinguishing such present-day items as jacket, coat, waistcoat, vest, sports coat, blazer, windbreaker, battle jacket, blouse, raincoat, overcoat, trench coat, topcoat, slicker, tuxedo, dinner jacket, and tails.

By mid-century the jacket had shortened to the courtepy, bringing down the wrath of the clergy and resulting in sumptuary laws which attempted to control it. The courtepy shared with all the other outer coat-like garments of the period full-topped sleeves which were extended by much padding, called mahoitres. The broadened shoulder line thus created served to make the pinched-in waist look even smaller and the abbreviated length showed off the legs in their silken hose to great advantage.

During the first half of the century the hair was cut in a bowl crop, level with the top of the ears to accommodate the very high collars. As the collars were gradually lowered the hair was worn longer. The early headdress was predominantly the chaperon, a fixed wound turban. Later in the century this gave way to the high sugar-loaf hat, which elongated the figure.

Pointed shoes of the fourteenth century continued in use, probably attaining their greatest length at the Burgundian court in the third quarter of the century. This was

another case where the opposition of the clergy and the law had little effect.

In the last quarter of the century the silhouette changed again, the fitted robe being replaced by a long loose gown with wide tubular sleeves through which the arms could emerge at conveniently placed slits. The pourpoint, which for so many decades had served to hold up the hose, gave up that function for the time being when the hose were at last merged into tights or trousers. The pourpoint then emerged from hiding and became the doublet—a waist-length, low-necked, smart outer garment, exposed for all to see. This radical change brought the shirt into the fashion picture. Judging from portraits they were well worthy of display. With the legs now revealed full length, the tight hose became more elaborate; slashing and purely decorative points or laces were added. Shoes changed from the elongated pike shape to the broad duckbill outline.

At the same time the high sugar-loaf hat gave way to either a flat bonnet with upturned brim or a wide-brimmed extravagant creation with a galaxy of plumes, held in place by a silk scarf passing under the chin.

Italy

In Italy, which was composed of rival city states, fashions were not uniform. However, because there was such variety and imaginative detail in Italian costumes and because of the sumptuousness of the fabrics employed, the excellence of jewelers' craftsmanship, the splendor created by Renaissance artists, and the material wealth resulting from Italy's foreign trade—which made all the rest possible—it seems fitting and proper to let the Italians present the main fashion story during this time.

The Gonzagas of Mantua, the Estes of Ferrara, the Montefeltros of Urbino, the Viscontis and Sforzas of Milan, and above all the Medicis of Florence produced the political, intellectual, and ecclesiastical leaders, who had the money, the taste, the appre-

FIG. 222. *Spinello Aretino, Scenes from the Venetian Campaign of Pope Alexander III against Frederick Barbarossa. Detail. 1408–1410. (Town Hall, Siena, Anderson Photograph— Alinari)*

FIG. 223.   Domenico di Bartolo, *Rector of Hospital Receiving Privileges from Pope Celestine III*. Detail. 1443. (*Hospital of Santa Maria della Scala, Siena, Anderson Photograph—Alinari*)

ciation, the family, and the civic pride necessary to stimulate creative activity in all the arts during the 1400s.

Not the least of Italian achievements at this time were in the field of textiles. Lucca, Venice, Genoa, and Florence vied in producing magnificent fabrics—velvets and brocades still wonderful to behold.

EARLY FIFTEENTH CENTURY

The smooth-shouldered, wide-sleeved Italian houppelande, reaching only to mid-calf, is well illustrated in Fig. 222, dated 1408–1410. Both wide-mouthed and bagpipe sleeves are shown, and dagging in a restrained form finishes the lower edge. Collars have been lowered and hair is of a moderate length. Only the second figure from the right has an unusually high hairline above the nape of the neck. The coif, popular in the thirteenth century, and a true hat, jeweled and plumed, appear side by side.

Figure 223, from di Bartolo's fresco in the Siena hospital, portrays the epitome of high fashion near the close of the exuberant first half of the fifteenth century. The knee-length houppelande, of white silk, patterned on a grand scale in green, is lined and banded in fur. The natural shoulder-line has been replaced by sleeve fullness massed at the armscye. Parti-colored hose carry out the heraldic theme. The curling hair and the elegant hat with upturned brim appear strikingly akin to styles of seventeenth-century cavaliers.

MID-CENTURY

By mid-century, as we have seen, much of the excess fullness of the houppelande and sleeves had given way to a shorter and less bulky fashion. For example, the Adimari-Ricasoli wedding procession includes dapper young men in surcoats above the knees, with open cape-like sleeves of matching length. The elaborately patterned sleeves of the courtepy (the abbreviated cotehardie) are

slightly full above the elbow, but fitted from elbow to wrist. The girdle is at the normal waistline.

Three of the party wear the chaperon, the final form of a headdress derived from the hood. Evidently the task of draping the distorted hood into a turban each time the gentleman wore it became tiresome, so some ingenious hatter designed the chaperon—a substitute that could be donned or doffed at will—the foundation of which was the roundlet, a head-fitting smooth roll. The cape of the earlier hood and lengthened liripipe were attached to the inside of the roundlet. It was fashionable to allow the cape portion to fall over one side of the roll, the liripipe over the other. Parti-colored

Fig. 224. *Costume Consisting of Pourpoint and Hose. Redrawn from the Painting, Civettino, Florentine School. 1445–1450. (Uffizi Gallery, Florence, Alinari Photograph)*

hose with soles of leather, slightly pointed at the toe, prevail.

A fashionable game of mid-century in Italy was civetta or civettino. Young sportsmen dressed for this by laying aside their cotehardies. The player reproduced in Fig. 224 shows the pourpoint and hose with the points which held them together. The pourpoint sleeves correspond in style to those of the cotehardies in the wedding procession referred to above. Note that the hose have not yet been joined to form trousers.

The frescoed walls of the chapel in the Riccardi palace, first built and occupied by the Medicis, provide another rich source of information regarding Italian fashions. Fig. 225 shows a detail from this chapel. Here the royal horseman, representing one of the three wise men, is modeled after the artist's memory of the Byzantine emperor who had visited Florence earlier in the century seeking help against the Turks. The short fur-banded sleeves of this style of houppelande appear often in Italian paintings.

The young men attending his majesty may well be corseted, so small are their waists and so sleek their body lines. Their pourpoints or doublets are made with standing collars, the upper edge of which forms a horizontal line instead of sloping upward toward the back as collars do today. Sleeves are full, puffed, and probably padded at the shoulders. The sleeveless jerkin or overjacket has a V-neckline in the back, deeply

Fig. 225. *Benozzo Gozzoli, Journey of the Magi. 1459–1462. (Chapel of Riccardi Palace, Alinari Photograph)*

FIG. 226. *Fiorenzo di Lorenzo, The Miracle of St. Bernardino. Detail. 1473. (Pinacoteca, Perugia, Anderson Photograph—Alinari)*

rounded armscyes, and a short skirt with bound scallops around the bottom. Jutting out below the scallops is a circle of organpipe pleating banded on the lower edge with embroidery.

The Brooklyn Museum collection of Russian costumes includes a jacket treated in somewhat the same way. Its outer silk fabric is lined and padded like a comforter. The three layers of which it is formed are shaped into columnar folds and then sewed into permanent position from the underside. The exactness and rigidity of much fifteenth-century pleating suggests that some such system must have been used. Common to costumes of both men and women throughout much of Europe, it also extends to the bases of the late fifteenth and early sixteenth century (Fig. 230).

The hose of this mid-century period still consist of two separate legs, which were not always perfectly fitted. The hose on the two lads at the left in Fig. 225 are certainly far from smooth. Boots finished with reversed scalloped tops are fastened with inside lacing. The porkpie hat on the young man at the right was a favorite with Italian men.

LATE FIFTEENTH CENTURY

It would be incorrect to assume that all well-dressed Italian men indulged in the extreme fashions of the day. That they did not do so is illustrated in Mantegna's painting of the family of Ludovico II of the House of Gonzaga. Ludovico was the grandfather of the future husband of Isabella d'Este, the most outstanding woman of the Italian

FIG. 227. *Cosima Jura and Francesco Cossa, The Triumph of Venus. Detail. 1470. (Palazzo Schifanoia, Ferrara, Anderson Photograph—Alinari)*

Renaissance. In this family group we can see moderation in the length of jacket, shape of shoes, and padding of shoulders. Tubular folds continue in use. Ludovico's robe is long, befitting the dignity of his position. Assuredly the fabrics are of the finest quality, and the fur of equal excellence.

The detail from the *Miracle of Saint Bernardino* (Fig. 226) shows youths who could be expected to be style conscious. The cyclas-like garments of the two men at the left were in fashion at the time of the Adimari-Ricasoli wedding (mid-century). But the young man shown in back view who wears a courtepy (shortened cotehardie) with its pendant sleeves caught under his girdle is following a fad current in his day. Sometimes the sleeves were looped over one another at the back. The young man at the right in doublet and hose and no overjacket at all is the fashion setter of the group. This is one of the earliest instances on record of doublet shortened to the waistline, combined with hose lengthened and joined into trousers, and fully exposed to view. Note that doublet and hose are still caught together with laces or points. Workmen had long worn only pourpoint and hose as a matter of practical common sense when the outer garment interfered with action or was too warm. But gentlemen did not adopt this undressed look until the latter part of the fifteenth century. The long slit down the outer fold of the sleeves was typical of Italian end-of-the-century fashions. While there is variety in the headdresses, they are not as eccentric as those of the Burgundians, as we shall see.

Figure 227 shows us back views of costume, which are so seldom portrayed. The sleeveless open-sided surcoat with tubular pleats similar to those of Fig. 226 is worn over doublet and hose. A painting in the same series, *The Triumph of Minerva*, shows older gentlemen in full ankle-length robes still wearing the chaperon. Shoes are quite normal in shape.

In the thirteenth century (see Fig. 189)

FIG. 228. *Giorgione, The Ordeal by Fire of Moses. Detail. c.1500. (Uffizi Gallery, Florence, Alinari Photograph)*

drawers reached below the knees, though as the hose lengthened and tightened this undergarment was gradually shortened. By the fifteenth century the breeches were brief indeed.

One of the most significant Italian paintings for the history of costume is Giorgione's *Ordeal by Fire of Moses*, reproduced in Fig. 228. The two men standing in front of the babe are dressed in the height of fashion for the end of the century. The shortened doublet appears in two forms, one with broad lacing down the front and the other with a surplice closing. The leg coverings have been elaborated. Vertical slashes, finished off by a broad horizontal border, appear on the left upper leg of the man at the left—forerunners of the paned and puffed trousers of the sixteenth century. Garters serving no apparent purpose are tied below the knees. Broad points are attached as decoration over the thigh section of the other gentleman's costume. His hose are not even attached to his doublet, the blousing of his soft shirt separating doublet and hose. One of the men at the right wears hose with long vertical slashes on both legs, their spreading edges brought together at spaced intervals by small points.

Carpaccio's series of paintings portray-

FIG. 229. Carpaccio, The Legend of St. Ursula. Detail from the English Ambassadors before King Maurus. c.1495. (Academy of Fine Arts, Venice, Anderson Photograph)

ing the Legend of St. Ursula, from which Fig. 229 is reproduced, also tells us a good deal about late fifteenth-century fashions. Many items of high style are shown here: low-necked shirt, scanty doublet laced across the front, doublet sleeve slashed both vertically and horizontally but held together by lacings, the short gown on the man at the left with open tubular sleeves and contrast-

ing revers, broad-toed footwear, shoulder-length hair, and low-crowned headdress.

There is great charm, as well as fashion, in the kneeling figure of the young son of Lodovico Sforza and Beatrice d'Este, shown in Fig. 230. His doublet sleeves are made in two sections, puffed on the upper arm but fitted and slashed on the lower; they are tied to the doublet, allowing the shirt sleeve

Fig. 230. *Bernardino de Conti, Lodovico Sforza and Son in Adoration of the Virgin. Detail. 1494. (Brera, Milan, Anderson Photograph— Alinari)*

to emerge through the openings of the armscye. His skirt, composed of conical shaped folds and supported by the matching doublet, is of the type called bases, which will be much in evidence in the sixteenth century.

The father wears a handsome knee-length damask gown with generous open sleeves. This new form of surcoat called the gown differed from the previous style in its wider sleeves and looser appearance. Where the fashionable mid-century surcoat emphasized slenderness and height, the late fifteenth-century outer garment either hung free or was loosely girdled. Lapels, often furred, marked the beginning of accent at the shoulder line and the generously cut sleeves increased the overall effect of bulkiness—a tendency carried to extreme in the following century.

Just as Italian men did not indulge in the long pointed poulaines so popular at the Burgundian court during the mid-century, neither did they adopt footwear of the extreme width which marked German men at the end of the century. The normal length and width of the shoes of Fig. 228 are indicative of Italian taste. One pair of shoes is cut out over the instep with a narrow strap; a slip-on one has a short pointed tongue.

The hair was worn long with a center part and either brushed to the back or dressed to radiate from the crown, forming bangs in front and rolled under at neck and shoulder. Young men were clean shaven, older men bearded (Fig. 228).

Most Italian men wore conservative headdress also. A small round cap, molded to fit the head snugly, was popular. Another style frequently seen had a higher crown with a more angular line than the cap and a sharply upturned brim two to three inches in depth. Only the young fops cocked a diminutive hat accented with two or three small feathers far forward or over one ear.

An official headdress worthy of note was that worn by the Doges of Venice (Fig. 231). The stiff rounded projection at the back was derived from the forward tilting soft crown of the Phrygian bonnet. Note the thirteenth-century coif worn beneath the symbol of office.

Burgundy and Flanders

HISTORICAL BACKGROUND

A brief summary of the relationship between France and Burgundy on the one hand and Burgundy and Flanders on the other will help explain the overlapping and interrelationship of fashions.

King John II of France, who ruled from 1350 to 1364, had four sons. The eldest, Charles V, succeeded his father as king and ruled from 1364 to 1380. The other three, all important, were Louis, Duke of Anjou, John, Duke of Berry, and Philip the Bold, upon whom his father bestowed the escheated Duchy of Burgundy.

Charles VI, son of Charles V, came to the throne as a minor in 1380, with Philip

FIG. 231. *Official Headdress of Doges of Venice. c.1476. Redrawn from Bellini, Doge Andrea Vendramin. (Frick Collection, New York)*

the Bold as regent. Each of the other three uncles exploited this opportunity to his own advantage. Later, when Charles VI became intermittently insane, Philip again acted as regent, a position which forwarded his ambitions. His marriage to Margaret, heiress of the last Count of Flanders, brought Flanders under the rule of the Dukes of Burgundy. By such shrewd marriages, inheritance, conquest, and purchase (when unavoidable), the Dukes of Burgundy eventually came to rule over not only the Duchy of Burgundy and Flanders, but also Artois, Brabant, Luxembourg (purchased), Holland, Zeeland, Friesland, and Hainault. Industry and trade made these provinces flourish. The dukes took heavy toll in taxes and disbursed the income as if it were their own private fortune.

As regent, Philip the Bold ruled both French and Burgundian holdings, for the most part from Paris. The capital city of the Dukes of Burgundy was moved from Dijon in Burgundy to Brussels in Flanders, though Dijon was retained as a ducal residence. Thus the affairs of Burgundy, France, and Flanders became almost inextricably interwoven. Fashion reflected these close ties. For succeeding Dukes of Burgundy, Flemish artists painted royal portraits and wedding festivities, illuminated manuscripts, and designed dozens of marvelous tapestries, replete with well-dressed courtiers and their ladies.

Naturally this acquaintance with Burgundian fashions was reflected in Flemish costumes and it is practically impossible to separate one from the other during their close association. Influence radiated from the court in Brussels, having least effect in Italy, where the native creative ability and taste held their own.

The ascendance of the Burgundian dukes lasted from 1361, when King John turned over the Duchy of Burgundy to his son, Philip the Bold, until the death of Charles the Bold at the battle of Nancy in 1477.

The break between France and Burgundy began in civil war and was abetted when Duke John the Fearless (1404–1419) refused to support the royal cause when Henry V of England invaded Normandy in 1415. The enmity was nurtured by John's repudiation of the Dauphin (the future Charles VII) and his subsequent murder at a conference called in an attempt to reconcile the opposing factions. Burgundy's separation from France became definite when the Burgundians under Duke Philip the Good (1419–1467) joined the English forces in 1428 in an attempt to secure the French throne for the infant son of Henry V of England. It was during these ominous proceedings that Joan of Arc was inspired to lead the French forces to victory and to effect the coronation of Charles VII as king of France. And it was the Burgundians who captured Joan and sold her to the British.

FASHION FEATURES

The most lavishly dressed court in Europe during the fifteenth century was that of the dukes of Burgundy, who had not only the requisite wealth, but love of splendor and exhibitionist impulses.

Philip the Bold, who is said to have possessed a mania for clothes, set the pattern for the era. On the occasion of a feast at Amiens in honor of the Duke of Lancaster in 1391, he is reported to have appeared in two dress suits. One was a wide black houppelande which reached the ground; its left sleeve was decorated with a sprig of gold roses, the 22 flowers composed of sapphires, rubies, and pearls. The second suit was a sort of cherry-red velvet coat embroidered with polar bears wearing jeweled gold collars and muzzles.

Until the very end of the Burgundian power in 1477, the apparel worn by succeeding dukes grew steadily richer until it became fabulous. A single example was a hat described as "yellow velvet ornamented with a gold coronet set with large pearls, sapphires and rubies as well as with a six strand pearl cord having a clasp of diamonds, rubies,

FIG. 232. *French School, John the Fearless of Burgundy. c.1410. (Louvre)*

and pearls. It was further adorned with a red and white dyed ostrich feather."[1]

The effect of richness came largely from the fabrics used, as was the case in Italy. Fine woolens and linens were available in the Low Countries and England, and cloth of gold, velvets, and brocades were imported in quantity from Italy. Furriers ordered skins by the thousand; the lavish use of fur appears over and over again in the paintings of the times.

The marriage of John the Fearless, Duke of Burgundy from 1404 to 1419, to Margaret of Holland, led to the Burgundian acquisition of that portion of the Low Countries. In one of his portraits (Fig. 232) he wears a handsome black houppelande lined and collared with fur; the red hood about his shoulders has interestingly dagged outer edges and a costly brooch. His hat probably originated from the early hood. Its face edge has been formed into a deep soft roll; the crown portion, tilted forward in a high soft pouch, is also adorned with precious stones.

A full-length figure in a Flemish tapestry toward the end of the first quarter of the century shows both the sleeves and the body of the houppelande falling in voluminous folds. The collar is high and fur-edged; in fact, the entire garment appears to be lined with fur. The feature which distinguishes it from the houppelandes of other countries at this time is the tremendous fullness at the top of the sleeves, which is mounted in deep round folds similar to the vertical folds in the body portion. The girdle is worn at the normal waistline. The hairline is natural, the hair soft at the sides, covering the ears but ending above the collar. A Van Eyck portrait of 1433 shows a similarly collared neckline and a huge turban draped of folded cloth instead of a hood.

The cosmopolitan costume shown in Van Eyck's portrait of Giovanni Arnolfini and his bride (Fig. 233) reflects the elegance of Burgundian-Flemish fashion. Arnolfini, a

merchant and agent for Philip the Good, wears an overgarment comparable to the early cyclas—front and back panels are open from shoulder to hem—but fuller and richer in its lavish use of fur than the crusader's garment. He poses proudly in a huge high-crowned beaver hat, a rare and costly status symbol of the well-to-do throughout Europe. His footwear, reaching above the anklebone, is conservatively pointed. The wooden galoches on the floor beside him are similar to those worn by Philip the Good of Burgundy. A Van Eyck portrait of Canon van der Paele, dated 1436, shows an accessory which is taken for granted today but was rare at the time: a pair of horn-rimmed spectacles.

The Rose Tapestries in the Metropolitan Museum collection, though dealing with a French subject, were designed and made in Flanders and should probably be considered Franco-Flemish (Fig. 234). The men's costumes represent a transition in style from the overabundance of fabric in the early part of the century to the long, lean look of the middle and third quarters. The courtiers wear surcoats, still designed with organ-pipe folds, but they end well above the knees and may be open on the sides as high as the hips. The sleeves are mounted in deep folds but are narrow compared to earlier ones and taper to a fitted wrist, where they are banded with fur. Some of the sleeves are slit from shoulder to below the elbow, revealing the sleeves of the pourpoint. Necklines are normal, with a narrow standing collar or fur band. The front closing is invisible but some of the surcoats are left open from neck to waist.

The chaperon is the uniform headdress, these examples having thick rolls, dagged cockades derived from the original shoulder capes, and liripipes reaching to the bottom of the surcoats. Silk hose and pointed shoes complete the costume.

Petrus Christus' *Portrait of a Young Man* (Fig. 235), though of the Flemish school, gives a clear picture of the houppe-

[1] *Ciba Review*, Ciba Ltd., Basle, Switzerland, no. 51, p. 1842.

FIG. 233. Jan van Eyck, Giovanni Arnolfini and Wife. 1434. (National Gallery, London)

FIG. 234. *Rose Tapestries. Detail. Courtiers with Roses. Franco - Flemish.* c. 1435 – 1440. *(Metropolitan Museum of Art)*

lande or robe that was fashionable in France at this time. Perhaps the most striking change that has occurred is the shortening and narrowing of the lower part of the sleeve to a trim line on the forearm. The chaperon is still slung by the liripipe over the right shoulder. Another important accessory, the purse, often handsomely mounted, is seen to good advantage in this painting.

The frontispiece of the *Chronicles of Hainault* by Jean Wauquelin, dated about 1450 but not pictured here, shows the author presenting his book to Philip the Good. The Duke and members of his court appear in the type of costumes which made Burgundian styles famous. The surcoats of the courtiers are of rich, boldly patterned brocades and velvets made in the broad-shouldered slim-waisted design which, in combination with the pleats extending from shoulder to hem and the long slim legs made to seem even longer by poulaines and needle-toed galoches, give the impression of imposing height and great elegance. Philip's rank is indicated not only by his bearing but also by the individuality of his costume

FIG. 235. *Petrus Christus, Portrait of a Young Man. 1450–1460. (National Gallery, London)*

which is entirely black—aristocratic because of its seeming simplicity.

Both Philip and his son, the future Charles the Bold, wear surcoats ending just above the knee but most of Philip's companions are dressed in long surcoats, a custom noted in the beginning of this chapter, which continued on occasion throughout the century. The sleeves have lost most of the length and volume of the early century and

are distinguished by their leg-of-mutton shape supported by mahoitres. The sleeves narrow down to modern width in the forearm. Surcoats and doublets are open from throat to waist, revealing the shirt; cords secure them at the necklines. The prevailing hair style is the bowl crop, cut well above the ears.

Philip's chaperon is more bulky than those of other countries and its liripipe is drawn snugly under the chin and fastened to the opposite side of the headdress. He and most of his companions wear the collar of the Order of the Golden Fleece.

The points of the poulaines had not reached their maximum length at this time but the galoche, described below, extended well beyond the poulaine. The pointed toes of fifteenth-century shoes were a revival of the poulaine of the late fourteenth century. Poulaines reached their maximum length in Burgundy during the third quarter of the century. The fifteenth century poulaine in the Victoria and Albert collection, shown in Fig. 236, measures 15 inches from heel to toe and is laced at the side. The long, soft, rather limp extension posed definite problems in walking. Each step had to be taken with a slight kicking motion to avoid stumbling over the toe of the shoe. Mud could quickly ruin a pair of these foppish, impractical points. Since roads were notoriously bad, even in cities, the answer was the patten or galoche, also a revival of fourteenth-century footwear. Authors differ widely in their use of the words poulaine, patten, and galoche. Poulaine is used to indicate both the pointed shoe and the beautifully crafted, metal-re-inforced leather sole fastened over it by means of straps. Patten and galoche are wooden-soled footwear worn to elevate the feet above the muck and mud. The thick soles were carved with higher sections at the

FIG. 237. *Thierry Bouts, Slaughter of the Innocents. Detail. Flemish. c.1470. (Musées royaux des Beaux-Arts de Belgique, Brussels)*

Fig. 238. *Loyset Liedet, Vasco de Lucena Presents Book to Charles the Bold of Burgundy. 1470.* (Bibliothèque Nationale, Paris)

heel and ball of the foot. They were held on by a broad band over the instep made to fit snugly over the foot or by a pair of straps which buckled in place. The Germans called this protective form an undershoe, the French a galoche, the English a patten. Made primarily for outdoor wear, during the reign of Philip the Good it was fashionable to wear them indoors. A very good representation of them is shown in Fig. 233.

Figure 237 is typical of the elongated look in Flemish-Burgundian styles about 1470. The doublet, of plain cloth, has slim velvet-patterned sleeves and the surcoat, of mid-calf length, is, in the original painting, of boldly patterned fabric also. The lines, however, fall close to the body, with a cen-

tering of full-length pleats at the back of the skirt. The narrow tubular sleeves with vertical openings add to the slenderizing effect. The sugar-loaf hat has lost its excess height. Brims are for the most part narrow and turn sharply upward, as in this case, or are omitted. The sock boots or pedules, though still pointed, are only slightly extended. Hair is chin length.

The wardrobe of Charles the Bold, last of the Burgundian dukes, surpassed that of his father in richness and extravagance. Something of the architectural setting in which the extreme Burgundian fashions were worn is suggested in a miniature by Loyset Liedet which depicts Vasco de Lucena presenting his book to Duke Charles the Bold

(Fig. 238). Here in the Burgundian court were seen the longest poulaines, the highest sugar-loaf hats, the broadest shoulders, the slimmest waists, the shortest courtepies and capes, and the tightest hose.

Two styles of hats were current at this time. The high sugar-loaf hat was so named because in size and shape it resembled the form in which sugar was marketed at that time: heavy syrup of the proper consistency was poured into cylindrical molds that were rounded at one end, and left to crystallize. The sugar-loaf hat found in Greenland has a short gusset set in from the edge at center back to accommodate the head size and to lengthen the back portion slightly.

The hat which alternated with the sugar-loaf model was the round crowned style with rolling brim worn by Charles the Bold. The man at the left in back view in the illustration is carrying a hat of this sort slung over his shoulder by a liripipe. Hair was

FIG. 239. *Dance of Mirth in a Garden. Flemish. Late Fifteenth Century. From Romance of the Rose. MS. 4425, Folio 14ᵇ. (British Museum)*

allowed to grow to chin length, but men continued to be clean-shaven.

Though the rule of the Dukes of Burgundy ended with the death of Charles the Bold in 1477, Brussels continued to be a center of fashion. The exotic high fashion of Flanders is shown in an illumination of a stately dance in a garden, one of the illustrations in Romance of the Rose (Fig. 239). A youth at the left is wearing doublet and hose; the wide V-shape of the front of his doublet is filled in with matching underbody, which forms a straight line across the throat. The sleeves are cut in two parts, the upper portion puffed, the lower fitted. The hose are startling; their upper section is striped in green, gray, pink, and white, and reaches to lower thigh, where the joining to the lower black section is masked with gold embroidery. Over these hose he wears high sock boots and mule-styled shoes with enormous bulging toes. A second young man wears the new gown or outer wrap. Reaching to the knees, it has wide full-length revers of fur which spread far apart at the neckline and are widened to extend over the shoulder. The long tubular sleeves falling below the hem of the gown to lower calf set these garments apart from the short houppelandes of the beginning of the century. Vertical slashes in the sleeves and deep bands of fur or other trimming at the lower edges are features common to most of the gowns in the scene. Two men wear gowns girdled rather loosely and have handsome tasseled purses suspended from their girdles. One in back view is ungirdled.

The hair is worn quite long, falling well down upon the shoulders. Two types of hats are shown. One is a small jaunty shallow red cap with narrow upturned brim; the other is the most spectacular hat of the century. It is of beaver with a broad crown and wide upturned brim. Soaring skyward is a great panache of feathers proportionally one-third the height of the wearer. The hat is anchored by a scarf which passes under the chin and through slits at the base of the crown, the ends being tied on top of the crown.

Figure 240 is typical of the gown which, with slight variations, became popular throughout Europe. In this instance the glowing costly fabric of gold background patterned on an imposing scale in velvet is luxuriously furred; its full-length revers extend into a collar and reversed cuffs finish the wide sleeves. The length—a few inches above the ankles—adds to its air of grandeur.

France

The first half of the fifteenth century

Fig. 240. *Flemish Gown. Detail from Scenes from Life of the Virgin by Master of Tiburtine Sibyl. Late Fifteenth Century. (John G. Johnson Collection, Philadelphia)*

Fig. 241. *Pol de Limbourg and His Brothers. 1409–1416. From Très Riches Heures du duc de Berri. April, The Betrothal. (Musée Condé, Chantilly)*

was a period of great strain for France. As we saw earlier, Charles VI, who ruled from 1380 to 1422, suffered from intermittent insanity and his unscrupulous uncles took full advantage of the situation, which thus provided an opportunity for the rapid rise to power of the Dukes of Burgundy. This period also marked a low point for France in the Hundred Years War. The coalition of England and Burgundy aroused Joan of Arc to her inspired leadership and led to the crowning of the weakling Charles VII in 1429.

John, Duke of Berry, one of the uncles of Charles VI, had one redeeming feature— at least as far as posterity was concerned— his love of fine books. The rarest and most beautiful of his manuscripts was the Très Riches Heures du duc de Berri, commissioned by him about 1409 but still unfinished at his death in 1416. The illuminations in this manuscript picture the rich attire of the

ducal court in glowing color, against a background of lapis lazuli blue, highlighted in
gold. Figure 241 reproduces one of its illustrations. Continuing the late fourteenth-century theme of exaggerated length, the
French houppelande of the betrothed gentleman in this picture sweeps the ground; his
dagged, fur-lined, embroidered sleeves fall
in harmonizing lines, their fullness arranged
in evenly spaced organ-pipe pleats—a signa-
ture of fifteenth-century costume. Two important hat styles are shown: the high-
crowned square topper with a small roll
encircling the head, and the softer, bulkier
turban, achieved by draping the hood. In the
feast scene, at which the Duke presides, he
wears a hat with a wide sharply upturned
brim of fur, a long houppelande of lapis blue,
and a broad gold collar.

FIG. 243. *French Cotehardie. Redrawn from
Harley MS. 4431, Folio 115. (British Museum)*

Guests of secondary importance at this
happy occasion wear shorter houppelandes
with low-slung belts, from which hang
sword and purse. The long silver band
running diagonally from right shoulder to
left hip (a baldric) is edged with bells. Fur
vies with dagging and embroidery for decoration.

A French manuscript in the British
Museum, dating about 1420, provides an
excellent record of French costume of this
time. Figure 242, taken from it, shows the
shortened, collarless houppelande with low-

FIG. 242. *French Houppelande. 1420. Redrawn
from Harley MS. 4431, Folio 143. (British Museum)*

FIG. 244. *Turban Draped from Hood. French. 1420. Redrawn from Harley MS. 4431, Folio 95. (British Museum)*

FIG. 245. *Straw Hat. French. 1420. Redrawn from Harley MS. 4431, Folio 95. (British Museum)*

ered waistline and dagged fur-lined sleeves, one or both of which might be embroidered. The leg wear is mi-parti. The hood, slung over the shoulder by the liripipe, is lengthened and widened almost beyond recognition. Bells are suspended from a necklace worn close to the throat. Only the collar and a portion of one sleeve of the pourpoint are visible. The bowl-crop hair style remained in fashion until mid-century. In spite of the disappearance of the high collar and the shorter length, the overall impression is still one of abundance of fabric.

Figure 243, from the same manuscript, illustrates the early fifteenth-century cotehardie with very wide flaring sleeves, evidently embroidered and lined with fur. The deep armscyes and the shape of the top of the sleeves indicate a method of cutting similar to that of the pourpoint of Charles of Blois (Fig. 194). The contour of the front indicates the rise of padding. The trim fitting at the waist seam adds to the feminine appearance of the costume. Mi-parti hose, soled with leather, perform the functions of both shoes and hose. His necklace of bells, broad ornate hip belt, and turban covered with overlapping leaf shapes assure him a place in the forefront of fashion. Note his small forked beard.

Another sleeve design worn quite gen-

erally in Europe at this time was the bagpipe or poky form. It varies from others previously noted in that the wrist opening is at wrist level, the lower part of the sleeve forming a pouch below it. The arm is thrust through the usual long vertical slit.

One manner of draping a French hood is shown in Fig. 244. The liripipe, bound about the head, is held in place by a large brooch. The shoulder cape covers the crown of the head, its edges falling symmetrically to right and left.

Another headdress, carefully drawn and illustrated in Fig. 245, is obviously a straw hat. A normal-sized crown fits the head nicely. The cock of the wide brim at one side is balanced by two waving plumes.

The nonchalant farmer in Fig. 246, dressing as he starts his round of morning chores, displays a hip-length shirt or pourpoint to which he is fastening his hose, a surcoat with outsize ball buttons down the front, plain rough shoes, and a hood on the order of the thirteenth-century coif.

Though the houppelande remained popular through the middle of the fifteenth century in France, its silhouette was altered. The broadening of the shoulders by mahoitres (padding), combined with slanting folds from shoulder to waist, emphasized the illusion of slenderness.

FIG. 246. *Farmer Fastening His Hose. French. 1420. Redrawn from Harley MS. 4431, Folio 115ᵇ. (British Museum)*

One of the most important documents of French fashion is King René's Book of the Tournament. In the painting from it reproduced here (Fig. 247), the king of arms presents to the Duke of Bourbon the blazons of eight gentlemen proposed as judges. Here high fashion is exemplified by mahoitred sleeves, pinched waist, set and rounded pleating, revealing brevity of the courtepy, sharply extended points of the footwear, longer hair, and high-crowned headgear. Only the Duke wears a brimmed hat, a fringed import from Portugal. The high cuffed boots reaching well above the knees are important fashion items, as is the greater exposure of the throat.

The French manuscript of Sir John Froissart's Chronicles of England, France, and Spain in the Bibliothèque Nationale in

Paris furnishes illustrations of French costume of the third quarter of the fifteenth century. Features just noted in the Book of the Tournament have now become sharpened. The courtepies of some of the young men are shorter, barely reaching the hipbone. The tops of their sleeves are wider and fuller and their long gowns appear to be tightly cinched at the waist. Mathematically exact rounded folds run from the shoulders to the center portion of the waist, then fall full-length to the floor, giving a tall lean look that was very popular. Hair is chin- or shoulder-length and rather bushy at the ends.

Hats have a high rounded crown not unlike our twentieth-century derby, but the brims are in the form of a level even roll all around the crown. Chaperons with long liripipes are worn by older citizens. Often a man wears a high-crowned hat and carries a second one slung over the shoulder by the attached liripipe.

Ankle-height shoes are pointed but not to the extreme set by the Burgundian court. There are instances of boots reaching almost to mid-thigh, where they are reversed into cuffs.

At the close of the century French costume changes were similar to those of other European countries. Waist-length doublets were combined with full-length skin-tight trousers. A sword belt worn around the waist served the purpose of a girdle. The French doublet differed from the Italian in that its sleeves extended outward from the waistline (dolman cut) and were either tapered to fit the wrist or gathered into a narrow wrist band. Figure 248 shows most of these features. The sleeve seam is left open, revealing the shirt sleeve. The neckline of the doublet was either square or rounded both back and front and quite low, allowing the shirt to show.

A front view of the doublet from the same source as the drawing shows the front unbroken, as if the doublet had been pulled on over the head. The hose, now really hose and trousers combined, are mi-parti, with

Fig. 247. *King René's Book of the Tournament. King of Arms Presents Blazons of Eight Gentlemen to Duke of Bourbon. 1460–1465. MS. 2695. (Bibliothèque Nationale, Paris)*

one or both legs striped or one or both plain. Decoration from waist to hip is similar to that of some of the Italian hose. Note the garter tied beneath the knee.

The shoes are spade-shaped with wide square toes and a strap to secure them.

The French contribution to sixteenth-century men's costume was the French bonnet: a low rather broad-crowned hat with an upturned brim slanting slightly outward.

Sometimes the front of the brim was cut away. More often a medal or brooch adorned the front as worn by Charles VIII in Fig. 249. Here the king is wearing one style of the late fifteenth-century gown. For men of high position the gown was full-length and often ungirdled. Often collarless, as in this case, they were usually worn with the upper front edges turned back to form revers. Sleeves were generously cut but shaped differently from early fifteenth-century sleeves, in that they were of even width from the armscye to the wrist. The royal sleeves in Fig. 249 have a horizontal slash over the elbow and are banded with fur at the wrist.

An anonymous French drawing in the Cleveland Museum of Art shows a lady with three suitors whose gowns vary in length from above the knee to the ankle. They have wide lapels. The sleeves are as wide or wider than those of King Charles VIII in Fig. 249. The visible portion of a doublet has a rather high wide neckline and no evidence of fastening. The brims of the French bonnets are cut away over the forehead. Their shoes are in the form of mules with broad rounded toes and thick soles. The hair is shoulder length.

FIG. 248. *Doublet and Hose. French. Late Fifteenth Century. Redrawn from Detail of French Gothic Tapestry, The Bear Hunt. (Art Institute of Chicago)*

Germany

Since a detailed account of German costume through the century would be repetitious, we shall confine ourselves for the most part to its variations from Italian, Burgundian, and French fashions.

The German houppelande of the early fifteenth century lacked the exaggerated fullness and length of French fashion in both the skirt and the sleeve. The houppelande was likely to be of ground length or just above the ankles, and the sleeve of wrist length or slightly longer and about 4 feet in circumference, instead of sweeping the floor.

Dagging was popular and hardly an edge escaped this scissored elaboration. As many as seven layers of petal-shaped dagges are shown on one skirt. The dagges themselves were often scalloped or even cut in leaf shapes. It was customary to sew a dagged band along the outside of the sleeve from armscye to lower edge, usually matching the color of the lining of the cotehardie or houppelande.

The bagpipe or poky sleeve was a favorite on surcoats but differed from those noted earlier in that it usually had no wrist opening. It varied in length from fingertip to lower calf, depending upon the formality of the garment. A small slit, often fur-trimmed, accommodated the arm.

The German cotehardie was much the same as in the rest of Europe, its chief distinction being in the design of the sleeve. Instead of ending at the wrist, a wide, deep trumpet-shaped extension covered the knuckles.

The natural hairline prevailed. Hair was cut short at the nape of the neck, but the combination of shaving above the ears and bowl-crop was seldom seen. Instead of the huge draped turbans and chaperons, the Germans wore smooth turbans of moderate size or round-crowned hats with upturned brims. Hoods continued to be worn in the normal manner.

A foible that was carried to extremes

Fig. 249. *Charles VIII of France Being Presented a Book by Its Author. End of the Fifteenth Century. French MS. 35320, Folio 3ᵇ. (British Museum)*

was the wearing of bells. Broad gold collars in round or deep V-shape were hung with round bells about 3 inches in diameter. From the girdle hung open bells 3–4 inches deep or one or two rows of large bells might be placed around the bottom of the cotehardie.

Mi-parti garments were also much in evidence, the contrasting colors of the hose often being reversed on the sleeves.

Shoes were moderately pointed, covered the anklebone, and were slit on the inside surface from the top downward to facilitate dressing.

A memorial plaque dated 1427 illustrates a fashion which seems to have been peculiar to Germany in this century. It shows a gentleman wearing a surcoat closely allied to the early form of the cyclas. Its deep armscyes, edged with fur, extend to the hips. The surcoat itself falls to lower calf; from about waist level its flared fullness is formed into organ pipe folds. A wide, loose metal girdle is worn below the great armscyes. The undergarment has full sleeves, confined at the wrists by narrow bands.

The headdress this gentleman wears, frequently seen in Germany, is probably a derivative of the hood. It differs from the chaperon in that the band or brim about the head is flat and the crown is in the form of a deep soft pouch which falls over the brim to the shoulder, either left or right. The traditional headdress of Santa Claus is not too far removed from this style. The man wears both beard and moustache and his hair follows the natural hairline. His shoes have points extending beyond the toes. They are higher than usual and are slit and laced on the inside surface.

By mid-century Burgundian fashions seem to have reached some parts of Germany, as Fig. 250 suggests. This engraving is from a playing card—a rich source of information on German costume. This young blood wears the sugar-loaf hat, differing from French and Burgundian styles both in shape and in the angle at which it is worn. His mahoitred sleeves and poulaines would pass muster even in Brussels. Other details shared with fashions elsewhere are his beaver hat, slung over the shoulder by a very long liripipe, full-length tight hose, and the rounded pleats in the skirt of the courtepy.

Another playing card of the same period pictures a man in a well-fitted and padded surcoat, with a dagged skirt reaching his knees, the shoulder cape of his hood deeply dagged, and on his head a broad-brimmed hat with a large bulging crown. The sleeves of his surcoat are moderate in size and taper to narrow wrist bands; they still have the dagged trimming sewn to the back edge, however. The garment is laced up center front. His shoes come well above the ankles, have a short point, and are slit down the center over the instep. A narrow band acts as a closure.

Figure 251 shows a young couple of this

Fig. 250. *German Playing Card. 1440–1460.* (*Metropolitan Museum of Art, Rogers Fund*)

period. The man wears hose of contrasting colors, ankle-height shoes with slender sharp points and laced on the outside, and a high-collared jacket which repeats the heraldic scheme of his hose. His softly waved hair falling to the shoulders is a style worn throughout the rest of the century. Note the elaborate jeweled band on his left leg.

The cyclas form of surcoat, with or without a girdle, continued to be worn as late as 1470.

A 1477 illustration shows the sons of a nobleman wearing matching doublet, courtepy, hose, footwear, and hat. Heraldic embroidery enhances their left sleeves, and they all wear long pointed boot hose, folded down to form a cuff. Their hats have high crowns and narrow, slightly flaring upturned brims. Their long curly blonde hair falls back of their shoulders.

By the end of the fifteenth century there is evidence of increasing awareness among the Germans of high style in other European countries. One amusing illustration shows an entertainer with a basket of puppets and a Jack-in-a-stein instead of a box. His jacket has the fashionable low wide V-neckline laced across the front of his shirt, and a hip-depth skirt with a bell attached at each side. Sleeves of even width

FIG. 251. *Swabian School, The Two Lovers, c.1470. (Cleveland Museum of Art, Delia E. and L. E. Holden Funds)*

have rolled-back cuffs and long slits. A red doublet shows slightly under the front lacing and through the opening of the outer sleeve. His waist-length, low-necked blue shoulder cape is fastened on the right shoulder. His hose are mi-parti: the right leg is striped in red, white, and blue and the left has horizontal bandings in those colors above the knee but is plain red below. His low-cut black shoes have points about 4 inches long. His little green hat with narrow rolled brim fits snugly on his head. He wears a moustache and short sparse beard, and his hair just covers his ears.

An illustration of the costume of a landsknecht, a professional soldier, shows affinity with late fifteenth-century Italian styles: waist-length doublet and hose, low-necked shirt, straight across the chest, and sleeves in sections, with horizontal slit at the elbow revealing the full shirt sleeves. The lower section of the doublet sleeve, however, bells over his hand. His small, plumed, flat, red hat is secured at a rakish angle by a band passing under the chin. His low shoes have a short rounded point.

In another illustration the gown of a Bavarian nobleman of 1497 is long, ungirdled, fur-lined, and collared. Its sleeves are narrower than those noted at this time in France.

In Fig. 268 the men of the two central couples are dressed in late fifteenth-century fashion: necklines of their shirts or false fronts are straight across the chest; their doublets are cut in a slanting line from about mid-shoulder to center front waistline, retaining a short skirt. Lacing across the front holds the doublet in position. The doublet sleeves have moderate ease and are open at the wrist. Their hose are sleek. The young man at the left retains the long needle point but the one at the right wears mules with the broad rounded toe of late fifteenth century. Hair is shoulder length or longer. Most of the hats are low-crowned with narrow upturned brims and boast one or more plumes, usually upright. One small figure in the upper left group wears a beaver hat tied with a narrow scarf in the manner seen in the illustration from the Romance of the Rose (Fig. 239).

Dürer's self portrait (Fig. 252) is a superb example of late fifteenth-century fashion. Note the very low-necked shirt, probably of the finest linen, shirred and embroidered with taste and precision; the wide curving edges of the front of the doublet, boldly outlined; the two-piece sleeve, similar in style to that worn by the young Sforza in Fig. 230, with the shirt sleeves visible at the elbow; and the long curling locks of hair topped by a soft low cap. Dürer's undoubted interest in style accounts for the wonderful fashion records he left to posterity.

England

England showed less deviation from prevailing continental fashions than was observed in Germany. The Hundred Years War took English armies to France, where they won success during the first part of the century. Henry V of England, following the treaty of Troyes, married Catherine, daughter of Charles VI of France and Queen Isabelle of Bavaria—a very fashion-conscious lady indeed. In one of the fluctuations of power during the war, Henry VI of England was acknowledged king of France at the age of 9 months. John, Duke of Bedford, brother of Henry V, acted as regent for him in France. The Duchess of Bedford was Anne, sister of Philip the Good of Burgundy. And in 1467 Charles the Bold of Burgundy took as his third wife Margaret of York, sister of Edward IV of England. Thus the English court became familiar with and was influenced by high fashion on the continent.

It is not surprising to find the heroic Henry V shown in a 1415 painting in a fur-lined trailing houppelande with equally long dagged sleeves. His low collar is covered with a band of ermine, which continues down the short center-front opening. He

wears a wide golden girdle at the normal waistline. The author in this painting, kneeling as he presents his book to the king, also wears a houppelande with a collar still high and very wide bagpipe sleeves. Both men wear the bowl-cut hair style reaching to the tops of their ears. This ceremonial style of houppelande was shown as late as 1445.

The custom of placing engraved brass plate memorials over burials within the churches of England continued throughout the fifteenth century and into the sixteenth. These contribute to the record of costume of both men and women. Illustrations of men's costume include both lay costume and armor. Though the latter is favored on these brasses, there are enough examples of men in customary dress to indicate the major fashion changes of the century. The brasses represent the nobility, the gentry, and, as time went by, the most successful of the merchant class. Their costumes are likely to be on the conservative side, because of both the serious purpose of the likeness and the age of the deceased.

No excessively long houppelandes are represented on the men of the early fifteenth century in these brasses. Instead, they show this popular garment in ankle-length, slit up center front, often fur-lined and with bagpipe sleeves and normal necklines. The hair covers the upper part of the ears. Footwear is usually of ankle height, with short pointed toes and inside lacing.

High fashion is certainly found in the Duke of Bedford's Book of Hours, begun in 1423 but not finished until 1430. This exquisite illuminated manuscript was probably a wedding gift to Anne, Duchess of Bedford. Here are gorgeous brocades in unstinted yardage, the designs accented with jewels, the linings of the finest fur. The colors glow. One man wears an apple-green hood, lapis-blue mantle, and vermilion surcoat over a blue pourpoint. His companion combines a chartreuse chaperon with a vermilion knee-length surcoat and mi-parti hose of blue and white. A third ensemble includes a rose-

FIG. 252. *Dürer, Self Portrait. 1498. (Prado Museum)*

colored hat with high crown and narrow upturned brim, lapis-blue knee-length surcoat, and vermilion hose.

The Duke of Bedford is shown in a costume closely akin to the French. His voluminous dagged and fur-lined houppelande resembles those worn by the banquet guests of the Duke of Berry. His bowl crop is high above his ears and his chaperon is slung nonchalantly over his left shoulder.

The high-crowned French hat in Fig. 241 is also represented in the Duke of Bedford's Book of Hours.

By the 1430s the houppelandes on the brasses are just above the ankles; the skirt is slit up center front; the flowing sleeves, smooth at the shoulder, widen to about 4 feet at the wrist. The collarless neckline is edged with fur and dips to a short V in front. The shaved portion of the head extends well above the ears, leaving a rim of hair resembling in size and shape a Frenchman's beret. Shoes are slightly pointed.

A drawing of Henry VI about mid-century shows him in a narrowed blue houppelande almost to the floor. Its sleeves are padded, but are not widened to excess, and taper to about 10 or 12 inches at the wrist. Its collar has disappeared, the neckline having widened a bit, allowing nearly all of the high stiff collar of the pourpoint to show. A narrow bright red girdle, from which is suspended a small gold purse, encircles the hips. Henry wears a large rose-red chaperon with a knee-length liripipe. His shoes are black with round points about 2 inches long.

Fashion leaders in England in the third quarter of the century adopted the long gown, slimmed to fit the waist and padded at the shoulders, along with the courtepy, though the latter was never as fantastic in England as it became on the continent. Long boots reaching the thighs were often worn with the courtepy. Points lengthened on both shoes and boots. Figure 236 shows a typical English poulaine of this period. There is little evidence of the sugar-loaf hat. Instead the round-crowned hat, slightly high, with narrow rolled brim and a feather curling over the crown from side or back, was preferred.

During the last quarter of the century the gown changed shape once more. The same free easy lines observed on the continent found favor in England. Sleeves became tubular and were lengthened to the knee or below, usually being slit for convenience. Later brasses show some sleeves which ap-

pear to be about 30 inches in circumference. The gowns were often fur-lined and had fur lapels. The shorter gowns, popular with young men, were often ungirdled.

In England also, as on the continent, doublet and hose were worn in public without a jacket. The same wide V-neckline observed on doublets of this period elsewhere was worn, laced across the shirt. Doublet sleeves, open from elbow to wrist, exposing the shirt sleeve, were caught together with narrow bands.

By the 1470s the hair had reached chin length; from 1480 onward, it radiated from the crown, forming bangs over the forehead, and was allowed to hang to the shoulders or below. The French bonnet was adopted in England as early as the 1470s. A shallow hat, fitting close to the head, with only a partial upturned brim, was worn with casual ensemble. Broad toes replaced the sharp points of the shoes, but again the English were

FIG. 253. *Carpenter Wearing Pourpoint and Hose. c.1430. Redrawn from MS. 11850, Folio 15ᵇ. Bedford Book of Hours. (British Museum)*

more reserved and designed their shoes more nearly to the shape of the foot.

The Working Class

Working class costume is illustrated in such scenes as the building of the Tower of Babel, shepherds tending their flocks, farmers in their fields or work sheds or, rarely, village dances. This costume changed little throughout the century. Long-sleeved tunics of approximately knee length and slit up the center from hem to hip level were common to nearly all workingmen. For strenuous work the tunic might be laid aside, revealing the pourpoint laced up center front, fitted quite closely, and reaching to hip or thigh where the hose were tied to it with points. Often the back points were left untied when the labor involved much bending (Fig. 253).

Leg wear showed some differentiation. A swineherd, for example, is shown wearing rough leggings tied below the knee and at the ankle. Shepherds often rolled the tops of their hose and secured them below the knees. A worker trampling the grapes in a huge vat at vintage time is shown stripped to pourpoint, shirt, and brief drawers. Farmers usually wore a short tunic and hose but the hose might be left to wrinkle below the knees, depending upon the season of the year and the occupation. Shoes were heavy and sturdy, shaped roughly to the foot.

Shepherds quite consistently wore hoods unchanged in form from those of the twelfth century. Farmers wore small brimless caps or hats with rolling brims.

11

Women's Costume of the Fifteenth Century

General Trends

In many respects women's costume in the fifteenth century incorporated features of the clothing worn by men. The feminine houppelande, for instance, was very similar to the masculine. The popularity of the man's chaperon was paralleled by the broad and often fantastic headdress of the women. Waistlines were raised and wide colorful belts created an empire effect. Both sexes were enamored of dagging and bells suspended from collars or girdles.

The high cone-shaped hennin, with a floating veil or an airy butterfly form soaring high above it, dominated women's headdress from about 1440 to 1470. This style was in keeping with, but far surpassed, the sugar-loaf hat in height. Pointed toes were common to the footwear of both sexes.

The neckline of women's cottes and surcoats, which had been wide and low in the late fourteenth and early fifteenth centuries, was modified to a deep V-shape on mid-century gowns, the decolletage being filled in with a stomacher or by an under-dress. Trains dominated skirts throughout the century, though the round length—a skirt of even length without a train—was introduced at the court of Burgundy about 1460, and sleeves became long and closely fitted.

Late in the century the fashion changed again and we find square necklines, widened bell-mouthed sleeves, and girdles with long pendants, the weight of which tended to create a pointed waistline. The greatest change was in the headdress. The high, tight, tortuous hennin gave way to the Brittany cap of Queen Anne of France, and a similar modification occurred in other European countries. Toes of shoes became wide and rounded.

Such were the main trends. National variations, of course, distinguished the styles of one country from another, and the upper classes strove constantly to excel their social inferiors. It was a century of great splendor as well as of vagaries which still astonish the modern observer. The physical inconvenience and discomfort which were tolerated would make our twentieth-century women quail.

Italy

On the predella of his *Presentation in the Temple*, Fabriano depicted a fashionable lady of the early part of the century (Fig. 254), the most arresting feature of whose costume is the voluminous, trailing, fur-lined, dagged sleeve of her houppelande. Its fullness, as well as that of the bodice, is controlled by matching rounded pleats. The white edge of the train suggests that the entire skirt is probably lined with fur. Her headdress, which is especially richly bedecked, is the great round turban which appeared with variations throughout the century.

An outstanding fashion artist of the period was Pisanello, whose studies of costumes are distributed among various museums. His sensitiveness to every detail is shown in his *Portrait of a Lady*, reproduced in Fig. 255. The lady's plucked forehead and shaved neck were the fashion in France and Flanders through most of the century, but the Italians exposed more of their hair than was the custom in other European courts. The bulk of the hair in the Pisanello portrait is confined by a very fine net, closely resembling our modern hair nets. The ends of the hair are wrapped neatly over the temples and held in place by pins. A spirally decorated padded roll gives an oriental flavor, which was much admired.

The lady's houppelande has the high standing collar of the late fourteenth century, but its light lining and an inner white collar add a fastidious note. The deep bluish green and gold of her gown are enriched by a golden girdle worn high, a double festoon of gold filagree beads, and a shaped, flexible collar of small patterned gold plaques at the base of the neck. If we could have a full-length view of her costume, the sleeves and skirt would probably resemble closely those of the Fabriano lady in the preceding illustration.

The full-length figures from di Bartolo's Siena hospital frescoes illustrate Sienese feminine fashion about 1440. Extravagant fur-lined sleeves which sweep the ground, and skirts so long they must be held up to avoid tripping over them, set them apart from other periods. Though the forehead is plucked or shaved, the hair is visible at the temples. A high melon-shaped headdress resembles those in several Pisanello drawings. In outline it somewhat resembles the headdress of German women toward the end of the century. The short cuffed outer sleeve, a significant Italian detail, is also represented.

The ladies of the Adimari-Ricasoli wedding procession furnish an example in Italian art of the high headdress typical in France, but the short vestigial sleeves of the outer garment are peculiar to Italy.

Italian ladies of the third quarter of the century were immortalized in a unique group of profile portraits. Pollaiuolo's *Portrait of an Unknown Lady*, now in the Poldi-Pezzoli Palace in Milan, is the most charming of these subjects (Fig. 256). The blending of the lady's hair and headdress is typical of Italian taste at that time. A wispy veil covers her ear and pearls and golden cords are entwined in her coiffure. Her forehead and neck have been depilated, but not excessively so. Her curving collarless neckline with its parallel border of white (probably her chemise) descends lower in back than in front. The sleeves of contrasting fabric were high fashion in Italy at this time.

Another *Portrait of a Lady*, this one by Uccello, hangs in the National Gallery in London. In this study more of the forehead is bared and the cap is a jeweler's masterpiece. A gossamer veil edged with pearls softens the severity of the headdress. The neckline and contrasting sleeve are like those of the *Unknown Lady* in Milan.

Francesca's *Queen of Sheba in Adoration* pictures the women in wide, rather high-waisted girdles and trained skirts falling in generous fullness to the floor. One full-length figure is wearing a version of the cyclas with dagged edges; another wears a surcoat with pendant sleeves, fur-lined, and open from the shoulder almost to the wrist.

Fɪɢ. 254.   *Fabriano, Predella of his Presentation in the Temple. 1423. (Louvre)*

FIG. 255. *Pisanello, Portrait of a Lady.* 1420–1424. *(National Gallery of Art, Washington, D.C.)*

FIG. 256. *Pollaiuolo, Portrait of Unknown Lady.* c.1460. *(Poldi-Pezzoli Palace, Milan, Alinari Photo)*

In the latter part of the fifteenth century, Italy produced some of the most remarkable women in history, the most famous being Isabella d'Este and her sister Beatrice. Caterina Sforza, Lucretia Tornabuoni, and Elizabetta Gonzaga were also women of great erudition and influence. It is interesting that with all their learning, their command of languages, and their interest and influence in politics they should be so concerned with fashion.

Isabella's feeling for dress is shown in a letter she wrote at the age of 17 to her agent before he departed for France in 1491:

I send you a hundred ducats and wish you to understand that you are not to return the money—if any of it is left, after buying the things which I want but are to spend it in buying some gold chain or anything that is new and elegant. And if more is required, spend that too, for I had rather be in your debt so long as you bring me the latest novelties. But these are the things that I wish to have: engraved amethysts, rosaries of black amber and gold, blue cloth for a camorra, black cloth for a mantle such as shall be without rival in the world, even if it costs ten ducats a yard; as long as it is of real excellence never mind! If it is only as good as those which I see other people wear, I had rather be without it.[1]

It is only fair to Isabella to note also that later on, when it came to a choice between personal vanity and the family good, her precious jewels went on the market.

Some of the best records of costumes of the time are in the frescoes of Ghirlandaio in the church of Santa Maria Novella in Florence, painted between 1488 and 1493. As was the custom of the time, the artist used leading citizens in his compositions—in this case members of the family who commissioned the frescoes.

In Fig. 257 the proud lady at the left is

[1] Julia Cartwright, *Isabella d'Este*, J. Murray, London, 1926, vol. I, p. 72.

FIG. 257. *Ghirlandaio, The Visitation. Detail. 1488–1493 (Santa Maria Novella, Florence, Alinari Photograph)*

Giovanna Tornabuoni. Although she wears a cyclas-like garment over a gown of diamond-patterned fabric, there is a real innovation in the design of her sleeves, which had wide acceptance in Italy. Vertical slashes above and below the elbow and a deep horizontal cut at the elbow reveal the soft white linen of the chemise. Another feature common to both men's and women's sleeves is illustrated in her costume: sleeves themselves were often separate from the garment, attached only by ties or points which allowed the skirt or chemise to emerge at the armscyes.

Giovanna's neckline is softly rounded, but the square neckline which was predominant in the sixteenth century was worn in Italy in the late fifteenth century. Girdling was usually inconspicuous or often absent. Giovanna's hairdress bears a striking resemblance to the hairdress that was popular in the reign of Louis XIII (1610–1643). Part of her hair hangs in soft curls at the sides of her face and what remains is brushed smoothly back and formed into a bun. Behind Giovanna stands a widow in a wimple and veil and a young woman in a sheer scarf headdress, the ends of which are fastened near the armscye.

The typical late fifteenth-century gown had a high, ungirdled waistline, deep V-neck filled in with a stomacher, separate sleeves more drastically slashed than in the preceding illustration, and long skirt with easy fullness falling from the waist.

Further elaboration of late fifteenth-century Italian costume is shown in a portrait by Ambrogio de Predis, about 1493, of Bianca Maria Sforza, sister of Beatrice d'Este's husband and second wife of Emperor Maximilian I of Austria. The painting shows Italian costume at its richest. Bianca wears a cap of gold network set with pearls and bordered with large precious stones—the work of a jeweler, not a milliner. A side ornament above her left ear, from which hang strands of coral, embodies the family device. A narrow dark band encircling her

head and crossing her forehead is like those worn by La Belle Ferronnière and other Italian beauties in other paintings. Bianca's hair hangs down her back, wrapped in cloth and bound spirally with a jeweled ribbon. From her necklace of pearls a pendant of great beauty and value is suspended. As if all this were not sufficient index of wealth, she wears also a massive girdle solidly set with jewels, worth a king's ransom. It is quite understandable that the family jewels could be pawned for enough to hire an army.

Beatrice d'Este, wife of Lodovico Sforza, is better known to us than her sister-in-law. In Fig. 258 she has arranged her hair in the same manner as Bianca's, but without the jewels on the encircling ribbons. However, she wears a small fortune in pearls which adorn her hair, edge the fashionable square neckline of her gown, and form her long necklace. Ribbons streaming from her sleeves tie them into the armscyes and close the slashes of the upper and lower sections. The kneeling figure of the bambino in swaddling clothes is endearing, though in sharp contrast to modern ideas of infant's wear.

Burgundy and Flanders

Before the extravagance of the Burgundian court had come into full flower, Flemish artists left such charming records as Jan van Eyck's painting of Giovanni Arnolfini and his bride (see Fig. 233). Here on a small scale can be seen reticulated horned projections at the temples. The hair is entirely covered. The kerchief edged with many ruffles explains the nebulé headdress shown on English memorial brasses of the late fourteenth century (see Fig. 219). Giovanna's houppelande (also in Fig. 233) is magnificent. By 1434, the high collar had given way to a flat neckline; vertical rounded pleats distributed the fullness, and there apparently was no limit on yardage, costly fur for bandings and linings, or painstaking but effective self-trimming on the luxurious sleeves.

FIG. 258. Bernardino de Conti, Beatrice d'Este in Adoration of the Virgin. Detail. 1494. (Brera, Milan, Anderson Photograph—Alinari)

Roger van der Weyden's *Portrait of a Young Woman* (Fig. 259) shows possible Italian influence in the treatment of the front of the bodice, but the headdress is characteristic of the Low Countries. In Italy the headdress often left the hair partially visible; in France and England the hair was concealed within cauls or rigid forms and topped by a bourrelet or one of the many bulky designs which preceded the hennin. In the Low Countries the traditional rectangular headcloth or veil was crisply laundered, folded neatly and cleverly, and pinned to the hair. The lines rising above the head were in the fifteenth-century mood but were distinctive in themselves.

The same opulence, novelty, and absorption in fashion that characterized Burgundian men marked the women as well. Fashion influence spread from that court the way it does from Paris today. Two women closely associated with these court fashions were Isabelle of Portugal, wife of Philip the Good, and Mary, daughter of Charles the Bold. Although Fig. 260 shows only a small part of Isabelle's figure, many of the high-style features are there. A stiff high headdress, elaborately jeweled, supports the thick bourrelet which slants sharply downward to a rounded point on the forehead and is covered with velvet-patterned cloth of gold which also is used for the pearl-edged drapery from the crest of the headdress. The V-neckline of the bodice is fur-collared, a flattering extension of sheer fabric showing beneath the fur. The handsome necklace is in keeping with the importance assigned this form of adornment.

Figure 261, Van der Weyden's *Portrait of a Lady*, illustrates the costume of Flemish gentry of mid-century. The eccentricities of the French and Burgundian modes were muted, but many modifications were adopted. As the portrait suggests, the hennin was severely truncated, some hair was allowed to show, and the V-neckline was brought close to the neck and filled in with layers of cloth. The high girdle had hand-

FIG. 259. *Van der Weyden, Portrait of a Young Woman. 1435. Redrawn. (Dahlem Museum, Berlin)*

some mountings of gold. Sometimes these girdles were buckled at side back, a long end falling almost to the floor. They were usually quite colorful, glowing Pompeian red being favored. The slim sleeves were knuckle length. The draping of the veil is reminiscent of that in Van der Weyden's earlier portrait.

When Mary of Burgundy married Emperor Maximilian I of Austria, she brought a rich dowry to that throne. In her portrait in the Vienna National Library she is shown in a high blunt-topped hennin small enough in circumference to reveal much of her shaved head. The hennin is embroidered with her monogram and is softened by veiling falling from the top and across the forehead. Her gown is of surpassing elegance. Its fur-collared V-neck, widened to curve over the shoulder bone, is pushed to a high point by the width of the girdle. Sleeves are as closely fitted as possible. The skirt has the ease and grace of a flared cut.

The pleasing study reproduced in Fig. 262 shows Flemish high fashion of the 1470s to have much in common with the French fashion illustrated in Fig. 265, the gown and

Fig. 260. *Flemish School, Isabelle of Portugal, Wife of Philip the Good of Burgundy. 1445. (Louvre)*

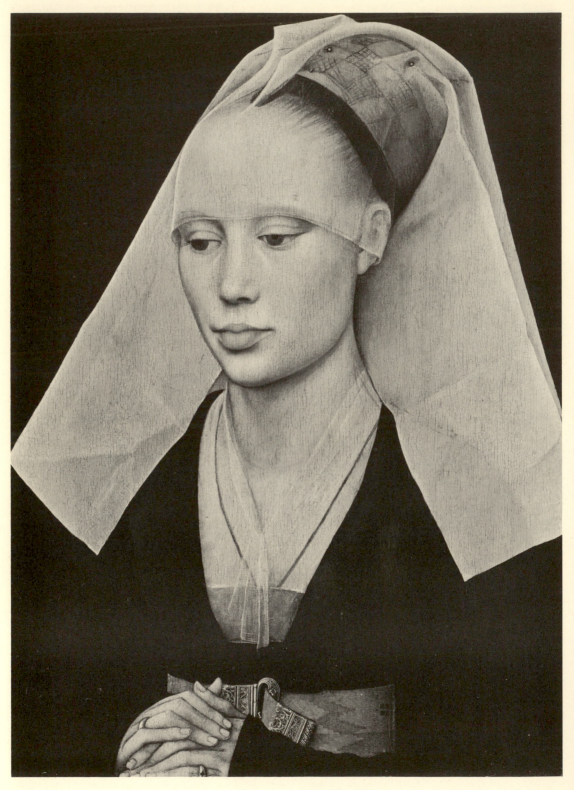

Fig. 261.   Van der Weyden, Portrait of a Lady. 1445. (National Gallery of Art, Washington, D.C., Mellon Collection)

the design of the jewelry being quite similar. The Flemish decolletage, however, is filled in almost to the neckline. The headdress varies also. Whereas the French hennin usually extended to quite a sharp point and formed an unrelieved line against the scalp, the Flemish hennin was usually blunted—in some cases decidedly lowered—and usually had a flattering band of velvet centered over the forehead and folded back against the

FIG. 262. *Memling, Virgin and Child with Donors. Detail. c. 1470. (National Gallery, London, Chatsworth Collection)*

hennin. The ends of the velvet in this painting fall behind the shoulders. The long gauze
veil placed over the hennin has a softening
effect. Flemish and Burgundian girdles seem
wider and higher than those of other countries.

Late fifteenth-century Flemish fashions
are illustrated in Fig. 239. The most eccentric
features have been replaced by designs and
accessories that will largely determine early
sixteenth-century styles. The high headdresses have been exchanged for hoods
which have a soft round crown covering the
back of the head with a flared extension
falling from the back neckline—much in the
manner of the American sunbonnet or a
child's hood with a ruffle at the back. The
front of the hood resembles the long velvet
fold worn with the Flemish hennin. The
long narrow front panels, lappets, figure
prominently in late fifteenth- and early sixteenth-century headdress.

The square neckline, which replaced the

V-shape, was sometimes made in modest
proportions, but gradually it became wide
and lower, dominating the bodice design of
much of the sixteenth century. On the
second lady from the left the bodice neckline
points sharply upward at center front. More
often it was a straight line and the low
square was usually filled in with contrasting
material. Bodices were snug, and skirts continued to fall with little fullness in front but
with excessively long trains. As shown in
Fig. 239, these were often lined with fur and
were long enough for the edge of the train
to be caught at the back of the waist and
still brush the ground.

The figure in the center foreground is
resplendent in cloth of gold. The young
woman at the far right has a deep border of
ermine on her skirt and the same precious
fur lines her looped-up train. The woman at
the left wears the new form of girdle, richly
jeweled and provided with a long pendant
down center front from which any of a

Fig. 263.   *Christine de Pisan Presenting Book to Queen Isabelle of Bavaria. c.1420. Harley MS. 4431, Folio
3. (British Museum)*

varied assortment of collector's items might be attached, a pomander being a popular one.

Another change, not illustrated, was a center front opening in the outer skirt from waist to hem, allowing the underskirt to share in the display. The relative slenderness of the skirt silhouette sets it apart from the sixteenth-century styles.

The broad toes of the shoes peep from beneath floor-length skirts.

France

The Duke of Berry's Book of Hours is as valuable as a source of French fashion as it is beautiful. Figure 241, reproduced from it, shows several different styles. Here the betrothed wears a gown with the great trailing sleeves and the low scooped neckline of the fourteenth century. Her hat resembles in contour that of the lady in Fabriano's Predella (Fig. 254), but is distinguished by being plumed. The woman at the right and the one kneeling directly behind her are wearing houppelandes of traditional cut, while the one at the rear is dressed more in the fashion of the fourteenth century, with long fur tippets depending from her elbow-length sleeves. The most significant part of her costume is her headdress. The round padded roll (bourrelet), of modest proportions, is placed over a rather simple hair arrangement. As the century advanced this feature increased in size and was worn on top of differently shaped foundations. It forms the heart-shaped headdress of Figs. 234 and 263.

Women's headdresses of the fifteenth century were among the most fantastic ever devised, rivaled only by the bizarre creations of the Marie Antoinette period. Figure 263 shows Christine de Pisan presenting her book to Queen Isabelle of Bavaria, wife of Charles VI of France, about 1420. The queen wears a typical houppelande. Her headdress has a set architectural form which must have required much time and skill to arrange—and must as surely have been conducive to head-aches. Queen Isabelle is credited with having introduced phenomenal millinery into France. In this painting her hair is enclosed above the temples by enlarged egg shapes covered with cauls. These cauls were often made of gold cord; later in the century they were set with precious stones. The bourrelet has already attained great width and is also jeweled. Christine de Pisan herself wears the fourteenth-century cotehardie in the painting and a horned headdress made of carefully folded linen placed over a wired or at least a rigid form.

Many survivals of these weird fifteenth-century headdresses were part of central European folk costume at least until World War II. In Čičmany, Czechoslovakia, women wore a pair of padded forms about the size and shape of goose eggs anchored above the temples. Indoors these were covered by a lovely filet lace cap. They served as supports for the high flaring scarf which was bound about the head for dress occasions. At the same time in Vrlika, Dalmatia, married women were still wearing a variation of the bourrelet, in the form of a thick sausage-like roll, constricted in five sections, and placed like a crown on the head. They were covered with flowing white kerchiefs.

Figure 264 is a drawing of a headdress from a painting of Jean Juvenal des Ursins, his wife and children, about 1445. Their costumes show the persistence of the cotehardie and sideless gown well into the fifteenth century. In fact, throughout the century it was occasionally used as a formal state costume. This painting also shows, in one of its most exaggerated versions, the heavy stiff jeweled contrivance which Norris[2] calls a reticulated headdress because of the net-like covering of the fixed form. All these later French headdresses concealed the hair completely. Foreheads and necks were shaved and eyebrows plucked to a thin arch.

By the middle of the fifteenth century,

[2] Herbert Norris, *Costume and Fashion*, Dent, London, pp. 437–442.

FIG. 264. *Detail of Headdress. c.1445. Redrawn from French School, Jean Juvénal des Ursins, Wife and Children. (Louvre)*

The cones themselves were covered with rich fabrics, including patterned velvets, brocades, and cloth of gold. Possibly to assist in adjusting the hennin, or as a detail of an undercap, a black loop often extends onto the forehead from under the front edge of the hennin. It is seen also in hooded headdresses in the Book of the Tournament. In some cases a sheer fold placed over the hair softened the baldness of the shaved head and contributed to the comfort of the wearer. Figure 266 drawn from an illustration in the

FIG. 265. *King René's Book of the Tournament. Review of Helms. 1460–1465. (Bibliothèque Nationale, Paris)*

French fashions, modeled closely on the Burgundian, had become more spectacular than those of Italy. Among its curiosities were the highest and most flamboyant headdresses of the century. Figure 234, taken from the Rose Tapestries, shows heightened egg-shaped excrescences covered with jeweled network and bearing in addition the thick padded rolls dipping to the forehead, the ends of which fall limp and free from the top of the construction. A liripipe has been attached to the right side.

Without a wisp of hair showing, towering cone-shaped hennins soared upward, sometimes with a long sheer veil flowing from the peak or with kerchiefs rising above them in a wired butterfly design. Figure 265, from King René's Book of the Tournament, is a classic illustration of the latter form.

FIG. 266. *Woman's Costume, with Extreme Form of Hennin. c.1470. Redrawn from Chronicles of Froissart, Marriage of Louis Anjou, King of Naples and Sicily, to Daughter of King Peter of Aragon. (British Museum)*

Chronicles of Froissart, shows one of the most extreme examples of the hennin. The heads appear almost entirely shaved, the hennins seeming to adhere by suction.

French gowns in mid-century quite consistently had deep V-necks plunging to the broad girdle. Fur collars, widening toward the shoulders, finished the necklines. This revealing cut was partially filled in with a stomacher or the horizontal neckline of an underdress. Nevertheless, the décolletage was daringly low. As the century progressed the V-line of the neck moved farther out on the shoulders. However, older matrons, either for modesty or for comfort, usually filled in the décolletage with contrasting material which came as high as the normal neckline.

The skirts of the ladies of the Rose Tapestry retained the fullness of the early part of the century, but after mid-century the cloth fell smoothly from the waistline over what may have been an abdominal pad (Fig. 265). However, with the waistline so tightly constricted the abdomen might have been forced outward to give that effect. Long trains were still in vogue, with deep borders of fur which matched the collars and often weighted and enhanced the hemlines. Sleeves, in contrast to those of the men, were slim and close fitting from shoulder to wrist. Here they widened into a funnel shape which either covered almost the entire hand or was turned back into a cuff.

Mid-century footwear followed the shape of men's footwear.

When the Burgundian power was destroyed in 1477, the French court again assumed leadership in fashion. The French queen, Anne of Brittany, is credited with several innovations, the most revolutionary of which was the headdress known to students of costume as the Anne of Brittany cap (Fig. 267). Hair again was allowed to show and the headdress of excessive height and burdensome weight disappeared. In the new headdress a white coif was fitted closely to the head, edged with a fluted ruffle—still to be seen in the headdress of some of the Catholic sisterhoods. Over the coif was placed the outer cap, which had a relatively wide band over the fore part of the head, reaching to the shoulders, and was usually lined with a rich band of contrasting color. For women of position and wealth the front edge might be jeweled. From temple to temple the band was folded back to reveal the lining. The back of the hood was often a simple half-circle, its straight edge mounted to the back edge of the front band, allowing the circular fullness to fall in soft folds. This portion is sometimes referred to as the curtain or veil, though it was often made of velvet.

Germany in the Late Fifteenth Century

Van Meckenem's *Dance of Herodias*

FIG. 267. *French School, Portrait of Lady.* 1499. *(Louvre)*

Fig. 268. *Israhel van Meckenem, Dance of Herodias. Late Fifteenth Century. (National Gallery of Art, Washington, D.C., Rosenwald Collection)*

(Fig. 268) presents a veritable kaleidoscope of end-of-the-century fashions. The woman at extreme left wears a fur-collared gown with long tubular sleeves, characteristic of the period. Three different necklines are visible on the lady of the next couple, but there is no indication of a girdle on either figure. Her full puffed sleeves, reaching a little below the elbow, are quite unusual. However, her piked shoes with pattens were seen much earlier in the century.

The third lady in the Van Meckenem painting is dressed in the high Flemish-Burgundian fashion which prevailed from about 1460 to 1480. The veil falling to the floor from the tip of her hennin contrasts with the shorter ones of the other dancers. The next lady in line wears a gown with a wide open front laced over an underdress similar to that of the child in Fig. 262. The lappets of her

hennin are folded upward and fastened at the temples, a detail which was to become very common in the coming century. The two women at the extreme right furnish rare back views of women's costumes, showing the deep V-neckline in back and concentrated fullness set in from just above the waistline. There seems to be no waistline seam.

Dürer's *The Promenade* (Fig. 269) provides an excellent illustration of the German high padded headdress with forehead veil. From the front, the headdress has a halo outline that is quite becoming. The lady's gown has a low neck, rounded in front and V-shaped in back, and the slashed sleeves so admired by the Germans. The two-piece effect, with an undersleeve showing at the elbow, is like the Italian style of the period. A closely set group of pleats adds fullness

FIG. 269. *Dürer, The Promenade. 1498. (Metropolitan Museum of Art, Mr. and Mrs. Isaac D. Fletcher Fund)*

FIG. 270. *English Hairdress and Headdress. 1405. Redrawn from Rubbing of Brass of Sir R. Drury and Wife. (Victoria & Albert Museum, Crown Copyright)*

over the protruding abdomen—a noticeable feature of many of Dürer's drawings. The lady's shoes are an odd compromise between the new broad blunt toe and the old-fashioned point.

England

Memorial brasses and effigies in England reveal major changes in women's fashions as the century passed, showing considerable correlation between the styles there and on the continent, as we noted in the preceding chapter.

Figure 270 illustrates the hairdress and headdress at the very beginning of the century. The hair is formed into a knot at each temple, where it is encased in a caul bound by a decorative band. A veil is simply arranged over the head. In this early style the ears are uncovered and the knots are the normal size formed by the woman's hair. The first changes which take place are in the size and shape of the caul-covered projections, which C. Willet Cunnington appropriately calls templers.[3] The rest of the lady's costume consists of an ungirdled cote-

[3] C. Willet and Phillis Cunnington, *Handbook of English Mediaeval Costume*, Dufour Editions, Albert Saifer, Philadelphia, 1952, p. 125.

hardie fitted smoothly through the torso and over the hips, then falling in flared fullness to cover her feet. Her fitted sleeves extend to the knuckles and are buttoned to the elbow.

The next illustration (Fig. 271) shows the English houppelande with two nicely

FIG. 272. *The Countess of Arundel. c.1416. (Church of the Trinity, Arundel, England) Photograph from Viollet-le-duc,* Dictionnaire du Mobilier Francais, 1858, *Vol. III, p. 320.*

proportioned flat collars, high, girdled waist-line and sleeves of length and width like those in early Italian and French styles. The sleeves of the lady's cotehardie or gown are similar to those of Fig. 221—full upper sleeve gathered into a deep fitted cuff. Her head-dress has spread outward and upward in a basket-work form far from the natural shape of the head. From this time (1416) onward for nearly 50 years, the hair and ears were covered.

Possibly the best-known example in England of the early reticulated headdress is that of the Countess of Arundel (1416) from her effigy in Arundel Cathedral (Fig. 272). These are among the widest templers on record. From their sides wires curve outward to support the veil, producing a horned effect. The countess' coronet rests

FIG. 271. *English Houppelande and Bulky Head-dress. c.1415. Redrawn from Rubbing of Brass of J. Peryent and Wife. (Victoria & Albert Museum, Crown Copyright)*

on the veil. Coronets and crowns were shaped to conform with the contour of the headdress instead of the head.

By the time of the Bedford Book of Hours in 1423, the templers had changed from the box-like form of Fig. 272 to that of the valves of a clam shell, greatly enlarged. They tilted outward and jutted above

FIG. 273. *English Woman's Costume. 1479. Redrawn from Rubbing of Brass of Anne Playters.* (Victoria & Albert Museum, Crown Copyright)

the head. The bourrelet followed the upward curving edges in what is often called the heart-shaped headdress. Both templers and bourrelet were jeweled if funds permitted. The houppelande with flat square-cornered collars and sweeping sleeves dagged and/or lined with fur reflected the fashion of the French court.

During mid-century the bivalvular form was reduced in scale but the heart shape was retained and a small veil was added. The houppelande, adapted and worn as a gown, had a narrow V-neck and a high waistline. The collar was graduated in width from a mere point at the waistline to 2 or 3 inches at the shoulder. Tubular sleeves with turn-back cuffs replaced the earlier wide effects. Tight sleeves of the undergown were visible at the wrists.

The English truncated hennin and butterfly veil are easily distinguished from the style of Flanders. The English woman pulled her hair tightly to the back of her head—the front of the head was still bared by plucking or shaving—and arranged the knot just below the crown. The short blunt cap, bearing little or no resemblance to a hennin, was placed over this knot in such a position that the base of the cap was upright, the surface usually visible from the front being in a horizontal position (Fig. 273). A folded sheer veil supported by visible wires completed the headdress.

The gown in this illustration is much more in the continental fashion than the headdress: the V-neck spreads the full width of the shoulders; the fur collar caps the shoulder bones; and the low horizontal line of the dickey partially bares the breasts. Skin-tight sleeves extend in deep funnels over the hands. The skirt of this costume, banded with fur, falls upon the floor in such generous length that it is necessary to hold it up in order to walk. The woman's girdle is indicative of the lateness of the costume. It is again below the waistline; unlike its fourteenth-century predecessor, however, a chain falls from the clasp, ending in a decorative pendant of some sort. The heavy necklace resembles those of Flanders.

About a decade later a hood somewhat similar to the hoods of Fig. 239 made its appearance (Fig. 274). The front section is fur-lined and turned back about the face. The crown is more firm and angular than the Flemish design just noted, and it can only be assumed that an extension falls down the back from the neckline edge of the crown.

The gown in this illustration is simplicity itself. A plain tight bodice, seamed or invisibly fastened down center front, has a square neckline slightly softened by shallow curves and a narrow underlay across the front; tight sleeves with fur-lined extensions turned back to form cuffs; and a flared skirt of moderate sweep falls upon the ground.

An exclusively English headdress appeared at the end of the century—a type

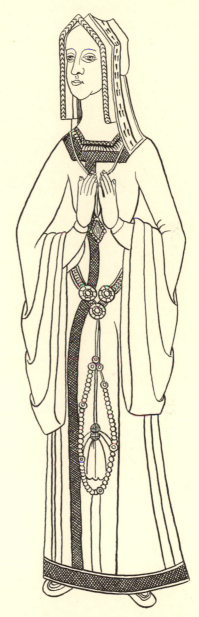

FIG. 274. *English Costume. 1487. Redrawn from Rubbing of Brass of Sir W. Mauntell and Wife. (Victoria & Albert Museum, Crown Copyright)*

FIG. 275. *English Woman's Costume. Late Fifteenth, Early Sixteenth Centuries (Great Cressingham Church, Norfolk) Redrawn from Cotman's Engravings of Sepulchral Brasses in Norfolk and Suffolk, Vol. I, Plate 34.*

referred to as the pedimental, kennel, or gable hood. The portrait of Lady Margaret Beaufort, mother of Henry VII, in the National Portrait Gallery, London, shows her wearing the gable hood in conjunction with a deep gorget which covers her bosom. Figure 275 from a memorial brass shows the hood as worn with the late fifteenth-century gown. Note the high square neckline, the flowing sleeves, the elaborate girdle, dipping to a low point in front, and the round-toed shoes.

Figure 276 shows Elizabeth of York, wife of Henry VII and mother of Henry VIII, wearing the gable hood in its earliest form, when the front hair was still visible.

FIG. 276. *Unknown Artist, Elizabeth of York, Wife of Henry VII. Late Fifteenth Century.* (*National Portrait Gallery, London*)

FIG. 277. *Pedro Garcia Bernabarre, Feast of Herod. Detail. Mid-Fifteenth Century. (Catalonian Art Museum, Barcelona, A.Y.R. Mas Photograph)*

(The shape of the pointed arch was changed from time to time but the distinguishing features were retained for about 50 years.) Her elaborately embroidered and jeweled lappets are separated from the semicircular curtain just above the shoulder level. She wears the square neckline fashionable on the continent.

FIG. 278. *Unknown Spanish Artist, Queen Isabella of Spain. Detail from Virgin of the Catholic Kings.* 1490. *(Prado Museum)*

Women's feet are seldom visible in the illustrations, but when glimpsed, their footwear conforms in design with that of the men.

Spain

Since Spain played such an important role in fashion during the sixteenth century, we should note some of the features of fifteenth-century Spanish costume which were to influence the dress of much of western Europe.

In a Spanish painting in the Metropolitan Museum (1450) Salome wears the bulky padded headdress with heart-shaped arrangement of the bourrelet and a beautiful brocaded gown slashed from hem to hip to reveal the underskirt—currently fashionable in Spain. The V-neck is higher than in France and the waistline is in its normal position. A sense of style is definitely conveyed, however.

The Spanish fashion which held Europe enthralled in the following century appears in another mid-fifteenth-century painting, based on the theme of the feast of Herod, Salome's stepfather. This painting, by Pedro Garcia Bernabarre is in the Catalonian Art Museum in Barcelona (Fig. 277). Salome is portrayed in Catalonian costume, the most startling feature of which is a series of six hoops, graduated in size from hip to hem and attached to the outside of her brocaded gown.

In the sixteenth century the hoops were concealed, but the rigid structure called the *vertugade* or *vertugardin* (*farthingale* in England) had its origin in this Spanish fashion. The word *vertugade* is said to be derived from the Spanish, meaning cane or wand. The hoops in Fig. 277 look as if they might be made of supple wood. Others worn by guests at the banquet seem to be covered with fabric contrasting in color with the gown.

A third painting dating from late fifteenth century in the Prado, Madrid, carries the fashion one step further. An overdress, open down center front, reveals a rich spreading underskirt held in architectural rigidity by rings of double hoops. In this costume the long-lasting formula of open cone-shaped overskirt, contoured by a hooped support, makes its debut.

Isabella of Spain, known to all Americans for the encouragement and help she gave Columbus, is shown in Fig. 278 kneeling in adoration of the Virgin. Her outer dress has long, open, pendant sleeves, which were retained in Spain throughout the following century. The center front opening of her skirt reveals an equally important underskirt. Her undersleeves show definite Italian influence. Her square neckline has softly rounded corners, into which her elaborate necklace fits harmoniously. She wears the simplest fifteenth-century hairdress and headdress.

12

High Renaissance:

Men's Costume of the Sixteenth Century

General Characteristics of the Period

During the sixteenth century, many streams of influence united to make some of the details of costume the most bizarre and the overall effect the most magnificent in history. French contact with Italian achievement in all the arts, brought about by Charles VIII's invasion of Italy, accelerated the spread of the Renaissance throughout western Europe. In fact, so impressed was Francis I with the work of Italian artists that he persuaded Cellini, Raphael, and Leonardo da Vinci to come to Paris to create for him.

The wealth and grandeur which had been concentrated at the Burgundian court had been dispersed after the defeat and death of the last Burgundian ruler, Charles the Bold. In 1477, during a Burgundian attack upon the Swiss forces at Nancy, the Burgundians were overwhelmed and Charles was left dead upon the battlefield. As was his custom even during campaigns, his tent was filled with tapestries, sumptuous silks, and gorgeous costumes, including jeweled accessories. This accidentally led to a new fashion; the war-worn Swiss soldiers, wildly excited by their conquest and having little true appreciation of the spoils, cut the beautiful textiles to bits, stuffing the pieces under and through the ragged holes in their own clothing. In this bizarre array they arrived back home. Adulation of the returning heroes led the people to copy the effect of these torn, puckered, polychromatic garments in civilian dress.

The German Maximilian I (1493–1519), who had married Mary, heiress of the Burgundian holdings, realizing the superior fighting ability of Swiss soldiers, secured their services as mercenaries and combined them with the German forces, where they became a famous contingent of the feared sixteenth-century landsknecht. Their slithered and slashed multicolored array was copied by the Germans and continued to influence styles throughout the century.

Another factor, too, helped create the opulence of high Renaissance costume. Exploration of the New World greatly increased the wealth of Europe, particularly of Spain; plundered treasure from Peru and Mexico made more gold and jewels available for enriching costumes. During this century

Spain reached the peak of her power and glory, and it was but natural that her fashions be widely copied.

Increase in trade via the new routes to the Indies, too, gave rise to a large wealthy merchant class throughout Europe, happy to proclaim their new status by conspicuous waste on costume.

Before the sixteenth century, trade goods were brought from the Far East to the markets of the Near East, largely by caravan, where they were transferred to Mediterranean ships. By the fifteenth century, Venice controlled most of this sea trade. The discoveries made during the latter part of the fifteenth and the early sixteenth centuries opened up new trade routes to the Far East. The Portuguese explored the African coast and, finally rounding the Cape of Good Hope, made their way to Calcutta. The discoveries of Christopher Columbus, followed by the voyages of the Cabots, Magellan, Balboa, and others, diverted the control of the world's trade routes from the Near East and Venice to the countries of western Europe.

The diverse and far-reaching effects of the Reformation, along with widespread acceptance of the philosophy of the humanists, made men willing to expend these newly available riches upon themselves—it was no longer necessary to place the best and finest of everything upon the altar.

A new adjunct of men's clothing had become necessary in the fifteenth century when the two separate legs of the long hose were finally joined together to form trousers. This was a small pouch in front called the codpiece. During the late fifteenth century it had remained functional and inconspicuous, but in most of the sixteenth century it became grotesque evidence of increased emphasis on the satisfaction of human desires, being enlarged into a bulbous, slashed, padded and puffed projection that baffles all understanding. In the seventies, however, because of the excessive proportions of pumpkin breeches it receded and

finally disappeared under the effeminate influence of Henry III of France.

Weavers and goldsmiths played a considerable role in creating this grand pageant. Skill in weaving and embroidery had long since reached perfection and craftsmen were well prepared to produce the sumptuous fabrics now in demand. The majestic scale of fifteenth-century patterns continued into the sixteenth, but apparently even many of the *nouveau riche* realized what a desecration it was to slash these masterpieces to ribbons. Plain fabrics, enriched with embroidery and gold and silver galloon also came into vogue; royalty and their courtiers must have seemed at times actually enveloped in cloth of gold. Glowing jewel-toned velvets were combined with lynx, marten, ermine, and sable. This more conventional manner of displaying wealth ran parallel with the eccentric slashing, which continued everywhere.

As if aware of the psychological moment, about the middle of the sixteenth century, lace made its debut in both Italy and Flanders. Openwork embroidery in the form of drawnwork and cutwork had long been produced in the Adriatic area, but both of these were based upon and grew out of a woven foundation. But true lace, a free and independent creation to be applied at will, *punto in aria* (literally, stitches in the air), was first made in the sixteenth century. It appeared upon the edges of ruffs and collars, adding to the airiness of the openwork embroidery; it graced the great wired curves of Queen Elizabeth's veils providing by contrast a note of relief to the heavy, padded, vise-like garments of the time. Lace was a new element of beauty in the sixteenth century. In the seventeenth century it was further developed and refined to become one of the wonders of the textile craft.

The display of jewels in all the courts of Europe in the sixteenth century was the richest in history, with the possible exception of the Byzantine period. Skilled designers and goldsmiths, with such artists as Cellini to inspire them, created mountings for precious stones that are still the wonder of all observers.

As travel and communication increased among all the countries of Europe, costume became less nationalistic. Innovations spread more rapidly and to greater distances than formerly. For example, the enthusiasm for Italian culture Charles VIII and Louis XII of France brought back passed on to Francis I and his court and was disseminated from there. In a similar manner the Germans, enamored of the possibilities they saw in the slashed apparel of the Swiss soldiers, carried that idea wherever their mercenaries fought or their emissaries traveled. By mid-sixteenth century, too, Spanish taste had attracted a wide following because of the power and prestige Spain then enjoyed. No single country dominated the fashion picture throughout this century. Though one country after another took the lead, similarities soon arose which make it difficult to isolate any one country from the rest of Europe. The three major influences in shaping men's costume during the sixteenth century came from Italy, Switzerland via Germany, and Spain.

Principal Influences on Costume

ITALIAN

Italian paintings of the late fifteenth century, such as Giorgione's *Ordeal by Fire of the Infant Moses* (Fig. 228), picture the universal garments of doublet and hose. Already there were modest cuts in the sleek full-length hose, accented by contrasting points which closed them. The low-necked, loosely fitting doublet revealed the shirt. The detail from Signorelli's *Last Judgment* reproduced here (Fig. 279) is a clear and faithful portrayal of the costume commonly worn in Italy at the beginning of the century, about 1500. These were the costumes Charles VIII and his soldiers found when they invaded Italy. The robes of the Italian dignitaries, fashioned from Florentine, Gen-

oese, and Venetian velvets and brocades, must have awed the invaders.

SWISS

The idiosyncrasies of Swiss garments have already been commented on. Parti-color itself was no new thing—it dated from the Crusades. What was new and incomprehensible was the multiplicity of slashes in all directions throughout the costume.

Underwear took on importance, since it now became an intrinsic part of the design, being pulled through the cuts to form puffing on the outer surface. Eventually this effect was approximated by appliquéing puffs of fabric to the uncut garment.

SPANISH

The discovery and conquest resulting from Isabella's foresight in subsidizing the explorations of Columbus poured wealth into the Spanish treasury. Marriages helped, too. Through the marriage of Joanna, heiress of Ferdinand and Isabella, to Philip the Fair, son of Maximilian I and Mary of Burgundy, the combined resources of Burgundy, the Low Countries, Austria, and Spain, were concentrated in the hands of their son, Charles V of Spain. He was the shrewdest and most powerful of the three great contemporary rulers of Europe, outwitting and overshadowing England's Henry VIII and Francis I of France.

Katherine of Aragon, sister of Joanna, aunt of the powerful Charles V, and first of Henry VIII's six wives, brought Spanish influence into England early in the century. Her influence and that of her ladies was responsible for much of the black work (delicate line embroidery on edges and borders in black) that adorned men's shirts and women's partlets (the accessory used to fill in the deep square neckline) and wrist ruffles during the sixteenth century.

Eleanor of Austria, sister of Charles V and second wife of Francis I, brought

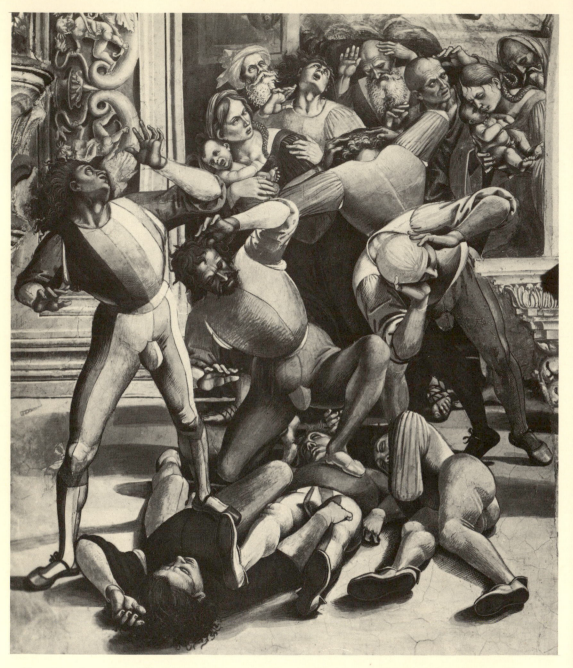

Fig. 279. *Luca Signorelli, Last Judgement. Detail. 1500. (Orvieto Cathedral, Alinari Photograph)*

Spanish styles to France. But even without these marriages Spain, in the early sixteenth century, would have led other countries to emulate her rich attire.

One predominant characteristic of Spanish costume throughout the century was rigidity. Fabric was stiffened in the weaving by gold thread or reinforced by row upon row of gold and silver braid: interlining, padding, and wiring gave garments a cast rather than a draped appearance. A black velvet doublet in the collection of the Metropolitan Museum (Fig. 280) has shoulder rolls stuffed with horsehair, collar and shoulder wings edged with silver braid and wire, and padded front sections (Draft 5). A girl's dress in the same collection has the front of its skirt made of white satin lined with two thicknesses of linen, all completely obscured by heavy silk and gold embroidery which makes it so stiff it could almost stand alone. The Metropolitan Museum also has a crimson and gold brocaded cape which is a fine example of the wrap which by the middle of the sixteenth century had captured the fancy of all of Europe (Fig. 281). Cut on a full circle, it has a swagger and dash that would inflate any wearer's ego. Characteristically these Spanish capes had deep hoods which, in paintings, are shown hanging down center back (Fig. 307). However, neither the cape of Fig. 281 nor the other one in the Metropolitan Museum collection has such a hood.

FIRST HALF OF THE CENTURY

Comparison of men's costumes of Germany, the Low Countries, France, Spain, England, and Italy reveals striking similarities, though certain variations or peculiarities serve to identify the costume of each country.

Kelly and Schwabe have given a clear and reasonable nomenclature to men's garments of the sixteenth century, somewhat as follows:

1. The shirt is suddenly important because so much of it is visible.
2. The doublet, formerly the pourpoint, again furnishes anchorage for the hose.
3. Stomachers or dickies might substitute for the doublet. These often make it difficult to determine exactly what garments the sitter was wearing as he posed for his portrait.
4. The jerkin or jacket is sleeved or sleeveless, longer than the doublet, and usually worn over it.
5. Hose are cut in one piece from waist to toe at the beginning of the century, but soon separated into upper or trunk hose and lower hose.
6. Bases, a skirt made in columnar folds, is worn as a separate skirt over armor or, when joined to a sleeveless body, often worn over the doublet.
7. The gown, a sleeved overgarment, is made long for dignitaries and professional men and short for men of fashion.
8. Cloaks or capes are popularized by Spanish grandees.[1]

Men's wear was by now on its way to becoming more or less identifiable with modern garments: shirt, vest, coat, trousers, and overcoat.

At the opening of the century, hose were form fitting, often gayly colored or striped, and frequently different on the two legs (Fig. 279). Before long, however, the Swiss idea of elaborate slashing was generally adopted. Dürer's *Triumphal Procession of Maximilian I* (Fig. 282) shows both the simple and the absurd in the costumes of his five landsknechts. By the time of this painting (1515), hardly any unbroken surface was left above the knees. So large were the openings that a second pair of plain hose were usually worn under the slashed ones, though soldiers are sometimes shown with the bare skin exposed. This was one reason for dividing full-length hose—which were really a form of trousers—into two parts during the sixteenth century. The trouser portion is referred to as upper stocks, upper hose or trunk hose; the stocking portion was called nether stocks or lower hose. The design of the trouser portion was changed frequently during the sixteenth century. The two sections were sometimes joined together for expediency in dressing. The Italian paintings of the first decade reproduced in Figs. 283 and 284 suggest a separation between upper and lower hose. In the second of these drawings the lower hose are rolled down and gartered low on the calf. Titian's 1533 portrait of Charles V shows him wearing upper

[1] Francis M. Kelly and Randolph Schwabe, *Historic Costume*, Batsford, London, 1925, p. 5.

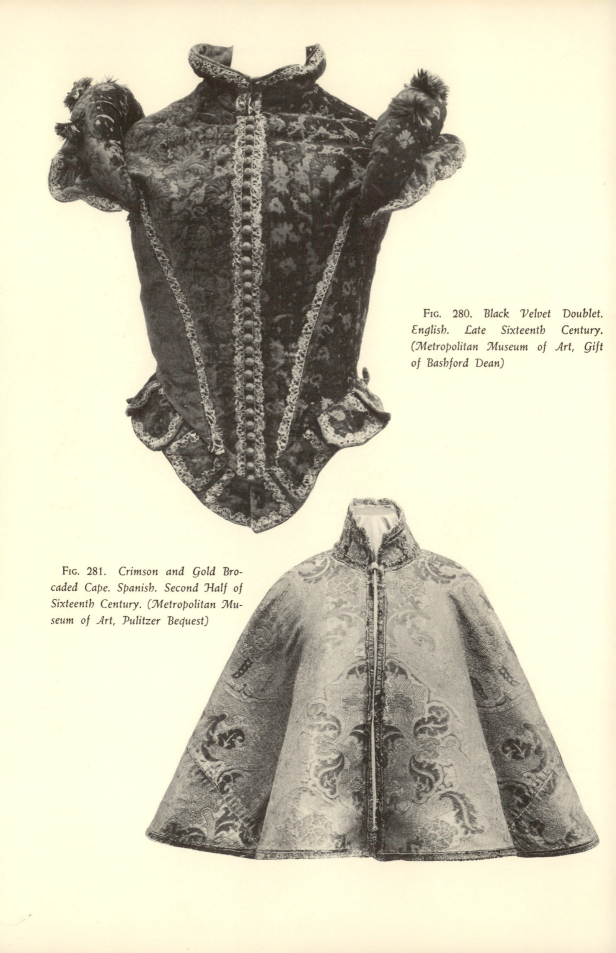

FIG. 280. *Black Velvet Doublet.*
English. Late Sixteenth Century.
(Metropolitan Museum of Art, Gift
of Bashford Dean)

FIG. 281. *Crimson and Gold Bro-*
caded Cape. Spanish. Second Half of
Sixteenth Century. (Metropolitan Mu-
seum of Art, Pulitzer Bequest)

FIG. 282. *Dürer. Triumphal Procession of Maxmilian I. Detail. 1514–1516. (Metropolitan Museum of Art, Gift of Georgiana W. Sargent in Memory of John Osborne Sargent)*

hose#5   *doublet*   *#2#*
                                  #3

hose sleek to the body, but decorated with numerous horizontal bands of vertical slits.

Slashing soon invaded every area of the doublet, with fantastic results. Sleeves might have as many as eight or more puffings from shoulder to wrist, or there might be fewer divisions but more varied patterns of cuts, either method producing voluminous expansion through the upper part of the body. Doublet necklines were consistently low and square, and both back and front surfaces were scissored in all directions. Most German doublets show no evidence of a center front closing, though in some cases a front panel is indicated. The jerkins of the landsknecht were often designed with diagonal closings and short scalloped skirts (Fig. 285).

Italian differentation of the doublet was in the design of the sleeves, which tended to be full and puffed or cut in vertical panes from shoulder to elbow, but fitted from elbow to wrist (Fig. 279). Doublets were frequently open to the waistline in a deep V, the edges left free or laced across the shirt front, or the space might be filled in with a stomacher (Fig. 286). By 1520 the edges met at center front.

During the first half of the century a skirt related to the fifteenth-century garments with organ-pipe folds was worn, sometimes tied about the waist like a separate garment over armor or attached to a sleeveless open-front top and worn in lieu of the jerkin. This garment is usually called bases.

doublet
#2 #3   *#6*

FIG. 283. *Italian Upper and Lower Hose. 1502–1509. Redrawn from Pintoricchio, Scenes in Life of Aeneas Sylvius Piccolomini (Pope Pius II). Detail. (Piccolomini Library, Siena Cathedral, Anderson Photograph—Alinari)*

FIG. 284. *Italian Upper and Lower Hose. 1502. Redrawn from Detail in Sodoma's Deposition. (Accademia, Siena, Anderson Photograph—Alinari)*

Dürer sketched Maximilian I in bases reaching to mid-calf. Holbein's portrait of Henry VIII reproduced in Fig. 287 shows him wearing bases of cloth of silver, further enriched with embroidery. The skirt portion is attached to a supporting top, sometimes referred to as a body, cut in a deep wide U-shape from near mid-shoulder to the waistline. An embroidered border, matching those on the skirt, accents the U-shaped edge. Descriptions of the costumes worn by Henry VIII and Francis I at their meeting on the Field of the Cloth of Gold, in 1520, give Henry's bases alternate folds of cloth of gold and cloth of silver, countercharged at the lower border.

A military skirt or bases in the collection of Arms and Armor at the Metropolitan Museum (Fig. 288) provides one answer to the problem of how these bases were constructed (Draft 2). Padding, evenly distributed as in a quilt or comforter, produced the rounded contour of the folds. The reverse folds on the back, equally spaced, were compressed and held in place by two parallel rows of braid.

Gowns, more frequently shown than bases in the paintings of the period, varied little from country to country (Figs. 286, 287, and 289). They alone were comparatively free from slashing. Made from sumptuous fabrics, often brocade, they were generously cut and magnificently furred. A broad deep collar and full sleeves extended in great width across the shoulders, so that the wearer of a short gown resembled a jack-in-the-box. The sleeves were provided with horizontal and/or vertical openings through which the arms might emerge, the lower part of the sleeve hanging free. Professional men, such as doctors, lawyers, teachers, and clergy, wore the full-length gown. The gown Luther wore is seen with little change in academic processions and in the pulpit today. Venetian senators were gorgeous in ruby-red double-pile velvet gowns similar to that of Fig. 289, their enormous wide-mouthed sleeves lined with fur. As robes of state, what could be more impressive?

The equestrian portrait of Francis I (Fig. 292) records another type of outer wrap—a rectangular mantle designed with center front opening and deep collar closely resembling corresponding features of the gown. In the portrait, the straight edge, which would normally fall to the hand or below, has been brought upward to the shoulder, revealing the sleeve of the doublet below the elbow.

FIG. 285. *Daniel Hopfer, Landsknecht and Wife. 1510–1530. (New York Public Library, Prints Division)*

FIG. 286. Bartolomeo Veneto, Portrait of Gentleman. c.1520. (Gallery of Antique Art, Corsini Palace, Alinari Photograph)

FIG. 287. *Hans Holbein, Henry VIII and His Father, Henry VII. Detail from Cartoon for Whitehall. 1537. (National Portrait Gallery, London, Formerly, Chatsworth Collection)*

Footwear harmonized with the rest of the costume; note the breadth of toe in Fig. 292 and slashing in Fig. 341c. Some German drawings show the toes of the shoes so broad and the uppers so shallow that one wonders how they were ever kept on the feet (Fig. 285). Those with ankle straps look somewhat more practical (Figs. 287 and 293). Riding boots are well fitted and well made, an outside lacing ensuring neatness of line and a snug grip. Footwear of men of the middle class is shown in Fig. 290.

Early in the century the hair was worn shoulder length, but by the twenties it was shortened to chin level and by the thirties it had quite a modern look. Beards and moustaches were seen in the twenties, though not universally worn. The earlier style of beard was broad, like that usually associated with Henry VIII (Figs. 287 and 289). Later the mode conformed more to the shape of the face.

Early sixteenth-century headgear is the offspring of the French bonnet (Figs. 286, 287, and 289). The self-assured Italian gentleman in Fig. 291 wears an enlarged version of it, with the customary medallion. Francis I preferred a flatter brim with an ostrich plume lying between brim and crown (Fig. 292). Fig. 293 illustrates a widespread fashion of confining the hair in a cap or caul, in this case of netted gold cord. The hat or bonnet was placed over it.

With their flair for exaggeration the Germans wore the widest brims, with the most slits, trimmed with the longest feathers (Figs. 285 and 294). Cranach painted many of them, even crowning Paris with a huge cartwheel dripping plumes, as he sits in judgment before the goddesses. Another version of the French bonnet frequently seen in Germany had the front of the brim cut away and the rest of it turned down over the ears and back of the head, rather like the

Fig. 288. *Bases (Military Skirt). Sixteenth Century. (Metropolitan Museum of Art, Rogers Fund)*

FIG. 289. *Hans Holbein, French Ambassadors. 1533. (National Gallery, London)*

knitted English cap (see Fig. 341*a*). A brimmed hat was often worn on top of it (Fig. 295).

MID-CENTURY FASHIONS

By the 1540s many changes in costume were heralded. For example, upper hose were made with panes or panels, often embroidered or pinked (small slashes), placed over or attached to a contrasting fabric.

They fitted quite smoothly over the hips but bloused moderately at mid-thigh or a little below. Lower hose were sleek (Figs. 296 and 298), and the sixteenth century witnessed a revolution in them. Formerly made of woven cloth, they probably seldom looked as unwrinkled as the paintings show them, but the introduction of knitted hose made the dream come true.

Doublets were closely fitted and had standing collar, normal sleeves, and slightly lowered front waistline. Decoration con-

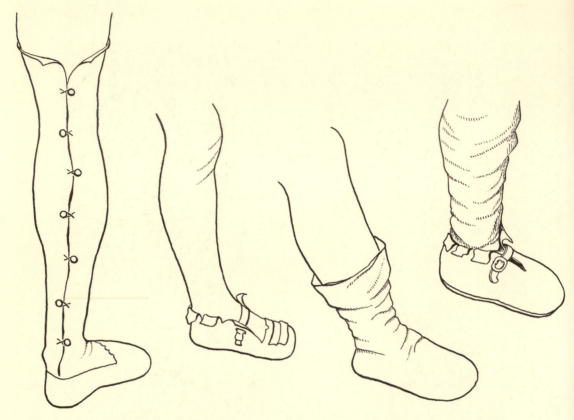

FIG. 290. *Footwear, Men of Middle Class. 1520. Redrawn from Details in Jan Mostaert, Ecce Homo.* (Musées royaux des Beaux-Arts de Belgique, Brussels)

sisted of small cuts and punctures in conventional geometric patterns. Skirts, if any, were short. Jerkins, with or without sleeves, synchronized nicely with the doublet; their skirts were nearly wrist length. Gowns for the fashion-conscious were shorter. A more harmonious use of color prevailed. The portrait, *Young Man in Red*, at Hampton Court (Fig. 296), gives us an excellent view of a monochromatic ensemble: all his garments excepting his shirt are red. Doublet and hose often matched. The hat brim of the young man in red is narrowed and the crown flattened like a pancake. In the fifties the crown became more spirited, softer, and fuller, and started on its upward rise. An ostrich tip was often substituted for the whole feather such as Francis I wore.

Footwear returned to moderate width

FIG. 291. *Italian Headdress. 1515. Redrawn from Raphael, Guiliano de Medici. (Metropolitan Museum of Art)*

FIG. 292. *Unknown Artist, Francis I on Horseback. 1524. (Musée Condé, Chantilly)*

and was now built to cover the instep. Slashes, however, were retained.

Evidence of knitting appears sporadically from the time of the Copts. The Victoria and Albert Museum has a pair of knitted socks dated fourth to fifth century. Pope Clement V wore knitted gloves in the mid-thirteenth century. A panel from the Buxtehude altar of the Virgin shows the Virgin knitting a garment for the Christ child.[2] In 1499 Princess Margaret Tudor, wife of James IV of Scotland, listed "two pairs of hosen, knit."[3] Latour cites three other important facts: "Locally knitted stockings are mentioned in the Records of

[2] A. Latour, *Ciba Review,* no. 106, pp. 3800–3801.
[3] Norris, *Costume and Fashion,* vol. III, book 1, p. 67.

FIG. 294.   *German Youth Wearing Plumed Bonnet. 1515–1520. Redrawn from Lucas van Leyden, Portrait of a Young Man with Skull. (New York Public Library, Prints Division)*

FIG. 293.   *German Costume. Early Sixteenth Century. Redrawn from Detail of Christ before Caiphas by Master of Kappenberg. (John G. Johnson Collection, Philadelphia)*

the city of Nottingham as early as 1519; the oldest known guild of stocking knitters was founded in Paris in 1557; about 1539, Henry VIII wore a pair of knit silk hose manufactured at Venice or Milan."[4]

Norris recalls that Edward VI received a gift of knitted silk hose, the source of which had been a Spanish merchant.[5] Evidently both Italy and Spain were producing knitted silk hose at this time. Once Queen Elizabeth had enjoyed their flattering texture, she would have no other. However, it was some time before they were commonly available.

Hairdress, too, changed dramatically from the womanish length of the early years to a short cut, very modern in appearance. Trimmed beard and moustache remained in favor.

By the middle of the century the neckline of the shirt, as well as that of the doublet, had been raised to a standing collar. In Germany, as early as 1514–1516, the shirt

[4] Latour, *op. cit.,* pp. 3800–3801.
[5] Norris, *op. cit.,* book 2, p. 392.

FIG. 295. *German Wearing Flat French Bonnet over Cap. 1527. Redrawn from Barthel Beham, Engraving of Leonart von Eck. (National Gallery of Art, Washington, D.C., Rosenwald Collection)*

easily sewed to the upper edge of the collar. Goffering or shaping this ruffle into regular convolutions gave it the appearance of a ruff.

Italy is usually credited with the invention of the ruff, and Catherine de Medici is supposed to have introduced it into France. However, the ruff was not a style suddenly launched and it would be most difficult to prove with certainty that it started in any one place. It seems rather to have evolved

FIG. 296. *Unknown Artist, Young Man in Red. 1548. (Hampton Court, by Permission of H. M. Queen Elizabeth II, Photograph by A. C. Cooper Ltd., London)*

was portrayed with a normal neckline and collar (Fig. 282). Other countries followed, but more slowly. Francis I wore the boat-shaped neckline as late as 1530, but by that date the newer fashion had become generally accepted.

Von Boehn[6] accepts the self-portrait of George Pencz, dated 1544, as documented evidence of the first appearance of the ruff. Its evolution follows the rise of the neckline frill, seen on the shirt in Dürer's self-portrait of 1498 (Fig. 252). Note the shirt of Veneto's *Gentleman* (Fig. 286). The collar of the landsknecht (Fig. 285) is clearly the result of extending the fabric of the shirt, and shirring and smocking it into a standing band to fit the neck. The familiar narrow ruffle is there. This method of making a collar is difficult and required an inordinate amount of fabric about the chest and shoulders. The obvious alternate was to replace the collar created by the smocking with a plain one. The flattering little ruffle was

[6] Max von Boehn, *Modes and Manners*, vol. II, Lippincott, Philadelphia, p. 125.

trunk hose

gradually, requiring many years before the enlarged, stiffened, and supported accessory usually referred to as the ruff appeared upon the scene.

necklines

The doublet neckline rose with that of the shirt. Figure 287 from the original cartoon by Holbein preserves a more reliable record of the various necklines than is to be found on later copies of it. We have already noted the deep U-shape of the neckline of the body supporting the bases. Note also the high horizontal neckline of the doublet and the standing shirt collar with its narrow frill (date, 1537, subject, Henry VIII of England). Compare the details of Henry's costume with those of Francis I (Fig. 292), 1524, where both shirt and doublet necklines are horizontal, and with the high neckline of both shirts and doublets of the French ambassadors, 1533 (Fig. 289).

Slashing was still used in mid-century but more conservatively, with smaller cuts and formal patterns (Fig. 297).

The trunk hose, now distinctly separate, still fitted closely to the hips but were loose and slightly puffed over the thigh. From the 1550s on the design usually consisted of numerous decorated panels over softer contrasting fabric. The portrait of Alessandro Alberti with a page (Fig. 297) clearly shows the cut and contour of the trunk hose at this time. The page is trussing the points; that is, he is lacing and fastening Alberti's hose to the doublet with points.

Other important fashion features shown in this portrait are the small hat with soft crown and narrow brim and the long slender gown with many small buttons closely set. Plain narrow sleeves wrinkle from shoulder to wrist. Rather wide flat wings extend the shoulder width. This type of coat or gown was apparently limited to Italy and appears in several portraits in the last half of the century.

A pair of trunk hose in the Metropolitan Museum shows one method of construction. In this case the panels are of leather, the intervening fabric of velvet. The two are seamed together with a French seam with the second stitching on the outside—just opposite to the usual procedure. This gives the effect of an overlapping edge, as the velvet is folded into an inverted pleat which lies back of the panels. This type of construction allowed the hose to be compressed neatly under armor, but the resilient materials rebounded when the weight was removed. There is no evidence of any kind of padding. However, many trunk hose were constructed with the panels free, attached to the underlying fabric only at the waistband and leg openings.

Titian's portrait of Philip II of Spain (Fig. 298) shows him dressed in the height of fashion in 1550, before the more eccentric features of the third quarter appeared.

3rd quarter of century

With the ascendancy of Spanish influence in the third quarter of the century the picture changed. Whatever ease there was of cloth or posture disappeared. The front of the doublet bulged, especially just above the waistline. This bulge was quite unobtrusive when it first appeared, at mid-century. However, it was gradually enlarged until it reached distended proportions (see Fig. 302). A doublet with this peculiarity is known as the peascod-belly doublet. By 1570 the protuberance was quite noticeable. Maximum distortion was reached among the landsknecht in the following decade.

Collars rose to brush the ear lobe. The modest ruffle widened to the proportions of the true ruff. The jerkin, following the contour of the doublet, was often sleeveless, with padded roll and wing at the armscye and lengthened skirt (Fig. 299). Trunk hose suddenly pushed outward in the form of pumpkin breeches. This name was obviously suggested by their shape. The legs of the breeches were enlarged to the shape and size of large pumpkins. The contour was maintained by various kinds of bombast

FIG. 297. *Northern Follower of Titian, Alessandro Alberti and Page. c.1557. (National Gallery of Art, Washington, D. C.)*

Fig. 298. *Titian, Portrait of Philip II of Spain. 1550. (Pitti Gallery, Florence, Alinari Photograph)*

(padding), such as tow (an inferior flax fiber) or horsehair. Usually the outer surface consisted of embroidered panels, or panes, which enriched the effect. The Spanish cape replaced the short gown. As hat crowns rose, brims all but disappeared.

Francis, Duke of Alencon, younger brother of Charles IX of France, is the perfect example of high fashion at this time (Fig. 300). Significant features of his costume are the padded, wrinkleless doublet with peascod-belly front and pickadils (edging of scallops or tabs) at the waistline, high collar and lace-edged ruff, pumpkin breeches with elaborately embroidered panes, sleek legs, slightly pointed, sophisticated shoes, high-crowned hat, jeweled chain and hat band, and lynx-lined cape slung from the left shoulder.

Ignoring the fashion of globular breeches, Germany and her northern neighbors adopted the loose but equally fantastic pluderhose of the landsknecht. Instead of 16 or 18 panes per leg, the pluderhose usually

FIG. 299. *Francois Clouet, Charles IX of France. 1569. (Hof Museum, Vienna, Photograph by Bruckmann)*

FIG. 300. *French School, Francis, Duke of Alencon. 1572. (National Gallery of Art, Washington, D.C., Samuel H. Kress Collection, Loan)*

had only 4; extravagant yardage of silk substituted for the horsehair or other form of
padding to produce the desired bravado.
Amman's illustrations of military pluderhose
show the silk cascading to the ankles.[7]
Townsmen were more conservative in their
dress. Figure 301 shows one of three 1567
costumes preserved in the Cathedral of
Uppsala, Sweden. A characteristic detail of
pluderhose is the constriction a few inches
below the waist which forms a puff between

[7] J. H. von Hefner-Altenect, *Trachten, Kunstwerke und Gerathschaften*, Heinrich Keller, Frankfurt am Main, 1888, vol. 9, plates 599, 600.

waist and hipbone level, a line which had
been noticeable even earlier (Fig. 297).

LAST QUARTER OF THE CENTURY

The decade of the seventies saw the
introduction of other varieties and combinations of upper hose, which, however, did
not entirely replace the styles already in
vogue. One very important type, introduced
from Venice and hence called Venetians,

FIG. 301. *Costume of Black
Velvet and Taffeta Worn by Erik
Sture. 1567. (Cathedral of Upsala,
Sweden)*

FIG. 302. *Gheyn, Standard Bearer. 1587. (New York Public
Library, Prints Division)*

was widely adopted at the time, reappeared at the end of the seventeenth century, lasted throughout the eighteenth, and as court costume even into the twentieth. They are usually known as knee breeches (Figs. 302 and 303). As Figs. 303 and 304a show, the sixteenth-century Venetians fitted rather loosely; they were sometimes padded around the hips, but were trimly fashioned about the knee.

Another variation of the hose consisted of abbreviated trunk hose supplemented by fitted tubular extensions, called *canions,* which reached to the knee (Fig. 305). Canions were usually made of contrasting fabric, often brocade or satin, the latter possibly slashed. Sometimes the trunk hose were so short—merely a padded roll at the top of the trousers—that one has to look closely at the paintings to distinguish between Venetians and canions. Occasionally vestigial trunk hose were worn with what we would call tights (Fig. 304b and d).

When the upper hose became so full that they resembled women's early gymnasium bloomers of our own century, they were called *galligaskins* (Fig. 306), the name being derived from Gascony, their place of origin. They might well have been developed from pumpkin breeches by omitting the bombast, from pluderhose by omitting the panels, or from Venetians by increasing the width at the knee.

Before the end of the century the contour of pumpkin breeches changed from a convex curve to an angular line which slanted outward from the waist to within a few inches of the knee, then turned sharply in toward the leg to form the square-based padded hose.

Garters in the form of wide strips of cloth, often fringed at the ends, were wrapped twice about the leg, above and below the knee, and tied in a bow. They played an important part in covering and securing the junction of upper and lower hose.

The Spanish cape in Fig. 307 remained

FIG. 303. *Unknown Artist, Portrait of James I of England as a Young Boy. 1574. Redrawn. (National Portrait Gallery, London)*

the most popular wrap throughout this period, but a second style, called the mandilion, was also often worn (Fig. 308). It had sleeves, but they were seldom used. Usually the mandilion was worn slung about the shoulders, in some cases with the right sleeve hanging down center front.

The overhanging snout of the peascod-belly doublet of the late sixteenth century reached the height of absurdity among German soldiers. Gheyn's engraving of a standard bearer (Fig. 302) demonstrates this. Throughout the last decades of the century the skirt of the doublet remained consistently short, the collar high, sleeves for the most part moderate but sometimes padded in conformity with women's styles, the armscyes accented with wings and/or pickadils.

A detail which has caused quite a little discussion and confusion is the tabbed decoration shown in Fig. 298 at the top of Philip's doublet collar, at his wrists, and on his shoes. These mark the beginning of the fashion of pickadils. At the same time, Maximilian II wore a leather jerkin with pickadils on the collar, wings, and lower edge. At first the tabs were merely an ornamental finish. As the ruffle grew into the ruff, however, the pickadils atop the collar were deepened to support the voluminous pleated material. A half-doublet of the late sixteenth century in

the Metropolitan Museum collection has tabs or pickadils about 2 inches in depth, stiffened with cardboard, which must have served such a purpose. As they appear on Claude de Beaune's costume (see Fig. 328), scalloped and edged with ermine, they are for diversion only.

Long before ruffs grew to shoulder width they required more than the usual pickadils to hold them in place. Beautifully designed frameworks of wire, sometimes gilded, sometimes wrapped with gold or silk thread, were pinned to the collar of the garment (doublet, jerkin, gown, or partlet) to hold the ruff at the admired angle. Figure 309, the original of which is now in the Metropolitan Museum, represents such a support. These accessories are referred to as *underproppers*, *supportasses*, or *rebatos*. Figure 336 shows the ruff of a woman's

FIG. 304. *Abraham de Bruyn*, Omnium Pene Europae, *Plate 105. 1581. (Metropolitan Museum of Art, Rogers Fund)*

FIG. 305. *Marguerite of Valois with Brothers, Duke of Alencon and Henry III. Flemish Tapestry. Fetes of Henry III. Detail. 1580–1585. (Uffizi Gallery, Florence, Alinari Photograph)*

FIG. 306. *F. Pourbus, Portrait of Henry IV. 1595.*
(Louvre)

costume resting on a supportasse which has
an elaborate gold fringe at the edge, definitely designed to be seen and enjoyed.

When the French adopted the high
standing band, usually called the Medici
collar, in the 1580s, they needed a firm support to maintain its upright position. This
device must have repeated the height and
shape of the collar. Medici collars were more
prevalent in the following century.

Neck treatment consisted of a ruff so
large that it required a wired support (Figs.
302 and 307) or a turnover collar, or falling
band (Fig. 308). Essex, Elizabeth's great
love, followed the fashion of wearing both
ruff and collar (Fig. 310).

FIG. 307. *Spanish Cape with Peaked Hood. 1590.*
(Metropolitan Museum of Art, Rogers Fund) Re-
drawn from Deutsches Leben der Vergangenheit in
Bildern, *Vol. II, Plate 1099.*

FIG. 308. *Mandilion, Sleeved Wrap Usually Worn*
as Cape. 1579. Redrawn from Marc Duval, The
Three Colignys. (Louvre, Department of Engravings)

Hats with high crowns prevailed, dandies wearing them as high as 8 or 10 inches (Fig. 311); but at the end of the century, in sharp contrast to this quixotic fad, hats had lower crowns and wider brims—forerunners of the cavalier hats of the seventeenth century. The profession of teaching was already indicated by a four-cornered cap which later became the mortar board. Figure 312 is a drawing from Moroni's portrait of Titian's schoolmaster.

Footwear took on a more familiar look, as extensions from the counters tied at the instep. Platform soles, perhaps suggested by the ladies' chopines, described in the next chapter, were seen occasionally; but the separate heel attached to the shoe to give height is a seventeenth-century contribution (Fig. 305).

During his reign, 1574–1589, Henry III of France himself was the fashion leader. Probably as ineffectual a king as France ever had, he devoted much of his time to his own personal appearance. Said to have been late at both his wedding and his coronation be-

cause of delay in the meticulous arrangement of his ruff, he was highly effeminate in both behavior and dress. In Fig. 305, Henry III wears the padded peascod-belly doublet, abbreviated trunk hose, and canions.

At the end of the century, ruffs were formed into fewer but larger, more open, convolutions (Fig. 311). This style had three advantages: it required less yardage, took less time to launder, and was lighter in weight.

Henry IV (1589–1610), one of the greatest of French kings, promptly set about repairing the damage done by his brother-in-law. Much less interested in clothing than Henry III, he spent little time on his appearance. Nevertheless his portraits point to certain fashion changes. In 1595 he appeared in full galligaskins, and at the turn of the century in square-based bombasted

FIG. 309. *Underpropper or Supportasse. Italian. Late Sixteenth Century. Redrawn. (Metropolitan Museum of Art, Gift of Mrs. Edward S. Harkness)*

FIG. 310. *Second Earl of Essex Wearing Collar (Falling Band) and Ruff. 1590's. Redrawn from Portrait by Unknown Artist. (National Portrait Gallery, London)*

FIG. 311. *Extreme Fashion of High Crowned Hat. 1578. (Miss P. Vansittart-Neale Collection) Redrawn from Portrait of Sir Edward Hoby by Unknown Artist as Published in Kelly and Schwabe, A Short History of Costume and Armour, B. J. Batsford Ltd., 1931, Plate 7.*

FIG. 312. *Academic Headdress. c.1575. Redrawn from Moroni's Portrait of Titian's Schoolmaster. (National Gallery of Art, Washington, D.C., D. C. Widener Collection)*

trunk hose (Fig. 306). He preferred a hat with modified crown and wider brim,

doublet with normal waistline, and ruff of medium size.

13

Women's Costume of the Sixteenth Century

The Century as a Whole

The modes of the 1490s were transitional; with little alteration they carried well into the sixteenth century. The typical gown consisted of a tightly fitted, square-necked bodice, its rapidly widening sleeves usually turned back to reveal their rich lining and the decorative undersleeve; the gently spreading skirt often opened down center front over a handsome petticoat. Distinctive caps or hoods differentiated one country from another.

Katherine of Aragon is reputed to have introduced the Spanish farthingale (a hooped underskirt) into England early in the century. The result was to convert the columnar skirt of the fifteenth century into the cone shape of the sixteenth. Both styles were worn in the early years of the century.

By mid-century many changes had occurred, paralleling those in men's costume. Spanish influence had introduced the hoop-supported skirt, smooth in contour, which was quite generally worn. Raised necklines were often collared, with a softening frill forecasting the ruff. Sleeves remained double: a wider and often longer outer sleeve was accompanied by an undersleeve which often matched the petticoat. Head-dresses became more homogeneous from country to country. The widened French cap was adjusted to the increasing volume of hair over the temples; the back curtain, or veil, bowed out in favor of the higher neckline treatment. Shoes assumed a natural contour.

The greatest absurdities marked the end of the century: the drum-shaped French farthingale became more popular than the Spanish cone; bloated leg-of-mutton sleeves came into fashion; ruffs spread to shoulder width and required wired support, pushing the hair to the top of the head.

All told, however, sixteenth-century costume is noted for its rich splendor. This was achieved to some extent by a super-abundance of jewels, mounted by goldsmiths who were real artists. Precious stones appeared in borders on the frontlets of caps. Wide carcanets (necklaces) encircled the throat; fur pieces, girdles, brooches, rings, and pendants glowed with diamonds, rubies, sapphires, and emeralds. Pearls, coral, and other stones formed allover patterns which must have made it practically impossible for the wearer to sit down. Cloth of gold, gold gauze, and silver tissue contributed to dazzling effects. Spreading over or edging the surfaces were splendid embroidered designs in black silk—a mark of Spanish taste—or polychromatic silks and gold. Lace added its ineffable touch.

FIRST QUARTER OF THE CENTURY

As we noted in the preceding chapter, the return of the French army of Charles VIII from Italy in 1495 and the campaigns of Louis XII in Italy during his reign (1498–1515) turned attention toward the south and resulted in emulation of Italian costumes. The low square neckline of the bodice, usually with a bare suggestion of gossamer drapery, provided an ideal setting to display gorgeous necklaces and pendants. Brooches or points were used to secure the popular separate sleeves, often made of contrasting material. Waistlines were relatively high and skirts fell with easy fullness, their joining being covered by a knotted sash or buckled girdle. The hair was simply dressed, as in the late fifteenth century. A narrow fillet encircled the head, sometimes accented by jewels or an ornament centered on the forehead. A snood resting at mid-shoulder often covered the hair.

Pinturicchio's painting of Emperor Frederick III and Eleanor of Portugal shows Eleanor with her hair in the pigtail fashion seen on Beatrice d'Este (Fig. 258). The low neck of Eleanor's gown is filled in with a sheer partlet; her sectional sleeves are elaborately treated, allowing the very full lingerie sleeves to fall in festoons. The skirt is slightly trained.

At the opposite end of the social scale are Carpaccio's two courtesans in Fig. 313. Though they appear extremely bored and disillusioned, they are well gowned. Their

gowns are especially interesting to the student of costume because in cut they resemble closely the early empire gowns of the nineteenth century. The treatment and the typical textile design, however, are unmistakably sixteenth century. The high coiffure is unusual.

Of greater significance for the period

FIG. 313. Carpaccio, The Two Courtesans. 1500–1510. (Civic Museum, Venice, Anderson Photograph —Alinari)

FIG. 314. *Anne of Brittany from Les Heures d'Anne de Bretagne. First Decade of Sixteenth Century. (Bibliothèque Nationale, Paris)*

is a pair of chopines (high platform-soled shoes) that appear in the original painting. Usually associated with Venetian women of fashion in the latter part of the century, it is of import to see them this early. Evidently they were in use throughout the century. Their appearance in Venice was the result of the close trade relations between Venetian merchants and the Near East.

The French mode at this time is illustrated in an illumination in a manuscript in the Bibliothèque Nationale (Fig. 314). Here Anne of Brittany, herself, models the headdress known by her name, described in Chapter 11. Already it has changed form. The white pleated frill of the under cap is now pushed farther back on the head. Instead of a band of cloth over the crown of the head, a jeweled band edges the veil of velvet which falls to the back. A supporting form (possibly the bulk of her hair arrangement) raises the top of her cap and tilts this portion slightly forward. Other late fifteenth-century fashion features still appearing are the square neckline, smooth bodice, and sleeves flared to a wide opening. The trained skirt of Anne's gown is cut with ample fullness at the back, and would fall softly and naturally when she arose.

One of the outstanding women of this period was Marguerite of Austria, Regent of the Netherlands and daughter of Maximilian I and Mary of Burgundy. Her portrait by Van Orley (Fig. 315) gives evidence of the continuance of the wimple in the pleated barbe, which originated in the fifteenth century. (The barbe was a piece of pleated linen attached to a band which encircled the face.) The barbe was worn over or under the chin during mourning or widowhood, according to the rank of the wearer. Over this nun-like accessory Marguerite wears the beguin—the Flemish hood—an immaculate rectangle of linen, carefully folded into a symmetrical headdress, and caught together at the nape of the neck. A center crease, turned downward, gives the heart-shaped contour to the front edge. Her gown has

the fashionable square neckline; the outer sleeves, lined with ermine, are turned back, the better to expose the lustrous fur.

By 1515 Italian ladies had made several changes in their costume. They filled in their décolletage by an embroidered partlet under a veiling of sheer fabric and edged their narrow collars with a goffered (carefully fluted) ruffle—an early appearance of the ancestor of the ruff. The greatest change, however, was in the sleeves, which by this time matched the gown and were sewed in. The upper section was generously cut, forming huge puffs, which were slashed in keeping with the rest of the dress. The lower sleeve was still relatively close-fitting. Wrist ruffles matched the collar edging.

The hairdress was varied by formal curls on the cheeks. In our own 1920s these were inelegantly known as "spit curls." The tire-shaped turban of the lady in the Luini portrait (Fig. 316), called by Vecellio[1] the *balzo*, is covered with shirred and puffed gauze which gives a feeling of lightness. Note the flea fur carried in her right hand. Much could be said concerning the low standard of cleanliness during the sixteenth century. The flea fur, usually a fur of fine quality elaborately mounted with gold and jewels, was so called in the optimistic belief that it would serve as a decoy for vermin.

In England, the Spanish Katherine of Aragon, first wife of Henry VIII, adopted the gable headdress of her mother-in-law, Elizabeth of York, which was illustrated in Fig. 276. Katherine's headdress, however, is modified by striped bands which fill in the open space between gable and forehead, completely concealing her hair (Fig. 317). The lappets which formerly fell forward onto the chest are now folded upward and caught in place. The square neckline of the queen's gown, as well as the frontlet of her hood, are embellished with precious stones, while two regal pendants add to her grandeur. Her furred sleeves are folded back to

[1] Cesare Vecellio, *Habiti Antichi et moderni*, Venice, 1958, vol. I, plate 46.

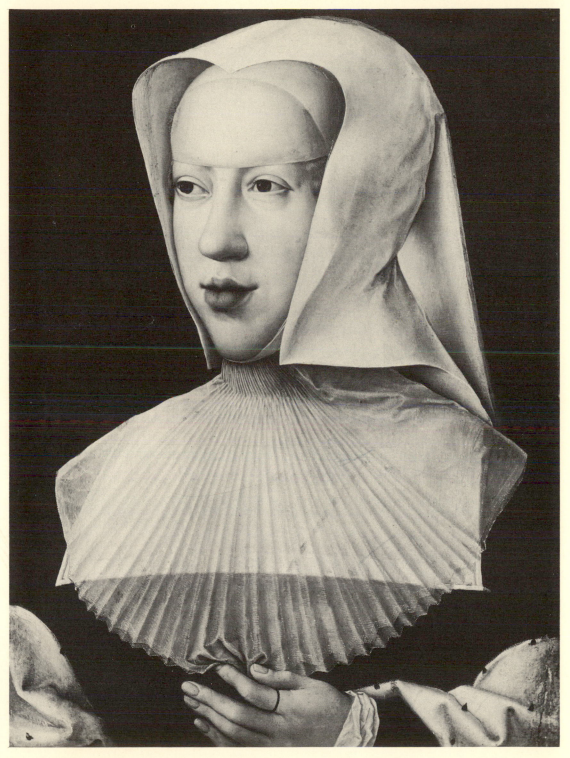

Fig. 315. Bernard van Orley, Portrait of Marguerite of Austria. 1515. (Musées royaux des Beaux-Arts de Belgique, Brussels)

Fig. 316.   Bernardino Luini, *Portrait of a Lady*. 1515. (*National Gallery of Art, Washington, D.C., Mellon Collection*)

FIG. 317. *Unknown Artist, Katherine of Aragon. 1520. (National Portrait Gallery, London)*

reveal the brocaded undersleeves and wrist ruffles. Figure 318 shows a rare back view of the gable headdress, after a Holbein drawing.

Claudia of France dressed much like her mother, Anne of Brittany. Eleanor of Austria, however, sister of Charles V and second wife of Francis I, brought to France a combination of Italian and Spanish influences (Fig. 319). The nonconformity of her bared head, with hair simply arranged, is refreshing in this era of ornate headdresses. However, magnificent jewels on her hair, pearl earrings, necklace, sleeve brooches, girdle, rings, and neckline border, all proclaim the wealth of her family. Her paned sleeves are designed in much the same manner as those of Frances I (Fig. 292). The enormous oversleeves of fur are caught at

FIG. 318. *Back View of English Gable Headdress. 1527. Redrawn from Holbein, English Noblewoman. (British Museum)*

armscye and elbow. Bodice and skirt are of sumptuous brocade.

SECOND QUARTER OF THE CENTURY

In the second quarter of the century trends of the first quarter crystallized. A more covered up look coincided with the rise of men's shirt collars. The Spanish farthingale was generally adopted. In its native country this produced a smooth, rigid, conical shape, but a softer outline developed in Italy and elsewhere, where the skirt fell from the waist with some fullness. Ruffles continue to appear at the tops of partlet collars, while waistlines dropped, sometimes with a decided point. Rich fabrics and jewels in grand array contributed to the Renaissance impression of splendor. Shoes narrowed to a normal contour.

In 1526 Titian portrayed the Spanish fashion in his painting of Isabella of Portugal, wife of Charles V (Fig. 320). The partlet and undersleeves of her costume are of sheer fabric, shirred and jeweled. Wrist and neck ruffles form gracious finishes. Her oversleeves are of the same material as the remainder of her gown. A wide band of pearl-studded embroidery ornaments all edges. A new feature is the arching of the neckline. The waistline slants downward to center front and is accented by a jeweled girdle, the long pendant of which was likely, in Spain at least, to terminate with a reliquary. In other countries a pomander containing fragrance of some sort took its place, playing the double role of perfume and deodorant. As Isabella's gown illustrates, skirts were cut to flare and fit over the farthingale, wrinkle-free. A petticoat of damask, brocade, or patterned velvet was usually displayed between the spreading lines of the overskirt.

The breastless effect of the metallic smoothness of Isabella's bodice was created by a tightly fitting vasquine, progenitor of our foundation garments, but more directly

FIG. 319. *Joost van Cleve, Portrait of Eleanor, Queen of France, Sister of Charles V, Second Wife of Francis I. c.1530. (Hampton Court, By Permission of H. M. Queen Elizabeth II)*

of the heavily boned and busked instruments of torture of the three following centuries. Sometime during the sixteenth century a clever blacksmith created an iron cage operated by means of hinges and bolts (see Fig. 341*b*). Empress Isabella's hairdress corresponds to that of her sister-in-law, Eleanor of Austria.

That the Italians gave their own interpretation to Spanish fashion is shown in Bronzino's portrait of Lucrezia Panciatichi (Fig. 321). Her bodice has more flexibility than its Spanish counterpart and her sleeves continue in the design of the Luini dress shown in Fig. 316. Cartridge pleats control and direct the fullness of Lucrezia's skirt.

FIG. 320.   *Titian, Empress Isabella of Portugal. 1526. (Prado Museum, A. Y. R. Mas Photograph)*

FIG. 321. Bronzino, *Lucrezia Panciatichi*. c.1532–1540. (*Uffizi Gallery, Florence, Alinari Photograph*)

FIG. 322. *Hans Holbein, Anne of Cleves. 1539. (Louvre)*

Intricately pleated gold gauze fills her decolletage but is low enough to set off her lovely pearl necklace. Her hair is arranged in a twisted coronet accented by a jeweled band which repeats the design of her girdle. One unmistakable Spanish detail is the use of points on the lower sleeve. By this time points usually served no purpose other than ornamentation, the tips or aiglets often being made of gold and even jeweled. This form of decoration continued far into the seventeenth century.

Flemish high fashion is well illustrated in Holbein's portrait of Henry VIII's fourth and most fortunate wife, Anne of Cleves (Fig. 322). Instead of the usual square neckline, the front edges of her bodice extend down to the waistline. Her underbodice, or plastron, is cloth of gold; it has a low neckline finished by a gold-embroidered and jewel-set border and it is filled in with an elaborately embroidered partlet extending upward into a standing collar. She wears a carcanet at the base of her throat. Her gown of glowing red velvet is lavishly trimmed with gold braid studded with pearls. Its unique sleeves are puffed at the top, constricted by bands of gold braid at mid-upper arm, and thence spread into great circular cut lower sections. Her waistline remains slightly high and is marked by a gold buckled girdle.

Her most outstanding accessory is her cap, which looks something like the melon-shaped headdress of Fig. 269, flattened at the top and back, leaving rounded extensions at the sides. A flattering transparent layer is placed directly over the embroidered band of her under cap, thus revealing the outer cap in all its grandeur of solid incrustation of gold and pearls. A large jeweled ornament with fringes of gold pendants further enhances the left side. This headdress alone must have warranted social security for the life span which Henry's divorce conferred upon her.

Catherine Howard, fifth of Henry's wives, was painted by Holbein near the middle of the century, at a time when English fashion was changing (Fig. 323). She had laid aside the gable headdress for the French hood, which now was designed with a short flat panel at back instead of the two long back panels and front lappets. Though her gown still shows the ubiquitous square neckline, this is merely indicated by a seam joining the black velvet yoke and collar to the satin bodice. This covered, collared fashion was worn by Queen Claudia of France as early as 1520 and is also associated with Queen Mary of England during her reign (1553–1558).

Catherine's sleeves also marked a point of departure from the double-sleeved smooth-shouldered effect of the earlier style. Here in embryo was the leg-of-mutton sleeve which would flourish in the last quarter of the sixteenth century. However, the fullness and crisp texture of the satin made these sleeves bouffant; a gold-embroidered rouleau stiffened and emphasized the seams. Points with gold aiglets (metal tag or tip of a lace or point) on the sleeve were a gesture to Spain, as was the black work—the silk embroidery on the wrist ruffles.

A portrait at Windsor Castle shows the young Princess Elizabeth wearing a magnificent rose-red costume, the bodice and skirt of which might well have been made in Spain (Fig. 324). In England at the middle of the century the exposure of neck and shoulders was a prerogative of the unmarried girl, a privilege which Elizabeth exploited as long as she lived. The sleeves of her gown are typically English. The outer sleeve, smooth and close as it drops off the shoulders, swells from the elbow to an inordinate width and length. The lower portion is folded outward and the edge lifted and invisibly secured high on the upper arm. This displayed both the rich lining of the outer sleeve and the inspired work of the under sleeve. A well-known portrait of Queen Jane Seymour shows a similar treatment. In Elizabeth's portrait the gown sleeve is self-lined but her undersleeves, which are un-

· ETATIS ·   SVÆ ·

FIG. 323. Hans Holbein the Younger, Portrait of Catherine Howard, Fifth Wife of Henry VIII. c.1540. (Courtesy, Toledo Museum of Art, Gift of Edward Drummond Libbey)

FIG. 324. *Flemish School, Princess Elizabeth. c.1547 (Windsor Castle, By Permission of H. M. Queen Elizabeth II)*

usually wide and regally jeweled, match the petticoat fabric of white and gold brocade. Her girdle (note the deep point at the waist), neckline, and cap borders reflect her life-long addiction to jewels. The French cap she wears was by now the accepted fashion.

Cranach's German ladies of the same period had a style all their own. Usually they were so heavily laden with huge neck chains that one wonders how they held their heads up. They also indulged in sleeves puffed and bound into numerous sections and wore skirts made in graduated organ-pipe folds crossed by multiple contrasting bandings, crowning it all with broad-brimmed plumed hats that could have challenged Gainsborough's dashing creations of the eighteenth century.

Cranach's portrait of Sibyl, wife of an Elector of Saxony (about 1548), illustrates most of these features (Fig. 325). Her hat, smaller than many of Cranach's, is smartly plumed and sits atop the elaborate cap which encloses her hair. Her pleated partlet has the now prevalent ruffled standing collar, and the bodice itself is also collared in the newer manner. Chains weigh upon her shoulders and chest, while her fingers display numerous rings.

FIG. 325. *Lucas Cranach, Sibyl, Wife of John Frederick, Elector of Saxony. c.1548. Facsimile. (Metropolitan Museum of Art, Dick Fund)*

THIRD QUARTER OF THE CENTURY

The third quarter of the sixteenth century was the period when the innocent looking little ruffle assumed the proportions and form of the true ruff. Waistlines became more pinched and pointed, and skirts jutted outward from the waistline before slanting toward the floor. In the first decade of this period sleeves retained the luxurious fur-lined character of the previous decades, but by the sixties they had slimmed down and were mounted with a puffed and scalloped treatment at the armscye.

Spain, enjoying great prestige at this time, contributed to the ensemble an open oversleeve which often fell to the floor. Beautiful aiglets tipped the nonfunctional bows which adorned the sleeves and skirt fronts.

A new hair style was inevitable as collar and ruff moved upward. In Spain a small high toque was popular. In France and England, where the hair was curled and fluffed above

FIG. 326. *Antonio Moro, Mary, Queen of England. 1554. (Prado Museum, A. Y. R. Mas Photograph)*

the temples, the cap was widened to accommodate the hairdress; the indentation we saw on the headdress of Marguerite of Austria (Fig. 315) was smoothed out into a modified heart shape which came to be identified with Mary, Queen of Scots. Jewels in superabundance remained a conspicuous part of the scene.

Two of the most famous queens in history began their reigns in this quarter-century: Catherine de Medici, wife of King Henry II of France (1547–1559), and Queen Elizabeth I of England (1557–1603). Later, as dowager queen-mother from 1559 to 1589, Catherine was the ruling force behind Francis II, Charles IX, and Henry III, her reigning sons. Both queens automatically exerted great influence on dress, and both are discussed later in this chapter.

The solemn, pious Queen Mary Tudor of England dedicated herself to restoring the Catholic Church to its former power in England. Indoctrinated by her mother, Katherine of Aragon, with sympathy for Spain, and sharing her devotion to the church, Mary married Philip II of Spain. Figure 326 is from a portrait of her painted in 1554, about the time of her marriage. Her costume retains many of the features we saw earlier on Catherine Howard. The bodice closing is raised a bit higher, the neck is covered, and the cap brought farther forward on the head, flattened and broadened at the top over the fuller hair arrangement. Her conservative sleeves are the same style worn by her mother and her half-sister Elizabeth. The jeweled brooch, a gift from Philip, contains a pear-shape pearl which was noted for its rarity, beauty, and value.

Figure 327 shows Catherine de Medici, Queen of France, in all her glory. She came to France richly dowered, as this costume testifies. She is credited with having introduced the ruff from Italy, a questionable point, but certainly the spreading collar springing from her partlet bears the widest and most carefully shaped ruffle seen up to this date (1555). Legend accuses Catherine

of having imposed a maximum waist measure of 18 inches on the ladies of her court, keeping her own at a record-setting 16. Metal would have had to have had real strength to achieve this standard.

In this portrait her waistline is constricted to little more than her spine, accounting at least partially for the arched form of the top of her skirt. The heavy jewel-laden fabric falls with architectural precision. Its reticulated pattern is formed of pearls, with sapphires at the intersections. It may have been at this time that the idea of stressing the width of the hips first took hold. Some padding was certainly necessary to create and maintain the rounded line at the top of the skirt. Her sleeves are in the tradition of the early part of the century. Her fan, comprised of a panache of plumes, is one of several forms introduced in the sixteenth century.

She is wearing the French hood, freed of its lower back portion, but has covered the top with a mosaic of pearls and precious stones. There is a gradual widening effect over the temples. The fabulous jeweled cross on the front of her bodice is almost lost against the background maze.

To her credit it should be said that at the sudden and tragic death of her husband she assumed deep mourning and continued to wear widow's weeds the rest of her life.

The costume Claude de Beaune wears in Fig. 328, about the same time, is, by contrast, elegant in its simplicity. Significant features are the high arch of the neckline of the bodice, the increased height of the collar of the partlet, and the compactly padded rolls at the armscyes combined with a double row of pickadils. The cap once again reaches the brow, but dips slightly in the center and curves sharply outward over the temples and back in again, covering the ears. A panel, as of old, falls from the back of this cap. This is the form Mary, Queen of Scots, wore as the widow of Francis II of France, and it is often referred to as the Mary Queen of Scots cap (Fig. 329). One other

FIG. 327. *Unknown Artist, Catherine de Medici. c.1555. (Uffizi Gallery, Florence, Alinari Photograph)*

FIG. 328. *Studio of Francois Clouet, Claude de Beaune. 1563. (Louvre)*

FIG. 329. *Mary Queen of Scots Wearing Widow's Barbe. 1561. Redrawn from Clouet, Mary Queen of Scots. (Reproduced by Permission of the Trustees of the Wallace Collection, London)*

feature of Claude de Beaune's gown which contributes to its beauty is the tasteful use of narrow strips of ermine in the trimming of bodice and sleeves.

LAST QUARTER OF THE CENTURY

Until 1580 women's fashions in Europe stayed within reasonable bounds, if we overlook Catherine de Medici's strictures and accept the idea of jewels unlimited. But during the eighties, features which had come into fashion as interesting innovations or natural developments were magnified or intensified into grotesque proportions.

In France, England, and the Low Countries, the A-shaped Spanish farthingale gave way to the French version, which produced a drum-shaped silhouette. Marguerite of Valois, daughter of Catherine de Medici and wife of Henry IV of France, is reputed to have introduced this distended form to camouflage her not too slender hips. She is also said to have been intensely interested in fashion and to have been blessed with a natural charm which canceled out the obstacles of the then-current mode.

A popular cartoon (see Fig. 378) suggests the tire-like roll which the ladies tied just below the waistline to create an outward thrust of the fabric. In many cases the farthingale must have been wired or caned to produce the desired right-angled break in the fabric, for the upper edge of the drum shape is usually sharply defined. On top of this shelf—which might well have served as a lazy susan—sometimes rested a pleated flounce of the same dimensions as the top of the drum—the so-called cartwheel ruff. Norris refers to the combination as the "wheel farthingale."[2] These skirts were of round length and shorter than the Spanish type.

Balancing this excessive girth were shoulder-width ruffs and huge padded leg-of-mutton sleeves. The ruff expanded to the point where it required a wired support. Ruffs could be either closed at the throat or open. The French, being the most daring, introduced the open high-standing ruff or collar springing from the deep V-neckline which plunged to the waist (Fig. 330).

The workmanship on these fantastic accessories is little short of marvelous. Anyone with the slightest understanding of drawn work and the variety of cutwork known in Italy as reticella must be awed by the tremendous patience, skill, and time required to complete the openwork of such a ruff as that shown in Fig. 336. Eight yards or more of this airiness, produced by such exacting proficiency, were used for one ruff, which must have been from 6 to 8 inches deep. The

[2] Herbert Norris, *Costume and Fashion*, Dutton, New York, vol. III, book 2, p. 618.

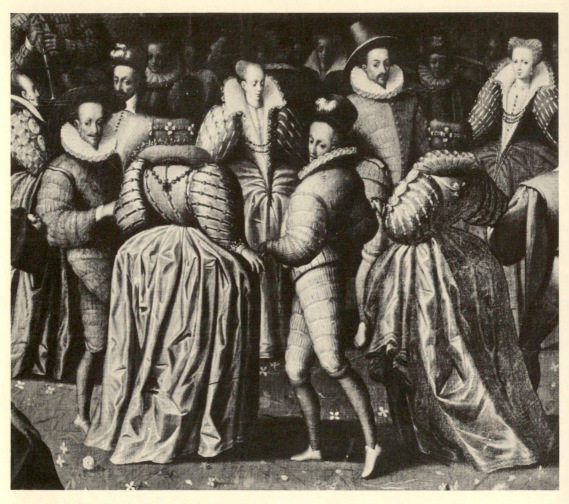

FIG. 330. *French School, Detail of Ball at Court of Henry III. c.1581–1582. (Louvre)*

same open lacy design formed the tilted wire support on which the ruff rested (Fig. 309). Notice the delicate floral pendants which fringe the outer edge of the support in Fig. 336.

The use of starch to give desired crispness was first perfected in Flanders, whence it spread to England. However, starch alone was insufficient for very deep ruffs. Colored starch is often mentioned, yellow particularly, but it is seldom recorded in paintings. Laundering the ruffs was a delicate operation, requiring time, skilled hands, and proper equipment. Poking sticks, first of wood but later of metal, were used in setting the ruffs. Toward the end of the century and into the seventeenth, the convolutions were larger and more open. Sometimes the ruffs were made in layers, carefully goffered to create a precise geometric design on the outer edge; sometimes they were haphazard, especially in the following century.

Eating habits and silver had to be altered to protect the ruffs from dribbled food. Even so, considering the other standards of hygiene then current, one questions their freshness and crispness at all times.

The blimp-like sleeves were in proportion to the width of the drum-shaped skirts and handicapped the wearer still further.

The Victoria and Albert Museum in London has a beautiful full-length sleeveless gown of the late sixteenth century, in which the fullness is controlled through the shoulder area by box pleats (Fig. 331). Two other incomplete gowns are in the collection: a velvet-patterned one with long sleeves and a sleeveless plush one with narrow wings. These gowns, though perhaps not wraps in the true sense of the word, doubtless were worn for extra warmth.

Draft 3, *a* and *b*, was taken from the velvet gown, enough of which remains to reconstruct an accurate pattern. In design it closely resembles Fig. 331, the difference being mainly that it has sleeves. These are definitely of Spanish origin—long, open along the front seam, stiff with lining and widened by a deep curve at the elbow. The open edges of the two sections of the sleeve differ in length because they do not meet at the armscye. The edge of the back section comes to a higher point on the armscye than that of the front section. The two edges are caught together only once on the lower portion of the sleeve.

Corsets by this time were truly iron cages with long sharp front points, which made possible the needle-like shape of the front waistline (Figs. 330 and 332).

Hair was brushed upward over pads into a high pompadour. Wigs were worn by such fashion leaders as Queen Elizabeth and Mary, Queen of Scots. The cap, for most occasions, practically disappeared. A two-piece hood was worn in England. Figure 341*d* pictures the one which accompanied Elizabeth's golden doublet. A drawstring was threaded through the loops at the nape of the neck to give it shape and secure it. The triangle evidently was worn on top of the hood proper, the wide base at the front. The Mary Queen of Scots cap acquired a graceful downward curve over the forehead, creating what was referred to as the shadow. Possibly the triangle could have been used to shade the upper part of the face when desired. Pins were used in abundance to fix various parts of the costume in position.

Illustrating many of the foregoing details are the costumes shown in Fig. 330, a detail of a ball given at the court of Henry III about 1581. The ladies all wear French farthingales. The back view of two of the dancers reveals the wire supports under the ruffs. Two ladies facing front are wearing the high-standing neckwear known as the Medici collar—called by Cunnington "the standing band."[3] All the sleeves are balloon-

[3] C. Willett and Phillis Cunnington, *A Picture History of English Costume*, Macmillan, New York, 1960, p. 36.

FIG. 331. *Sleeveless Gown. Late Sixteenth Century. Back View. (Victoria & Albert Museum, Crown Copyright)*

Fig. 332. *Crispin van de Passe, after Isaac Oliver, Queen Elizabeth I. Facsimile. Original, 1588. (Metropolitan Museum of Art, Gift of Robert Hartshorne)*

like, their outer surfaces still broken by slashes and puffs. Note the extremely sharp attenuated front waistlines and the diminutive waists. The hairdress harmonizes with the bulbous look of the sleeves.

The salient features of Spanish costume toward the end of the century are shown in the portrait of the Infanta Isabella Clara Eugenia and her dwarf companion, Fig. 333. The Infanta's ruff practically covers her ears; her bodice is cut to the normal neckline, covering her upper body fully; her trained skirt has the typically Spanish smooth cone-shaped contour; handsome aiglets cascade down center front. Probably most important at this time is the sleeve treatment: the inner sleeves are long, closely fitted, with horizontal braiding running the full length; the outer sleeves, slit from armscye to wrist, sweep majestically to the floor. Upon her pompadour hair-do rests a high-crowned bonnet, plumed and jeweled. She is apparently wearing a fair share of the family wealth in her carcanet, girdle, and beautifully set jewels.

The engraving reproduced in Fig. 332 shows Queen Elizabeth, proud, vain, intelligent, shrewd, indomitable, standing in full panoply of state with crown, orb, and scepter. This likeness was drawn in 1588 but not engraved until 1603. Her wardrobe, estimated at her death at from 500 to 3000 robes, must have been a gorgeous array.

In this engraving we find her upholstered in a French farthingale, with a petticoat occupying almost half of the skirt surface. A portion of her cartwheel ruffle is visible between the petticoat and over skirt. The very long pointed stomacher, with its allover pattern of applied puffs and jewels, matches her petticoat and leg-of-mutton sleeves. Her outer gown fits like a vise through the bodice. Her skirt, with ornamental banding along its open edges, is only slightly longer than the petticoat. Falling under and back of the true sleeves are long, open false sleeves, inspired by Spanish style.

In many of her portraits Elizabeth wears a great, high, arched veil, wired, and edged with lace which forms the background for her crowned head and then falls from her shoulders into a train. Jewels sparkle in her wig, hang from her ears, encircle her neck, and form rope-like festoons across her chest and bodice before they drop to a curve framing her stomacher. A small but important detail is the flaring turned-back cuff which replaced the wrist ruffle. Of significance also is the skirt length, short enough to show her feet, shod with embroidered or brocaded shoes.

The Boston Museum of Fine Arts is the proud possessor of the golden doublet presented to Elizabeth about 1578 (Fig. 334 and Draft 4). The fabric of the doublet is fine, firm white linen, obviously from the loom of a superior weaver. The surface is covered with gold and silver embroidery in an endless scroll design enclosing a stylized flower. The background is thickly sewed with minute gold sequins. Gold lace finishes the lower edge. The doublet is breathtaking in its gleaming splendor and awe-inspiring in its historical implications. Almost 400 years old, it is in near-perfect condition, a real sixteenth-century masterpiece. Actual measurements of the doublet indicate that the queen was a small person but her grand manner left no such impression.

Another garment exciting to hold in the hand is a Spanish child's garment which is one of the gems of the Metropolitan Museum collection (Fig. 335 and Draft 6a and b). This rare example of Spanish fashion provides a unique opportunity to study the method of reinforcement, construction, and decoration which produced the characteristic silhouette and rigidity of Spanish costume at the court of Philip II. Although it has been altered, possibly to be placed on a statue in a shrine or cathedral, enough of the basic structure remains to convey much information.

An examination of the under skirt, for instance, showed it to consist of a layer of heavy slipper-weight satin backed by sized

FIG. 333. *Sanchez Coello, Infanta Isabella Clara Eugenia with Magdalena Ruiz.* c.1584. (*Prado Museum, A. Y. R. Mas Photograph*)

FIG. 334. *Golden Doublet of Queen Elizabeth I. c.1578. (Courtesy, Museum of Fine Arts, Boston, The Elizabeth Day McCormick Collection)*

linen and completely covered with closely placed silk embroidery done through both thicknesses. This surface, in turn, is overlaid with a heavily padded design couched in gold. Gold-embroidered borders down center front and across the bottom of the skirt, combined with silver braid, act as a metallic foundation and support, which look inflexible on the figure. An added lining of sized linen to the embroidered fabrics increases the firmness. The back of the under skirt, which is covered by the overdress, is made of linen.

The front of the bodice and visible portion of the sleeve are of gray-blue satin embroidered in gold and silver and chartreuse, green, and gold silk. The sleeve is lined with blue linen with eyelets worked at the wrist opening, through the linen only, for lacing the edges together. A peplum attached to the bodice is of plain satin in the back. The lower band of the flared front section

matches the front bodice; the upper portion is of true blue satin. The embroidery is a repeat of the pattern of the bodice.

The overdress is like those seen on numerous portraits of Spanish women of the late sixteenth and early seventeenth centuries. Ungirdled, it hangs free from the shoulders and spreads to display the marvelous decorative effect of the underdress. The sleeves, vestigial as far as any practical purpose is concerned, are closed at the normal wrist opening and are slashed both vertically and horizontally to provide outlets for the arms. Deep wings of gray satin are stiffened with numerous rows of silver braid, an effect repeated on the cuffs of the pendant sleeves. A panel of linen has been added down center back of the underskirt and overdress. The dimensions of these are not shown, since they were probably not part of the original costume.

Correlated with this dress, and exhibited

FIG. 335. *Young Spanish Girl's Costume. Late Sixteenth Century. (Metropolitan Museum of Art, Fletcher Fund)*

beside it at the Metropolitan, is Coello's 1590 portrait of the Infanta Isabella Clara Eugenia (Fig. 336), mentioned earlier in connection with the ruff and the supportasse. The Infanta's costume also includes an underbodice with ruff and wrist ruffles attached. Her overdress is closed down the front. The tabs forming her sleeve wings are similar to those which finish the lower edge of her bodice. Her outer sleeves are fashioned much like those of the child's dress, with both vertical and horizontal cuts. Her pompadour, bangs, and high pointed hair ornament are important late sixteenth-century fashion features. Unlike most Spanish dresses of this period, her skirt is pleated at the waistline.

All during this quarter-century, Italian ladies went their comfortable way, their plump bodies (they added padding if their own forms were not sufficiently rounded) clothed in bulging bodices, their waistlines slanting downward from the underarm seam to form a broad yet deep, rounded point. In Venice the horizontal neckline was level with the armpits, the decolletage being filled in with a revealing low-necked sheer yoke, finished with a limp double ruffle which bore little resemblance to the northern ruff. However, Vecellio drew a Venetian noble woman wearing a Medici collar.[4]

Skirts were full, rounding outward from the waistline and ending in a slight train.

The hair as usually portrayed on Venetian women was softly curled and arranged with an upstanding peak on each side of the center part. Boissard's drawing shows a wider, more formal style, with the points appearing as apexes of triangles when viewed from the side. His drawings of companion figures of a noble Venetian matron and a courtesan (not shown here) also illustrate this hair style. The matron has a long sheer finely pleated veil floating from the back of her head. The gown of the young bride differs from that of the noble woman only in the fact that her bodice has a stomacher

front. The courtesan is dressed in a looser, mannish-cut gown, buttoned all the way down center front and girdled with a sash. Wings mask the armscyes, and vestigial open sleeves of the same brocade as the gown hang back of close-fitting sleeves of plain fabric slashed in an early-century manner.

Abraham de Bruyn recorded the fashions of Roman women in 1581. They dressed much like the Venetians, but with round-length gowns, puffs or padded rolls with pickadils at the low armscye line, and collars edged with narrow ruffles. Voluminous veils of the size of Queen Elizabeth's were arranged to fall from just back of the front hairline. None of these Italian dresses had the open-front skirt.

Blond hair had long been admired in Italy. Legend has it that even in ancient Rome ladies experimented with bleaching their hair. Vecellio[5] is responsible for the drawing of Fig. 337, the style-conscious Venetian who was willing to spend hours on the balcony in the sun—not to induce a sun tan—heaven forbid!—but to expose her hair to the sun's bleaching rays. To protect her fair complexion she wore a broad-brimmed crownless hat. She seems to be giving some cosmetic encouragement to the process. Note the chemise and the chopines.

The Metropolitan Museum possesses the underlinen of a Sicilian bride's trousseau of this period. A camisia (chemise), shirt, drawers, and footless hose comprise the set. Elegant enough for a royal bride, they are of fine white linen embroidered in gold, silver, and silk embroidery.

Outer Wraps of the Century

We have little pictorial evidence of what protective clothing—outer wraps—were worn by women of the sixteenth century. In Germany, as early as 1516, Dürer drew the figure of a woman wearing a goller —a smartly shaped little shoulder cape— which must have furnished welcome warmth

---

[4] Vecellio, *op. cit.*

[5] Vecellio, *op. cit.*

FIG. 336. *Sanchez Coello, Infanta Isabella Clara Eugenia.* c. 1590. *(Metropolitan Museum of Art)*

FIG. 337. *Venetian Woman Bleaching Her Hair.* *1590. Redrawn from Vecellio,* Costumes Anciens et Modernes, *1598, Vol. I, Plate 119. (University of Washington Library)*

FIG. 338. *German Shoulder Cape, the Goller.* *1551. Redrawn from Pourbus, Adrienne de Buuck.* *(Musée Communale, Brussels)*

FIG. 339. *Anne Boleyn. 1527. Redrawn from Bartolozzi Engraving of Holbein's Drawing of Anne Boleyn. 1797. (Author's Collection)*

over the low-cut neckline (Fig. 338). Holbein painted a middle-class lady of Basle (1520) wearing a slightly deeper cape. His drawing of Anne Boleyn (Fig. 339) shows her wearing a fur-collared outer garment which must have served the purpose of a wrap. The flea fur, often of marten or sable with costly mountings, served the same purpose.

For colder weather indoors an overdress, sleeved or sleeveless, had widespread popularity (Fig. 331). Cut to hang from the shoulders and usually ungirdled, it was a favorite garment in Spain (Fig. 335). Catherine of Austria, Queen of Portugal, wears a sleeved surcoat in a portrait of 1552 not included here. A mantle brought up over the head was used by young Spanish girls to mask the face, as well as to give protection from the weather.

A little-known portrait of Queen Elizabeth I, dated 1563, which hangs in the castle of Gripsholm, Sweden, shows her wearing a fur-lined and collared surcoat with elbow-length sleeves puffed at the top. Her headdress, consisting of a rather saucy little mannish hat over a jeweled cap which completely covers her hair, indicates that she is dressed for travel.

Short coats on the order of the mandilions worn by the Coligny brothers in Fig. 308 are on record. Accompanying hats were also similar to those of these men.

A memorial brass dated 1557 (not shown) illustrates the most practical-looking surcoat of the century.

Accessories of the Period

Shoes were quite normal in shape from mid-century onward. They were often cushioned with a cork-filled platform sole. Fabric as well as leather was employed. Wooden-soled protective overshoes called *pattens* were strapped over the fragile footwear for outdoor use.

High chopines like those shown in Figs. 337 and 340 are most closely associated with Venetian ladies, but they were worn in

FIG. 340. *Venetian Chopine. Late Sixteenth Century. (Brooklyn Museum)*

Spain also. In a Vecellio drawing of a prostitute of Venice the skirt reaches only to the woman's feet, leaving the platform of the chopine exposed. This platform was made of wood or cork, covered with leather or fabric, and painted or sometimes even gilded. Perforated leather usually formed the upper part, into which the wearer slipped her feet. These chopines were introduced into Italy from the Near East, where Venice had acquired holdings and carried on a thriving trade. European chopines were copies or adaptations of harem footwear.

Chopines in the costume collections of the Brooklyn and Boston Museums range in height from about 6 to 15 inches; we read of their being as high as 18 inches. Travelers returning from Venice reported that Venetian women had to be supported when they appeared on the street wearing them.

Gloves, which were a fashion necessity for both men and women, have had a long and honorable history, dating at least from the well-shaped ones found in King Tutankhamen's tomb. The gloves of early sixteenth century were rather short, with a fold at the wrist; they were subject to the slashing inflicted upon all other garments. Cuts occurred especially on the fingers, to accommodate numerous rings. In mid-century the gloves were finished with pickadils.

The man or woman who sat for a portrait often wore one glove and carried the other. Made of the softest leather and permanently perfumed, they were a fastidious and cherished part of the wardrobe. They could be a pledge of love or a challenge to combat. During the latter part of the century, deep cuffs were added to both men's and women's gloves, usually elaborately embroidered in gold and colored silks (Fig. 341e). The Victoria and Albert Museum has a charming pair of red velvet mittens with deep embroidered gauntlets.

A fashionable accessory, which entered more or less by the back door, so to speak, was the apron. Parmigianino's portrait, *La Bella,* displays a long narrow white apron

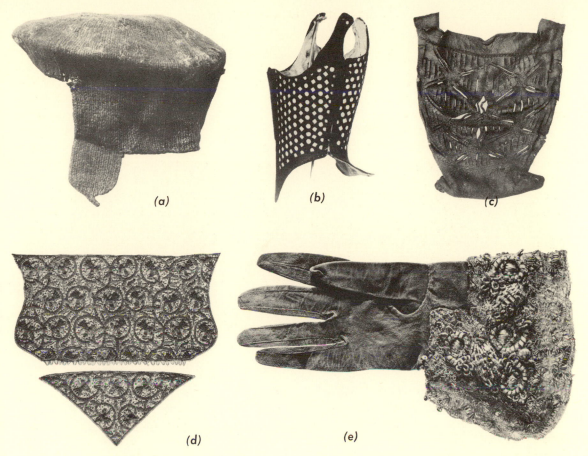

FIG. 341. a. *Knitted Cap. English. Sixteenth Century. (Metropolitan Museum of Art, Bashford Dean Memorial Collection) b. Iron Corset. French or Italian. Seventeenth Century. (Victoria & Albert Museum, Crown Copyright) c. Upper Front of Shoe. First Half of Sixteenth Century. (Metropolitan Museum of Art, Bashford Dean Memorial Collection) d. Two-piece Cap that Belonged to Queen Elizabeth I. c. 1578. e. English Glove with Cuff Decorated with Metal Braid and Embroidery. Late Sixteenth Century. (d and e, Courtesy, Museum of Fine Arts, Boston)*

with horizontal bands of colored outline embroidery. In the late years of the century, apron masterpieces of cutwork and lace sometimes vied with the ruff for attention.

Fans and handkerchiefs were seen frequently in the latter half of the century. Attention was called earlier to the beautiful feather fan of Catherine de Medici. Queen Elizabeth carried a very modern looking folding fan in one of her portraits. The Venetians were partial to a fan of a stiff flag-shaped design.

Handkerchiefs were large and often edged with lace or weighted with beads or buttons at the corners.

14

The Baroque Period:
Men's Costume of the Seventeenth Century

Spain's domination of the fashion world diminished with her loss of power. Under Charles V and Philip II she had prospered from the vast wealth brought back from her discoveries in the Americas. However, much of this was dissipated in warfare, such as in the "Invincible Armada," shattered by storms and defeated by England in 1588. Charles V practically eliminated the Moorish population in southern Spain, the most industrious class in the country; Catholic Inquisition forced many Jews and Moors to flee; finally even Christianized Moors were persecuted. The Thirty Years' War (1618–1648) weakened Spain along with the remainder of Europe, but her contest with France lasted another decade, ending with the Peace of the Pyrenees in 1659, which was sealed with the marriage of the Infanta Maria Theresa, daughter of Philip IV, to Louis XIV of France. This treaty left France in the ascendancy in Europe, and Spain never recovered her lost glory.

Through the wisdom, tolerance, and farsightedness of Henry IV, who reigned from 1589 to 1610, France began to regain the prestige she had lost in the sixteenth century. During the period when Cardinal Richelieu was virtual ruler of France (1624–1642), and after that when Cardinal Mazarin was the chief minister of Louis XIV (1642–1661), she reestablished her leadership.

Germany, the principal battleground of the Thirty Years' War, was left devastated and decimated by the time it ended. England, too, went through revolution and civil war, precipitated by Cromwell. Furthermore, the great plague of 1665 and the great fire of 1666, which burned 450 acres of London, temporarily destroyed any concern England might have had for fashion. France, however, avoided revolution for another 140 years.

Christian IV, of Denmark, being a Lutheran, entered the Thirty Years' War in 1625 on the side of the Protestants, but was also moved by the desire to add territory to his small domain. Later Gustavus II, Adolphus the Great, led his Swedish troops into the fray with a similar mixture of religious conviction and yearning for greater power. Having already acquired territory around the Baltic Sea in a series of three wars, he needed only a foothold on the German coast to give Sweden complete control of this waterway. In 1630 he invaded Germany; though he fought a brilliant and successful campaign, he was killed in the Battle of Lutzen in 1632. Thus deprived of strong leadership, Sweden's gain was fleeting but both Sweden and Denmark emerged from the war as powers to be reckoned with. Their new position was reflected in the smartness of their fashions.

Holland also reached the peak of her glory in the seventeenth century. Her mercantile enterprises flourished around the world, through the Dutch East India Company founded in 1602, and the Dutch West India Company, founded in 1612. At the same time she produced a galaxy of artists: Rubens, Hals, Rembrandt, Ter Borch, Peter de Hooch, and Vermeer, to name only a few. They were rivaled only by Van Dyck, a Flemish artist at the English court, and Velasquez, Zurburan, and El Greco in Spain. Unlike the arrogant aristocrats portrayed by Van Dyck, the Dutch artists painted scenes and subjects which are friendly and communicative.

Fashion illustrators increased in number in this era. Leaders in this field were Hollar in England, and Callot, Bosse, I. D. de St. Jean, Arnoult, and the Bonnarts in France.

Especially important for our understanding of the seventeenth-century fashion pageant is the considerable documentary evidence we have in the form of actual garments of the period. Such collections as those of the Victoria and Albert Museum, the Royal Armoury in Sweden, and the Rosenborg Palace in Denmark are invaluable in reconstructing the scene. Unfortunately for the completeness of the story, while from 1620 onward the story of men's wear in this century is quite clear, little has been preserved of women's costumes.

The high Renaissance of the sixteenth century expanded and burgeoned into the baroque style in art and architecture of the seventeenth, which has been called dazzling, undulating, sinuous, complex, florid, unrestrained, emotional, among other terms. Everything was done on a grand scale: larger, more flamboyant, more voluptuously curved than in the preceding century. This is apparent in costume as well as in art and architecture.

The overlay of jewels of the sixteenth century gave way in the seventeenth to buttons, bows, and lace. This is the century of lace par excellence. During these hundred years needle-point lace evolved from the early simple geometric patterns of *punto in aria* which enhanced ruffs, to deeply scalloped designs, often referred to as collar lace, and thence to the bold and magnificent relief effects of Venetian *gros point* beloved by Charles I. This design, in turn, was reduced to the scale of Venetian rose point. By the end of the century, Venetian needle-point lace had become the finest and most incredible product of the needle: grounded Venetian point, so fragile it seems weightless. Bobbin lace followed the same style changes. The late seventeenth-century *point d'Angleterre* of Brussels has never been excelled.

THE FIRST PERIOD, 1600–1620

The seventeenth century had advanced some years before fashion asserted itself as distinct from its immediate predecessor. There was very little change during the first decade, except that the more fantastic features of the late sixteenth century were modified: the peascod belly was reduced to a rounded point; the ruff shared the limelight with a widening collar, referred to in costume double-talk as the falling band; the skirt of the doublet began to deepen; sleeves became unassumingly natural in outline, the armscye seam still masked by projecting wings. A trim body line persisted, and the front closing was effected by small buttons, closely spaced.

Upper leg covering in the late sixteenth

FIG. 342. *Unknown Artist, Henry Frederick, Prince of Wales, and Sir John Harrington. English. 1603.* (Metropolitan Museum of Art)

century, as we saw in Chapter 12, included bombasted (padded) and paned trunk hose (pumpkin breeches), Venetians, short trunk hose combined with long nether hose or with canions and knee-length stockings, galligaskins, and open-legged short trousers. All of these persisted in the early seventeenth century.

Figure 342 shows Henry, Prince of Wales, and his friend, Sir John Harrington, wearing the doublet described above and rather loose Venetians with stockings drawn up over them. The plumed hat of the young prince, with brim of medium width and

FIG. 343. *Costume Worn at Coronation of James I of England. Peascod Belly Doublet and Hose with Canions. (Victoria & Albert Museum, Crown Copyright)*

rather high crown, is typical. Note the sheer collars (falling bands), lace-edged; these will predominate over the ruff in the second quarter of the century. At the same time Henry's father, James I of England, was painted in open-legged, straight-cut breeches. Boots in this early phase were slender, with turned-back cuffs.

Contemporary with the portrait of Prince Henry is a remarkable costume, rather recently acquired by the Victoria and Albert Museum (Fig. 343), and a most valuable addition to research material. Its documentation indicates that it was worn at the coronation of James I in 1603. It consists of a very rare example of the peascod-belly doublet and trunk hose with matching canions, made of deep burgundy-red voided velvet (the pattern only in pile weave) with background in satin weave. Forty-one buttons close the doublet. The standing collar is 5 to 6 inches high and therefore necessarily flared. The back portion of the collar and the back section of the doublet are cut in one piece.

The trunk hose of this costume are excessively full but not paned, having more in common with galligaskins than with pumpkin breeches. The costume is also unique in that the canions match the trunk hose, probably a more common practice than paintings portray.

In another portrait of the period (Fig. 344) Richard Sackville, an English dandy painted in 1616, exhibits further fashion changes. By this time the peascod outline has completely disappeared, but his waist is sharply pointed in front. His full trunk hose maintain their silhouette by the weight of the fabric and interlining, not by bombast. They appear to be constructed in the same manner as the trunk hose in the Metropolitan Museum collection. Sackville's lower hose are bright blue with elaborate clocks and his shoes are neatly turned, with a well-shaped heel, cutaway instep, and a shoe rose, which replaces or covers the ties which fasten the instep strap.

FIG. 344. *Isaac Oliver, Richard Sackville. English. 1616. (Victoria & Albert Museum, Crown Copyright)*

The whisk—or golilla, as it was called in Spain—was another substitute for the ruff. Beautifully embroidered and often lace-edged, it lay flat on the tilted wire frame (underpropper) which originally supported the ruff. Philip IV decreed that the golilla should replace all other neckwear in Spain; he himself wore it in numerous portraits, one of which is reproduced in Fig. 345.

An earlier portrait of this same Philip

(Fig. 346) illustrates the conservative tendencies of Spanish dress at this period. The huge ruff has not yet been replaced by the golilla, and his padded trunk hose and cape show little change from the preceding century. The lengthened skirt of his doublet and the squared toes of his shoes are the most notable innovations.

Note the sword belt in Fig. 346, which remains unchanged. In the more robust period to follow it will be replaced by the baldric (see Fig. 369b).

DENMARK

A portrait of Denmark's revered Christian IV shows the costume which prevailed over most of Europe during the 1620s. Pinked slashes in the fabric form regular patterns. His doublet is like that in Fig. 344, the skirt still narrow and tabbed, the front flat and closely buttoned. His trousers are the galligaskins of the sixteenth century, very full and bloused in bloomer fashion. Again and again these appeared in country after country, as the predominating style.

The huge military sash was an important accessory, and not only in Denmark. Chris-

FIG. 345. *The Gollila. 1625. Redrawn from Velasquez, Portrait of Philip IV of Spain. (Metropolitan Museum of Art)*

FIG. 346. *Rodrigo de Villandrando, Philip IV of Spain. c. 1615–1620. (Prado Museum, A. Y. R. Mas Photograph)*

FIG. 347. *Prince Christian of Denmark. c.1620. Redrawn from Portrait of Prince Christian by Unknown Artist. (National Historic Museum, Frederiksborg, Denmark)*

tian's son, Crown Prince Christian, wore his tied high in the back (Fig. 347). The huge loop of the bow extends well above his left shoulder and the ends fall almost to his knees. A photograph of one end of the military sash Charles I of England wore in 1642 is shown in Fig. 369e.

SWEDEN

Gustavus II, Adolphus the Great, to give him the title used in Sweden—won his

FIG. 348. *Purple and Gold Costume of Gustavus II, Adolphus the Great. 1620. (Royal Armoury, Stockholm)*

Fig. 349. Frans Hals, Laughing Cavalier. 1624. Reproduced by Permission of the Trustees of the Wallace Collection, London.

country's enduring respect both by his leadership in war and by his progressive policy in government at home. It was, then, with both deference and excitement that the present author measured and recorded his truly regal costume, dated 1620, in the Royal Armoury in Stockholm (Fig. 348 and Draft 7).

The trousers and jerkin of this costume are of purple broadcloth embroidered in gold, the doublet of matching purple satin. Their perfect synchronization here accounts for the difficulty we often have in distinguishing one from the other in sixteenth- and seventeenth-century portraits. In the photograph reproduced here the doublet sleeves emerge through the open front seams of the jerkin sleeves. The closing of the jerkin is unique in its diagonal direction from center front to underarm. Shapes and proportions are best delineated by the scale drawing of the pattern draft. (Figure 369d shows a collar worn by Gustavus Adolphus.)

1620–1630

In addition to the ruff, the golilla and the falling band, a fourth variety of neckwear (shown in Fig. 349) was a limp or unstarched ruff, which must have been a great relief from the older style. The cavalier costume in this Frans Hals painting is closely associated with England also. New too, is the vertical slashing of the doublet over the chest, the shoulder blades, and the upper part of the sleeve. Draft 8 is the pattern of a similar doublet in the Museum of Decorative Arts of the Louvre. This slashing exposed the shirt to view once more, thus giving it greater importance. The cavalier's deep lace-trimmed cuffs are shown turned down over the hand. His military sash is of fashionable dimensions. His broad-brimmed hat, cocked and set at a rakish angle, was worn also by cavaliers of England and musketeers of France (Fig. 350).

A 1629 portrait of Charles I of England

FIG. 350. *Back View of Cavalier. 1629. Redrawn from Bosse, French Male Costume. (Victoria & Albert Museum, Crown Copyright)*

(Fig. 351) shows further development of the costume of the cavalier. The trousers are slimmed down more nearly to the dimensions of the sixteenth-century close Venetians and the knee-length breeches which appear later, in the eighteenth century. Points passed through eyelets of both lower hose and breeches hold them together.

It was the fashion at this time to wear the hair long falling upon the shoulders; still longer strands on the left made the "love

FIG. 351. *Daniel Mytens, Charles I of England.* 1629. *(Metropolitan Museum of Art)*

lock." This hair style is variously accounted for. One reason often cited for the fashion is that Louis XIII of France had beautiful hair and fancied it in flowing waves. When it was no longer either beautiful or flowing he resorted to a wig, thus starting another fashion which gained momentum through the century and endured for yet another one. Only when the limp ruff and falling band replaced the starched ruff and whisk was it really feasible to wear the hair long.

As evidenced in many paintings of the period, a pointed beard, ranging from the small tuft on Hals' cavalier to much larger ones on other men, was often combined with a mustache. Van Dyck's subjects wore this fashion so often that the pointed beard is still referred to as a Van Dyck.

The seventeenth century is marked also by the popularity of boots, which were worn indoors as well as out, and were spurred whether or not their wearers ever went near a horse. The large quatrefoil spur strap worn by Charles I in Fig. 351 draws attention to the boot; the turned-down top reversed on itself foretokens even greater emphasis upon footwear in succeeding periods. Figure 369f shows an English shoe of the reign of Charles I.

1630–1650

THE DOUBLET. During the 1640s several changes occurred in the doublet that persisted until mid-century. First of all, it took on an easy appearance. The waistline was raised and straightened somewhat. The rosette-like arrangement of the points around the waistline was purely decorative, the breeches being supported by hooks on the trouser band which engaged eyelets on an

FIG. 352. *Abraham Bosse, The Ball. 1635. (Metropolitan Museum of Art, Whittelsey Fund)*

inside belt of the doublet. Doublet skirts lengthened noticeably and were cut in fewer sections. The deep front point disappeared. Sleeves shortened and widened, the front seam often being left open to reveal the shirt. In the 1640s, as the doublet shortened, the upper part of the trousers was more exposed, and they were given a smoother, more professional fit. In general, they straightened, lengthened, and widened slightly in the leg.

THE SHIRT. Shirts became more important as they became more visible. They were cut with much fullness through both body and sleeves. The one worn by Charles I at his execution (by his request a warm one, so that he would not shiver from the cold and thus give the impression that he was shaking with fear) is of firm linen embroidered with openwork and embellished with tiny ribbon bows.[1]

DECORATION. These three decades were a period of excessive trimming, in the form of rows and rows of braid or dozens of buttons placed along the sides of the trousers, the edges of the doublet, and sleeve openings (see Fig. 352). Wider and more elaborate lace glorified the enlarged collars and cuffs; as boot tops spread and boot hose became an important accessory, lace lay incongruously against the leather.

FOOTWEAR. Indoor wear on more formal occasions was chiefly the low-cut shoe, more open, square-toed, with blocky, heightened heel and elaborate shoe rose over the instep. But boots competed with these low shoes in popularity, even at the ball painted by Abraham Bosse (Fig. 352). The widened boot top, folded down and reversed, must have forced an awkward gait in the wearer, but it was nevertheless favored as an added surface for the display of elegantly trimmed boot hose (Fig. 353). A Swedish portrait shows circles of scalloped

[1] Mary Symonds Antrobus, *Needlecraft Through the Ages*, Hodder, London, 1928, p. 288.

FIG. 353. *August, Duke of Brunswick, 1636. (Metropolitan Museum of Art) Georg Hirth, Kulturgeschtliches Bilderbuch aus drei Jahrhunderten, Vol. III, Plate 1136.*

organdy lying layer upon layer within the boot top.

THE BALDRIC. The narrow sword belt worn earlier was now replaced by the baldric. This was a long wide strap, often embroidered, worn over the right shoulder to support the sword under the left arm (Figs. 369b, 354, and 359). Spur straps reached their zenith in this period (Fig. 354). With spurs jangling and swords clattering, a group of night revelers must have been a raucous lot.

in place.[2] Though some of these wrapped garments had short sleeves they are seldom shown in use (Fig. 354).

Figure 355 shows another form of mantle, an actual garment in the Rijksmuseum, Amsterdam. Here the sections covering the arms can be unbuttoned from the back and front panels, and the whole rebuttoned to form a sleeved overcoat.

The seventeenth-century cassock from the Cooper Union collection, shown in Fig. 356, is a long, practical overcoat which was probably widely worn by all classes. Certainly the swaggering blade of Fig. 350 would have been quite uncomfortable in zero weather.

Soldiers were provided with buff coats made of deerskin of various lengths, sleeved or sleeveless. These would surely have furnished excellent insulation against wind and cold. Like the cassock, they no doubt, formed a functional part of many laymen's wardrobes.

[2] Kelly and Schwabe, *Historic Costume*, Batsford, London, 1925, p. 126.

FIG. 354. *Henry II of Lorraine. c.1640. Redrawn from His Portrait by Van Dyck. (National Gallery of Art, Washington, D.C., Gift of Cornelius Vanderbilt Whitney)*

OUTER WRAPS. Capes remained the most popular outer garment all during these decades. They were longer than the sixteenth-century Spanish capes and some, at least, were cut on a full circle (see Fig. 357). They were usually worn resting naturally upon both shoulders, as Fig. 353 shows. In fine weather, however, Frenchmen preferred slinging it over the left shoulder and under the right arm, as shown in Fig. 350; cords attached to the underside secured it firmly

FIG. 355. *Outer Wrap. Seventeenth Century. Redrawn from Photograph of Original Dutch Garment. (Rijksmuseum, Amsterdam)*

FRANCE

Figure 352 gives a remarkable picture of high fashion in France during the mid-thirties. Among the features to observe are the doublet with raised waistline, longer skirts, numerous decorative points, and profusion of buttons; the wide falling band with deep collar lace; the open sleeve seam revealing the shirt; deep lace-trimmed cuffs (still known as cavalier cuffs); wide sash-like garters knotted in large bows below the knee; square-toed low dress shoes with fluffy shoe roses; boots with spurs held in place with quatrefoil straps; pantofles—the protective footwear worn by the gentleman at the right; longer hair in loose curls, with love locks accented by ribbon bows; slashing of center back, sleeves (upper or lower), and front of the doublet; dashing, plumed broad-brimmed hats, definitely cocked on one or both sides. Baldrics and sleeved cloaks are also in evidence.

FIG. 356. *Cassock. Seventeenth Century. Redrawn from Original Garment. (Cooper Union Collection)*

ENGLAND

Figure 357 shows a chartreuse satin costume from the Victoria and Albert Museum collection, dated about 1630. Draft 9 is the pattern for it. This is a handsome ensemble, remarkably fresh in appearance. The cape is cut on a full circle; a straight square-cornered collar, now missing, was originally mounted to the neckline. A residue of the old Spanish rigidity persists. The doublet is interlined with heavy green satin and lined with chartreuse satin. The stiff high-standing collar is $\frac{1}{4}$ inch thick. Three doublets of this period, carefully inspected and drawn to scale by the present author, all have triangular pieces of stiffening along the lower front edges of the doublet; in tailor's language these were called belly pieces. In the doublet of Fig. 357 this stiffening was about $\frac{3}{16}$ inch thick and slightly flexible, like heavy cardboard. In a black serge doublet dated between 1630 and 1640, wood provided the stiffening. Draft 9 shows its size and position.

The trousers of the chartreuse costume of Fig. 357 are shaped for comfort through the crotch and smoothness in the lower leg. The most astonishing feature of the costume as a whole is the infinitely detailed strap work which encrusts the entire surface of the doublet and hose and covers most of the surface of the cape. Draft 9 shows this detail.

A portrait of the Duke of Brunswick dated 1636 (Fig. 353) suggests some approaching fashion changes. The doublet, for instance, is cut without a waist seam and fits easily. The trousers are shorter and open-legged; loops of ribbon finish the lower edges. Boot tops, emphasized by lace-trimmed boot hose, are more swashbuckling.

Van Dyck's portrait of Henry II of Lorraine, Duc de Guise, made about 1640, shows him wearing a jerkin or doublet with no waist seam (Fig. 354). The front edges are laced together over his chest but spread apart the rest of the way. This is about the

FIG. 357. *Verney Costume of Chartreuse Satin. c.1630.*
(Victoria & Albert Museum, Crown Copyright)

earliest evidence of uncovering the waist portion of the shirt. Henry's triple-layered cuff is also new. His collar, capping the shoulder, effaces the armscye wing, which has finally disappeared, after serving for nearly a century to mask the juncture of sleeve and garment. Henry's spur straps must have set a record for size. His barbering is impeccable, and he wears a two-color ribbon bow on his love lock. His hat has the proper elements of elegance and bravado.

DENMARK

The magnificent costume collection in Rosenborg Palace contains an example of some further evolution of the mode of the moment (Fig. 358). This handsome ensemble, made of light-blue satin and dated 1645, was in the wardrobe of Crown Prince Christian. It is so completely covered with rows of contiguous silver braid that the satin is all but obscured. Linings are of blue silk woven with silver, and silver lace highlights all edges. A noticeable change has occurred in the design of the doublet and trousers. The former is much shorter, tending toward a high waistline but still retaining a short tabbed skirt. The sleeves are decidedly abbreviated. The prince's breeches resemble those of Fig. 357 except that they are wider in the leg. They are supported by hooks

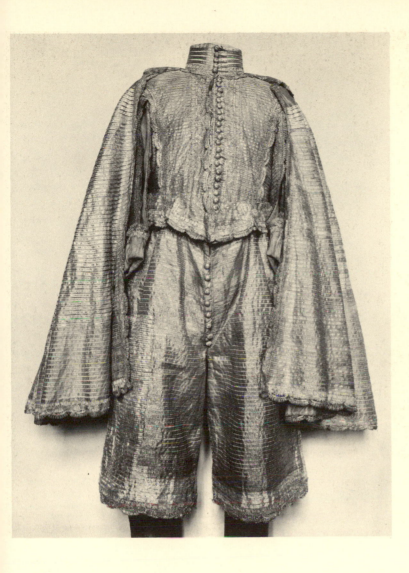

Fig. 358. *Costume of Prince Christian. 1645. (Rosenborg Palace, Copenhagen)*

which connect with four pairs of straps attached to the waistband of the doublet. The front closing is plainly apparent.

Another costume of the same year in the collection is similar in form. It is made of black silk, brocaded in gold, with doublet and cape lined with reddish violet satin. Edges and seams are finished with gold lace.

GERMANY

The portrait of Gustav Adolph, Prince of Mecklenberg-Bustrow (Fig. 359), illustrates the German interpretation of the mode in the middle fifties, a transition to the following period. Although tentatively dated 1655, his costume is more in the spirit of the late forties. The new cut of his doublet is accompanied by spreading breeches which now reach only to the knees. A huge triangle of ribbon loops covering the front opening and bulky rosettes of loops at the sides of the legs indicate the increasing importance of such decoration.

His small, square-cornered collar is notable only for the ornate tasseled cords which fasten it. Here again is the baldric, broad and splendidly embroidered, in keeping with the lavish and technically perfect needlework on doublet, breeches, and gloves. Boots, boot hose which appear to be finished with two ruffles of wide Flemish lace, and

FIG. 359. *Broder Matthiesen. Prince Gustav Adolph of Mecklenborg-Gustrow. c.1655. (National Historic Museum, Frederiksborg, Denmark)*

silk stockings exhibit concern for high fashion. The prince's richly plumed high-crowned hat with jeweled band is cradled carefully in the crook of his arm.

1650–1670

In 1650 we face the moot question as to whether men actually wore skirts at this time. So far as the author has been able to determine, no specimen of a true skirt has been preserved, though there are several examples of very full breeches. These were called Rhinegraves because they originated along the Rhine; they were also called petticoat breeches because of their appearance. Whether constructed as a divided skirt or not, the garment is fantastically unmasculine.

Until well after World War I, a related form of trouser survived in Hungary, especially in the village of Meskovesd, where the older men still wore long white linen trousers, so full they could easily have passed for skirts. Upon the occasion of the rededication of the Cathedral of Djakovo in northern Jugoslavia in 1937, dozens of young men appeared in white trousers trimmed with embroidery and lace and similarly decorated shirts falling in full folds about their hips. In neither case was there anything feminine about the character of the wearers. Both folk costumes seem to be vestigial forms of mid-seventeenth-century high fashion. On the other hand the fustanella—a short very full white skirt of Albania and Greece, still in use—is a true skirt, measuring as much as 36 yards around the lower edge.

The baroque trousers style of the seventeenth century had the appearance of a full short skirt varying in length from above the knee to the lower calf; or of a shorter skirt below which a trousered undergarment or extension was gathered in to fit the leg, giving the effect of bloomers showing below the outer garment (Figs. 360, 361, 362, and 363).

As we have noted, full gathered trousers known as galligaskins or Dutchmen's breeches were familiar in the late sixteenth and early seventeenth centuries. Petticoat breeches, however, were totally different, due not only to the open leg but also to the texture, color, and trimming used. Enthusiasts speak of hundreds of yards of ribbon used on a single costume.[3] The amount used on the Verney costume of 1660 in the Victoria and Albert Museum (Fig. 360) is

[3] Von Boehn, *Modes and Manners*, Lippincott, 1932, vol. III, p. 139.

Fig. 361. *German Petticoat Breeches. c.1650. (Metropolitan Museum of Art, Rogers Fund) Redrawn from* Deutsches Leben der Vergangenheit in Bildern, *Vol. II, Plate 1101.*

Fig. 360. *Verney Costume with Petticoat Breeches. c.1660. (Victoria & Albert Museum, Crown Copyright)*

certainly impressive. Here the ribbons vary in color, width, and weave; but all are subtle and beautiful and the tailor was not niggardly in the amount used. The long loops are massed at the waistline and on the sides of the legs. The fabric is deep beige and ivory

Fig. 362. *Flemish Petticoat Breeches. c.1670. (Metropolitan Museum of Art, Dick Fund) Redrawn from Romeyn de Hooghe,* Figures à la Mode, *Plate 9.*

FIG. 363. *Flemish Costume. c.1670. (Metropolitan Museum of Art, Dick Fund) Redrawn from Romeyn de Hooghe,* Figures à la Mode, *Plate 3,* Cavalier Walking.

nized with the prissy look of the petticoat breeches. Doublets were curtailed to bolero proportions—a form still worn in Moravia, Czechoslovakia, prior to World War II. Sleeves shrank to elbow length, allowing the ruffled sleeves of the shirt to puff over the forearms.

The wig increased in volume and in length, and hence necessitated a change in the shape of the collar. Since the neckwear had to be visible in order to be appreciated, the pattern was altered from the even width of the old form to a narrow section across the back with rectangular tabs of varying depths extending downward in front. Those

figured silk; the ribbons are white, beige with pink and black center stripes, lavender with beige design, grayed chartreuse, pale blue, and grayed orange. There can be no doubt about the cut of the costume, which is shown in Draft 10. Each leg measures 61½ inches in circumference, the two together having a sweep of at least 3 yards, after discounting the distance between the legs. The breeches of two costumes in the Rosenborg Palace collection in Copenhagen are similar in cut to those of the Verney collection.

The remainder of the costume harmo-

FIG. 364. *Young Man in Simplified Costume. German. 1662. Redrawn from Christian Wolfgang Heimback,* Young Man. *(National Portrait Gallery, London)*

of Venetian *gros point* were handsome indeed (see Fig. 369*a*).

The high-crowned narrow-brimmed hats, even when plumed, lacked the dash of their predecessors. Shoe roses were now retired in favor of a very wide stiff bow, while the display of finery within the bucket-topped boots was replaced by deep gathered cannons—wide ruffles sometimes edged with lace or made entirely of lace. These hung down from the kneecap over the calf of the leg. Masculinity in costume reached an all-time low at this time (see Fig. 366).

However, there were also those who dressed more simply—the Puritans, for example. Figure 364, dated 1662, presents a less exotic spectacle. A German youth is shown in a steeple-crowned hat, prim collar, elegant in its simplicity, and a plain doublet. He wears his mantle in French fashion.

HOLLAND

The Dutch have documented this period richly in such paintings as Vermeer's *Glass of Wine*, Van den Temple's *Nobleman and Wife in their Park*, Jan Steen's *The Dancing Couple*, R. de Hoogh's *Signing the Treaty of Breda*, Van Tilborgh's *The Repast*, Rembrandt's *The Syndics of the Draper's Guild*, Van der Helst's *A Young Couple*, and Ter Borch's *The Letter*, *The Concert*, and *The Suitor's Visit*. Probably the best example is Ter Borch's *Portrait of a Gentleman* in the National Gallery in London (Fig. 365). From the tip of his hat crown to his square-toed shoes, every detail of this gentleman is in the approved fashion.

FRANCE

The rich French tapestries of the era give many glimpses of the court life of Louis XIV, whose love of splendor and elaboration in costume is legendary. This has been explained as compensation for an inferiority complex, induced by neglect during

Fig. 365. *Terborch, Portrait of a Gentleman. c.1660. (National Gallery, London)*

his early childhood.[4] The ostentation of the Sun King's court is clearly revealed in a 1660 Gobelin tapestry which records his meeting, accompanied by his entourage, with Philip IV of Spain at the Isle of Pheasants (Fig. 366). Here Louis is arrayed in full wig, bolero-like doublet, vast expanse of shirt, petticoat breeches with masses of ribbon loops, cannons of ridiculous proportions, and the high-heeled shoes with broad flat bows which had caught his fancy. He carries his flat-brimmed plumed hat, no

[4] Sisley Huddleston, "Louis XIV in Love and in War," *The Book League Monthly*, May, 1929, pp. 31, 59.

doubt in deference to the occasion; but the habit of carrying hats became increasingly popular as wigs burgeoned in height and bulk. Other innovations deserving notice during this period and evident in the tapestry are the square-tabbed collars worn by the French courtiers, the lengthened cape of the gentleman immediately back of the king, and the long straight coat on the second figure from the left.

The French costume in this scene is in marked contrast to the old-fashioned apparel of Philip IV of Spain, and provides an eloquent comment on the changing political positions of the two countries.

The coat of the French courtier just cited in Fig. 366 is the new mode in its initial phase as high fashion. Narrow in cut

and reaching almost to the knees, it differs drastically from the doublet except for its abbreviated sleeves. A closer study of the record than can be detailed here reveals that a similar coat, much like the cassock shown in Fig. 356, had been in use continuously since 1630. The most exciting example of this early long coat encountered by the author was again in the Rosenborg Palace collection (Fig. 367 and Draft 11). Dating about 1655, it belonged to King Frederick III of Denmark. It is made of handsome brownish-gray wool fabric with embroidered borders and lace of gold thread; its full-length sleeves are entirely covered with vertical rows of gold embroidery. The breeches are short and wide, similar to those of Figs. 358 and 359.

FIG. 366.   Detail from Gobelin Tapestry: Meeting of Louis XIV of France and Philip IV of Spain on Isle of Pheasants. 1660. (Versailles National Museum)

FIG. 367. *Costume of King Frederick III of Denmark. c.1655. (Rosenborg Palace, Copenhagen)*

During a comparatively brief period—from about 1650 to 1665—the short doublet enjoyed considerable popularity among high-fashion addicts. It could never have served the functional purpose of warmth, however, and when its novelty wore off, the more practical coat came forth again—not as martial as the leather buff coat or as unpretentious as the cassock, but a garment of great style, made of fine fabric and richly decorated.

About this same time, 1666, Charles II of England made an unsuccessful attempt to introduce a looser, more flowing outer garment based on Persian robes. There was a certain relationship between the French and English modes, however, and out of this trend came the coat and waistcoat of the last decades of the seventeenth century. These persisted through the entire eighteenth century with easily traceable permutations. The suit coat and vest of the nineteenth and twentieth centuries are their direct descendants.

THE SEVENTIES

With the course toward coat and waistcoat set during the sixties it remained for the following years to give them definite form. Quite straight, short-sleeved, and collarless at first, they depended for attraction upon richness of fabric and ornamentation.

Ter Borch's portrait of Francois de Vicq dated 1670, (Fig. 368), documents the transition from mid-century to late seventeenth-century men's wear. The lengthened coat is still short-sleeved and has contrasting up-turned cuffs. Dozens of buttons lie along the front closing but the coat is worn unfastened, with the edges folded back to form long slender revers. These early coats were provided with horizontal pockets of the slashed type without flap or welt. The usual position was low, within a few inches of the bottom of the coat. Nonfunctional buttonholes were placed above the opening, buttons below. The waistcoat, a fashion revived from the fourteenth century when the pourpoint was worn under the cotehardie, and from the early seventeenth century, when the doublet was paired with the jerkin, once again assumed a major role. In the early phase of its revival illustrated here it is buttoned closely from neck to waist and reaches well down over the hips; its sleeves are slightly longer than those of the coat. The ruffled lace-trimmed cuff covers the bend of the elbow, leaving a generous amount of the shirt sleeve on view. The lace is repeated down the front.

FIG. 368. *Terborch, Francois de Vicq. 1670. (Rijksmuseum, Amsterdam)*

ACCESSORIES. The cravat, a linen strip usually ending in lace, encircled the neck and was held in place by a ribbon bow at the throat. Figure 368 shows it in its simplest form. The cravat[5] is said to have been adopted from the neckwear of a regiment of Croatian soldiers—cravat being an old form of Croat—enlisted since 1636 in the service of the French crown. In the villages near Zagreb, Croatia, until at least World War II, men's neckties consisted of a square kerchief folded in half diagonally and then repeatedly folded parallel to the first fold until a narrow tie was formed. This was placed around the neck and tied neatly into a bow knot.

Fairholt[6] says that the "cravat succeeded the ruff and band [collar] and was generally

[5] Von Boehn, *op. cit.*, p. 144.

[6] F. W. Fairholt, *Costume in England*, G. Bell, London, 1896, vol. II, p. 295.

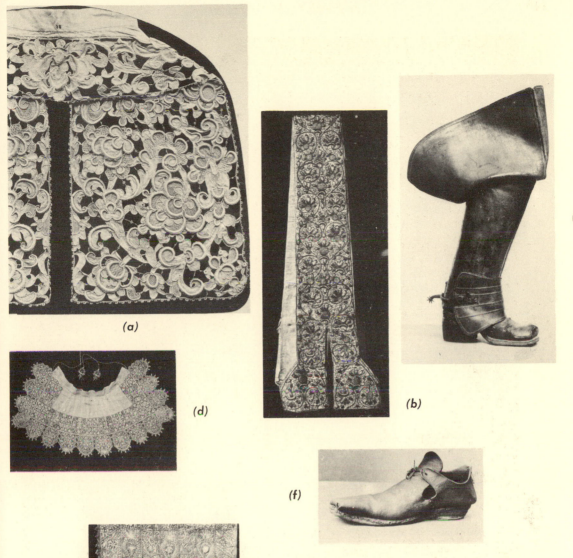

FIG. 369. *Men's Accessories. a. Collar, Venetian Gros Point. Italian. Third Quarter, Seventeenth Century. b. Embroidered Silk Baldric. Seventeenth Century. c. Leather Boot with Broad Top. English. Middle or Second Half of Seventeenth Century. (a, b, and c, Victoria & Albert Museum, Crown Copyright) d. Collar Embroidered with Reticella and Edged with Punto-in-aria Lace, Worn by Gustavus II, Adolphus the Great. c.1630. (Royal Armoury, Stockholm) e. English Military Scarf of Purple Silk Embroidered with Silver Gilt and Silver Threads and Colored Silks, Worn by Charles I. 1642. f. Leather Shoe with Latchets. English. Reign of Charles I, 1625–1649. (e and f, Victoria & Albert Museum, Crown Copyright)*

worn during the reign of Charles II [1660–1685], by whom it was introduced from France." He adds a quotation from Evelyn to the effect that this took place during the 1660s.

An ivory-topped cane, flat-brimmed hat with lowered crown, and narrow sash complete the visible part of the gentleman's costume. Note his natural hair, worn long and softly waved.

Cannons remained in use for some time. The shoes retained the flat bow into the early seventies (note the boot in Fig. 369c). The hat, not always as restrained as the one in Fig. 368, continued to sport jaunty plumage. The cocking of the brim which produced the tricorne began at this time.

THE EIGHTIES

Sir Thomas Isham's wedding suit of 1680, now in the Victoria and Albert collection (Fig. 370), suggests the coat's simplicity of cut in its earlier years. Sir Thomas' narrow sleeves are longer than those in the preceding decade, and his cuffs assume impressive proportions, a characteristic which endured well into the next century. The horizontal pockets of his coat are still quite low and are generously provided with buttons, as are the front opening and side vents (Draft 12).

The trousers of Sir Thomas' suit are unique in that the wide legs are finished with flared cuffs cut in three sections, which are turned up and caught at the points of their outer edges. Pattern Draft 12 shows how this was accomplished. Additions at the bottoms of the trouser legs extend under the hose and create a bloomer effect. In the light of this authentic example of a separately cut extension attached to the lower edge of the trousers which would create a bloused or bloomer effect when worn, is it not possible that a comparable combination might have produced the skirt and bloomer look of Figs. 361, 363 and 366 (man at left)?

By the mid-eighties the lines of the coat were further altered, the waistline being indicated and the skirt flared by additional width at the side seams of the front and back sections. This is illustrated in St. Jean's portrait of Louis XIV (Fig. 371). This extra fullness was formed into fan-shaped pleats which were steadied by stitching that was hidden by a large button. Descendants of these buttons are still to be seen on men's formal wear.

FIG. 370. *Sir Thomas Isham's Wedding Suit. 1680. (Victoria & Albert Museum, Crown Copyright)*

FIG. 371. *J. D. de St. Jean, Louis XIV. 1680's. (Metropolitan Museum of Art, Whittelsey Fund)*

Long vertical pockets made their appearance in the mid-eighties and the coat was seldom closed except at the waistline. Sleeves usually ended at mid-forearm, thus making the huge cuffs more manageable while still allowing a display of shirt sleeve.

ACCESSORIES. Several other details of the King's costume shown in Fig. 371 are worthy of note. His hat is cocked on two sides and the plumes either lie flat against the inside of the brim or the fronds are attached in such a way that they rise above the lace- or braid-trimmed edge. The lace ends of his cravat emerge from under the spreading multiple loops of ribbon at his throat. A plain baldric supports his sword. His gloves have wide flaring gauntlets finished with deep fringe; fringe also edges the front and bottom edges of the waistcoat, which has lengthened perceptibly.

Breeches have all but disappeared from view, with the hose covering the knees in reversed folds.

The great King's shoes are more ornate than is usual, but their contour is in the current mode—square toes, high reversed tongue, lowered blocky red heel (a color restricted to the court), and narrow instep straps fastened by small buckles.

A novelty of the eighties was a coat cuff that was relatively narrow against the inner portion of the sleeve but widened rapidly at the elbow in a circular flare which fell in deep folds to the wrist (Fig. 372).

An alternate to the exposed shirt sleeve was a long fitted sleeve on the waistcoat, like that worn by St. Jean's Homme de Qualité. A man of obvious status, he wears a striped wool suit with fashion features which will continue for many years: a decided increase in the sweep of the coat, echoed by greatly

Fig. 373. *Costume of King Frederick IV of Denmark. 1695. (Rosenborg Palace, Copenhagen)*

enlarged cuffs; upright tongue of the shoe; disappearance of the baldric in civilian attire; shirt following the trousers into obscurity, with only wrist ruffles remaining in view; the waistcoat only slightly shorter than the outer coat and provided with buttons its full length. There is harmony among the component features of the costume and a pleasingly less cluttered surface.

THE CLOSING DECADE OF THE CENTURY

In the nineties the final seal was set upon the style which was to continue with only slight variations during the following 20 to 25 years.

The suit pictured in Fig. 373 was worn by King Frederick IV of Denmark during

Fig. 372. *Detail of Coat Cuff. 1684. Redrawn from H. Bonnart, Le Cavalier bien mis. (Metropolitan Museum of Art, Dick Fund)*

the ceremonies marking his marriage to Princess Louise of Mecklenburg in 1695. This suit gives us an appreciation of the grandeur of the late baroque period. His coat and breeches are of red velvet, the coat being lavishly embroidered in silver in pure baroque design. Its lining of light-blue silk and silver cloth harmonizes with the waistcoat of blue and silver brocade. Horizontal pockets on both coat and waistcoat are provided with elaborate flaps. There is a great increase in the flare of his coat, which is controlled by deep fan pleats. His full-length sleeves gradually increase in width toward the wrist, ending in deep, wide, solidly embroidered cuffs. A more magnificent ensemble is difficult to imagine.

THE CRAVAT. Inspired by an event of 1692, a new method arose of arranging the cravat. At the battle of Steinkirk, French soldiers, caught by surprise in an early dawn

FIG. 375. *French Costume. 1678. Redrawn from N. Bonnart, Homme de Qualité en Manteau. (Bibliothèque Nationale)*

attack, knotted their cravats quickly, twisting the ends and tucking them through a high buttonhole of the coat. Planché[7] says: "In commemoration of the victory achieved by the Mareschal of Luxembourg over the Prince of Orange on that day, a similar negligent mode of wearing the cravat obtained for it the name of a 'steinkerque'" (Fig. 374). Even the ladies wore it. In this fad the cravat was lengthened to give it proper éclat and it was often lace-trimmed. A Largillière portrait in the Wallace Col-

FIG. 374. *Steinkirk, 1690's. Redrawn from N. Bonnart, Louis, Marquis de Bade. (Metropolitan Museum of Art, Dick Fund)*

[7] J. R. Planché, *Encyclopaedia of Costume*, Chatto & Windus, Ltd., London, 1876, vol. I, p. 143.

Fig. 376. *French Costume. 1689. Redrawn from J. D. de St. Jean, Homme de Qualité. (Victoria & Albert Museum, Crown Copyright)*

Fig. 377. *Overcoat Called Brandenburg. 1675– 1679. Redrawn from N. Bonnart, Casaque à la Brandebourg. (The Pierpont Morgan Library)*

lection (eighteenth century) shows one that seems to be made entirely of lace, ending in tassels of pearls (see Fig. 412).

THE WIG. The beautifully dressed full-bottomed wig worn by the gentleman in Fig. 374 represents close to the largest size

wigs ever reached. However, Fairholt[8] quotes a comment of the day which is enlightening: ". . . one whose periwig 'was large enough to have loaded a camel and he

[8] F. W. Fairholt, *Costume in England*, 4th ed., G. Bell, London, 1885, vol. I, p. 346.

bestowed upon it at least a bushel of powder'; he adds that his long lace cravat 'was
most agreeably discolored with snuff from
top to bottom.' "

Thus by the nineties the fashion of
powdering the wig was established. Much
criticism was leveled at the practice, with
the usual negative result. The untidy dredg-
ing of the shoulders came under fire also.

THE HAT. The perfectly formed tricorne hat will persist throughout the next
century. The coat sleeves having reached the
wrist, gloves became less spectacular and
were subordinated to the huge cuffs.
Tongues of shoes subsided to more rational
dimensions also.

OUTER WEAR OF THE LATE
SEVENTEENTH CENTURY

In the late seventies Bonnart drew a
gentleman wearing a cape with rounded collar, its front edges richly embroidered (Fig.
375). Figure 376, dated 1689, shows a Beau
Brummell wearing a somewhat fuller cape
with the right side lifted and thrown over
the left shoulder, muffling his face and
throat. This gesture may have been for
warmth (he wears a muff suspended from
his belt, a possible indication of cold
weather), a form of disguise, or sheer brag-
gadocio.

A more popular wrap was the Brandenburg, illustrated in Fig. 377. Extending to
the calf and providing easy fullness, it was
a comfortable, practical overcoat, modestly
ornamented with braid. It was adopted
during the seventies from the great coat
worn by soldiers from Brandenburg, a powerful province in Germany. The typical
braiding which formed its closing device
came in time to be called a brandenburg, re-
gardless of the garment or the use.

With the aging of Louis XIV and the
dampening influence of the extreme piety,
assumed or real, of Madame de Maintenon,
his second wife, the varied diversions which
earlier had kept the noble guests at Versailles
entertained and the king in a perpetual round
of activity tended to disappear. Colors became somber, with black predominating.
There was little incentive to create new
fashions and a curious quiet closed a tur-
bulent century.

15

Women's Costume of the Seventeenth Century

1600–1630

SKIRTS AND BODICES. For women as for men, the sixteenth century passed into the early seventeenth with little change in modes. Enormous skirts were either drum-, dome-, or cone-shaped. Drum-shaped skirts were supported by a series of hoops mounted to firm fabric and anchored at right angles to the waistline. A pleated cartwheel ruffle often extended from the waistline to the drum-like edge (see Fig. 383). A dome-shaped skirt was created by fastening a padded roll resembling an automobile tire around the body just below the waistline (Fig. 378). In Spain the cone shape, based on a hooped petticoat of that form, persisted through this period.

The rigid bodices fitted like skin over closely boned or metal corsets (Figs. 379 and 411*a*). Padded leg-of-mutton sleeves were worn until about 1610, when a more slender sleeve became fashionable. However, the Spanish mode of long free-hanging sleeves was retained in Spain, Italy, and the Lowlands. Though Spain was rapidly losing the race for power, she still maintained her prestige in fashion, especially in Italy. Paolo

Adorno, illustrated in Fig. 380, and other Genoese ladies by Van Dyck, show strong Spanish influence.

The front of the waistline was definitely modified during these years by the abrupt jutting of the skirt; with the dome-shaped skirt it dipped to a sharper point than with the other skirt styles. The conical outline retained by ladies under Spanish influence permitted a long extension of the waistline, as illustrated in Fig. 380. The dominant feature of the Dutch costume was a long, broad stomacher of lighter, richer fabric than that of the gown or else splendidly embroidered (Fig. 381).

By 1620 hoops and rolls began to lose their charm. For the first time in a hundred years the fabric was allowed to fall naturally from waist to hem. In the transition from enormous to normal, the outer skirt was often pulled up and caught casually about the hips, providing extra volume but adding a bit of zest by deliberately exposing the underskirt as on the lady on the right in Fig. 382. These petticoats—of satin or other silk fabrics, lined with contrasting colors and in some cases trimmed with gold lace—

FIG. 378. *Caricature of Feminine Costume. Dutch. 1610. Detail Redrawn from Anonymous Engraving. (Metropolitan Museum of Art)*

were worthy of being on parade and during the next century and a half they played an increasingly important role. In Hollar's drawing, *Winter* (see Fig. 394), the proud lady displays two underskirts quite impartially. The fad offered great color possibilities and the women of the first half of the century enjoyed it and indulged their liking for it.

NECKWEAR. The first half of the seventeenth century is noted for the infinite variety of its ruffs, collars, and kerchiefs, most of them lace trimmed and all artfully contrived as flattering frames for the wearer's head.

The ruff was designed in a number of ways: in large open convolutions (Fig. 380), in smaller and closer folds like those seen in some Dutch portraits, and in layers of scalloped and pleated organdy (Fig. 383). At least three competitors of the closed ruff appeared by 1620:

1. The open ruff, which spread in a great slanting arc from the open neckline of the gown (Fig. 384).

2. The whisk, a replica of men's neckwear, but often exceeding it in size (Fig. 385). It was closed at center front. In a portrait at Gripsholm, Sweden, Amalia, Princess of Orange, wears three whisks simultaneously.

3. An open standing collar, similar in outline to the open ruff but without any pleating. This, the true Medici collar, is seen in its most perfect form in the portrait of Marie de Medici, reproduced in Fig. 386 and on the lady at the right in Fig. 382. It could have been a modification of either the underpropper, some of which were handsome, or the open ruff.

Necklines were lowered in this period; even Anne of Denmark, Queen of England, appeared in a deep round decolletage which

FIG. 380. *Van Dyck, Paolo Adorno. c.1621–1625. (Frick Collection, New York)*

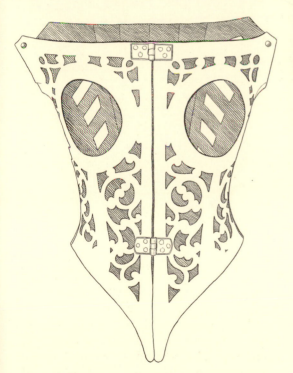

FIG. 379. *Steel Corset. Seventeenth Century. Redrawn from Photograph of Original. (Reproduced by Permission of the Trustees of the Wallace Collection, London)*

would cause eyebrows to lift today (Fig. 387). Square and V-shapes also appeared. Married women usually filled in the exposed space with a simple arrangement of sheer cloth (Fig. 382) or more elaborately as in Fig. 385.

Neck treatments at this time were correlated with wrist treatments.

HAIRDRESS AND HEADDRESS. Women's hair styles, like men's, reflected the rise

Fig. 381. Frans Hals, *Catharina Booth van Dereen.* 1620. (*Louvre*)

FIG. 382. *Willem Buytewech, Two Couples.*
c.1620. *(Rijksmuseum, Amsterdam)*

FIG. 383. *François Pourbus, Marie de Medici.* 1617. *(Prado Museum, A. Y. R. Mas Photograph)*

Fig. 384. *Francois Pourbus, Marie de Medici. Early Seventeenth Century. (Louvre)*

and fall of neckwear. In the early years of the century the hairdress reached its extreme height. Stretched upward over a firm foundation, it became a setting for jewels (Figs. 387 and 388). Hats and caps apparently were superfluous.

Flemish and Dutch women kept to a more natural hair arrangement, like that

FIG. 385. *Unknown Artist, Unknown Lady in Gray. 1607. (Courtesy of the Honorable M. L. Astor)*

shown in Fig. 382, and retained their attractive caps (Fig. 381). Frithjof van Thienen,[1] in his excellent discussion of Dutch caps, calls this the "diadem cap." Isabella Brant even managed a high-crowned hat on top of her coiffed head (Fig. 389). Another

portrait shows Anne of Denmark in hunting costume—indicated more by the presence of horse and dogs than by anything she wears—with a plumed hat perched atop her pompadour. In Fig. 380 Paolo Adorno wears a cap-shaped ornament of pearls over her bun of hair.

ACCESSORIES. Where Spanish fashion prevailed, jewelry was used quite lavishly;

[1] Frithjof van Thienen, "The Great Age of Holland," *Costume of the Western World*, Harper & Row, 1951, p. 260.

FIG. 386. *Unknown Artist, Portrait of Marie de Medici. c.1617. (Pitti Palace, Alinari Photograph)*

careful examination of the paintings of the era, however, shows that pearls replaced most other jewels.

From a practically heelless slipper of 1600, heels of moderate height became fashionable. Shoe roses appeared as early as 1610. A French patten of this period is shown in Fig. 411*e*.

Expertly cut and finished gloves of the early seventeenth century are included in several museum collections. Their deep, elaborately embroidered cuffs might be lace-edged, fringed, or tabbed with ribbon loops. They were worn or carried by both men and women.

In the complete drawing of which Fig. 378 is a detail, a customer is holding two masks and being fitted with a third. Masks

FIG. 387.   *Anne of Denmark, Queen of England. c.1610. Redrawn from Portrait by Unknown Artist. (National Portrait Gallery, London)*

FIG. 388.   *Hairdress of Young English Girl. Early Seventeenth Century. Redrawn from Gheerhaert, Portrait of a Young Lady. (Metropolitan Museum of Art)*

FIG. 389.   *Hat Worn over Cap. c.1610. Redrawn from Rubens, Self Portrait with Isabella Brant. (Alte Pinakothek, Munich)*

FIG. 390. *Michiel Miereveld, Portrait of Woman with Red Hair. 1631. (Metropolitan Museum of Art, The Theodore M. Davis Collection)*

were a generally accepted accessory in England, France, and Italy.

Some of the aprons of this period are masterpieces of needlework (see Fig. 411*c*).

In Fig. 383 Marie de Medici carries a beautiful lace-edged handkerchief.

MOURNING COSTUME. Figure 383 shows Marie de Medici wearing the approved head-dress for French widows. The deep point encroaching upon the forehead (the widow's peak) is an extension of a black cap to which a long sheer black veil is attached, its edges wired to enclose the back of the ruff. From the shoulders the veil falls down the back, partially covering the sleeves, and its lower corners are brought forward and caught to the center front of the skirt.

Widow's weeds showed great variation throughout Europe. In Scandinavia white predominated in the costume. In other countries the enshrouding fabric was more opaque than Marie's veil and was gathered to a small cap-like form which shadowed the forehead. The wrap fell over the body in abundant folds, enveloping the entire figure. Whatever the custom in a country, it was adhered to religiously. Only within the twentieth century has the rigidly set observance of mourning tended to disappear. The University of Washington's collection of costumes includes two tiny black taffeta jackets, muffled in black crepe, in which a 2-year-old child mourned the death of her grandmother in 1842.

THIRTIES AND FORTIES

Paralleling the decided change which took place in men's costume during the 1630s, women's clothing also made a bid for freedom. The rigid cast-iron appearance of the bodice became softened. The typical ensemble consisted of a skirt, moderately full and falling unhindered from waist to floor, a short-waisted bodice with basques (tabs), resembling men's doublets of the period, and an open overdress.

THE OVERDRESS. The overdress descended from the Spanish overdress of the sixteenth century, had short sleeves, open on the inner seam but caught together with a ribbon bow just above the elbow. Usually the overdress contrasted sharply with the garments beneath it. Thus, Miereveldt's *Lady With Red Hair* (Fig. 390) wears white, patterned in red velvet, under black.

THE BODICE. During the thirties the French bodice characteristically had large paned sleeves, caught at the elbow into two puffs, and ending 2 inches or more above the wrist. Upturned flaring cuffs bordered with deep lace echoed the style of the neckwear (Fig. 352). In some portraits the central section of the bodice, extending in a rounded point which is longer than the squared tabs, is an integral part of the bodice itself; in others a separate stomacher is indicated. A bodice in the Victoria and Albert collection requires a stomacher to fill in the front (Fig. 391).

A narrow girdle was usually worn outside the overdress, tied into a bow or primly finished at the joining with a rosette.

NECKWEAR. The neckwear of this era was so involved one almost needs X rays to probe its mysteries. The simplest arrangement was a falling or fallen collar accenting the neckline, now spread to greater width at the shoulders. As the neckline became more open, the exposed area was covered in various ways with lace-trimmed lingerie. Figure 392 dated 1633, after the edict prohibiting the use of lace and more elegant fabrics, shows a French woman wearing a plain guimpe with lapels and collar which we would call today a convertible style. In Fig. 390, however, three different necklines are discernible: an outer square one, to which the woman's large wired slanting collar is attached; a V-shaped one, also collared; and under that a dickey with a lace-edged center closing reaching to the normal neckline, where it is enhanced with a double turnover of lace. The woman is Dutch, the date 1631.

FIG. 391. *Bodice of Cream Colored Satin. Second Quarter Seventeenth Century. Redrawn from Photograph of Original. (Victoria & Albert Museum, Crown Copyright)*

A new accessory that became popular in this decade was a folded square of sheer fabric adorned with lace worn about the neck and shoulders (Fig. 393). The square shape is quite evident in some portraits, folded diagonally a bit off center, the better to display all of the lace edging. In others, if the artist has been realistic, there would of necessity have been some careful shaping to produce the deep double cape collar, where the cloth lies smoothly below a high closed neckline.

WRAPS. For outdoor wear the cape was generally popular. It readily accommodated the full sleeves. The overdress, too, gave added warmth and was worn more during the winter months. Busier, less fashion-minded women probably wore an unsophis-ticated coat cut on the lines of a man's cassock.

HAIRDRESS AND HEADDRESS. Hairdress was quite uniform throughout Europe during this period. In the early thirties the hair was dressed low with a fringe of bangs. A part ran from above the temples to the nape of the neck, from which the side hair fell in curls over the ears. The rest of the hair was braided or rolled in a round bun placed high at the back of the head. This was a favorite focal point for jewels (Fig. 390). In the forties the bangs tended to disappear and the side locks lengthened to rest upon the shoulders.

Hats were worn mostly for riding and travel. A loose, dark, snood-like cap appears on many of Bosse's French models (Fig.

FIG. 392. *French Fashion after Edict of 1633 Banning Use of Lace and Other Trimmings. Redrawn from Bosse,* The Reformed Lady. *(Metropolitan Museum of Art, Whittelsey Fund)*

392); Hollar's figure, *Winter*, wears a closer hood (Fig. 394). The Dutch cap, edged with lace, rested far back on the head.

Another headdress that should be noted is the English wide-brimmed steeple-crowned hat of 1640 which appears in the drawing from Hollar reproduced in Fig. 393.

ACCESSORIES. Muffs were common and comforting accessories in cold weather. At this time they were of quite generous proportions, made of fur and fabric. Evidently they were worn by both men and women, for Pepys tells of buying a new muff for his wife and taking her old one for himself. Fur scarves often accompanied the muffs (Fig. 394). Surprisingly enough, fans were carried in both winter and summer. Folding fans became popular, but not to the extent of

FIG. 393. *English Woman's Hat. 1640. (Courtesy of the Museum of Fine Arts, Boston) Redrawn from Figure in Hollar's* Ornatus Muliebris.

displacing feather fans entirely (Fig. 390). Masks continued in use (Fig. 394). In Hollar's drawing, *Winter*, the mask seems to be worn for protection. It was also worn at carnival time as a prank or disguise. Heavy make-up, including patches, characterized this period. A code developed by which the shape and position of the patches conveyed secret messages between lovers.

Figure 411*d* presents a smart shoe from this part of the century and gloves remained

FIG. 394. *Winter Costume. English. c.1640. Redrawn from Engraving Symbolizing Winter by Hollar. (Victoria & Albert Museum, Crown Copyright)*

an essential accessory for gentlewomen; their cuffs were still fringed and embroidered.

From the woman's waistline hung a hand mirror, a pomander (a perfumed ball usually enclosed in an attractive case), and toilet articles (Fig. 392).

Pearl earrings, necklaces, and bracelets were the favorite jewelry.

HOLLAND

In Holland change came more slowly than in some of the other European countries. A broad, thick ruff of fine convolutions, peculiar to Holland, is seen frequently in the paintings of Frans Hals. It was called the millstone ruff because of the compactness of its folds and the similarity of its proportions to those of a real millstone. Voluminous skirts and long, wide, ornate stomachers are familiar details in portraits by Moreelse, Hals, and Cornelis de Vos. By 1637, however, Hals portrayed Dorothea Berck in a simplified costume with pleasing lines of kerchief and cuffs, emphasized only by self-binding. The 1640s were rich in portraits showing broad collars which cap the sleeves, folded kerchiefs, and deep cuffs, all with displays of lace that must have contributed much to the wearer's social standing. The charming little caps were shaped to cover the bun of hair and rest lightly on the crown of the head.

ENGLAND

English costume was more restrained during this period than it had been earlier. In 1637, for example, the Marchioness of Worcester wore a bodice almost exactly like one noted a moment ago in the Victoria and Albert Museum (Fig. 391). It was worn with a stomacher which was laced with strands of beads. The English sleeve was usually soft, full, and without paneling or double puffs. The overdress was seldom worn.

In her portrait (1633) by Van Dyck (Fig. 395) Queen Henrietta Maria, wife of

FIG. 395.   *Van Dyck, Queen Henrietta Maria with Her Dwarf. 1633. (National Gallery of Art, Washington, D.C.)*

Charles I, wears a costume typically English. Her bodice with basques (separate sections forming the peplum) is worn with a stomacher. Her full uncluttered sleeves are shorter than the French and Flemish ones of the same period. The cavalier collar so closely associated with her husband covers much of her open neckline. A gossamer fichu or pelerine ends with ribbon loops at the waist. Her lovelock and her dashing hat are obviously borrowed from men's attire. In another portrait of about the same time she wears a costume with a broad low square decolletage filled in with a lace partlet to which a wide-spreading lace collar is at-tached. Her tabbed bodice is smooth and un-broken across the front, indicating a back closing. Another royal portrait illustrates a third variation: the front edges of the tabbed bodice are laced with ribbon across the stomacher.

THE FIFTIES AND SIXTIES

SPAIN

Of all western European countries Spain was the last to succumb to the spell of France. Accustomed to leadership, she continued throughout most of the seventeenth century to devise her own fashions, which seem very strange by comparison with other mid-century modes.

About 1655 an unknown artist painted the portrait of the jewel-laden Duchess of El Infantado reproduced in Fig. 396, which gives a good idea of Spanish costume at this time. More tightly corseted than ever, if possible, the flat front of the Duchess tends to confirm the story that girls were bound from childhood to prevent the development of their breasts. (When fashion again sponsored the boyish figure in the 1920s the supposedly enlightened modern women did much the same thing.) The Duchess' arms are practically immobilized by the bandaged effect of her shoulders and her cumbersome bolster-like sleeves. The farthingale was still being worn, though here increased in size and changed in shape. The front waistline is shortened and sharpened in response to the new hip width. The open front of the Duchess' overskirt, her pointed waistline, and her broad neckline bear a resemblance to the mode of other European countries, but the total effect is vastly different. She obviously has not heeded the fashion decree that only pearls are to be worn at this time. Her chandelier earrings, enormous brooch, hair and shoulder ornaments, ring, bracelet, and watch are all ornate in the Spanish tradition.

The Velasquez portraits of Queen

Fig. 396. *Unknown Artist, Duchess of El Infantado. c.1655. (Courtesy of the Hispanic Society of America, New York)*

Mariana and the princesses display the most exaggerated phase of Spanish style. His charming young Infanta Margarita (Fig. 397), whose outstretched fingertips barely touch the rim of her skirt, is typical. Her gown is a combination of shimmering silver and light-coral silk. A horizontal effect is given to her costume by her broad wig-like hairdress, which rivals that of the Egyptians; the boat-shaped neck of her gown, accented by black; the widespread ellipse of her peplum, which lies almost flat over the top of the skirt; and the extreme width of the skirt itself, made more pronounced by its deep band of silver braid. Her paned sleeves relate back to the sixteenth century, but the reversed sleeve ruffles come from more recent modes. That the child could smile in this fantastic outfit is almost miraculous (this is more than her stepmother and sister managed to do under similar circumstances). The little one grew up to be an empress, marrying the Holy Roman Emperor, Leopold I of Germany.

FIG. 397. *Velasquez, Infanta Margarita. c.1660. (Prado Museum, A. Y. R. Mas Photograph)*

In spite of the discomfort it imposed, this was a fascinating style, unique, dramatic and, in its own way, magnificent.

General Trends in Europe

THE BODICE. Farther north, fashion followed a simpler trend. Bodice and skirt, either joined together or worn with the point of the bodice overlapping the skirt, comprised the basic body garment. The bodice fitted smoothly and usually fastened in front, either with a stomacher or, as so often observed in Lely portraits of English women, with the front edges caught together at intervals with brooches, allowing the chemise to emerge in narrow puffs. Alternately it opened in the back.

The center front of the pointed bodice, stomacher, or corset was stiffened by a removable ornamented busk, a broad rigid stay of metal, ivory, or wood (see Fig. 411*b*). The stomacher might be covered by a series of ribbon bows, called an eschelle

(Fig. 398). It might be handsomely embroidered, or, as Queen Maria Theresa's portrait shows covered with ermine. Six jeweled bands cross the ermine, holding the edges of her bodice in place (Fig. 399).

NECKWEAR. The popular but indiscreet decolletage of this era was treated in several ways. La Vallière, Louis XIV's first important mistress (for whom the delicate jeweled pendant we know is named) depended upon the lace frill of her chemise to give an air of modesty. His queen, Maria Theresa, wore a fitted fold of sheer fabric set

FIG. 399. *Detail of Bodice. Third Quarter Seventeenth Century. Redrawn from Nocret, Portrait of Queen Maria Theresa. (Versailles National Museum)*

FIG. 398. *Terborch, Portrait of a Lady Standing. 1660–1665. (Cleveland Museum of Art, The Elizabeth Severance Prentiss Collection)*

above her neckline (Fig. 399). Her stepmother, Queen Mariana of Spain, used a much higher and more opaque pleated extension of fabric. Ter Borch's *Lady* (Fig. 398) wears both guimpe and lace-trimmed sheer capelet. The portrait of Hortense Mancini, Duchess of Mazarin (Fig. 400), one of Cardinal Mazarin's intelligent and much sought-after nieces, shows her wearing only an attractive narrow edging of Venetian lace at her neckline. Madame de Sévigné, whose home, wherever she might be, was the gathering place of literati, artists, and wits, draped a fluff of gauze below her revealing off-the-shoulder neckline.

SKIRTS. The skirt at this time, sans hoops, was longer than floor length in front, slightly trained in back, and either closed or open down center front. If closed, panels of fine embroidery or jeweled clasps lent an air of elegance; if open, the petticoat provided the enrichment. Fullness was mounted in carefully set pleating, often a decorative feature in itself.

HAIRDRESS AND HEADDRESS. Hairdress

changed gradually in style. Bangs disappeared; the volume of hair at the sides of the face was increased by curling and frizzing, and finally, in the 1660s, by wiring (Figs. 400 and 401). Curls made from the back hair were brought forward over the shoulder. The arrangement of most of the hair in a bun was characteristic of much of the seventeenth century.

For riding and travel women wore broad-brimmed steeple-crowned hats patterned after those worn by men. Loose hoods similar to those of the previous period gave protection in inclement weather. Flemish and Dutch maidens kept to their little bun-fitting caps indoors, with larger, more concealing models for outdoor wear

FIG. 401. *Elaborate Hairdress. c.1670. Redrawn from Portrait of Bertha Ahlefeldt by Unknown Artist. (National Historic Museum, Frederiksborg, Denmark)*

(Fig. 402). Netscher's *Lace Maker*, working indoors (Fig. 403), wears a beautiful embroidered cap. Her jacket, with its cartridge-pleated sleeve, was the poorer woman's version of the elegant satin garments so realistically rendered in many of the Dutch and Flemish paintings of the time.

Vermeer's lovely *Girl With a Pearl Necklace* wears a wrist-length jacket bordered with fur (in this case soft yellow silk trimmed with ermine) that must have been widely worn as a wrap or indoor winter garment. Shoulder capes of varying lengths appeared.

FOOTWEAR AND OTHER ACCESSORIES. The design of the well-worn shoes of the *Lace Maker* had been fashionable a generation earlier (Fig. 403). At the period we are discussing my lady's shoe had a more tapered toe, though still blunted at the tip; the heel was higher and more slender, and the material, of course, much more elegant—the softest leather and brocaded and embroidered silks were employed (see Fig. 411f). Note the skates in Fig. 402.

FIG. 400. *Unknown French Artist, Hortense Mancini, Duchess of Mazarin. Third Quarter Seventeenth Century. (Metropolitan Museum of Art)*

Fig. 402. *Romeyn de Hooghe, Figures à la Mode. c.1670. (Metropolitan Museum of Art, Dick Fund)*

Patches became increasingly popular during the entire last half of the century. Handkerchiefs took on undue proportions (Figs. 396 and 397). Gloves and parasols were important accessories.

END OF THE CENTURY,
1670–1700

During the remaining years of the century a new fashion for women gradually evolved, in which sympathetic treatment of fabric gave way to overmanipulation. From lines which followed the natural contour of the body, the silhouette again became distorted, this time in the form of the bustle. Ornamentation, restrained in mid-century, went completely out of bounds. Madame de Maintenon, Louis XIV's last mistress and second wife, is credited with having imposed modest necklines and somber colors at court, but she cannot have had much influence esthetically, as the overdecoration and unnatural silhouette indicate.

THE BUSTLE SILHOUETTE. The process of change began subtly enough with draping

Fig. 403. Netscher, The Lace Maker. 1664. (Reproduced by Permission of the Trustees of the Wallace Collection, London)

Fig. 404. *J. D. de St. Jean, Madame la Dauphine. 1670. Arnoult, Bonnart, and Trouvain, Costume Plates, Seventeenth Century. (The Pierpont Morgan Library)*

FIG. 405. *Gold Embroidered Wool Gown. c.1690. (Metropolitan Museum of Art)*

back the edges of the overskirt. The brooches or bows that secured the folds called more attention to the skirt (Fig. 404). By the 1680s the reversed lower front edges met at center back, producing a cascade of cloth which thickened the figure decidedly when viewed from side or back. By the nineties, the front edges of the overskirt were pulled abruptly to the waistline at center back, leaving little visible from the front and creating the bustle effect without any extraneous means. Bustles were not wanting, however. Fashion drawings show the skirt arching out abruptly from the waistline. A remarkable gown in the Metropolitan Museum collection dates from about 1690. Cut with an outward curving side seam to accommodate some sort of padding (Fig. 405 and Draft 13*a* and *b*), it is made of warm gray broadcloth, striped predominantly in royal blue and dull gold, and embroidered in gold so skillfully that it is completely reversible. The wool has been so expertly fulled that the raw edge of the overskirt has not raveled perceptibly in 250 years. The skirt is cut in one piece with the bodice; the underskirt, of the same material and also profusely embroidered, gives a far

FIG. 406. *Trouvain, Madame la Princesse de Conty Douairiere. 1690's. Arnoult, Bonnart, and Trouvain, Costume Plates, Seventeenth Century. (The Pierpont Morgan Library)*

more harmonious effect than those observed in fashion drawings. The flat banding or robing bordering the neckline is becomingly shaped and embroidered (see draft for actual cut). As always, the photograph is a very poor substitute for the original. One must see it to appreciate it, and the more closely it is examined, the greater the admiration and respect it arouses.

THE UNDERSKIRT. As the exposed petti-

coat gained in importance it became the focus of all kinds of ornamentation, usually horizontal in direction. For example, the skirt worn by Bonnart's lady, *La Dame du Grand Air*, has three flounces of lace upon a patterned fabric. Imaginations ran riot in these years, employing deep fringes, tassels, braid, and/or self-fabric flounces, one above the other from hem to waist (Fig. 406).

THE BODICE. The bodice changed

Fig. 407. *Arnoult, Fille de Qualité à sa Toilette. 1690's. From Costumes, Epoque Louis XIV, Seventeenth Century. (The Pierpont Morgan Library)*

FIG. 408. *Unknown Artist, Queen Mary II of England.* c.1694. *(Victoria & Albert Museum, Crown Copyright)*

FIG. 409. *French School, Madame de Maintenon. 1690's. (Metropolitan Museum of Art, Whittelsey Fund)*

more slowly than the skirt and underskirt. The low off-the-shoulder line persisted into the eighties, bringing with it the short sleeve and multiple ruffles and puffs of the chemise (Fig. 404). However, possibly because of Madame de Maintenon's insistence upon a more modest decolletage, the stomacher-front bodice took precedence, the front edges of the bodice continuing in a vertical direction up over the shoulders, thus creating a square neckline (Figs. 406 and 409).

The whole character of the shoulder

and sleeve mounting was altered by this new fashion. Sleeves became narrower and longer. Usually they were cuffed, but sometimes the chemise sleeve was allowed to show. More often, however, they had their own multiple ruffles attached (Fig. 406).

HAIRDRESS AND HEADDRESS. Hair styles, as always, responded to dress design. The wired out coiffure of the sixties gave way in the next decade to a short, carefree, allover-curled effect known as the hurly-burly or hurluberlu (Fig. 404). In the later seventies and eighties this was followed by a more disciplined arrangement, with a center part and curls placed above the temples.

The vertical lines of the 1690 bodice were repeated in the famous fontange head-dress (Fig. 406), named after Madame Fontange, one of Louis XIV's mistresses who is said to have bound her hair with her garter when her coiffure became disheveled while riding. This story has been discounted, how-ever, since it seems that the lady died before the fashion started. Nonetheless, it bears her name. The fontange headdress was an elabo-ration of the little white lingerie cap which had been part of a lady's wardrobe for some time. To the front of this cap were now added tiers of ruffles, lace, and ribbons, ex-tending higher and higher until a wire frame-work was required to keep it erect. Cunning-ton[2] distinguishes between the fontange—the cap itself, with its toppling superstruc-ture—and the commode, the wire support. The piled-up curls arranged in front of the tiers (Fig. 407), not infrequently false, con-stitute the tower. Lappets of lawn and lace fell back on the shoulders. Some of these are now highly prized items in museum lace collections. A portrait of Queen Mary of England shows her wearing the most at-tractive fontange on record (Fig. 408).

By the end of the century the use of patches reached the ridiculous. One observer

FIG. 410.   *Seventeenth Century Stole from Valder-marslot, Denmark. c.1690–1700. (Danish National Museum, Copenhagen)*

reports having seen as many as 15 on one individual.[3]

ACCESSORIES. A scarf or loose hood knotted under the chin, an embroidered shoulder cape, and a smaller muff were pre-ferred toward the end of the century (Fig. 409). Fur neckpieces took the form of flat tippets, or a long, slender, tubular scarf looped at the throat.

Cape stoles were favorite wraps, and much time, artistry, skill, and money were invested in them (Fig. 409). The National Museum in Copenhagen is the fortunate

[2] C. Willett Cunnington and Phillis Cunning-ton, *Handbook of English Costume in the Seven-teenth Century*, Faber, London, 1955, p. 181.

[3] *Ibid.*, p. 187.

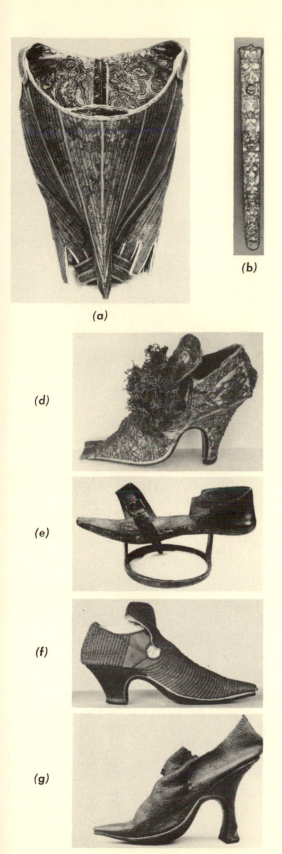

Fig. 411. *Women's Accessories, Seventeenth Century.* a. *Woman's Corset. French. c.1620. (Courtesy, Museum of Fine Arts, Boston)* b. *Busk. French or Spanish. Seventeenth to Eighteenth Century.* c. *Italian Apron. Reticella Embroidery and Punto-in-aria Lace. Early Seventeenth Century. (b and c, Metropolitan Museum of Art)* d. *Woman's Shoe. First Half of Seventeenth Century. (Nordiska Museet, Stockholm)* e. *French Patten. Early Seventeenth Century. (Courtesy, Museum of Fine Arts, Boston)* f. *Shoe of Leather Trimmed with Braid. Reign of Charles II (1660–1688). (Victoria & Albert Museum, Crown Copyright)* g. *French Shoe of Black Leather. Late Seventeenth to Mid-Eighteenth Century. (Metropolitan Museum of Art)*

possessor of the unique example shown in Fig. 410. The upper folded edge is center back; the widest section, just below, falls over the shoulders; the narrowest part is at the waistline. The glowing, sumptuously embroidered panels spread over the skirt front.

Shoes had become truly French, with slender pointed toes and high, slim, curving heels, set well forward (Fig. 411g). Tongues were high, straps narrow, buckles small. The clog, made to harmonize and synchronize with the shape of the slipper, was a clever and attractive means of protecting delicate footwear.

Aprons, which had been in fashion more or less throughout the century, now received more attention and became a definite part of the ensemble. Though some of them were really elegant, their beauty was lost in the melange of furbelows (Fig. 407).

Elbow-length gloves, as sleek as if they had come from a modern shop, are illustrated in Fig. 408. Women adopted the steinkirk as a fashionable and patriotic accessory. Parasols, masks, fans, and muffs were essentials in their wardrobes. Jewelry alone was simple and unassuming. A choker necklace, often with pendant cross, was most popular (Figs. 407 and 408).

16

Eighteenth-Century Fashions for Men

Historical Background

The eighteenth century witnessed a gradual transition from the grand and opulent designs of the baroque period to the light, delicate, colors and patterns of the rococo style. The imposing and almost overpowering setting which Louis XIV considered appropriate for His Supreme Majesty would have been incongruous for a Pompadour or a Marie Antoinette.

Increased trade with the Middle and Far East during this century resulted in frequent contact with that civilization, which had a profound influence in western Europe. This could be seen throughout the century in textiles in the form of textures of lighter weight, patterns of smaller scale and colors both more subtle and more light-hearted. The great popularity of printed cottons stemmed from that source. Prohibiting the import of such fabrics to protect native industries merely whetted the desire for them, since gowns made of them became a symbol of exclusiveness—something which was becoming more and more difficult to achieve.

Interest in classic art was stirred at this time by the excavations at Pompeii and Herculaneum, as well as by publications of the great German archeologist, Johann Winckelmann, especially his *History of Ancient Art* (*Geschichte der Kunst der Altertums*) in 1764, and by Robert Adam's study of Diocletian's palace in Spalato (the city previously known as Spalato is now called Split). An eighteenth-century Renaissance in architecture developed. Nearly every state in the United States and all of the eastern states bear witness to this classical revival with the columns and domes of their state capitol buildings. Chinese and classic sources blended to produce Chippendale furniture, and upholstery materials were inspired by Persian fabrics.

Pompadour, a woman of good taste, helped to direct the trends of mid-century styles by her encouragement of arts and artists. Fickle Marie Antoinette, the dominant personality at the French court during the seventies and eighties, tired of the pomp and ceremony and exactions of court life and turned to such diversions as amateur theatricals and her Swiss village. In this way she was influential in fostering a mood for less formal and dignified furnishings. However, some designers continued to work in the grand manner, such as Philippe de La Salle whose designs, though in naturalistic forms and Persian-inspired coloring, are truly magnificent.

In the middle of the century such men as Voltaire and Rousseau led an intellectual revolution which more or less paralleled the fight for liberty and independence in America and was influential in bringing on that in France. The catastrophic upheaval in France in the closing decades of the century led to changes in costume as decisive as those in government.

FIRST HALF OF THE CENTURY

As Louis XIV aged (he died in 1715 at 77) the tempo of change slowed practically to a halt, especially as far as men's fashions were concerned. Largillière's portrait of Louis with members of his family, done in 1710 (Fig. 412), near the close of his reign, shows him wearing coat and waistcoat made to button all the way down the front, though actually his coat is fastened only at the waistline. Its cuffs are both deep and wide. The waistcoat is but a few inches shorter than the coat. Though his sleeves are lengthened they still expose a puff of shirt sleeve and wrist ruffle. In this portrait Louis is wearing

FIG. 412. *Largillière, Louis XIV and Members of His Family. 1710. (Reproduced by Permission of the Trustees of the Wallace Collection, London)*

FIG. 413. *Wedding Costume of King Frederick V of Denmark. 1743. (Rosenborg Palace, Copenhagen)*

while two additional pleats in back give it generous fullness. The off-grain cut of the back provided a smoother fit and afforded a little more elasticity under strain. The back has a waistline seam which controls the hang of the skirt. The back of the sleeveless waistcoat is made of linen.

Figure 413 shows the wedding costume of King Frederick V of Denmark, about 20 years later than the one just described. The Rosenborg Palace collection of royal costumes, of which this is one, is proof of the splendor that was achieved with rich fabric and superb workmanship. However, this should not delude the observer into assuming that ordinary people dressed that way. Nevertheless, in style, cut, and decoration, these costumes are typical of the period in which they were produced.

The wedding suit, including the trousers and the entire waistcoat, is made of cloth of silver. There is no faking or substitution. The coat is remarkable for the amount of fabric employed in its pleats. The extension of the front is so large that it overlaps the armscye, necessitating a piecing, as indicated in Draft 14. This represents the ultimate in skirt fullness of men's coats. The garment worn at Frederick's wedding by his father, King Christian VI (Fig. 414), was made of deep-violet silk, brocaded with floral pattern in silver, and overlaid with broad borders of finely executed gold embroidery. The back view shown illustrates the fall of the fan pleating. The skirts of these two royal garments, woven with metal thread, are so stiff that they would stand out from the body of their own accord, especially Frederick's where the coat lining is woven of blue silk warp and silver weft. In addition, the suit is heavily padded and interlined throughout, both skirt and body parts. No indication of boning was found in any of the costumes examined by the author. Notice that the male silhouette tended to resemble that of the ladies in the breadth of its skirt.

Figure 415 illustrates a typical French

his cravat simply looped; however, the steinkirk continued to be worn—it appeared in Hogarth's series of paintings, "Marriage a la Mode," as late as 1745.

A few fine costumes of the early part of the century can be seen in European collections. The Victoria and Albert Museum has an outstanding ensemble of the period of George I (1714–1727). The fabric is a grayish-green silk faille with a self-color floral pattern woven to shape (*en disposition*) on the cuffs, around the pockets, and down the front edges. The edges of the fronts are cut slightly off grain; an extension on the skirt is sufficient to form four pleats,

Fig. 414. *Costume of King Christian VI, Worn at His Son's Wedding in 1743.*
(Rosenborg Palace, Copenhagen)

costume of the period. Note the style of wig, the plain neckband called the stock, which replaced the cravat, the frills of lace down the front opening constituting the jabot, the large open cuffs, the imposing spread of the skirt, the stockings still gartered over the knees.

Since people who have their portraits painted usually want to be immortalized in their best raiment, overcoats are seldom seen in portraits. Longhi's *The Visit* (1746) includes a good representation of a well-shaped full cape of the type called the roquelaire (Fig. 416). Slits were usually provided toward the front to allow the arms to emerge. The rather wide flat collar is a type that was seen on the cassock of the seventeenth century—a garment which had been, and continued to be, worn by the lower classes. In the eighteenth century this garment was

FIG. 415. *Quentin de la Tour, Duval de l'Epinoy. 1745. (Gulbenkian Foundation)*

FIG. 416. *Eighteenth Century Cape Called Roquelaire. 1746. Redrawn from Longhi, the Visit. (Metropolitan Museum of Art)*

referred to as a frock coat and it was widely enough adopted by fashion leaders to attain recognized standing. Because of its source it became known as a wrap rascal. This garment should not be confused with the fashionable gentleman's frock coat of the nineteenth century.

The great coat or redingote of about 1730, shown in Fig. 417, repeats the style of the justacorps or suit coat in its fitted waist and flaring skirt. The upper collar is shown buttoned for greater protection.

WIGS. One of the most important changes in men's fashions in the eighteenth century concerned wigs, of which there was a great variety, depending upon occasion and vocation. The full-bottomed wig, outmoded by 1730, was retained for court wear and continued to be worn by professional men and elderly conservative gentlemen. These full-bottomed wigs lent an imposing air but must have been burdensome to wear. Note in Fig. 412 that Louis' wig is

unpowdered, the wig of the Dauphin standing behind him is powdered, while the grandson at Louis' left seems to be wearing his own natural hair, carefully curled. The more comfortable practice of lifting the side hair back to the nape of the neck and controlling it there in one of several ways was generally followed. Kelly and Schwabe list some of these styles:

1. The tie—a mere bunch of curls caught together by a black tie.
2. Square black bag, trimmed with bow at the top, in which the hair was encased.

FIG. 417. *Great Coat or Redingote. c.1730. Redrawn from Leloir,* Histoire du Costume, *Vol. XJ, Figure 11B.*

FIG. 418. *Hogarth, The Marriage Contract. 1745. (New York Public Library, Prints Division)*

3. Ramillie—braid of plaited hair with bow at the top and often at the end.
4. Pigtail, encased in a spiral black ribbon case.[1]

Several other types of wigs were also worn, including the major wig, with queue, formed in one curl; the brigadier, a wig that ended in two curls; and the catagon, a wig with a club arrangement of the back hair. The latter was one of the affectations of the Macaronies, a group of English fops of the 1770s.

Hogarth's *Marriage Contract* (Fig. 418), the first of his series known as "Marriage a la Mode," shows the older gentlemen wearing reduced versions of the full-bottomed wig, powdered; the father of the bride, still clinging to the steinkirk, is noticeably more simply dressed and more old fashioned; the ends of his wig are folded up in club fashion.

[1] Francis Kelly and Randolph Schwabe, *Historic Costume*, Batsford, London, 1925, pp. 199–200.

The bored bridegroom wears a bag wig with outsized bow at the back and a black ribbon, called the solitaire, knotted into a small bow in front. In the breakfast scene, a guest appears with his hair in curlers. When relaxing indoors the men removed their wigs and substituted caps, many of which were beautifully embroidered; winter ones were even fur-trimmed.

The tricorne was the predominant hat style, and remained so until the 1780s. Note in the portrait of Louis' family (Fig. 412) both the Dauphin and the grandson carry their plumed tricornes; this was correct in the presence of the king, but doubtless at other times they carried them instead of wearing them, to avoid disheveling their hair.

By 1730 the tongue of the shoe had diminished and the heel was lowered, though it continued to be painted red for court wear until 1750. By mid-century the tongue projected less than an inch above the buckle, which had increased noticeably in size. Heels corresponded to the height men wear today. Figure 418 shows shoes of this type.

Snuff boxes became an important accessory and conversation piece. Many of them were choice examples of the jeweler's craft.

THE FIFTIES, SIXTIES, AND SEVENTIES

In the three decades from 1750 to 1780 a certain homogeneity gave some continuity to fashion. Typical of the fifties is the costume shown in Fig. 419, with fur-lined coat and elaborate braiding on both coat and waistcoat. The thigh length waistcoat was retained as late as the 1770s.

Coats were cut along the same general lines as in the first half century, but were altered in neckline, cuffs, and skirt volume. By the sixties the neckline had become higher and closer and had acquired a collar—either a narrow standing band, as shown in Fig. 420 or a flat collar borrowed from the frock coat of the working class (Fig. 421).

In the general slimming of the silhouette which took place at this time the broad cuffs of the sleeve became narrower and closed in the fifties; a new form was added in the sixties (Fig. 421, center figure). This cuff of stepped height known as the mariner's cuff is shown here embroidered to match the rest of the coat; it was also often braided. The sleeves on the figure at the right are made with a deep opening which is bound and buttoned, giving a trimmer and leaner effect. The coat sleeve finally reached the wrist, with only the shirt ruffle or, for informal wear, a narrow wristband showing.

The skirt of the coat lost much of its volume, both in the pleating and by cutting away the front edges below the waistline. By the seventies pleats had disappeared from the back skirt, and side-seam pleats were moved farther toward the back.

At this time the upper classes adopted the frock coat for casual wear. Made of a fine grade of fabric, it had looser, more comfortable lines than the dress coat and was especially suitable for riding, travel, and general outdoor wear. Figure 421 shows it as a gentleman's garment.

As more surface of the breeches became visible, more attention was paid to fitting. Legs below the thighs were encased smoothly. Openings above the knee were fastened neatly with buttons, and the well-shaped knee bands were buckled (Fig. 420).

Figure 419 illustrates the fashion during the fifties of beautiful braids applied in intricate designs on coat and waistcoat. Note also the use of fur on cuffs, pocket flaps and front edges of the coat.

The portrait of the Marquis D'Ossun reproduced in Fig. 420 is also highly significant of the period. His powdered wig is closely dressed with two side curls. He wears a suit of matching coat, waistcoat, and trousers. The coat has the new standing collar and hangs naturally without stiffening. His waistcoat is shortened to mid-thigh. The small-scale open-embroidery design is a reflection of Madame Pompadour's influence upon the taste of the day. A similar feeling is evident in the airiness of the lace pattern of the Marquis' jabot and wrist ruffles. His trousers overlap the hose in a new sleekness, with buttons and buckles at the knee. The rounded toes of his shoes and enlarged curving shoe buckles are in keeping with the latest mode. From head to heels he is a fashionably dressed gentleman of the third quarter of the eighteenth century.

The plain costume worn by the barber in the cartoon reproduced in Fig. 422 is not without a certain amount of style. Its high turnover collar and cuffs, which follow the contour of the sleeves, continued to be seen throughout the 1780s. Securing the cocks of his hat by buttoned tabs is significant, as are also the smaller tricorne and broadened curls of the gentleman sketched on the wall. The "shave-for-a-penny" sign is really historic.

FIG. 419. *François-Hubert Drouais, Le Comte de Vaudreuil. 1758. (National Gallery, London)*

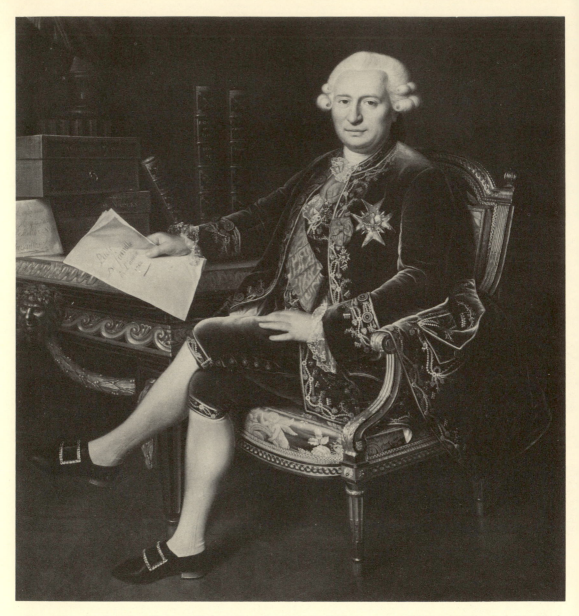

Fig. 420. *Attributed to Francois-Hubert Drouais, Marquis D'Ossun. 1762. (National Gallery of Art, Washington, D. C., Gift of Mrs. Albert J. Beveridge)*

Figure 423 is typical of handsome costumes in many outstanding collections. Dating probably from the 1770s or 1780s, this one is from the Design Laboratory of the Brooklyn Museum (Draft 15). A comparison of Drafts 14 and 15 will emphasize the radical change in the volume of the skirt of the coat. It is made of plum-colored Jacquard woven silk, magnificently embroidered in polychromatic silks. The waistcoats worn with these costumes were often of lighter silks, sometimes embroidered with harmonizing motifs, sometimes in smaller, more delicate patterns (Fig. 424).

FOOTWEAR. Shoes at this time had a normally rounded toe, but tongues disappeared and buckles were enlarged, being

Fig. 421. *Sir Joshua Reynolds, The Hon. Henry Fane and Guardians. 1766. (Metropolitan Museum of Art)*

curved to follow the shape of the foot (Fig. 420). Many of these buckles were handsome; some were of silver, wrought with restraint; some were set with paste, occasionally with precious stones for the favored few. Heels showed little change.

Jockey boots with their tops turned down were popular for outdoor wear (Fig. 421). Spatterdashes (leggings) buttoning up

the outside of the leg furnished similar protection. Heavier boots, covering the knee but cut away beneath it, were worn by country folk and in general for more rugged use. Hose for dress wear were often clocked (Fig. 420).

HAIRDRESS AND HEADDRESS. The new designs in wigs of these decades harmonize with the general tendency toward natural lines. The center part disappeared, the hair being brushed back smoothly from the forehead. The side hair was arranged in one or two horizontal curls above the ears (Figs. 419 and 420). For dress wear the bag wig was the accepted mode, though its back bow became smaller. The solitaire—the black ribbon extending from the bag wig to center front—was at first tied but later it was tucked inconspicuously into the shirt front. In the sixties it disappeared entirely, leaving a plain stock fastened in the back (Fig. 420). After two centuries of absence the shirt collar now reappeared as a narrow turnover at the top of the stock. For a brief while wigs fell

FIG. 423. *Man's Silk Costume. c.1770–1780.* (*Brooklyn Museum*)

FIG. 422. *Cartoon of English Barber. 1771.* (*New York Public Library, Prints Division*)

out of favor. In Fig. 421 all three English gentlemen are coiffed in their own hair, unpowdered.

The cartoon of 1771 reproduced in Fig. 422 is a valuable document of fashion at this time. The barber himself wears a short-bob wig which was probably the most generally popular of all the prevailing styles. In his hand he carries a tie wig with queue in the form of a single curl. The increased bulk of this wig parallels the increase in volume in women's hairdress (see Fig. 458). Note

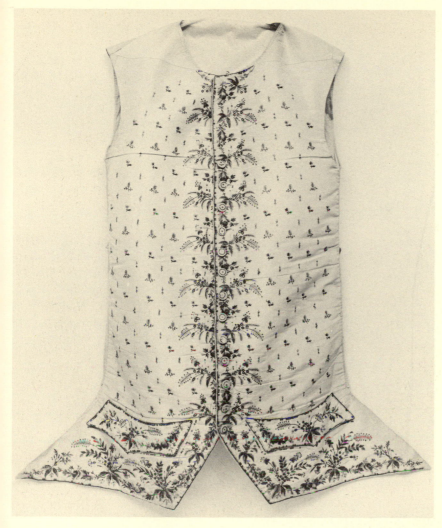

FIG. 424. *Embroidered Waistcoat. French. Second Half of Eighteenth Century.*
(*Courtesy, Museum of Fine Arts, Boston*)

the huge catagon of the hairdresser on the ladder.

THE EIGHTIES

The eighties witnessed numerous changes in fashion, one following quickly upon another, with many different styles existing side by side. The eccentric clothing of the fop in France and the Macaronies in England reflected the unrest of the times. The more conservative element adopted changes more slowly and in less extreme versions.

The most noticeable feature of the costume worn by the young man in Fig. 425 is the skimpiness of the coat, as compared, for example, with Prince Frederick's wedding costume in Fig. 413. In the later coat the lower corners of the fronts swerve sharply to the back of the knee. The buttons probably could not be fastened. Back pleats have vanished. Sleeves are tight and cuffless. A high turnover collar finishes the neckline.

FIG. 425. *Young Man in Fashionable Costume of 1782. From La Galerie des Modes, Vol. I, Plate 16. (New York Public Library, Art and Architecture Division)*

The waistcoat is reduced to a short extension below the waistline, which it will soon lose. The wig is dressed in the famous catagon style, a club-shaped arrangement originating in the stables. The tricorne is now well on the way to becoming a bicorne.

Trousers, now quite fully exposed, were fitted so closely that suits with two pairs of pants were in order: one pair for standing at state occasions, a looser pair for more active pursuits. The desire for a tight yet wrinkle-free appearance partly accounts for the popularity of leather breeches. Leather was about the only material with enough elasticity to stand the strain of such tightness. (Not until the nineteenth century did knitted trousers come into vogue.) The guards at St. James' Palace in London still wear these eighteenth-century styles; their snow-white leather breeches fit them like their own skin.

In the eighties the impending change from knee breeches to ankle-length pantaloons, or trousers as they are known today, was perhaps forecast by the riding breeches. In the eighties the breeches, though tight, came well down the calf of the leg to tuck into the half boot or buskin.

Hose and shoes underwent little change in the early eighties. Double watch fobs, sometimes ending in tassels and often dangling several seals, became the rage. Even if the wearer did not possess two watches, the bisymmetric balance was pleasing. The tasseled cane was considered an indispensable accessory for the gentleman.

A fashion plate from *Cabinet des Modes*, dated 4 years later than Fig. 425, presents a different picture. Here the coat is cut with a notch at the low waistline. The front edges expose the embroidered waistcoat, which has been shortened again and straightened on the lower edge. The same sleeve as in Fig. 425 is finished with mariner's cuffs. Frogged buttonholes borrowed from military dress simulate a fastening. The broad high-crowned hat, startlingly different from either tricorne or bicorne, presages a new style. Without the hat the wig would appear broad, high, and bushy. The striped hose also introduce a bit of novelty. Toes of shoes are once more becoming decidedly pointed.

A more extreme costume of the same year was portrayed by Debucourt in *The*

Bride's Minuet. Here the coat is so scanty that it brings to mind the present-day tail coat, which, of course, derives from it. No one would think that it was supposed to fasten. Buttons were enlarged, though never to the extent the Macaronies favored. The wig resembles women's hair styles, being dressed upward and outward in great volume.

Figure 426 presents an American gentleman whose attire is typical of the conservatively dressed citizen. His coat, curving sharply toward the back, has a high standing collar. Its buttons are moderately large, its buttonholes probably faked. The gentleman's trousers are as tight as feasible. His shoes and hose show no change. He wears a bow tied cravat above his pleated shirt frill. He leans lightly upon an ivory-topped tasseled cane and carries his cocked hat in his hand. His powdered hair, which might be his own, is of normal bulk. One watch fob bearing two seals suffices for him.

THE CRAVAT. The cravat, which was popular in the late seventeenth century, reappeared as neckwear in this decade, but in a different guise, closely resembling that of the Croatians who started the idea and gave it its name, as we noted earlier. In the 1780s

FIG. 426. *Ralph Earl, Daniel Boardman. 1789. (National Gallery of Art, Washington, D.C.)*

FIG. 427. *Redingote. 1783. La Galerie des Modes, Vol. II, Plate 157. (New York Public Library)*

the Macaronies revived it in its original form. From this modest adaptation, the cravat, through the following decades, assumed a form and proportion that its originators would never have recognized.

THE REDINGOTE. An important garment of the 1780s was the redingote. In Fig. 427 the triple-collared coat is of olive-green wool. Its multiple collar and outsize lapel are in the forefront of fashion. The double-breasted effect is high style also.

CAPES. Long full capes remained in use through most of the eighteenth century. In 1775 Zoffany painted an ankle-length model with a flat collar of moderate width and buttoned closing. The Costume Institute possesses a swaggering red-wool original, cut on a full circle, a deep shoulder cape adding a smart touch. It is dated late eighteenth century.

The Closing Decade of the Century

The nineties were characterized by wide lapels on both coat and waistcoat, tight breeches fastened well below the knee with strings instead of buckles, shoes resembling pumps with pointed toes and slight heels, and natural hair worn long in the early decade, but cropped short à la Brutus by the turn of the century (see Figs. 428 and 432).

Although reliable accounts stress the danger of appearing well dressed on the streets of Paris during the years of the Revolution, Debucourt's *Public Promenade* of 1792, showing the foppishness of men's clothing at that time, is as much of a caricature as Vernet's *Incroyables* of 1796. The difference of course is that they represent extreme opposites in sleekness of attire and grooming.

Details of historic significance of the Debucourt dandies are the collars—one of new grotesque height, the other of greatly extended width; tightness of both coats and breeches; bunches of loops at the outside of the knees, replacing buckles; double-breasted

effect of coat and waistcoat; huge buttons; conspicuous watch fobs; cravats which brush the ear lobes and cradle the chin; gypsy-like earrings.

One of the men wears a powdered wig with a cropped bushy crown known as the hedgehog, and one large stiff curl circling the back of his head from ear to ear. The other figure is possibly wearing his own unpowdered hair dressed as a wig.

The low pointed pumps with bows seem in character with the rest of the man's costume. A booted individual, presumably dressed for riding, is wearing a redingote with long narrow tails, flat brimmed high crowned hat, and riding crop.

Goya's Don Sebastián Martínez (Fig. 428) is in strong contrast to the Debucourt fops. Here is a gentleman of the same year, calm, composed, natural, at ease, and fashionably dressed. This painting is a valuable guide to the manner in which cloth was cut for the fronts of the coat. Note the direction of the stripes, which indicates the engineering of the boldly projecting curve over the chest and the rapidly receding line of the tails. The same clue reveals the curve at the elbow of the sleeve as much sharper than the style in use today. Draft 16 shows the disposition of grain very clearly. The turnover collar is high but does not touch the ears; the lapel is quite pointed; the buttons are large but not obtrusively so. The waistcoat of contrasting fabric is rich in texture and has visible lapels. The modest cravat shifts emphasis to the frill of the shirt. Breeches are close fitting without seeming ready to burst. The strap below the knee is still buckled. Don Sebastián's wig of powdered hair is arranged close to his head, with a single curl over his ears. (See also Fig. 475.)

David's portrait of M. de Sériziat (Fig. 429) is one of the most familiar illustrations of 1790 costume. Dressed in riding costume, this gentleman is much more convincing than the Debucourt poseurs. His riding coat—double-breasted, with wide lapels and high

Fig. 428.   *Goya, Don Sebastián Martínez. 1792. (Metropolitan Museum of Art)*

FIG. 429. David, Monsieur de Sériziat. 1795. (Louvre)

Fig. 430. Gerard, Portrait of J. B. Isabey and Daughter. 1795. (Louvre)

turnover collar—is quietly and beautifully tailored. (Draft 17 was taken from a similar coat.) The flat cuffs of his sleeves are moderate in width. His double-breasted waistcoat has the fashionable lapels of the era. The bow of the cravat rests above the shirt frill. His trousers are again tight, resembling leather in texture, and are fastened below the knees with string ties. Note that his boots and trousers do not meet. His natural hair is arranged in a soft upward roll over the ears. The gently rolling brim and high

crown of his hat have the smart form of the new hat style.

THE SPENCER. Gerard's portrait of the painter Isabey and his daughter (Fig. 430) shows still another, and more casual, type of outdoor costume. Legend had it that Lord Spencer, while riding, was thrown from his horse and in the tumble the tails of his riding coat were torn off. Possibly to cover his chagrin, he boasted that he would make the mutilated garment fashionable. In this way

FIG. 431. *Vernet, Incroyables. 1796. (British Museum)*

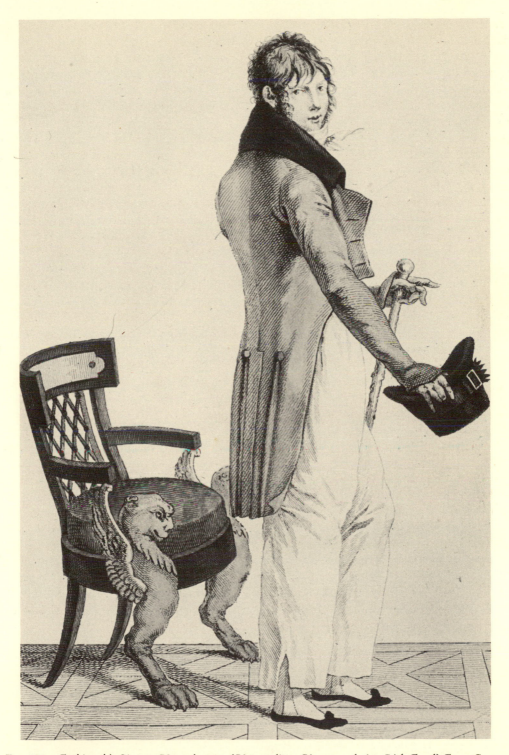

FIG. 432. *Fashionable Young Man of 1800.* (*Metropolitan Museum of Art, Dick Fund*) *From Cos-*
tume Parisien, *Plate 237.*

the spencer entered the wardrobe. Isabey's coat is short and of even length—the spencer as worn by men. Although it is seldom illustrated in men's wear, it is frequently recorded in women's fashion plates. Draft 18 was taken from an original in the collection of the Costume Institute of the Metropolitan Museum.

The remainder of Isabey's costume conforms with those already noted, though it is more conservative. The widened collar of his shirt shows up by its turnover at the upper edge of the cravat. The shirt itself is full but without a frill. His breeches extend down into his boots and are held in place below the knee by ties passing through loops on his boots. His hair is in the new style, cut short all over the head and slightly waved in imitation of the Greek mode.

THE INCROYABLES. The two extroverts (beatniks of their time) shown in Fig. 431 are obviously caricatures of fashions of the nineties. Some ensembles of this type were so fantastic that their wearers were called the "incroyables" (incredibles), their feminine counterparts being known as the "merveilleuses." Vernet recorded many of these phenomena, the men shown in Fig. 431 being his best known. The disheveled, slept-in look was considered safer than being well groomed and certainly upkeep was no problem. These men deserve their epithet—their hair unkempt, cravats sloppily bulky and colorful, lapels ridiculously large, and an overall contrived carelessness. The wrinkled buskins on the man at the left would appear on the fashionably dressed male as

sleek well-fitted footwear. His hat will emerge as the aristocratic high silk hat of the nineteenth and twentieth centuries. The spyglass of his companion performs the role of the snobbish monocle and his club proclaims his disdain of the popular cane.

Transition to the Nineteenth Century

A plate from *Costume Parisien* (1800), reproduced in Fig. 432, illustrates the typical fashion of the close of the eighteenth century and the beginning of the nineteenth. The gentleman's cutaway coat is by now fully developed, retaining the high collar which persisted for some time. His cravat is worn high and loose and overlaps his chin, a vagary of the beaus of the era. His haircut à la Brutus reflects classical influence. His hat, cane, pumps, and clocked hose are correct accessories of the day.

The most newsworthy garment of the end of the century is the long, loose trousers, or pantaloons, another contribution from the peasantry. During the French Revolution revolutionists of the poorer class were known as sans-culottes—literally, without breeches (the knee breeches of the aristocracy). For centuries the working class had worn this type of leg covering for very practical reasons. Pumpkin breeches, rhinegraves, and satin culottes had little place in fields or farm yards. Once in power, the sans-culottes became respected and finally accepted, as indicated by this fashion plate. It is interesting to note that our patriotic symbol, Uncle Sam, dated from and was inspired by, the fashions of this period of French unrest.

17

Women's Costume of the Eighteenth Century

After a lull at the beginning of the eighteenth century, women's fashions quickened. Beginning with the 1760s the accelerated pace of fashion change produced one of the most quixotic periods on record. The bizarre creations of the last 30 years of the century were largely the result of, first, Marie Antoinette's craving for diversion, and, after her downfall, to the chaotic political situation in France. English styles were more conservative but exerted great influence in France during the eighties and nineties.

In the early eighteenth century, Watteau painted French men and women in idyllic surroundings, dancing, conversing, engaged in theatricals, or as in *Gersaint's Signboard* (Fig. 433) examining works of art. His painting highlights the change from the ceremonial grandeur of baroque art, which was commissioned and designed for formal palatial settings, to the more informal, more natural, and more intimate atmosphere of the rococo period which followed. Costume was quick to reflect the change. Fabrics of rich heavy texture and large-scale designs were still popular in the first quarter century, but intermingling with them even then

were more buoyant silks, plain or patterned in smaller motifs. Coloring was modulated from the darker, more dignified, tones to lighter values and tender colors, as the French describe them. Pompadour was the sponsor and exponent of this taste in dress.

SKIRT FASHIONS. Since skirts experienced the greatest alterations, a brief summary of the successive silhouettes should help to place individual costumes in their proper niches. Six basic forms appeared during the century, in the following order:

1. The bustle was a continuation of the 1690 mode.

2. The bell or dome shape resulted from the reintroduction of hoops; in England by 1710, in France by 1720.

3. The ellipse, the second phase of the hoop skirt, was achieved by broadening the support from side to side and compressing it from front to back. It had a long run of popularity, from 1740 to 1770, the extreme width being retained in court costumes. In France it persisted until the revolution, except that skirts were allowed to curve outward in back again. English court costume

411

FIG. 433. *Watteau, Antoine Gersaint's Signboard. Print. 1720. (Metropolitan Museum of Art, Gift of Mr. and Mrs. Herbert N. Straus)*

followed this fashion well into the nineteenth century.

4. The dairy maid, or polonaise, style could be achieved either by pulling the lower part of the overskirt through its own pocket holes, thus creating a bouffant effect, or by planned control of the overskirt, through the cut or by means of draw cords, ribbons, or loops and buttons, which were used to form the three great "poufs" known as the polonaise (see Fig. 452). These diversions appeared in the late sixties and became prevalent in the seventies. They were much like the familiar styles of our own Revolutionary War period.

5. The return of the bustle in the 1780s.

6. The tubular form, drawn from classic art, in the 1790s.

BODICES. Bodices showed less variation than skirts. The vast majority were tight, with pointed waistlines. The chief differences lay in the manner of closing, of which the principal ones were the following:

1. The open or stomacher front which had characterized late seventeenth-century dress continued practically throughout the eighteenth century.

2. Front closings might be invisibly laced or hooked down center front. A less prevalent closing was an overlapping of the two sides in a surplice line (see Fig. 442).

3. Back closings were used on most of the wide-necked gowns of mid-century.

Basic Composition of Costumes

In the eighteenth century the costume we refer to today as a "dress" was composed in four different ways.

1. A combination of overdress and underskirt was by far the most popular (Fig. 434).

2. A costume more in line with our modern concept of a dress had bodice and skirt cut separately and joined with a waist seam. Sometimes only the back waist portion was closed, the remainder being left free to allow lengthened front bodice sections to overlap the skirt (see Fig. 455).

3. A flowing robe, commonly called the sacque, fell freely from the shoulders in both back and front.

4. A combination of jacket and skirt also made a costume. These appear in Lancret's painting, *Camargo Dancing;* in ladies' riding habits, which borrowed tricorne hat, stock, jabot, and gloves, as well as waistcoat, from men's wear; and in the caraco costume of the 1770s (see Fig. 456).

Eighteenth-century gowns are also classified in another way:

1. When the back fullness was formed into box pleats at the neckline, falling freely from there to the floor, the gown is referred to as a *robe à la francaise* (Fig. 433).

FIG. 434. *Green and Gold Brocade Gown. 1710.* (*Danish National Museum, Copenhagen*)

2. When the back bodice portion fits closely to the body, either by edge-stitching the pleats to the underbody or by seaming, the gown is known as a *robe à l'anglaise* (Fig. 435).

1700–1730

As we have noted earlier, Madame de Maintenon's restraining influence discouraged novelty in costume during the last years of Louis XIV's reign. Typical of fashions at this time is a magnificent green and gold brocade gown of 1710, still remarkably fresh and shimmering which is the pride of the costume collection of the National Museum in Copenhagen (Figs. 434 and 435). Note the similarity of its cut to that of the late seventeenth-century dress in Fig. 405 (Metropolitan Museum) described earlier. In the overdress and petticoat category, its front closing is a handsome stomacher. Its back fullness is controlled by stitched pleats, which identifies the costume as a *robe à l'anglaise*. The sleeves, in particular, are typical of this period. Quite a lot of fullness in the back portion is fashioned into vertical pleats. Watteau's enlightening drawings corroborate this feature. The cuffs also are sig-

FIG. 435. *Back View of Fig. 434. Redrawn from Photograph. (Danish National Museum, Copenhagen)*

Draft 21, is of greenish-brown faille embroidered in a baroque design in white, both designs and techniques being legacies from seventeenth-century needlework. The museum dates it as of the reign of Queen Anne, 1702–1714. It is of special interest to students of costume because it illustrates the skirt and jacket ensemble. The sweeping skirt, nearly 3¼ yards around, is cut in straight widths, the length being determined by the curve at the waistline. The jacket has a very full saucy peplum, like those seen on some of Watteau's ladies.

The second dress (Fig. 437) also comes within the first quarter of the century. It

FIG. 436. *Embroidered Brown Faille Costume. Queen Anne Period. 1702–1714. (Courtesy, Museum of Fine Arts, Boston)*

nificant: cut generously in the form of a long narrow rectangle, they are joined at the ends and shaped by cross-pleating at the inner surface of the elbow; extra girth extends in a sort of wing beyond the sleeve. This cuff style lasted into the 1740s. The lingerie ruffles below the cuff might be attached to the chemise or sewn to the dress sleeves.

Two rare gowns in the Museum of Fine Arts, Boston, throw much light on this period. The first, shown in Fig. 436 and

FIG. 437. *Blue and White Brocatelle Costume. Second Quarter of Eighteenth Century. (Courtesy, Museum of Fine Arts, Boston)*

is of blue silk patterned in white, its open, net-like portion being taken from lace designs. It is made with the free floating back of the *robe à la française*. The fitted front of the bodice calls for a stomacher (Draft 22a and b).

WATTEAU PLEATS. A disputed point regarding eighteenth-century costume is the aptness of applying the name of the great artist, Watteau, to the double box pleats which, from 1720 on, often hung in a long free sweep from a straight back neckline to the hem of the skirt. His *Gersaint's Signboard* (Fig. 433) illustrates such an arrangement, the box pleats here being formed by a single pleat at each edge. Often the pleats were stacked or spaced slightly apart in an arrangement of two or three folds at each side of the box pleat. It is this graceful, flowing treatment of the back that characterizes the *robe à la française;* the means by which it is achieved is popularly called Watteau pleats. It seems a small but appropriate tribute to the artist in return for all the information his paintings and drawings provide about the costume of his era.

THE SACQUE. Occasionally, but perhaps more often than the records indicate, the dress hung uninterruptedly from shoulder to floor in both back and front, resembling nothing so much as a tent—especially when worn with a hoop petticoat. This is the sacque. Von Boehn[1] says that it was also called a contouche or andrienne—a name derived from Terence's comedy, *Andria*, in which the actress Mme. Dancourt wore it as a maternity dress. It was considered proper for travel as well as for casual at-home wear. It is the one robe of the first three-quarters of the century that looks comfortable, and it must have been convenient during pregnancy.

THE RETURN OF HOOPS. Although France is considered the chief source of European fashion during the eighteenth century, England contributed several fashion firsts, one being the reintroduction of hoops. By 1710, hoops were calling forth acrimonious comments in England; by 1720 at the latest they had found favor with the French.[2]

Silhouettes of the eighteenth century were determined by the types and shapes of the gown's substructure. For example, the Danish gown shown in Figs. 434 and 435 was designed to be worn with a bustle. The return of dome-shaped hoops marked the century's first important innovation in contour. At first the hoops were quite modest in size. About 1730 they began to increase in circumference at the hemline, possibly inspired by the shortened and widened ballet skirts of Mlle. Camargo, the idolized ballerina of her day.

In Hogarth's 1729 painting of a wedding scene his ladies wear true dome-shaped skirts, closed all around in the manner of the *robe à l'anglaise*. Their bodices have narrow stomacher fronts, the square decolletage being filled in with gauzy neckerchiefs. Their sleeves, including the cuffs, have been reduced in volume since 1710. Three of the lace-edged caps in the painting are worn with falling lappets and all are shaped to a dipping point at center front. Folding fans and gloves complete the visible accessories.

FOOTWEAR. Footwear became more sophisticated in line than in the previous century; the heels, though still rather blocky, were slimmer and higher and the toes more pointed. Figure 438d is a fine example of a shoe made largely of brocade, with a matching clog for protection out-of-doors. (Note also 438e and f.)

1730–1750

In the thirties, skirts increased in volume,

---

[1] Max von Boehn, *Modes and Manners*, Lippincott, Philadelphia, 1932, vol. IV, pp. 176–177.

[2] *Ibid.*, p. 162.

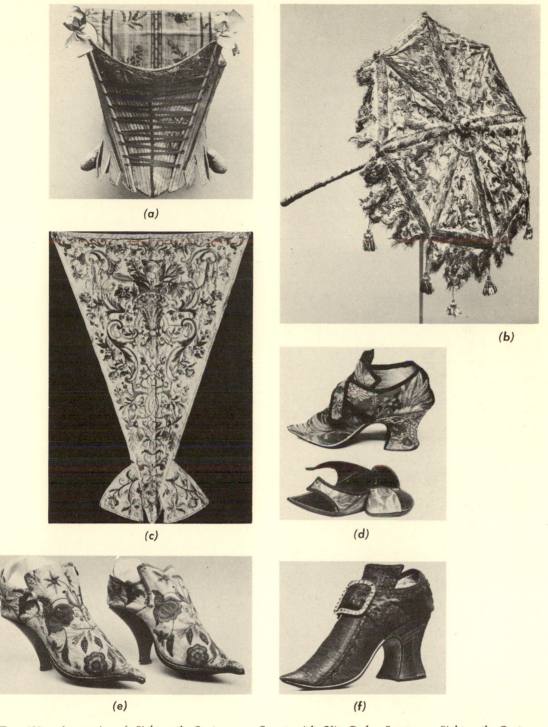

Fig. 438. *Accessories of Eighteenth Century. a. Corset with Hip Pads. European. Eighteenth Century. b. Embroidered Parasol. Italian. Eighteenth Century. (a and b, Metropolitan Museum of Art) c. Embroidered Stomacher. Italian. Early Eighteenth Century. d. Shoe with Matching Clog, Eighteenth Century. (c and d, Courtesy, Museum of Fine Arts, Boston) e. White Kid Shoe Embroidered with Silk. French. Eighteenth Century. (Metropolitan Museum of Art) f. Satin Shoe Trimmed with Braid. English. Early Eighteenth Century. (Victoria & Albert Museum, Crown Copyright)*

being worn over enlarged hoops. Necklines widened to harmonize with increased emphasis upon horizontal lines. Sleeve ruffles called *engageantes* provided feminine froth at the elbows. Bodices were long, smooth, and sharply pointed, bespeaking a heavily boned, tightly laced corset beneath (Figs. 439, 440 and Draft 26*a*, *b*). All of these costumes have closed skirts over round hoops, the last one showing pronounced increase in size.

NECKLINE TREATMENT. All necklines were more open in the thirties and forties. Camargo's broad, low, curved decolletage is the same as that of the court costume of Queen Marie Leczinska shown in Fig. 439. In Nattier's paintings of the royal princesses, sisters of Louis XV, this neckline also prevails. It continued as a feature of court costumes into Marie Antoinette's reign (see Fig. 449). The characteristic finish of this open neckline was a band of exquisite lace.

FIG. 439.   *Louis Toqué, Queen Marie Leczinska. 1740. (Louvre)*

FIG. 440. *Gown Worn Over Elliptical Hoop Petticoat. 1745. Redrawn from Arthur Devis, Portrait of Countess of Egremont. (California Palace of Legion of Honor)*

Closings were usually down center back. The smooth front of the dress was decorated with lace, flowers, ribbon, and/or jewels.

A significant fashion detail which persisted through much of this century and into the nineteenth was the separate frilled neckband, which was introduced as early as 1730.

SLEEVES. The thirties and forties witnessed a revival, not only of the mid-seventeenth-century neckline, but also of the sleeves of that period. The court costume of Marie Leczinska shown in Fig. 439 has these features. The fabric of the gown is used only in a tiny sleeve cap; below it is a sleeve made of ruffles of lace on puffed, delicate fabric, ending with a double ruffle at the elbow. This sleeve design persisted in court costume as late as Marie Antoinette's reign (see Fig. 449).

Other types of sleeves include a long tight sleeve seen on the jacketed costumes and the soft loose sleeve reaching just below the elbow, ending in ruffles of lace (Fig. 441).

FRONT CLOSINGS. Contemporaneous with broad necklines and back closing bodices were gowns with front closings of several types:

1. The most prosaic was the fastening down center front. The front bodice sections were either cut to meet at center, or extensions were sewed to the slanted line from shoulder to waist; these were hooked or otherwise fastened.

2. An alternate front closing was made by overlapping the two sides in surplice fashion, as shown in Fig. 442. Here the decolletage is filled in with a dickey, above which appears a soft ruffle, possibly from the chemise.

3. The third and most popular design was the front with robings—flat folds of materials which finished the slanting edges of the fronts from shoulder to waist or lower. Robings were introduced in the seventeenth century and remained in the fashion scene quite continuously through the eighteenth. This type of front required some sort of accessory to complete the bodice, the most usual one being the stomacher, shown in Fig. 434. Many elaborately embroidered stomachers are in museum collections; of these Fig. 438c is outstanding. These were often pinned in place to the corset by tabs along the sides.

Sometimes the corset itself, covered with damask or embroidered silk intended for display, took the place of a separate stomacher (Draft 26a, b). Sometimes the ends of a fichu or neck scarf held in position by

FIG. 441. *Hogarth, Miss Mary Edwards. c.1742. (Frick Collection, New York)*

ribbons which spanned the opening, covered the void. In the painting by Hogarth (Fig. 441) Miss Mary Edwards uses a long narrow brooch for this purpose.

Another method of securing the robing edges was to lace them together over the corset by tapes or cords threaded through vertical strips of eyelets attached to the lining of the bodice. Figure 455, although of a later period and different design, illustrates

FIG. 442. *Surplice Closing. 1740–1750. Redrawn from Unknown Artist, Portrait of Duchess of Marlborough. (National Portrait Gallery, London)*

the technique involved and is typical of the inside structure of many eighteenth-century gowns. Note the back lacing also.

Still another device was bows of ribbon in graduated widths extending from top to bottom of the elongated V. This arrangement, known as an *eschelle*, first appeared in the seventeenth century (Fig. 398) and was a favorite accessory of Madame Pompadour.

DRESS WITH PETTICOAT. A bodice with robings was often combined with an open skirt and worn over a petticoat—a garment which gained in importance as the century progressed. The material of the petticoat often matched the gown, but frequently during this period it was of contrasting material (satin was a favorite) elaborately quilted.

NEW SHAPE OF HOOPS. During the 1740s, hoops unlimited seem to have been the order of the day. They spread to enormous proportions, rivaling the seventeenth-

century gowns of the Spanish Infantas, as suggested by the gown worn by Queen Maria Leczinska in Fig. 439. But the hoops of the eighteenth century were brought under control in one dimension; the great circle was flattened into an ellipse. This characteristic distinguishes it from other periods. Figure 440 shows how slender the figure appeared from front to back.

WRAPS. Evidence of eighteenth-century wraps is slight but the few illustrations of the period and the rare original garments in museums point up the prevalence of capes. Among the fashion drawings of 1729 is a voluminous full-length collared cape with matching hood, buttoned all the way down center front and provided with openings for the arms.

A portrait by Nattier in the Wallace collection (Fig. 443) shows a silk cape of perhaps hip length with hood attached. It is tied at the throat with ribbons and finished on all edges with bands of fur.

Leloir[3] describes a winter costume consisting of full skirt and wrist-length jacket, both padded and beautifully quilted.

[3] Maurice Leloir, *Histoire du Costume*, Henri Ernst, Paris, 1938, vol. XI, p. 53.

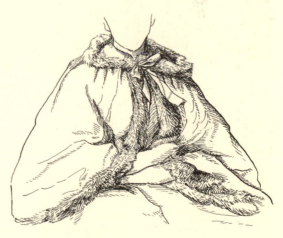

FIG. 443. *Short Cape Trimmed with Fur. 1750. Redrawn from Nattier, Portrait of Comtesse de Tillières. (Reproduced by Permission of the Trustees of the Wallace Collection, London)*

HAIRDRESS AND HEADDRESS. During the thirties and forties the hairdress was softened. Women wore loose curls at the back of the head beneath a tiny lingerie cap, or longer curls falling forward over their bared shoulders (Fig. 439). In England the cap became larger and more enveloping. The cap worn by Miss Mary Edwards in Hogarth's painting (Fig. 441) is lavishly trimmed with precious lace. Lace ruffles form a slight peak above her forehead and curve downward to rest upon her shoulders.

At this same time a broad-brimmed low-crowned hat was very popular. Joseph Highmore showed it in his illustrations for Richardson's *Pamela*, which date from 1744. Country folk wore it over their round-eared caps. In Boucher's portrait Madame Bergeret carries hers by its ribbon ties. Some paintings show the ties on the upper surface of the

FIG. 444. *Middle-Class Costume. 1739. Redrawn from Chardin, The Governess. (Metropolitan Museum of Art, Dick Fund)*

hat; when the ribbons were tied under the chin, this would pull the brim down over the ears. The Elizabeth Day McCormick collection in the Boston Museum has several fine examples of these hats (Fig. 437).

FOOTWEAR. Heels became much more slender and higher at this time, and pointed toes were elongated. As on men's shoes the buckles were curved to the contour of the instep.

ACCESSORIES. Aprons continued to be a fashionable accessory, even for quite important occasions. They varied from the simple, functional, bibbed garments of Chardin's middle-class subjects (Fig. 444) to the elegance of one made entirely of Argentan lace and worn by a princess. A taffeta apron in the Boston Museum collection, embroidered in colored silks and edged in gold lace, was by no means designed for housework.

Jewelry on the whole was kept simple, Miss Edwards' resplendent display of diamonds in Fig. 441 being an exception. Note also her pearl necklace, rings, and the chatelaine with watch hanging from her waistline. Queen Marie Leczinska concentrated her wealth of jewels on the front of her bodice (Fig. 439).

Flowers were an expression of the rococo style. As we have seen, the sixteenth century was identified with a profusion of jewels and the seventeenth with lace; the eighteenth retained the lace and added flowers. In Lancret's portrait Camargo wears garlands of flowers around the hem of her skirt and scarf, at the neckline, on her sleeves, and in her hair. Corsages were so popular that pockets were often provided in the lining of the bodice or corset for small vials of water to keep the blossoms fresh. They were also worn on the shoulder and attached to ribbons round the throat. One of the best-known drawings of Marie Antoinette's reign shows the great wedding-cake skirt of the court gown decorated from waist to hem with festoons of flowers.

All in all, it was a feminine century for the ladies.

THE FIFTIES AND SIXTIES

Corseting was a fine art in the eighteenth century. It required exact measuring, accurate cutting, sturdy stitching, a knowledge of boning apropos to stress, strains, and curves, and no conscience about the sufferings of the wearer. Garsault made a series of drawings in 1769 depicting corsets for the pregnant woman, the horseback rider, the lady at court, the young girl, the young boy, and the little boy with his first culottes, which were held up by buttons and buttonholes. The Victoria and Albert collection includes a wonderful example of a small boy's corset, which, to the uninitiated, is indistinguishable from a woman's garment. Corseting was accepted from youth on and its demands taken for granted. Every woman knew that the impeccable smoothness of her bodice depended upon her stays (Draft 26).

Some of the corsets which have come down to us were obviously intended as underwear; those covered with damask or, as in an example in the National Museum of Denmark, with cherry-colored faille, deserved to be seen and often were partially visible. The broad, low, curving neckline of Fig. 438a belongs to mid-century. It is covered with beautiful brocade and metal lace, and even the quilting which encases the boning is decorative. The front of this garment might well have substituted for a stomacher. The fat little hip pads provided a shelf for hoops to rest upon. Note the direction of the staying and the outward thrust which it gives to the front of the garment. This corset might also have been worn with undress—loose flowing garments worn over stays and petticoat and donned in the intimacy of the home or even to receive guests. Plain linen or leather corsets were worn under costumes which were closed in front, though the corsets themselves might fasten down either front or back. A wide rigid removable stay called a busk was often inserted down center front (Fig. 411b).

Madame Pompadour's Influence on Fashion

Mid-eighteenth century costume, as well as the settings in which they were worn, owed much to the taste of Madame Pompadour. Trained carefully and thoroughly for the career of mistress to the King, she managed by one means or another to cross the path of Louis XV, catch his attention, be introduced, and attain her goal. Since hers was an enviable position, highly respected, and vested with power, she became first lady of the land and took full advantage of her opportunities. (Her eventual successor in Louis XV's affections, Du Barry, lacked the social background and training of the grand mistress, and had litttle or no influence on fashion.)

Madame Pompadour's name has come down in costume history by way of such terms as the pompadour (which refers to a hairdress much higher than shown in any of her portraits), and pompadour taffeta, which usually connotes a warp print silk with floral design.

Figure 445 shows her in 1755, at the age of 34, in the light, airy costume she favored. The skirt silhouette is not as distorted as those of Figs. 439 and 440 referred to earlier. The buoyant silk fabric seems to float of its own accord—an illusion, but a pleasant one. Femininity seems to have reached its ultimate expression in dress at this time. In this portrait the bouffant nature of the fabric is aided and abetted by ruffling, ruching, lace, ribbons, and flowers. Here is the perfect interpretation of the rococo style in costume: light in feeling, subtle in coloring, a composition of continuously curving lines with infinitely intricate detail.

Every item of Madame Pompadour's costumes became fashion news. Her widened but square neckline prolonged the popularity

FIG. 445. *Francois Boucher, Madame Pompadour. 1755. (Reproduced by Permission of the Trustees of the Wallace Collection, London)*

of that style in competition with the broad curved decolletage of the court costume. Following her example, gradually widened flutings adorned the front edges of the overdress in fashionable circles, replacing the flat robings. Three of her most important portraits show her stomachers covered with eschelles. The swirls and flounces of her petticoats suggest both the ascendency of the overdress-and-petticoat costume and the elaborate decoration bestowed upon undergarments.

The sleeves of this period were more closely fitted than earlier and ended in a froth of full, delicate, multiple, ruffling called *engageantes*. The winged cuff was replaced by graduated ruffles of the dress fabric, usually two, edged with fringe, metallic lace, or colorful openwork silk braid. Beneath these spread the engageantes: two, or if possible, three, shaped ruffles, also graduated in width, of the finest lace the exchequer could provide. Less opulent folk substituted plain or embroidered muslin.

In the portrait by Boucher (Fig. 445) Pompadour has added a fluffy bow of ribbon near her inner elbow. Her neck frill is not new but she gave it the cachet of authority by wearing it. Like her many imitators, she restricted her jewelry largely to pearls. They appear in her hair, earrings, a choker worn high above her neck frill, and a pair of four-strand bracelets. Her hairdress resembles the twentieth-century style named for her only in that the hair is brushed back from the forehead. This close but soft and becoming style gave way in the sixties to an increase in bulk rising in an egg shape above the forehead and employing stiff, set curls and powder (see Fig. 457).

Other Fashion Features

Shoes were now more rounded at the toe and had a high slender heel and a large buckle, most frequently set with paste.

Figure 446 shows the magnificent coronation robes of Queen Louisa Ulrica of Sweden. The fabric is silver brocade, woven for her in Stockholm. Her broad neckline

FIG. 446. *Coronation Robes of Queen Louisa Ulrica of Sweden. 1751. (Royal Armoury, Stockholm)*

and horizontally trimmed sleeves echo the court fashions of the French royal family. Draft 23a and b shows the pattern of the dress and its accompanying court train. The mechanism which created the contour of her skirt was built into the petticoat, as shown in Draft 23c, the pattern of the white silk faille petticoat worn under her coronation robe.

An alternate support for the very wide skirt of this era was the pannier. One example of this is in the Metropolitan Museum collection. A complicated but more flexible framework in the Cluny Museum is shown in Fig. 447. This one is provided with hinges which made it possible to collapse the lateral extensions when passing through doorways or entering a vehicle.

In all of these types the spring of whalebone or caning was regulated by pairs of tapes on the inside of the garment which could be tied to whatever front-to-back depth the wearer desired. This elliptical form remained in fashion during the fifties and sixties.

WRAPS. The collection of costumes in the Nordiska Museet, Stockholm, has wonderful surprises for the student of costume, such as a damask coat cut to fit over the projecting hoops worn in the middle of the eighteenth century (Fig. 448).

The Brooklyn Museum, too, is justly proud of its rare, pink, uncut velvet wrap of the same period. The Museum of Fine Arts, Boston, is rich in examples of long

hooded capes and capelets of about the same date, made of cotton fabrics, often chintz, some of them trimmed generously with chantilly lace.

Various portraits reflect the popularity of fur-edged velvet capes. Muffs continued as a popular accessory, and although seldom seen in paintings, parasols were also carried. A handsome embroidered one of Italian workmanship is in the Metropolitan collection (Fig. 438b).

Fabrics

When we consider the magnificence of Queen Maria Leczinska's gold and silk brocade, Queen Sophia Magdalena's cloth of silver, and Pompadour's exquisite taffetas and richly glowing damasks, it seems almost incongruous that cotton fabrics, which we are apt to consider rather ordinary, should have been so fashionable and so important in the economy of eighteenth-century France. Laws were made (and later repealed) controlling the importation and manufacture of printed cottons. At one time when such imports were contraband, Pompadour had her rooms decorated with them. Two circumstances undoubtedly whetted the desire for them: when first introduced their price was exorbitant, making them real luxuries; and when importation was forbidden, their possession inflated the ego and bestowed a certain enviable eminence upon the owner.

This craze for cotton fabrics would have been of purely ephemeral importance,

FIG. 447. *Collapsible Panniers. c.1760. Redrawn from Leloir,* Histoire du Costume, *Vol. XI, Figure 38. (Cluny Museum)*

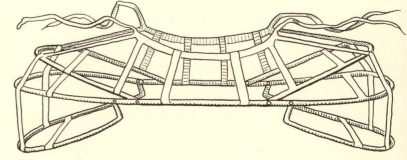

FIG. 448. *Damask Coat. Mid-Eighteenth Century. (Nordiska Museet, Stockholm)*

except for the fact that it stimulated the establishment of the cotton industry in France and led to the production of printed cotton fabrics which, as a result of continuous efforts to improve methods of printing, quality of dyes, and designs, are now treasured with other rare textiles in museum collections.

At the same time, however, trade with the Orient continued and contact with India, Persia, and China familiarized Europeans with oriental art in many of its expressions. Chinese porcelains and Persian and Indian miniatures adorning the rooms of Schönbrunn formed part of the background of Marie Antoinette's Vienna childhood.

Oriental architecture and furnishings had a telling effect upon European artists and craftsmen. The term *chinoiserie* describes the style imparted to many textile designs by quaint pagodas, figures in pointed hats and pigtails, and other Chinese motifs. Chippendale, one of the great eighteenth-century English cabinet makers, borrowed heavily from Chinese sources.

Persia and India also contributed much to color appreciation; Persian fabric designs of the eighteenth century were practically duplicated in the delicate floral striped silks of Louis XVI's reign.

Imported Indian cotton prints became popular for men's morning robes, a much more important article in men's wardrobes at that time than at present. Women's dresses, too, were made of them but, unfortunately for the historian of costume, were not popular in portraiture. The Nordiska Museet in Stockholm has a jacket made of Indian cotton embroidered in polychromatic silks so fine in both stitchery and filament that close examination is necessary in order to distinguish the technique.

Importation of such fabrics increased in England in the eighteenth century, when the refinement of India muslin was truly appreciated, and later in both France and England when the revival of classic styles created a demand for a soft, sheer, clinging fabric for their construction. At the end of the century the incomparable shawls of India happily substituted for the Greek himation.

THE SEVENTIES

At first sight pictures of the fashionable ladies of the seventies look unreal to us, their costumes incredible— for masquerade perhaps, for daily wear never. Louis XVI succeeded to the French throne in 1774. The undisciplined deportment of his queen, Marie Antoinette, held somewhat in check during the old regime, now had free play. Since her taste ran to dancing, theatricals, and masked escapades, her costumes and those of her court exhibited quixotic tendencies toward absurdity and exaggeration.

Her amusement with the Swiss village she built at Versailles and the peasant theme it dramatized led to shorter skirts and emphasis upon the polonaise, a mode which resembled the milkmaid's tucked up skirt. She became obsessed with her hair and engaged an expert, Leonard, to keep her coiffure at the forefront of the mode.

Court costume retained the hooped silhouette at its greatest expansion, and resumed a rounded contour in the back. Garlands of flowers, swags of diaphanous gauze, flutings and plastics (padded appliqué) of self fabric, intricate and ingenious silk fringes and/or fur, helped to give these gowns a fairy tale atmosphere. Figure 449, one of the many portraits of Marie Antoinette, was made by Mme. Lebrun in 1775.

Necklines of this decade were scandalously low, according to French prints. They were, however, often softened by a frill of lace or fluting and sometimes by an upright ruffle of lace which echoed the Medici collar or standing ruff, though it is neither as wide nor as elaborate as the seventeenth-century original (Fig. 450).

For daily wear panniers were worn, like those of mid-century (Fig. 447). However, another type of pannier, more closely related to the true meaning of the word (basket), was also worn. This consisted of a pair of caned or boned pouches, their inner surfaces curved to the contour of the hips, the outside extending well beyond them (Fig. 451). The Nordiska Museet has a pair of these made of chamois. The tendency in

FIG. 449. *Mme. Vigée-Lebrun, Marie Antoinette. c.1775. (Versailles National Museum)*

FIG. 450. *Young Woman of Quality Wearing Victory Headdress. 1778. La Galerie des Modes, Vol. J, Plate 7. (New York Public Library, Prints Division)*

everyday wear was toward a narrower, closer silhouette than during mid-century, possibly due to the peasant influence promoted by Marie Antoinette.

These panniers provided ideal supports for the polonaise—the overskirt draped in three great puffs over the back and sides of the petticoat (Fig. 452). Various devices were used to create this draped effect. Usually the overskirt was cut on grain, quite full and of even length; for more formal occasions it was trained. Cords threaded through rings sewed on the underside could be drawn and tied to hold the fabric at the desired level. At other times ribbons fastened at the waistline were looped under the overskirt, shaping it into the familiar festoons. Tasseled cords also appeared on the outside. lifting the cloth high at the sides. The polonaise could also be fashioned by pleating or shirring along the side seams.

Figure 453 reproduces a French fashion drawing of a *robe à l'anglaise* with a polonaise jutting abruptly from the waistline.

FIG. 451. *Woman Wearing Panniers. c.1775. Redrawn from Joseph von Göz, Old Coquette. (New York Public Library, Prints Division)*

Note the revealing decolletage, the lengthened waist with sharply dipping point, and the shortened skirt. This is the first time in European fashion that so much of the foot and ankle has been exposed.

Figure 450 shows a court costume typical of the seventies: long, pointed bodice, excruciatingly tight, closing down center front; low square neckline with standing frill inspired by early seventeenth-century neckwear; sleeves in broken areas of ruffles and puffs, ending in double or triple *engageantes;* enormous hoops, arching upward from the waistline; matching petticoat, the front sections of both skirts paneled with ruchings and swags accented with nosegays; the tow-

ering hairdress of apparently sculptured solidity topped by a pouf encircled by laurel and crested with plumes. Elbow-length gloves and large folding fans, some painted by fine artists, were ubiquitous accessories.

Fortunately not everyone indulged in such absurdities. A realistic but remarkable testimonial of this is a gown in the Brooklyn Museum, the richness and beauty of which is almost entirely lost in a photograph (Fig. 454 and Draft 27*a* and *b*). It is made of glowing gold-colored silk of luxurious texture and embroidered with polychromatic silks in varied but carefully balanced floral designs which cover the entire overdress and petticoat. Some alterations have doubtless been made but the basic structure remains intact. Originally it was probably worn with a different neck frill and engageantes to match.

A back view of the gown presents an excellent example of Watteau pleats or *robe*

FIG. 452. *Polonaise. 1780–1782. Redrawn from La Galerie des Modes, Vol. II², Plate 135. (New York Public Library)*

FIG. 453. *Robe à la Anglaise with Polonaise and Therese. 1770's. (Author's Collection)*

the attached strips with eyelets for the front closing. The skirt and bodice are joined at the back only. The fronts of the bodice are free to cover the waistline of the front of the skirt as in Fig. 454.

PLASTICS. The sausage-shaped trimming on the overskirt of Fig. 450 which stands out in relief from the fabric of the dress is padded to give a three-dimensional effect—a type of garnishment used frequently in the third quarter of the century and called plastic decoration or plastics. The design was frequently far more elaborate than this example.

THE CARACO. Another innovation of

FIG. 454. *Embroidered Gold Silk Costume. 1770's. (Brooklyn Museum)*

à la francaise. Figure 455 is a drawing of the inside of one of these gowns. A complete inside bodice, which functioned as both lining and reinforcement, could be adjusted by the lacing down center back. This arrangement accounts for the sleek look of the bodice when worn and the retention of the precise form of the Watteau pleats. Note

the seventies was the caraco, illustrated in Fig. 456. The word *caraco* refers to the jacket, which looks almost like a polonaise cut off at hip level and finished with a double ruffle. The Costume Institute of the Metropolitan Museum has a golden-yellow satin costume which almost duplicates Fig. 456 (Draft 24*a* and *b*). The caraco remained in fashion throughout the eighties and into the nineties.

HAIRDRESS. The feature which dominates all 1770 portraits and fashion plates is the hairdress. In the sixties the hair began to be built up in volume and was generally powdered. In Fig. 457, taken from a 1771 portrait of Queen Charlotte of England, the mushrooming is already apparent.

The combination of circumstances which brought about the monstrous constructions of the seventies is difficult for us to comprehend. The inception of these fashions depended upon the existence of a leisure class and involved a repulsively low standard of hygiene. They could have evolved only during a period when every aspect of dress was fantastic, when personal appearance mattered more than impending political cataclysm and helped to hasten it.

Figure 458, from a cartoon of the seventies, gives some idea of the extreme to which the caprice was carried. In order to erect such a structure and keep it upright, much padding of crinkled crinoline, false hair, etc. had to be placed inside. The hair itself was stiffened with a flour paste which gave the desired whiteness of powder and, when dried, assumed a texture somewhat akin to papier-maché. In the cartoon the balloon-shaped skyscraper seems to be composed entirely of hair, but Fig. 450 suggests a variety of objects which might be added. The most famous of these bizarre creations was one in which a ship in full sail, designed to commemorate a naval victory during the American war for independence, rode the

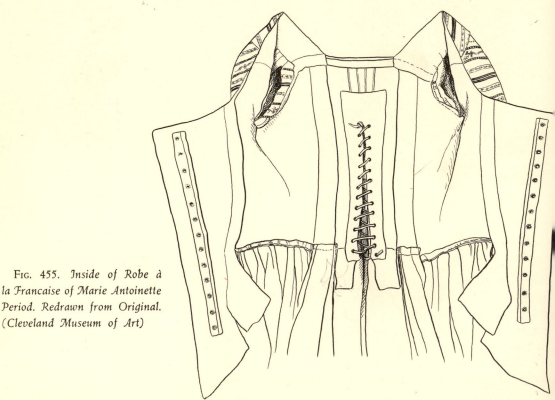

FIG. 455. *Inside of Robe à la Francaise of Marie Antoinette Period. Redrawn from Original. (Cleveland Museum of Art)*

consequently they were built to last. If 3 or 4 weeks intervened between appointments, as often happened, the victim's endurance met a real test. Since the coiffures were fragile, though stiff and heavy, one wonders how ladies so handicapped managed doorways, chandeliers, entering and leaving their sedan chairs (they often knelt in transit), and most of all, how it was possible to sleep. Through the long intervals between renewals, vermin held high holiday. If they became too active the headdress was opened —that is, slits were made through the hardened paste and lively hunting ensued. Robert Burns' poem "To a Louse," written in 1786, was inspired by watching a creature scuttling about on the hat of a lady in front of him in church. The lines most often quoted are:

Oh wad some Power the giftie gie us
To see ourselves as others see us.[4]

[4] *The Poetical Works of Robert Burns*, Lee and Shepard, Boston, 1873, pp. 120–121.

FIG. 456. *Caraco Costume. 1778. La Galerie des Modes, Vol. J², Plate 51. (New York Public Library)*

FIG. 457. *Early Stage of High Hairdress. 1771. Redrawn from Zoffany, Portrait of Queen Charlotte of England. (Victoria & Albert Museum, Crown Copyright)*

crest of the waves (Fig. 459). Figures of people, carriages, gardens, anything suggested by the latest gossip or current event, might be enshrined upon a towering mass of hair.

These conglomerate affairs required long hours of patient work by professionals and

FIG. 458. *Cartoon of Woman's Hairdress of 1770's. (New York Public Library, Prints Division)*

*Cœffure
à l'Indépendance ou le
Triomphe de la liberté.*

FIG. 459. *Coiffure of Independence. 1770's. (Musée de Blèrancourt)*

FIG. 460. *Robe à la Francaise. c.1780. (Metropolitan Museum of Art)*

Wigs would have been far more hygienic than the built-in fixtures of this decade. In this respect men enjoyed a great advantage. The amount of flour consumed in hairdressing by both men and women reduced markedly the supply available for

food and increased the discontent among the peasantry. These features tend to destroy the glamour often associated with court costume.

Personal cleanliness received short shrift at any level of society. Marie Antoinette is said to have considered daily washing of the hands sufficient observance. A present-day resident of England's Hampton Court, a woman steeped in the history and lore of England, was recently asked where the ladies of the court bathed. She replied, "Oh, they paddled in a pudding pan."

The stench from body odors must have been almost overpowering—perhaps this was why perfumes were considered a necessity. Powder and rouge were almost a ritual. Fans were indispensable, both for masking expressions and for keeping air in circulation.

OUTDOOR WEAR. The therese of this period (a voluminous head covering) was designed to give protection to the top-heavy hairdress (Fig. 453). It was of light-weight material and would have served chiefly as a windbreak. For more rugged weather a more practical head covering was the collapsible calash, made of heavier fabric and ribbed and hinged somewhat like a carriage top.

Wraps continued much as in the previous decade; the pelisse—a cape, often hooded, with armhole slits—was a favorite. Fur applied to all edges gave it warmth and beauty.

The footwear of the seventies is illustrated in Figs. 453 and 456.

THE EIGHTIES

During the eighties, panniers decreased in size and finally disappeared, leaving skirts with rather a limp, deflated look. Court costume, however, retained the large hoops and elaborate ornamentation of the previous decade.

Rose Bertin was one of the first great dressmakers to be identified and noted for her creations. Her story is a book in itself. She planned and worked closely with Marie Antoinette on her wardrobe. She is largely responsible for the general style of the formal costumes of this period and the gauzy festooned trimming, caught with flowers or

dainty braids and fringes, which gave the whole a delicate air. The costume in Fig. 449 illustrates many of these features. Figure 460, a photograph of a dress of about 1780 in the Metropolitan Museum, is probably the work of the great Rose—at least it is very much in her manner. The diminutive scale of the floral pattern, the narrow stripes, the delicate colors, and the lightness of the silk denote the final phase of the rococo style in dress.

FIG. 461. *Plum Colored Caraco Worn with Rose Colored Skirt. 1786.* Cabinet des Modes, *August 15, Plate II. (University of Washington Library)*

THE BUSTLE SILHOUETTE. A new silhouette, produced by shifting the emphasis from the hips to the bust and the bustle, replaced that made by hoops. The costume shown in Fig. 461, from a French fashion plate of 1786, achieved the new look by a ruffled and puffed neckcloth which contributed to the front projection and a perky flip of the peplum of the caraco out from the back waistline over the bustled skirt. This became the dominant style of the late eighties and early nineties. Figure 462 illustrates a caraco of the eighties from the Museum of Decorative Arts in Paris; Draft 25 shows its smart cut.

Other ways of creating this silhouette included full fichus tucked into the neckline or crossed at the breast and tied at the back waistline, a corsage posed at the perimeter of the bustline, and large overlapping lapels worn in combination with fabric piled up over a bustled foundation.

SLEEVES. A noteworthy change in sleeve design was the introduction of plain full-length fitted sleeves, scarcely seen since the fifteenth century. Marie Antoinette, as usual, set the pace, but these sleeves appear in both French and English portraits.

THE REDINGOTE. In contrast to the ultrafeminine feeling of Bertin's gowns, redingotes were quite revolutionary in appearance. A fashion innovation from England, they were tailored, trim, and efficient looking (Fig. 463). Heretofore masculine influence upon women's clothing had been largely restricted to the riding habit. Now the English riding coat or redingote, full length, with deep collars and wide lapels, assumed the role of overdress or wrap. From this time on, the redingote held an important place in women's wardrobes. It became the smart enveloping wrap of the empire period in the next century and may well be the ancestor of women's coats of today.

Classical Influence

Another English contribution to the fashion of the eighties was the sheer white muslin dress familiar to us from the paintings of Reynolds, Romney, and Lawrence. In this respect the English fell under the spell of classic Greek influence sooner than the French did. Lacking the restrictions imposed by Marie Antoinette's court, the English were free to adapt costume designs from the source which was inspiring their architects and draftsmen. Happily, one of these gowns has been preserved in the collection of the London Museum. Its simplicity and understatement is refreshing after the grotesque artificiality of the seventies. The diaphanous muslin from India was a sympathetic medium for the interpretation of the mode.

That the French were not entirely unaware of this movement is proved by a

FIG. 462. *Striped Satin Caraco. 1780's. (Musée des Arts Decoratifs, Palais du Louvre)*

Vigée-Lebrun portrait of Marguerite de Jancourt, who posed in a long-sleeved white dress in pleasing contrast to the court costume, though maintaining the fashionable silhouette. Also, for informal wear, the *Cabinet des Modes* of 1786 included the casual-looking costume of Fig. 464, describing it as a *robe en chemise* of mousseline fastened down the back and belted with a black ribbon. The fabric being transparent, the underskirt and corset are of rose taffeta (evidently the gown was not quite as relaxed as it appears). The fichu is of linen gauze.

Other Fashion Features

The most striking feature of the eighties, as is evident from the illustrations already

FIG. 464. *Robe en Chemise. 1786. Redrawn from* Cabinet des Modes, *April 15, Plate 1. (University of Washington Library)*

FIG. 463. *English Redingote. c.1790. Redrawn from Morland,* The Squires Door *in Von Boehn,* Modes and Manners, *Vol. IV, Page 288.*

cited, was the headdress. Hairdress necessarily became subordinate to the millinery. Emphasis was transferred from the hair to the hat or headdress. Often these headdresses were great soft poufs of cloth, embellished with garlands and plumes as in Fig. 461. Sometimes they assumed a mushroom effect that all but overwhelmed the wearer. Figure 465, *The Fair Dorine*, is from a drawing published in *La Galerie des Modes* about 1785. This was the decade of the wide, sweeping, plumed masterpieces Gains-

FIG. 465. *Hat of 1785. Redrawn from* La Galerie des Modes, *The Fair Dorine, Vol. JJJ², Plate 203. (New York Public Library)*

FIG. 466. *Parisian Costume. 1792. Redrawn from Debucourt,* Public Promenade. *(Louvre)*

borough painted so often, and which have borne his name ever since. They were certainly among the most dramatic creations of all millinery. To keep such imposing headdresses balanced, the hairdress had to be broad and substantial. Natural hair made a welcome reappearance. In France, in keeping with the trimmer costume of the period, the headdress became more recognizable as a hat with a wide brim and real crown.

Figure 466, from Debucourt's *Public Promenade*, although dated 1792, gives quite a true picture of the transitional fashions of the decade. The skirt is simple and unadorned, its fullness increased at the back and molded into an outward curve by a bustle; the long-sleeved bodice has a tailored collar and "pouter pigeon" front, achieved by yards of crushed gauze. The unpowdered hair is treated quite simply.

Figure 467 is an excellent illustration of the most popular outdoor costume of the mid-eighties: a hooded, fur-trimmed pelisse, accompanied by a long fleeced muff of generous proportions and a plumed pouf.

Jewelry played a minor role in these years. The real novelty was a pair of watch fobs borrowed from men's wear and usually worn with the English-inspired tailored costume.

THE NINETIES IN ENGLAND

England went through no such upheaval in the nineties as France did. English portraits of this decade continue to feature the unpretentious white dress with long sleeves, normal waistline, and fichu crossed in front with ends tied at the back. A portrait of the Countess of Derby in the Metropolitan Museum shows her wearing a pelisse over her white gown and carrying a huge muff which matches the fur of her wrap.

The tailored redingote of 1790 (Fig. 463) was mentioned earlier (see page 438).

HEIDELOFF's *Gallery of Fashion*

The fashion plates published by Heideloff in London from 1794 to 1803, the *Gallery of Fashion,* are not only a sheer delight, but of great import to students of fashion. It is impossible to do justice to them with only one or two plates and without the color and the gold highlights. The overall impression they convey is that English women were modestly covered in the early nineties, often in overdress and petticoat; that heavier fabrics with more pattern and color were used; and that for a while hairdress remained more elaborate and headdress more involved than in France. Hoops were retained in court costume, producing a silhouette entirely at variance with accepted fashion.

Figure 468 from Heideloff's *Gallery of Fashion* is representative of English costumes of the mid-nineties. A brief glance reveals little evidence of Greek influence. Only the raised waistlines and unobstructed fall of the skirts may be traced to that source. The following descriptions, which accompany the figures, help bring them to life (see Fig. 468):

[Left] The hair combed into light curls; plain chignon, white bouffant around the head. Bonnet of black velvet lined with pink satin; the cawl [crown] of pink satin spotted with black, the top fastened and crossed in several parts with black velvet riband, fastened with a button on top, trimmed with pink riband made into one large bow in front and behind. One black ostrich feather in front. Round gown of chintz, with long sleeves, and trimmed at the bottom with a narrow flounce. Full cravat around the neck. Black satin short cloak trimmed with broad lace. Isabella bearskin tippet and muff. Red morocco slippers.

[Right] Hair in light curls and ringlets; white satin riband round the head and tied with

FIG. 467. *Woman Wearing a Pelisse. 1785.* Cabinet des Modes, *December 1, Plate 1. (University of Washington Library)*

a bow in front. Bonnet of black velvet and lined with yellow satin; cawl of yellow satin spotted with black, the top flattened; trimmed with yellow satin riband, forming a large bow in front and behind; one small bow of black riband on the left side. Petticoat of worked muslin with a Vandyke scallop at the bottom. Spencer of dark blue cloth edged with scarlet. Ruff of white lace around the neck. Plain muslin handkerchief. York tan gloves. Purple shoes. Fur muff.[5]

[5] N. Heideloff, *Gallery of Fashion,* London, 1795.

Fig. 468. *English Outdoor Costumes. 1795.* Heideloff, Gallery of Fashion, *Figure 45 (New York Public Library)*

The following excerpts from the *Gallery of Fashion* suggest some of the popular colors:

[Figure 3, April, 1794 is described as wearing a] Circassian robe of purple and orange striped satin.

[Figure 194, Oct., 1798] Military habit of superfine scarlet cloth, turned up with blue, gold buttons and gold epaulettes. . . . Crimson sash. Purple shoes. Buff gloves.

[Figure 211, March, 1799] Pelisse of Turkey light green silk lined with purple. The cape and cuffs [purple] trimmed with black fringe.

Note that the outer garment—spencer, pelisse, or overdress—carried the dominant color. The appearance of the spencer as early as 1795 is also of moment.

In September, 1800, Heideloff published the costume of Fig. 469. With little adaptation, it could appear today in the best-dressed circles. His description is worth repeating:

Hair short and in ringlets. Sun shade, bonnet of green silk, trimmed round and on the crown with lace and a loose bow of green riband. Round gown of yellow muslin; short sleeves, trimming of lace round the neck. Short round jacket of black gauze; short loose sleeves with a broad hem. White net gloves. Purple shoes.

Another fashion popular at this time should be mentioned: the tunic or overdress. This was cut with a surplice closing of the bodice but the front edges of the skirt slanted in the reverse direction, thus exposing the underskirt. Heideloff records them, sometimes with the overskirt trained. The newer idea, however, was a tunic length much shorter than the underskirt. The Boston Museum has a handsome example of the trained overdress, cut without a waist seam, girdled high, and worn over a sequined mull petticoat. This was worn in Massachusetts in 1799.

A yellow and white silk striped overdress in the collection of the Costume Insti-

FIG. 470. *Overdress of Yellow and White Striped Silk. 1795–1799. (Metropolitan Museum of Art, Costume Institute)*

FIG. 469. *Yellow Muslin Gown. 1800. Redrawn from Heideloff, Gallery of Fashion, Figure 274. (New York Public Library)*

tute of the Metropolitan Museum is almost a duplicate of the one published by Heideloff in January, 1795 (Fig. 470). Draft 28 explains the cut of the overdress which differs from the Heideloff drawing chiefly in that its sleeves are of white linen, completely covered with an irregular matelassé effect achieved by an overlay of shirred Dacca muslin. This costume seems to be a descendant of the widely spread overskirts of previous decades.

HAIRDRESS AND HEADDRESS. The manner of arranging the hair in 1795 has been described in a number of Heideloff quotations. Upright ostrich plumes formed the most striking feature. Often the bulk of the hair was allowed to fall in a heavy strand to the shoulder blades, where it was reversed, the ends being caught at the nape of the neck. By the late nineties, when Greek influence was in the ascendant, the hairdress had undergone a remarkable change, becoming reduced in bulk and less startling in appearance. Another hairdress of Heideloff's *Gallery* was described as follows: "Headdress à la antique. The front hair and sides in ringlets, the hind hair turned up plain and short, ornamented with two bandeaux."[6] The bandeaux are red, patterned in a black Greek key design. A later figure had "Toupee [top] cut short and combed in feather curls, hind hair turned up in loops."[7]

By December, 1798, the new style had emerged. Heideloff's Figure 201 had "Toupee cut short and combed straight; hind hair cropped and dressed in easy curls." Thus the style of short hair all over the head evolved. Irene Castle reintroduced it in 1918 as a boyish bob, and it was as revolutionary then as it had been in 1798.

Headdress followed much the same story as hairdress. Early plates of the period show involved arrangements of scarf, beads, and upstanding plumes intermingled with the hair, as in Fig. 468. By the late nineties the close cap of Fig. 471 (Heideloff Figure 250) was fashion news. The cap is made of embroidered muslin trimmed with lace and has pleated lace across the throat. The small kerchief tied over the cap matches the grayish fuchsia of the jacket.

Other Fashion Features

FOOTWEAR. Gayly colored footwear is a notable feature of many costumes of the nineties. Mention is made in fashion notes of

6 *Ibid.*, March, 1798, Fig. 172.
7 *Ibid.*, October, 1798.

FIG. 471. *English Costume. 1800. Redrawn from Heideloff,* Gallery of Fashion, *Figure 250. (New York Public Library)*

shoes of purple satin, green satin, red morocco, white, gold embroidered, blue and white striped satin, olive color, purple Spanish leather, purple embroidered with gold, and green morocco. White gloves and shoes, however, were worn with many of the later costumes. (Gloves, in general, harmonized with the shoes.)

ACCESSORIES. It had been the usual practice during the eighteenth century to wear a pair of pockets, often attractively embroidered but never visible as they were worn over the true underskirt. Pocket slits in the overdress and accompanying petticoat gave access to them. Until the nineties this added bulk was desirable, but the Greek ideal of dress permitted no room for bulging pockets. Therefore the custom arose of carrying bags called *reticules* (a word later popularized as *ridicules* or changed to *indispensables*).

With so much emphasis on the classic in costume and elsewhere, it is hardly surprising that jewelry reflected this influence also. Josephine found a style ready at hand in the cameos of Italy and introduced them upon her return to France in 1797. They proved to be a long-lasting and widely worn ornament. Two- or three-strand bead necklaces, as well as a single strand with a suspended cross, were popular in England. Pendant earrings of pearls, gold, or diamonds are mentioned in fashion notes, large gold or gold hoop earrings predominating.

THE NINETIES IN FRANCE

The decade of the nineties in France covered most of the French Revolution (1789–1799), including the Reign of Terror (1793–1794) and the Directory (1795–1799). This was a period of great turmoil and contrasts. During the early years, when fashionable clothing was supposed to be taboo, Debucourt's satiric painting *Public Promenade* (Fig. 466) shows the people in ridiculously foppish costume and poses, a far cry from what we think of as the era of the guillotine. (Louis XVI was beheaded in January, 1793; Marie Antoinette in October of the same year.)

The shocking stories of wild conduct during the French Revolution stem largely from the period of the Directory. Notorious conjugal infidelity in France was incited in part by women's near nudity. We read of their discarding all underwear, wearing pink tights under transparent muslin dresses, going barefoot except for rings on their toes. At the same time, gossip of the day reported that two women who appeared for a stroll in the Tuileries in nothing but sheer gowns were promptly jeered back under cover.

Octave Uzanne gives a typical account of Parisian society during the Directory:

Everything—habits, traditions, language, throne, altar, manners and customs—had been swallowed up in the Revolution. . . . Good society went by preference to the Hotel Longueville, where the lovely and voluptuous Madame Hamelin did not scorn to exhibit her indolent charms, and show off her never-to-be-forgotten undress.[8]

However, it is doubtful that this mania for undress reached all classes of people or was indulged in to the same extent in other European countries.

David, the outstanding French artist of the decade, an ardent classicist, had many followers. His ideas and his paintings helped persuade people that ancient Greece was the fountainhead of the finest expression in every medium of creative art. England had already simplified her fashions in response to an awakened interest in classic art, and the charm of her costumes had been felt in France.

Moreover, after every major war there is a sharp reaction to the repressions, austerity, and emotional strain imposed by the conflict. In our day Christian Dior was well aware of the propitious timing of the "New Look" he launched after World War II. So in France, after the Revolution and its accompanying Reign of Terror, Greek dress, as well as Greek architcture and philosophy, was all the more acceptable because it differed so radically from the artificial, cumbersome, restricting fashions of the hated court. The public was ready to celebrate. Chiton and himation, sans stays and chemise, seemed fitting costumes in which to stage festivities, and David was available to design the fetes for them.

Without our abundant sources of information relative to Greek and Roman dress, some of the reconstructions of the nineties might seem a bit whimsical. Certainly, how-

[8] Octave Uzanne, *Fashion in Paris*, William Heinemann, London, 1898, p. 7.

ever, this classic movement had a direct effect upon fashion for the following 25 years. Furthermore, we have been copying, adapting, and borrowing from it through much of the twentieth century.

Debucourt's *Public Promenade*, of which Fig. 466 is a detail, shows women wearing the pouter pigeon front, bustle back, puffed fichu, and a new hat form, with tall crown and flat brim.

In David's portrait of her (Fig. 472), Mme. de Sériziat's costume retains elements of previous costumes. Her soft, clinging, unlined, unboned dress, with its drawstring neckline filled in with a fichu, is far from being a Greek chiton, though it does achieve a pleasing simplicity. The lady, by the way, has not discarded all of her underwear. The sheerness of the fabric of her dress and its absence of decoration, except in accessories,

FIG. 473.   *Baron Gros, Christine Boyer, First Wife of Prince Julien Bonaparte. 1800. (Louvre)*

FIG. 472.   *French Costume. 1795. Redrawn from David, Portrait of Mme. de Sériziat. (Louvre)*

suggest a relationship to the Greek, but her cap and hat would have caused astonishment on the Acropolis.

Figure 473 shows a costume of Christine Boyer, first wife of Prince Julien Bonaparte, which is far more in the mood of its classic source than the David portrait, and is probably a more realistic picture of what was

FIG. 474. *Directoire Gown Worn with Sleeveless Spencer. 1799. (Metropolitan Museum of Art, Dick Fund) Redrawn from* Costume Parisien, *Plate 234.*

fabric known. It is form-revealing, and the presence of underwear is unmistakable. The drawstring neckline is still in vogue, the girdle of silk cord is placed high in emulation of the girdling of the late Ionic chiton, and an Indian shawl makes a beautiful and popular substitute for the himation. Christine's hairdress reflects its ancient origin with its fringe of curls, fillet, and veil. Non-Greek features of her costume are the train and the fragile slippers, though footwear in the style of sandals was fashionable.

The skirt of this column-like gown is often described as narrow; certainly it is by comparison with any other eighteenth-century silhouette. However, in surviving costumes of the period the skirts, while falling close to the body, are never tight. Much fullness is concentrated at center back. A close inspection of the hemline of Christine's train suggests the sweep of the skirt. Draft 32 provides a pattern of a skirt of this type.

OUTDOOR WEAR. Reports have come down to us of overexposure from insufficient clothing resulting in illness and an increase in the death rate, and this may well have happened in the first exuberance of freedom. We have all seen women too thinly clad on a chilly Easter morning, and certainly uncomfortable on a summer day with mink about their shoulders. Fashion has a strange power and often has little to do with health. However, protection was available at that time and used. For those who wished to imitate the Greeks as closely as possible, superb Indian shawls did nicely. Costly and limited in supply, they could not have had wide distribution—at least for some time. Meanwhile, smaller shawls or scarves, often fur-trimmed, were worn, comparable to the stoles of the 1950s. Figure 474, taken from a *Costume Parisien* fashion plate of 1799, supplements the information provided in Fig. 473. The same basic dress is shown, with accessories suitable for outdoor wear. The little jacket which is part of this costume in Fig. 474 is a sleeveless spencer, the feminine

worn in high society at the end of the century than lurid reports would have us believe. Price[9] claims that the fashion of no chemise lasted exactly a week. Christine's dress is made of sheer white soft fabric, probably Dacca muslin, the finest cotton

[9] Julius Price, *Dame Fashion*, Sampson Low, Marston and Co., London, 1913, p. 33.

FIG. 475. *Costume of Directoire Period, Including a Spencer. (Metropolitan Museum of Art, Costume Institute, Gifts of Mr. Lee Simonson, Miss Alice McMahon, Miss Ethel Frankau and Miss Alice Bernstein)*

FIG. 476. *Charlotte Corday Cap. Directoire Period. Redrawn from Hauer, Portrait of Charlotte Corday. (Versailles National Museum)*

counterpart of the man's abbreviated coat. Usually sleeved, they contributed needed protection, alternating with shawls in that respect (Fig. 475 and Draft 19).

ACCESSORIES. The headdress in Fig. 474 is a type of straw bonnet which had innumerable variations during the next 25 years. This one is small and shaped much like the cloches of the 1920s; however, it is distinguished by a very long lace veil—a coy addition, which recurs in numerous fashion drawings. Figure 476, the Corday cap, is taken from a portrait of Charlotte Corday at Versailles. The cap gained a certain popularity in 1793, when its wearer murdered Marat, a revolutionary leader, in his bathtub. Caps of related design appear in fashion drawings as late as the empire period.

Long gloves, reaching well above the elbow for formal wear, were a prominent feature of the mode. Folding fans, reduced in scale from the days of Marie Antoinette, and delicate slippers usually tied with narrow ribbons crossed over the instep completed the costume of the well-dressed lady at the close of the century.

18

Men's Wear in the Nineteenth Century

Following the fall of the monarchy in France, men's fashions changed more markedly than women's, never again attaining their old color and magnificence except as they were fostered at Napoleon's court.

Historical Background

The Industrial Revolution, with all its ramifications, was largely responsible for this lasting transformation. Although clothing manufacture was still a handcraft industry at the close of the eighteenth century, ready-to-wear shops had begun to appear in America by 1800. Tailors made up extra stock in their spare time to sell over the counter. The famous firm of Brooks Brothers was founded in 1818. By 1825 many tailors were selling garments manufactured by pioneers in factory production. However, the real transition to factory-made apparel was slow. Even as late as 1860 custom-made clothing still represented 80 percent of the sales volume in men's clothing, and in 1890 it still constituted 50 percent.

Mass production necessarily means standardization, with the sacrifice of variety of design and individual fitting. Pattern making and grading, cutting and pressing equipment, specialized machines and skilled labor to operate them were either lacking or in experimental stages in the early years of the clothing industry. It is not surprising that much of the merchandise produced during the latter half of the century was shoddy. The industry would like to forget that period of its history.

Other influences on men's clothing in the early days of the Industrial Revolution were the dirt and soot from factory smokestacks, train travel (no electricity, Diesel engines, or air conditioning), and urbanization generally, with its accelerated tempo. Embroidered satin, lace jabots, and delicate colors hardly fitted into the picture.

Although the clothes of the first few decades of the nineteenth century seem foppish and absurd to us, by the end of the century business suits and their accessories had assumed a dull, drab, uniform, but practical, cast.

Napoleon deliberately sponsored extravagance in dress, both to encourage French textile industries and to increase the prestige of his court. Court dress continued much in the mode of the eighteenth century, with little restraint in decoration. Embroidered silk coats were ostentatious in both scale of design and lavish use of gold (see Fig. 498). Napoleon's coronation robes of white satin embroidered in gold set the pace.

For daily wear, in both France and England, the story was quite different. In England, particularly, this was the period of fine fabric, expert cutting and skillful tailoring, fastidious grooming and debonair comportment, making it one of the most pleasing periods in the history of men's clothing.

George Bryan Brummell, familiarly known to history as Beau Brummell, deserves much of the credit for this gleaming perfection. A graduate of Eton and Oxford and an officer in the Prince Regent's own regiment, he was noted for his excellent taste and mastery of the art of being well dressed. He became the Emily Post of men's fashions and companion and advisor to the Crown Prince. The Beau's sartorial reign lasted from 1796 to 1816, when he fled the country to escape his gambling debts. During those 20 years he introduced such novelties as shoe polish, fresh linen at least daily (he sometimes changed as often as three times a day), and starched cravats. No creator of fashion himself, his reputation was built upon his comprehension of and insistence upon faultless line, perfect fit, and superb construction. He was conservative in the use of color, preferring blue, which he wore almost exclusively.

The age of dandyism introduced by Beau Brummell was prolonged by Count D'Orsay (see Fig. 482), a Frenchman who spent much of his time in England and who set the standard for the gentleman's wardrobe of the 1830s and 1840s. D'Orsay, tall and handsome, was a man of keen wit, as well as a respected artist and sculptor.

Louis Napoleon III, Emperor of the French from 1852–1870, by his invariably smart appearance, had as much influence as anyone during the mid-century. Prince Ed-

ward of England, later Edward VII, commanded a following in the latter part of the century.

THE FIRST TWO DECADES: 1800–1820

As we have seen, one result of the turmoil and confusion in France at the end of the eighteenth century was the passing of leadership in men's fashions to England; here it has remained ever since.

During this century military costume of one country or another became a source of inspiration for decorative details for both men's and women's apparel. In Central Europe and the Balkans such ornamentation continued well into the present century. Heavy elaborate gilding on the jacket is considered a vestige from the days of armor. In Dalmatia, plaques of solid silver were still to be seen on men's coats in 1940.

The portrait reproduced in Fig. 477, once considered to be of Louis Charles Mercier Dupaty (identity of both artist and painter is questioned), displays an ensemble Beau Brummell would have approved: crisp high shirt collar, faultless cravat, freshly pleated ruffles, high-collared white waistcoat under a coat with smartly shaped, smoothly rolling collar and lapels. The double notch formed at the joining of collar and lapel was a cherished detail.

TROUSERS. One notable change in men's costume grew directly out of the French Revolution. The peasant class had for centuries worn long rather shapeless pantaloons. When the revolution began it became imprudent to appear in rich attire. Knee breeches, symbol of the aristocracy, became suspect and disappeared. During the 1790s trousers were lengthened to the calf, and by 1800 to the ankle (Figs. 432 and 503). For court wear, however, knee breeches remained obligatory until 1830, and conservatives continued to wear them much later.

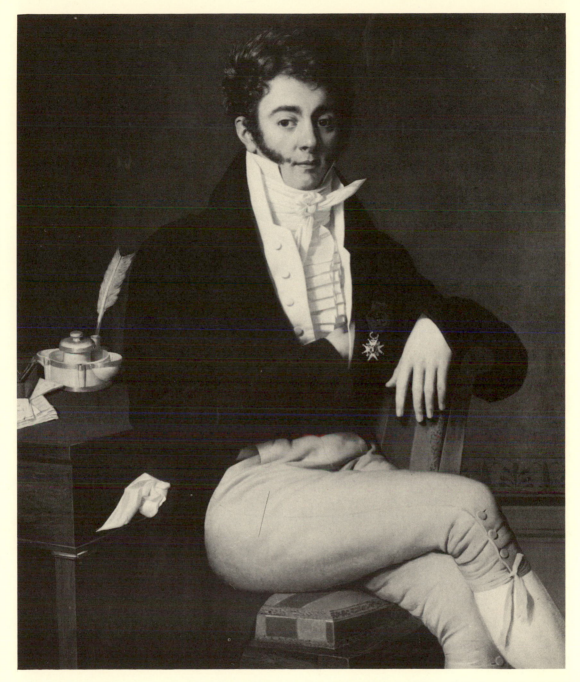

FIG. 477. *Unknown Artist, Portrait of Gentleman. c.1805–1810 (John G. Johnson Collection, Philadelphia)*

During the first third of the century, trousers were often so tight that only knitted fabric or soft leather was elastic enough to render them wearable. The *Index of American Design* records a pair of black jersey trousers from the collection of the Museum of the City of New York.

By 1815 a looser cut of trousers had been

introduced, with straps under the boots and single front closing. At the close of this period another innovation appeared, in keeping with the new idea of a small waistline: fullness at the top of the trousers. A Cruikshank cartoon of 1818 shows the corseted fop in the process of donning his stays. Figure 478 illustrates the finished product. Here the fullness of the trousers is formed into many small pleats which project outward toward the hips.

SHIRTS. The double ruffle down the front opening of the shirt was still in evidence at this time, though without the lace of the eighteenth century. Portraits like that shown in Fig. 477 show these ruffles fluted and turned toward the left. Collars brushed the ear lobes, framing the chin. With all the thicknesses of the folded cravat encircling the neck twice, the head must have been wellnigh transfixed (Draft 20).

An announcement in Ackermann's *Repository of the Arts* of 1813 reads almost like a modern advertisement:

Imperial cotton thread shirting, brought out by Mr. Milliard, the proprietor of the East India Warehouse. Its excellence consists in its desirable property of preventing the taking of cold, its superior durability and its great economy, being of a fineness and quality equal to and nearly half the price of Irish and foreign linens. The most skillful and eminent faculty will hold it in high estimation, being of a nature to prevent a too profuse perspiration, which flannel is liable to create at the same time that it does not too severely check that vital principle of health.

The sample submitted is of firm, closely woven, lustrous cotton akin to fine cambric.

WAISTCOATS. Waistcoats remained the one gay, colorful, individual article in men's wardrobes long after the rest of the costume had been neutralized. High-collared white waistcoats were fashionable until 1815. The Brooklyn Museum collection includes two early nineteenth-century waistcoats, one of buff satin with an open pattern in black velvet, the other of black velvet with a narrow cream satin stripe. Both have 3-inch standing collars, no lapels, and a rather low singlebreasted closing.

FIG. 478. *Man's Costume. 1820.* Journal des Dames et des Modes. (*Author's Collection*)

Waistcoat collars were lowered along with the coat collar at the end of this period. Figure 478 shows the new trend: a shawl collar on a waistcoat made of pale-pink silk, with an allover pattern in rose, worn over a second plain rose one. Throughout the period the waistline was straight and near normal position.

FIG. 479. *Garrick with Five Cape Collars. 1813.* Le Bon Genre. *(Author's Collection)*

COATS. Coats present a more varied picture in these decades. Ingres' young men are usually clad in double-breasted coats reaching only to the waistline across the front and falling sharply to knee length at the sides and back—one more step in the evolution of the tail coat. Double-breasted coats, often cut too small to be fastened, were also designed with the front skirt edges curving toward the back from waist level, the panels narrowing as they dropped to within a few inches of the knees. These scanty coattails, as they were later called, were in startling contrast to the flared and pleated coat skirts of the early eighteenth century, though the line of descent is unbroken.

The 1820 dandy of Fig. 478 wears the most cut away coat of all, with the outlines of the true tail coat. Its waistline rises slightly above that of the waistcoat and its slender tails fall below the knees. Today these coats are restricted to formal wear but at this time they were daytime clothes.

OVERCOATS. The overcoat called the *garrick* is familiar to us from carolers and coachmen in English scenes (Fig. 479). *Le Bon Genre*, in its bantering way, drew it too long, too full, too deeply collared, but in the main true to its nature. Though this particular garrick has five cape collars, the number varied from three to five. The tabbed closing and the stiffened, quilted, high standing collar are both typical. The garrick was one of the smartest greatcoats of all time and designers of women's coats have gone to it repeatedly for inspiration.

Figure 480, from the *Index of American Design*, shows a topcoat of the second decade of the century, of light-tan broadcloth with a collar of golden velvet. Note the seam at the waistline, which allows freedom in designing the flare of the skirt.

The Polish overcoat of this era had a fitted waistline, flaring skirts, and braided detail on chest and back. The French redingote was a topcoat of medium weight, long, fitted, and collared with velvet, much in the manner of Fig. 480 but lacking its smartness.

Probably more commonly worn than fashion plates indicate was the more practical medium-length, double-breasted coat. There must have been long seasons when an intermediate garment between tails and topcoat was in great demand. These coats appeared in bright blue, celestial blue, slate blue, olive green, toast, and reddish brown as well as in the favorite blue of Beau Brummell.

FOOTWEAR.　As in the seventeenth century, boots were in high favor and for decades were preferred to shoes for outdoor wear. At this time there were three general types: the Hessian, with heart-shaped top and tassels; the Wellington, a boot with a higher top, cut away back of the knee, and the jockey boot, with a turned down top of lighter leather (Fig. 502), which was the correct riding boot throughout the century.

Incongruous as it seems today, boots were worn under trousers, which were strapped beneath the instep (Fig. 478). Gaiters continued their useful role (Fig. 502). For indoor and formal wear slippers were worn. Conservative men wore low

FIG. 480.　Topcoat, 1810–1820. (National Gallery of Art, Washington, D.C., Index of American Design, Original in Museum of City of New York)

shoes and long hose with knee breeches (Fig. 502).

HAIR AND HAT STYLES. Hair styles varied from Napoleon's familiar bangs to the carefully casual locks of the gentleman in Fig. 477. Sideburns extending downward toward the chin appeared by the first decade (Fig. 502).

The high top hat, usually black or dark

FIG. 481. *Men's Costumes. 1826.* Journal des Dames et des Modes. (*Author's Collection*)

gray, had reached its characteristic shape by 1798 and dominated the entire nineteenth century. The *chapeau bras* or bicorne remained in use for both general wear and more formal occasions. The coachman and the man at extreme left in Debucourt's drawing (Fig. 502) wear bicornes, a frequent accessory in Ingres' portraits.

ACCESSORIES. Gloves were as important in the wardrobe of the gentleman as of the lady. A foible that appealed to many men was a cluster of fobs or seals attached to the watch and hanging from the watch pocket on the right side (Fig. 478).

1820–1850

In line with the trend toward the bizarre in women's wear, expressed by diminished waist, bulging bustle, broad shoulder lines, and giddy hats, men now turned with enthusiasm toward an effeminate figure, characterized by pinched waist, rounded hips, and bosoming chest. Corseting for men continued throughout these 30 years. The greatest change came in the forties, when the waistline dropped considerably below its normal position.

In the coat, these ladylike contours were achieved by throwing more length and outward thrust on the front edges from shoulder to waist, raising the double-breasted closing to emphasize the chest line, and by the bulk formed by the cravat, the overlapping of lapels, and the double waistcoat. The shoulder seam was lengthened. Leg-of-mutton sleeves followed the mode of women's wear. Coat skirts increased in spread so that shoulders and hem, by contrast, made the waist appear smaller (Fig. 481).

Count D'Orsay's sartorial supremacy is reflected in the sketch shown in Fig. 482. The harmony of lines created by the curve of his shawl collar, the fall of his watch chain, and the crease and lapel lines of his

frock coat is pleasing enough to warrant modern adaptation. The style with which he wears his impeccable tailoring is admirable. It is difficult to conjure up a more dashing figure.

COATS. During the early part of the twenties tail coats occupied first place among coats. Cut in both single- and double-breasted styles and fitted closely at the waist, they were unique because of the leg-of-mutton sleeves which tapered to a narrow

FIG. 482. *Unknown Artist, Count D'Orsay. 1834.* (*New York Public Library, Prints Division*)

FIG. 483. *Men's Costumes. 1848.* Fashion et Theorie. (*Author's Collection*)

wrist and extended to the knuckles. The collar, rolling high at the back, still joined the lapels in a W-notch.

By the mid-twenties the frock coat was as popular as the tail coat for daytime wear. Its front edge was continuous from lapel to hem, which was well down toward the knees. This cut added to the svelte appearance of the waist. Probably because of its more practical nature it eventually relegated the tail coat to evening and formal wear. This was largely accomplished by mid-century and the frock coat remained an important item in the man's wardrobe throughout the century. A feature of the design of coats and waistcoats in the forties, as in women's fashions, was the obvious lowering of the waistline (Fig. 483).

In the late forties the frock coat faced competition with a more conservative garment—the suit coat. An 1849 print in the Victoria and Albert Museum shows the idea quite well developed, and by 1855 it had arrived (Fig. 484).

The topcoat, or redingote, as it continued to be called in France, was styled like the frock coat but was lengthened to midcalf (Fig. 481). The loose, boxy, comfortable looking overcoat of Fig. 483 would be quite at home on the street today. Many of these coats were velvet collared. Colors such as plum, mulberry, brown, bright blue, and bottle green are mentioned—a transition from rich and brilliant silks to the dark, drab uniformity to follow.

WAISTCOATS. The last bit of splendor of past centuries to disappear was the waistcoat, ancestor of the modern vest. During the twenties and thirties men had the satisfaction of wearing two at a time, and we had such combinations as white velvet over rose-colored silk brocaded in gold (Fig. 481). Stripes, colored velvets, plaids, and figured silks also added a touch of gaiety to the scene. In the thirties the neckline was lowered and rounded and a rolling collar added (Fig. 482). This shawl collar lasted

into the forties, when a more tailored collar and lapels appeared.

TROUSERS. The design of trousers in the twenties contributed to the effeminate figure. Massing small pants pleats at the waistline made the fabric slant sharply outward in a peg top outline. Trousers held taut by straps under the instep were fashionable in the twenties, lost favor in the thirties, were revived in the forties, and disappeared by the fifties. The fop of the twenties wore trousers almost skin-tight below the knee, ending 2 or 3 inches above the anklebone (Fig. 481). Trousers of the thirties still tended to be closely fitted (Fig. 482), but in the forties they were eased some. Plaids enlivened the scene at this time. Knee breeches continued in use as court dress.

NECKWEAR. The all-enveloping cravat was sobered in the twenties into a flat surfaced layer, still high and stiffened, and finished off with a formal flat bow (Fig. 481). By 1827 separate collars became available, thanks to the ingenuity of a blacksmith's wife who tired of providing a clean shirt each day for her fastidious husband (Draft 20).

In Fig. 482 Count D'Orsay wears a high, lustrous black cravat, which manages rather magically to cover the whole expanse of shirt that otherwise would be exposed by the lowered neckline of his waistcoat. Photographs and detailed drawings indicate that the form of the new cravat was long and wide; it hid the shirt from view by studied knotting, folding, and pinning. (Prince Albert wore a pearl-headed tie pin to secure the ends of his cravat.) This rather unique feature remained in fashion through the forties. Not all neckwear was black, however. Fashion plates show such variety as flowered patterns, polka dots, and green and gold stripes, in addition to plain colors. White continued to be correct for evening wear.

FOOTWEAR. Half boots were worn under the wide-legged trousers of the early

FIG. 484. *Men's Costumes, 1855.* Le Lion, Supplement to l'Elegant. (*New York Public Library*)

twenties, though such trousers as those of the dandy of Fig. 481 could hardly have accommodated them. Figure 481 shows pumps with bows. The square-toed boot sponsored by Count D'Orsay remained in vogue through the forties.

HAIR AND HATS. Curls in abundance

adorn the beau of Fig. 481 and sideburns meet the edges of his high collar. A surprising advocate of this hair style in 1833 was young Disraeli.[1]

In general men wore their hair rather

[1] Herbert Norris and Oswald Curtis, *Costume and Fashion*, Dent, London, 1933, vol. VI, p. 64.

Fig. 485. *Sack Coat. 1859. Gazette of Fashion. (New York Public Library)*

full and long—certainly by modern standards. Curls took up the length. Arranged in a forward movement in front of the ears, they merged with the sideburns. The hair was usually parted on the left.

The chin was often clean-shaven. Rather small mustaches with upturned curled ends were a fashion of the forties.

The high silk or beaver hat reigned supreme during this period, varying from year to year in height and flare of crown and width and roll of brim. The peculiar high straight stovepipe crown is seen as early as the thirties (Fig. 482).

In brief, 1850 closed a period marked by pleated frills, rich color, and smart tailoring, but spiced with foppishness and dandyism. From then on, color was restricted to waistcoat and tie. Expert tailors were patronized by a diminishing clientele. Business im-

Fig. 486. *Men's Fashions. 1859.* Gazette of Fashion. (*New York Public Library*)

posed restrictions; the popularity of sports fostered specific and functional designs for each recreation.

1850–1870

Coats. The all important contribution of the fifties to men's wear was the matched suit, consisting of coat, waistcoat or vest, as it is known today, and trousers. Called "ditto" suits at first, they remained a novelty for some time but gradually gained popularity through the rest of the century. An early suit in dark gray that seems particularly pleasing is shown in Fig. 484. It retains the fitted waistline and long skirt of the frock coat.

By 1859 the sack coat appeared, approaching still more closely the look of men's wear today (Fig. 485). The coat is boxy in outline and the sleeve has increased in girth. A single issue of the *Gazette of Fashion* showed two striped ditto suits (Fig. 486), both semifitted through the waistline, their separately cut skirts producing a little more flare in the lower part of the coat. Sleeves show the same increase in proportion noted in Fig. 485. The fashion news was the decreased size of coat collar and lapels and the accompanying high closing. Only the upper buttons were fastened. During the sixties and seventies collars and lapels shrank still more, the latter disappearing at times. It became the smart thing to fasten only the top button, allowing the rest of the coat to swing backward.

Following this trend of the high single-button closing, cutaways started to slant well above the waistline, revealing much of the waistcoat. Frock coats and tail coats were still worn with contrasting trousers, either striped, plaid, or in plain colors (Figs. 486 and 487).

WAISTCOATS. With sack coats and cutaways the waistcoat still contributed a bit of dash. Brocades, striped satin with floral pattern, raised matelassé designs, dotted velvet, and paisley printed piqué are among the fabrics used for the mid-century waistcoats in the Brooklyn Museum collection. Note the designs in Figs. 486, 487, and 488.

TROUSERS. Trousers of the fifties and sixties became easy in cut, in harmony with the fuller sleeves of this period. They were long enough to reach the heels of the shoes. They continued in the traditional lighter tones, such as grayish blue, aqua, and pearl gray for summer, and steel gray and brown, brown and black, and green and black mixtures for winter. For daytime wear and informal occasions checks and plaids were still favored, however. A good example, shown in Fig. 488, is a costume of Prince Albert who had a reputation for being well dressed. Here he gives his stamp of approval

to the combination of checked waistcoat and plaid trousers with the frock coat.

OVERCOATS. Another garment which made a definite break with the past in the sixties and filled a lasting need was the overcoat. Its diminutive collar followed the trend of daytime coats; its ease of cut was similar to the sack coat.

SHIRTS AND COLLARS. A typical dress shirt of 1850 in the costume collection of the Brooklyn Museum has a shirt front of handkerchief linen with eight 1-inch ruffles stitched on in vertical lines. It is designed to be tied securely in place with tapes at the shoulders and sides. Striped shirts were worn for sporting occasions.

Neckwear was definitely lower and there was greater choice available. Most collars were still standing, but even Prince Albert wore the turnover type in a relaxed mood and casual costume (Fig. 488). In the sixties disposable collars made of linen bonded to paper and stamped to imitate stitching became available. These collars inspired the following glowing notice in *Godey's Ladies' Book* for January, 1860:

Have any of our subscribers heard anything of this new, beautiful and useful appendage called "patent enameled collars?" The price is not more than one half as much as the price of washing it. There are the D'Orsay, the Byron, the English and a host of others.

Narrow bow ties predominated, sometimes patterned, but white prevailed for formal wear.

SPORTSWEAR. The sixties saw Mrs. Bloomer's influence extend to men's clothing. The hunting costume was one of the early gestures toward suitable clothing for active sports. These first knickers were quite full, clearly reflecting their relationship to women's wear.

HATS. Figure 488 shows Prince Albert holding another important innovation—the low-crowned wide-brimmed soft hat. Note

Fig. 487. *Men's Fashions.* 1870. *Gazette of Fashion.* (*New York Public Library*)

also Figs. 484 and 486. Its counterpart for summer wear was the straw hat worn by the man at the left in Fig. 486. Straw hats had been worn by farmers for centuries (remember the thirteenth-century harvesters of the Morgan Library's Maciejowski Bible), but only late in history were they accepted by townsmen. It has been suggested that their appearance in America at this time was an aftermath of the Mexican War, 1846–1848. The G.I.'s of that day probably brought many straw hats home with them as souvenirs and discovered their advantages.

From the fifties onward the top hat shared the scene with one new style after another. Instead of disappearing after a brief run of popularity, each new style found its particular function and remained to give versatility to the wardrobe. A case in point is the high-crowned cap of Fig. 486, which became the headgear of both workmen and sportsmen and is still worn.

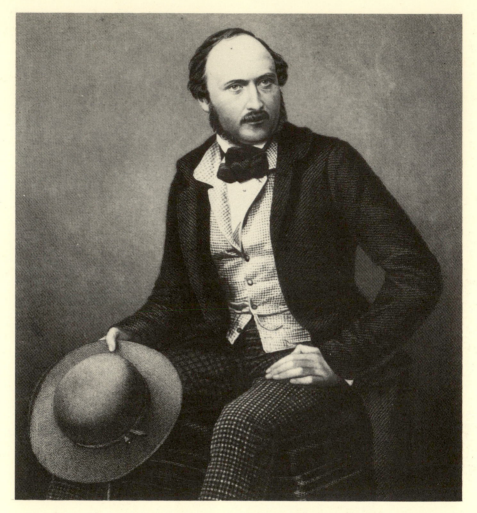

FIG. 488. *Prince Albert of England. 1855. From* Illustrated News of the World. (*New York Public Library, Prints Division*)

Another newcomer, the bowler, was also introduced in the sixties. This early form of what eventually became known as the derby has retained its hard rounded crown and narrow brim throughout its long history.

HAIR STYLING. There was no great change in hair styling in the sixties or seventies. The hair was worn full and waved over and in front of the ears and neatly trimmed at the neck. The side part curved into a center part as it continued to the back hairline (Fig. 484), an effect that might appeal to some of today's beatniks.

Sideburns descended to the jaws in this era and became Dundreary whiskers. Full beards were worn, but the clean-shaven look also had quite a following. Mustaches were popular, their ends waxed and curled, probably in imitation of Napoleon III.

FOOTWEAR. Footwear of the fifties included square-toed and bowed pumps for occasions which today would seem inappropriate. For example, note the man in street attire in Fig. 484. Half boots, or what we would call shoes, were worn with most daytime costumes. Elastic insets, which made fastening unnecessary, left a smooth un-broken surface over the front of the foot. However, buttoned shoes were introduced in the sixties, for men as well as for women. Laced shoes were also available. The small boy in Fig. 484 wears leggings buttoned over his shoes, an indication that his father did also, since children's clothing aped that of their elders. Half boots, laced on the inside, were worn over buttoned leggings for sports wear.

ACCESSORIES. Watch chains, less con-spicuous than in the heyday of Count D'Or-say, constituted the principal jewelry. Canes, though still carried, were seen less often than in previous periods.

THE SEVENTIES

The last thirty years of the nineteenth century witnessed marked increase in factory production of clothing, with corresponding decrease in quality. One history of men's costume says of this period: "Generally speaking, men were more inelegantly and more shabbily dressed during this period than any other time previous. It was a period of great industrial progress with more atten-tion paid to business than to clothes."[2] Poor taste seems to have prevailed simultaneously in both men's and women's clothing.

The contributions of the seventies were less numerous than those of the preceding decade, yet the styles presented by an out-standing firm in London were quite diverse. In many cases they are identifiable with modern dress. These, it should be noted, were designed for custom tailoring.

COATS AND WAISTCOATS. Figure 487 shows one man wearing a well-cut cutaway or morning coat. It is double breasted, but still reveals a triangle of the lower part of the waistcoat, with seaming at a lowered waistline, larger lapels than during the sixties,

[2] *Men's Wear: History of Men's Wear Indus-try, 1790 to 1950.* Fairchild, New York, 1950.

and a velvet collar. The other man wears a shortened frock coat with many of the same details. The ditto suit of Fig. 489 is more casual, the coat retaining most of the features of the sixties. The front edge is cut away to such an extent that only the top button could possibly have been fastened. The natty double-breasted seaside costume of Fig. 490 shows a new type of coat, loose, boxy, com-fortable in cut, and appropriate for holidays and outings.

The tail coat, faultlessly tailored, re-mained correct wear for evening and formal occasions. Its very low closing was auto-matically accompanied by widened lapels. The inset of contrasting fabric, illustrated in Fig. 491, usually heavy silk, is superbly done.

FIG. 489. *Man's Suit. 1871. Redrawn from Gazette of Fashion. (New York Public Library)*

Fig. 490. *Seaside Costume. 1873. Redrawn from Gazette of Fashion. (New York Public Library)*

The waistcoats shown in Fig. 487 were worn with an underlay of white; in the ditto suit the neckline of the waistcoat rose above that of the coat. In the seventies a notable change in evening attire was a matching black waistcoat (Fig. 491). White remained the proper color for the most formal occasions.

TROUSERS. Trousers showed little change in cut. However, the boldness of the plaid pattern and vibrant stripes of Fig. 487 echo the combinations of unrelated textures, colors, and patterns of women's fashions of the same period.

SHIRTS AND NECKWEAR. Figured shirt fabrics were accepted in the seventies. More

informal and less soil revealing, they were a concession to the business world. Polka dotted shirts were worn with both the frock coat and the ditto suit (Figs. 487 and 489).

As we have seen, the low turnover collar had been favored in the 1850s. In the seventies high standing collars were made more comfortable by turning back the corners (Figs. 487 and 489). This winged effect, known colloquially as "gates ajar," was destined for a long life.

The bow tie was largely replaced by the four-in-hand for daytime wear, but retained with evening dress.

OVERCOATS. The familiar chesterfield coat continued through the seventies. A more luxurious model, longer, collared, cuffed, and completely lined with fur was designed for the upper income bracket (Fig. 492). Another overcoat with a modern air was a long belted model of rough-surfaced fabric with matching hood.

SPORTSWEAR. Hunting outfits of the seventies had shorter jackets and more closely cut knickers than in the sixties. Knickers with long hose and low-cut shoes served for less strenuous sports.

HAIR AND HATS. The haircut of the seventies was shorter and brushed closer to the head than in the sixties. Short beards gained in popularity; mustaches were common.

Top hat and bowler shared honors with straw boaters like that worn with the seaside costume of Fig. 490. With its stiff, sharp-edged low crown and straight wide brim, it differed markedly from the early straw hat of the fifties. By the seventies the boater had assumed the shape it was to retain for decades.

FOOTWEAR. Shoes followed a conservative bent, continuing the square-toed, noticeably heeled, smooth, polished look of the previous decade. The low laced shoe of the seaside ensemble—forerunner of the sneaker or tennis shoe—was new. Rubber woven into

FIG. 491. *Men's Formal Attire. 1875. Gazette of Fashion. (New York Public Library)*

cloth had been used as insets in both men's and women's shoes since the early forties, but not until the sixties was a method perfected for attaching rubber soles.

THE EIGHTIES

By the last decades of the century, men's wear had many features which are almost indistinguishable from today's fashions; the double-breasted sack suit, the single-breasted summer suit with its lower closing, and many overcoats have a modern look. Sports clothing became more specialized.

Innovations of the eighties included a return to slim trousers and smaller top hat and introduction of the fedora, the deerstalker cap, and a higher crowned straw hat with a bold broad band, slightly reminiscent of Coney Island in effect.

COATS. Suit coats, accompanied by the affectation of fastening only the top button, retained their high closing into the early eighties. By the late eighties the usual front closing was resumed. The formal tail coat was designed with a higher closing, however, necessitating three buttons instead of the traditional one. A new type of coat, a com-

FIG. 492. *Men's Winter Fashions. 1872. Gazette of Fashion. (New York Public Library)*

promise in formality between the tail coat and suit coat, was introduced: the dinner jacket or tuxedo, still a favorite today.

When coats were again buttoned, the waistcoat or vest practically disappeared from view. Where visible they were single-breasted, with a closing in keeping with that of the coat.

NECKWEAR AND FOOTWEAR. Straight standing collars, winged or turnover, were worn with stiff-bosomed shirts which opened down the back. These turnover collars indicate a trend toward casual and comfortable neckwear. Increasing informality is indicated by the collegiate stripes of four-in-hand ties.

Footwear was slim in design with narrower and higher heels than are customary today. Patent leather buttoned shoes worn with spats were fashionable.

SPORTSWEAR. The eighties brought the belted Norfolk jacket (Fig. 493), usually plaid, with its characteristic box pleats from shoulder to hem.[3] With matching knickers, heavy shoes, and leggings it was suitable for hunting; with oxfords or laced shoes and hose, it served for walking, golf, or other light exercise. The deerstalker cap accompanied the hunting outfit.

OVERCOATS. The knee-length topcoats of this period were classic in design, often

[3] Norris and Curtis, *op. cit.*, p. 200.

double-breasted, with velvet or fur collars. Overcoats, cut straight, and with fly closings, were a bit of novelty.

The Inverness cape and deerstalker cap, inseparably associated with Sherlock Holmes, were frequently seen on less famous citizens. An original Inverness cape in the Costume Institute collection is made of heavy double-cloth wool with a brown, tan, and green plaid outer surface and a still more colorful inner surface in which red predominates. The upper cape, instead of being continuous and free all the way around, springs from seam lines dropped from the back armscyes.

ACCESSORIES. Gloves, cane, and mon-

ocle were esteemed accessories, especially of the English man about town, during the latter part of the century.

THE CLOSING DECADE: THE NINETIES

Sack suits of the nineties have a rather familiar appearance, possibly due to broadened collar and lapels. Morning coats, with their rounded front skirts, remained an essential and constant feature of the urban scene. Vests, still much in evidence, were often made of contrasting fabric. The white silk waistcoats for formal wear were truly elegant. Daytime models were made in both single- and double-breasted styles, with or without collar and lapels.

Shirt collars retained the styles of the eighties, the turnover type being more popular among the fastidious. The four-in-hand tie became a center of attention because of its excessive bulk and pronounced pattern. Pretied ascots shared this emphasis on neckwear, though more modestly scaled bow ties were still worn, especially by men in public service.

TROUSERS. Trousers returned to more comfortable proportions as the century waned, and center leg creases appeared for the first time. Prince Edward of England, later Edward VII, is credited with having initiated this fashion. Legend has it that he tried on at his tailor's shop a pair of trousers that had been folded for some time so that creases had formed down the centers of the legs, front, and back. Their slenderizing effect pleased the Prince and he wore them in that condition. The fashion quickly gained general acceptance. Figure 494 shows the Prince in daytime attire in 1898: single-breasted sack suit, wing collar, four-in-hand tie, and carrying a fedora. The flower in his buttonhole and the inch of visible shirt cuff are both significant details. Correct attire for more formal daytime wear consisted of

FIG. 493. *Norfolk Jacket and Knickers. 1899. Redrawn from Laver,* Nineteenth Century Costume, *Figure 99. (Victoria & Albert Museum, Crown Copyright)*

white waistcoat, Prince Albert frock coat, striped trousers, high silk hat, and cane.

Typical French end-of-the-century fashion is worn by Count Boniface de Castellane in Fig. 495. The Count, who married the American Anna Gould in 1895, looks quite debonair in his bold shepherd's checked trousers, morning coat, cane, and high silk hat.

Costume Changes

Topcoats ranged from single-breasted

Fig. 495. *Count Boniface de Castellane. 1895.* Harper's Weekly.

Fig. 494. *Edward, Prince of Wales, 1898.* Harper's Weekly. (*New York Public Library, Prints Division*)

finger-tip length coverts to long fur-lined and fur-collared overcoats that radiated opulence. August Belmont was photographed in such a status symbol in 1895.

By 1900 the derby or bowler, top hat, fedora, and summer straws had nearly attained their present forms, though during the nineties straw hats had rather narrow brims and wide fancy bands. Caps were popular for casual wear.

The clean-shaven look finally prevailed, though the mustache was often seen and more conservative and older men were bearded. Steel-rimmed and pince-nez glasses were functional accessories.

Sportswear. As the century closed, a modern phase of both men's and women's wear was the emphasis on suitable clothing for active sports. The Norfolk jacket, introduced in the eighties, became the most popular outdoor garment in the nineties (Fig. 493). In conjunction with knickers it was worn for hunting, fishing, golfing, and bicycling. A surprising addition to the sportsman's wardrobe was shorts for mountaineering, probably inspired by Tyrolean leather shorts, but more closely cut. The accompanying long underwear or knitted knee protectors gave them the sign and seal of the nineteenth century. For tennis, a flannel shirt was popular. Laced up the front, and with its own low collar, it was worn with white knickers.

Heavy hunting boots, reaching well up the calf, were sometimes worn, but lower shoes worn with buttoned leggings served the same purpose. Spiked boots were available for mountain climbing.

Illustrations of this decade in *Harper's Weekly* are impressive in the diversity of sports represented. By the nineties specific garments were designed and worn for individual sports, including polo, hockey, baseball, track, and rowing, as well as tennis, bathing, and bicycling. Of all of these, the bathing costumes seem most quaint today. Swim suits, including socks and underwear, came in bold horizontal stripes. A catalogue of the eighties lists among undershirts "men's anti rheumatic scarlet cashmere shirts, heavy and medicated, all wool and highly recommended. $1.50."

A glance through books illustrated by Charles Dana Gibson gives a kaleidoscopic view of men of the nineties and their attire. They are all there: old and young, brash and staid, dull and dandified. At the lower income levels, men look rumpled and ill at ease in their poorly cut, factory made clothing. Those more successful are trim, smart, and assured in their custom-made garments. The portrait of Mr. Stokes reproduced in Fig. 564 is a fine example in real life of the latter group.

As the nineteenth century closed, practically all of the peacock qualities of previous centuries and cultures had been obliterated from men's wear. The perfect escort of that day served as background and foil for the scintillating colors and rich textures worn by his partner—and he still does. The twentieth century has brought relatively minor changes in men's day and formal evening wear, though an increasingly casual air has invaded clothing in all walks of life and more color is being introduced, some of it subtle and beautiful.

19

Women's Fashions
of the Nineteenth Century

In spite of widely different political backgrounds, fashions of the early nineteenth century in England and France were remarkably homogeneous. Greek inspiration dominated both areas. As we have seen, England had yielded to the classical spell in the eighteenth century while France was still bound by the traditions and leadership of her royal court. Not until after the French Revolution, when David was at the height of his career and all things having the slightest taint of royalty were repudiated, did the French wholeheartedly abandon brocade for muslin.

Portraits by Reynolds, Gainsborough, and Romney display a marked simplicity of dress in England after the 1780s, and the ladies of fashion there stepped quite naturally into the roles of Greek maids and matrons. As noted in the previous chapter, French feminine costume during the Directory, at the very end of the eighteenth century, was patterned after classical styles. By 1820 France had resumed her fashion leadership and has held it ever since, except for short wartime intervals.

THE FIRST DECADE OF THE CENTURY

By 1800 outer garments had assumed the chief characteristics they were going to maintain until 1820: tall, slender, willowy silhouette; abnormally high waistline; light, supple, clinging fabrics; heelless footwear; addiction to scarves, stoles, and shawls; and an amazing and engaging variety of headgear inspired by many lands as well as by topical events.

Though underwear was supposedly reduced to a minimum, there are plenty of illustrations of corsets, which were obviously necessary to mold figures into fashionable svelte lines. Figure 496 illustrates a type of corset in which when the straps were cinched in front, the breasts would be held high, the position observed in so many portraits of the time. Another type of corset extended below the hips in the manner of modern foundation garments, thus inducing a sleek skirt contour.

FIG. 496. *Underwear, Including Corset. 1803. Redrawn from* Costume Parisien, *Plate 467. (Metropolitan Museum of Art, Dick Fund)*

Classical Influence

Throughout this first decade inspiration from classic sources ruled fashion. Drawstrings in the hems or facings of necklines or front edges crossing on diagonal lines shaped the decolletage. In France the neckline was revealingly low, and either square in contour or a deep V. Figure 497 shows a square neckline diverted into a shallow V across the front—one of the most revealing decolletages on record. Draft 29 was made from Betsy Bonaparte's costume in the collection of the Maryland Historical Society. Its center front depth from neckline to waistline is about ½ inch! When Betsy received from her suitor, Jerome Bonaparte, the Paris fashion news that necklines were shockingly low, she is alleged to have re-

marked that if Josephine and her sisters-in-law wore such gowns, she would follow suit. This little bodice seems to prove her determination.

Though bodice and skirt may at first have been cut in one piece, with a drawstring controlling the waistline (Fig. 472), by 1804 a seam joined the two, often covered by a narrow sash, as in Fig. 497. The skirt fell straight and flat to the floor in front, its fullness being concentrated at the center back. Most of the dresses illustrated in fashion plates and portraits of this period have trains. The outstanding characteristic which marks the styles of the first few years of the era is utter simplicity, especially in the most elegant fashion circles. Madame Recamier, Madame Hamelin, and the Empress Josephine are portrayed in gowns with a minimum of dressmaking and ornamentation, the first two wearing no jewelry even when sitting for their portraits.

The early Greek-inspired gowns had short sleeves, sometimes set in, often, by shirring and buttons, simulating the sleeves of Ionic chitons. However, the two-sectioned sleeve with puffed upper portion and long fitted extension reaching to the knuckles soon made its appearance. Josephine's coronation robe of 1804 was so designed (Fig. 498). Fashion plates of the time show numerous examples of short puffed sleeves, as well as fitted ones of medieval length, for court designers were already borrowing from periods other than the classic. Thus the standing lace frills at the necks of the robes Josephine and her attendants wear at the coronation have a sixteenth-century origin. Note also the neck frill of Fig. 497. Before the end of the decade short puffed sleeves were paned in the manner of the early seventeenth century.

Other Features of Dresses

An intriguing feature of actual dresses of this period examined by the author in various museums was the method of fasten-

Fig. 497. *Gerard, Pauline Borghese and Maid of Honor.* c.1804–1807. (*California Palace of Legion of Honor, San Francisco, Lent by Prince and Princess Metternich*)

FIG. 498. *David, Coronation of Napoleon and Josephine.* 1806–1807. *(Louvre)*

ing. Nearly all of them depended upon draw tapes or cords, the latter adding a note of interest. The dress shown in Fig. 499, though worn in New England instead of France, nevertheless embodies many fashionable features. The incredibly narrow back section necessitated a sleeve totally different in shape from sleeves today (Draft 32). The puffed upper section gave essential ease; the lower portion has the extended length of the Middle Ages. The bodice is cut with a high front and standing collar with shirred muslin sewed on to simulate a ruff. The skirt is separated from the bodice across the front but would have required pinning or fastening in some manner to achieve and hold the high empire line. The side seams of the skirt are open quite a distance from the waist downward to allow the front edges to be drawn to the back, where they are tied with tasseled cords. The fabric is a firm white cotton with woven stripes. This unpretentious dress is probably far more typical of garments worn by the majority of women during this decade than the gossamer, exquisitely embroidered creations worn by Pauline Bonaparte Borghese in Gerard's painting.

WRAPS. Large Indian shawls worn in this first decade of the century were substitutes for the Greek himation, increased trade with India having made them available on the European market. Those painted in early nineteenth-century portraits are long and colorful; they are decorated with narrow borders along the edges and deeper ones across the ends (Fig. 497). Smaller shawls the size of stoles, made of kitten-soft cashmere and embroidered in polychromatic silks, were worn when less warmth was needed.

However, since imported shawls were expensive and in short supply, plain shawls of solid color, fringed or weighted with tassels, were also worn. Long, floating scarves attached at the armscyes of the dresses could be draped at will about the shoulders.

As far back as 1795 women had found the spencer a charming and convenient accessory (see Fig. 475 and Draft 19) and it continued in use through the 1820s. Draft 30 shows the cut of Betsy Bonaparte's coral velvet sleeveless spencer, a jewel-like accent for a sheer muslin gown.

For colder weather, the redingote, an English riding coat, came into favor. Made full length, with long sleeves and cape collar, and smartly tailored, it graced many a wardrobe (Fig. 500). In a letter written in 1820 by an Englishwoman residing in Paris the redingote is synonymous with the pelisse: "We still wear pelisses or as we call them,

FIG. 499. *White Cotton Dress. c. 1806. (University of Washington,. School of Home Economics)*

FIG. 500. *Redingote. 1806. Redrawn from Costume Parisien, Plate 677. (Author's Collection)*

FIG. 501. *Short Hair Style. 1803. Redrawn from Costume Parisien, Plate 474. (Metropolitan Museum of Art, Dick Fund)*

redingotes."[1] As we have seen, the redingote first appeared in French fashion as far back as the 1780s. It came back into practical

[1] *Ackermann's Repository of the Arts,* London, February, 1820.

everyday service in England as the pelisse—a fair exchange.

HAIRDRESS AND HEADDRESS. Hairdress and headdress continued to intrique nineteenth-century women. We noted earlier that by the end of the eighteenth century their hair was cut short and worn in curls all over the head (Fig. 501). Having shorn her hair, the next step, woman-like, was to add a wig. This accessory is recognizable in fashion plates and paintings as a close, compact coiffure, intertwined with many small braids, and often finished off with a bouquet of flowers above the forehead (Fig. 502, far right).

Powdered hair had been largely abandoned in England in the 1780s, in France in the 1790s. When wigs were adopted they were made in a varied range of colors. The lady of fashion could, and did, change the color of her hair as easily as she did her hat. In portraits, however, one is often aware of

FIG. 502. *Debucourt, Les Courses du Matin. 1805. (Courtesy, Museum of Fine Arts, Boston)*

FIG. 503. *Prudhon, Rutger Jan Schimmelpennick and Family. 1801–1802. (Rijksmuseum, Amsterdam)*

natural hair parted in the center, with a few curls about the face and a chignon high on the head or just above the hairline in back (Figs. 497, 498, 503).

In a Proudhon portrait of Josephine the Empress wears three fillets in Greek fashion. On the other hand, in David's portrait of Madame Hamelin in the National Gallery of Art, her straggly locks look as if she hadn't given a thought to her hair for some time—a studied carelessness.

As the result of simplifying the remainder of the costume the headdress became the focal point of fashion interest. It ranged from a copy of the Greek sphendone (Fig. 504), wreathed with vines, to a Polish

FIG. 504. *Headdress Adapted from Greek Sphen-done. 1806. Redrawn from* La Belle Assemblée. *(Author's Collection)*

FOOTWEAR. Footwear played a role in fashion more by its color than by its design. Fashion plates of the decade show slippers of turquoise, buff, bright red, almond green, and yellow, as well as of white. The majority have pointed toes, are cut out deeply over the vamp, and are decorated with small bows. By 1806 there was more coverage, with lacing over the vamp and a more rounded toe (Fig. 507). In Fig. 497 Princess Pauline Borghese and her maid of honor wear slippers with higher vamp and square toes. Note the openwork stockings worn by the Princess.

ACCESSORIES. Gloves usually matched the shoes, and with daytime dresses they reached the elbow or above; for evening wear they were longer, coming well up toward the shoulders. Dangling earrings were the most noticeable jewelry of the decade. Necklaces usually consisted of a single strand of beads. Combs placed well forward of the chignon were often a focus of attention. A much greater display of precious jewels was worn at French court functions (Fig. 498). Josephine's tiara is indicative of

inspired beret, tasseled, and circled with fur. It included the upright plumes, sometimes combined with a caul, of English court costume; delicate embroidered and frilled lingerie caps (Figs. 496 and 499), worn both in and out of doors; turbans from India (Fig. 502); and, as the decade advanced, straw hats (Fig. 505), with both wide and narrow brims, trimmed with ribbon; and bonnets tied beneath the chin. One handsome chapeau of black velvet, reflecting Napoleon's military activities, was made in the form of a helmet crested with plumes. Another of similar origin had a cocked brim corded in gold and a burst of varied feathers and plumes shooting in all directions. (Figures 500 and 506 show a velvet hat and a straw poke bonnet.)

FIG. 505. *Straw Hat. 1809. Redrawn from* La Belle Assemblée. *(Author's Collection)*

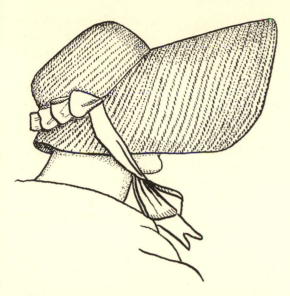

FIG. 506. *Straw Poke Bonnet. 1807. Redrawn from Costume Parisien, Plate 804. (Metropolitan Museum of Art, Dick Fund)*

her new rank. The diadems of her sisters-in-law are also regal.

THE SECOND DECADE

The second decade of the nineteenth century inherited the slender silhouette and high waistline of the early empire period, but classic influence was soon forgotten. Fabric became increasingly opaque and firm; patterned yardage appeared again; decoration on the lower skirt attained greater depth and intricacy, utilizing borders, ruffles, rouleaus, and flowers. The ruff, after dallying tentatively in the earlier years, turned into a major accessory and held its popularity well through the thirties.

Shawls, though still widely used, made way for the spencer, redingote, and mantle. By the end of the decade bonnets were the dominating style of headdress.

By 1810 colorful fabrics were frequently part of the fashion scene. Indian shawls, which were as popular in England as they were in France, were sometimes made into dresses, their wide borders forming the hem-line. *Ackermann's Repository of the Arts* in 1812 included actual samples of chintz, cambric, merino, printed batiste, chinese crepes, and heavier muslins, in addition to the gossamer nets, gauzes, and India muslins of the early empire period. Merino, a fine soft wool, provided warmth for winter. Early in the decade a new wool fabric in diagonal weave was said to "possess the useful property of never creasing in wear."[2]

Satin was used for both pelisses and spencers; velvet appears in portraits. Printed muslins and ginghams were recommended for intermediate wear. Ackermann's magazine contained many examples of fine silky cottons in plain or fancy weaves with delightful diminutive printed or woven patterns.

Colors indicate the general mood of the fashions: white remained a great favorite for dresses, though rose, blossom (a pale pink), amber, marigold, sea green, primrose, lilac, cerulean blue, sage green, and fawn were in vogue also. Daytime costumes were apt to be in these light subtle tones, while white remained correct for formal wear.

[2] *Ibid.,* November, 1812.

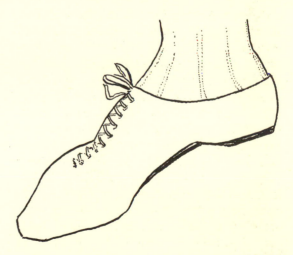

FIG. 507. *Laced Shoe. 1806. Redrawn from Costume Parisien, Plate 730. (Metropolitan Museum of Art, Dick Fund)*

BODICES. A distinction was made in morning, walking, and carriage attire as well as in evening, ball, and court dress. At the extremes were the domestic style, invariably high at the throat, and the ball gown, "formed to display rather too much of

FIG. 509. *Draped Bodice. 1817. Redrawn from* Le Bon Genre, *La Corbeille de Mariage. (Courtesy, Museum of Fine Arts, Boston)*

bosom, back and shoulders."[3] The Marquise Visconti posed for the painter Gerard in a ball gown that could hardly have been more revealing. Traces of Greek influence are visible in her sleeves of Ionic origin and the palmette border at the hemline.

A marked contrast is the daytime dress illustrated in Fig. 508 with its modest neckline and long full sleeves, spirally bound with a fine cord. With few exceptions the waistline remained high, like that shown in Fig. 509, seemingly achieving the impossible— even higher under the arms and breasts than previously (Figs. 502 and 503).

Figure 510, though a French drawing, illustrates an English bonnet and spencer. Presumably the low waistline was an English fashion. The color scheme includes a cherry spencer, neck scarf of pink with cherry stripes, and yellow shoes.

A functional feature of a gown in the Brooklyn collection, recorded in Draft 33, is a bodice evidently designed for the nursing mother. Cunnington shows a similar dress (of 1812) advertised for this purpose as follows: "It enables ladies to nourish their

FIG. 508. *Manches en Spirale. Profusion de Garnitures. 1811.* Le Bon Genre, *Plate 54. (Author's Collection)*

[3] *Ibid.,* July, 1813.

infants in the most delicate manner possible, when full dressed."[4] The horizontal drapery on the front of the bodice shown in Fig. 509 suggests an important change in the designing of bodices, modifications of which persisted during the next two decades.

Draft 34, made from an early empire period Italian gown of gold-colored raw silk, rich in texture, illustrates the drawstring neck, which was a feature of many gowns of the consulate and early empire periods.

SKIRTS. The skirts of this period underwent more radical changes than the bodices, two of which were soon apparent: deeper and more involved trimming around the bottom of the skirt, and a gradual increase in its sweep. The stiffening effect of the former emphasized the latter. Skirt fronts were quite smooth and flat, the extra width being controlled by pleats concentrated at the back (Fig. 511). At the same time side seams were slanted, changing the outline from a tubular one to a slender cone (Fig. 510).

Trimming assumed many forms. Figure 508, one of the most charming of the *Le Bon Genre* series, shows in its "Profusion of Garnitures" four deep ruffles, one of which is double, and gives ample evidence of the increased circumference of the skirt. A dress of 1818 has five ruffles of eyelet embroidery mounted with embroidered bandings; that of Fig. 511 has a band of rich gold embroidery. Most skirts were ankle length or slightly longer. In Fig. 510 the artist Vernet presents the shortest version among the illustrations given here though he included still shorter ones in his series, "Les Incroyables et les Merveilleuses."

WRAPS. Spencers and pelisses continued in use during the second decade of the century, gaining preference over shawls. Spencers performed an important function in those days of light-weight fabrics and minimum heat in stone-cold buildings. Fig-

[4] C. Willett Cunnington, *English Women's Clothing in the Nineteenth Century*, Faber, London, 1937, p. 33.

ure 510 suggests the preference for knuckle-length sleeves. This spencer with its lowered waistline hints of the styles of the 1820s.

A pelisse drawn by Vernet illustrates the lavish use of fur on winter garments. A fashion plate of January, 1820, pictures a pelisse of blue velvet with collar, cuffs, epau-

FIG. 510. H. Vernet, Les Incroyables et les Merveilleuses. c.1814. Plate 21. (Metropolitan Museum of Art, Dick Fund)

Fig. 511. *Ball Dress. 1818. La Belle Assemblée. (Author's Collection)*

lettes, front bandings, and deep bottom border of chinchilla. For milder temperatures
pelisses were made of silk with braid or self-
trimming, or of light-weight wool, sometimes with cape collars like the man's overcoat pictured in Fig. 512 called the garrick.
Corded loops were sometimes used as
fastenings.

Capes as outer wraps, sometimes having
a definitely military air, were introduced as
early as 1811. A cape published in *Journal
des Dames et des Modes*, 1820, of purple-
blue taffeta lined with rose was designed for
evening wear and has a hood. The bonnet
beneath the hood is of tulle with rouleaux of
blue satin.

The pelerine, a name used in *Ackermann's Repository of the Arts*, was a small,
shaped, shoulder scarf, sometimes as filmy as
muslin, sometimes sizable enough to serve as
a shoulder cape. Larger ones were made of
firm material and had long panels hanging
down the front. Another term, *canezou*, apparently covered a wide variety of accessories, from a bit of neck lingerie to a
blouse.

Large muffs were still in the fashion
picture at this time.

HAIRDRESS AND HEADDRESS. Hairdress
remained unchanged during this second decade of the century. A center part with curls
over the temples and high chignon was the
prevailing style. A comb placed over or in
front of the chignon was a decorative feature (Fig. 509).

Frilled muslin caps were worn indoors
at all times of day and were sometimes visible
under bonnet brims with outdoor costumes.

In the early years of the decade hats
predominated. The high-crowned hats of
Figs. 508 and 512 are excellent examples.
Later the bonnet became popular—a charming and flattering feminine artifice, engag-
ingly ruched and plumed. With only slight
changes it remained in the fashion picture
for 40 years. The little straw bonnet of Fig.
510 is especially effective. Turbans continued
to be worn with evening dress (Fig. 511).

FOOTWEAR. Footwear followed a practical bent during this decade. The sandal
was discarded and except for evening wear
so was the very fragile slipper. A Parisian

FIG. 512. *Woman's Garrick. 1817.* Journal des
Dames et des Modes. (*Author's Collection*)

pedestrian was shown wearing the seventeenth- and eighteenth-century iron-ringed patten of Fig. 513; another was shown wearing buttoned spats during the winter months (Fig. 512). A high front laced shoe of the era is shown in Fig. 510. Similar shoes with side lacing were fashionable also. Fur-trimmed footwear adapted to wear with skates was available. Note, too, the slippers in Fig. 511. Footwear usually repeated the color of another part of the ensemble.

ACCESSORIES. The role of gloves in this part of the nineteenth century cannot be overemphasized. Through much of the century they were worn both indoors and out, being removed only when eating. Short-sleeved dresses demanded long gloves, but short gloves accompanied all other costumes. Even though the craft of glove making is an old and proficient one, it is surprising to note the finesse with which gloves of the empire period were cut and finished. For example, a pair of short gloves in the University of Washington collection, made in Germany around 1810, are of fine closely woven cotton and are cut entirely on the bias for flexibility. The small insets at the base of the fingers, fourchettes, and hinged thumbs are as well shaped as in the gloves of today. The minute hand seaming is still intact.

Figure 510 illustrates the parasol, carried like a cane when closed.

The Betsy, a pseudo ruff, enjoyed a long reign and appeared in different forms; one of six layers is shown in Fig. 508 and a double-layered one in Fig. 510. The high

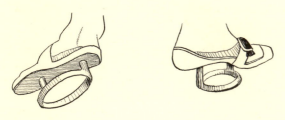

FIG. 513. *Pattens. 1811. Redrawn from* Costume Parisien. (*Author's Collection*)

pleated frill attached to the neckline of court costumes and ball gowns is related to the standing ruff, Fig. 511. A neck scarf is shown in Fig. 510.

Jewelry was relatively inconspicuous in these years, little or none being worn during the day. The use of decorative combs has already been mentioned. In a portrait of this period Betsy Bonaparte wore a beautiful comb ornamented with gold and set with amethysts. Both portrait and comb are in the collection of the Baltimore Historical Society.

THE TWENTIES

By 1820 the classical influence on costume was pretty well played out. There then ensued a series of swellings and protuberances that lasted the rest of the century.

Earlier in the century sleeves had shown a tendency toward fullness, and this feature was accented during the twenties. If we examine fashion plates of these years in chronological order we note a steady increase in sleeve volume; by 1830 the breadth across the upper part of the body was gargantuan. To keep the costume somewhat in balance the skirt was widened also, but the top-heavy look was accentuated by some of the most unique and startling millinery in history. Loaded to capacity with ribbons and feathers, these broad-brimmed hats appeared ready to take off in flight at any moment, their windmill sails revolving like propellers. In fact the whole costume had a nervous, restless air, though there were elements of charm and beauty. At their best, costumes of the early twenties had a feminine grace, pleasing combinations of color and texture, and variation in decoration without exaggeration. Draft 31, the pattern of a bodice of an 1820 gown, is indicative of the detailed cut of some gowns of the post empire period. It was taken from an exquisitely embroidered white muslin costume in the Brooklyn Museum collection.

FIG. 514. *Corset and Bustle of Late 1820's. Redrawn from William Heath, The Bustle. (New York Public Library, Prints Division)*

During the latter half of the twenties, however, taste took a holiday. The bustle reappeared and this distortion gave the final grotesque touch to costumes (Fig. 514). Shirtwaists and skirts divided the figure. To add to the disparity, skirts were often plaid, blouses white, and hats unrelated to either (Fig. 515).

For evening wear the hairdress was as mannered as a gown. The hair was brushed sleek, drawn up to the crown of the head, and manipulated by separate strands and braids into standing loops which required wire, hairdressing, and high-backed combs

to hold them erect. Flowers and feathers were generously intertwined (Fig. 516).

Fabrics

The tendency toward more colorful fabrics than those of the empire period continued. Muslin declined in popularity, in favor of satin, velvet, gros de Naples, lutestring, Irish poplin, and machine-made lace. Bobinet, a machine-made fabric resembling the net background of lace, had been produced successfully in 1809, and patterned lace within the next decade. Flouncing and even entire dresses were made of it in the 1820s.

Popular colors during the twenties were richer in tone than their immediate predecessors: dark green, purple, bright rose, cherry, and dark ruby are mentioned on fashion plates of the era. Plaids were made in combinations of red, green, and black.

Fashion Features

MOURNING COSTUME. English fashions of 1820 were affected by the deaths, in rapid succession, of the Duke of Kent and King George III. Since mourning was then a matter of strict observance, a brief discussion of it is in order here. Court mourning was officially regulated, but mourning was also generally worn throughout the century. In fact, as late as the 1920s a shop on New York's Fifth Avenue dealt exclusively in mourning clothes.

The degree and period of mourning were determined by the nearness of the relationship. Ackermann describes the first stage of mourning clothes for King George III thus:

A walking dress of black bombazine ornamented with narrow pipings of crape. Long sleeves (to knuckles) of easy width and surmounted by full epaulettes. Headdress consisted of cornette or cap of white crape and bonnet of black crape over black sarsenet trimmed with a black crape rose. Black leather

FIG. 515. *Walking Dresses.* 1826. Journal des Dames et des Modes. (*Author's Collection*)

FIG. 516. *Full Dress Evening Costume (Left). Ball Dress (Right). 1828. La Belle Assemblée. (Author's Collection)*

half boots; shamoy gloves. [Even ruffs were made of black crape.] Evening dress should be of black crape over a black sarsenet slip. Corsage low but with tucker of black crape. Black crape toque with black plume; jet jewelry. Black velvet pelisse with black crape trim. Fan of black crape.[5]

The second stage of court mourning called for plain black silk, the third added colored flowers and ribbons. Queen Victoria, overwhelmed with sorrow at the death of her consort, Prince Albert, continued to wear some form of mourning for 20 years or more. This truly sincere expression of her sorrow cast a shadow over state festivities.

George III had been mentally ill the last 10 years of his life and George IV had had to act as regent. Because of these circumstances he agreed to a shortened period of full mourning for George III, in the interest of trade.

SKIRTS. Spreading contours and the conspicuous horizontal decoration of court dress were typical of skirts throughout the decade. Ornamentation might be provided by gathered or pleated ruffles, appliquéd designs in self- or contrasting fabric, tucks, or rouleaus of silk or fur. For example, one extravagant winter frock had a patterned border of chinchilla at the hemline, matched by a long pelerine and muff.

As the decade advanced, skirts continued to widen. At first this was accomplished by goring, later by gathered or pleated fullness at the waistline. With the introduction of large bustles like those shown in Figs. 514 and 517, skirts inevitably had to have longer and much fuller backs. As they jutted outward with the lift of the bustle and increased their sweep, they shortened also, thus exposing the ankles. Ball gowns, perhaps in response to the vogue of more sprightly dancing, were shorter than any other costume. Dancing slippers were tied ballet fashion, with ribbons crossing the instep (Fig. 516).

[5] Ackermann, *op. cit.*, March, 1820.

Although English court costume during this decade retained the high waistline, the normal waistline prevailed for other dress, usually marked by a straight belt of medium

FIG. 517. *Underwear. 1825–1835. White Lawn Petticoat; Three-flounce Bustle, 1833; Cotton Sleeve Puffs Filled with Down; White Cotton Cap; White Cotton Pockets. (Gallery of English Costume, Manchester)*

Fig. 518. *Morning Visiting Dress. 1826.* La Belle Assemblée. (*Author's Collection*)

width. Toward the end of the period the belt dipped sharply downward in center front, inaugurating another cycle of pointed waistlines (Fig. 516).

SLEEVES. As though in competition with the fussiness of the skirt, sleeves gradually gained the spotlight. Already swollen at the top by 1820, they continued to grow until they required support of some kind, usually down filled forms or stiff linings (Fig. 517). Though sleeves displayed considerable ingenuity in shape, the majority were of the leg-of-mutton type: largest at the top, diminishing gradually to the wrist (Figs. 515 and 518). An offshoot of this style was a sheer tapering sleeve worn over a short but very full puffed sleeve (Fig. 519). Sleeves called "gigots" were very full to the elbow and smoothly fitted from there to the wrist. Others, with the charming name of "imbecile sleeves," were full from armscye to wrist, finished there with fitted bands of varying depth. Naturally, deviations occurred in each

FIG. 520. *Wide Neckline with Bertha. 1829. Redrawn from German Fashion Plate. (Author's Collection)*

style. All three types became more sharply differentiated in the early thirties.

NECKLINES. Necklines took a new turn in this period, by the addition of a bertha, a falling ruffle, or a shaped band mounted to the widened edge (Fig. 520).

Lengthening and dropping of shoulder seams, and straightening and widening of necklines contributed further to the expansiveness of the shoulder area (Figs. 515 and 518). Where the neckline was high, wide cape-like collars outreached the sleeves. Extensions remotely related to the wings of the sixteenth and seventeenth centuries, often bearing their full share of ruffles, braid, and/ or embroidery, capped the sleeves (Fig. 518).

High necks also continued to display the Betsy of the previous decade, often made in two or three tiers.

FIG. 519. *F. Westin, Josephine, Queen of Sweden 1826. (Gripsholm, Sweden)*

Figure 521 reproduces a lovely gown of green and gold silk brocade worn at a ball given in honor of General Lafayette in 1825 —evidence that eccentricity did not hold complete sway in the twenties. Its well-cut scooped neckline is becoming. Here the designer allowed the pattern of the cloth to dominate the style, using a narrow silk fringe on the diminutive sleeve as the only trimming (Draft 35).

A feature in blouse designing, first noted in Fig. 509 (1817) reappears in Fig. 516: a separate piece of material, probably cut on the bias, gathered at both ends and at the center and attached just below the front neckline from armscye to armscye. The dress at the right has two such pieces slanted from shoulder to waistline, where they meet. This use of overlaid sections of fabric to give emphasis to the bust was further exploited during the 1830s and 1840s.

FASTENINGS. Practically all of the dresses of this era fastened down center back with buttons, lacing, or concealed closings of hooks and eyes. Pelisse robes and walking dresses were closed down center front and often decorated with bows which did not necessarily function.

WRAPS. The redingote or pelisse, which was comparable to our modern coat dress, continued in use during the twenties. In this decade it evolved into two distinct garments: the walking or carriage dress made of firm material and appropriate for outdoor wear, and a true outer wrap of warm fabric, more voluminous in cut than earlier. A traveling coat pictured in the *Index of American Design* was made of quilted gray silk lined with gray calico. Leg-of-mutton sleeves and large cape collar accented its shoulder breadth. Figure 522 shows a Parisian redingote of brown wool.

Spencers, which gave as much warmth as was needed for mild weather, lengthened as the waistline dropped. The one illustrated in Fig. 523 is from the Brooklyn Museum collection.

Shawls, fur pelerines, and boas contributed variety in wraps.

HAIRDRESS. The hairdress of the early twenties was a relatively subdued affair, with curls from the center part concentrated over the temples. By 1826 sausage curls, reminiscent of the formal arrangements of the eighteenth century, were massed at each side of the forehead (Fig. 519). By 1828 hair stylists had reached the ultimate in manipulating the hair and from that time on, novelty was a matter of choice and anchoring

FIG. 521. *Gown Worn at Lafayette Ball. 1825*
(*Brooklyn Museum*)

FIG. 522.   *Redingote. 1822.* Journal des Dames et des Modes. (*Author's Collection*)

hats followed much the same curve as hair-dress (Fig. 522). Bonnets differed little from those observed earlier. By 1826, however, the brim had been lifted and the crown brought forward; once more the wide-brimmed hat was in the limelight (Figs. 518 and 520). At first these hats were moderately trimmed with ribbons and flowers but, like all other parts of the costume, they were soon affected by the mania for exaggeration—with results like the structure shown in Fig. 524. Bulky turbans, like that worn by Queen Josephine of Sweden in Fig. 519, were seen frequently in the latter half of the decade.

FOOTWEAR.   Shoes showed little change, the low slipper and the side-laced shoe carrying through the decade. In describing costumes of the early twenties *Ackermann's Repository of the Arts* mentions both boots and shoes of purple leather and black kid for daytime wear and white satin shoes with diamond buckles for evening.

The low heelless slipper, square-toed in the earlier years of the decade, became more pointed at the end. For sturdier wear shoes with leather toe caps and slight heels had practical advantages (Fig. 515).

of extraneous decoration (Fig. 516). Mechanical supports and hair dressing of some sort must have been employed.

HATS.   In the early years of this decade

FIG. 523.   *Spencer of Late 1820's. Redrawn from Photograph of Original.* (*Brooklyn Museum*)

ACCESSORIES. The wearing of jewelry increased during these years, but was still within modest bounds as compared with the sixteenth century. Matched bracelets and rings were now worn, as well as the earrings and necklaces of previous years. Cameos continued in favor.

Parasols and gloves remained indispensable. Note the lorgnette in Fig. 522.

The 1820s were really a transition stage between the tubular silhouette of the empire period and the grotesquely abnormal figure of the thirties. Signs in that direction were in evidence in the late twenties: diminutive pointed waistline, extreme width at the shoulders, ballooning sleeves balanced by spreading skirts, intricate manipulation of the hair, and spectacular headdresses.

THE THIRTIES AND FORTIES

Styles of the late 1820s, which lasted well through the thirties, are distinct and recognizable wherever encountered. Shoulders spread to their greatest width ever, while skirts widened to maintain an appearance of balance. The diminutive waistline, by contrast, emphasized the exaggerated horizontal dimensions. Caprice reigned in both hairdress and headdress.

The enormous sleeves of the era were supported by boning or down cushions. Artists working on the project of the *Index of American Design* reported finding the latter in dresses. Figure 517 illustrates the English device of down-filled sleeve puffs worn to maintain the desired outline. To further emphasize sleeve breadth various sorts of projections were extended out over the sleeves from the neckline or armscye. A perfect exmple of this is a gown in the Smithsonian collection. It is of crisp dove-gray silk with a hairline stripe of lavender which gives it a misty, luminous quality. Self-bound layers of the fabric wing out over the sleeves. In all kinds of costumes collars, capes,

canezous, pelerines, and berthas were used to attain this fashionable width.

At the same time, additional widths of dress fabric were used to bring the skirt into balance with the upper part of the costume; even at that, a fashionable contour required more petticoats. Waistlines, already minimized by optical illusion, were further diminished by excruciatingly tight lacing.

The thirties and forties marked the romantic period at its height. Ladies were adept in swooning at the slightest provocation; they were also conditioned to affect an attitude of distaste, at least in public, at the sight of food. It took the acute food shortages of a world war almost a hundred years later to bestow respectability upon a cleaned plate.

Actually, the volume and weight of the garments which fashion dictated might well

FIG. 524. *Hat of 1827. Redrawn from* La Belle Assemblée. *(Author's Collection)*

have caused ladies to droop from fatigue, but one wonders if they ever looked as boneless as the fashion drawings of the day suggest!

In his book on French costume Uzanne emphasizes that the clinging, sighing, swooning prototype of the high romantic period was soon replaced by a far different model.[6] He claims that the woman of the forties, of whom George Sand is an extreme example, was much more independent, assertive, and efficient, and her costume was suited to her new role. George Sand, it will be remembered, startled everyone by wearing men's clothing.

Queen Victoria, who came to the throne in England in 1837, had a sobering influence on society. Well trained by her mother, she established a novel moral tone at court; after her happy marriage to Prince Albert she set a pattern for domesticity as well as for state affairs. *Godey's Ladies' Book* of April, 1840, describes the wedding dress of Queen Victoria, which is on display at the London Museum, as follows:

> Her Majesty's dress was of rich white satin, trimmed with orange blossoms. The headdress consisted of a wreath of orange blossoms and over this a beautiful veil of Honiton lace. . . . The cost of the lace alone on the dress was one thousand pounds [about five thousand dollars] . . . more than 200 persons were employed on the lace from March to November. Lace which formed the flounce on the dress measures four yards and is three quarters of a yard in depth. The veil is one and a quarter yards square.

Evening gowns varied little during the thirties and forties. Low broad necklines and draped sections over the bosom were fashionable, as they were in the twenties (Fig. 525). Cleverly designed self-fabric trimming adorned necklines and sleeve edges. A typical evening gown of the forties, in the collection of the Drama School of the University of Washington, is made of lightweight aqua

[6] Octave Uzanne, *Fashion in Paris*, William Heinemann, London, 1898, pp. 104–107.

FIG. 525. *Evening Gown of Silvery Gray Damask. c.1835. (University of Washington, School of Drama)*

damask. Its draped folds lead to a narrow pleated panel which extends upward from the waistline. Blonde lace, in high favor at the time, forms an appropriate finish of sleeves and neckline.

Fabrics

Throughout the thirties dress fabrics

Fig. 526. *Striped Silk Dress. 1840's. (Brooklyn Museum)*

FIG. 527. *Morning and Carriage Dress. 1830. La Belle Assemblée. (Author's Collection)*

tended to be light and buoyant; organdy, mousseline de soie, tarlatan, printed cambric, and muslins in summer; foulard, challis, cashmere, peau de soie, satin, and gros de Naples in winter. Colors were muted: fawn, straw, dust, azure, lilac, apple green, cabbage green, claret, and chocolate. During the forties red, fuchsia, purple, bright blue, plum, dark green, and dark gray were more favored. Taffeta was manufactured in lovely combinations of changeable colors as well as in dominant stripes and plaids.

Major Costume Features

BODICE AND SKIRT. As we have noted, most of the costume features of the early thirties made their debut in the late twenties: swelling sleeves, broad collars, wide hats, and spreading skirts. The thirties carried these features to their climax. The bodice was closely fitted and slightly lengthened, with diagonal lines often extending from shoulder to waist. This V-shape emphasized shoulder width and helped to minimize waists. Skirts were full, but without the heavy decoration of the twenties, and shortened, especially for evening wear.

With the pivoting of directional emphasis in the forties, waistlines were lowered, actually as well as seemingly. Diagonal lines from shoulder to center waist, produced in various ways—slanting darts, gathered folds in the bodice itself, or overlaid panels—together with pointed waistlines and full-length closings, intensified this lengthened effect.

Concurrently with this change in the bodice, skirts lost some of their volume and buoyancy; for a few years they, too, emphasized a vertical line. Elaborate hemline embellishment disappeared, and when the skirt swept out again, flounces provided the emphasis.

The wine-red and silvery-gray striped satin gown shown in Fig. 526, now in the Brooklyn Museum collection, illustrates several characteristics of the forties, especially the V-neckline, long, closely fitted sleeves, and the lengthened waistline extending into a point. The bertha-shaped application gave way later to emphasis upon a diagonal line from shoulder to waist (Draft 38).

SLEEVES. Morning and carriage dresses illustrated in *La Belle Assemblée* for August, 1830, show three prevalent types of sleeves: (1) full to the elbow but fitted from elbow to wrist, (2) full from shoulder to wrist and mounted there to a tight cuff, and (3) fullness at the top formed into puffs (Figs. 527, 528, and 529). The extremely long, sharply slanted shoulder line of the costume on the seated figure in Fig. 527 is characteristic of fashion drawings of the thirties. Incidentally, this pose would be difficult to assume, especially by today's healthy and sportsminded young women.

Figure 528, from the *Gazette des Salons*, shows the maximum spread sleeves attained at this time. Figure 529, from the same journal, shows the collar resting on the outermost limits of the sleeve. This is the unique feature which sets 1830 dresses apart from all others.

Figure 525 shows a pale-gray damask gown in the collection of the Drama School at the University of Washington. The fabric is light, soft as down, and highly lustrous. Blonde lace finishes its neckline. Pattern Draft 36 explains its cut and construction; nothing else could make one believe the amount of material required for these mammoth sleeves, or their exact shape.

The excessive sleeve volume began to diminish by 1837. However, this did not immediately affect the yardage required because the first change in the sleeve was only in the control of its fullness—by vertical pleats about 4 inches down from the armscye (Fig. 530). There was still much ease over the elbow, but the wings which once extended outward now became short cap sleeves or broad tucks.

By the early forties sleeves were narrowed and straightened, almost as if the excess had been stripped away by stroking it downward over the elbow and off the

FIG. 528. *Brocade Satin Dress. c.1835. Gazette des Salons. (Author's Collection)*

FIG. 529. *Gown of White Cashmere. 1835. Re-drawn from Gazette des Salons. (Author's Collection)*

FIG. 531. *Bodice with Fitted Sleeves. Spaniel Curls and Bonnet. 1845. Redrawn from Monthly Belle Assemblée. (Author's Collection)*

FIG. 530. *Diminished Upper Sleeve. 1839. Re-drawn from Monthly Belle Assemblée. (Author's Collection)*

hand (Fig. 531). In the very last years of this decade the lower part of the sleeve was shortened and widened slightly to permit a lingerie undersleeve to show. As we shall see, this was the signal for the sleeve to take off upon another tack for the fifties and sixties.

NECKLINES. During the forties necklies changed from a predominantly lateral direction to a V-shape. Figure 527 shows a ruffled guimpe and Betsy filling in the plunging V; in Fig. 528 a visible chemisette creates a wide rounded neckline. Figure 529 also suggests the tendency toward a higher neckline at this time. Furthermore, in the new social climate of the decade, a prim closing, starting at the normal neckline, replaced previous styles for daytime wear (Fig. 531).

UNDERGARMENTS.   Corset models of this era changed little from the preceding period.

Cords gave firmness through the midriff, gussets were let in at the bust area, lacing controlled the waist measure, and long metal stays maintained the front posture (Fig. 532c).

Underskirts, made of all manner of

(a)

(b)

Fig. 532. *Accessories. a. Pelerine of 1830's. (University of Washington, School of Home Economics) b. White Organdy Morning Cap. Mid-Nineteenth Century. (Metropolitan Museum of Art) c. Corset of 1830's. (Gallery of English Costume, Manchester)*

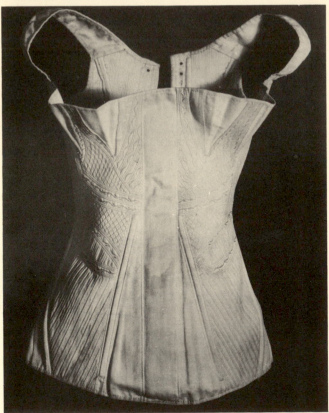

(c)

fabrics, multiplied. Wadded, quilted petticoats furnished both warmth and width. One device for spreading cotton petticoats out was solid cording at the lower edge to a depth of 6 to 8 inches. Real crinoline, a fabric woven of flax and horsehair, was considered progressive because it was wiry enough to replace two or three cotton petticoats. In general, starched and ruffled petticoats formed the outer layers of the burdensome structure which supported the skirt.

WRAPS. During the thirties, when the mass of the sleeves made a fitted wrap all but impossible, shawls and capes served the purpose of protection and wamth. Many varieties of capes appeared, from light ones for summer wear to such long, full, interlined, double caped models as the one in Fig. 533 (Draft 37a and b). This is an original garment from the Brooklyn Museum collection which proves that the fashion plates were realistic. This mantle is made of light-weight sand-colored wool, lined with quilted rose taffeta, and embroidered in silk of related tones. Here the sleeve problem is met by the use of a full upper cape. This is an excellent historic record in every way.

With the narrowing of sleeves in the forties it again became possible to mold wraps to the body (Fig. 534). However, shawls and capes had so ingratiated themselves by this time that they lingered on through the fifties and sixties.

HAIRDRESS AND HEADDRESS. During the first part of the thirties hairdress continued to be as exotic as it had been in the previous decade, but hats were replaced by bonnets which spread above and away from the face, giving a demure and helpless look in keeping with the fashionable romantic ideal.

As late as 1835 the hair was still manipulated into weird shapes like that in Fig. 535. By the end of the decade the upward direction of these creations was reversed. From a center part the hair was combed downward in front of the ears, drawn under them, and

knotted at the nape of the neck. Sometimes the front hair was braided in two side plaits which were looped under the ears (Fig. 536).

FIG. 533. *Double Cape of 1830's. (Brooklyn Museum)*

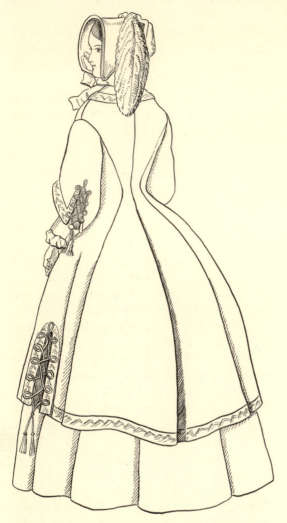

531 was made shows a bonnet in rose color with matching plume, a purple one harmonizing with a dress worn under an emerald-green mantle, and a teal-blue bonnet which makes a pleasing accessory for a gray dress

FIG. 535. *Hair Style of Early 1830's. Redrawn from Fashion Plate showing Coiffure by M. Seigneur, Paris. (Author's Collection)*

FIG. 534. *Back View of Long Fitted Coat. 1845. Redrawn from Monthly Belle Assemblée. (Author's Collection)*

In the forties groups of curls hung down like spaniel's ears at each side of the face. Elizabeth Barrett Browning and George Sand are inseparably associated with this mode (Fig. 531).

The bonnets of the forties shrank in size to the modest proportions seen in Fig. 531. They were flat over the crown of the head and trimming was kept close to the frame. Their interest lay principally in the color and richness of the fabric used. For example, the complete plate from which Fig.

FIG. 536. *Hair Style of Late 1830's. Redrawn from Winterhalter, Queen Victoria. (National Gallery of Art, Washington, D.C.)*

enriched with brown fur. In each case matching ribbons tied under the chin.

FOOTWEAR. The low square-toed slipper, still heelless and tied with ribbons about the ankle, was a perfect prop for the clinging-vine pose. They were made in black satin, white kid, and many colors of leather. The Brooklyn Museum collection includes an elaborate pump of 1840, decorated with chain stitch embroidery, cut steel beads, and an intricate bow of ribbon centered with a silver buckle. Another gay little pair, made of red and white candy-striped leather, gives the first evidence that square toes are about to be replaced by a rounded shape.

Soon after Queen Victoria's coronation in 1838, her shoemaker made her a low boot with elastic insets at the sides. Known as gaiters, these later became an important item for both men and women. In the forties the side-laced boot with leather toe and counter remained the prevalent form of footwear. Note the two-toned shoe in Fig. 527.

ACCESSORIES. Delightful accessories of the era, which must have been dear to the feminine heart, were sheer embroidered and ruffled white caps and various forms of neckwear essential to a real ladylike appearance. The lady on the left in Fig. 527 shows a typical pelerine worn with a Betsy. Betsies remained in fashion during the 1830s but were seldom seen after 1840. Figure 532*b* shows a cap from the Metropolitan Museum collection and *a* shows a pelerine from the costume collection of the School of Home Economics, University of Washington. The finest caps were made of India muslin, adorned with handmade lace. No wonder the ladies wore them everywhere! The embroidery on such lingerie items, including the chemisettes often visible above low necklines, is wonderfully fine and beautiful.

Lace mitts were worn as well as the usual leather gloves. Cunnington calls attention to the use in 1833 of knitted gloves for morning wear and mittens of black silk net worked on the back with gold or mittens of white silk net or white kid for dinner parties.[7] He also quotes a fashion note to the effect that by 1841 mittens of black silk were indispensable for all parties.[8]

Aprons, once more quite elegant, came out of the kitchen and became an accepted part of morning costumes.

THE FIFTIES AND SIXTIES

Historical Background

In 1853 Louis Napoleon III, nephew of Napoleon I and grandson of Josephine, married Eugénie de Montijo of Spain. This marriage brought a fresh new personality to fashion leadership. By her beauty, grace, and charm the Empress won a large following and exerted a great influence upon fashions of the second empire.

Charles Worth, the Englishman who founded the first of the great couturier houses of Paris, had the great good fortune to secure Empress Eugénie as a client. Her endorsement and patronage did much to further his success. With his genuine appreciation of fine fabric, Worth was largely responsible for the revitalization of the fabric industry of Lyons. The most striking feature of the famous Worth gowns and cloaks throughout the last half of the nineteenth century was the magnificence of the materials he employed.

By mid-century a dress reform movement which must have been brewing for some time found leadership in Amelia Jenks Bloomer, publisher of *The Lily*, a monthly woman's magazine devoted to temperance and literature. There is a general impression that she and her "bloomers," as the garments came to be called, received nothing but ridicule in the United States and abroad. Certainly when she appeared in London in 1851, *Punch* made the most of the occasion and Cruikshank gave his active imagination full play in his cartoon of bloomers in Hyde Park.

[7] Cunnington, *op. cit.*, p. 113.
[8] *Ibid.*, p. 139.

However, the *Illustrated London News* referred to Mrs. Bloomer as "a lady of rare accomplishment and beauty" and said that her costume "appears far neater and more tasteful than that generally worn."[9] It devoted a full column to a quotation from a Boston doctor in defense of the costume. Figure 537 taken from the issue of September 27, 1851, shows the lady wearing the bloomers she advocated. Incidentally, she did not design them—she merely endorsed and promoted them.

Although this particular dress reform failed of adoption, it did have a lasting effect: bloomers (the word itself is a memorial) appeared in the bathing dress of the sixties, and were revived and adapted again and again as women engaged in one outdoor sport after another. The movement for more sanitary and functional clothing for women was carried on for at least 60 years, and while no single spectacular success marks its history, the freedom of modern dress owes quite a debt of gratitude to the gallant ladies who led the revolt.

Influence on Costume

REAPPEARANCE OF HOOPS

Two events of the 1850s had a far-reaching effect upon costume, one immediate and temporary, the other revolutionary and lasting. The first was the introduction of the hooped petticoat as a substitute for the many garments required to inflate skirts to the desired contour; the second was the invention of the sewing machine. There were many points in favor of the hooped petticoat: it was much lighter than the previous accumulation of padded, crinoline, and starched muslin petticoats, which must have been both heavy and a real impediment to freedom of motion. And although it did not solve the laundry problem, it alleviated it. Furthermore, fewer waistbands enhanced the slimness of the waistline.

[9] *Illustrated London News*, Sept. 27, 1851.

At the time the idea seemed a great boon to womankind. The first hoops were made of strips of cane or whalebone inserted in casings in the muslin petticoat. Later an American device was universally accepted: circles of watch spring steel, protected by rubber, riveted to vertical tapes.

But while solving some difficulties hoops also presented new ones. In an era when modesty reigned supreme, when women were even supposed to be devoid of ankles—not to mention legs—a lady could lose her

FIG. 537. *Amelia Jenks Bloomer. 1851.* Illustrated London News. (*New York Public Library*)

social standing by an accidental flip of her springing hoop. The decade from 1855 to 1865, when hoops were *de rigueur,* saw a constant battle between mores and fashion, which fashion usually won. Recognizing the fact that feet and legs would inevitably be exposed, shoemakers gave thought to aesthetics when they designed footwear, and stockings took on a new gaiety. Petticoats, now revealed, became more colorful and provocative. Dresses were even equipped with mechanical devices to lift the hem of the skirt, the better to ensure the sight of the petticoat.

The size of these hoops often made life difficult for their wearers. Even spacious ballrooms and drawing rooms were easily overcrowded. A factor that must have given pause to many a woman was the fire hazard. Normal exits could not accommodate panicked wearers of these highly inflammable skirts, and the holocaust in public conflagrations was horrible. Empress Eugénie is given some credit for the abandonment of hoops by discouraging their appearance at her large functions. As always, too, there comes a time of boredom with any fashion— a longing for change, and with it designers' answers to the challenge.

INVENTION OF THE SEWING MACHINE

The second and far more momentous event in the dressmaking world of the fifties was the introduction of the sewing machine. Elias Howe patented his machine in 1846; by 1855 it was sufficiently perfected to be mass-produced for the market. From then on there has been a steady decline in handmade garments, until today the craft is almost extinct.

For some time, however, production was relatively slow and the price was high, so that for decades hand sewing remained the only method of construction in poorer homes and hand finishing accounted for at least 90 percent of the time spent in producing custom-made clothing. Today many mothers have never owned a machine or felt the need for one, buying, as they do, everything ready-made.

THE INDUSTRIAL REVOLUTION

The invention of the sewing machine was only one phase of the Industrial Revolution, which began in the eighteenth century and is still in progress. Such inventions as the steam engine in 1770, which could be used to power Hargreave's spinning jenny of the same year, and Whitney's cotton gin of 1794, speeded up the manufacture of fabrics enormously. Furthermore, steam transportation by both land and sea, which came in the early nineteenth century, balanced distribution with production. The pace has been accelerating ever since, creating new environments in every sphere of man's being. Men's wear reflected this new way of life much more quickly than feminine fashions did. Women still had the struggle for women's rights ahead of them before they could assume public positions and concern themselves with costumes suitable to their new world.

Fabrics

Fabrics of the fifties and sixties were rich in variety and interesting in texture. Materials were often woven or printed *en disposition,* that is, with designs planned for definite parts of the costume. These appeared in both sheer organdies and heavy silks. Dimity, lawn, chambray, gingham, chintz, piqué, Irish poplin, and nankeen were among the summer choices; cashmere, merino, challis, flannel, foulard, taffeta, brocade, velvet, moiré, and barathea were available for winter use. Gauze, mousseline, barege, and grenadine supplemented tulle for evening wear. Velvet, plush, and fur, as well as braiding, were used for trimming on outer wraps.

Designs from India appeared on fabrics varying all the way from lawn to flannel, while plaids were a favorite theme for taffeta. Fringes were made in great variety, sharing with lace the finishing of dresses and mantles.

An important innovation of the early sixties was the introduction of aniline dyes, the first ones available being in the range of violent red-purples such as cerise. Much has been said of the raucous result, but museum collections and fashion magazines of the period show little evidence of their general acceptance.

IMPORTANCE OF LACE. Empress Eugénie's love of lace resulted in a marked increase in the use of that lovely, delicate fabrication (Fig. 538). Lace lent itself to the airy mood of the costume of the day. It was lavished upon sleeves, hats, capes, and handkerchiefs. Entire flounces, parasols, jackets, and shawls of lace were created by skilled lace makers of Europe. Figure 539 shows a shawl and parasol of Chantilly lace.

Fashion Features of the Era

The comparatively minor fashion changes of the early fifties were the result of trends already noticeable in the forties. The sleeve widened into the full pagoda, a name given to an open sleeve which flared widely below the elbow. This design drew attention to the lingerie under the sleeves, sometimes separate accessories tied securely above the elbow but often part of a chemisette or underblouse sometimes referred to as a *canezou* (Fig. 540). Until hoops were reintroduced in 1854, skirts depended for bouyancy upon the airy projection of flounces. Many skirts were double, some triple. For the most part, however, ruffles varying in number from the usual three to

FIG. 538. *Winterhalter, Empress Eugénie and Ladies in Waiting. 1855. (Compiègne)*

FIG. 539. *Day Dress with Accessories. 1862–1864. (Gallery of English Costume, Manchester)*

eleven or more for evening wear were sewed to an already full foundation.

For day wear bodices were frequently cut separately, with tabbed extensions to preserve the long waistline of the forties. Often they were closed with buttons from the throat down. For evening wear shoulders were still bared.

Inevitably the hooped silhouettes of a century evoke comparison with the court costumes of Louis XV and Louis XVI. Many details reminiscent of those fashions were revived on mid-nineteenth-century gowns. Festoons of gauze, artificial flowers in sprays or bouquets, open and spreading overskirts, pointed waistlines, which became extreme in

FIG. 540. *Flounced Costume. 1850. Redrawn from* Monthly Belle Assemblée. (*Author's Collection*)

FIG. 541. *Two-Piece Costume. 1857. Redrawn from* Magazin des Demoiselles. (*Author's Collection*)

the second decade of this period, all can be traced to Madame Pompadour and Marie Antoinette.

Other influences were also in evidence in the fifties. The smart two-piece costume shown in Fig. 541 has quite a long jacket, the skirt of which juts out from the waist—a design reminiscent of costumes of Spanish Infantas of the seventeenth century. The Spanish bolero reappeared later in an 1860 adaptation. Separate semifitted fur-edged jackets recall the women in Vermeer's paintings.

The Italian war of independence, 1848–1849, launched new fashions: the Zouave jacket, inspired by the colorful uniforms

of a branch of the French infantry, and the Garibaldi red shirt and braided pillbox cap. These items were taken over almost intact. Adoption by women of this mannish shirt marks the beginning of such influence. To be sure, riding costumes throughout the century had been quite tailored and the blouses worn with them had aped men's shirts and neckwear of the period. Nor was the blouse and skirt idea new—witness Fig. 515 showing a style typical of the late 1820s. But those blouses were definitely feminine. The Garibaldi shirt was of a different mood and served a different purpose; its descendants are still with us.

Zouave uniforms caught the fancy of

the fashion minded and led to an assortment of jackets with braid trimming and fur edging. Braiding, which soon spread to all manner of garments, came to be identified with the second empire period (Fig. 541).

Figure 540 illustrates the moderate sweep of the skirt at the beginning of the fifties, the basqued bodice, pagoda sleeves, already definitely shaped, and the embroidered ruffles on the undersleeves of the canezou. Contrasting tabbed jackets appeared at this time, fastening from throat to waistline. Shoulders were rounded and smooth, with the armscye already drifting downward a bit. The bonnet was pushed back, revealing more of the hair. Spaniel curls were no longer in evidence.

Figure 541 shows how the pagoda sleeves had increased in size by 1857, their accompanying undersleeves, longer jacket peplum, and wider skirt jutting out from the waistline. The only part of the costume which had diminished by this time was the bonnet, the brim and crown of which appear to be blended into one. It is worn with the rim far back on the head.

A charming costume of the period, now in the Brooklyn Museum collection, can be converted into an evening gown by a second bodice which has a broad neckline and short sleeves (Fig. 542). Modern in its versatility, it is nevertheless a typical example of its time, as its pagoda sleeves, pointed waistline, and full-length front closing proclaim (Draft 39). One of its remarkable features is that three differently designed fabrics were woven for the one ensemble, all employing the same colors and the theme of stripes, but varying in grouping and proportions for the two bodices and the skirt. The misty look of the flowers was no doubt obtained by the warp print process, though many of the plaids so popular at the time were woven of tie-dyed yarn. The color scheme here is chocolate brown in the moiré and satin stripes, and white as the background of the rose, lavender, and green floral design.

Another remarkable costume in the

FIG. 542. *Striped Taffeta Costume. c.1855.* (Brooklyn Museum)

same collection, of subtle apple-green silk with a light silvery-gray pattern woven *en disposition*, is provided with three tops: a daytime bodice, an evening bodice, and an artful little jacket of matching green in plain fabric.

Figures 543 and 544, drawn by the master fashion artist Pauquet, idealize the hoop mode. They date from the early sixties. Figure 543 shows evening costumes with skirts at their extreme extension, floating in a mist of lace and net. The gown at the left is rose taffeta with Chantilly flounces; the other is black net over white satin. The eve-

FIG. 543. *Ball Gowns. Early 1860's. Petit Courrier des Dames. (Author's Collection)*

ning headdress consists of a spot of tulle with lace or fluted tulle edging, a dash of gay ribbons, and flowers. The attenuated point of the first bodice is significant, as is the disposition of the fullness of the skirt.

During the thirties, forties, and fifties skirts had been cut in full lengths of fabric, the fullness being distributed quite evenly by gathers or cartridge pleating around the waist. This feature, coupled with the same treatment in the petticoats, produced the familiar bell shape. With the sixties the extra fabric was folded, usually into wide box pleats, often stacked three deep, and proportioned to form six such groups, radiating from the waistline. This treatment gave a less jutting, more angular line—the bell was on the way to becoming a cone. Inseparable from the outer aspect of the skirt was the controlling support beneath. To ensure the skirt's flattening in front, the hoop structure had to be changed. As the process continued

FIG. 544. *Day Costumes. Early 1860's.* Petit Courrier des Dames. *(Author's Collection)*

fewer and fewer circles of steel were used in the top of the hoops, finally disappearing entirely from the front. By the late sixties they were engineered to create a narrow width from side to side and a sharply angled line from the back waistline to the floor.

The Pauquet drawing of 1863 (Fig. 544) shows shockingly short skirts, made more liable to censure by a looped up lower edge which revealed the petticoat. Both women in this drawing wear high-heeled shoes, the one on the left tan, the other blue with light stockings. Two types of wraps are shown, a long lace-trimmed cape and a somewhat tailored, semifitted, sleeved coat.

Far less elaborate than fashion plate models, Fig. 545 illustrates the average interpretation of the mode. The handling of the fitting, the slope and length of the shoulder seam, and the clever method of creating the pagoda sleeve comprise an authentic record of the practice and style of the time.

By 1868 the front of the skirt was usually perfectly straight and flat. Goring removed all excess material from the front waist mounting, but an abundance of fabric was still massed at the back, where it flowed upon the floor in a train. Sometimes an overskirt swept back repeated the story of the late seventeenth century.

A fashion plate of August, 1868 (Fig. 546) shows a revival of the polonaise. The seated lady in the illustration is wearing a skirt of pale fuchsia. Her overdress is of white and lighter fuchsia, and its borders and ribbons match the skirt. The fact that the overdress is cut without a waist seam, the material falling free from the shoulders,

FIG. 545. *Emerald Green-and-Black Striped Wool Dress. 1865. (Brooklyn Museum)*

may have some bearing on the princess style of the next decade. This costume shows marked affinity with eighteenth-century modes in both fabric and design, but could never be confused with them. Instead, the bulkiness of the fabric, pushed to the back and bunched into puffs and folds, foretells the modes of the early seventies.

Godey's Ladies' Book for May, 1853, faithfully reports descriptions of the wedding dresses Eugénie wore at the cathedral and civil ceremonies:

It is in uncut velvet with a train and covered with point d'Angleterre. The corsage is a basque, decked with diamonds. The head-dress consisted of a diadem and of a crown of diamonds and sapphires, mixed with orange blossoms. At the dinner, the Empress wore a parure of diamonds and rubies. For the civil marriage she wore rose colored satin, covered with point d'Angleterre, ornamented at the bottom with agrafes of white lilac, with a corsage drape, ornamented in the same way.

Her trousseau included a full dress of rose-colored moiré with very long basques ornamented with fringe and lace; one in blue velvet with Alencon lace; one of black velvet with gold braid; one of pearly gray satin with nine flounces of Brussels lace; a blue evening gown in tulle and satin, with feathers and roses; one of white tulle with tufts of violets and ribbons. Most of her gowns were made with long basques and draped corsages. Eugénie is said to have made tulle the standard evening fabric.

Lingerie items in the form of under-sleeves, fichus, canezous, collars, and cuffs continued their long popularity; they ranged in fabric from India muslin to handkerchief linen of somewhat heavier weight. A more tailored type of lingerie appeared during the sixties.

WRAPS. Wraps multiplied in type throughout these two decades. Shawls were traditional cashmeres from India, cleverly woven Paisleys from Scotland, light printed silks of France, embroidered silks from

are also employed as cloaks but this is too un-becoming a fashion to be adopted by any person of taste."

The Crimean War in 1854 brought into vogue the burnoose, a voluminous hooded mantle of the Near East, often in its original handsome form. This garment was admirably suited to spreading over the billowing skirts (Fig. 547).

BATHING COSTUME. Another highlight of the sixties from the Brooklyn Museum collection is the bathing costume shown in Fig. 548. Public mixed bathing is pictured in *Godey's Ladies' Book* of 1849, but long before that ladies went down to the sea in roving cabanas. Heideloff's *Gallery of*

FIG. 546. *Overdress in Polonaise Style. 1868. Re-drawn from Il Mondo Elegante. (Author's Collection)*

China, and gossamer Chantilly and rose point laces (Fig. 539). There were Talma cloaks—circular capes of silk, velvet, merino, or other wool; mantillas, cape-like in the back, with long front panels; mantles, fashioned with full circular cut and flaring sleeves. Fitted cloaks appeared in the sixties.

Godey's Ladies' Book for August, 1856, cautions ladies as follows:

The fashion of appearing in the street without scarf, shawl or mantilla is not considered lady like, nor is it the fashion. There is no excuse for it now, when lace, tissue and muslin mantles of every variety, light enough for the extremest heat of summer, are to be had.

Mink-minded moderns would certainly find incredible a Paris report in the *London Illustrated News* for January, 1850: "Furs

FIG. 547. *Burnoose Worn with Eugénie Hat. 1860's. Redrawn from Petit Courrier des Dames. (Author's Collection)*

Fashion for September, 1797, shows wheeled bathing carriages on the shore. Among costume plates showing styles for men, the one shown in Fig. 485 explains the use of these traveling cabanas. The bather could dress at home in privacy and be taken to the beach in a closed horse-drawn vehicle, where steps at the back door allowed her to descend into the waves practically unobserved.

It should not be surprising that specialized costumes were designed for bathing by the late sixties. The model shown in Fig. 548 is a long way from a bikini, but it does indicate advancement over the water-logged dresses in the Godey sketch. This one is made of black wool poplin trimmed with red

FIG. 548. *Bathing Costume of 1860's. (National Gallery of Art, Washington, D.C., Index of American Design, Original in Brooklyn Museum)*

flannel and black soutache braid. The bloomers, heritage from Amelia, differ notably in cut from our present shorts (Draft 40*a* and *b*). The cape is made of black and red plaid homespun. This bathing costume is one of the first straws in the wind indicating the eventual break with tradition regarding concealment of the body and the evolution of garments appropriate for varied activities.

HAIRDRESS AND HEADDRESS. Eugénie influenced hair styles as well as costumes. Her naturally beautiful auburn hair became the envy of everyone. Much bleaching and dyeing went on in the hope of achieving a similar richness of color. Fashion magazines advertised hair dyes and one shudders to think of some of the results. The hairdress the Empress preferred, and which was commonly adopted, was an outward sweep from the temples (Fig. 538). Large meshed snoods often encased the low chignon and since bulk was admired, the addition of false hair met with approval.

The small concealing bonnet of the forties gave way first to a curtailed brim which exposed much of the hair (Fig. 541) and then to the various types of hats associated with Empress Eugénie. One of the latter is the broad-brimmed, lace-edged model seen in Fig. 485; another is the beautiful hat in the Winterhalter portrait of the Empress and her ladies in waiting (Fig. 538, far right). Figure 547 pictures the small coquettish, tilted, and plumed hat that was revived in the twentieth century as the Eugénie hat. An innovation of the early sixties was the spoon bonnet (Figs. 544 and 545) with its jutting crown and deep bavolet (back extension below the crown). Worth's son, in a biography of his father,[10] says his mother was the first woman to wear a bonnet without a bavolet, thus initiating the fashion of the diminutive bonnet that was a hallmark of the seventies and eighties.

[10] Jean Philippe Worth, *A Century of Fashion*, Little, Brown, Boston, 1928, pp. 33–34.

FOOTWEAR. With shoes exposed to view in the early sixties by either swinging hoops or shortened skirts, more attention was paid to their design, and heels reappeared. Rich fabrics were employed in the uppers, the top edge was fashioned into interesting curves, and front lacing replaced side lacing. The buttoned shoe became popular in the sixties.

THE SEVENTIES

The Franco-Prussian war, with the resulting fall of the second empire, paralyzed the French fashion industry for a time. That fact is sometimes cited as the cause of the conglomerate costume creations that ensued. However, the general course had already been set, and it was almost inevitable that the bustle with all its attendant vagaries would follow the curve of development and decline. Although costumes of the seventies have been execrated as the worst in history, there were also some distinguished gowns.

On the negative side there were the preposterous bustle and the use of two or more colors in one dress, which unless done with real artistry, created a garish effect. Furthermore, the multiplicity of textures and patterns used in a single ensemble offends our sense of unity, and the opposing directions pursued by these competing themes confounded the confusion. Seldom during this decade was the body free to move with ease and grace, encumbered as it was in the early years, and constricted almost to immobility in the later years by tight lacing and narrow skirts. However, not all gowns were multicolored or multitextured. The looms of Lyons turned out magnificent fabrics, and Worth handled them with an appreciative touch.

The silhouette of the seventies passed through three phases. The bulky residue of the very full skirt of the sixties, banked at the rear of the costume and supported by a sturdy substructure, produced the high bustled contour of the first few years. Following this came a compromise in which the bodice was extended downward to the hips, creating what is referred to as the "cuirass bodice"; the accumulation of fabrics and trimmings fell from this lowered line. Pleased with this beginning, designers prolonged the lines of the bodice to the knees, and then to the floor. Thus the princess dress came into being, and for a few years the tubular silhouette held the center of the stage.

The most extreme examples of this last phase are said to have been so tight about the knees that walking was difficult. The ideal of a very slender figure led to the discarding of all underwear that could possibly be dispensed with. The corset, of course, was indispensable for molding and maintaining the desired curves; the chemise was reduced in bulk by darts and seaming; and tight chamois drawers made other underwear unnecessary below the waistline. Dust ruffles sewed to the inside of skirt bottoms functioned like petticoats in sweeping the streets and protecting hemlines of gowns from abrasion.

THE BODICE. Tightness was a feature of the bodice throughout the decade. Necklines for daytime were either a modest V or square, or the bodices were buttoned from the throat downward. A standing band replaced the flat embroidered or lace collar of the sixties. The shoulder line was soon shortened, and, with the slender look as the objective, the armscye was moved to its normal position. For formal wear necklines were much lower; during the first few years of the decade they retained the broad curved cut of the sixties. As the whole figure narrowed, the decolletage changed to a rather deep V both back and front. If it was too daringly plunging, it was filled in with lace, ruffling, or some other confection.

Sleeves were comparatively simple: straight and smooth regarding fit, but embellished in keeping with the trimming of the rest of the garment. Sleeves were usually

FIG. 549. *Blue-Purple Silk Day Dress by Worth. Early 1870 s. (Hair Style not Nineteenth Century.) (Brooklyn Museum)*

wrist length for daytime wear but shorter for special occasions.

SKIRTS. The skirt was the showplace for all the ingenuity designers could command in complicated drapery and combinations of textures. Swags of material, matching or violently contrasting, were draped from waist to hem in straight, curved, diagonal, or zig-zag lines. Throughout the decade there was a penchant for endless detail. Hundreds of variations, it seems, were played on the theme of pleated flounces and in the treatment of edges of drapery and hemlines—a practice which also marked the eighties. Fringe abounded.

That the result was sometimes less awful than it sounds is proved by the fine examples that have been preserved. The dignity and elegance of the gown shown in Fig. 549, from the Brooklyn Museum collection, demonstrate the genius of Mr. Worth. Dark blue-purple satin is combined with a soft heavy, matching silk, patterned with chevrons alternating in satin and ribbed weaves. In cut this two-piece costume is more complicated than it appears. There is a foundation skirt, to which three swags of fabric are mounted across the front. Each is folded into uneven pleats, both vertically and horizontally, draped to the precise curve and position desired, and then immediately sewed into place by hand (no mass-production there). Worth's restraint left the back widths free to fall in unbroken grandeur.

The bodice has the usual open square neckline but the basque is unique. The front dips into a squared tab. Under the arm it just covers the waistband, but at the back it drops again into a graceful rounded point. The most noteworthy detail of the whole bodice is the organ-pipe pleated extension of this back peplum, which may give us a clue to the puzzling tubular construction of the fifteenth century. Space does not permit including the draft of the cut of this costume, which required 12 pages of graph paper to construct! No two gores of the layered skirts are alike; each piece of horizontal drapery across the front differs from its neighbor; each mounting line looks like a different mountain trail. But it was this individual handling that made a Worth gown unique, right for the individual, and usually compellingly beautiful.

The School of Drama of the University of Washington possesses an exquisite wedding dress, in which design, fabric, and expert needlework all contributed to produce a masterpiece. Diaphanous handmade lace and shirred organdy in alternating strips compose the fitted basque bodice. To achieve the proper shaping, the organdy sections are tapered proportionally from shoulder to bust, from bust to waistline, and thence onward again to the lower edge, narrowing at the waistline to $1/2$ inch. They are rolled, whipped, and gathered their entire length. The front of the polonaise is constructed in the same fashion. The basic skirt, which spreads into an impressive train, is weighted with five flounces edged with lace. Frills of wider lace finish all edges of the bodice and are used in generous profusion on the tablier and the great pouf of the polonaise.

Figure 550 reproduces a costume fashion plate of the middle seventies, in a most pleasing monochromatic harmony. Bodice and skirt are a rich brown, the train is of middle brown, and the plaid is a combination of ivory and the two tones of brown. The ball fringe, too, repeats the three values. The only other hues used are green plumage on the hat and a corsage of red roses. This model is a good example of the cuirass bodice. Its square neckline is softened by a frill of lace and a fluting of the dress fabric. The flat bow of multiple loops shows the same detail as the Worth sleeve in Fig. 549. Drapery, ruffles, shirring, and bows are typical of skirt design in this decade.

In the late seventies a sleek slim line dominated costumes for all occasions. This is the era when daytime skirts became so narrow that walking was greatly inhibited. The princess line seen frequently in evening wear spread at the hemline into a train.

WRAPS. The wrap in keeping with the pencil-slim mode of the seventies was the dolman (Fig. 551), its sleeve cut so that the wearer's arms were practically bound to her body. Dolmans were made of all sorts of material: wool or silk, lined, furred, braided, fringed—in fact, all the trappings bestowed upon gowns. For evening wear over the bustled back they might stop short at the waist, thus avoiding the problem of covering such an obstacle. For daytime wear they varied from hip to ground length. Dolmans enjoyed a prolonged vogue extending through the nineties. (See Draft 41 for the pattern of a comparable dolman.)

FIG. 550. *Day Costume in Tones of Brown. 1875.*
La Mode Artistique, *Number 152. (Author's Collection)*

HAIRDRESS AND HEADDRESS. Throughout the seventies the mass of hair hung down between the shoulders. It might be confined in a snood, formed into a large loose braid caught back at the nape of the neck, or arranged in falling curls. The latter was preferred for evening wear.

Hats were charming, employing all the feminine wiles of lace, ribbon, velvet, flowers, and feathers. They remained small throughout the decade and only toward the end showed the tendency toward height of crown which was to follow. Both hats and bonnets were worn, the latter distinguished by ties knotted under the chin. Bonnets were considered the more formal of the two.

FOOTWEAR. Buttoned shoes remained in vogue, while slippers took on new interest. White satin pumps were correct for weddings and evening wear.

The Gallery of English Costume possesses a pair of brown kid ties with comfortable-looking rounded toes and medium heels which probably represents the type for general wear. In the Brooklyn Museum collection an attractive pair of white satin slippers is banded by narrow black ribbon from tip of toe to instep, where pompoms of black and white ribbon repeat the theme. Heels are covered with black satin.

A pair of French white satin wedding slippers in the Metropolitan Museum collection, dated 1872, has a large rosette of ribbon loops covering the instep and reaching almost to the tip of the rounded toe.

ACCESSORIES. Drop earrings, pairs of

FIG. 551. *Braided White Serge Dolman. French. 1875–1880. (Metropolitan Museum of Art, Gift of Mrs. Philip Rhinelander)*

bracelets, and modest necklaces continued in vogue. Folding fans, gloves, and elaborately decorated parasols completed the ensembles.

THE EIGHTIES

As the eighties opened, the pencil silhouette, which relied upon intricate manipulation of fabric for interest, was dominant. By 1881, however, the back skirt was beginning to bulge again and by 1884 it had reached its maximum extension. In this extreme form it endured through the mid-years, declining gradually toward 1890.

As in the previous decade, the contour

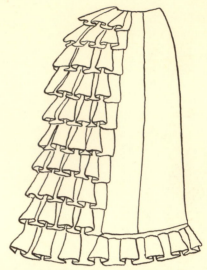

FIG. 553. *Ruffled Support Called Crinoline Pannier, 1884. Redrawn from Catalog of Cooper, Conard Co., Philadelphia. (Metropolitan Museum of Art, Costume Institute Library)*

was maintained by various forms of bustles and boned underwear (Figs. 552 and 553). The artifice of Fig. 552 consists of a shaped panel of white cotton almost full length, banded by 12 horizontal curved steels controlled by 4 pairs of ties. An additional boned and laced cage at the top supplies the necessary sturdiness required for the 1880 silhouettes. Often the foundation skirt itself had boning inserted in casings across the back. Tapes attached at terminal points were tied together to form the desired arcs and hold them in place. Linings, crinoline facings, and dust ruffles contributed both to contour and to weight. Jet passementerie often encrusted the outer surface, and beaded and chenille fringes decked the edges.

One of the objectives of the dress reform movement of the eighties was to reduce the crushing weight of women's clothes. One woman who participated in this effort related that after listening to a lecture on the subject she weighed the garments she had worn to the meeting. They tipped the scales at 40 pounds!

The eighties did, however, tend toward

FIG. 552. *Bustle. 1884. (Gallery of English Costume, Manchester)*

of this figure incorporates explicit features of the 1880 bustled contour. Built upon the princess foundation, the clean-cut closely fitted waistline curve was retained, thus lowering the level of the bustle projection. In its most extreme form the outward direction of the bustle of the eighties was more nearly a true horizontal, and the extension even greater, than in the seventies—almost as if

Fig. 554. *Ball Gown with Fashionable Bustle Silhouette. 1884. Redrawn from* Le Moniteur de la Mode. *(Author's Collection)*

simpler tailored effects. This was a natural outgrowth of increased participation in sports and a more active life generally outside the home.

The Silhouette

Why bustles, so recently taboo, were so quickly reinstated in a form more preposterous than before, is one of the mysteries of historic costume. By 1884, *Le Moniteur de la Mode* was showing the fantastic costume illustrated in Fig. 554. The silhouette

Fig. 555. *Eyelet Embroidered Costume by Worth. 1880 s. (Brooklyn Museum)*

the wearer had inadvertently become attached to an overflowing pushcart. The costume of Fig. 554 is predominantly ruby-red
in color; the lace flounced overskirt is white
patterned with red and yellow flowers. Garlands of artificial roses in matching colors
adorn the posterior structure.

Worth designed a summer costume of
grayish-green eyelet embroidered cotton
(Fig. 555), now in the Brooklyn Museum
collection, that is lovely by any standard.

FIG. 557. *Ball Gown by Worth. 1887. (Metropoli-
tan Museum of Art, Gift of Mr. Orme Wilson and
Mr. R. Thornton Wilson in Memory of Their Mother,
Mrs. Caroline Schermerhorn Astor Wilson)*

FIG. 556. *Checked Taffeta Day Dress from Bon
Marché, Paris. 1885. (Brooklyn Museum)*

Consistent throughout in color and texture,
its air of daintiness is enhanced by pleated
white frills at neck and center front. Another beautiful Worth dress in the same collection, made of white handkerchief linen,
has three flounces graced by delicate pink
and white appliqué, their scalloped edges
finished with a narrow line of rose embroidery. Cut in princess style, it buttons down
the front.

The day dress shown in Fig. 556 of
checked taffeta, presents a somewhat
chastened expression of the 1880 style.

Labeled "Bon Marche, Paris," it employs a moderate bustle silhouette and a short draped front overskirt above a series of pleated flounces. The back overskirt, however, is unbroken in line. The openwork embroidery is the only incompatible note (Draft 42*a*, *b*, *c*).

Many evening gowns of the eighties were less bizarre than that of Fig. 554. A ball gown by Worth, dated 1887 (Fig. 557), shows restraint and good taste. The bustle has collapsed or disappeared and a sunburst of embroidery replaces the usual involved drapery. Its lines are softened by multiple ruffles of chiffon.

Prophetic of the coming decade, a brown wool princess dress of 1887, monochromatic in color, uncluttered in line, and rich in texture, is another gem of the Brooklyn Museum collection. It too stands the test of time. Its long sleeves are slightly enlarged at the top. Its decoration consists of appliquéd brown velvet leaf patterns in a narrow border at the wrist and the same patterns in larger scale radiating from the neckline and bordering the hem. The standing collar and the edges of the wrist line and bottom of the skirt are of brown sealskin. The effect is that of sleekness and elegance.

The business-like tailored ensemble of the eighties was a practical contribution to women's wear. Figure 558 is an example of this type of costume. Though the preposterous bustle is still present, this two-piece costume of brown cashmere has no extraneous fringes, flounces, beading, or braid. The plaid underskirt harmonizes with the dress. The prim streamlined hat is brown, the shoes black with brown uppers. In a few years, when the wearer lays aside her bustle, she will be ready to commute to the office.

Fabrics

While colors were more subtle in the eighties than in the seventies, the practice of combining many colors and textures within one costume continued. Handkerchief linen and eyelet embroidery appeared in summer costumes. All stops were out on winter fabrics: gorgeous velvets in dark rich colors with ciselé (uncut loops) patterns, satins of slipper weight, brocades and failles which

FIG. 558. *Tailored Cashmere Serge Costume. 1886–1887. Redrawn from Fashion Plate. (Author's Collection)*

FIG. 559. *Fashions for Women and Children. 1892. Le Moniteur de la Mode. (Author's Collection)*

almost stand alone all are vital to the 1880 scene.

Fashion Features

HAIRDRESS AND HEADDRESS. In this decade the hair was brought in soft waves to the top of the head, and frizzed bangs fringed the forehead. Flowers and high combs were added for evening festivities. Bonnets continued to be seen throughout the eighties, but hats increased in general use. Crowns mounted upward to accommodate the new coiffure; brims were tilted rakishly; plumes curled over the edges and stuffed birds nested against the ribbon bows.

FOOTWEAR. Shoes in the eighties grew more varied in line. A pair of black laced boots in the *Index of American Design* is trimmed with gold kid appliqué and tassels. Pumps with pointed toes were made in the fabrics of the gowns: satin, faille, and brocade.

WRAPS. The dolman was the leading wrap in the eighties, as it had been in the seventies. Short or long, silk or wool, its sleeves continued to be mounted so low on the body that the arms were almost immobilized (Fig. 551 and Draft 41). Wraps designed for dressy occasions were ornately trimmed with jet and chenille fringe or braiding; more practical coats were also available. The Brooklyn Museum collection includes a wool coat striped in beige, tan, and a hairline of brown, cut on princess lines, with standing collar and well-drafted two-piece sleeves. It is smart looking and not far from the modern conception of a topcoat. The Brooklyn Museum collection is rich in magnificent wraps of this period.

During this decade Worth designed a sealskin cape with a 7-inch flare extending from the bottom of the long front panels across the back. Its Medici shaped collar and front edges were of beaver.

THE NINETIES

The phrase, "the gay nineties," evokes an atmosphere of carefree waltzing, frou-froued ladies, and correct and attentive escorts. To many citizens of the United States who lived through the panic of 1893 and the depression which followed, life was anything but gay. But as one surveys the parade of fashion through those final 10 years of the century, one notes a lightening of the earth-bound trappings of the two previous decades. The evidence in museum collections points toward a more active, more gregarious, less cloistered life for women.

By 1890 the main features of end of the century fashions had crystallized. The focus of attention was diverted from the skirt to the sleeves. The small, tightly corseted waist-line remained the ideal. Soon the skirt fabric, no longer contrived into puffs, swags, and cascades, fell unhampered from waistline to floor, induced by skillful cutting to fit smoothly over the hips and then slant outward to the hemline (Fig. 559). There also persisted, however, an obsession for trimming of all sorts, with lace, usually machine made, taking the lead (Fig. 560). Beading continued, but in smaller scale and lighter patterns. Cut steel beads competed with jet.

Collars increased in height and were stiffened by crinoline or boning. Often the outer layer was satin ribbon harmonizing with the main color of the costume.

There was much borrowing from pre-

FIG. 560. *High Style. 1895.* La Mode de Style. (*Author's Collection*)

vious periods. For example, Worth turned to the seventeenth century for inspiration for an elaborate gown with paned and puffed sleeves, tabbed peplum, and off the shoulder neckline, enriched by a deep fall of real *punto in aria* lace. There are obvious similarities between the sleeves of the 1830s and the 1890s. Ruchings and pleatings at the neck are reminiscent of sixteenth-century ruffs.

The fashions of 1891 were transitional in character. Bodices with full sleeves had a newer look than skirts, which retained some of the draped effects of the eighties. By 1892, however, the distinctive form of the nineties was well developed. Figure 559 suggests the important changes, especially the bulging leg-of-mutton sleeve (the puffed sleeves of the two children at the left could be 1895 models) and the skirt with its closely fitted hipline and widening sweep. This princess dress is made of dove-gray wool with yoke, collar, and jabot of white.

The costume of Fig. 560 illustrates the idiosyncrasies of the decade full blown. The dress is white silk with wine-red stripes. Sleeves, collar, bows, bag, hat, and hem border match the stripes. The sleeve has reached its maximum volume; the bosom is full and emphasized with added lace; the waistline is elongated, pointed, and laced to the point of distress; the skirt is smooth over the hips, gradually swinging out to sweep the floor. This is the much vaunted hourglass figure.

Balloon-like sleeves were popular for evening as well as daytime wear. Sargent caught the essence of the festive mood of 1895 ballgowns in his portrait of Mrs. Chamberlain (Fig. 561). White satin forms the main portion of her dress. Her sleeves and the wrap which she holds in her left hand are pale blue, tending toward turquoise. Her soft pompadour hair style, tilting plume, long gloves, and fan are essential details. The absence of jewels and the comparative simplicity of the entire ensemble testify to the lady's good taste.

A gown by Worth combined a chartreuse velvet top, with a broad, low decolletage and a rather sharp-pink brocaded corsage and skirt. The large scale of the patterned fabric is typical of these regal materials. The amount of lace and beading is modest compared with that of the previous decade.

Worth had a marvelous time with color. In one notable costume he used olive-green satin to frame white faille with a warp printed design of flamboyant red roses and deep-green foliage. In an opposite mood he created a gown of silver and muted tones ranging from hyacinth blue to soft grayed rose. For a light-hearted and seductive evening gown of white taffeta with a warp-printed design of cherries, he made an under-bodice of white taffeta, a modesty of lace and pink chiffon with chiffon ruching edging the low decolletage. Over the front he draped the cherry fabric, with pleats radiating upward from the center front waistline to create a neckline much larger than the figure. This neck edge, stiffened by a deep fold of the fabric and fine wire, could be manipulated at will, up or down, in or out, as the wearer chose.

In 1895 Maggy Rouff did a stunning, albeit impractical, gown of heavy ivory satin. Its low square-necked bodice was covered with pearl beads the size of peas. The outward swing of the lower skirt was effected by a flared extension which deepened from 15 inches at center front to 48 inches at center back. This entire section was beaded to match the bodice. The gown was lined throughout with gold-colored taffeta which enhanced the warm glow of the satin.

Coming down to earth and into the daylight, the suit and coat of Fig. 562 are indicative of the changing role of women. The suit of heathery tweed, now an accustomed part of the wardrobe, was vastly different from the morning and carriage dresses of the earlier part of the century.

SLEEVES. Of all the 1890 leg-of-mutton

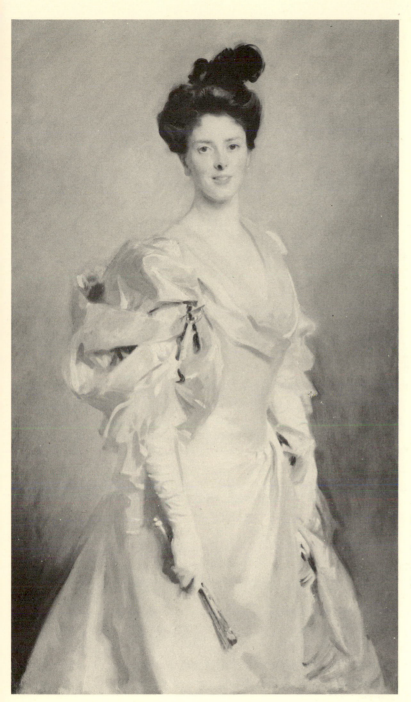

sleeves examined by the author, none have had any padding or boning, but some have had as many as four layers of fabric. Most frequently there was a basic fitted sleeve of either cambric, light silk, or the fabric of the garment. To this was mounted a puffed sleeve, which usually had a crinoline interlining cut exactly the same size and shape, the two layers being treated as one. If chiffon was used, it formed a fourth layer, over a taffeta, crinoline, and cambric base. A characteristic gesture of an 1890 belle was to

Fig. 562. *Two Costumes of 1895.* (*Brooklyn Museum*)

CAREER AND SPORTS WEAR. Two types of costumes which had been appearing tentatively in previous decades assumed an important place in the overall picture of the nineties. One was the tailored ensemble, a beginning of which we saw in the sixties and again in the eighties; the other was the sports costume. In the nineties women's tailoring became an important business. Suits were popular with the increasing number of wage-earning women, and there was a trend toward more functional and healthful clothing.

There was also an earnest effort to develop appropriate costumes for tennis, bicycling, and bathing. Though a far cry from today's shorts and bikinis, they were a vast improvement over the bustled and boned conceptions of the past. Parisian women boldly took to jacket and bloomers for bicycling, but the English waited for a lowered bicycle frame which would accommodate skirts. A compromise was made in the form of a flared knee-length skirt.[11] Bathing suits became more daring, with shorter sleeves and skirts which allowed much greater freedom of movement. The tennis costume of Fig. 563 was revolutionary for its day. Sailor blouses had a long run in high schools, college halls, and gymnasiums, and in fact they are still with us.

Riding habits, accepted and consistently smart and well turned out for centuries, continued as such in the 1890s.

Fabrics

Fabrics for the privileged were sumptuous: slipper satins with the hand of fine kid and brocades and satins in patterns of regal scale were used. Lyons velvets, crisp, glowing, alive to the touch, were perfect for ballooning sleeves, and lustrous broadcloth was worthy of its silk associates. Chiffon insinuated itself into the picture via bodice

fluff out her sleeves upon removing her wrap. The fabrics were of a texture to obey the hand.

SKIRTS. Worth's skirts were provided with bands of elastic to keep the folds in their proper position. Tapes attached to side or back seams could be tied to contain the back fullness, thus guaranteeing an unwrinkled front. Skirts were lined with cambric or taffeta and trained gowns were weighted and disciplined by facings of horsehair which might be as deep as eighteen inches at center back. In addition, a generous silk facing, velvet binding, or silk cord, and pleated, lace-edged dust ruffles added to the finish. Nothing was left to chance.

[11] Herbert Norris and Oswald Curtis, *Costume and Fashion, The Nineteenth Century*, Dent, London, 1933, vol. VI, pp. 229–230.

fronts, sleeve ruffles, and ruchings. Faille and taffeta, supported, lined, trimmed, or constituted the main part of the costume. In summer there were piqué, linen (plain or printed), dimity, lawn, dotted swiss, organdy and printed fine-textured cottons such as we never see today.

In the lower price bracket, and for daytime wear, foulard was a prime favorite. Wool voile appeared, along with printed challis. For the housewife stores were stocked with factory made printed calico frocks, complete with machine made buttonholes.

Other Features

WRAPS. Wraps of this decade also showed modern tendencies. The wonderful resiliency of fabrics of the nineties made it possible to wear coats over the huge sleeves. Figure 562 pictures such a garment. With modification of the sleeves and hemline it could be shown in a modern collection with assurance of wide acceptance. It is both smart and practical, being in fact a raincoat. The hood is one of its unusual features. Its pattern (Draft 43a and b) throws light on the enlarged sleeves of the nineties.

For more glamorous occasions there were appropriate wraps. Worth designed an olive-green velvet jacket with leg-of-mutton sleeves, brocaded silk lining and wool interlining, and cut steel beading.

More often the lady wore some form of mantle or cape; designs of the latter are unending. They are made of all sorts of fabric, usually beaded or embroidered, almost invariably with high flaring collars forming a flattering frame for the head. They occur in different lengths and have a charm and grace all their own.

From Baltimore came a cape of the late nineties made of embroidered black broadcloth with three ruffles of velvet-edged taffeta encircling the entire garment. Wired petal shapes of taffeta substituted for the standing collar.

Long velvet evening coats with large open sleeves and quilted silk linings contributed to the grandeur of the scene. One in the Brooklyn Museum collection has a collar and full-length bandings of ostrich fronds.

FIG. 563. *Tennis Costume. c.1895. Drawn from Photograph of Original. (Brooklyn Museum)*

A sleeved opera cloak dating from the end of the century when sleeves had subsided was made of lustrous heavy black damask lined with white satin. The inside surface of the Medici shaped collar is shirred white chiffon and the wide revers are formed of black lace over white silk. Long accordion pleated and ruffled panels of black chiffon are suspended from the chest—for no accountable reason other than their added feminine touch. This also came from Baltimore, where society women were proud of being well dressed.

UNDERWEAR. The corset of the nineties, with its inflexible front and narrow waist, had a built-in uplift feature, the upper portion being longer than the lower. Underwear became pretty in the true sense of the word and feminine as never before. The finest was made of silky batiste, embroidered in delicate designs, and made alluring by unlimited yardage of frothy lace and pastel ribbons.

Drawers were shortened, widened, and elaborately decorated. Petticoats were made to be seen. A lady was adept in lifting her trained skirts and holding them so that the satin-edged pleated chiffon froufrou was visible. Taffeta was the preferred basic fabric, both because of the aria it sings when in motion and because it was indicative of the bank account. Women in lower income brackets are said to have sewed paper inside their petticoats in an effort to achieve the rustle of silk, though an acute ear would never have been fooled.

HAIRDRESS AND HEADDRESS. The tall flower pot hats and tiny bonnets of the eighties gave way to a flattened crown and wide brim in the early years of the nineties (Fig. 559). The boy's hat, copied from his father's, was adopted by mother and sister as an appropriate accessory for bicycling costumes. The small hat remained fashionable for afternoon and dinner wear. In fact, the one on the lady in Fig. 560 could be worn today without attracting undue notice. At the

FIG. 564. *John Singer Sargent, Portrait of Mr. and Mrs. Newton Phelps Stokes. 1897. (Metropolitan Museum of Art, Bequest of Edith Minturn Stokes)*

close of the century daytime hats were large again.

Hair styles changed little, the hair being brushed upward and knotted on the crown of the head.

FOOTWEAR. Shoes acquired a narrow attenuated look, with very pointed toes and medium heel. High-topped shoes combining patent leather with fabric or kid were made in both buttoned and laced models. Bronze kid slippers with matching or cut steel beading were popular. A true oxford was designed for the tailored ensemble. For more festive wear there were slippers of white kid with one or more straps, and pumps with small pearl buckles. Elegant carriage boots, certainly a boon in freezing winter weather, were made of black velvet, edged in fur, and lined with quilted satin, just right for the after the ball journey home.

Precursors of twentieth-century developments are the costumes of a young couple painted by Sargent in 1897 (Fig. 564). The lady, Mrs. Stokes, posed in a mannish shirtwaist, plain skirt, tailored jacket, and what could almost have been her husband's hat. No doubt she possessed a wardrobe which included beautiful gowns for both day and evening, but it seems significant that both artist and subject agreed upon the simpler costume as appropriate for the spirit of the time.

Pattern Drafts

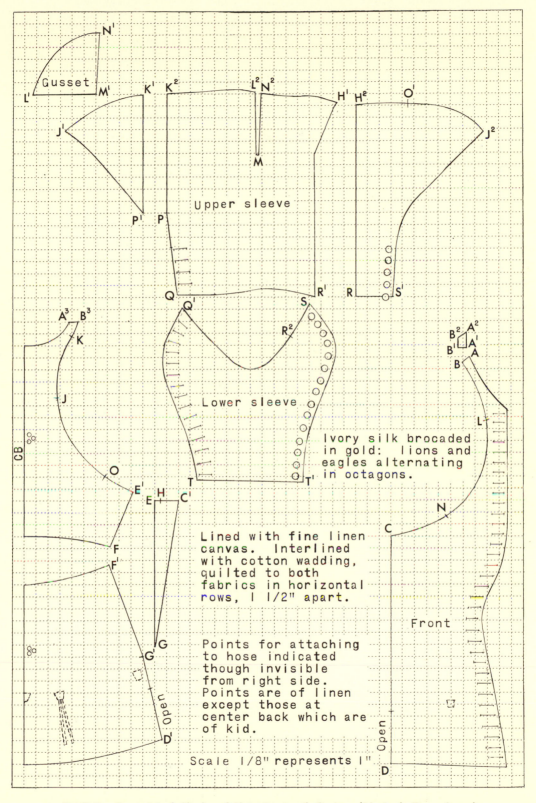

Labels visible in the drawing:

Gusset

Upper sleeve

Lower sleeve

Ivory silk brocaded
in gold: lions and
eagles alternating
in octagons.

Lined with fine linen
canvas. Interlined
with cotton wadding,
quilted to both
fabrics in horizontal
rows, 1 1/2" apart.

Points for attaching
to hose indicated
though invisible
from right side.
Points are of linen
except those at
center back which are
of kid.

Front

Open

Open

CB

Scale 1/8" represents 1"

Draft 1. Pourpoint of Charles of Blois. Fourteenth Century. (Musée de Tissus, Lyons)

539

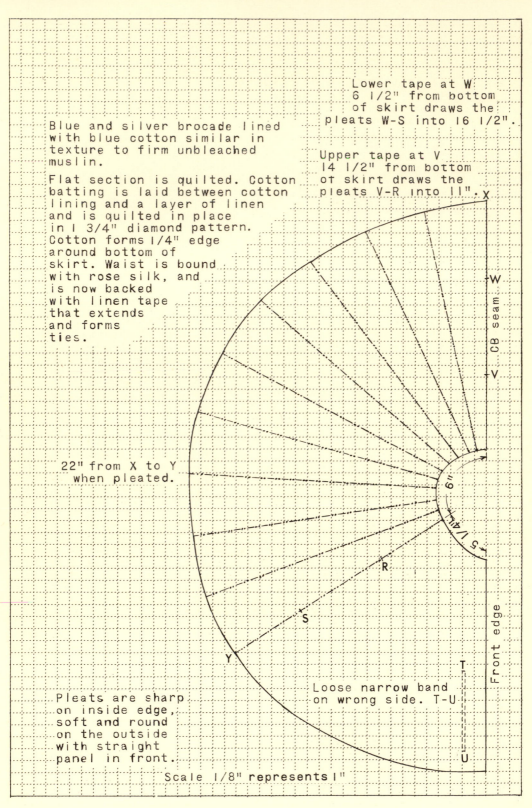

Blue and silver brocade lined with blue cotton similar in texture to firm unbleached muslin.

Flat section is quilted. Cotton batting is laid between cotton lining and a layer of linen and is quilted in place in 1 3/4" diamond pattern. Cotton forms 1/4" edge around bottom of skirt. Waist is bound with rose silk, and is now backed with linen tape that extends and forms ties.

Lower tape at W 6 1/2" from bottom of skirt draws the pleats W-S into 16 1/2".

Upper tape at V 14 1/2" from bottom of skirt draws the pleats V-R into 11".

22" from X to Y when pleated.

Pleats are sharp on inside edge, soft and round on the outside with straight panel in front.

Loose narrow band on wrong side. T-U

CB seam

Front edge

W

V

X

5 1/4"

6 1/2"

R

S

Y

T

U

Scale 1/8" represents 1"

Draft 2. Bases (Military Skirt). Early Sixteenth Century. (Metropolitan Museum of Art, Arms and Armor Collection)

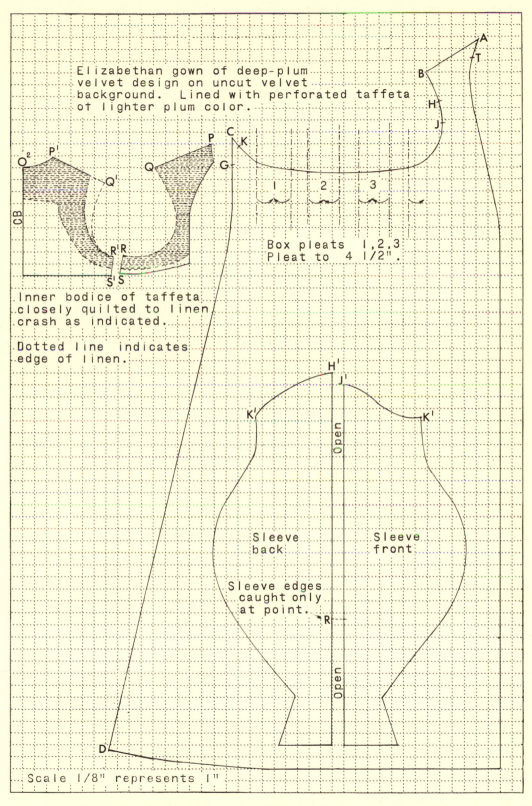

Elizabethan gown of deep-plum velvet design on uncut velvet background. Lined with perforated taffeta of lighter plum color.

CB

Box pleats 1, 2, 3
Pleat to 4 1/2".

Inner bodice of taffeta closely quilted to linen crash as indicated.

Dotted line indicates edge of linen.

Open

Sleeve back

Sleeve front

Sleeve edges caught only at point.

Open

Scale 1/8" represents 1"

Draft 3a. Overdress. Late Sixteenth Century. (Victoria & Albert Museum)

541

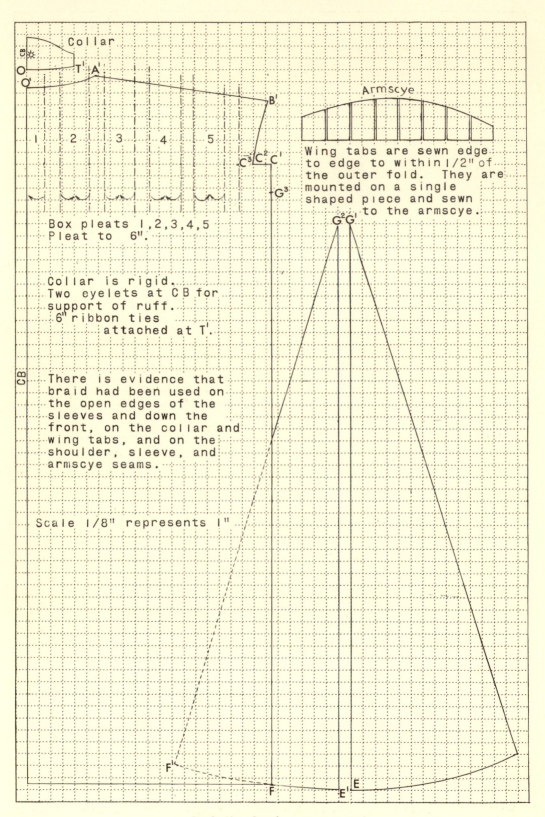

Collar

Armscye

Wing tabs are sewn edge
to edge to within 1/2" of
the outer fold. They are
mounted on a single
shaped piece and sewn
to the armscye.

Box pleats 1,2,3,4,5
Pleat to 6".

Collar is rigid.
Two eyelets at CB for
support of ruff.
6" ribbon ties
            attached at T'.

CB

There is evidence that
braid had been used on
the open edges of the
sleeves and down the
front, on the collar and
wing tabs, and on the
shoulder, sleeve, and
armscye seams.

Scale 1/8" represents 1"

Draft 3b. Overdress *(Continued)*

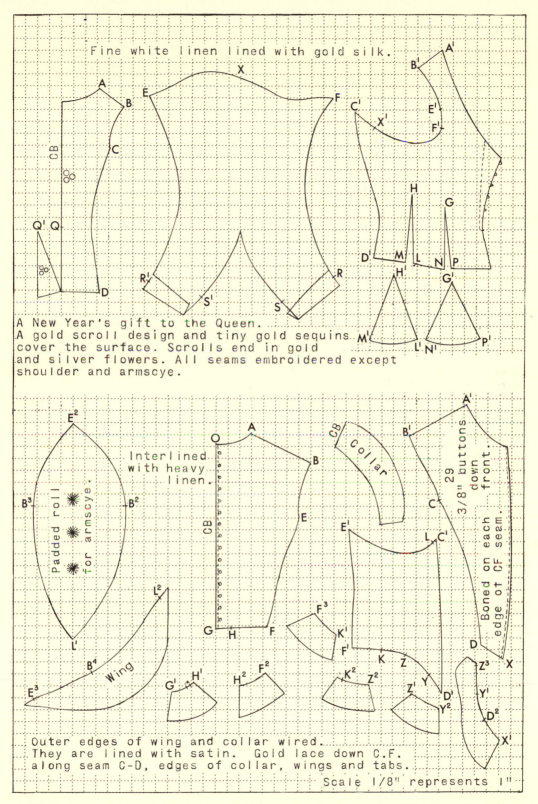

Fine white linen lined with gold silk.

CB

A New Year's gift to the Queen.
A gold scroll design and tiny gold sequins
cover the surface. Scrolls end in gold
and silver flowers. All seams embroidered except
shoulder and armscye.

Interlined
with heavy
linen.

Padded roll
for armscye.

Wing

Collar

29 3/8" buttons down front.

Boned on each
edge of CF seam.

Outer edges of wing and collar wired.
They are lined with satin. Gold lace down C.F.
along seam C-D, edges of collar, wings and tabs.

Scale 1/8" represents 1"

Draft 4. *(Top)* Queen Elizabeth's Golden Doublet. 1578. (Museum of Fine Arts, Boston) **Draft 5.**
(Bottom) Black Voided Velvet Doublet. Late Sixteenth Century. (Metropolitan Museum of Art)

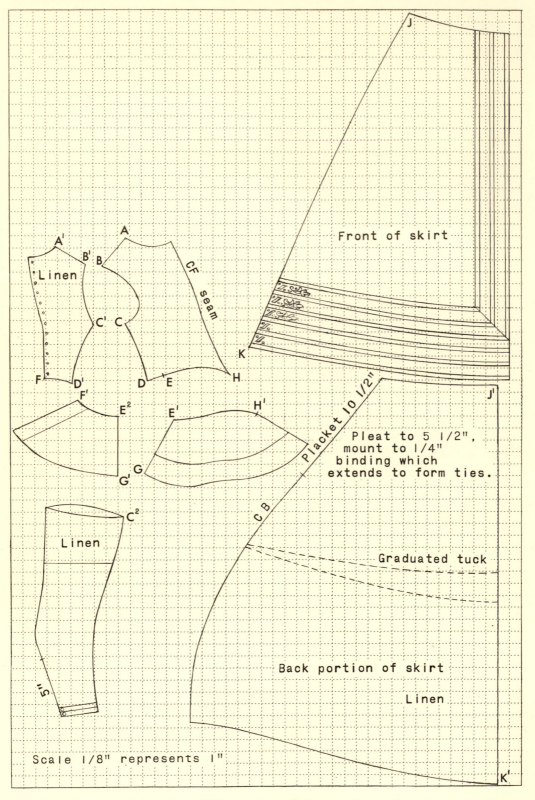

Front of skirt

Linen

CF seam

Pleat to 5 1/2",
mount to 1/4"
binding which
extends to form ties.

Placket 10 1/2"

Graduated tuck

Back portion of skirt

Linen

Linen

5"

Scale 1/8" represents 1"

Draft 6a. Spanish Dress for a Child. Late Sixteenth Century. (Metropolitan Museum of Art)

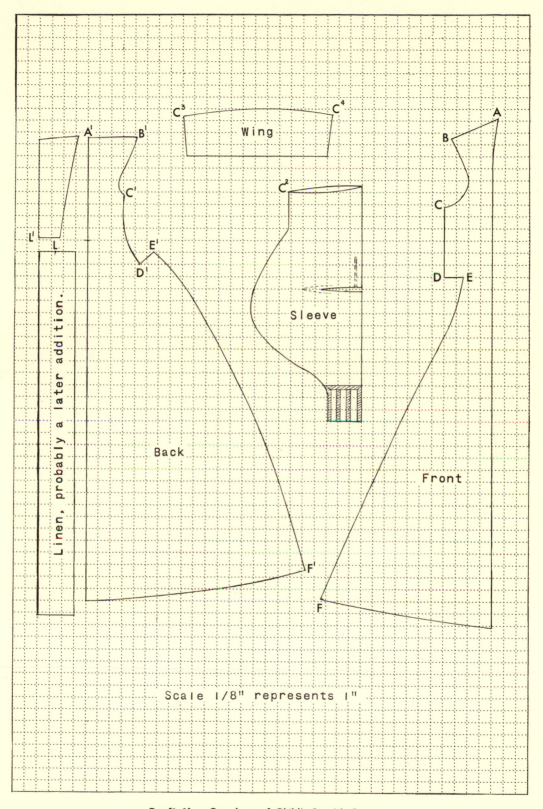

Draft 6b. Overdress of Child's Spanish Costume.

545

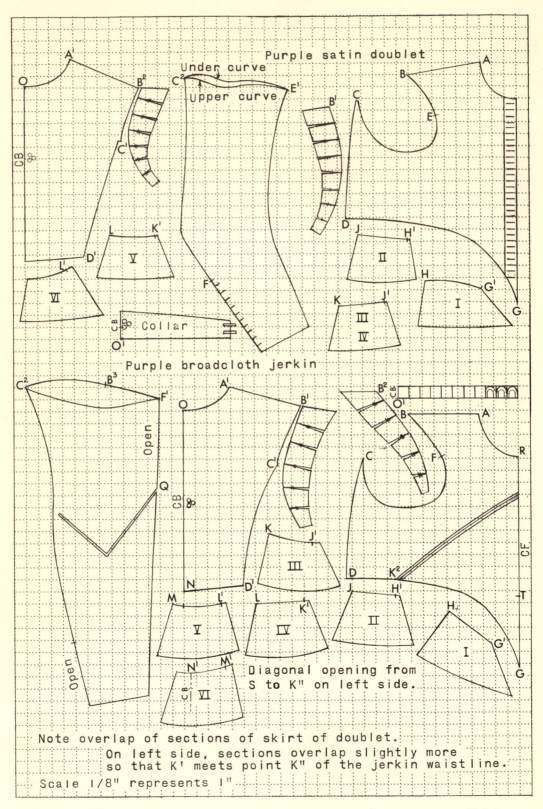

Purple satin doublet

Purple broadcloth jerkin

Note overlap of sections of skirt of doublet.
On left side, sections overlap slightly more
so that K' meets point K" of the jerkin waistline.

Scale 1/8" represents 1"

Draft 7a. Costume of Gustavus II, Adolphus the Great. 1620. (Royal Armoury, Stockholm)

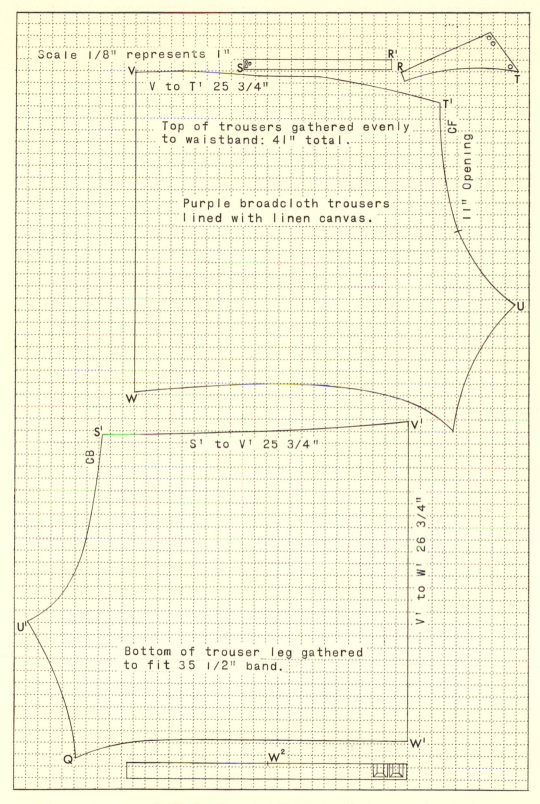

Scale 1/8" represents 1"

V to T' 25 3/4"

Top of trousers gathered evenly
to waistband: 41" total.

Purple broadcloth trousers
lined with linen canvas.

11" Opening

CF

CB

S' to V' 25 3/4"

V' to W' 26 3/4"

Bottom of trouser leg gathered
to fit 35 1/2" band.

W²

Draft 7b. Costume of Gustavus II *(Continued)*

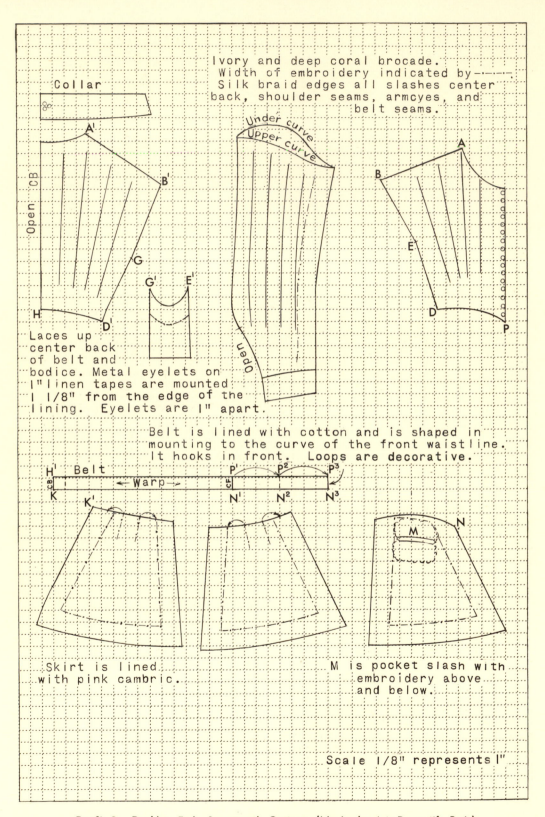

Ivory and deep coral brocade.
Width of embroidery indicated by —·—·—.
Silk braid edges all slashes center
back, shoulder seams, armcyes, and
belt seams.

Collar

Under curve
Upper curve

Open CB

A'
B'
G
G' E'
H
D'

A
B
E
D
P

Laces up
center back
of belt and
bodice. Metal eyelets on
1" linen tapes are mounted
1 1/8" from the edge of the
lining. Eyelets are 1" apart.

Open

Belt is lined with cotton and is shaped in
mounting to the curve of the front waistline.
It hooks in front. Loops are decorative.

H' Belt
CB
← Warp →
CF
P' P² P³
K K'
N' N² N³

K'
M
N

Skirt is lined
with pink cambric.

M is pocket slash with
embroidery above
and below.

Scale 1/8" represents 1"

Draft 8. Doublet. Early Seventeenth Century. (Musée des Arts Decoratifs, Paris)

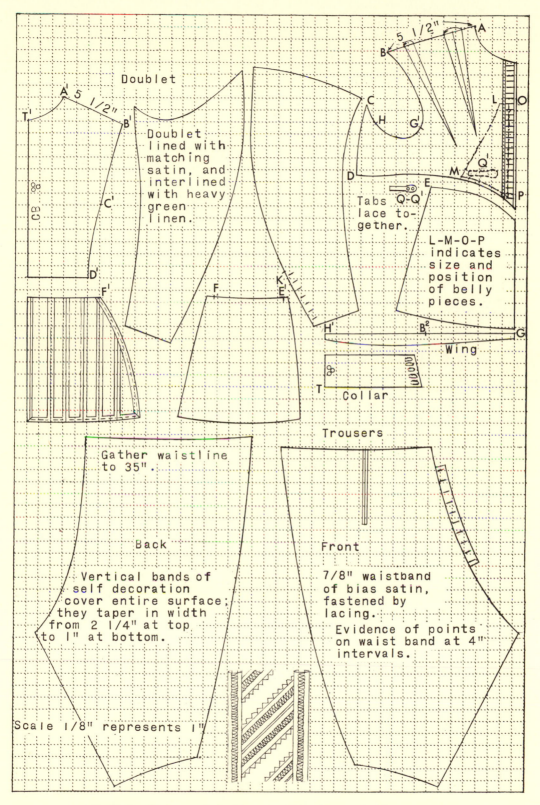

Doublet

Doublet lined with matching satin, and interlined with heavy green linen.

5 1/2"

5 1/2"

Tabs lace together.

Q-Q

L-M-O-P indicates size and position of belly pieces.

Wing

Collar

Trousers

Gather waistline to 35".

Back

Vertical bands of self decoration cover entire surface; they taper in width from 2 1/4" at top to 1" at bottom.

Front

7/8" waistband of bias satin, fastened by lacing.

Evidence of points on waist band at 4" intervals.

Scale 1/8" represents 1"

Draft 9. Chartreuse Satin Costume. c.1630. (Victoria & Albert Museum)

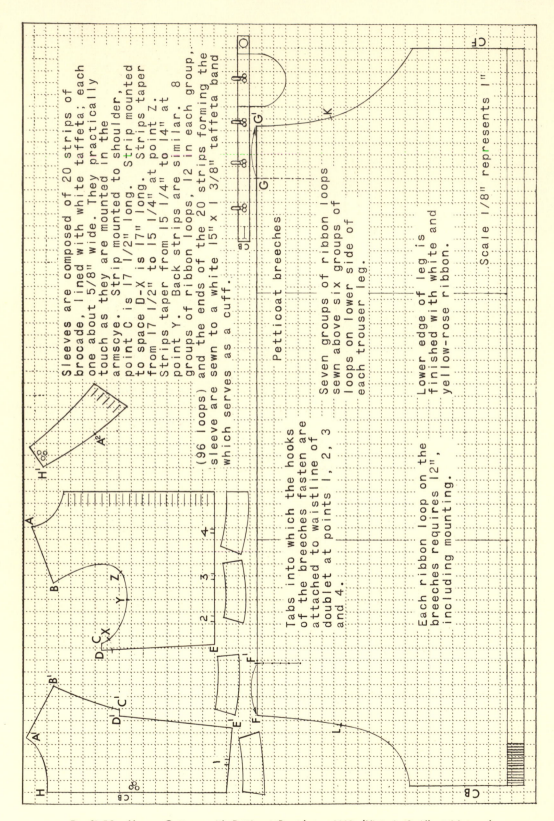

Sleeves are composed of 20 strips of brocade, lined with white taffeta; each one about 5/8" wide. They practically touch as they are mounted in the armscye. Strip mounted to shoulder, point C is 17 1/2" long. Strip mounted to space D-X is 17" long. Strips taper from 17 1/2" to 15 1/4" at point Z. Strips taper from 15 1/4" to 14" at point Y. Back strips are similar. 8 groups of ribbon loops, 12 in each group, (96 loops) and the ends of the 20 strips forming the sleeve are sewn to a white 15" x 1 3/8" taffeta band which serves as a cuff.

Petticoat breeches

Seven groups of ribbon loops sewn above six groups of loops on lower side of each trouser leg.

Tabs into which the hooks of the breeches fasten are attached to waistline of doublet at points 1, 2, 3 and 4.

Lower edge of leg is finished with white and yellow-rose ribbon.

Each ribbon loop on the breeches requires 12", including mounting.

Scale 1/8" represents 1"

Draft 10. Verney Costume with Petticoat Breeches. c.1660. (Victoria & Albert Museum)

550

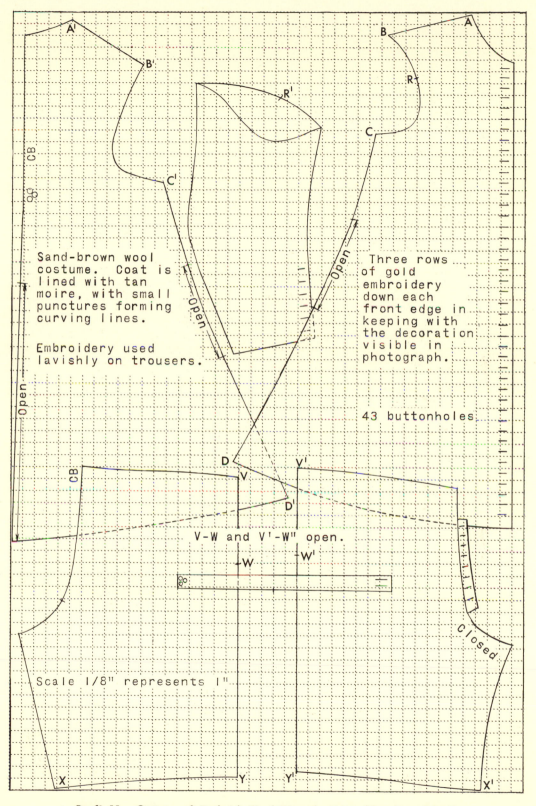

Sand-brown wool costume. Coat is lined with tan moire, with small punctures forming curving lines.

Embroidery used lavishly on trousers.

Three rows of gold embroidery down each front edge in keeping with the decoration visible in photograph.

43 buttonholes

V-W and V'-W" open.

Scale 1/8" represents 1".

Draft 11. Costume of Frederick III of Denmark. c.1665. (Rosenborg Palace)

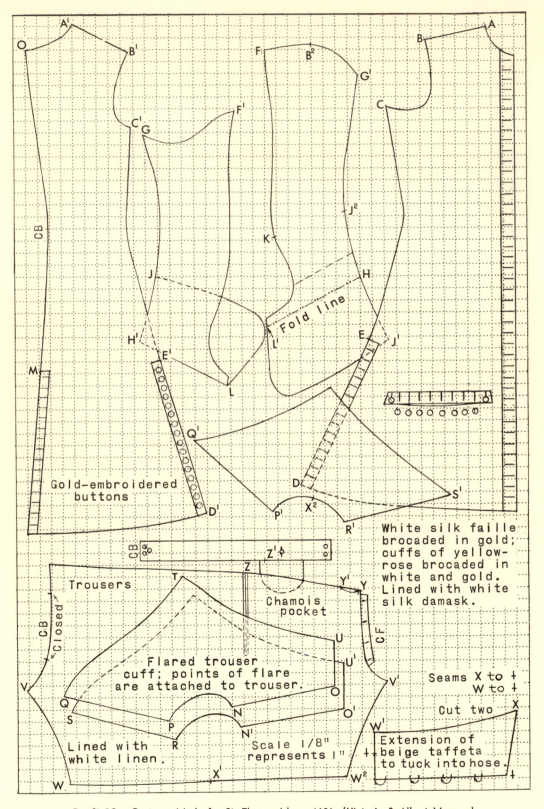

Within the figure, the following labels appear:

A', O, B', F, B², A, B, G', C, C'G, F', J², K, J, H, Fold line, H', E', L', E, J', M, CB, Q', D, S', D', P', X², R', Z'

Gold-embroidered buttons

White silk faille brocaded in gold; cuffs of yellow-rose brocaded in white and gold. Lined with white silk damask.

Trousers

CB Closed

T, Z, Y', Y, U, U', CF, V, Q, S, P, N, N', O, O', V'

Chamois pocket

Flared trouser cuff; points of flare are attached to trouser.

Seams X to ✝
W to ✝

Cut two

X, W', W²

Extension of beige taffeta to tuck into hose.

Lined with white linen.

Scale 1/8" represents 1"

Draft 12. Costume Made for Sir Thomas Isham. 1681. (Victoria & Albert Museum)

552

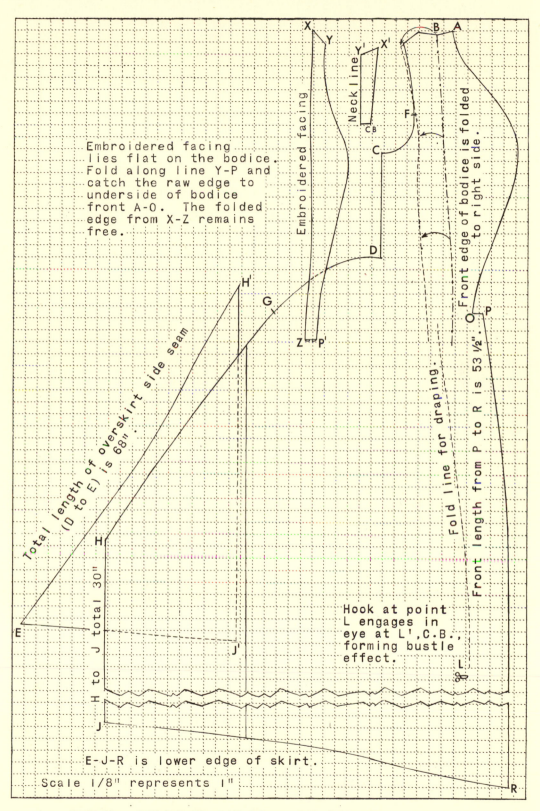

Embroidered facing lies flat on the bodice. Fold along line Y-P and catch the raw edge to underside of bodice front A-O. The folded edge from X-Z remains free.

Neckline

Embroidered facing

C B

Front edge of bodice is folded to right side.

Total length of overskirt side seam (D to E) is 68".

Fold line for draping.

Front length from P to R is 53 ½"

H to J total 30"

Hook at point L engages in eye at L',C.B., forming bustle effect.

E-J-R is lower edge of skirt.

Scale 1/8" represents 1"

Draft 13a. Gold Embroidered Wool Dress. c.1690. (Metropolitan Museum of Art)

553

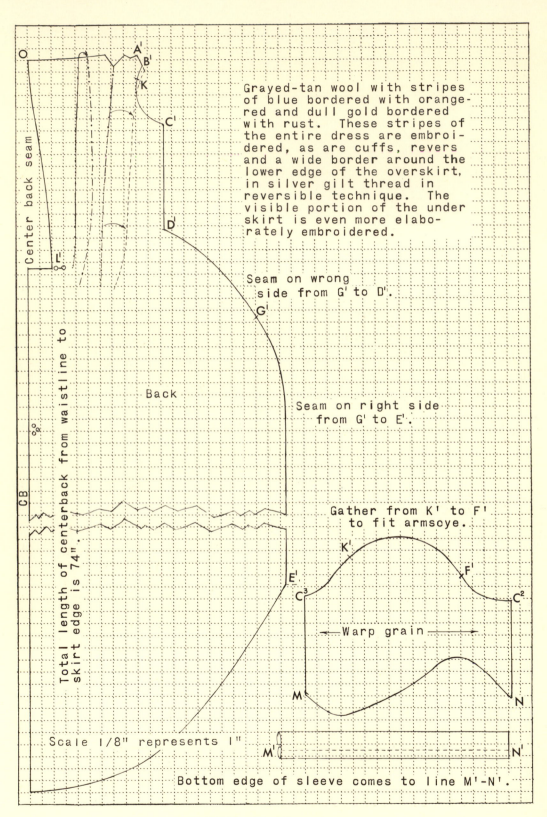

O

A'

B'

K

C'

D'

Center back seam

Grayed-tan wool with stripes
of blue bordered with orange-
red and dull gold bordered
with rust. These stripes of
the entire dress are embroidered, as are cuffs, revers
and a wide border around the
lower edge of the overskirt,
in silver gilt thread in
reversible technique. The
visible portion of the under
skirt is even more elabo-
rately embroidered.

L'

Seam on wrong
side from G' to D'.

G'

Total length of centerback from waistline to
skirt edge is 74".

CB

Back

Seam on right side
from G' to E'.

Gather from K' to F'
to fit armscye.

K'

F'

E'

C³

C²

←Warp grain→

M

N

Scale 1/8" represents 1"

M'

N'

Bottom edge of sleeve comes to line M'-N'.

Draft 13b. Wool Dress *(Continued)*

554

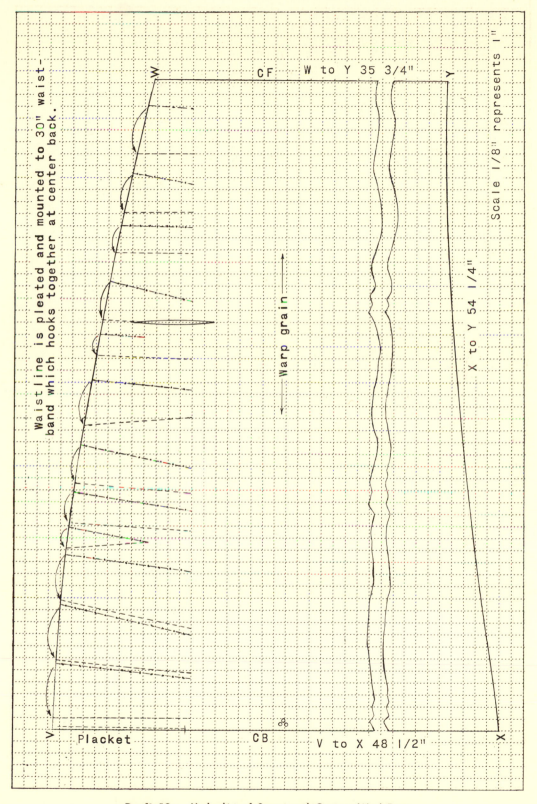

Waistline is pleated and mounted to 30" waist-band which hooks together at center back.

W   CF   W to Y 35 3/4"   Y

Scale 1/8" represents 1"

← Warp grain →

X to Y 54 1/4"

V   Placket   CB   V to X 48 1/2"   X

Draft 13c. Underskirt of Seventeenth-Century Wool Dress.

555

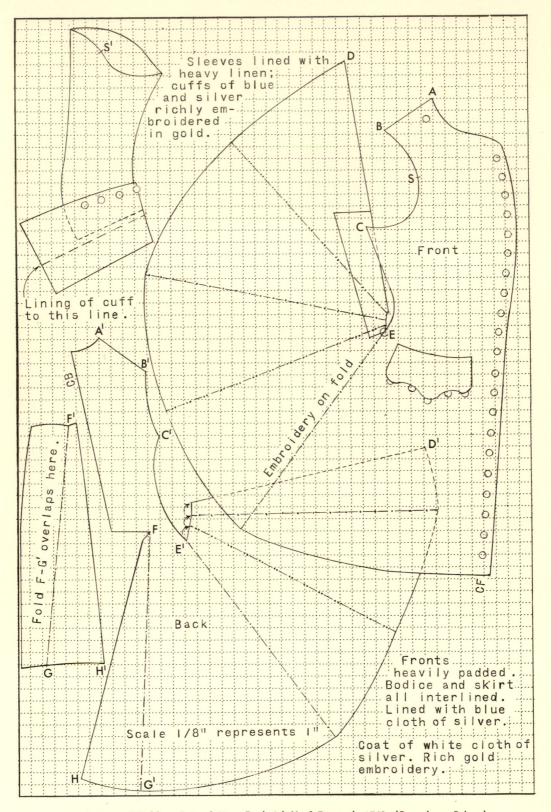

Within the figure the following labels appear:

S'

Sleeves lined with
heavy linen;
cuffs of blue
and silver
richly em-
broidered
in gold.

D

A

B

S

C

Front

Lining of cuff
to this line.

A'

B'

CB

C'

E

Embroidery on fold

F''

D'

Fold F-G' overlaps here.

F

E'

G   H'

Back

CF

Fronts
heavily padded.
Bodice and skirt
all interlined.
Lined with blue
cloth of silver.

Scale 1/8" represents 1"

Coat of white cloth of
silver. Rich gold
embroidery.

H   G'

Draft 14a. Wedding Suit of King Frederick V of Denmark. 1743. (Rosenborg Palace)

556

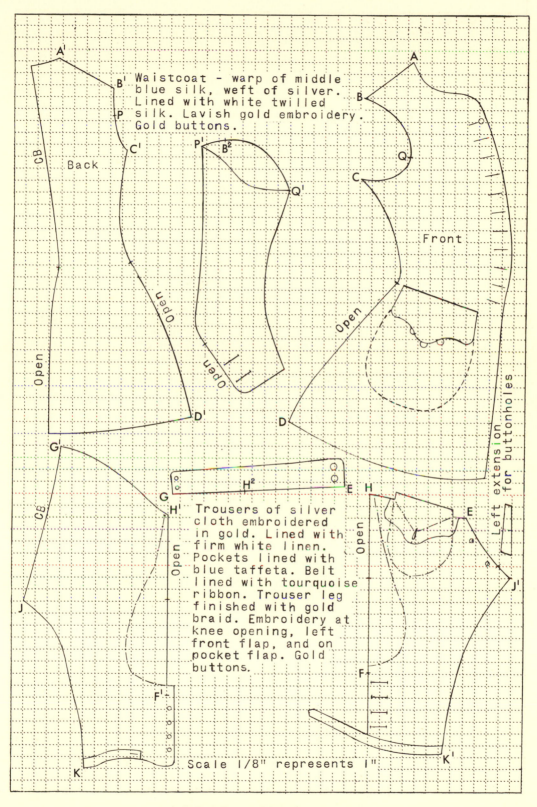

Waistcoat - warp of middle
blue silk, weft of silver.
Lined with white twilled
silk. Lavish gold embroidery.
Gold buttons.

Back

Open

Open

Front

Open

Left extension
for buttonholes

Trousers of silver
cloth embroidered
in gold. Lined with
firm white linen.
Pockets lined with
blue taffeta. Belt
lined with tourquoise
ribbon. Trouser leg
finished with gold
braid. Embroidery at
knee opening, left
front flap, and on
pocket flap. Gold
buttons.

Open

Open

Scale 1/8" represents 1"

Draft 14b. Wedding Suit *(Continued)*

557

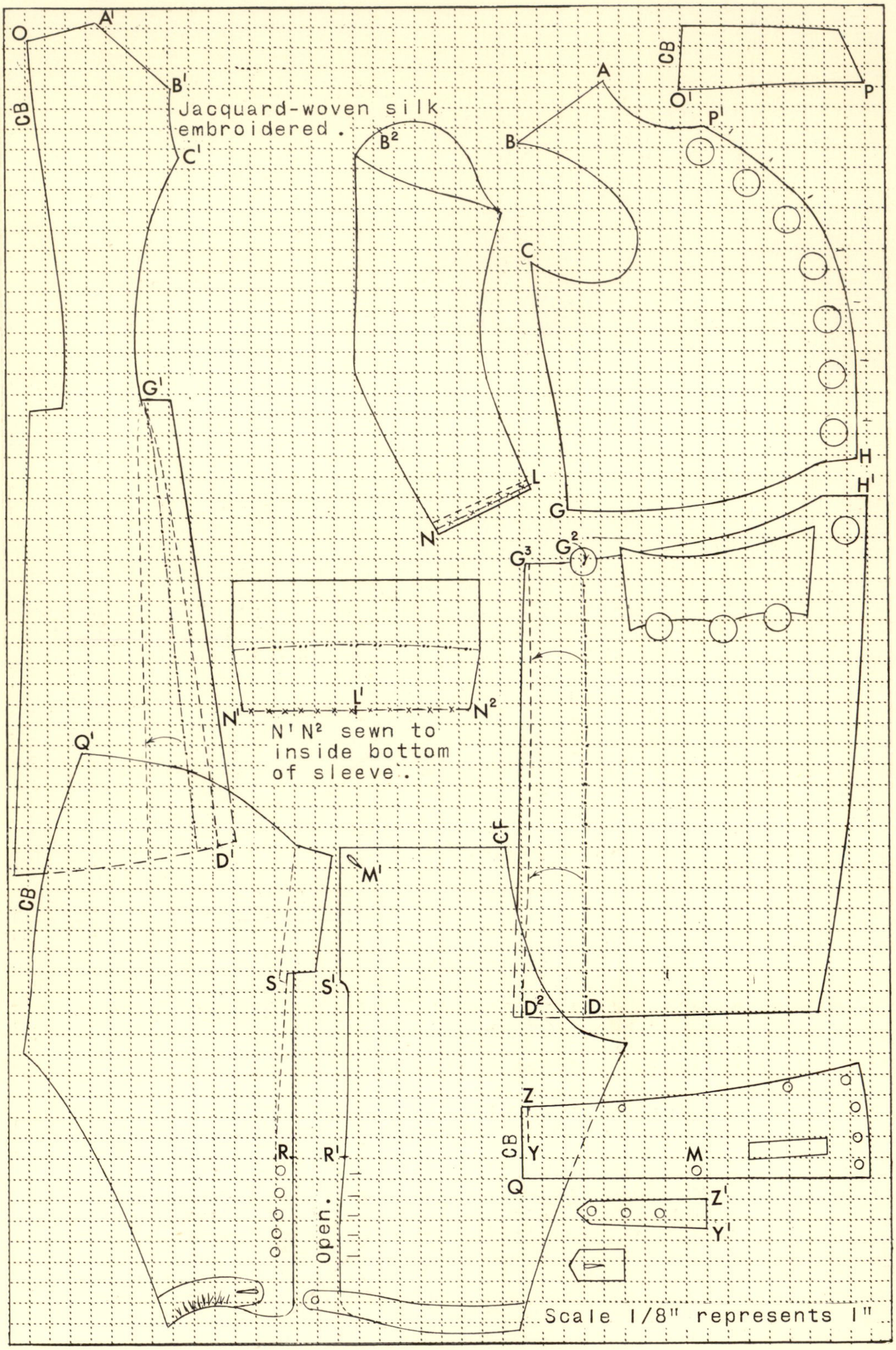
Jacquard-woven silk embroidered.
N' N² sewn to inside bottom of sleeve.
Open.
Scale 1/8" represents 1"

Draft 15. Man's Plum-Colored Silk Suit. Late Eighteenth Century. (Brooklyn Museum)

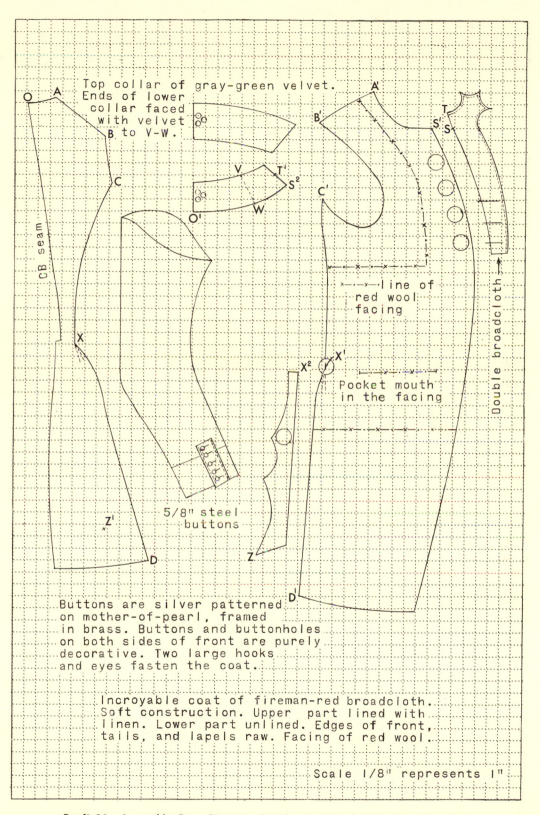

Top collar of gray-green velvet.
Ends of lower collar faced with velvet B to V-W.

line of red wool facing

Pocket mouth in the facing

CB seam

Double broadcloth

5/8" steel buttons

Buttons are silver patterned on mother-of-pearl, framed in brass. Buttons and buttonholes on both sides of front are purely decorative. Two large hooks and eyes fasten the coat.

Incroyable coat of fireman-red broadcloth. Soft construction. Upper part lined with linen. Lower part unlined. Edges of front, tails, and lapels raw. Facing of red wool.

Scale 1/8" represents 1"

Draft 16. Incroyable Coat. Directoire Period. 1795–1799. (Musée Carnavalet, Paris)

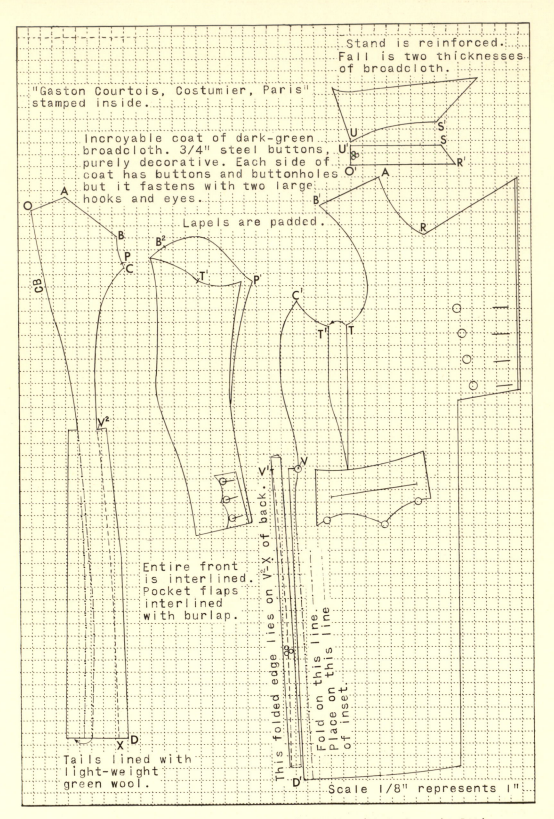

Draft 17. Incroyable Coat. Directoire Period. 1795–1799. (Musée Carnavalet, Paris)

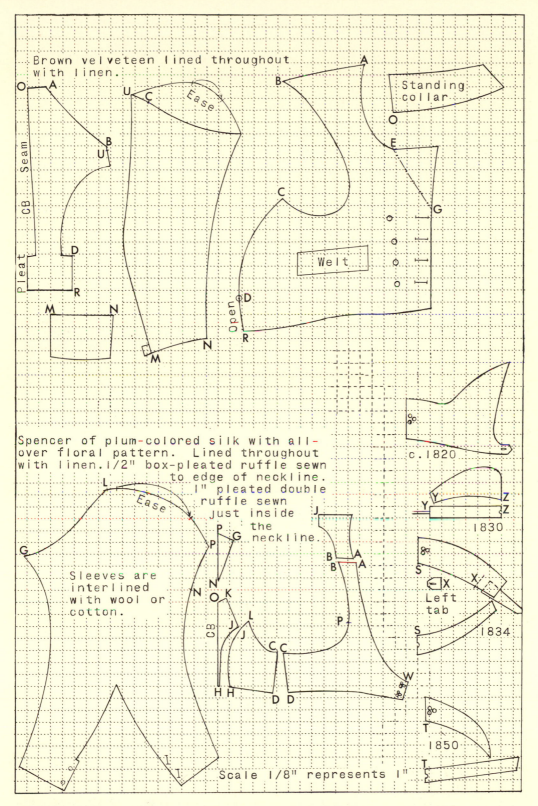

Brown velveteen lined throughout with linen.

Ease

Standing collar

CB Seam

Pleat

Welt

Open

Spencer of plum-colored silk with all-over floral pattern. Lined throughout with linen. 1/2" box-pleated ruffle sewn to edge of neckline. 1" pleated double ruffle sewn just inside the neckline.

Ease

Sleeves are interlined with wool or cotton.

CB

Left tab

c.1820

1830

1834

1850

Scale 1/8" represents 1"

Draft 18. *(Top)* Man's Spencer. Empire Period. 1795. (Metropolitan Museum of Art, Costume Institute)
Draft 19. *(Bottom left)* Woman's Spencer. Early Empire. (Metropolitan Museum of Art, Costume Institute) **Draft 20.** *(Bottom right)* Men's Collars. Nineteenth Century. (Brooklyn Museum)

561

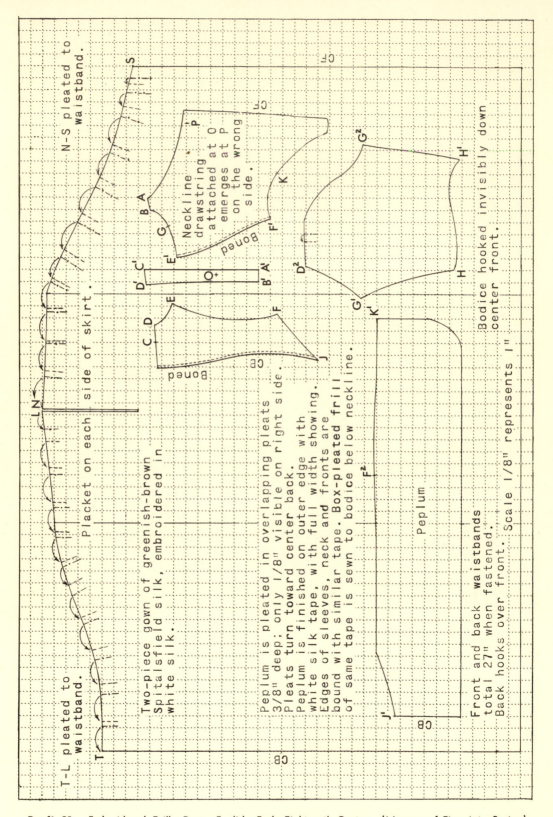

The text labels within the diagram include:

N-S pleated to waistband.

T-L pleated to waistband.

Placket on each side of skirt.

Two-piece gown of greenish-brown Spitalsfield silk, embroidered in white silk.

Neckline drawstring attached at O emerges at P on the wrong side.

Boned

Boned

CB

CF

CF

Peplum is pleated in overlapping pleats 3/8" deep; only 1/8" visible on right side. Pleats turn toward center back. Peplum is finished on outer edge with white silk tape, with full width showing. Edges of sleeves, neck and fronts are bound with similar tape. Box-pleated frill of same tape is sewn to bodice below neckline.

Peplum

Bodice hooked invisibly down center front.

Front and back waistbands total 27" when fastened. Back hooks over front.

Scale 1/8" represents 1"

CB

CB

Draft 21. Embroidered Faille Dress. English. Early Eighteenth Century. (Museum of Fine Arts, Boston)

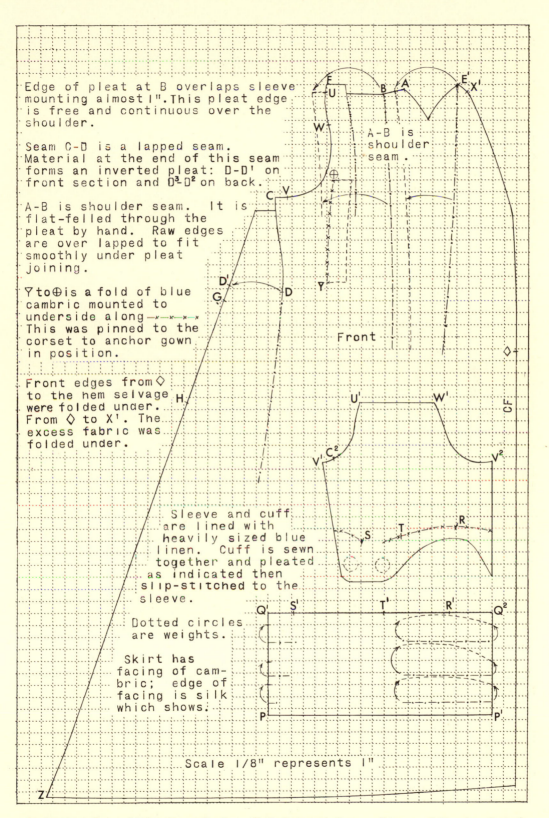

Edge of pleat at B overlaps sleeve
mounting almost 1". This pleat edge
is free and continuous over the
shoulder.

Seam C-D is a lapped seam.
Material at the end of this seam
forms an inverted pleat: D-D' on
front section and D³-D² on back.

A-B is shoulder seam. It is
flat-felled through the
pleat by hand. Raw edges
are over lapped to fit
smoothly under pleat
joining.

Υ to ⊕ is a fold of blue
cambric mounted to
underside along —×—×—×—×
This was pinned to the
corset to anchor gown
in position.

Front edges from ◇
to the hem selvage
were folded under.
From ◇ to X'. The
excess fabric was
folded under.

A-B is
shoulder
seam.

Front

Sleeve and cuff
are lined with
heavily sized blue
linen. Cuff is sewn
together and pleated
as indicated then
slip-stitched to the
sleeve.

Dotted circles
are weights.

Skirt has
facing of cam-
bric; edge of
facing is silk
which shows.

Scale 1/8" represents 1"

Draft 22a.   Blue and White Brocatelle Gown. Early Eighteenth Century. (Museum of Fine Arts, Boston)

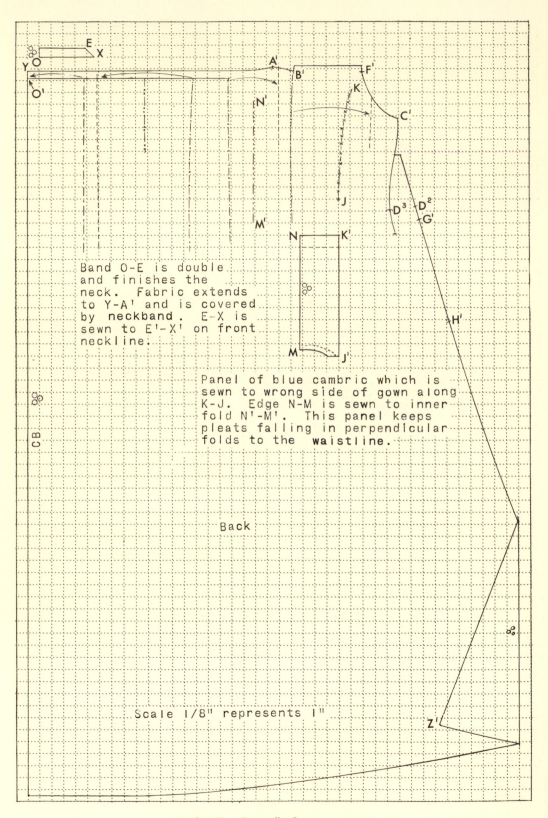

Band O-E is double
and finishes the
neck. Fabric extends
to Y-A' and is covered
by neckband. E-X is
sewn to E'-X' on front
neckline.

Panel of blue cambric which is
sewn to wrong side of gown along
K-J. Edge N-M is sewn to inner
fold N'-M'. This panel keeps
pleats falling in perpendicular
folds to the waistline.

Back

Scale 1/8" represents 1"

Draft 22b. Brocatelle Gown (Continued)

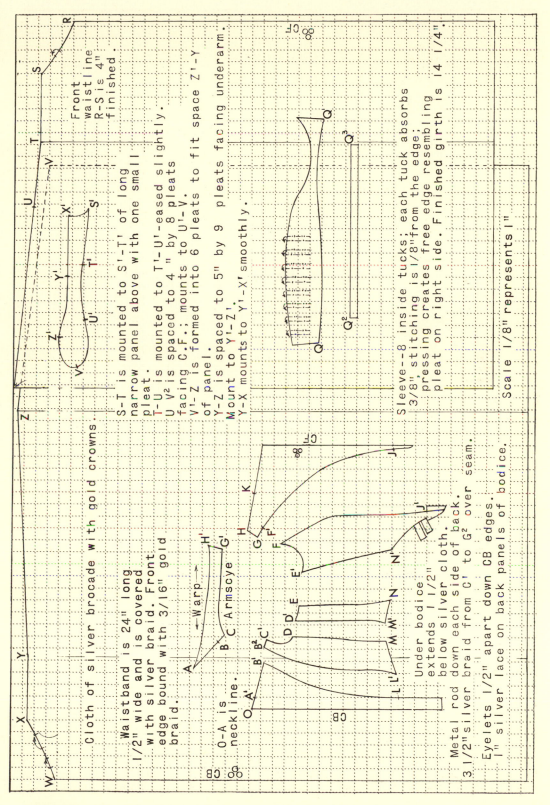

Cloth of silver brocade with gold crowns.

Front waistline R-S is 4" finished.

Waistband is 24" long, 1/2" wide and is covered with silver braid. Front edge bound with 3/16" gold braid.

S-T is mounted to S'-T' of long narrow panel above with one small pleat.
T-U' is mounted to T'-U'-eased slightly.
U-V² is spaced to 4" by 8 pleats facing C.F.; mounts to U'-V.
V'-Z is formed into 6 pleats to fit space Z'-Y of panel.
Y-Z is spaced to 5" by 9 pleats facing underarm.
Mount to Y'-Z'.
Y-X mounts to Y'-X' smoothly.

Warp →

O-A is neckline.

C Armscye

Under bodice extends 1 1/2" below silver cloth.

Metal rod down each side of back.
3 1/2" silver braid from C' to G² over seam.

Eyelets 1/2" apart down CB edges.
1" silver lace on back panels of bodice.

Sleeve--8 inside tucks; each tuck absorbs 3/8" stitching is 1/8" from the edge; pressing creates free edge resembling pleat on right side. Finished girth is 14 1/4".

Scale 1/8" represents 1"

Draft 23a. Coronation Robes of Queen Louisa Ulrica of Sweden. 1751. (Royal Armoury, Stockholm)

565

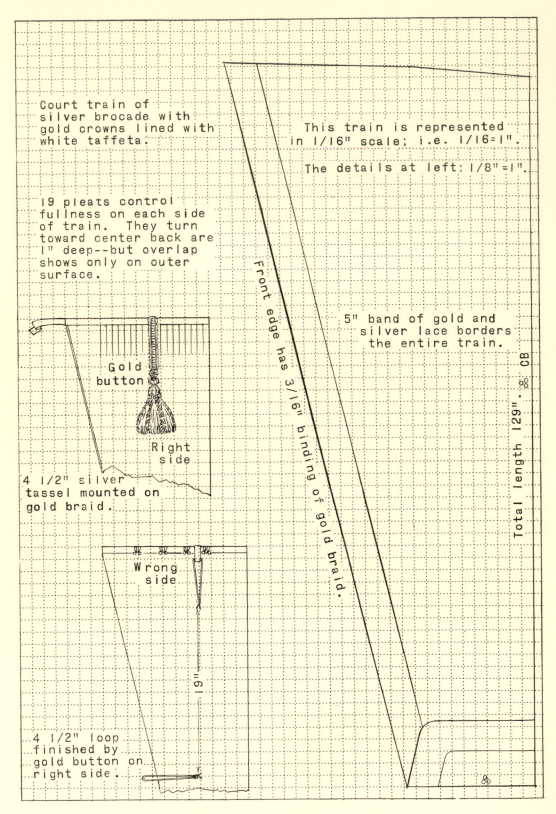

Court train of silver brocade with gold crowns lined with white taffeta.

This train is represented in 1/16" scale; i.e. 1/16=1".

The details at left: 1/8"=1".

19 pleats control fullness on each side of train. They turn toward center back are 1" deep--but overlap shows only on outer surface.

Gold button

Right side

4 1/2" silver tassel mounted on gold braid.

Front edge has 3/16" binding of gold braid.

5" band of gold and silver lace borders the entire train.

Total length 129". CB

Wrong side

19"

4 1/2" loop finished by gold button on right side.

Draft 23b. Queen Louisa Ulrica's Court Train.

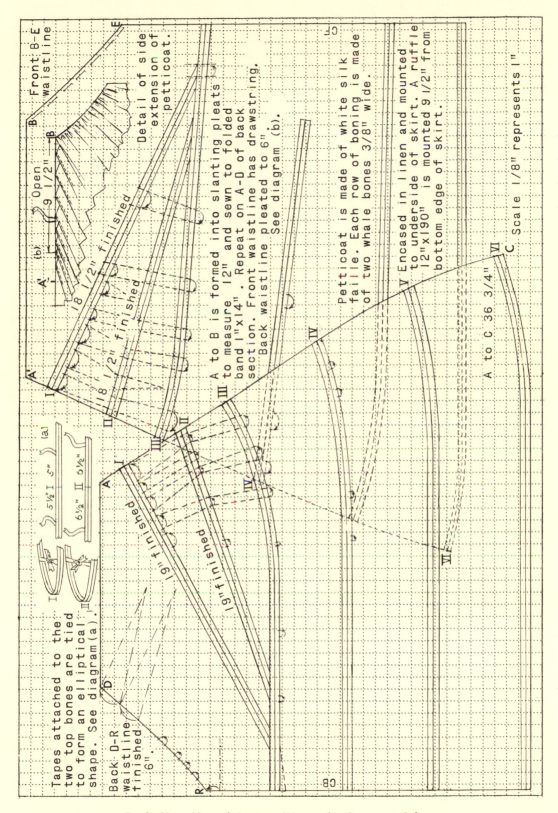

Front: B–E waistline

B

A': Open 9 1/2"

18 1/2" finished

(b)

Detail of side extension of petticoat.

E

18 1/2" finished

A'

I

II

II

III

III

II

IV

IV

I

A

V

VI

VI

C

A to C 36 3/4"

CF

A to B is formed into slanting pleats to measure 12" and sewn to folded band 1"x14". Repeat on A–D of back section. Front waistline has drawstring. Back waistline pleated to 6". See diagram (b).

Petticoat is made of white silk faille. Each row of boning is made of two whale bones 3/8" wide.

V Encased in linen and mounted to underside of skirt. A ruffle 12"x190" is mounted 9 1/2" from bottom edge of skirt.

Scale 1/8" represents 1".

Tapes attached to the two top bones are tied to form an elliptical shape. See diagram(a).

(a)

5 1/2" I 5"

6 1/2" II 5 1/2"

I

II

19" finished

19" finished

Back: D–R waistline finished 6".

D

CB

R

Draft 23c. Hooped Petticoat Worn under Coronation Robe.

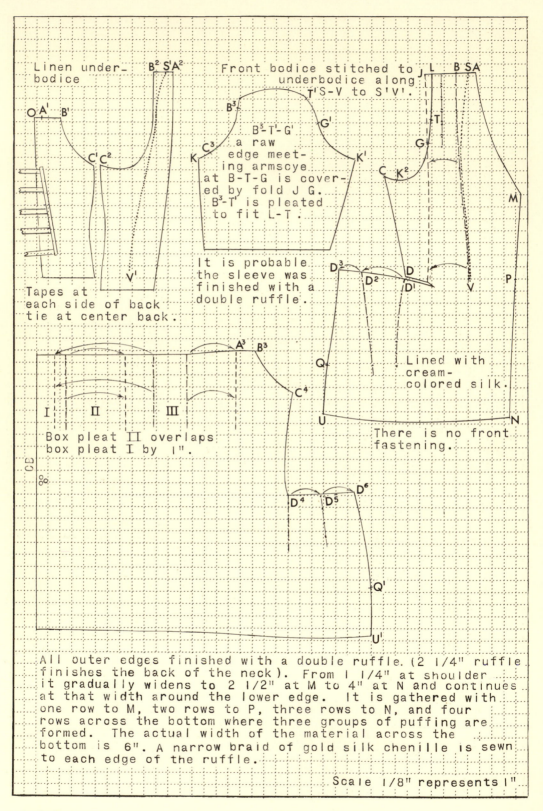

Linen under-bodice

B^2 S'A^2

Front bodice stitched to underbodice along T'S-V to S'V'.

J L B SA

O A' B'

B^3

G'

T

C' C^2

K C^3

B^3-T-G'
a raw
edge meet-
ing armscye
at B-T-G is cover-
ed by fold J G.
B^3-T' is pleated
to fit L-T.

K'

G

C K^2

M

V'

It is probable
the sleeve was
finished with a
double ruffle.

D^3 D

D^2 D'

V P

Tapes at
each side of back
tie at center back.

A^3 B^3

Q

Lined with
cream-
colored silk.

C^4

I II III

U

N

Box pleat II overlaps
box pleat I by 1".

There is no front
fastening.

D^4 D^5 D^6

Q'

U'

All outer edges finished with a double ruffle. (2 1/4" ruffle
finishes the back of the neck). From 1 1/4" at shoulder
it gradually widens to 2 1/2" at M to 4" at N and continues
at that width around the lower edge. It is gathered with
one row to M, two rows to P, three rows to N, and four
rows across the bottom where three groups of puffing are
formed. The actual width of the material across the
bottom is 6". A narrow braid of gold silk chenille is sewn
to each edge of the ruffle.

Scale 1/8" represents 1"

Draft 24a. Caraco Costume of Gold Satin. c.1778. (Metropolitan Museum of Art, Costume Institute)

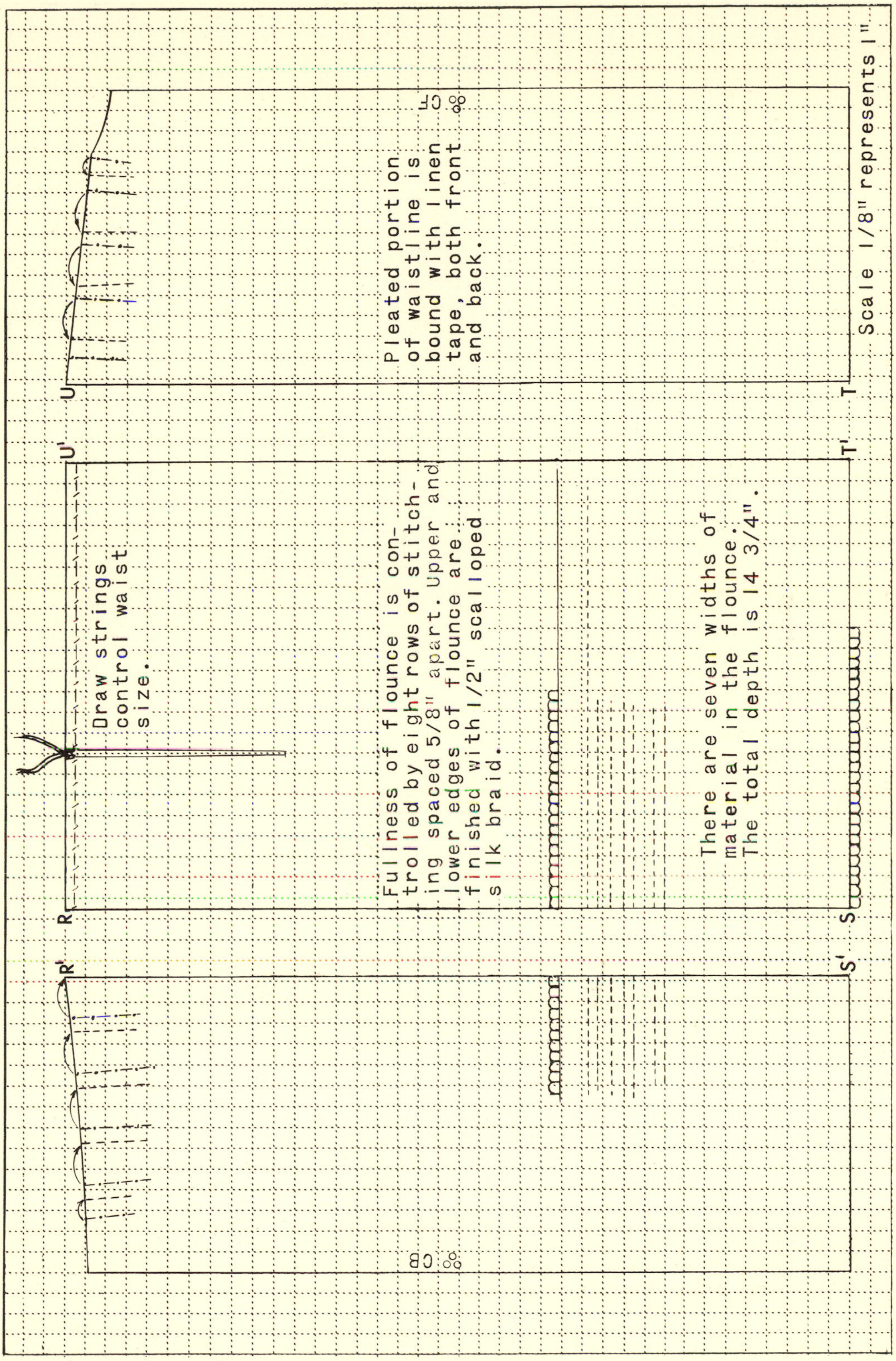
Scale 1/8" represents 1"
U
T
Pleated portion of waistline is bound with linen tape, both front and back.
CF
U'
T'
Draw strings control waist size.
Fullness of flounce is controlled by eight rows of stitching spaced 5/8" apart. Upper and lower edges of flounce are finished with 1/2" scalloped silk braid.
There are seven widths of material in the flounce. The total depth is 14 3/4".
R
S
R'
S'
CB

Draft 24b. Skirt of Caraco Costume.

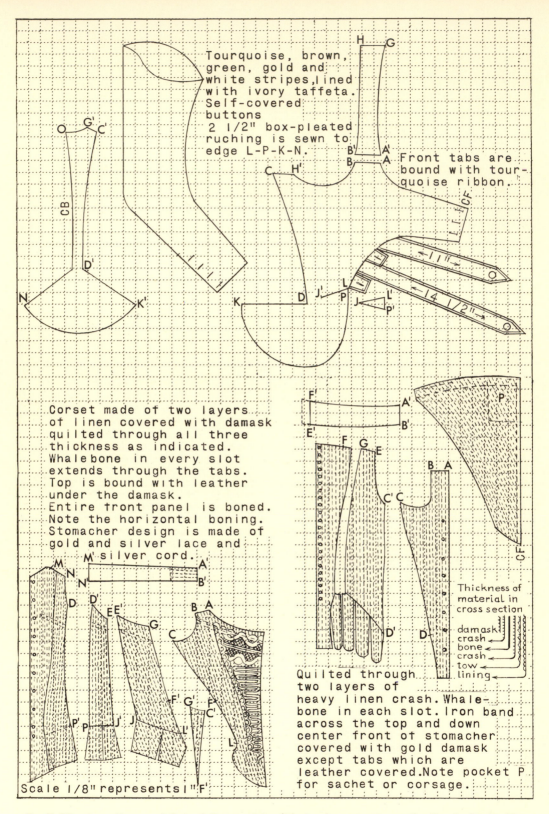

Tourquoise, brown, green, gold and white stripes, lined with ivory taffeta. Self-covered buttons 2 1/2" box-pleated ruching is sewn to edge L-P-K-N.

Front tabs are bound with tourquoise ribbon.

Corset made of two layers of linen covered with damask quilted through all three thickness as indicated. Whalebone in every slot extends through the tabs. Top is bound with leather under the damask. Entire front panel is boned. Note the horizontal boning. Stomacher design is made of gold and silver lace and silver cord.

Thickness of material in cross section

damask
crash
bone
crash
tow
lining

Quilted through two layers of heavy linen crash. Whalebone in each slot. Iron band across the top and down center front of stomacher covered with gold damask except tabs which are leather covered. Note pocket P for sachet or corsage.

Scale 1/8" represents 1"

Draft 25. *(Top)* Caraco of Striped Satin. 1780s. (Musée des Arts Decoratifs, Paris) **Draft 26a.** *(Bottom left)* Bohemian Corset. Eighteenth Century. (Brooklyn Museum) **Draft 26b.** *(Bottom right)* Venetian Corset. Eighteenth Century. (Metropolitan Museum of Art)

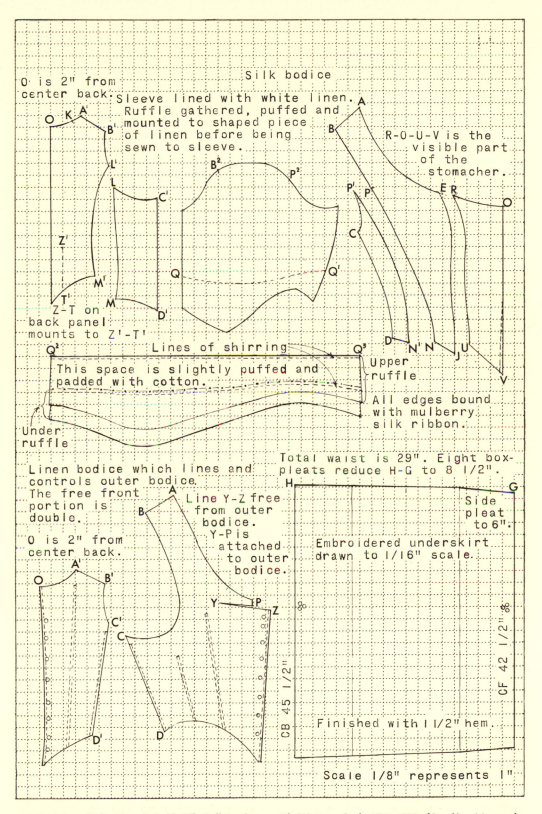

Silk bodice

O is 2" from center back.

Sleeve lined with white linen. Ruffle gathered, puffed and mounted to shaped piece of linen before being sewn to sleeve.

R-O-U-V is the visible part of the stomacher.

Z-T on back panel mounts to Z'-T'

Lines of shirring

This space is slightly puffed and padded with cotton.

Upper ruffle

All edges bound with mulberry silk ribbon.

Under ruffle

Linen bodice which lines and controls outer bodice. The free front portion is double.

O is 2" from center back.

Line Y-Z free from outer bodice. Y-P is attached to outer bodice.

Total waist is 29". Eight box-pleats reduce H-G to 8 1/2".

Side pleat to 6".

Embroidered underskirt drawn to 1/16" scale.

CB 45 1/2"

CF 42 1/2"

Finished with 1 1/2" hem.

Scale 1/8" represents 1"

Draft 27a. Embroidered Gold Silk Taffeta Gown with Watteau Back. 1770–1780. (Brooklyn Museum)

571

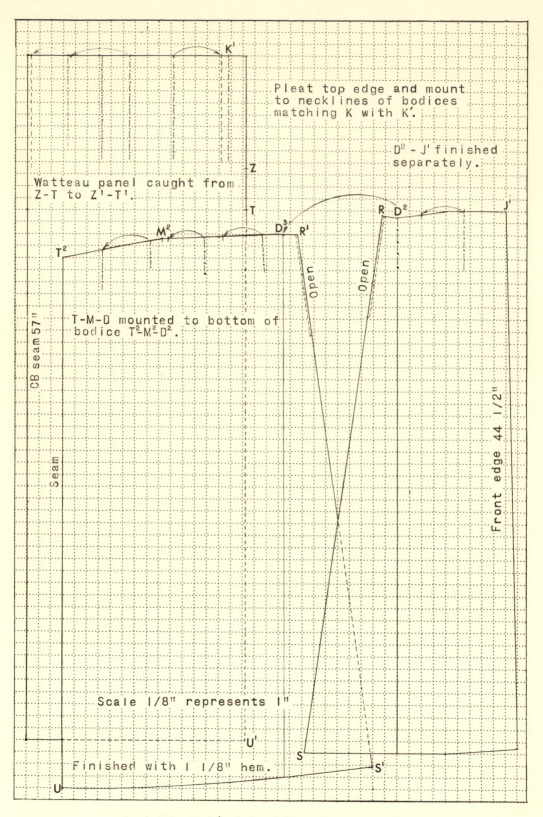

K'

Pleat top edge and mount
to necklines of bodices
matching K with K'.

D² - J' finished
separately.

Z

Watteau panel caught from
Z-T to Z'-T'.

T

R D²   J'

M²   D³ R'

T²

Open   Open

CB seam 57"

T-M-D mounted to bottom of
bodice T²-M²-D².

Seam

Front edge 44 1/2"

Scale 1/8" represents 1"

U'

Finished with 1 1/8" hem.

S

S'

U

Draft 27b. Wattéau Back and Skirt of Gold Taffeta Gown.

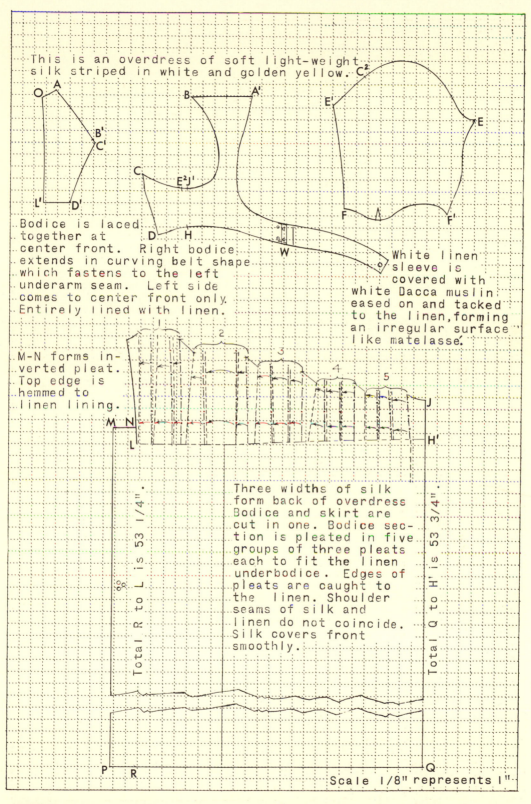

This is an overdress of soft light-weight silk striped in white and golden yellow.

Bodice is laced together at center front. Right bodice extends in curving belt shape which fastens to the left underarm seam. Left side comes to center front only. Entirely lined with linen.

M-N forms inverted pleat. Top edge is hemmed to linen lining.

White linen sleeve is covered with white Dacca muslin eased on and tacked to the linen, forming an irregular surface like matelassé.

Three widths of silk form back of overdress Bodice and skirt are cut in one. Bodice section is pleated in five groups of three pleats each to fit the linen underbodice. Edges of pleats are caught to the linen. Shoulder seams of silk and linen do not coincide. Silk covers front smoothly.

Total R to L is 53 1/4".

Total Q to H' is 53 3/4".

Scale 1/8" represents 1".

Draft 28. Overdress of Directoire Costume. English. 1795-1801. (Metropolitan Museum of Art, Costume Institute)

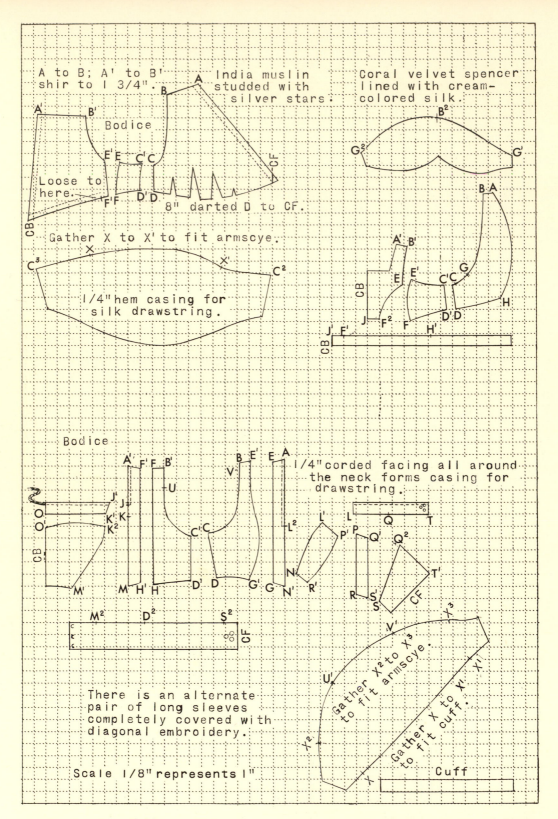

A to B; A' to B' shir to I 3/4".
India muslin studded with silver stars.
Coral velvet spencer lined with cream-colored silk.

Bodice

Loose to here.

8" darted D to CF.

Gather X to X' to fit armscye.

1/4"hem casing for silk drawstring.

Bodice

1/4" corded facing all around the neck forms casing for drawstring.

There is an alternate pair of long sleeves completely covered with diagonal embroidery.

Gather X² to X³ to fit armscye.

Gather X to X¹ to fit cuff.

Cuff

Scale 1/8" represents I"

Draft 29. *(Top left)* Bodice of Betsy Bonaparte's Wedding Gown. 1804. (Baltimore Historical Society)
Draft 30. *(Top right)* Spencer of Betsy Bonaparte. **Draft 31.** *(Bottom)* Bodice of White Muslin Gown. c.1820. (Brooklyn Museum)

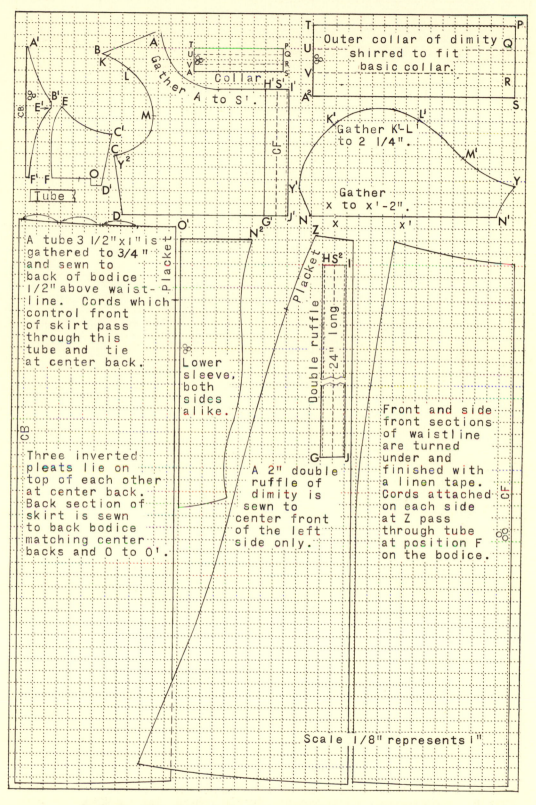

A'
B
K
L
A
T U V A
P Q R S
Gather A to S'.
Collar
Outer collar of dimity shirred to fit basic collar.
T P
U Q
V R
A S

CB
E' E
B'
M
H'S' I'
Gather K'-L' to 2 1/4".
K' L'
M'

F' F
O
C'
C
Y²
D'
D
Tube
CF
Y'
J' N
Gather x to x'-2".
x x'
N'
Z

O'
N²G'

A tube 3 1/2"x1" is gathered to 3/4" and sewn to back of bodice 1/2" above waist-line. Cords which control front of skirt pass through this tube and tie at center back.

Placket

HS² I

Placket

Double ruffle 24" long

Lower sleeve, both sides alike.

CB

Three inverted pleats lie on top of each other at center back. Back section of skirt is sewn to back bodice matching center backs and O to O'.

A 2" double ruffle of dimity is sewn to center front of the left side only.

G J

Front and side front sections of waistline are turned under and finished with a linen tape. Cords attached on each side at Z pass through tube at position F on the bodice.

CF

Scale 1/8" represents 1"

Draft 32. White Cotton Empire Dress. c.1808. (University of Washington)

575

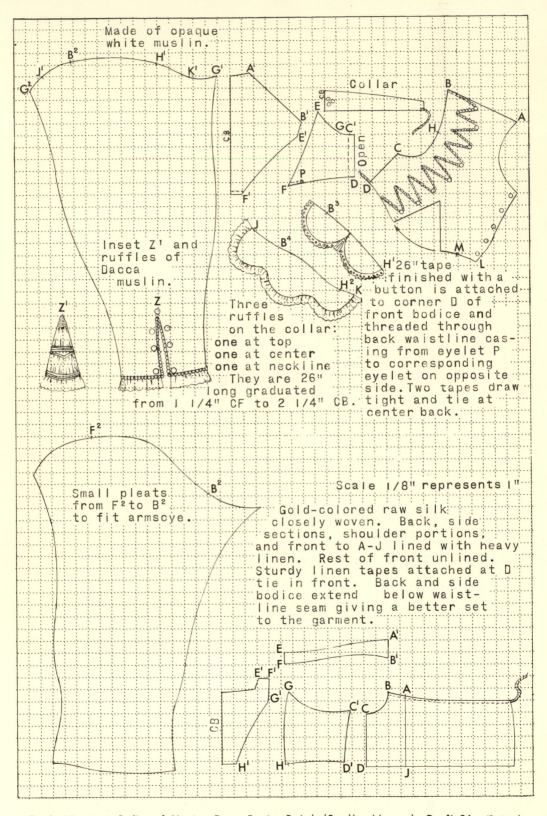

Made of opaque white muslin.

Collar

Inset Z' and ruffles of Dacca muslin.

Three ruffles on the collar: one at top one at center one at neckline They are 26" long graduated from 1 1/4" CF to 2 1/4" CB.

H'26" tape finished with a button is attached to corner D of front bodice and threaded through back waistline casing from eyelet P to corresponding eyelet on opposite side. Two tapes draw tight and tie at center back.

Small pleats from F² to B² to fit armscye.

Scale 1/8" represents 1"

Gold-colored raw silk closely woven. Back, side sections, shoulder portions, and front to A-J lined with heavy linen. Rest of front unlined. Sturdy linen tapes attached at D tie in front. Back and side bodice extend below waistline seam giving a better set to the garment.

Draft 33. *(Top)* Bodice of Nursing Dress. Empire Period. (Brooklyn Museum) **Draft 34.** *(Bottom)* Italian Silk Dress. 1805–1810. (Metropolitan Museum of Art, Costume Institute)

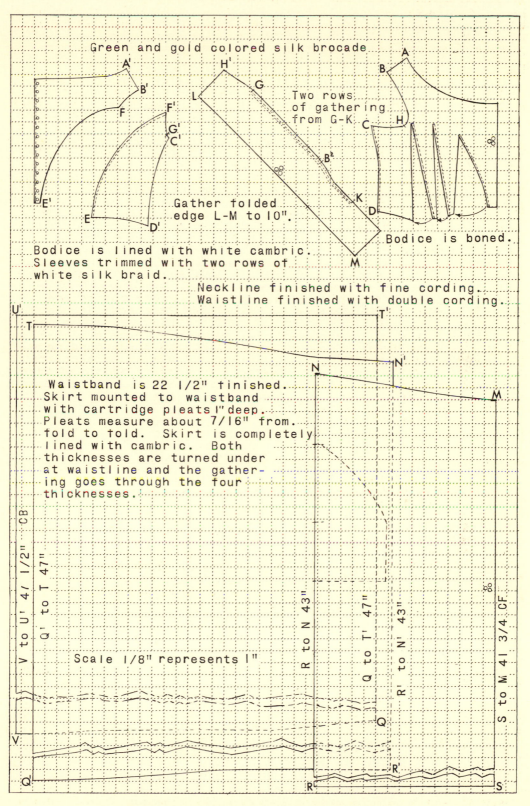

Green and gold colored silk brocade

Two rows of gathering from G-K

Gather folded edge L-M to 10".

Bodice is boned.

Bodice is lined with white cambric.
Sleeves trimmed with two rows of
white silk braid.

Neckline finished with fine cording.
Waistline finished with double cording.

Waistband is 22 1/2" finished.
Skirt mounted to waistband
with cartridge pleats 1" deep.
Pleats measure about 7/16" from
fold to fold. Skirt is completely
lined with cambric. Both
thicknesses are turned under
at waistline and the gathering goes through the four
thicknesses.

Scale 1/8" represents 1"

V to U' 41 1/2"   CB

Q' to T 47"

R to N 43"

Q to T' 47"

R' to N' 43"

S to M 41 3/4 CF.

Draft 35. French Ball Gown. 1825. (Brooklyn Museum)

577

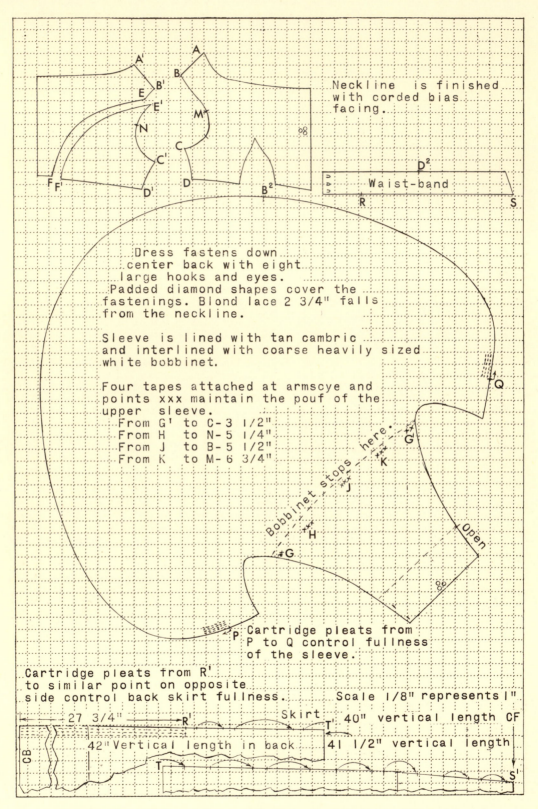

Neckline is finished
with corded bias
facing.

Waist-band

Dress fastens down
center back with eight
large hooks and eyes.
Padded diamond shapes cover the
fastenings. Blond lace 2 3/4" falls
from the neckline.

Sleeve is lined with tan cambric
and interlined with coarse heavily sized
white bobbinet.

Four tapes attached at armscye and
points xxx maintain the pouf of the
upper sleeve.
  From G' to C- 3 1/2"
  From H to N- 5 1/4"
  From J to B- 5 1/2"
  From K to M- 6 3/4"

Bobbinet stops here.

Open

Cartridge pleats from
P to Q control fullness
of the sleeve.

Cartridge pleats from R'
to similar point on opposite
side control back skirt fullness.   Scale 1/8" represents 1"

Skirt   40" vertical length CF
27 3/4"

42" Vertical length in back   41 1/2" vertical length

CB

Draft 36. Gray Silk Damask Gown. c.1835. (University of Washington, School of Drama)

578

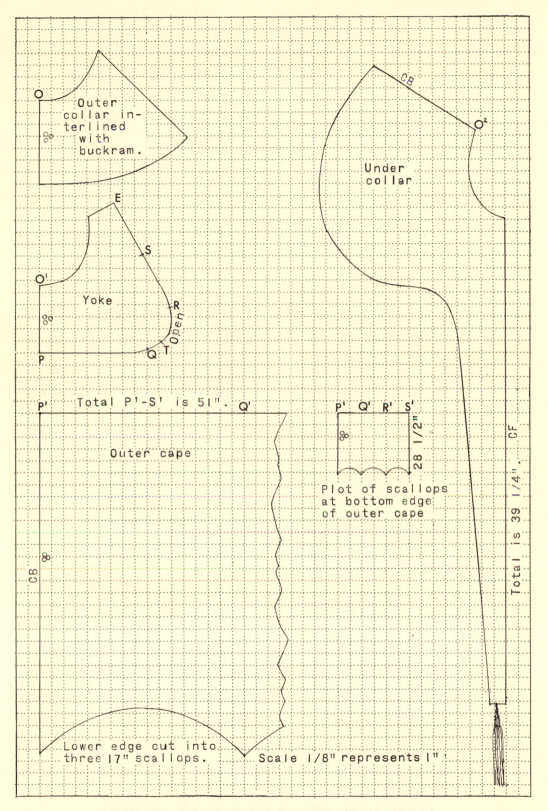

O

Outer
collar in-
terlined
with
buckram.

CB

Under
collar

O²

E

S

Yoke

O'

R

Open

P

Q

T

P'   Total P'-S' is 51".   Q'

P'   Q' R' S'

Outer cape

28 1/2"

Plot of scallops
at bottom edge
of outer cape

CB

Total is 39 1/4".   CF

Lower edge cut into
three 17" scallops.

Scale 1/8" represents 1".

Draft 37a. Embroidered Wool Cape. 1830s. (Brooklyn Museum)

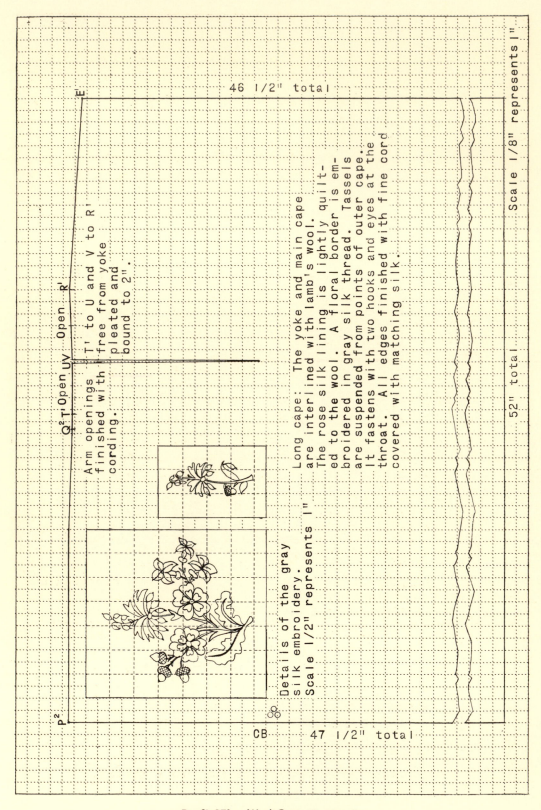

46 1/2" total

E

Q²T'Open UV Open R'

Arm openings T' to U and V to R'
finished with free from yoke
cording. pleated and
bound to 2".

Long cape: The yoke and main cape
are interlined with lamb's wool.
The rose silk lining is lightly quilted to the wool. A floral border is embroidered in gray silk thread. Tassels
are suspended from points of outer cape.
It fastens with two hooks and eyes at the
throat. All edges finished with fine cord
covered with matching silk.

Details of the gray
silk embroidery.
Scale 1/2" represents 1"

P²

CB   47 1/2" total

52" total   Scale 1/8" represents 1"

Draft 37b. Wool Cape *(Continued)*

580

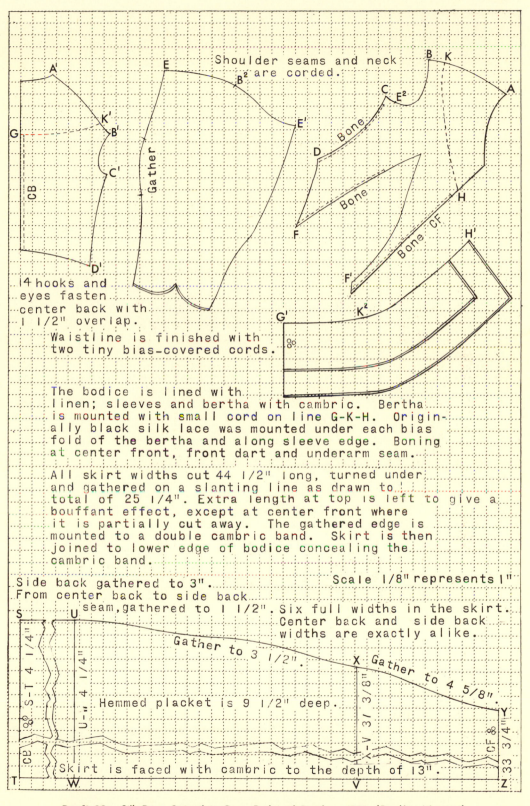

Shoulder seams and neck are corded.

Gather

Bone

Bone

Bone CF

CB

14 hooks and
eyes fasten
center back with
1 1/2" overlap.

Waistline is finished with
two tiny bias-covered cords.

The bodice is lined with
linen; sleeves and bertha with cambric. Bertha
is mounted with small cord on line G-K-H. Originally black silk lace was mounted under each bias
fold of the bertha and along sleeve edge. Boning
at center front, front dart and underarm seam.

All skirt widths cut 44 1/2" long, turned under
and gathered on a slanting line as drawn to
total of 25 1/4". Extra length at top is left to give a
bouffant effect, except at center front where
it is partially cut away. The gathered edge is
mounted to a double cambric band. Skirt is then
joined to lower edge of bodice concealing the
cambric band.

Side back gathered to 3".   Scale 1/8" represents 1"
From center back to side back
seam, gathered to 1 1/2". Six full widths in the skirt.
Center back and side back
widths are exactly alike.

Gather to 3 1/2".

Gather to 4 5/8"

S-T 4 1/4"

U-" 4 1/4"

X-V 31 3/8"

CF 8"

33 3/4"

Hemmed placket is 9 1/2" deep.

CB

Skirt is faced with cambric to the depth of 13".

Draft 38. Silk Dress Striped in Gray, Red, and Purple. c.1840. (Brooklyn Museum)

581

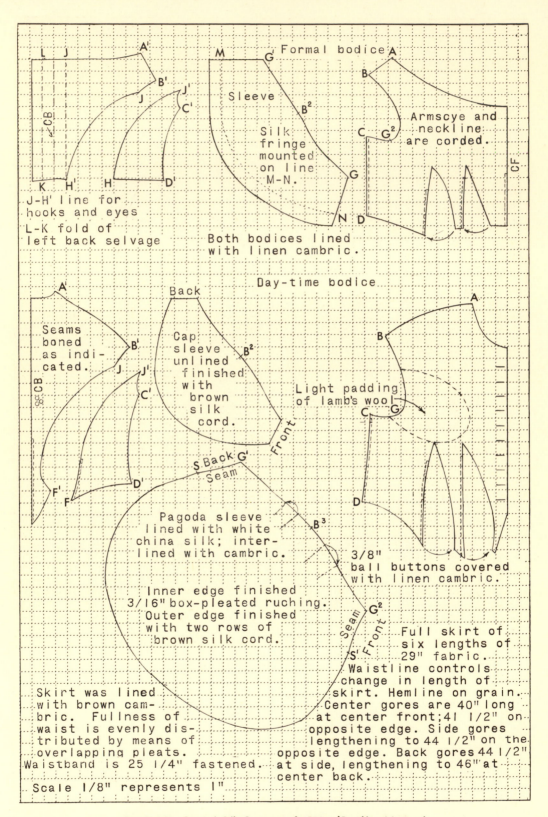

L J A'
M G Formal bodice A
B'
Sleeve B
J' J
← CB B²
C'
Armscye and
neckline
Silk are corded.
fringe
mounted C G²
on line
M-N. G
K H' H D'
J-H' line for N D
hooks and eyes
L-K fold of Both bodices lined
left back selvage with linen cambric.

Day-time bodice

A' Back A
Seams Cap B
boned sleeve B'
as indi- unlined B²
cated. J' finished
J with Light padding
C' brown of lamb's wool
silk
CB cord. C G
∞ Front D
S Back G'
Seam

F' D'
F B³ 3/8"
Pagoda sleeve ball buttons covered
lined with white with linen cambric.
china silk; inter-
lined with cambric.

Inner edge finished
3/16" box-pleated ruching. G²
Outer edge finished Seam
with two rows of S' Front Full skirt of
brown silk cord. six lengths of
29" fabric.
Waistline controls
change in length of
Skirt was lined skirt. Hemline on grain.
with brown cam- Center gores are 40" long
bric. Fullness of at center front;41 1/2" on
waist is evenly dis- opposite edge. Side gores
tributed by means of lengthening to 44 1/2" on the
overlapping pleats. opposite edge. Back gores 44 1/2"
Waistband is 25 1/4" fastened. at side, lengthening to 46" at
center back.
Scale 1/8" represents 1"

Draft 39. Striped Silk Costume of 1850s. (Brooklyn Museum)

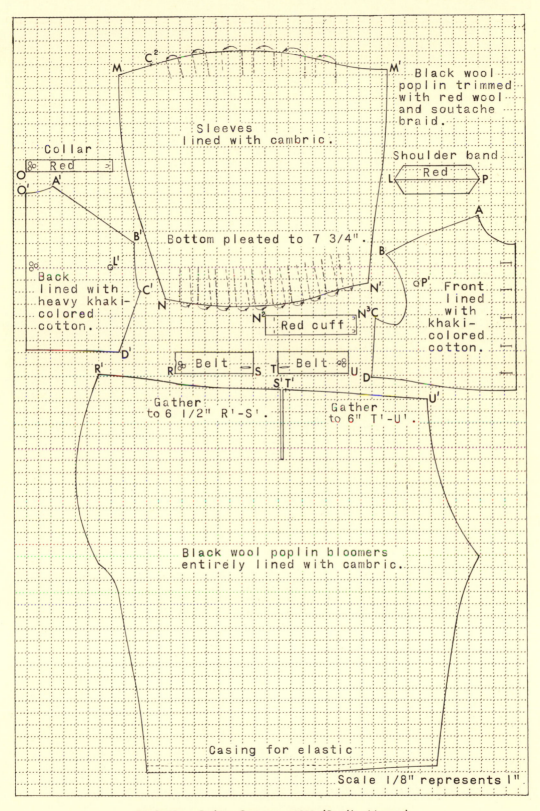

Collar

Red

Black wool poplin trimmed with red wool and soutache braid.

Sleeves lined with cambric.

Shoulder band

Red

Bottom pleated to 7 3/4".

Back lined with heavy khaki-colored cotton.

Front lined with khaki-colored cotton.

Red cuff

Belt

Belt

Gather to 6 1/2" R'-S'.

Gather to 6" T'-U'.

Black wool poplin bloomers entirely lined with cambric.

Casing for elastic

Scale 1/8" represents 1"

Draft 40a. Bathing Costume. c.1860. (Brooklyn Museum)

583

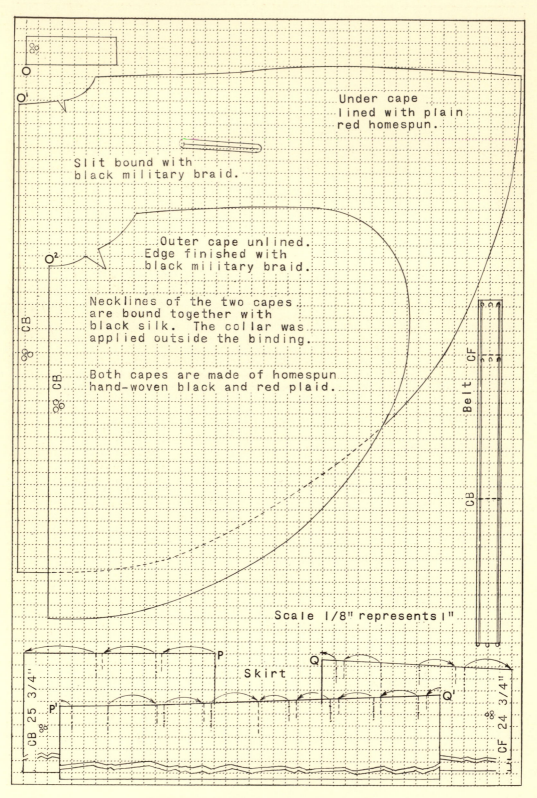

Under cape
lined with plain
red homespun.

Slit bound with
black military braid.

Outer cape unlined.
Edge finished with
black military braid.

Necklines of the two capes
are bound together with
black silk. The collar was
applied outside the binding.

Both capes are made of homespun
hand-woven black and red plaid.

Scale 1/8" represents 1"

Draft 40b. Double Cape of Bathing Costume.

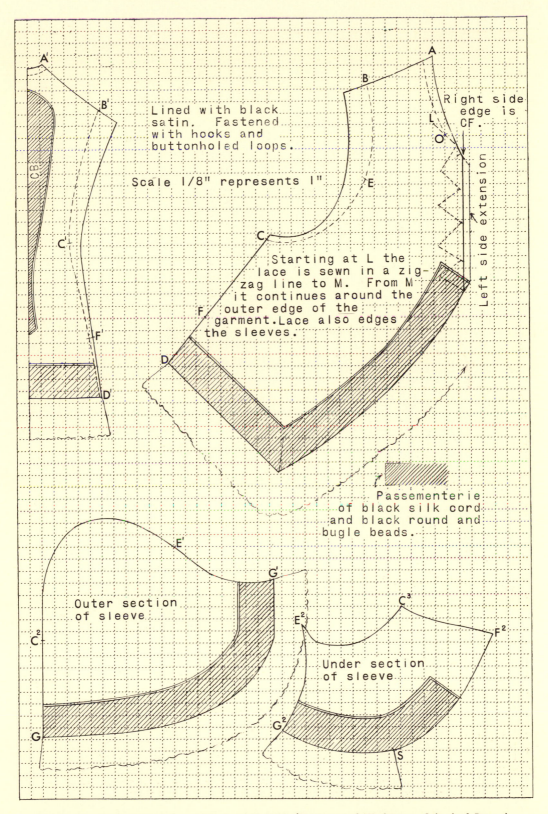

Text labels within the figure:

A′ B′ CB C′ F′ D′ D F C E B A

Lined with black satin. Fastened with hooks and buttonholed loops.

Scale 1/8" represents 1"

Right side edge is CF.

L O

Left side extension

Starting at L the lace is sewn in a zig-zag line to M. From M it continues around the outer edge of the garment. Lace also edges the sleeves.

Passementerie of black silk cord and black round and bugle beads.

E′ G′ C³ E² F²

Outer section of sleeve

C²

Under section of sleeve

G G² S

Draft 41. Black Satin Dolman Wrap. 1870–1880. (University of Washington, School of Drama)

585

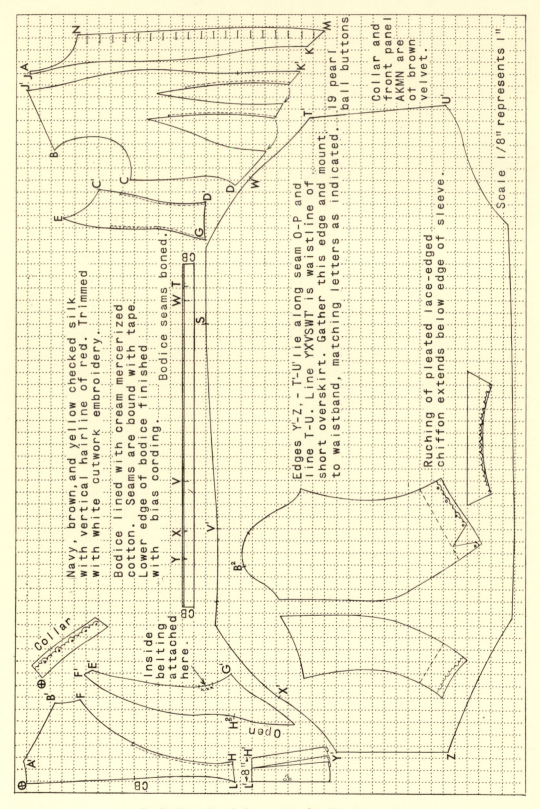

Navy, brown, and yellow checked silk with vertical hairline of red. Trimmed with white cutwork embroidery.

Bodice lined with cream mercerized cotton. Seams are bound with tape. Lower edge of bodice finished with bias cording.

Bodice seams boned.

Edges Y'-Z, - T'-U'lie along seam O-P and line T-U. Line Y'XVSWT is waistline of short overskirt. Gather this edge and mount to waistband, matching letters as indicated.

19 pearl ball buttons.

Collar and front panel AKMN are of brown velvet.

Ruching of pleated lace-edged chiffon extends below edge of sleeve.

Scale 1/8" represents 1"

Inside belting attached here.

Collar

Open

Draft 42a. French Gown. 1885. (Brooklyn Museum)

586

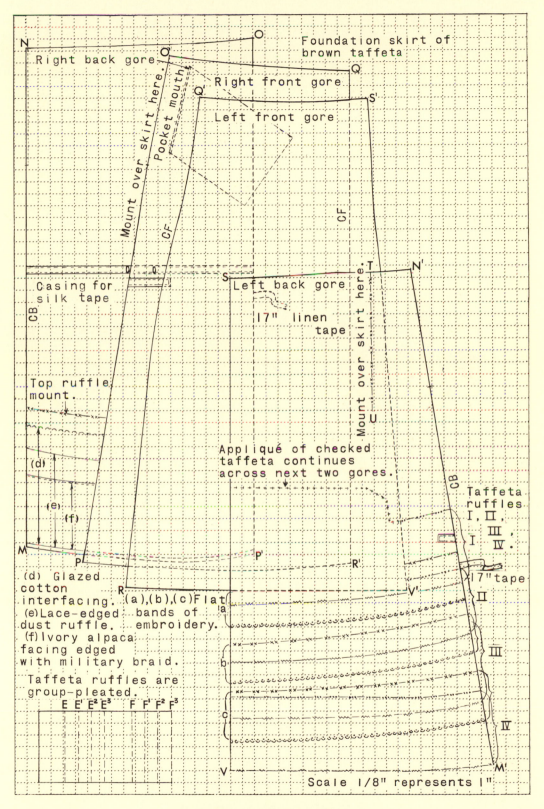

Draft 42b. French Gown *(Continued)*

587

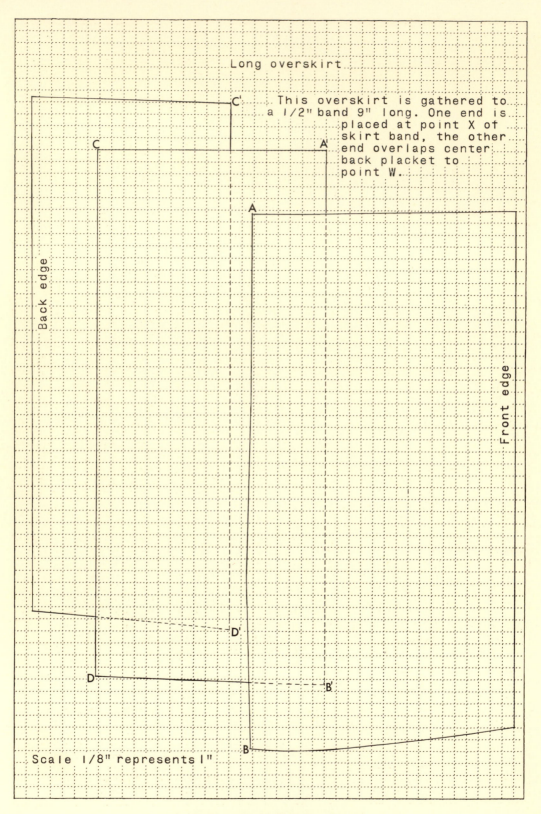

Long overskirt

This overskirt is gathered to a 1/2" band 9" long. One end is placed at point X of skirt band, the other end overlaps center back placket to point W.

Back edge

Front edge

Scale 1/8" represents 1"

Draft 42c. French Gown *(Continued)*

588

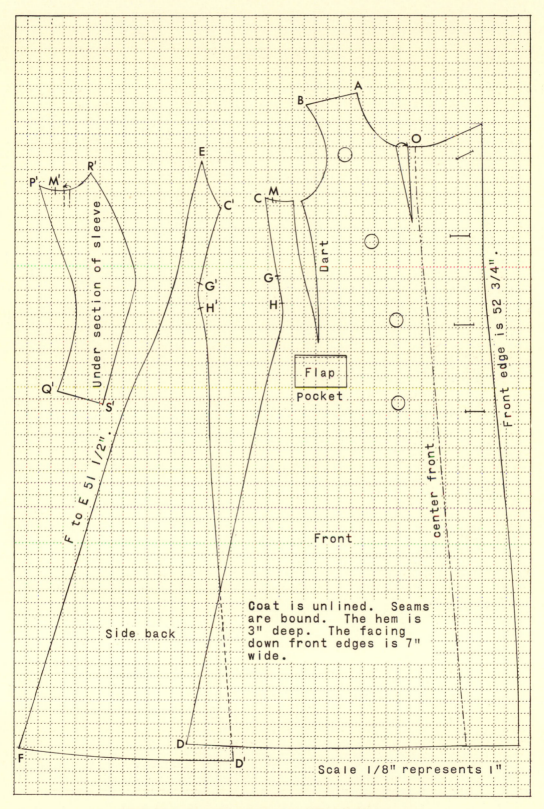

Text labels within the figure:

A, B, O
E, R', P', M', C', C, M
Dart
G', H', G, H
Under section of sleeve
Q, S'
Flap
Pocket
F to E 51 1/2".
Front edge is 52 3/4".
center front
Front
Coat is unlined. Seams
are bound. The hem is
3" deep. The facing
down front edges is 7"
wide.
Side back
F, D', D'
Scale 1/8" represents 1"

Draft 43a. Black Serge Raincoat. c.1895. (Brooklyn Museum)

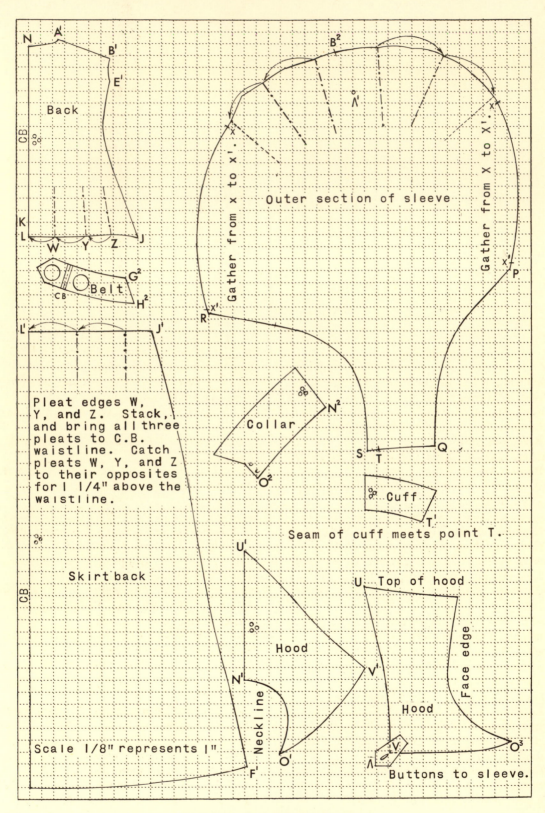

N A'
    B'
    E'

Back

CB

K
L
W Y Z J

Belt
CB G²
H²

Gather from x to x'.

Outer section of sleeve

Gather from X to X'.

B²

Λ

x'
P

L'   J'

Pleat edges W,
Y, and Z. Stack,
and bring all three
pleats to C.B.
waistline. Catch
pleats W, Y, and Z
to their opposites
for 1 1/4" above the
waistline.

Collar
N²

O²

R x'

S T Q

Cuff
T'

Seam of cuff meets point T.

Skirt back

U'

U Top of hood

Hood

N'

Neckline

V'

Hood

Face edge

CB

Scale 1/8" represents 1"

F' O'

V
Λ
O³

Buttons to sleeve.

Draft 43b. Black Raincoat *(Continued)*

590

Bibliography

Books

Abrahams, Ethel Beatrice. *Greek Dress*. London: J. Murray, 1908.

Alford, Marian M. (Lady). *Needlework as Art*. London: Sampson Low, Marston, Searle, and Rivington, 1886.

Barton, Lucy. *Historic Costume for the Stage*. Boston: W. H. Baker, c.1935.

Bell, Quentin. *On Human Finery*. New York: Wyn, 1949.

Bernstein, Aline. *Masterpieces of Women's Costume of the Eighteenth and Nineteenth Centuries*. New York: Crown, c.1959.

Binetti-Vertua, Caterina. *Trine e Donne Siciliane*. Milan: Ulrico Hoepli, 1911.

Boas, Franz. *Primitive Art*. New York: Dover, 1955.

Boehn, Max von. *Modes and Manners*. Philadelphia: Lippincott, 1932, 4 vols.

Boehn, Max von, and Oskar Fischel. *Modes and Manners of the Nineteenth Century*. New York: Dutton, 1927, 4 vols.

Boutell, Charles. *Monumental Brasses and Slabs*. London: G. Bell, 1847.

British Museum. *A Guide to the Babylonian and Assyrian Antiquities*, 3rd ed., London: Harrison and Sons, 1922.

Broholm, Hans C. and Margrethe Hald. *Costumes of the Bronze Age in Denmark*. Copenhagen: Nyt Nordisk Forlag, 1940.

Brown, Margaret W. *Dresses of the First Ladies of the White House*. Washington, D.C.: Smithsonian Institution, 1952.

Buck, Anne Mary. *Victorian Costume and Costume Accessories*. London: Jenkins, 1961.

Calthorp, Dion Clayton. *English Costume*. London: A. & C. Black, 1907.

Carleton, Patrick. *Buried Empires*. London: E. Arnold, 1939.

Carter, Howard, and A. C. Mace. *The Tomb of Tut-ankh-amen*. New York: Doran, 1923–1933, 3 vols.

Cartwright, Julia. *Isabella D'Este, Marchioness of Mantua*, 2nd ed., London: J. Murray, 1903.

Challamel, M. Augustin. *History of Fashion in France*. London: Sampson Low, Marston, Searle, and Rivington, 1882.

Cotman, John Sell. *Engravings of Sepulchral Brasses in Norfolk and Suffolk*. London: Henry G. Bohn, 1939, 2 vols.

Crawford, M. D. C. *One World of Fashion*. New York: Fairchild, 1946.

Cunnington, C. Willett. *English Women's Clothing in the Nineteenth Century*. London: Faber, 1937.

——. *Feminine Attitudes in the Nineteenth Century*. London: Heinemann, 1935.

Cunnington, C. Willett, and Phillis Cunnington, *Handbook of English Costume in the Eighteenth Century*. London: Faber, 1957.

——. *Handbook of English Costume in the Seventeenth Century*. London: Faber, 1955.

——. *Handbook of English Costume in the*

Sixteenth Century. Philadelphia: Dufour Editions, 1954.

————. *Handbook of English Mediaeval Costume*. Philadelphia: Dufour Editions, 1952.

————. *The History of Underclothes*. London: M. Joseph, 1951.

————. *A Picture History of English Costume*. London: Longacre, 1960.

Davenport, Millia. *The Book of Costume*. New York: Crown, 1948.

Davies, Nina. *Ancient Egyptian Paintings*. The University of Chicago Press, 1936.

Dio, Cassius. *Dio's Roman History*. Translated by Herbert Baldwin Foster. Troy, New York: Pafraet, 1906, 6 vols.

Earle, Alice Morse. *Two Centuries of Costume in America, 1620–1820*. New York: Macmillan, 1903, 2 vols.

Einhard and the Monk of St. Gall. *Early Lives of Charlemagne*. Translated and edited by A. J. Grant. London: Chatto & Windus, 1922.

Erman, Adolf. *Life in Ancient Egypt*. London: Macmillan, 1894.

Evans, Sir Arthur. *The Palace of Minos*. London: Macmillan, 1921–1935, 4 vols.

Evans, Joan. *Dress in Mediaeval France*. Oxford: Clarendon Press, 1952.

Evans, Lady Maria Millington. *Chapters on Greek Dress*. London: Macmillan, 1893.

Farcy, Louis de. *LaBroderie*. Angers: Belhomme, Libraire-Editeur, 1890.

Fairholt, F. W., *Costume in England, A History of Dress to the End of the Eighteenth Century*, 4th ed., Revised by H. A. Dillon. London: G. Bell, 1896, 2 vols.

Floerke, Hanns Florian. *Die Moden der Italienischen Renaissance von 1300 bis 1500.* Munchen: Georg Muller, 1917.

Flügel, John Carl. *The Psychology of Clothes*, 3rd ed., London: Hogarth, 1950.

Frankfort, Henri. *Sculpture of the Third Millennium B.C. from Tell Asmar and Khafaje*. The University of Chicago Press, c.1939.

Fürtwangler, Adolf, and Karl Reichhold. *Griechische Vasenmalerei*. Munich: Brüchmann, 1904–1932, 3 vols.

Gallery of Fashion 1790–1822. Plates by Heideloff and Ackermann. Notes on plates by Doris Langley Moore. London: B. T. Batsford, 1949.

Gardilanne, G. de, and E. W. Moffat. *Les Costumes Regionaux de la France*. Paris: Les Editions du Pegase, 1929, 4 vols.

Gibbs-Smith, Charles H. *The Fashionable Lady in the Nineteenth Century*. London: Her Majesty's Stationery Office, 1960.

Giglioli, Giulio Quirino. *L'Arte Etrusca*. Milano: S. A. Fratelli Treves, 1935–1943.

Goldscheider, Ludwig. *Etruscan Sculpture*. Phaidon Edition. New York: Oxford, 1941.

Gorsline, Douglas. *What People Wore*. New York: Viking, 1952.

Grabar, André. *Byzantine Painting*. Geneva: Skira, 1953.

Harmand, Adrien. *Jeanne d'Arc ses Costumes son Armure*. Paris: Librairie Ernest Leroux, 1929.

Hefner-Alteneck, Jacob Heinrich von. *Trachten Kunstwerke und Gerathschaften*. Frankfort: Heinrich Keller, 1879–1889, 10 vols.

Huezy, Léon and Jacques Heuzey. *Histoire du Costume dans L'Antiquité Classique l'Orient*. Paris: Les Belles Lettres, 1935.

Hiler, Hilaire. *From Nudity to Raiment*. London: Simpkin Marshall, Ltd., n.d.

Holland, Vyvyan. *Hand Coloured Fashion Plates, 1770–1899*. London: B. T. Batsford, 1955.

Hope, Thomas. *Costume of the Ancients*. London: William Miller, 1812, 2 vols.

Houston, Mary G. *Ancient Egyptian, Mesopotamian and Persian Costume and Decoration*, 2nd ed., London: A. & C. Black, 1954.

————. *Ancient Greek, Roman and Byzantine Costume and Decoration*. London: A. & C. Black, 1931.

————. *Medieval Costume in England and France, the Thirteenth, Fourteenth and Fifteenth Centuries*. London: A. & C. Black, 1939.

Hurlock, Elizabeth. *The Psychology of Dress*. New York: Ronald, 1929.

Kelly, Francis M., and Randolph Schwabe. *A Short History of Costume and Armour 1066–1800*. New York: Scribner, 1931.

————. *Historic Costume, A Chronicle of Fashion in Western Europe, 1490–1790*, 2nd ed., New York: Scribner, 1929.

Kendrick, A. F. *Catalogue of Textiles from Burying Grounds in Egypt*. Victoria and Albert Museum. London: His Majesty's Stationery Office, 1920, 3 vols.

Kohler, Carl, and Emma von Sichart. *A History of Costume*. New York: G. Howard Watt, 1933.

La Mesangère, Pierre, *Le Bon Genre*. Paris: Les Editions Albert Levy, 1931.

Langer, William. *An Encyclopedia of World History*. Boston: Houghton Mifflin, 1948.

Lassaigne, Jacques. *Spanish Painting from the Catalan Frescoes to El Greco*. Geneva: Albert Skira, 1952.

Laver, James (ed.). *Costumes of the Western World*. New York: Harper & Row, 1951.

Laver, James. *Taste and Fashion*. London: Harrap, 1945.

Leloir, M. Maurice. *Histoire du Costume*. Paris: Henri Ernst, 1933.

Le Musée du Caire. *Encyclopédie Photographique de l'Art*. Paris: Editions Tel, 1949.

Le Musée du Louvre. *Encyclopédie Photographique de l'Art*. Paris: Editions Tel, c.1936–1948, 3 vols.

Lester, Katherine Morris, and Bess Viola Oerke. *Accessories of Dress*. Peoria, Ill.: Manual Arts, 1940.

Linthicum, Marie Channing. *Costume in the Drama of Shakespeare and his Contemporaries*. Oxford: Clarendon Press, 1936.

Lutz, Henry F. *Textiles and Costumes among the Peoples of the Ancient Near East*. Leipzig: J. C. Hinrichs'sche Buchhandlung, 1923.

Macquoid, Percy. *Children's Costumes from the Great Masters*. London: The Medici Society, 1923.

Marinatos, Spyridon. *Crete and Mycenae*. New York: Harry N. Abrams, 1960.

Men's Wear. *History of Men's Wear Industry, 1790–1950*. New York: Fairchild, 1950.

Morse, Mrs. Harriet K. *Elizabethan Pageantry; A Pictorial Survey of Costume and Its Commentators from 1560–1620*. London: The Studio, 1934.

Murphy, Arthur. *The Works of Cornelius Tacitus*. London: Printed for John Stockdale, 1811, 8 vols.

Norlund, Paul. *Viking Settlers in Greenland*. London: Cambridge, 1936.

Norris, Herbert. *Costume and Fashion*. London: Dent, 1925, vol. I; 1940, vol. II. New York: Dutton, 1938, vol. III, 2 books.

Norris, Herbert, and Oswald Curtis. *Costume and Fashion*. London: Dent, 1933, vol. VI.

Pallis, Svend Aage. *The Antiquity of Iraq*. Copenhagen: Ejnar Munksgaard, 1956.

Palliser, Fanny. *History of Lace*. London: Sampson Low, Marston, 1902.

Parrot, Andre. *Sumer*. London: Thames and Hudson, 1960.

Pauquet Fréres. *Modes et Costumes Historiques*. Paris: René Pincebourde, Libraire-Editeur, n.d.

Pierce, Hayford, and Royall Tyler. *L'Art Byzantin*. Paris: Librairie de France, 1932, 2 vols.

Piton, Camille. *Le Costume Civil en France*. Paris: Ernest Flammarion, Editeur, n.d.

Planche, James Robinson. *Cyclopaedia of Costume*. London: Chatto & Windus, 1876.

Powys, Marian. *Lace and Lace Making*. Boston: Branford, 1953.

Price, Julius. *Dame Fashion*. London: Sampson Low, Marston, 1913.

Quicherat, Jules E. J. *Histoire du Costume en France*. Paris: Hachette, 1877.

Racinet, Albert Charles. *Le Costume Historique*. Paris: Firmin-Didot, 1888, 6 vols.

Ramsay, William. *A Manual of Roman Antiquities*. New York: Scribner, 1895.

Rice, David Talbot. *The Art of Byzantium*. London: Thames and Hudson, 1959.

Richter, Gisela. *Red Figured Athenian Vases in the Metropolitan Museum of Art*. New Haven: Yale, 1936, 2 vols.

———. *Handbook of Greek Art*. London: Phaidon, 1959.

———. *The Sculpture and Sculptors of the Greeks*. New Haven: Yale, 1950.

Riefstahl, Elizabeth. *Patterned Textiles in Pharaonic Egypt*. Brooklyn Institute of Arts and Sciences. Brooklyn Museum, 1945.

Rohrback, Carl, and Albert Kertschmer. *Die Trachten der Volker (The Costumes of the People)*. Leipzig: Adolph Schumunn, 1906.

Rosenberg, Adolf. *The Design and Development of Costume from Prehistoric Times up to the Twentieth Century*. London: W. and G. Foyle, 1925, 5 vols.

Rudofsky, Bernard. *Are Clothes Modern?* Chicago: P. Theobald, 1947.

Schmidt, Erick Fredrich. *Persepolis*. The University of Chicago Press, 1953.

Shaw, Henry. *Dresses and Decorations of the Middle Ages*. London: William Pickering, 1843, 2 vols.

Skira, Albert (ed.). *The Great Centuries of Painting: Roman Painting*. Geneva: Editions Albert Skira, 1953.

Speed, John. *The Historie of Great Britaine under the Conquests of the Romans, Saxons, Danes and Normans*, 3rd ed., London: John Dawson, 1632.

Sronkova, Olga. *Gothic Woman's Fashion*. Prague: Artia, 1954.

Stenton, Sir Frank Merry. *The Bayeux Tapestry*. London: Phaidon, 1957.

Stow, John. *The Annales of England*. London: George Bishop and Thomas Adams, 1605.

Strutt, Joseph. *A Compleate View of the Manners, Customs, Arms, Habits, etc. of the Inhabitants of England from the Arrival of the Saxons till the Reign of Henry VIII*. London: Benjamin White, 1775, 3 vols.

Symonds, Mary (Mrs. Guy Antrobus). *Needlework Through the Ages*. London: Hodder, 1928.

Tacitus, Cornelius. *The Germany and the Agricola of Tacitus*. The Oxford translation revised with notes and introduction by Edward Brooks, Jr. New York: McKay, c.1897.

Uzanne, Louis Octave. *Fashion in Paris, 1797–1897*. London: Heinemann, 1898.

Vecellio, Cesare. *Habiti antichi et moderni*. Venice, 1598.

Victoria and Albert Museum. *Catalogue of Rubbings of Brasses and Incised Slabs*. London: The Ministry of Education, 1929.

Victoria and Albert Museum. *Nineteenth Century Costume*. Introduction by James Laver. London: The Ministry of Education, 1947.

Viollet-Le-Duc. *Dictionnaire Raisonné du Mobilier Francais*. Paris: Bance, Editeur, 1858, vols. III, IV.

Weibel, Adele Coulin. *Two Thousand Years of Textiles*. New York: Pantheon, 1952.

Wilson, Lillian May. *The Clothing of the Ancient Romans*. Baltimore: Johns Hopkins, 1938.

———. *The Roman Toga*. Baltimore: Johns Hopkins, 1924.

Woolley, C. Leonard. *Ur Excavations*. Oxford: University Press, 1934, 2 vols.

Worth, Jean Philippe. *A Century of Fashion*. Boston: Little, Brown, 1928.

Periodicals

Ackermann's Repository of the Arts. London: Rudolph Ackermann, 1809–1829.

Almanach des Modes. Paris: 1814–1822.

La Belle Assemblée or Bell's Court and Fashionable Magazine Addressed Particularly to the Ladies. London: John Bell, 1806–1869.

Cabinet des Modes. Paris: Chez Buisson, 1785–1789.

La Galerie des Modes. Paris: Jacques Esnauts and Michel Rapilly, 1778–1787.

The Gallery of Fashion. London: Nicolaus Wilhelm von Heideloff, 1794–1803.

Godey's Ladies' Book and Magazine. Philadelphia: Louis A. Godey, 1830–1898.

Journal des Dames et des Modes (Costumes Parisiens). Paris: De Carpentier-Mericourt, 1797–1839.

Le Journal des Demoiselles. Paris: Au Bureau de Journal, 1833–19—.

Les Modes Parisiennes. Paris: 1843–1875.

Petit Courrier des Dames. Paris: 1822–1865.

Articles

Hamilton, Edith. The Greek Way. *The National Geographic Magazine*, March, 1944.

———. The Roman Way. *The National Geographic Magazine*, November, 1946.

Hayes, William C. Daily Life in Ancient Egypt. *The National Geographic Magazine*, October, 1941.

Gentili, Gino Vinicio, and Duncan Edwards. Roman Life in 1600-Year-Old Color Pictures. *The National Geographic Magazine*, February, 1957.

Speiser, E. A., and H. M. Herget. Ancient Mesopotamia: The Light that Did Not Fail. *The National Geographic Magazine*, January, 1951.

Index